Denial of Violence

Denial of Violence

Ottoman Past, Turkish Present, and Collective Violence against the Armenians, 1789–2009

FATMA MÜGE GÖÇEK

OXFORD
UNIVERSITY PRESS

OXFORD
UNIVERSITY PRESS

Oxford University Press is a department of the University of Oxford.
It furthers the University's objective of excellence in research, scholarship,
and education by publishing worldwide.

Oxford New York
Auckland Cape Town Dar es Salaam Hong Kong Karachi
Kuala Lumpur Madrid Melbourne Mexico City Nairobi
New Delhi Shanghai Taipei Toronto

With offices in
Argentina Austria Brazil Chile Czech Republic France Greece
Guatemala Hungary Italy Japan Poland Portugal Singapore
South Korea Switzerland Thailand Turkey Ukraine Vietnam

Published in the United States of America by
Oxford University Press
198 Madison Avenue, New York, NY 10016

Library of Congress Cataloging-in-Publication Data

Göçek, Fatma Müge.
Denial of violence : Ottoman past, Turkish present, and collective violence against the Armenians,
1789–2009 / Fatma Müge Göçek.
pages cm
Includes bibliographical references and index.
ISBN 978-0-19-933420-9 (hardcover : alk. paper) 1. Armenians—Turkey—History.
2. Ethnic conflict—Turkey—History. 3. Political violence—Turkey—History. I. Title.
DR435.A7G63 2015
956.100491′992—dc23
2014003287

3 5 7 9 8 6 4
Printed in the United States of America
on acid-free paper

CONTENTS

PREFACE

This book is the end result of a very long journey, one that was not only scholarly but also intensely personal. I will share the journey with you through two separate yet entangled narratives. The personal narrative I commence with emphasizes more the negotiation of meaning, while the academic narrative stresses the patterns that form across events. Personally, it was my life chances that led me to generate particular meanings in relation to minorities and the collective violence they experienced. I was born and raised in İstanbul, Turkey, into an upper-class business family, one that ensured I received the best education the country had to offer. Another significant aspect of my childhood years was how accepting my immediate family was of others, that is, how they did not define people through difference. For instance, I was not aware that I was raised in a multiethnic and multicultural space with many Greek Rum, Armenians, and Jews around me. To me, they were all honorific aunts and uncles or my playmates and later classmates. I was never made aware by my parents of their ethnic and religious difference; it was much later, when I came to the United States for my graduate work and started to get interested in minorities in Turkey, that I realized the people around me had been different.

Then, looking back, I did become aware of small signs of difference that I had evidently stored in my memory only to forget eventually, instances that moved to the surface when I started to work on minorities. The first instance of prejudice and discrimination occurred within my own extended family. During the summer months, my family and the families of my paternal grandmother and paternal uncle all vacationed in a summer mansion on an island off of the city. When my brother was in his early teens, among his best friends were two boys who were Jewish. Interestingly enough, I was not even aware of their religion until I heard my paternal uncle tell his son, who was about the same age as my brother, that his son should not become close friends with these two boys because they were Jewish. Also around the same time, I remember going to pick up groceries from the corner market, where I was told by the grocer that he was honored to serve my family because we were Turkish, not like the other riffraff—namely, non-Muslims—who populated the island. At the time, I was jolted into thinking what made us different and, failing to come up with an answer, simply refused to go to that grocer from that point on. At the private club that my family belonged to, the situation seemed reversed. Prominent non-Muslims who were also members not only seemed richer and more cultivated, but I could sometimes sense that they looked down at us Turks, considering us less civilized. Throughout my teens, as I attended Robert College for nine years, I was surrounded by many non-Muslim students, once again not at all registering their difference.

I also witnessed prejudicial and discriminatory behavior around me that did not explicitly stand out but was rather embedded and naturalized in everyday interactions. I distinctly remember my mother's actor friends entertaining at parties by imitating non-Muslim dialects, especially of Armenians. I also recall some of my parents' Turkish friends forcing their Jewish and/or Armenian friends to explain the actions of Israel or Armenian terrorist attacks against Turkish diplomats, as if they knew anything more than we did. Discriminatory phrases such as comments that non-Muslims were secretive and untrustworthy, or did not love the country as much as we did, seeped through the fragments of my memory here and there. Yet, at the time, none was enough to alert me to their difference.

What I thought—and was taught—about the past was shaped around the same discourse. Basically, during the Turkish independence struggle, many people had betrayed us, including the non-Muslims, Balkan peoples—especially Greeks—and Arabs. But we had persevered, establishing our republic in spite of it all. Whatever collective violence in the past had occurred because others had provoked us, the Turks, first; subsequent violence and suffering were therefore mutual and had been necessary for the Turkish nation's survival. After college and before coming to the States for my graduate work, I studied French in Paris for a term in 1981; I remember being terrified, along with most of the Turkish diplomatic community living there, that the Armenians were going to assassinate us all. Every time we went out, my cousin who was living there at the time made me check to ensure there was no bomb placed under their car. And the Turkish ambassador's driver entertained me with stories about how diplomatic cars had been tested with guns to make sure they were bulletproof with many failing the test.

Things changed when I arrived in the United States and started my graduate work at Princeton University. I still remember in vivid detail one student I met at the sociology department lounge who had been very friendly to me until he found out I was Turkish. He told me he was Armenian, a piece of information that did not affect me in any particular way. Yet to this day, I still see in my mind's eye the revulsion with which he started looking at me, demanding to know in a voice trembling with anger why I had murdered his grandparents. Recalling the infinite care and moral propriety with which my family had raised me, I was shocked to think that I or anyone in my family before me could have committed such a crime. I do not remember how I responded, but I can still recall the disgust in his eyes. I also remember wondering what he was talking about, and why I knew nothing about it. During my graduate studies at Princeton and my subsequent job as an assistant professor at the University of Michigan, most of my work focused on the Westernization of the Ottoman Empire because I wanted to figure out why Turkey had such a problematic relationship with the West. It was my mentor at Princeton, Bernard Lewis, who first alerted me to the role non-Muslim minorities had played in the empire, a role that was hardly acknowledged in the literature at the time. My own dissertation research also articulated the pivotal role they had played in the transformation of the empire. Yet, not only was the role of non-Muslim minorities unrecognized, but their presence and participation had gradually dissipated during the ensuing republican years.

And this was not the only silence I noticed. After receiving tenure and teaching many theory courses on critical theory in general and on gender, race and sexuality in particular, I became increasingly aware of the significance of silences in Turkey's own past, roads that were not taken, and choices that were not made. What impact did such decisions and ensuing silences have on Turkey's democratization process, I wondered. Focusing on the marginalized locations of women, ethnic and religious minorities, leftist intellectuals, and the Islamists in Turkey led me to research in turn the instances of collective violence they experienced in the past in the hands of the state. I organized such instances temporally to arrive at the foundational violence that had not only triggered but also normalized the subsequent practices: it was through this line of inductive reasoning that I arrived at what had happened to the Armenians in the past, in 1915 to be exact, because this was the earliest instance of collective violence that had still not been accounted for by the Turkish state and society.

Initially I had no idea how difficult researching this research question was going to be. While I was trying to figure out what had happened then and why, fierce politicized debates took place on disparate interpretations of official documents located in the Ottoman archives. I had worked with such archival documents in my earlier research when my training as a sociologist had enabled me to assess their epistemological limitations. Drawing on insights offered by critical theory, I decided instead to immerse myself in the contemporaneous literature and its remnants at present, reading newspapers, novels, and memoirs. In addition, beginning in 2002, I also visited eastern Turkey for five consecutive summers to see for myself the ancestral lands of Armenians. It was then that I decided to recover my own roots as well. I had noticed that whenever I gave talks on collective violence committed against the Armenians, radical

Armenians and radical Turks reacted in exactly the same manner, both claiming that I must be Armenian myself. Radical Armenians were sure of the existence of some Armenian blood in me because they could not fathom that a mere Turk would take the stand I did, conjecturing that Turks could not possibly be so civilized and sophisticated. Radical Turks were also certain my blood was tainted by Armenian blood because no pure-blooded Turk in her right mind would take such a critical stand in relation to the past, betraying all Turks in the process.

Such remarks made me realize that my lineage was going to be closely scrutinized once this book came out, and that I should look into my family tree before others did so. I knew that three branches of my family tree—those of my paternal grandmother, paternal grandfather, and maternal grandfather—were ethnically Turkish without any doubt. Yet my maternal grandmother's origin was somehow suspect. In 1903, her father had moved to the imperial capital from a village near the town of Eğin. The republican state had since changed the names of both the town and the village, as it had also done with thousands of places of Greek, Armenian, or Kurdish origin. Eğin, known to Armenians as Akhn, had become Kemaliye, and the village of Başvartenik, "main rose bush" in Armenian, had turned into Başpınar, "main water spring" in Turkish. In 2002, I decided to take my first trip to that village, almost a century after my great-grandfather had departed from it. At the time, I invited my friend Hrant Dink to accompany me there, but he could not due to a prior commitment. Instead, he suggested I go with Baron Sarkis Seropyan, the owner and Armenian section editor of the *Agos* newspaper.

I retold my story to Baron Seropyan, and he, in return, explained why he wanted to visit Eğin. In 1915, his grandfather, who had been an Ottoman army surgeon at Gümüşhane along the Black Sea coast, had gotten into trouble with the staunch Unionist governor there for treating civilians for free during his spare time. As a consequence, the governor had placed him in one of the Armenian deportation caravans passing through the city, never to be heard from again. His wife had just given birth to a son, and to help her with the young infant, her mother and sister were visiting her from their native Adapazarı near the imperial capital. Yet before they could figure out what was going on, they too, along with the other three children including Baron Seropyan's mother, were put into the next deportation caravan on its way to the desert of Deyr Zor. During the arduous journey, the women spoke Greek among themselves when they did not want others to understand; they all knew Greek because initially, during the Byzantine times, the Armenians were only permitted to do their liturgy in Greek and therefore ended up learning the language. Some had later on continued to attend Greek schools at major cities as well.[1] When the guards heard them speak in Greek, they reacted by stating that the Greek Rum imperial subjects were not supposed to be deported. Upon being asked if they were indeed Greek Rum, the latter of course responded in the affirmative. It was then decided that the family should stay at Eğin, one of the stopping places on the forced march to Deyr Zor, until this matter was cleared up through an investigation. On the way there, however, the baby and the grandmother perished, and the aunt committed suicide by throwing herself into the Euphrates River. The rest of the family, now comprising the mother and her three young children, stayed in Eğin for a couple of months until the end of the investigation, which proved inconclusive, leading to their eventual return to the imperial capital, thereby escaping certain death. Baron Seropyan's mother would always recall her time in Eğin, especially the walnut and mulberry trees, the rushing waters, and the way they stole food from abandoned Armenian houses in town in order to survive. She told her children that what they did was not stealing because they did it for survival, and these were once members of their own community who would have gladly given them the food had they still been there. Baron Seropyan wanted to see this place his mother had talked about, and to pray for the souls of those who had perished during the deportation, especially his great-aunt and great-grandmother.

I have told Baron Seropyan's story in such detail because I want to draw attention to how our searches into the past and what we recovered were so dramatically different. Upon arriving at my great-grandfather's village, I was able to locate some distant relatives still living there who showed me around the village, pointing out the house my great-grandfather had been born in, the religious primary school he had attended, the water fountain the family had built for the village, and the huge brass candleholders they had endowed to the mosque. All was intact. I found out that our family of Sunni Turks had originally come to the region from the Caucasus in the sixteenth century. The village was initially Armenian, but the inhabitants had vacated it centuries ago on their own volition, moving on to the larger town of Eğin for trade. After a very pleasant visit, we too proceeded to Eğin, this time to recover what we could of Baron Seropyan's past. There were no visible signs of Armenian presence in the town that, prior to 1915, had at least been 30 percent Armenian. The one remaining church had been transformed into a museum, the priest's house into a municipal building, and a mansion into the military recruitment center. As we walked around, Baron Seropyan taught me how to identify the buildings of Armenian origin through their stonework and ornate iron doorknobs, two skills the Armenians had once excelled in. When we inquired about the Armenian cemetery, we were directed to the town dump, only to discover a single broken *khachkar* (Armenian tombstone) buried in the garbage.

The two distinct ways in which our two pasts had survived, mine totally intact through the centuries and his almost fully destroyed, demonstrated to me dramatically that history is always written by the victors. And the destruction of the losers was not only physical but also social, spatial, and cultural. This vivid difference stayed with me throughout the following four summers as we visited one former Armenian settlement, monastery, and church after another, always to find them in ruins. As I watched Baron Seropyan trying desperately to capture with his camera the image of every broken stone once carved by the Armenians, I started to surmise what it must be like for him to now live as a minority on what was once his ancestral land, witnessing from one year to the next its continuously dwindling physical remains. During the five summers we traveled, he never once pointed this out to me or complained about what had happened or why, leaving me to infer everything on my own. To this day, I owe Baron Sarkis Seropyan deep gratitude for graciously accompanying me on these trips, thereby enabling me to envision for myself what life must have once been like only to be thoroughly destroyed.

While in Istanbul, I collected all the books I could find about the past, chancing in the process upon the Aras publication company, which since the first couple of years of the 2000s had been translating and publishing Armenian-language books into Turkish and Turkish books into Armenian. Aware of my growing interest in their communal history, the publishers, who were of Armenian origin, asked if they could help me in any way. I replied that the one vital thing they ought to do was interview as many of their elderly as possible in order to capture their past. "Don't you think we have tried?" they responded, "but our grandparents refuse to talk about the past to us, their own grandchildren. They decline to talk about 1915 and instead want to tell us about happy things that would not get us into trouble, like the establishment of the Turkish republic." This selectivity in the victims' memory reveals how hard it is to remember the collective violence embedded in one's own past, especially when one is the victim. Such remembrance not only brings back sorrow and suffering but also undermines one's own faith in humanity. Turkish state and society's denial of this collective violence was the last blow, which the Armenians of Turkey could handle only by harshly repressing their own memories.

Yet, I wondered, what about the memories of the Turks? Could there be remnants of that past collective violence in their accounts as well? It was then that I started to systematically collect and read all contemporaneous memoirs. In the hundreds of memories I thus accessed, I found ample evidence that I could—thanks to computer technology—link them to discern patterns throughout. I ended up translating into English the pertinent parts of 356 texts penned by 307 memoir writers, leading me to generate a historical database that was a thousand pages long. These are the data on which I base this book. For the more contemporary period, I realized that I too was a participant in those events, transforming the last empirical chapter into almost a memoir of my own journey uncovering and negotiating collective violence. Hence, I decided it was crucial for me as a scholar to bring my own voice into the book at particular junctures.

Even though such a move is most welcome by gender, race, and queer theorists, it is not practiced much in sociology. Yet in this specific case, I think it adds rather than subtracts from the narrative. Unlike official documents, memoirs had not been employed by scholars working on the Ottoman Empire and the Turkish republic to recover and renarrate past collective violence. No one had attempted to study them systematically because they had been published over very wide spans of time and space, often by small printing presses that immediately went out of business. It took me ten years to collect an amount sufficient to reveal social patterns running across the memoirs. I employed only those memoirs that had been published in Turkey in Turkish and therefore had been publicly available to Turkish state and society. Here I share what I found.

Turning to the academic narrative, I should first note that the research process was unlike many social scientific endeavors I had previously undertaken. All too often, the focus of social science research is on the context of scientific validation where results are judged by the community of scholars. The context of discovery during which the research question emerges is rarely discussed. In the case of this book, however, I would argue that the context of discovery was just as significant as the context of scientific validation, particularly due to the highly politicized nature of the research topic. While the Armenian Diaspora and the international scholarly community regard what happened to the Armenians in 1915 as genocide, contemporary Turkish state and society fail to acknowledge the inherent collective violence as genocide, insisting instead that what violence occurred took place during war conditions in which as many Turks as Armenians lost their lives. My initial research question was to decipher the roots of such denial: Why did contemporary Turkish state and society still deny the collective violence committed against the Armenians in their past?

It was extremely difficult to research this question. I found it especially challenging to differentiate empirical fact from fiction, knowledge based on sources from rhetoric, and historical events from their mythified recollections. Every individual and/or collectivity engaged in the debate had their own interpretation, refusing straight out to consider anything else. Hence, all was destabilized at the level of epistemology (what constituted knowledge), ontology (what constituted social reality), and ethics (what the nature of good and evil was). I therefore had to first literally reconstruct what constituted my research field before engaging in the process of making sense of it. In the course of the book, I shall discuss in detail these challenges and my attempts to overcome them.

Here I want to focus on the particular challenges I encountered during the course of my research, since I realized how unprepared I had been for them academically. In his presidential address to the American Sociological Association in 2004, Michael Burawoy outlined the virtues of engaging in public sociology. "The standpoint of sociology is civil society," he remarked, "and the defense of the social... interests of humanity."[2] I heartily concurred with the idea of taking such a humanist position. After all, in my research, I was trying to understand why a particular state and society vehemently denied what has been defined by Western scholarly community as the first historical instance of "a crime against humanity." Such an understanding would indeed positively contribute, I thought, to the defense of the "social interests of humanity." Yet deciding to study such topics came at significant personal cost. As Douglas Massey astutely pointed out in the same volume, "personal vilification heaped upon scholars for expressing heterodox views dissuaded many from undertaking research on contentious topics."[3] Even though I was not dissuaded, I nevertheless want to share what taking a scholarly "heterodox" stand on a contentious topic entails.

When I started this research project, I had received tenure, with two sole-authored books and some edited volumes and articles under my belt. With tenure, my professional stand had thus been confirmed, and I subsequently tried to contribute to the development of my field by taking on administrative duties. Yet I also had to identify a new research topic in my subfield of comparative historical sociology and in my specialty of social change in the Middle East in general and Turkey in particular. Understanding the reasons behind the political success of religiously conservative parties in Turkey around that time emerged naturally as a great research topic. The ensuing frequent military interventions in politics made me realize quickly, however, that the course of social change was dictated not by political parties but instead by officers and their officials. Given the high level of danger involved in researching Turkish state and military activities that were often secret, extralegal, and paramilitary in nature, and given the ensuing impossibility of studying the course of social change in Turkey merely from what was publicly known and discussed, I decided to alter my focus from social change to the collective violence inherent in this political process. Hence, the political violence committed by state and military officials through their frequent interventions in the democratic process directed me to probe instead into why such violence seemed endemic to Turkish state and society, thereby preventing Turkey from becoming a true democracy.

I therefore turned to analyzing the history of collective violence in Turkey, identifying as the first instance of such violence that which occurred in 1915 to 1917, right before the establishment of the Turkish republic. This was the foundational collective violence committed against the Armenian subjects of the Ottoman Empire,[4] when hundreds of thousands had been deported, thus forcibly and violently removed from their ancestral lands, a violent act commonly referred to as the Armenian Genocide. And this collective violence was still denied by Turkish state and society, almost a hundred years after its occurrence. As such, the research question enabled me to study how such collective violence embedded in the past was still negotiated at present. I also surmised that such denial somehow accounted for the current lack of democratization in contemporary Turkey. As I slowly started to research this collective violence and its contemporary denial, I lost many old friends and met and made many new ones.

Because I resided in the United States while working on this topic, the Diaspora Armenians figured prominently among my new friends. Their first reaction to me was often one of skeptical disbelief. Having never met any Turks except in the narratives of their grandparents, they were initially certain that I must be an agent of the Turkish state, there to challenge the veracity of their narratives filled with grief and suffering. What followed for years was an incessant series of tests I had to pass in their eyes. I had to prove to the Diaspora Armenians that in spite of belonging to the social group of the Turks that had perpetrated violence against them in the past, I too was a moral human being, and that it was indeed possible for me to arrive at that ethical stand without having suffered the violence that their ancestors had experienced and they in turn had inherited. That was a lot for some to take in, but most Diaspora Armenians I encountered eventually did. In the end, as I charted my way through this last decade, I had the amazing benefit of single-handedly constructing a whole new set of like-minded friends from all over the world. I now realize that the common thread that unites us is that we define each other not first as Turks or Armenians but rather first as human beings. Simple as that may sound, I have learned through experience how difficult it is to live in accordance to that principle, especially because difference is the hardest obstacle for contemporary humanity to overcome.

It was especially difficult for me because I had to constantly engage in self-reflection: Could I truly understand and relate to the Armenian suffering, especially since I was a member of the social group of Turks that had produced it? Would I be able to chart my research so that I did not fall into the vicious cycle of overempathizing with one group while totally disparaging the other? How should I include in my research the moral implications of what I investigated? While struggling with such questions, I had to strip myself down to the core and question my entire identity as a scholar, as both a Turkish and an American citizen, and as a moral human being. I also visited Armenian ancestral lands to get a better grasp of the geography, mobilized scholars working on the Armenian issue, organized letter-writing campaigns to protect the rights of public intellectuals working on the topic in Turkey, and learned to deal with various death threats I received in the process. I had incessant arguments with family members living in Turkey, since they worried about my personal safety and asked me to study something else. Many of my Turkish friends from high school and college either gently warned me about how I had to think about my children first and give up working on this dangerous topic, or harshly pointed out that through my work, I was personally betraying them and "their"—no longer "my"—country.

Hence I lost many old Turkish friends who decided that I had turned into a pawn of, alternately, the Armenian Diaspora, the United States, or the West; only a few acknowledged the significance of such work for rekindling our common hope in humanity. Some Turkish government officials I met rudely declared straight out that I was not fit to be a Turkish citizen, since I did not voice the official state position on the Armenian issue; others quietly told me to continue my research because it would, they argued, benefit everyone by enhancing the possibility of a peaceful solution in the end. All the while, I constantly questioned myself in line with the criticisms I received. I relentlessly reflected on my research to make sure that I processed all I learned impartially and critically.

When I look back, I now realize that one particular experience in 1998 emotionally committed me to writing this book. At the University of Michigan, Ann Arbor, where I teach, I was asked on the seventy-fifth anniversary of the foundation of the Turkish republic to organize a panel discussion on a relevant topic. Given the Turkish state's controversial stand on many social issues, staying away from contentious topics proved difficult, but I finally came upon the relatively safe one of "Turkey and the European Union." In selecting panelists, I decided to invite a former college classmate of mine from Turkey whom I had recently run into at a conference. It so happened that my former classmate was now the Turkish consul general of Los Angeles. I naively thought that it would be appropriate to have him articulate the stand of the Turkish state on the topic while I presented the academic view. On the day of the panel, I arrived to find the entire administrative staff in a panic: the building where the panel was to take place was surrounded by large numbers of protesting Diaspora Armenians holding signs about the Armenian Genocide. Until then, it had not occurred to me that my former classmate was of course also a representative of the Turkish state, one that the Diaspora Armenians took issue with for denying the genocide. As we entered the lecture hall among protests, I apologized to my former classmate about this dramatic turn. He graciously pointed out that on a previous occasion in Germany, Diaspora Armenians had thrown their shoes at him; here they were peaceful, he said, so there was nothing to worry about. The panel proceeded without any disturbances; we all delivered our talks to an almost exclusively Armenian audience, making no references to the Armenian Genocide.

The ensuing discussion period started, however, with a question asked by an elderly Armenian woman who stood up with tears streaming down her face: How, she wanted to know, did the Turks think it would be possible for them to ever join the European Union, when they had so cruelly murdered most of her own family on the way to Deyr Zor? My friend the consul general immediately responded by pointing out that his Kurdish mother's entire family in the eastern provinces of the Ottoman Empire had also been murdered by Armenian militia; he wanted to know who was going to account for *their* murders. Even though we had been friends for decades, this was the first time I had heard about his family tragedy. Later, reflecting upon this past silence, I realized that we almost never talked about the past in Turkey, always focusing instead on either the present or the future.

Given the ensuing tension, I intervened, addressing them both by pointing out that I was lucky because I did not have such violence and trauma embedded in my own family's past. Then, turning to the elderly Armenian woman, I stated that as a young mother, I could certainly understand how painful it must be to lose one's family. I asked what I could do to ease her pain and suffering because it was clear that she still hurt so much after all these years. I still vividly remember the incredible shock and emotional relief on her face, and the sudden ease of tension in the lecture hall brought about my acknowledgment of the Armenians' suffering. Without thinking, I had simply related to her emotionally as a human being; I was just as surprised as the audience by the positive consequences my action produced. Looking back, I now realize that it was also at that moment that I comprehended the cruelty and injustice of denial. I understood that denial refused human beings the very basic need to reconcile with their emotions, a reconciliation that would then generate the possibility of healing. Failure to do so, however, emotionally stunted and maimed humans for life as their open wounds kept festering. And the first and only step that I as a moral human being and a scholar could take to counter this particular denial was to study, understand, and hopefully disarm it.

Another emotional experience that has been just as significant concerns a special person who is unfortunately no longer with us. I first met Hrant Dink, a Turkish journalist of Armenian origin, during the Workshop on Armenian Turkish Scholarship (WATS) that my colleague Ronald Grigor Suny and I organized at the University of Michigan in 2002. We had decided to invite Dink because the Armenians living in Turkey had not been represented at our previous workshop, held at the University of Chicago in 2000. The Turkish state miraculously issued him a passport for the first time in his life, thereby allowing Dink to attend the second workshop. I was thus given the opportunity to become friends with and observe firsthand an outstanding journalist who not only tackled the many difficult social and political issues in Turkey with fortitude but did so in spite of his precarious social location in Turkey as a member of a minority group. What Dink said at the workshop was certainly not what those with set political agendas wanted to hear, those people in Turkey and throughout the world who only seek disciples and, when rejected, often turn into enemies. And when the gusty winds of politics turn into tumultuous tornadoes, they start to threaten those who do not think like them. In Turkey, even though we, that is, the public intellectuals and liberal scholars, including Hrant Dink, all kept delivering similar messages in relation to the origin and course of collective violence, Dink got singled out as the target of all ire because of his minority status. He was assassinated in front of his newspaper office in İstanbul on 19 January 2007.

Hrant Dink's presence in our scholarly community had enabled us to envision the impossible in Turkey, a society in which people from all walks of life participated equally and democratically, regardless of their religion, race, or ethnicity. I still hold this vision instilled by Hrant dear to my heart. Living with the reality of his murder remains extremely difficult for me, especially because the perpetrators who instigated the assassination have still not been brought to justice in Turkey. Recalling my many discussions of this book with Hrant and his enthusiasm for the project has kept me going, albeit with immense difficulty.

At this point, I wish to acknowledge all who made this book a much better one through their questions, comments, and feedback. Not surprisingly, the list is extremely long, given the time it took for me to complete the book. Still, members of the online WATS listserv I ran for a decade deserve special thanks, as do my audiences at many university campuses including Pennsylvania, Columbia, NYU, CUNY Graduate Center, and Delaware on the East Coast; Chicago in the Midwest; UCLA, UC Davis, UC Berkeley, and Stanford on the West Coast; Oxford, Cambridge, and SOAS (School of Oriental and African Studies at the University of London) in England; and Boğaziçi in Turkey. I am grateful to all friends and colleagues who provided feedback, and I recognize here in particular those who were brave enough to read and give written comments on the initially very lengthy manuscript. They are, in alphabetical order, Donald Bloxham, Dzovinar Derderian, Fuat Dündar, Gerard Libaridian, Anahid Matossian, Martin Murray, Nora Nercessian, Jeffery Paige, Anne Pitcher, Dan Stone, Ron Suny, Kiyoteru Tsutsui, Tom de Waal, and Genevieve Zubryzcki. Of course, the remaining mistakes in the text are mine alone. I am also indebted to my editor at Oxford University Press James Cook, assistant editor Peter Werger, copy editor Susan Ecklund, project manager Jayanthi Bhaskar, and marketing manager Cherie Hackelberg for doing an outstanding job in printing this very complex book—it has been a great joy to work with such an amazing team of professionals. And my special thanks go to my friend, colleague and amazing artist Helin Anahit who once again designed a very striking and apt book cover, one that combines the locked door of an Armenian property with the title deed of a massacred Armenian. I am grateful for the symbolism she has been able to capture so well.

This book is dedicated to five special human beings: to my children, Alexander and Shira, who literally grew up while I was writing this book and still cannot believe it is finished; and to Hrant Dink's grandchildren, Nora, Nare, and Saren, who unfortunately will never see, as I have, that wonderful, joyous twinkle in their grandfather's eye every time he would have seen them. May Alexander, Shira, Nora, Nare, and Saren have the opportunity that neither our ancestors nor we have yet had, that is, to live in a world where people finally learn to relate to one another first as human beings.

Denial of Violence

Introduction

On the Denial of Collective Violence

The words of truth are always paradoxical.

Lao Tzu, Chinese philosopher, 600–531 B.C.E.

I. Complexity of Denial

To this day, the Turkish state officially denies that what happened to the Armenians in 1915 was genocide. Based almost exclusively on official state documents located in Turkey, as well as a few select oral histories and foreign documents, it instead claims that what occurred then was the mere relocation from the eastern war front to other regions of seditious Armenian subjects threatening military security. It also contends that Armenian revolutionary committees caused this turn of events by forming armed bands that killed substantive numbers of Turks, the total number matching and sometimes even exceeding that of the Armenian deaths. Ultimately, the current official Turkish state narrative asserts that approximately 300,000 Armenians perished during the relocation in 1915 not because of genocidal intent but primarily due to unfavorable conditions of war that also caused the deaths of at least a million Turks. Every year, the Turkish state spends millions of dollars throughout the world, making many international political, economic, and military arrangements and compromises to sustain and promote its official narrative. Such an official stand is also strongly supported by the majority of Turkish society.

The Western scholarly community is almost in full agreement that what happened to the forcefully deported Armenian subjects of the Ottoman Empire in 1915 was genocide, with approximately 800,000 to 1.5 million Armenians perishing. Scholars based their interpretation on oral histories of the survivors; eyewitness accounts of Western travelers, journalists, missionaries, and professionals; and contemporaneous reports of European state representatives. They often embed this case in comparative studies of collective violence across time and space. In order to prevent the recurrence of this first instance of a crime against humanity, scholars also advocate worldwide acknowledgment of moral responsibility as well as political, economic, and legal accountability for this violent act. Their stand is in turn strongly supported by many Western states and societies.

Those representing the official Turkish state position often rely on official documents from the Ottoman archives, including the contemporaneous confiscated documents of Armenian revolutionary committees, formal state and government correspondence, and some Western sources that support, or at least do not challenge, the official Turkish state position. Because these sources are interpreted in a manner that backs the official denial, the current Turkish state and government as well as most members of Turkish society continue to refuse to recognize this past historical act as genocide. Because of this partial use of sources, the Western scholarly community finds the ensuing Turkish official discourse unscientific, propagandistic, and rhetorical and therefore does not address or engage it. As a consequence, the Social Science Citation Index does not, for instance, contain a single reference to the works of those advocating the Turkish official stand. Interestingly enough, the official Turkish state discourse likewise totally fails to acknowledge the stand of the Western scholarly community on totally different grounds: it defines such discourse as Eurocentric, imperialist, and self-serving.

Yet denial has been and still is extremely costly for all concerned. Internationally, the Turkish state annually spends millions of dollars to prevent other countries from employing the term "genocide." In doing so, the economic concessions it makes often extend to military ones. In the case of the United States, for instance, when the American president delivers his annual genocide commemoration speech on 24 April 1915, he often ends up not employing the "G" word as a consequence of last-minute concessions negotiated with the Turkish state. In addition, the border between the Turkish and Armenian republics remains closed, since Turkey has the nonrecognition of the Armenian Genocide as one of the preconditions for reestablishing relations and opening the border. The closed border saps economic and social growth in Armenia, Turkey's eastern provinces, and the entire region, leading to political instability. Additional pressure is also brought by Turkey's possible European Union membership, which would necessitate Turkey's coming to terms with its violent past, including a reexamination of the Armenian issue. As the Turkish state fails to confront the past and the violence contained therein, denial remains normalized, reproducing itself throughout Turkish state and society. True democracy therefore remains a constant challenge for Turkey as its failure to acknowledge the collective violence embedded in its past keeps reproducing such violence in the present.

Likewise, many Armenian Diaspora organizations annually expend millions of dollars to promote Armenian Genocide recognition throughout the world. They do so while Turkey, the one country whose recognition would actually enable Armenians to start healing, adamantly refuses to do so. In addition, the Armenian republic cannot focus on its own domestic and international issues because Armenian Genocide recognition constantly complicates matters, including its domestic and foreign policy. As a consequence, the Armenian republic cannot strive toward a true democracy either. Meanwhile, the Turkish denial prevents all Armenians scattered throughout the world from adequately mourning, grieving, and thereby eventually coming to terms with their own tragic past. Remaining emotionally trapped in the violence of their past, none can move on to the present or have confidence in a better future, losing hope in humanity during the process. Hence, Turkish denial traps both Turks and Armenians, reproducing the cycles of violence in different ways: Turks steadily refuse to remember that past, and Armenians continually refuse to forget it.

Yet such denial and its subsequent cycles of violence are not limited to Turks and Armenians. Many states and societies throughout the world struggle with similar issues, such as the United States in relation to the scope of violence committed against Native Americans and African Americans; Great Britain with respect to the various massacres in India, Kenya, and elsewhere; France's collective violence in Algeria; Japan's stand in relation to what happened in Korea and China during World War II; and, unfortunately, many others, including contemporary practices such as the violence in Bosnia and Chechnya. So the question posed is not specific to Turkey alone but a more general one. The vast spectrum of such empirical instances, as well as variations in meaning and the larger context, explain why it has been so difficult to develop a social science theory of denial.

This chapter contains three sections. In section I, I discuss the complexity of denial as a concept, highlighting its public display through silence, secrecy, and the subversive. I then develop an alternate approach to the denial of collective violence, one that conceptualizes denial as a process generated through the intersection of structural and affective elements. In section II, I move on to the use of 307 memoir writers' accounts of what transpired during the 220 years of history from 1789 to 2009 that I cover. For the contemporary period, I also include my own memories of growing up in Turkey to becoming a social scientist studying Turkey. Memoirs enable me to traverse the undue emphasis on the state as the primary actor of denial, bringing in social groups, including the minorities, on their own terms. Section III applies the theoretical framework I develop to the empirical case of the Ottoman Empire and the contemporary Turkish republic. I demonstrate that denial of collective violence is layered through history, covering the imperial, Young Turk, early republican, and late republican periods, with each contributing yet another dimension to the denial of the collective violence committed against Armenians. As such, my main argument comes in three parts. First, the denial of collective violence against the Armenians is not restricted to the 1915–17 period of genocide that many scholars focus on but actually has encompassed a much longer span, from 1789 to the present. Second, the historical construction of denial varies in relation to the particular interaction of structural and affective elements, constituting, in this particular empirical case, four distinct periods of collective denial. Third, denial persists across time for more than two centuries because it involves the interaction of state *and* society, becomes multilayered across time, and keeps on selectively and successfully drawing on events for legitimation. Finally, let me reiterate that even though the Ottoman Empire and contemporary Turkey form the empirical case here, I think the analytical framework can be employed to understand the persistence of autocracy and the lack of democracy throughout the world.

History of and Approaches to Denial

Why do states and societies insist on denying the acts of collective violence embedded in their pasts and their present? The social scientific history of the concept of denial can be traced back to the emergence of psychoanalysis in early twentieth-century Europe in general and to Sigmund Freud in particular. Freud first used the concept social scientifically in 1923, and his daughter, Anna Freud, later explained it more fully by approaching it as a mechanism individuals generate for defense of the ego and coping with stress. This individually based conception acquired a collective dimension in the aftermath of the Holocaust; Theodore Adorno and Stanley Milgram,[1] among others, tried to understand how and why people denied afflicting violence on others even when they observed the suffering. By articulating people's inclination to obey authority at all costs to self and others, such studies highlighted the characteristics of authoritarian personalities in general and the nature of autocratic regimes in particular. Finally, as the Cold War waned, minds throughout the world colonized by national security concerns—instilled by the two superpowers of the United States and the Soviet Union—were freed to consider what past violence had been denied due to security concerns and how such denial continued into the present. Hence the renewed study of denial with the push for apology and acknowledgement moved to the forefront of human concerns.

This brief history of the concept of denial is also concomitant with the development of three current approaches to denial, based on the individual (social psychological approach), on the practice of discrimination (critical racism approach), and on international concerns over human rights (world polity approach). Stanley Cohen and Eviatar Zerubavel are the two major representatives of the social psychological approach.[2] While Cohen tried to meticulously categorize all aspects of denial emanating from people's interactions, Zerubavel instead began with the consequences of such interactions, especially ones that produced "an elephant in the room" that no one acknowledged, and worked his way back to the origins and nature of interactions. Also significant in this context was Albert Bandura's concept of "moral disengagement," which highlighted how blaming the victim or circumstances on the one hand and minimizing the damage done by the in-group on the other lead to this unethical state.[3] The critical racism approach emerged after the end of the Cold War from the critical studies of Teun Van Dijk on the denial of racial discrimination and then expanded to studies of the denial of AIDS, first peoples, animal suffering, industrial pollution, and global warming, thereby covering all discriminatory acts against specific social groups on the one hand and against specific social issues on the other.[4] The world polity approach emerged at approximately the same time in the aftermath of the Cold War; it is predicated on the notion of a global world culture that emphasizes progressive Western values such as adherence to democracy, respect for human rights, and aspiration for world citizenship. John Meyer is the leading scholar of this approach, articulating through his voluminous work specifically, in this empirical context, the significance of Western pressure for acknowledgment of past violence.[5] The subsequent work that follows this approach emphasizes the structural and the political, especially highlighting the connection between denial and the infringement on human rights in, for instance, Argentina, Ireland, and Japan as these countries interact with the now universally accepted or at least globally exercised principles.[6]

Two studies among these approaches focus specifically on Turkey. One, by Rezarta Bilali,[7] adopts the social psychological approach to examine the relationship between the national narrative and the social psychological influences in Turks' denial of the mass killing of Armenians as genocide. Bilali, who conducted interviews with Turkish students at an American university, argues that in-group glorification, perceived in-group threat, and positive attitudes toward war increased the practice of denial measured as less willingness to support reparations to Armenians. The other study, by Başak Çalı,[8] takes the world polity approach to denial, focusing on cases from southeast Turkey (read Kurdish) before the European Court of Human Rights during the decade from 1996 to 2006 to argue that supranational human rights litigation does not lead to local acknowledgment of Turkish state violence because the intervention is only technical-bureaucratic and as such can be easily obfuscated by the state. How does my analysis mesh with these approaches? Although all articulate different dimensions of denial extremely well, there are three additional dimensions that need further articulation, specifically power, narrative, and history. Postcolonial criticisms put forth the first two; Nicos Trimiklinoitis[9] points out the shortcomings of Christian-centric and western/northern traditions that hegemonize the articulation of denial and subsequent possible reconciliation. And Victoria Margree and Gurminder Bhambra[10] discuss the power of literary narratives in denying the agency of certain groups. I concur with these criticisms and add a third one: all these approaches are ahistorical in that they do not treat denial as a *process* that transforms through time and across time; they instead often focus on the immediate or the past only as a snapshot, not taking into account changes over time.

Regarding the empirical literature on denial, the case of Holocaust denial is probably the most frequently documented because of its being the first and only publicly acknowledged collective violence to date, followed by Armenian denial due to the constant refusal of the Turkish state to acknowledge the collective violence delivered upon the Armenians as genocide. Scholars have also written about the unacknowledged atrocities of the twentieth century,[11] including work on Robert Mugabe, the 1964 Zanzibar revolution, the Mau Mau Rebellion in Kenya, the Biafran war of independence in the 1960s, the Algerian Harkis, the Spanish Civil War, the Allied bombing of Dresden, the expulsion of ethnic Germans from Czechoslovakia and Poland after World War II, the Ukrainian Holodomor, the Hama massacre in Syria, the Palestinian massacres during Israeli nation-building, the 2002 massacre of Gujarati Muslims in India, the 1965 Indonesian coup, and the Japanese military's use of Korean comfort women. The sheer length of the list demonstrates the hold denial wields over states and societies, a power that may be best understood empirically by delving further into the two best-documented cases of Holocaust and Armenian denial. The most significant study on Holocaust denial is by Deborah Lipstadt,[12] who carefully analyzes the emergence and current state of denial to reveal that by employing denial as a tool, marginalized radical groups legitimate their hatred of minorities around them, and that by attempting to present their claims as an alternate approach to knowledge that should be included on grounds of freedom of thought and expression, the same groups delegitimate academic knowledge.[13]

The literature on the denial of the Armenian Genocide comes together around three bodies of work. The monumental work Richard Hovannisian has produced on the topic ranges from comparing Armenian and Holocaust denial to articulating the transformation in the nature of official Turkish denial "from absolute negation of intentional mass killing to that of rationalization, relativization, and trivialization."[14] He notes that negators and rationalizers of both the genocide and the Holocaust emphasize the same points, specifically the emergence of alleged violence either as a part of wartime propaganda or as a product of war and national security, the assumption of provocation by alleged victims, the rationalization of the perpetrators' intent to destroy, the contestation of number of victims, the presumption that trial of war criminals absolves all violence and destruction, the relativization of the inherent violence and suffering by arguing that portrayers of academic freedom and truth need to discuss all sides, including falsified narratives, and finally the trivialization of violence by minimizing the numbers or making incongruent comparisons.[15] Hovannisian then summarizes the difference between the Armenian experience and the Jewish one in three points, namely, "The Armenians were still living in their historical homelands, had passed through cultural and political movements to the formulation of social, economic, and administrative reforms in the Ottoman Empire, and were perceived as an obstacle to the realization of designs espoused by some members of the [ruling] party."[16] Hovannisian also discusses various Turkish official attempts to prevent genocide recognition, such as thwarting the Hollywood filming of Franz Werfel's novel *The Forty Days of Musa Dagh* first in 1934 and then in 1938, as well as attempts during the Cold War and on the fiftieth anniversary of the genocide in 1965 and the seventieth anniversary in 1985 to avert the promulgation of resolutions at the United Nations and the United States to recognize the genocide.

The second scholar who has taken a comparative stand between the Holocaust and Armenian Genocide is Israel Charny,[17] who approaches denial psychologically to determine the motivations of the people who deny; he identifies the five categories ordinary people resort to in denial as follows: (i) innocence and self-righteousness; (ii) scientism in the service of confusion; (iii) practicality, pragmatism, and realpolitik; (iv) idea linkage distortion and time-sequence confusion; and (v) indirection, definitionalism, and maddening.[18] It is important to note that both Hovannisian and Charny were mobilized into action to discuss the Turkish denial when the Turkish government asked their Israeli counterparts not to include the Armenian Genocide in the 1982 International Conference on the Holocaust and Genocide held at Tel Aviv. Scholars had already arrived at the conference site when the Israeli government attempted to stop it, based on the information provided by the Turkish state that it would threaten the well-being of the Jews in Turkey.[19]

The third set of scholars comprises Roger Smith, Robert Jay Lifton, and Eric Marcusen, who approach the academic discussion of genocide denial in the United States. They try to understand how and why certain professionals and scholars take a denialist stand, and they criticize these individuals for their lack of professional ethics.[20] In the process, they document the manner in which the Turkish state and its governments attempt to control the agenda in the United States by establishing and funding research institutes to monitor and discredit scholarship on the Armenian Genocide. Another important conjecture I would like to make in this context is that one reason the Turkish state engages in denial may be due to historical conjuncture of the Turkish republic: Turkey did not participate in World War II and was therefore never impacted by the ensuing discussions of moral responsibility and by the principles of critical social theory of the Frankfurt school that emerged in the aftermath of the Holocaust.[21] Even though these three bodies of work certainly articulate the Turkish denial, they do so without differentiating the agency of state and society in the process.

Displaying Denial: Silence, Secrecy, and Subversion

I will conclude this section with a discussion of the indicators of denial that emerge from the literature, namely, silence, secrecy, and subversion. Zerubavel articulates silence, stating that "the most public form of denial is silence," and then expounds on the silence of the victim by arguing that there is often "a double wall of silence" when the survivor suppresses telling and the descendant represses asking because of fear of finding out. In addition, silence breakers often generate deep resentment, disturbing cognitive tranquility, and are therefore often unwilling to stand out.[22] Another crucial element in sustaining the conspiracy of silence are bystanders who enable denial by refusing to take a stand. This interpersonal approach to silence is complemented by Malin Akerstorm, who discusses public silence actively produced by those in power with the intent to limit the spread of information that will harm them; he argues that the powerful prevent public access to such information through restrictive laws.[23] A case in point is the promulgation of laws in the Turkish civil code such as Article 301 issued in 2008 according to which acknowledging the genocide can be tried under the act of denigrating Turkishness, with a possible prison sentence ranging from one and a half to three years. This legal threat also promotes self-censorship as intellectuals refuse to approach certain topics, thereby reproducing silence. Michel-Rolph Trouillot takes silences to the level of historical production, contending that silences occur at four crucial moments, namely, "the moment of fact creation (the making of *sources*); the moment of fact assembly (the making of *archives*); the moment of fact retrieval (the making of narratives); and the moment of retrospective significance (the making of *history* in the final instance)."[24] A case in point is the lack of any discussion in Turkish history textbooks of the collective violence Armenians suffered first as Ottoman subjects and then as republican citizens.

Secrecy is yet another form of denial. This occurs, Zerubavel argues, when the powerful control the scope of information others can access, as well as what they can pass on, leading to "various forms of forced blindness, deafness, and muteness."[25] Hence people see and hear but cannot speak. Another strategy would be to convey information informally, thereby enabling both the deliverer and the recipient "to feign ignorance later and avoid being held accountable if possessing the information becomes a liability."[26] A case in point is what happened during the rule of the Committee of Union and Progress (CUP).

During the forced deportations of the Armenian subjects in 1915–17, many CUP members knew what was going on but were sworn to secrecy and deferred the decision regarding what to divulge to the central committee. Likewise, orders for massacring Armenians were either given orally or were written down but with instructions to destroy the paper after reading it. Other practices of secrecy are discussed by Simon Hallsworth and Tara Young, who describe how those in power create states of exception and engage paramilitary bands to illegally murder those who speak.[27] The activities that the CUP engaged in before, during, and after coming to power in 1908 with the constitutional revolution provide a case in point. Initially formed as a secret committee against the sultan, the CUP sustained secrecy throughout its rule by making all members take a vow of total obedience, agreeing to the punishment of death upon violating the secrecy code.

Subversion of texts is the third and final form of denial. In this case, unlike what is withheld to produce silence or censored to sustain secrecy, perpetrators actually produce a text but do so by subverting what actually occurred and producing half-truths. Jovan Byford states that "denial is represented as self-evident, based on common sense that does not require verification. . .. it does not just involve 'defensive rhetoric,' that is the construction of one's own position as factual, true, unprejudiced, but also 'offensive rhetoric,' namely the undermining of alternate views as products of strategy or interest."[28] An example of this occurred whenever I gave talks on this research project. I was told by some audience members that I had developed an alternate stand either because "Armenians" had bankrolled my research or because "Americans" had granted me tenure with the intent to have me produce research that would destabilize Turkey.

In discussing the strategies and mechanisms of distortion, Roy Baumeister and Stephen Hastings have articulated seven tactics: "selective omission, fabrication, exaggeration and embellishment, linking versus detaching, blaming the enemy, blaming circumstances, and contextual framing."[29] Most of these tactics are self-evident. Linking means fabricating links among events or actors when there are none, and detaching means obliterating existing links; contextual framing refers to reducing the many factors and variables that constitute an event to only a few through selective interpretation. Throughout this book, I will provide ample examples of each tactic; I will not do so here because one can only detect these tactics if one is able to construct as much of what happened as possible.

II. An Alternate Approach to the Denial of Collective Violence

The alternate approach I develop here builds on the social science literature by introducing three additional dimensions of denial, as an interactive process of the structural and the emotional, one that is layered across time and space, and one that ultimately brings destruction upon the perpetrators.

Production and Reproduction through State-Society Interaction

I do not focus solely on official Turkish denial of the collective violence against the Armenians but instead emphasize the interaction and inherent collaboration of state *and* society because that joining of forces is what sustains and reproduces denial over time and across space. The generation of collective memory that equates state interests with the interests of society and that engages in active remembering through adorning all streets, buildings, and bridges with the names of prominent state leaders is especially significant in this context. Such a carefully orchestrated state-society relationship also necessitates the creation of two separate official narratives, one for the domestic audience and the other for the international audience; information generated for the domestic audience tends to be much more nationalistic and symbolically violent. Yet the proliferation of communication technology has gradually changed the nature of this domestic-international divide; now, especially the younger generations throughout the globe have direct access to both, making this nuanced distinction null and void. Still, this possible accountability within or outside the country has often pushed state and government officials and especially the military to resort to extralegal means of violence through the employment of paramilitary bands or symbolic violence by listening in on all citizens at the expense of infringing on their right to privacy. This state-society interaction also complicates the possibility of acknowledgment of collective violence in the future. Who should acknowledge to whom on whose behalf, fully assuming the responsibility that comes with such acknowledgment, is hard to determine. Given the strength of state tradition in Turkey, it is always assumed that society will follow whatever the state and its governments see fit. Yet, as I try to demonstrate here, the fragmentation that first set in in the Ottoman Empire and then the Turkish republic due to the inherent tension between expanding the boundaries[30] of collective action (progress) on the one hand and sustaining the coherence of local meaning and morals (freedom) on the other undermines the validity of that assumption, underscoring once again the need to give agency to society in all state and government transactions.

Destructive Impact of Denial on Perpetrators

Denials in the past and present in general and denial of the Armenian Genocide in particular mostly focus on the destructive impact on the survivors, who die a second time when their memory is not allowed to survive. And the impact passes through generations as the descendants of survivors are also caught in a constant state of emotional upheaval: the wounds cannot heal, imprisoning all in the past and undermining their faith in humanity and justice. I do not doubt that denial is indeed the last stage of genocide, and it makes the lives of survivors and their descendants nightmarish. Yet here I concentrate on the impact of denial on perpetrators to counter the widespread popular belief in Turkey that acknowledgment has been, and still is, forced upon the Turkish state and society by Western powers in general and the Diaspora Armenians in particular, and that acknowledgment will ultimately only benefit the Armenians. I instead contend that the Turkish state and society have also paid and continue to pay an enormous price for sustaining denial.

What has been the cost of denial to the Turks? Eviatar Zerubavel carefully articulates the impact of denial at the individual level by stating that "it distorts one's sense of reality, a problem that is further exacerbated when others collude in it through their silence. . .. it tends to heighten fear . . . makes one emotionally numb . . . triggers feelings of loneliness . . . causes people to expend large amounts of effort to avoid noticing and speaking about what is denied." Most important, "denial is morally corrosive, as it inevitably opens the door to abuse."[31] All these points can be illustrated by the tincture of public discourse in Turkey, as many claim that "all countries are after the lands of the Turks (distortion of reality); Turkey can be destroyed in the brink of a moment if one lets defenses down (heightened fear); Turkey has to steel itself against all attacks (emotional numbness); Turks have no friends except each other (loneliness)."

Also, the most significant loss in Turkey is that of a moral compass as the moral fabric of society frays and people lose hope in each other, claiming that "everyone only looks after their own interests, their own people and no one else." I would further contend that the most destructive consequence of denial has been the normalization of collective violence within the Turkish state and society. As former perpetrators transitioned into the republic to assume the role of leaders, they kept applying the same violence to social groups, once again with impunity. Because society was unable to confront its violent past, people lost faith in each other and in the possibility of an ethical system that went beyond narrow individual material interests. And such adverse impact passed on from one generation to the next.[32] In discussing the impact of such denial on perpetrators, Zerubavel concludes that the silenced and the self-censored "came to embody the type of citizen who makes the authoritarian regime possible: not speaking, not looking, not even asking once afterward, not once curious."[33]

Contextualization of Structural and Affective Elements

It is in this context that two interesting insights emerge. One is the "circle of denial" described by Samantha Power,[34] who argues that because the public is not alerted to the collective violence by governments worldwide, governments then claim there is no public support to legitimate their inaction, which, in a vicious cycle, reduces the chances of public awareness. The other is the idea of "boomerang justice" suggested by Jane Curry,[35] who contends that pressure from outside the country splits the domestic populace, alienating both sides and thereby reducing the efficacy of change, which, in turn, decreases international influence. What differentiates these insights is that rather than treating denial ahistorically, they focus on the process of negotiation, albeit in the different contexts of the United States and El Salvador.

Also important here are two observations by Gary Alan Fine,[36] one made in the context of analyzing social problems across time and space, and the other in developing classification strategies in relation to whether events belong together. In the context of the first discussion, Fine proposes the concept of "chaining of social problems" to refer to how attempts to solve social problems generate opportunities and constraints that in turn generate other problems, thereby endorsing a path-dependent analysis of problems. The second discussion focuses instead on how two events separated in space and time can either belong to the same cognitive category or speak to the same issues. Fine refers to this as "historical equivalence," since the events belong together cognitively and in terms of collective memory. Such theorizing across time allows me to once again theorize denial across time and space as a process that unfolds over 220 years as the Ottoman Empire transitions into the Turkish republic, identifying denials of historical equivalence that are chained together, with each one becoming layered upon and impacting the next one.

I thus analyze denial here as a complex process, as a collective stand that emerges through the interaction of structural (collective violence and modernity) and affective (collective emotions and events) elements over time and across space. The most significant characteristic of denial is silencing, namely, the absence of portions of information regarding past and present events. Such absence is due to the affective component of denial that leads to the suppression of knowledge contrary to one's own stand, and it is this absence that makes it methodologically challenging to study denial sociologically.

How can one recover that which has been suppressed through time and across space? The insights provided by critical feminist and race theories as well as postcolonial theory recommend reading hegemonic texts against the grain on the one hand and utilizing "informal" intermediaries of interpretation that are captured in literature, songs, stories, and material artifacts on the other. Hence the whole realm of culture, that is, the negotiation and interpretation of the world and the simultaneous and subsequent creation of social meaning, can be systematically employed to counterbalance the "formal" documents created by the state and its elites. Such critical and cultural exploration would reveal what is not said not only in formal documents but also in many of the informal discourses as well.

i. Structural Elements

My own work on the topic of denial combined both structural and affective elements. I experienced the affective element of denial when I started working on this topic. During the talks I gave on my research, some audience members would always take an emotional stand, either fervently opposing or passionately embracing the argument. Accustomed to the Durkheimian and Weberian emotionally distancing "objectivity" that academics practice, I was struck with their passion until I remembered the work of Albert Hirschman,[37] who commented on the relationship of passions and interests. I had no trouble identifying the structural and ideational interests of various state and societal actors that coalesced around legitimacy: those acknowledging collective violence challenged the material and normative status quo, while those denying it were instead set on maintaining it. Yet what was missing in my academic analysis was what I had experienced as an academic, namely, the role of emotion, especially anxiety and fervor, in the expression of these disparate interpretations. And while the parties shared the passion, they could not recognize what they shared because their interests separated them. In terms of analyzing denial, however, this observation helped me realize that I needed to combine these disparate elements.

I therefore focus specifically on the interaction and intersection of structure, idea, and emotion in the production and reproduction of denial by state and society, and do so by approaching denial as a process that transforms by selectively combining disparate elements at different junctures across time and space. This selectivity draws on what was previously there yet mixes these elements into a new permutation that is ultimately shaped by what prevails in the larger context. The denial ultimately includes and excludes certain elements to create a semblance of the truth; indeed, this quality of "half-truth" makes denial rigorous. The half-truth highlights the elements that favor the interests of the perpetrators while silencing, dismissing, or subverting those factors that undermine perpetrator interests by revealing clues leading to the inherent collective violence. What are these elements, and how do they come together to produce and reproduce denial?

The most significant structural element is the collective violence that the denial is predicated on; the composition, boundaries, and intent of this collective violence transform through time and across space in accordance with local conditions. Modernity forms the other structural element in that both the nature of collective violence and the composition of denial alter to encompass entire societies after the advent of modernity.

a. Collective Violence

In this section, I discuss one of the two structural elements that produce denial, namely, the element of collective violence, by first discussing its definition, history, and approaches, then analyzing in more detail two components that are inadequately covered in social science literature, namely, the employment of *extralegal* collective violence, and the occurrence of genocide as the foundational violence of nation-states.

Definition, History, and Approaches

In terms of the history and approaches to the academic study of violence, sociologists often trace the analysis of violence back to initial analyses of individual acts of crime, thereby equating violence with crime.[38] What often follows is a functional explanation, underscoring how crime contributes positively to the functioning of society by generating moral solidarity and by reinforcing dominant norms and values. Scholars who approach collective power in and of itself instead draw attention to structural factors such as power inequalities within society on the one hand and the concentration of power in the political institution of the state on the other; social scientists like Barrington Moore and Charles Tilly therefore highlight the role of the state in monopolizing and executing collective violence, where two forms of collective violence, war making and state making, reinforce one another.[39] Likewise, Hannah Arendt differentiates power from violence, arguing that "the rule of law resting on the power of the people (read power) would put an end to the rule of man over man (read violence)."[40] Once again, the state and its legal institutions are highlighted as always overpowering the temporary insanity of collective violence. Mark Mazower criticizes the assumption that is inherent in this structuralist analysis that collective violence emerges temporarily during periods of transition in all states and societies but eventually disappears once peace is established.[41] Such criticism leads to the question of why collective violence has not been adequately analyzed in and of itself, not as a state of exception but perhaps as an inherent aspect of human existence. In summary, then, the initial individual focus on crime and the structural focus on the state eventually lead to the contemporary depiction of collective violence as *inherent* in human life in general and in ethnicity in particular.

Dan Stone[42] and Giorgia Dona[43] best articulate this contemporary stand of collective violence as a principal component of states and societies. Stone conjectures that collective violence was marginalized in the study of modern societies because "violence that serves no profitable purpose is believed to have been eradicated. Although this is not actually the case, it means that when violence ... does occur, it explodes.... Then, however, it disguises itself because perpetrators of violence cannot admit that they have deviated from the aspirations of their society. . ..

because of modernization's rhetoric of self-styled civility, it refuses to admit the fact."[44] As what we aspire to clouds over the violence immersed in the actual nature of all societies, we are blinded to collective violence. Dona takes this approach a step further by arguing that "violence has been a neglected topic in sociological research because of the dominant pacifist stand of western modernity."[45] Hence, Dona systematically analyzes Stone's blinded cognition back through another route, emphasizing the lineage of Marx, Durkheim, Weber, and Simmel through alienation, anomie, the iron cage, and anonymity.[46] Even though these social thinkers were initially ambivalent about living in modern society, the second half of the twentieth century in general and the Cold War era in particular, we are told, witnessed emphasis only on the positive sides of modern societies, in the process turning violence into an abnormality that soon would be eliminated. That is why, Dona contends, most sociologists omit collective violence from their central problematic. Also significant at this juncture is the postcolonial criticism of Jörg Meyer,[47] who posits that contemporary Western protagonists of modernity naturalize the violence that they commit in non-Western contexts in the name of the peace they are supposed to be pursuing. In this case, they are blinded to collective violence that they themselves commit elsewhere in the world in the name of peace.

There are two exceptions to this pattern in sociology, however: Zygmunt Bauman,[48] who argued the Holocaust was not an aberration but instead a direct product of the rationalization process of modernity, and Andreas Wimmer,[49] who posited that ethnic conflict was the basis of modernity itself. I will be discussing the relationship between modernity and violence in more depth later, so I specifically focus here on the connection of ethnicity to violence. In my discussion, I add to Wimmer's work that of Rogers Brubaker[50] and Michael Mann[51] because I think they complement each other. While Wimmer focuses on the politics of ethnic boundary making in general and the emergence of exclusions with the transition from empire to nation-state in particular, Mann problematizes the concept of ethnicity by arguing that even though common culture and common descent are often given as the two characteristics that ethnic groups share, what these mean, how important they are, and how they connect to power change across time and space. Brubaker takes the discussion a step further by arguing that ethnicity does not involve only social construction but also cognition—it is a way of seeing, interpreting, representing, and processing the world. What I want to emphasize in this discussion is the significance of process on the one hand and the transformation of meaning and cognition on the other.

Hence, collective violence broadly refers to a range of human activities one social group engages in and carries out against another with the intent to inflict physical, material, or symbolic harm.[52] The most significant part of the definition is the intent to inflict harm, and the collective nature draws from the involvement of two social groups, one transforming into perpetrators and the other into victims through the act. Most scholarly discussion on collective violence privileges physical harm because of the high degree of human suffering, ranging from murder to rape or maiming the body in other ways. Material harm involves the plunder of the wealth a social group has labored to create during their lifetime or inherited from their ancestors, including lands, properties, commercial shops and equipment, jewelry, cash, and other valuables. Since Pierre Bourdieu's introduction of the concept of symbolic violence to articulate the inherent modes of cultural domination in everyday life, however, symbolic harm has also been studied in depth.[53] Such symbolic harm covers everyday practices of discrimination against a particular group, infringing on their rights to live equally with others. I propose to expand symbolic harm to also cover the violence inherent in the production of knowledge,[54] especially in relation to one social group censoring and limiting information by destroying another group's contributions to the cultural and social fabric by tearing down their houses and religious buildings, changing any street, neighborhood, or region named after them, forcing them to change their names and to speak in a language other than their own.

I thus expand the definition of collective violence by multiplying the range of activities that produces harm on a social group. In the empirical case of the collective violence against the Armenians under study here, the 1894–96 massacres and the 2007 assassination of the Armenian Turkish journalist were both primarily acts of physical harm with the inherent or actual threat of material and symbolic harm; the pogroms of 6–7 September 1955 primarily inflicted material harm with the inherent threat of physical and symbolic harm. What distinguishes the 1915–17 violence, leading scholars to term it "genocide," was the intent to inflict the *entire* repertoire of physical, material, and symbolic harm; the intent was only partially carried out during that period. Interestingly, the most important indication that the intent was genocidal is the subsequent republican treatment of non-Muslim minorities in general and Armenians in particular: republican administrations kept practicing the same violence with the same intent, reducing the non-Muslim population to its current level of 0.02 percent of the total population. I conclude the discussion of collective violence with two insights I incorporate into the study of denial: the use of extralegal collective violence in all cases of collective violence I study in the context of the Ottoman Empire and the Turkish republic, and the observation that the Armenian Genocide constitutes the foundational violence of the Turkish nation-state.

Employment of Extralegal Violence

Although the scholarly literature covers the connection between the state and collective violence, only recently have scholars started to differentiate extralegal violence executed by paramilitary groups that are either directly but secretly or indirectly supported by the state, government, the military, or locally powerful persons or communities. Such collective violence is not adequately discussed because it falls outside the realm of murders that are legally sanctified either as casualties during warfare, or shootings by security forces during peacetime, or death sentences delivered during trials, or cases assigned to and executed by secret services. Even though these may be considered individual acts of violence, their systemic character and the support provided by an organization make them collective in impact. Another reason for lack of discussion is that their existence undermines the public image states and governments want to convey in terms of the legitimacy of their political power and control. None wants to recognize such violence as anything more than individual aberrations, exceptions to the peaceful, fully functioning system of rule.

Few studies that have started to appear after the end of the Cold War focus on violence within the context of national security, terrorism, or human rights violations. For instance, one[55] critically examines the issue of collusion, that is, the engagement of "state agents (military, intelligence, police) ... with non-state agents in wrongful acts often of (or linked to) non-state political violence." Not only are such acts a part of a continuum of state practice, but the perpetrators engage in violence with total impunity and lack of accountability. Another[56] contends that political assassinations in particular that occur within this continuum constitute a "particular form of social control within an alternative system of informal justice." The informality of justice implies that certain groups challenge the legal authority of the country not only by taking the interpretation and delivery of justice into their own hands but by doing so with total impunity. Still another[57] focuses on how forms of assassination are positioned within the West, where the idea of ambivalence is introduced as a framework to justify the inherent political violence.

The employment of such extralegal violence is especially significant in the empirical case I study here because it was used in all four instances of collective violence against the Armenians. In the 1894–96 massacres, the Hamidiye regiments formed by the delegation of the sultan's authority to prominent tribal leaders and their men carry out most of the murders; in the 1915–17 genocide, the paramilitary Special Organization (Teşkilat-ı Mahsusa) of the Young Turks execute most of the massacres of the men, women, children, and the elderly in the deportation caravans outside cities and towns; in the 1955 pogroms, plain-clothes military special operation members and policemen mobilize, direct, and oversee the mob that is set out to destroy; and in the 2007 political assassination, radical elements within the state, government, and the military conspire to eliminate any challenges to their vision of control. What unites all these instances is that almost no one is ever held accountable and punished. As such, the study of extralegal violence warrants closer scrutiny in Ottoman and Turkish history, and at present only Ryan Gingeras[58] has conducted research revealing its continuation from the empire through the independence struggle into the republic.

Genocide as the Foundational Violence of Nation-States

It is a truism that all states that engage in nation-building commit collective violence, and it is also the case that such violence is often the most destructive in a nation's history. What is not discussed as often is the connection between such violence and denial by states and societies. I argue here that among all acts of violence committed directly or indirectly by states and their governments, those that are temporally closest to the nation's creation myth are silenced and denied the most and the longest because they constitute a foundational violence. It is foundational because any discussion is framed as a direct threat to the legitimacy and stability of the state and society in question. The shift from empire to nation-state leads to ethnic exclusion, Andreas Wimmer argues,[59] as the ruling elite actively attempts to enforce ethno-national homogeneity. What such violence should be called is significant but contentious; recently, there have been attempts to employ the term "genocide" to underscore that it is a crime against humanity, a crime that is without a statute of limitations. Yet such employment often undermines reconciliation and acknowledgment efforts, since it escalates the resistance of state and society. A case in question is what recently happened in Argentina, where the narration of past violence and the replacement of the term "state terrorism" by "genocide" intensified the divides within adversarial groups, stymieing the reconciliation process.[60]

The term "genocide" is also contentious in that it has an inherent moral judgment; as Christian Gerlacht states in his study of extremely violent societies in the twentieth century, "Genocide is an action-oriented model designed for moral condemnation, prevention, intervention or punishment. In other words, genocide is a normative, action-oriented concept made for the political struggle, but in order to be operational it leads to simplification, with a focus on government policies."[61] In the case of the destruction of Armenians, he employs the term "persecutor" rather than "perpetrator," since it refers to economic profiteering. Yet that is an oversimplification, as I have argued earlier that the Armenian Genocide was a process that combined physical, material, and symbolic harm. The other term that comes close to capturing the enormity of destruction is "ethnic cleansing," which is "an effort to render an ethnically mixed country homogenous by expelling a particular group of people and turning them into refugees while demolishing the homes they were driven out from."[62] Yet the Armenians were not only driven out of their homes and expelled; they were also massacred by paramilitary bands and the gendarmerie. In addition, the ensuing Turkish republican policies revealed the intent to literally eliminate the Armenians from their ancestral lands through a policy of attrition, one that has managed to decimate their population from 20 percent to less than 1 percent of the total population.

When I started this research project, I objected to the use of the term "genocide" to refer to the 1915–17 collective violence against the Armenians not because I did not think what had happened was genocide. As my earlier discussion indicates, I certainly think that was the case, especially in terms of the long-term consequences; the existence of Armenians as a social group in their ancestral lands was certainly destroyed. What I objected to was the almost total ignorance of contemporary Turkish society about what had happened to the Armenians in the past due to the nationalist educational system that whitewashed all such violence on the one hand and the perception this was imposed by the West with the intent to only appease the Armenians on the other. I argued that I would start employing the term after I had personally written and informed the Turkish public about what I think happened. With this book, I believe I have fulfilled that obligation and can therefore employ the term, although I concur that it contains an inherent value judgment, one that privileges the morality of the victims over the perpetrators. If the intent is acknowledgment and reconciliation, it is necessary to address the ethical framework of the perpetrators, giving them agency in repairing the consequences of the destruction they initially created. Regardless of the negotiation over the term employed, however, what makes 1915–17 genocidal both then and since is, I argue, closely connected to its being a foundational violence in the constitution of the Turkish republic. After all, when Mustafa Kemal Atatürk set out to lead the independence struggle, he did so on 19 May 1919, four days after the Greek occupation of Smyrna, and because of this close connection, many historians have singled out the occupation as the main factor. Yet Mustafa Kemal did not go anywhere near western Anatolia, but instead landed in Samsun with the intent to travel to Erzurum in eastern Anatolia, and the declaration issued after the first congress held there addressed not the Greek threat but instead the possibility of the establishment of an Armenian state. Hence the independence of Turkey emerged in direct opposition to the possible independence of Armenia; such coeval origins eliminated the possibility of acknowledging the past violence that had taken place only a couple years earlier on the one hand, and instead nurtured the tendency to systemically remove traces of Armenian existence on the other.

In summary, then, the most significant element of denial is the collective violence that is not acknowledged; as a consequence, the perpetrators who committed the violence are not held accountable and therefore are not punished. I define "collective violence" as the physical and symbolic harm and destruction that are directed against a social group by the state and its extralegal forces and indirectly supported by other groups in society that stand by and do not intervene. Even though the main form of collective violence that contemporary states and societies engage in is warfare, this is often very public and rarely denied. The collective violence that is denied almost always takes the form of aggression against a social group or groups within the country; its only connection to warfare is that it tends to escalate during periods of war. Even though physical destruction ought to be easier to track and reveal, its unaccountable nature necessitates rapes, secret torture, undocumented mass burials, and other such clandestine measures. Symbolic destruction is conceptualized following the work of Michel Foucault and Pierre Bourdieu; it emphasizes the harm and destruction of individual and communal property belonging to the group, such as houses, shops, tillable land, and factories, as well as seizure of all valuable assets, including art, jewelry, produce, and the like; the names of streets, places, and any aspect of everyday life that evokes memory of the group are also systematically replaced, and the legal system is informally altered with the intent to infringe on the rights of the group. In this particular empirical context, the first instance of collective violence against the Armenians occurred in 1894–96, when approximately 100,000 to 200,000 Armenian subjects were massacred, mostly in the Anatolian provinces. This imperial violence was followed in 1915–17 with the forced deportation and subsequent destruction of almost the entire Armenian population of Asia Minor. This genocidal act of Young Turk violence reduced the non-Muslims from about 20 percent to 4 percent of the total population. Non-Muslims no longer posed a physical threat, but they nevertheless continued to control significant wealth. As a consequence, the third instance of early republican violence occurred on 6–7 September 1955, when pogroms in large cities were directed at non-Muslims with the intent to destroy their material wealth and force them to leave the country. The fourth and final form of late republican violence occurred on 19 January 2007, when Hrant Dink, a Turkish journalist of Armenian origin, was assassinated in front of his office.

How do these elements illuminate the four instances of collective violence against the Armenians? The perpetrators in all four instances were formally or informally connected to the state, and they were never punished for the collective violence they committed against Armenians. The primary culprits in the 1894–96 massacres were the Hamidiye regiments established by the reigning sultan Abdülhamid II; these regiments were made up of armed local Kurdish tribal leaders and their men. During 1915–17, it was the secret paramilitary organization of the reigning Committee of Union and Progress, the Special Organization, that carried out most of the mass killings outside of settled areas. The pogroms of 1955 were secretly organized by the Turkish military with the tacit consent of the government; military operators recruited and transported hundreds of "common men" to totally destroy everything that belonged to non-Muslim citizens. Hrant Dink's assassination was secretly planned by nationalist elements within the military with the support of clandestine civilians. It is important to note that the nature of destruction changed after the transition from empire to republic in that it initially spread to other non-Muslim groups and then to groups defined as non-Turkish by the state and military. The victims in all four instances were non-Muslims; they were specifically Armenians with the exception of the pogroms, which targeted all non-Muslims but especially the Greek Rum. The location of the violence was determined by where most Armenians were initially concentrated, namely, rural areas in 1894–96, to all urban and rural places in 1915–17, to urban locations in 1955 and 2007—the last determined by the fact that almost no one was left in rural areas.

The particular nature of violence differed as well, as local massacres gave way to almost total ethnic cleansing, followed by a pogrom and assassination during the republican eras. This change is significant because imperial violence never intended to exterminate all Armenians but rather to punish them as unruly subjects; yet Young Turk violence explicitly intended to ensure that Armenians no longer had a viable presence in their ancestral lands. The republican instances of violence did not have to be as physically destructive because Armenians were no longer a significant threat in numbers; instead, symbolic violence took over to destroy what was left of them in the cultural fabric as they were forced to speak Turkish, were identified as traitors in history textbooks, and witnessed the systematic destruction of almost all their churches and cemeteries. In addition, the boundaries of violence expanded with the transition from empire to the republic as the same violence began to be directed at all groups defined as "other." The bystanders in all cases were Muslims, none of whom demonstrated any reaction other than tacit complicity except in the case of Hrant Dink's assassination in 2007, when about 100,000 people marched in protest. This societal complicity was due, I conjecture, to state control over society through fear and retribution, a control that only began to abate around the year 2000 with Turkey's possible European Union membership and subsequent easing of the legal hold over rights. In all, then, collective violence against the Armenians emerged as a lack of state protection over the community combined with the overt or covert employment of extrastate elements to execute the destruction. This discussion leads to the question of how and why such collective violence originated at a particular juncture, steering the focus to the concept of modernity.

b. Situated Modernity

At the moment, "modernity" is an overdetermined term employed to refer virtually to anything that is contemporaneous, from art and architecture to lifestyle to individuals to institutions. In addition, there is still wide-ranging debate on its origins, spread, simultaneity, and multiplicity across time and space as well as in meaning. In this section, I first discuss the history of and approaches to modernity, articulate its connection to time and violence, and then introduce the concept of "situated modernity" that I employ in this empirical study.

History and Approaches to Modernity

Modernity is a complex and overdetermined phenomenon that can be described as some combination of "rapid social, economic and technological change; industrialized mechanized production and the growth of cities; individualism as a basic resource of cultural expression, political rights and public and private identities; struggle over popular sovereignty; the power of states organized as nations and based on mass mobilization; bureaucratic routinization and governmental interference in life; tension between a worldview based on reason and science, and one based on feeling and religion; nationalism as the primary source of public loyalty and cohesion."[63] It is a particular combination of almost all elements that have constituted the human experience in the last three centuries. The only point all scholars agree on is that the components of change coalesced in the eighteenth and nineteenth centuries; the particular combination of political and economic changes in Western Europe has dominated the world since then.[64] The rest of the literature on modernity is marked by disagreement over its temporal, spatial, and epistemological boundaries.

The expansion of Western Europe after the eighteenth and nineteenth centuries led, in the twentieth century, to mass violence and bloodshed of the two world wars in 1914–18 and 1938–45. During the subsequent Cold War (1946–91), the modernity "project" was constructed positively in terms of development and was exported from the West—now also including the United States—to many non-Western states and societies. The assumption was that all would modernize following the Western trajectory to eventually converge on the "original" Western European model.[65] In the 1970s and 1980s, however, dependency and world system theories amply demonstrated that the initial advantages Western Europe had accumulated had so skewed the power distribution in the world—with the 20 percent of the world population that resided in the West controlling 80 percent of the world's resources—that such universal modernity was impossible to achieve. With the end of the Cold War, the view that the West had employed the modernity project to sustain its hegemony gained more analytical weight, leading many to decenter the West by arguing that Western Europe had initially become dominant either because of contingency and conjuncture,[66] or due to the exploitation of the rest of the world by stripping its natural and labor resources.[67]

Such decentering led instead to a proliferation of terms. A case in point is the emergence of the following five models of modernity each with its own particular qualifier. The "multiple" modernities model[68] acknowledges that there are many different, culturally distinctive formations other than the classical Western model; by doing so, however, it silences and naturalizes the continuing power and dominance of the Western European model. The "alternative" modernities model[69] focuses instead on how modernity takes place within specific locations, and such different starting points lead to different outcomes; such an approach challenges the inherent Western European origins by studying "alternate" formulations, but it still reproduces the epistemological weight of the original Western model by acknowledging that the others are merely "alternatives." The "entangled" modernities model[70] instead privileges the inherent time orientation, arguing that several different, competing master narratives of the past and future remain entangled at any given time; such an orientation captures the complexity of any given moment but does so ahistorically, that is, without acknowledging how, why, and if some master narratives dominate over others.

The "connected"[71] or "interconnected"[72] modernities model that prioritizes the connected histories among colonizing and colonized state and societies with the intent to capture the continually transforming power inequalities probably comes closest to overcoming the previous criticisms I have raised of the other models: it takes historicity into account, approaches the original Western modernity critically, and brings in the rest of the world equally, yet it also is aware of inherent inequalities. Yet one can argue that all such modernities are still embedded in states and societies and, as such, privilege structures over meaning on the one hand and spatial parameters over ideas on the other.

It is in this context that the conceptions of modernity by Amartya Sen, Jerrold Siegel, and Partha Chatterjee warrant discussion. Sen specifically concentrates on the "mobile" elements of modernity,[73] whereby modern ideas such as democracy reside in mobile constitutive elements that emerge and are negotiated discursively throughout a wide spectrum; hence they do not originate in the monopoly of a particular state or society. In relation to the empirical case analyzed here, such a conception enables, for instance, the inclusion of local, inherently democratic elements that exist in the idea of *cemaat* (religious community), one of the earliest formulations of a public sphere in the context of Islam, alongside the attempts to establish parliamentarian rule from the 1850s onward. Siegel also frees modernity from an association with a particular state and society by depicting it as a "style of life" created by a particular group of people through market, state, and communication networks.[74] So the mobile elements of modernity freed by Sen acquire further organization and practical meaning through the introduction of networks on the one side and lifestyles on the other.

Chatterjee's conception of "our" modernity[75] frees the elements of modernity culturally by providing agency to each culture's particular interpretation. Basically, modernity is only constituted through the interaction among abstract ideas, technological tools, and material resources on the one hand and local histories, practices, and ideas on the other. In such cases, all states and societies end up framing modernity in relation to what they have constructed through such an interaction. Yet, this discussion still does not address the impact of modernity on states and societies, and I turn to that issue next.

Modernity, Time, and Violence

Two aspects of modernity are significant in illuminating the process of denial, the conception of time, and the imminence of violence. Scientific research, technological developments, and industrialization produce machines that are able to go beyond speeds produced by the natural forces of wind and fire; steam- and coal-operated engines—the force of which is still measured in horsepower—cause ships, trains, and, after the invention of electricity, planes to circumnavigate the world and accelerate the experience of time. As a consequence, time folds into the future, and the past becomes devalued. Past traditions, practices, and ideas are shed and replaced with future expectations; the best times of states and societies are no longer sought in the past but instead promised in the future.

One scholar notes the acceleration of time with modernity and argues that "a consciousness of time and the future begins to develop in the shadows of absolutist politics, first in secret, later openly, audaciously combining politics and prophecy."[76] Hence the future orientation empowers those leaders who acquire legitimacy through their mastery of rhetoric, and the diminished status of the past, its absence and distance, delegitimates the value of history. Interestingly, the modern legal system also assumes time to be fully reversible in trying cases, in that a crime committed in the past can be "reversed, annulled or compensated by the correct sentence or punishment."[77] Yet, because things that become a part of the past are already distant and ambiguous, retributive justice can never fully reverse the damage. This ambiguity of the past and the accompanying tendency to forget[78] also enhance and help sustain the denial practices of states and societies.

Among the many scholars who have discussed the connection of modernity to violence, Zygmunt Bauman and Stuart Hall stand out. For Bauman,[79] violence is inherent in modernity's attempt to contain and order everything through the use of science, rationality, and bureaucratization. That which could not be cataloged, classified, and contained was marginalized and excised from the system. Just like the conception of the past, social groups that did not fit in what was envisioned became distant and ambiguous, and they could be destroyed without any compunction by those who belonged. For Hall,[80] modernity and violence are one and the same; all that is not made public and celebrated in modernity is repressed and archaic—this dark side is the other side of the coin that constitutes modernity. Yet what is viewed and publicly acknowledged in Western

Europe is only the peaceful side of the metropole, without taking into account the colonies where the violence of modernity is practiced.

Other scholars bring this divide back to the center by arguing that much occurs at the metropole that is violent as well, yet such violence is either normalized,[81] and thereby silenced, or all that lies outside the realm of what is considered to constitute modernity "is made invisible, excluded from the real, disdained, even unnamed."[82] One such practice that is inherently violent is displacement of humans, but it is so widely practiced that it is rarely commented upon.[83] In summary, then, time and violence are not only interconnected, but both are inherent elements of modernity, certainly escalating the structural and emotional tendencies toward denial. In all, then, what the recent literature on modernity articulates is the challenge of including the Western along with the non-Western formations, including but not limited to noncolonized non-Western contexts on the one hand and doing so in a manner that is not totally bound by local parameters on the other.

Dialectics of Situated Modernity

It is because of these concerns that I have formulated a "situated" modernity model to analyze the empirical case here, one that unites the global, regional, and local forces of change around the inherent tension between autonomy and progress,[84] a tension that translates into practice as disparate impact on institutions structurally and on individuals culturally.[85] While institutions shape state and society, individuals fragment the same project as they develop disparate interpretations. Among all institutions, the economic and the political ones became dominant over others due to the development of the conception of democracy based on nation-states and capitalism predicated on markets and labor. The intersection of the economic and the political also undergirds, I argue, the conceptualization that modernity is situated; this is the case because it is ultimately the specific location of institutions and individuals within states and societies that settles and shapes the result of the tension between progress and autonomy. It is the attempt to apply human reason to both that generates the tension in the first place; while progress necessitates the mobilization of all forces to expand human mastery through the employment of reason to dominate the world, autonomy of the individual in overseeing this process requires freedom and liberties that ultimately challenge the project of progress. I conjecture that a worldwide transformation regarding the elements of progress and autonomy took various configurations at disparate temporal and spatial junctures. In operationalizing progress and autonomy, however, I include emotions in addition to reason, thereby capturing the "dark sites" of modernity, including violence, an inclusion that destabilizes the Western model.

The modernity occurring in Western Europe in general and France and England in particular, I conjecture, gained ascendance over others during the eighteenth and nineteenth centuries due to Europe's systematic exploitation of the world's natural and labor resources during the previous, concomitant, and subsequent centuries on the one hand and the particular conjuncture at which they came to being on the other. And because this Western modernity then hegemonized the world first through imperialism in the nineteenth and twentieth centuries and then through modernization during the twentieth and twenty-first centuries, it became analytically challenging to distinguish its particularity behind the normalized dominance it maintained with the intent to sustain its political, economic, and social power over the world.

Such dominance began to crack, however, in the aftermath of the Cold War as many other countries started to reproduce especially the technological tools of dominance. The wide lens of analyzing the dynamics of modernity through three centuries, across an empire and republic, enables me to identify patterns that are much harder to identify otherwise. Crucial among these is the differential impact of the autonomy-progress tension on institutions and individuals. In the Ottoman and Turkish context, progress is defined in terms of dynastic, communal, party, and military interests, and when the checks and balances attempting to preserve institutions while protecting the subjects no longer work, modernity generates violence and continues to generate it from the empire to the republic.

Before further developing and putting my model into practice, however, I will briefly review the most recent works on Ottoman and Turkish modernity. Two that stand out are an edited volume[86] on rethinking modernity, published in 1997, and two more recent studies, published in 2004[87] and 2011,[88] that formulate new models of modernities. The 1997 edited volume by Sibel Bozdoğan and Reşat Kasaba, in analyzing whether it would be possible to "critically engage with the modern project and [explore] options beyond without falling back into an antimodern 'return to tradition' or getting lost in the postmodern 'global theme park,'" assumes a broad, interdisciplinary perspective to argue that the Turkish project of modernity conceived from its inception "under the sponsorship and the priorities of the nation-state has been flawed and problematical" and suggests that the future trajectory would be structured by the recent shift of power from state to society at large.[89] Hence the main contribution of the volume is to include society in the debate on Turkish modernity, one that has been so far almost totally dominated by state modernity projects.

The 2004 book by İbrahim Kaya develops the concept of "later modernities" to capture the plurality of histories, civilizations, modernizing agents, and projects of modernity, nevertheless assuming that the Ottoman and Turkish modernities were not contemporaneous with their Western European counterparts and instead developed "later." According to Kaya, the inherent tension is between globalization and localization; such tension, however, inherently naturalizes the power inequalities among different locales, thereby indirectly reproducing the Western European domination over globalization. Nevertheless, Kaya ably captures the complexities and contradictions within Ottoman and Turkish modernities, pointing out, for instance, that secularization had indigenous roots in Turkey (thus the secularizing modernity project of the state was not fully determined by the Western European model), and that at various junctures, there were competing and opposing projects of modernity instigated by the state and its governments on the one hand and various social groups within society on the other.[90]

Finally, the 2011 article by Ayhan Kaya and Ayşe Tecmen approaches Western European modernity from the vantage point of the Turkish case, arguing that in Turkey, spatial modernity was equated with Europe; this made the operationalization of modernity rather straightforward in that it was defined as the systematic observation and absorption of what occurred in Europe. Yet I would argue that the locally formulated syntheses continued to contain local and regional elements as well, and the articulation of such elements awaits future study.

In summary, then, I define "modernity" as a gradual, worldwide transformation from a divinely ordained world to a human-centered one. Such a transformation engendered the reorganization of state and society, as human-produced, quantifiable, and measurable knowledge became increasingly privileged as the guiding principles of social action over religious beliefs and wisdom; social reality based on the observable and the knowable was prioritized over the intuited and the surmised; and ethics started to favor human interests before all else, including the divine. This transformation occurred throughout the world, taking disparate forms as it interacted with local structures. Among such interactions, the one occurring in Western Europe gradually began to dominate others because of the auspicious coalescence of three factors at a particular conjuncture: mass exploitation of the world's natural and human resources, mass mobilization of masses into governance through democracy and human rights, and mass recruitment of labor into the market through capitalism and industrialization. The most significant challenge of this new combination was legitimacy: power was no longer embedded in the divine the ruler emanated; it had to be actively collected from the masses. This active collection generated a new, vastly expanded public sphere for which knowledge was specifically produced: for the first time, there was the necessity to produce different kinds of knowledge for disparate interests. Knowledge constructed for internal consumption for leaders, domestic consumption for citizens, and external consumption for all foreigners varied. Eventually, this magical merger of global exploitation with concomitant political and economic mobilization unleashed a human-produced force that began to dominate the world.

It is significant to recognize that Western European modernity as such was Janus-faced in that it presented itself to domestic and foreign audiences separately. As Western European modernity acquired power, it legitimated and normalized its hegemony domestically by claiming that its achievements were all locally and consciously produced, thereby silencing both its exploitation of world resources and its magical conjuncture of factors. Externally, Western European modernity emphasized its superiority over all other global forms by arguing its version could be easily transported to the rest of the world. Soon thereafter, specific elements of Western European modernity such as mass-produced consumer and industrial goods started to circulate the world alongside new forms of knowledge such as the social and natural sciences imparted through formal, often secular education. These elements interacted with local modernities throughout the world, generating new formations that resembled the Western European version but were never fully like it. I approach Ottoman and Turkish modernity within this analytical framework, differentiating the negotiation process of the Western European and local versions across time and space and in meaning as imperial, Young Turk, early republican, and late republican modernities.

In this particular empirical context, two parameters differentiate the various modernities: the nature of the interaction of the economic and political spheres, and the differentiation of the institutional and individual levels. Imperial modernity was marked by the profane administration of disparate resources by a divinely ordained ruler who tried to constantly maximize his resources while minimizing domestic conflict through local governance. In the eighteenth century, increasing Ottoman military defeats eventually necessitated adoption of Western European practices, including formal education, year-round training, and a separate treasury for expenses in imported arms and ammunition. Hence the sultan defined the political sphere in terms of the increased public participation of soldiers that happened to be almost exclusively Muslim due to the local ethnic division of labor. Non-Muslims who paid a special poll tax in return for being excused from military service were relegated to the initially less significant economic sphere. The centuries-long ethnic divide institutionally precluded the fusion of the political and economic spheres; the sultan did not trust his non-Muslim subjects enough to let them gradually become industrial entrepreneurs locally producing arms and armaments for his state. And non-Muslims could only accrue economic resources insofar as they did not translate these into political assets. While urban-based Armenians prospered through trade and commerce with Europe, those in the rural areas suffered; while those educated along the Western European model of formal education wanted to participate in communal governance, the religiously educated traditional leaders tried hard to protect the status quo favoring the latter. In all, then, imperial modernity was marked by the ascendance of military institutions in the political sphere and the fragmentation of non-Muslim communities in the economic one. The fragmentation and ensuing rebellions produced the first instance of collective violence against the Armenians.

The ensuing Young Turk modernity witnessed the emergence of the first Western-style educated military graduates who favored their acquired knowledge over the wisdom attained through age and practice. Intent on preserving the state through the repromulgation of the constitution and parliament, they carried out a revolution that marginalized the sultan. Yet replacing the divinely ordained body of the ruler with the abstract body of the constitution undermined their legitimacy, leading the committee leaders to engage in extralegal violence that did not formally challenge their government. They attempted to monopolize their control over the political and economic spheres by resorting to such violence, assassinating their political opponents and forcefully removing non-Muslims from the economic sphere. Hence the committee defined the political sphere in terms of increased public participation of Muslim subjects through elections; in the process, Muslim subjects officially and symbolically evaluated as family households rather than individuals had a rough time transitioning into individual citizens. Non-Muslims who were used to paying an individual poll tax and also participating in communal self-governance were much more aware and active. The committee also attempted to monopolize the economic sphere through establishing state-sponsored banks, companies, and organizations staffed solely by Turks. While taking such actions, however, it was challenged by Muslims who instead wanted to preserve the imperial framework; fragmentation among the Muslim majority between the Western-oriented "reformers" and imperial "traditionalists" ensued. The latter also wanted to include the non-Muslims in the body politic. When they were forcibly removed from power by the committee supported by the military and extralegal forces, non-Muslim Armenians active in the political and economic spheres were destroyed without much opposition. In all, then, Young Turk modernity was marked by the ascendance of political institutions and the forced consolidation of the political and economic spheres with the violent elimination of the Armenians who posed a political challenge in terms of their large numbers throughout the empire and an economic challenge due to their financial prominence.

The early republican modernity that emerged after the successful independence war was set on creating a unified national body politic. Intent on creating a nation, the former Young Turk leaders who had transformed into the military commanders and civilian bureaucrats of the republic first established full control over knowledge production by secularizing and monopolizing all public instruction. Hence they defined the political sphere through the participation of all citizens in education. Yet the educational institutions privileged as ideal citizens only those who were secular yet initially religiously Sunni Muslim, and ethnically Turkish; all others like the Kurds, Alewites, and the religious were systematically excluded. Hence the social fragmentation translated from the majority to the rest of society, thereby posing secular republicans against the rest of the population. In the economic sphere, the leaders set to produce Sunni Muslim Turkish entrepreneurs strictly loyal to the republic; these too could not initially transform their economic power into a political asset, and when they tried, the military executed a series of military coups with the intent to secure control over the political and economic spheres. At this juncture, non-Muslim minorities were too few in number to pose a political challenge, but they continued to possess economic resources. Their economic hold necessitated the use of extralegal force in the form of pogroms clandestinely organized by the military, as a consequence of which much of the non-Muslim economic wealth was summarily eliminated. In summary, then, early republican modernity was marked by the privileging of educational institutions and the coalescence of the political and economic spheres under state control; the symbolic exclusion of non-Turkish, non-Sunni citizens from the body politic was accompanied by pogroms targeting non-Muslims with the intent to remove their economic wealth.

Late republican modernity emerged when the state's hold over the economic sphere started to wane because managing the economy with the intent to maximize state security rather than profits did not yield productive results. There were finally enough Turkish entrepreneurs to successfully manage the economic sphere, gradually pulling the country out of the hundred-year-long economic standstill launched by the systematic decimation of the imperial Armenian subjects by the Young Turks. Many economic institutions were able to generate wealth through directly participating in the world market; their socially conservative owners in the provinces that had been marginalized by the secular republicans not only accumulated capital outside state control but also invested it to gain political influence. With their financial and social support, the Justice and Development Party that is still in government today came to power. Structurally, this was the closest Turkish modernity came to the Western European version as the political and economic spheres could now work in tandem, albeit without the exploitation of the world's natural and human resources. Yet, there was another significant difference: fragmentation finally set into the core of the state as secular republican officials clashed with the religiously conservative new appointees. The proportion of non-Muslim minorities had dwindled to 0.02 percent of the population at this point (from a high of 20 percent during imperial modernity). No longer existing as a significant force in the economic and political spheres, the few non-Muslim minorities left behind joined the attempts of Turkish and Kurdish liberal intellectuals to further democracy in the political sphere. Yet the secular republicans united with the religiously conservative to practice violence against the least protected elements in society, the non-Muslims, to covertly execute assassinations where the perpetrators were never caught and brought to justice by the government. In total, then, late republican modernity was distinct in prioritizing the economic institutions over all else, as the state's control over the economic sphere dwindled. Now the totally diminished non-Muslim minorities joined forces with the liberal segments of society, only to face violence once again in the form of assassinations covertly executed by radical Turkish nationalists within the state and the military.

ii. Affective Elements

Affective elements are significant in that they capture the meaning-making processes that inform not only the norms and values of social groups but also their social actions. Even though such processes are often studied under the general rubric of culture, in this case culture gets hijacked by affective elements: emotions and selected events help social groups quickly crystallize and distill the repertoire of meanings available to them. Hence social groups certainly draw upon the cultural tool kit in determining the course of action, but the engagement of emotions quickens that selection process, helping them focus on very few options with great intensity. In the context of this empirical case, emotions and events are consistently utilized to mobilize Muslims in general and Turks in particular against the Armenians.

a. Collective Emotions

In this section, I first discuss the significance of collective emotions and then delve into the connection of emotions with nationalism and trauma in particular, two dimensions that have not been adequately articulated in the social sciences. I finally introduce the concept of publicly manufactured emotions to capture a phenomenon I observed in my analysis.

Significance of Collective Emotions

Like violence, emotions have been inadequately analyzed within the context of social life due to the focus of Western European modernity on the public, visible, rational, and quantifiable.[91] Yet emotions in general and collective emotions in particular play a significant role in the process of denial at two junctures: the transformation from the social segmentation generated by modernity to the actualization of collective violence, and then, during and in the aftermath of violence to the selection of the legitimating event, followed by the declaration of denial. Especially in relation to the collective violence against the Armenians, these junctures are marked by stigma,[92] namely, the extreme dislike directed at a person or group on the basis of social characteristics that distinguish them from others. I can personally attest that Turkish identity also draws a similar stigma especially in Western Europe due to the denial of genocide on the one hand and the unfavorable location of Turkish migrant workers within societies on the other. Yet, thankfully, it has not reached the level of violence in my case. Collective emotions also play a significant role in two additional and interrelated contexts: trauma, that is, the emotional response to a deeply distressing and disturbing experience like violence; and nationalism, that is, an ideology and practice predicated on visualizing and emotionally responding to the imagined community of the nation. Trauma often precedes, accompanies, and succeeds violence, leading to the privileging of some emotions over others with often destructive consequences to the self and others. There is likewise a close connection between nationalism and violence, especially due to the mobilization of emotions to validate the boundaries of the imagined nation, monitoring to determine, often by force, those who have to be included or excluded.

Emotions are "a relatively short term evaluative response essentially positive or negative in nature involving distinct somatic (and often cognitive) components."[93] Hence they provide a lens for individuals and social groups to utilize in processing the world around them, and they form through a process, starting with the cognitive perception of a situation, the stimulation of a physiological response, the labeling of that response by culturally available tools, and the social expression of the feeling negotiated by the cultural framework.[94] It is important to differentiate emotion from affect. Affect is a disposition without a particular targeted object, such as anxiety; it becomes an emotion, such as jealousy, when it is directed at a specific object.[95] The specific content of the emotion is determined by a combination of personal and structural factors. The personal factors include individual personality dispositions, knowledge and information available about the particular situation, and evaluation, including a moral component, undertaken in relation to particular norms and values.[96] The ethical component is especially noteworthy because it ultimately decides how to negotiate emotion to what ends, that is, it chooses whether to take action, including in the form of violence or not. Scholars highlight the significance of this ethical dimension of emotions by underscoring how emotions impact state and institutional activity,[97] and have the capacity "to prevent fear and anxiety from turning into murderous action."[98] The structural factors include the political force of state formation, the economic impact of market expansion, and the social influence of continuous technological change and increased perception of risk associated with modernity. Power and status relations in a society also play a role in that one's own or another's power and status impact the manner in which emotions are negotiated; one's own increased power and status decrease negative emotions, whereas the same structural variables increase negative emotions when they pertain to the power and status of another.[99] Similar to personal factors, structural factors also form a frame through which to interpret emotions. Needless to say, the two factors continually interact, as in the case of emotional socialization.[100]

The shift from individual to collective emotions has not yet been adequately studied, but the personal and structural factors discussed earlier probably determine the parameters of collective emotions as well, with the addition of the communal level in terms of cultural expectations, norms, and values. An important aspect that needs to be further highlighted is the role of social, economic, and political power in the production and expression of emotions; those with more resources have a better opportunity to provide their own framework for the processing of emotions. The state actively promotes its own institutional agenda in setting up the emotional habitus for its citizens, stressing, for instance, the need for continual national security concerns through ongoing discussion of what might happen if this concern loses its prime location in the emotional repertoire of its citizens. Such emotional messages are often relayed by "state institutions of shame," such as the military in Turkey, that highlight the dangers that will result from such abandonment of national security concerns. It is difficult to discuss the full spectrum of universal collective emotions because the content is always socially, culturally, and historically mediated. Still, fear seems to be the most significant political emotion,[101] predicated on the Hobbesian argument in the *Leviathan* that humans enter into a social contract to eliminate the state of fear they experience in nature, where they are without protection. In the case of denial, such fear is complemented by the emotion of shame[102] that is felt by victims and perpetrators in coming to terms with the collective violence. To these two emotions, one can also add guilt, remorse, hurt, and anger.[103]

In trying to ascertain which emotion among these is significant in a particular case, it may be best to briefly discuss the history of emotions in social science literature.[104] Sociological analyses point out the initial removal of emotions by Max Weber to the realm of the private and the irrational and highlight Émile Durkheim's study of how collective emotional responses solidify moral sentiments of a social group. Georg Simmel and later Erving Goffman instead focus on the nature of everyday interaction, highlighting the public presentation of the group in which emotions are often silenced to save face. At the collective level, the initial focus on the crowd by Gustav Le Bon in 1896 led to the creation of the field of social psychology and the formulation of how frustration, upon reaching a certain level, leads to aggression and violence. Historical approaches to the study of emotions term this the "hydraulic" view, which, it is argued, no longer holds, especially given the more recent cognitive and social constructionist views. I should also mention in this context the analysis of emotions in non-Western contexts. While emotions are often fully silenced in Western contexts, since they are assumed to be negotiated and removed outside the public realm, the opposite is often true in analyses of non-Western contexts, where it is assumed all public decisions are predicated not on reason but on emotion alone.[105]

Emotions, Nationalism, and Trauma

The gradual loss of the power and authority of imperial rulers eventually leads to the formation of nation-states in which legitimacy no longer draws from the sacred body of the ruler immersed in divine power but instead from the people's participation in and approval of the political system. With the transition from subjects to citizens, people need to adopt and assume a national identity that symbolically and emotionally connects them to each other and to the abstract concept of the nation, making them feel they belong. This is not at all a pre-condition in an imperial setting because all subjects are considered to belong symbolically to the household of the ruler. New emotional needs emerge with the transition to nation-states. As one scholar argues, "Nationalism... the ruling passion of our age... [is] political sentiment seeking to establish self-determined nation-states... social mobilization to realize and defend nations... and passionate loyalty and devotion to one's nation."[106] Hence emotions help create such an imagined community; within the country, a shared past and traumas embedded within can be utilized to generate collective emotions through, for instance, the commemoration of momentous events in the nation's history and the daily celebration of the national flag.[107] The subsequently generated attachment is the emotion of patriotism. In addition to such processes of inclusion, nation can cohere emotionally through exclusion as well: certain domestic groups that do not belong to the body politic can be excised through violence, indirectly increasing coherence within the dominant majority. Likewise, the nation and its state can define external enemies and, better still, fight them, a process that once again leads to the cohesion of the imagined nation.

Hence nationalism is a cognitive and affective framework through which citizens interpret the world around them. Such a tightly connected, emotionally wound network among citizens exacerbates volatility, especially over the political issues of who belongs to the nation or who should speak on its behalf, quickly leading to collective violence. Indeed, after the 1789 French Revolution, most of the nineteenth century was spent in systemic violence as social groups attempted to determine the boundaries of nations. When the expectations of equality raised by the revolution were not met, when people's newly constructed conceptions of justice were offended, the emotional reaction was one of rage that translated into violence as the quickest solution. Hence, oddly enough, perpetrators also explain their decision in terms of the anger they felt; the issue here is not to question the authenticity of the perpetrators' emotions but rather the mechanism by which they target an object as the source of their emotions. In the case of the Ottoman Empire and the Turkish republic, this process commences with the 1839, 1856, and 1876 reform efforts and culminates in the 1908 constitutional revolution of the Young Turks. It is not accidental that the gravest collective violence against the Armenians was committed specifically by these Young Turk leaders during their attempts to build a nation.

In the aftermath of collective violence, the discontent continues, this time taking the form of trauma suffered by the victims and perpetrators. Because the empirical focus here is on the denial of such collective violence by perpetrators, I will analyze in depth the emotions of the latter. Such analysis is not, of course, in any way undertaken with the intent to justify the violence but rather to delve into the convoluted emotions that result in denial. One expects the emergence of collective guilt, that is, "the remorse that is felt when one's group has illegitimately harmed another group and not repaired the damage done."[108] Such remorse is morally necessary for the perpetrators as well as the victims to sustain their trust in humanity and justice. In the absence of such remorse, however, knowledge and truth become totally relative, and the moral compass breaks down, enabling the perpetrators to distort what happened to such a degree that perpetrators turn into victims. Bernhard Giesen provides the most astute analysis of the trauma of perpetrators,[109] arguing that "traumas and triumphs comprise the 'mythomoteurs' of national identity. They stand for experiences and ultimate horizons for the self-constitution of a collective subject." This integration of trauma into national identity formation, of foundational collective violence into political consciousness, makes it especially challenging for perpetrators to acknowledge the trauma. Giesen argues that, in addition, the inherent atrocity "would have been alleviated by the moral triumph of a collective project that could have persisted even after a defeat and could even have earned the tacit respect of the victors—a heroic war of liberation and independence, for example." Unlike in the German case, this is exactly what happened in the aftermath of the Armenian Genocide when the struggle for independence changed the emotional landscape; as former perpetrators became republican heroes, they whitewashed their past sins in the righteousness of the independence struggle.

Publicly Manufactured Emotions

The preceding discussion reveals the great significance of emotions to the nation-building process especially in the creation and subsequent legitimacy of the abstract conception of the imagined community of the nation. Such collective emotions initially emerged unfettered, predicated on and structured by the particular temporal, spatial, and cultural context in which they came into being. Once the state and its governments realized the verve of emotions in sustaining nation-states, officials soon succeeded in manipulating their citizens' emotions to continue their legitimacy. Such manipulation took many forms, ranging from controlling the patriotic content of textbooks in education and newspapers and periodicals in the public sphere, to promoting frequent commemorations of significant events in the nation's history, to employing extralegal paramilitary bands to create a state of emergency and the ensuing increased reliance of the citizenry on the state to secure their protection. This is indeed the exact foundation stone of the idea of a national security state whereby the state and its governments manufacture emotions to convince the citizenry to relinquish their rights and responsibilities.

As one scholar argues in the case of waging war, "One of the principal ways emotions affect the decision to wage war is through the creation of public support for governmental violence.... To the extent that individuals idealize the government and national leaders ... they will follow the leaders' cues to displace their anger onto those defined as enemies of the nation."[110] In the empirical case under study here, it is with the coming to power of the Young Turks that one starts to witness the creation of manufactured emotions. Because the Young Turks needed to reinforce their legitimacy, they were not loath to formulate their own Special Organization to assassinate their opponents, destroy the Armenian presence on the latter's ancestral lands, and mobilize large groups of porters at the capital, for instance, to storm and plunder shops, buildings, and properties of social groups they did not consider a part of the emerging Turkish nation.

In summary, then, the social science literature on emotions concentrates mostly on individual emotions in relation to their impact on interpersonal interactions; the focus on collective emotions is largely limited to social movements, where they are analyzed in terms of their positive mobilizational potential. In the empirical case under study here, however, collective emotions often play a more negative, often destructive role. Here, I define collective emotions as the public expression of affective states toward particular social groups. Methodologically, cultural sites that avail information regarding affective states include individual memoirs, diaries, and chronicles; contemporaneous novels, plays, poetry, songs, and military marches; and newspaper editorials, columns, and political cartoons. Throughout the 220-year period analyzed here, fear and anxiety emerge as the prominent collective emotions that were then skillfully channeled by political leaders into anger toward weak, unprotected domestic targets like the Armenians, often as a proxy for the larger, stronger, and therefore not easily challengeable marks such as Western powers. During this period, imperial generations began to be socialized with fear and anxiety when the empire started to physically shrink during the nineteenth century; the succeeding generation not only inherited and expanded upon this emotional state as it fought in wars for eleven years straight (war in Tripoli in 1911, the Balkan Wars in 1912–13, the First World War in 1914–18, and the independence war in 1919–22), but became even more agitated by the worry of racial extinction. The ensuing three republican generations also experienced such fear and anxiety, this time artificially induced by political and military leaders constantly identifying domestic and external enemies that threatened national security.

Collective emotions during the imperial era were often locally monitored; the sultan acted as the patriarch over his fictive household of administrators that in turn watched over self-governing communities and social groups. Non-Muslim communities were controlled by their religious leaders, who had a somber emotional tone; Muslim villages and urban neighborhoods were controlled by their elders, who played a similar role. The respect granted the decisions of such wise men was complemented by a legal system that included Muslim and non-Muslim communal courts. Within this framework, collective emotions surged mostly during times of war, especially because campaigns involved the accumulation of large numbers of soldiers at the capital to receive orders. Discontent often originated among the soldiers over unpaid wages and was either settled by direct negotiation by the sultan or led to the sultan's removal and replacement by another male successor from the same dynasty. Other instances took place mostly at urban centers, where social groups such as artisans, shopkeepers, and religious students protested rising prices, or in rural contexts, with villagers complaining about taxes or compulsory services.

Many such expressions of collective emotions were successfully contained until the second half of the nineteenth century until the wars with Russia in 1853–56 and 1877–78; the first one placed a heavy financial burden on the treasury, and the second produced large land losses in the Caucasus and the Balkans, leading to a huge influx of Muslim refugees into the empire. The gradually emerging print media also fostered such fear and anxiety in spite of strict censorship by the sultan. During this period, Armenian subjects in the rural areas were increasingly frustrated due to the failure of imperial social and legal reforms to recover their lands and enact their legal rights; their frustration made them amenable to the incitement of Armenian revolutionaries to rebel against the state. Unlike his kind treatment in the case of the rebellions by Muslims, the sultan reacted more harshly, permitting collective violence and delegitimating the Armenian rebellions by shifting the blame from domestic discontent over failed reforms to external incitement of the Great Powers.

Collective emotions were much more volatile during the Young Turk era, since the Committee of Union and Progress initially came to power through a revolution against the will of the sultan. The committee leaders then became actively involved in manipulating the collective emotions, especially of the Muslim populace of the capital, to garner legitimacy for their actions. Such manipulation escalated during wars as the CUP actively promoted domestic boycotts of

Austrian goods and stores when the Austro-Hungarian Empire annexed Bosnia and Herzegovina in 1908, and boycotts of Italian goods and stores when Italy invaded Tripoli in 1911. Likewise, on the eve of abolishing the capitulations in 1914, it secretly organized the urban crowds of the capital to storm Western establishments. Collective fear and anxiety especially among the dominant Muslim Turkish majority reached a new high during the Balkan Wars when the empire suffered a traumatic loss, withdrawing in a couple of weeks from the entirety of the Balkan Peninsula that had been under their rule for almost four centuries; another large influx of traumatized Muslim refugees followed, often fleeing with nothing but the clothes on their back. The CUP was infuriated by the duplicity of the Great Powers, which had feared an imminent Ottoman victory at the advent of the war and therefore declared that no land would change hands due to the war, only to renege on their declaration when the Ottomans lost, allowing Balkan states to keep the territories conquered from the Ottomans. This "Western betrayal" was widely covered in fierce newspaper articles that incited vengeance, once again indirectly monitored by the CUP.

The journalists had no accountability for inciting hatred, and this collective surge of emotions carried over to World War I, where wartime censorship over the press guaranteed even fuller control to the CUP. During the war, demoralized through a series of defeats and anxious that the pincer movement with the British attack through the Dardanelles in the west and the Russian assault through the Caucasus in the east would result in Turks' racial extinction, the CUP started to incite hatred toward Armenian subjects on the grounds of potential collaboration with the enemy. Hence, when some Armenians joined the Russian forces in the east, rather than punishing those few and/or peacefully removing the rest inland, the CUP instead decided to destroy all Armenian subjects with a vengeance. It could thus exact proxy vengeance on unarmed Armenians instead of the regular troops of the Allied forces. Such destruction, however, not only destroyed the social and economic fabric of Asia Minor for a century but also ruined the moral fabric of the Turks; the perpetrators of the genocide had lost their moral compass and with it their society's trust in justice and humanity prevailing over all else. For decades to come, the republic inherited this damaged moral fabric as state interests easily prevailed, destroying whatever attempted to challenge it.

During the early republican period, the people who had suffered through eleven years of continuous war and witnessed the genocide of Armenians, Assyrians, and the Pontus Greeks were initially too traumatized to resist the increased control of the state and its government dominated by former military commanders. The emerging republican leaders, most of whom were former CUP members and perpetrators of collective violence against non-Muslims, continued to act with impunity, directing hatred against the remaining non-Muslims.

The state's mismanagement of economic enterprises that rewarded party loyalty over profits and economic decisions based on military concerns instead of financial stability led to severe economic crises, especially during World War II, when Turkey did not enter the war but mobilized a vast army that it had to feed for years as the war dragged on. Both during and after the war, rather than relinquishing control over the economy through liberalization, the republican leadership targeted, raided, and forcefully depleted the economic resources of non-Muslim minorities, inciting hatred against them through newspaper articles. It was also during this time that non-Muslims were aggressed upon to send indirect messages to Western powers who were their coreligionists; they were there locally, and they were the weakest in terms of legal and political protection—they had only limited economic power, and that was targeted next. Turkey's conflict with Greece over Cyprus led to the incitement of hatred toward the Greek Rum citizens of Turkey; when the military organized Muslim masses to raid the Rum establishments, *all* non-Muslim enterprises, houses, and churches were destroyed within a couple of days. Such systematic persecution of non-Muslim citizens led to the dwindling of their population during the republican period to less than 1 percent of the total population. Hence, by fostering and sustaining fear and anxiety on the one hand, and anger and hatred against non-Muslim minorities on the other, the republic symbolically finished the genocidal acts the Young Turks had initiated.

The late republican period likewise sustained the fear and anxiety of the populace as the republican civilian and military leadership, intent on building a nation through fear, constantly generated domestic and external enemies. Such an emotional state justified the military to appropriate half of the annual operating budget taxes for its expenses; the secular, ethnically Turkish urban entrepreneurs and industrialists who gradually emerged through state subsidies and protection sustained their wealth insofar as they did not engage in any political activity. During the Cold War, the military engaged in covert operations, assassinating prominent intellectuals and inciting political divides within the populace with the intent to legitimate military coups that occurred directly in 1960, 1971, and 1980 and indirectly forcing government change in 1993 and 1997. Toward the end of the Cold War, as Turkey opened to world markets, the republican leadership started to lose its grasp on the political and economic spheres for the first time; the frustrated and marginalized religiously conservative provincial businesses prospered and successfully challenged the republican leadership in 2003. Their political slogan was putting the happiness and prosperity of citizens before the state, and also eliminating rule based on fear by advocating transparency.

This electoral victory agitated the radical groups among republicans to clandestinely mobilize with the intent to provoke the populace to overthrow the legitimately elected government. As many liberal intellectuals took a political stand against the radical elements, it was a journalist of Armenian origin who was assassinated among them because of his ethnicity and lack of proper protection by the state. Yet the assassination did not repress the populace but instead enraged many in İstanbul, as about 100,000 took to the streets in protest. Yet neither the newspapers, periodicals, and television programs that fomented hatred toward this journalist, accusing him of treason, nor those radical leaders who gave the orders to the underage assassin were tried and punished by the government.

b. "Legitimating" Events

William Sewell Jr.'s seminal work on eventful analysis focuses on historical events to comprehend both the production of meaning and the generation of change.[111] After reviewing the existing temporalities in contemporary historiography, Sewell argues that the most analytically rigorous one capturing the complexities of history is the "eventful approach" that focuses on the process through which events defined as the transformation of structures shape and reshape people, meaning, and social action across time and space. The eventful approach concentrates on the narrative process through which historical events as well as global contingencies come to being.[112] Sewell articulates the significance of historical events in the construction of social meaning in great detail.[113] In emphasizing the event as opposed to mere facts in historical transformations, the eventful approach builds upon the work of Gilles Deleuze;[114] in employing the narrative mode to examine the temporality of such events, it relies on the works of Andrew Abbott[115], Ron Aminzade,[116] and Larry Griffin.[117] Sewell predicates his formulation of the historical event on the example of the French Revolution, one of the most momentous structural transformations in recent history.[118] Historical events of such large scope are, as Sewell also notes, rare, and the logic behind them "uneven, lumpy and contingent."[119] The issue of the event's uniqueness raises questions about the nature of its impact on other similar instances elsewhere, on whether and to what degree one can claim that such a transformation is universal or whether the eventful approach is specifically predicated on explaining the historical processes of modernity.

The application of the eventful approach to the analysis of Ottoman and Turkish collective violence and denial generates significant insights especially into the construction of denial. Unlike the liberating mode in which Sewell's events work in the French context, however, events in the Ottoman and Turkish contexts operate in a confining, restrictive, and conservative setting: rather than acknowledging violence, they instead lead to its denial. By thus rationalizing the denial of contemporaneous collective violence, these events do not challenge but instead legitimate the status quo.[120] During the four time periods, four events occur that are then employed by state and society to rationalize and justify their collective violence against the Armenians. Building upon Sewell's insights, I argue that emotions play a significant role in which events are collectively selected as pivotal not only by societies but also by states.

Selection of Pivotal Events through Emotions

The extensive literature on emotions contends, in relation to the focus here, that emotions play a significant role in determining "selective attention and perspectival selectivity,"[121] and this selectivity is especially triggered when one is faced by unpleasant emotions that one intends to reject. Such desire to avoid already available information accompanied by the unpleasant emotions the information would provide leads social groups to the practice of "emotional management" whereby social groups decide to choose certain events while silencing others. Another level of selectivity takes place not due to emotions but instead to narration. Even though people have ample information about events—especially if they have personally experienced them—they also select certain features while narrating particular events, giving them a superficial consistency in the process. Put differently, "When an event is retold by means of a language, it inevitably acquires a structural unity. This unity, which in fact belongs only to the level of expression, inevitably becomes transferred to the level of content too. So the very fact of transforming an event into a text raises the degree of its organization."[122]

Yet another dimension of narrating events, especially regarding traumatic ones, concerns the silencing and suppression of certain aspects. As some scholars, argue, in relation to events within collective memories, "Silent events that no one wants to talk about may be the most potent in the development of collective memories because when people are to avoid talking or thinking about an event that event becomes even more deeply ingrained in their memory."[123] Hence, events that are suppressed and silenced often ingrain themselves the most in collective memory, especially because one is not permitted to make them public, reflect on their impact, and heal.

Scholars have often engaged in textual deconstruction to capture that which is privileged, silenced, or suppressed. They often do so by reading the text against the grain and bringing in other sources on the particular events narrated in the text. In addition to bringing in the academic scholarship on Ottoman imperial and Turkish republican history, I overcome the issue of textual voice, silence, and suppression by immersing myself in contemporaneous memoirs, systematically analyzing as many accounts of particular events as I could find. This captures and hopefully overcomes the issue of personal idiosyncrasies and political tendencies. In addition, the frequency of mention of certain events juxtaposed to and coupled with the discussion of the Armenian issue points out which events memoir writers employ to legitimate the collective violence. When I thus analyzed hundreds of contemporaneous memoirs, actors narrating the violence did indeed bring up particular events to legitimate their investment in denial instead of acknowledgment. All these events not only gave negative, destructive agency to non-Muslims in general and Armenians in particular but also were incorporated into the denial narrative as selective half-truths.

I would argue in addition that the selection process involved in identifying such "legitimating" events is not a rational but rather an emotional one. Actors often searched not for truths but for events that would justify the particular course of action they personally or their society collectively took. I should highlight here once again that the intent was not an academic one to engage and learn but rather an emotional one to bolster one's stand, in this case, denial of what transpired. Such perverted selectivity and implied causality of events was not, I am sure, what Sewell had in mind when he constructed the eventful approach, but it certainly helps explain how the path from collective violence to acknowledgment gets subverted. In relation to the period analyzed here, that is, from the systematic reforms of Sultan Selim III commencing in 1789 to the contemporary period of 2009 when I ended my research project, four pivotal events stood out in terms of how frequently the memoir writers discussed them within the context of the collective violence against the Armenians. These events occurred in 1896 during the imperial period (1789–1907), in 1912–13 during the Young Turk period (1908–18), in 1920 during the early republican period (1919–73), and in 1975–86 during the late republican period. I next discuss these pivotal events that "legitimated" collective violence and thereby subverted possible acknowledgment in depth.

Event I: 1896 Ottoman Bank Raid by Armenian Revolutionaries

This first pivotal event takes place on 26 August 1896 at the imperial capital during the reign of Sultan Abdülhamid II. On this day, twenty-eight armed members of the Armenian Revolutionary Federation (also known as the Dashnaksutiun) storm and take over the Ottoman Bank that largely employs French and British personnel. The intent is to draw the attention of the Great Powers to the 1893–96 Armenian massacres to possibly trigger their military intervention in the Ottoman Empire. The fourteen-hour-long seizure results in the deaths of a few Ottoman soldiers as well as some revolutionaries. Upon the diplomatic—and not military—intervention of the Great Powers, however, the rest of the revolutionaries are given amnesty by the Ottoman sultan. They are then escorted out of the building into a private yacht that gives them safe passage to France.

The immediate consequence of the bank raid is the massacre at the capital of approximately 6,000 minorities comprising mostly, but not exclusively,

Armenians. Contemporaneous accounts penned by Ottoman Turkish officials reveal other, less noted consequences. In the collective memory of the dominant Ottoman Turkish majority, this event is repeatedly mentioned as the first instance of how they became aware of the seriousness of the Armenian issue, which had until then remained mostly confined to the provinces. They especially remark upon how there had never been any significant challenge to the long authoritarian rule of Sultan Abdülhamid II, certainly not at his well-fortified imperial capital. Members of the then secret Young Turk political organization start to discuss how they could likewise initiate action against the sultan, a course that had not occurred to them until then as a viable option.

Another significant impression registered in the collective conscience is the shock and astonishment at how the Armenian revolutionaries escaped "scot-free" without any punishment because of Western protection. As such, the event vividly demonstrates to the Muslim populace the power Western states had started to wield within the empire with the potential to intervene on behalf of the Armenians. Sultan Abdülhamid himself employs the event most creatively as he first underlines the seriousness of the Armenian issue and the ensuing European intervention to imperial sovereignty. He then takes the additional step of drawing a causal connection between these two factors by stating that the event demonstrates how Western powers actually *created* the Armenian issue in the first place. In doing so, the sultan initiates the process of officially "othering" the Armenian subjects by raising doubts about their intents and ultimate allegiance. He indirectly legitimates the past as well as possible future violence against the Armenian subjects by removing them from his symbolic protection to the dubious one provided by European powers.

Event II: Disastrous Defeat during the 1912–13 Balkan Wars

After the Young Turks oust Sultan Abdülhamid II from power in 1909, the empire plunges into a war in 1912 with the Balkan League[124] comprising the former subjects—and therefore the minorities—of the Ottoman Empire. The empire suffers a swift and devastating defeat as hundreds of thousands of Turkish Muslim refugees, who had settled in the Balkans since the thirteenth century, flee in disarray amid massacres toward the capital, leaving everything they possessed behind them. Haunted by enemy fire audible at the capital, the Young Turks, who are then not in government, increasingly blame the current administration. The pivotal event is the fall, after a six-month siege, to the Bulgarian forces on 26 March 1913 of Adrianople/Edirne, a former Ottoman capital that had been in Ottoman possession since 1363.

The siege leading to the fall triggers in January 1913 the first successful military coup in Ottoman history: the Young Turks under the leadership of Enver

Bey storm the Ottoman Assembly and unlawfully seize power. In the aftermath of the coup, the Young Turk government curbs existing freedoms by effectively eliminating political opposition, and the military assumes a significant role in politics that has continued unabated to this day. In relation to the fall of Adrianople, even though the Ottomans are initially defeated, the subsequent infighting among the Balkan League over the spoils once again enables the by then war minister Enver Bey to recapture the former capital on 21 July 1913. The Young Turk propaganda during the process constantly highlights the atrocities the Balkan states committed against Muslim Turks; it also maintains the hypocritical silence of Western powers to Muslim suffering. Even though they would raise many questions about every non-Christian minority killed in the Ottoman Empire, Western powers remain mute during the massacres of tens of thousands of Balkan Muslims.

Along with these historically visible consequences of the siege and fall of Adrianople, other less-discussed outcomes abound. The mass flight of Balkan refugees significantly alters the ethnic and religious composition of the empire to the advantage of Muslim Turks, who rearticulate their position in society as the dominant majority. In addition, as these refugees vie for land and shelter in Anatolia, they put tremendous pressure especially on the minorities who have resided there for centuries, further polarizing social relations. Yet perhaps the most significant impact is emotional. For the first time in Ottoman history,[125] contemporaneous newspaper articles, songs, poetry, and fiction mostly penned by the dominant Turkish Muslim majority express the fear of biological extinction. The discussed apocalyptic scenario predicts the penetration of the empire in a pincer move, from the west by Balkan states supported by the West and from the east by the Russians aided by the Armenians; before they unite at the Anatolian core, they massacre all the Muslim Turks in their path. This apocalyptic vision that fosters and legitimates radical ideas in the empire parallels the rise to power of Enver Bey, and with him a radical militant segment within the Young Turks, including the two major perpetrators of 1915, namely, Dr. Nazım and Dr. Bahaeddin Şakir. During this process, Enver Bey is first promoted to the rank of pasha and then ends up commanding the Ottoman army during World War I to a disastrous 1915 eastern defeat against the Russians at Sarıkamış. Officially, the Young Turk government first subverts the blame for this disastrous defeat to the activities of the Armenian militia and then employs it to justify the ensuing deadly Armenian deportations throughout the empire.

Event III: 1920 Mistrial of Nusret Bey as a Perpetrator

In the aftermath of World War I, the Allied forces that occupy the capital insist on bringing to justice those who had perpetrated the collective violence against the Ottoman Armenians from 1915 to 1917. An imperial decree issued on 21 November 1918 declares the establishment of military tribunals, and one begins to operate within two months. During the course of 1919, many prominent Ottoman officials are arrested on charges of perpetrating the Armenian massacres, and the executions of Boğazlıyan district governor Kemal Bey and Urfa subdistrict governor Nusret Bey lead to widespread protests. Even though the first execution, of Kemal Bey, is legally sound in that it is legitimated by the emerging evidence during the trial, Nusret Bey's execution on 5 August 1920 is legally not as sound: he is literally tried twice for the same alleged perpetration.

Nusret Bey is at first investigated and cleared of possible crime; he is then retried and sentenced to fifteen years of hard labor. Yet after the dismissal and replacement of the dissenting juror, this decision is converted to execution by hanging, which is carried out within twenty-four hours. The manner of the execution scandalizes especially those prominent Ottoman officials who were imprisoned alongside him. The military court of appeals later reconsiders and retries the execution decision on 18 January 1921 to find all jurors in the case, including the head judge, Mustafa Pasha, guilty of miscarriage of justice against Nusret Bey. They are all sentenced to prison terms ranging from three to seven months, but the sultan grants them amnesty.

This mistrial is pivotal because it is employed by the dominant Muslim Turkish majority to delegitimate the entire legal process of bringing to justice the perpetrators of the collective violence against the Armenians. It enables this increasingly nationalist dominant Muslim majority to declare that *all* decisions reached by the tribunal as well as *all* instances of Armenian massacres have been unsound and therefore incorrect. Contemporaneous newspaper accounts reveal how this legal skepticism gradually extends to Armenian complaints at large. The veracity of Armenian testimonies in court comes under doubt as well. The mistrial is framed as yet another ploy of Western powers based on unfounded accusations of Armenian subjects to destroy the empire and, through it, all Muslim Turks. The impassioned protests of the Muslim populace of the capital to the few executions lead the British to hastily remove the rest of the perpetrators to the island of Malta to face trial at a later date. Yet, as the Turkish independence struggle gains momentum and achieves success, these imprisoned officials are all released to the victorious nationalist forces in exchange for the same number of captured British nationals.

In the end, many of these perpetrators not only escape justice and are never held accountable for the atrocities they committed, but some become prominent members of the new Turkish national assembly, eventually serving as ministers, prime ministers, and even as president.

Event IV: 1975–86 Assassinations of Turkish Diplomats by Armenian Terrorists

After the military tribunals, the newly founded Turkish republic—joined in its leadership ranks by former perpetrators—considers the Armenian issue closed. Yet collective violence against all non-Muslims persists, gradually reducing the minority population even further through outmigration from 20 percent to its recent level a century later of 0.02 percent.[126] The Turkish state and military systematically destroy historic Armenian sites and silence their contemporary presence in Turkey, thereby burying the Armenian issue in the past. World War II and the ensuing Cold War enable the Turkish state to retain its own parochial version of history, sanitized of all its collective violence. The Armenian issue once again gains international prominence, however, in 1973, as Gurgen (Karakin) Mgırdıch Yanikian, a seventy-seven-year-old American Armenian immigrant from Turkey, assassinates the Turkish consul general of Los Angeles, Mehmet Baydar, and his deputy, Bahadır Demir. According to the long text Yanikian had prepared and mailed to major American newspapers two days before the murders, he has resorted to such violence in order to avenge the events of 1915. Stating that "it was about time that someone accounted for what had been perpetrated," Yanikian urges all Armenians to follow his example.[127]

Two radical Armenian groups are indeed formed to follow suit—the Justice Commandos of the Armenian Genocide (JCOAG) and the Armenian Secret Army for the Liberation of Armenia (ASALA)—and over a decade execute the murder of forty-two Turkish officials. Initially, when Western prosecutors ask the Turkish state for literature on its official standpoint on 1915, all the Turkish Foreign Ministry can come up with is one short brochure. Retired diplomats are then commissioned by the Turkish state to write an official account of what transpired in the past and why. The ensuing end product of these amateur historians further mythifies the Armenian issue, drawing a causal line from the present aggressive violence of a few to the culpability and violence of all the Armenians against the Turks from time immemorial. The recent "martyrs" are situated along a long line of Ottoman Turkish officials who perpetrated the Armenian genocide in 1915 and who as a consequence were assassinated by Armenians around 1919. This official literature grows domestically through self-referencing as commissioned academics and research institutes devoted their time to further develop this mythified version of 1915 in which all the responsibility for collective violence is placed squarely on the Armenians, with Turks emerging as the ultimate victims.

All this Turkish official denial literature develops as a consequence of this decade of violent assaults by the JCOAG and ASALA as they execute a total of 110 acts of terror against the Turkish republic in thirty-eight cities of twenty-one countries. Of these, 39 are armed attacks, 70 are bomb attacks, and 1 is an occupation. During these attacks, 42 Turkish diplomats and 4 foreign nationals are murdered, and 15 Turks and 66 foreign nationals are wounded. This violence against Turkish targets turns into organized action in 1975, escalating in 1979 and finally abating in 1986. According to contemporaneous Turkish newspaper accounts, the initial reaction of both the Turkish state and the dominant Turkish Muslim majority is one of total disbelief; both constantly search for Western duplicity in instigating these murders. Hence, both the Turkish state and the dominant majority draw upon existing denials to place the blame squarely on Western powers and their Armenian henchmen attempting to bring down the Turkish republic. In summary, all four historical events reify the power of the state and dominant Muslim Turkish majority, legitimating their violence against domestic minorities and their subsequent denial.

III. Memoirs as an Empirical Source Documenting Denial

Collective repertoires of meaning that survive culturally exist scattered across many sites such as literature, songs, stories, and material artifacts. The most significant concept that enables us to access the system behind this cultural selectivity across time and space is that of memory: humans are bombarded by thousands of stimuli every day, processing these and then retaining only those that they deem significant while promptly forgetting and/or naturalizing the rest. On a larger scale, societies engage in a similar activity, handling many ideas and practices daily only to distill some among them over time and across space. Sites of memory in general and memoirs in particular are an ideal empirical source for analyzing denial because, unlike official spaces and documents, they contain knowledge on the informal and emotional aspects of life, thereby allowing access to meaning production in society.

Here, I employ memoirs as the primary site of knowledge about the past and present; I specifically approach them as social constructions that actively include and exclude contemporaneous information. By doing so, I am able to identify in the construction of past and present the structural and affective elements on the one side, and silences as well as hegemonic rhetoric on the other. I also assume that the manner in which I exhaustively collected all memoirs I could find with relevant information on minorities through Ottoman and Turkish history enables me to treat my population as representing contemporaneous collective memory. As such, collective memory not only enables the articulation of collective identity over time but also is imbued with moral imperatives, thereby revealing the elements of the moral order at large.[128] In addition, collective memory provides access not only to knowledge that is filtered in accordance with certain claims of truth at the expense of others but also to emotions and feelings that were awakened in the past and are rekindled at present upon remembrance.

Collective Memory, Emotions, and the Selective Remembrance of the Past

Collective memory comprises one of three ideal types: (1) homogeneous, when all share the same past, an outcome that is often produced by close state control over the construction of public memory, where official and national memory become one and the same; (2) complementary, when different members have disparate recollections but all still complement one another, sharing the basic parameters of knowledge and information; and (3) contested, when the different perspectives do not function reciprocally but instead often contradict one another.[129] In the Ottoman and Turkish cases, I argue, collective memory is complementary during the imperial period, become contested during the Young Turk period, and settle into homogeneity during the early republic, to once again become contested in the late republican period. The empirical analysis of memoirs is significant in that they are one of the few sources through which one can recover how the perpetrators negotiated what happened. In the case analyzed here, the perpetrators committed their violence in the name of the larger collectivity to which they belonged whose will and intent they took upon themselves to define. In addition, they never had to personally come to terms with the consequences of their violent actions because they were not punished throughout the imperial and republican periods. Their violence has only recently started to be documented in the aftermath of the Cold War.

It is significant to further note that the memories contained in the memoirs I study here are not official but instead episodic in nature. Episodic memory is produced by individuals when their personal experiences intersect with the larger events going on around them, whereas official memory is constructed by institutions controlled by the state and its governments, where state interests ultimately determine the particular interpretation of events.[130] Episodic memory is also referred to as either autobiographical[131] or "flashbulb" memory[132] to highlight the manner in which the mind captures the exact intersection of personal experience and historical events. It is not accidental that cohorts, namely, people banded together by sharing the same historic events who often belong to the same generation as well, often have similar recollections. And their cohort memories are especially shaped by events they have witnessed and experienced during early adulthood, from the ages of fifteen to twenty-five.[133] In the case of Ottoman and Turkish history, the cohort born in the 1880s that lived through the transition from empire to republic wrote the largest number of memoirs in order to share the historic times they experienced; as such, they could be termed the "canonical"[134] generation of the Turkish republic, a generation whose historic imprint has been difficult to overcome.

What do such generations collectively remember in their memoirs? More significant still, what do they forget? According to the literature, remembering and forgetting exist in a dialectical relationship in that whenever collective remembering occurs, something is often intentionally forgotten, and whenever collective forgetting takes place, the memories still exist, albeit layered away from public recognition.[135] Hence, what is forgotten is rarely lost. In addition, remembering and forgetting are also fluid in that they shift over time, with the larger societal context influencing the process.[136] Gary Alan Fine and Larry Griffin are prominent sociologists who have studied patterns of remembrance in depth. Fine examines the manner in which the impact of an event transcends its actual occurrence to serve as memory templates later on, arguing that memory templates have two subtypes, interpretive templates that contribute to how the public recalls the past, and action templates that aid in developing strategies for action.[137] Fine states that for templates to have effects, "they need the sponsorship of individuals, groups, and organizations, and need to be spread through forms of media and institutional affiliation."[138] Taking this argument a step further, those who are in positions of power act as "memory entrepreneurs," deciding what to remember and what to forget in a manner that privileges the status quo and their location within it. Hence, what is remembered and forgotten is often determined by those in positions of power. In analyzing the same selectivity of events to remember, Larry Griffin[139] underscores the significance of norms and values that frame the remembering in that people often recall events that agree with their ideological orientation. This sociological insight can be extended beyond political divides to the ideology of nationalism, which systematically extinguishes the memory of all social groups that did not contribute to the nation's formation. In this context, the reputational trajectories of historical figures of a national struggle impact later memory in a path-dependent manner, revealing once again the manner in which nationalism ideologically privileges some heroes over others and does so over time.[140] In remembering, then, people self-censor the past in accordance with the ideological and cultural parameters of their present.

What is remembered in Turkey in relation to past collective violence, and why? In dealing with its difficult past of committing collective violence against the Armenians, Turkish society has recently moved to "fragmented commemoration" in that there are now "multiple times and spaces in which different discourses of the past are aimed at disparate audiences."[141] While the Turkish state sustains its denial and silence by only undertaking commemorations that stereotype and portray Armenians as the perpetrators and Turks as the victims, civilian human rights organizations instead hold public vigils remembering the Armenians destroyed during the genocide. Given this record and decades-long suppression in Turkey, it is useful to next analyze forgetting.

Forgetting, that is, removing selected events and peoples from memory, often takes a multiplicity of forms. While narrative forgetting entails the formation and dissemination of a historical narrative, symbolic forgetting is "the creation of a new symbolic geography of new places and street names."[142] Such forgetting was practiced by the Young Turks and subsequent republican regimes in obliterating the memory of non-Muslims in Anatolia by systematically destroying churches, confiscating lands and residences, and changing *all* names of Armenian and non-Muslim origin, from street names and provinces to names of plants and animals. The same forgetting also occurs in the memoirs. Over time, especially after the foundation of the republic, the mention of non-Muslims in general and Armenians in particular disappears not only from the social fabric but from memory as well. Yet, according to the literature, such forgetting is not final but probably is one way of dealing with traumatic memories in the short term.

Forgetting is institutionally fostered by states and governments, and ideologically supported by modernity. Official responses throughout the world are predicated on encouraging permanent forgetting because the intent is to reproduce the existing power relations that would be undermined through remembrance. Indeed, countries like Germany, Italy, France, Spain, Argentina, Chile, and Uruguay have all engaged in such forgetting, but they are now gradually willing to consider confrontation with their violent pasts.[143] They do so in order to achieve permanent peace and democracy. The Turkish republic has not started this process yet. One way in which past violence can be remembered and acknowledged is through getting the social groups of perpetrators and victims to interact and reconstruct the culture and meanings they once shared; studies indicate that the smaller the cultural distance between the two groups, the bigger the chance of remembrance and the smaller the chance of recurring violence.[144] Yet this has not been possible between the Turks and Armenians because the number of Armenians in Turkey has been decimated almost to extinction.

Forgetting is also fostered by modernity because its dual ideals of progress and autonomy necessitate the elimination of structures and practices from the past that are viewed as holding state and society back from "progress." Likewise, the autonomy of the individual in modernity also privileges total control over life chances, destroying in the process the hold of past status and class hierarchies.[145] As historical memories are often determined for the citizens by political elites and the institutions the latter control,[146] such memories quickly transform into official memories that highlight the positive while silencing the negative and the destructive. Such silencing thus normalizes and contains difficult pasts, leaving generations of citizens either totally ignorant or barely aware of past collective violence. Then, as official memory keeps circulating through the educational system, media, museums, public monuments, commemorations, street names, coins, and banknotes,[147] it gradually begins to prevail over and erase alternate, contentious memories. Hence elites as social actors and the institutions they control shape what is remembered and forgotten, a process that ultimately promotes, as one scholars puts it, "structurally instigated amnesia."[148] Yet there is also built-in resistance. Unofficial memories percolate through the social system informally, either orally or in the written form of memoirs, which I employ here. In this context, then, memoirs constitute a significant source of private, informal knowledge about the past that traverses the narrow confines of public, formal documentation. I now turn to a fuller discussion of the memoirs I employed in this work.

Memoirs as a Source for Ottoman and Turkish History

Autobiographical writing or first-person narratives are among the most ancient writings in the world. A society's reflection on its dominant norms and values, on what it chooses to remember and also forget, is best revealed through memoirs, autobiographies, and, within Islam, chronicles (*tevarih*), diaries (*yevmiyyat*), biographies (*tercüme-i hal*), books of adventures (*sergüzeşt*), or books of conversation or companionship (*sohbetname*) and any other media such as personal miscellanea and scrapbooks (*mecmu'a*) through which individuals experience and interpret the world around them.[149] In the Ottoman case, initially biographical dictionaries are significant, interspersed with travel literature, especially that occasioned by the Muslim pilgrimage. The nature of these works changes in the Ottoman Empire with the advent of modernity in the eighteenth century; they assume a more public and political tone in the nineteenth century.[150] In the Young Turk period, the genre expanded as former elites wrote memoirs "in order to exclude themselves from the sins of the old era" on the one hand, and to prove they contributed to the proclamation of the constitution on the other.[151] Also significant was "the emergence of an interval of freedom of expression and publication."[152] Later, many continued to write of their experiences and service during numerous wars, including the Balkan Wars, World War I, and the independence struggle. Likewise, many wrote after the 1960 military coup.

This pattern becomes especially prominent during the republican period (1923–2009) as more and more public figures write memoirs to legitimate not only the Turkish republic but also their particular role in it. A case in point is Yakup Kadri Karaosmanoğlu's autobiographical writings, in which he describes his rebellion against the world in his teens and twenties, his obsession in bodily pleasures in his thirties, and finally his discovery of "the love of nation" that "turns into a divine order" once he discovers Mustafa Kemal as "the guide of the nation."[153] He forms a part of the "transitional" generation (from empire to republic) who are permitted to have a voice; "others" become the domestic dissenters of the independence movement as well as the "vicious," "hypocritical," and "imperialist" Europeans who are not only "the enemy of the Turks, [but] whose main objective is to wipe out the Turkish people from world history."[154] Another intersecting genre that emerges during the nationalist period of Turkish history is what Hülya Adak terms "misanthro-biography" as the works of those who either do not support and/or become excluded and marginalized by the dominant official republican narrative based on Mustafa Kemal's famous *Speech* (*Nutuk*).[155] These texts are not only relational but also intertextual in that they all have to interact with the *Speech* that has become the official dominant narrative of the republic. As such, they all challenge the myth of Mustafa Kemal as the sole prophet of the Turkish nation.

In general, historians in Turkey had shunned autobiographies as a source for historical analysis for fear that they "might not tell the truth," while literary scholars considered the genre a "generic hybrid of history book and novel."[156] Yet, autobiographical writings as well as biographical sketches and essays that first appear in print media to be then collected and published in book form reveal the community of intellectuals, poets, writers, journalists, and artists as "a memory community... who write their history by conversational memorizing."[157] In these sketches, the authors describe meetings, reconstruct conversations and dialogues, and also tell anecdotes; they also recount their banishment, exile, and imprisonment as they are sanctioned by the state during the Ottoman and republican periods.

Memoirs as an Empirical Site of Knowledge, 1789–2009

I shall first discuss the empirical database of memoirs in terms of their temporal boundaries, specifically in relation to how far back I went in my analysis and why. It was easier to determine the end point because it had to be the present, namely, 2009, when I concluded my study, because denial still existed then. Establishing the point of origin was more difficult. I had to trace the process to the first instance when the execution of such collective violence became possible. This meant delving into the past, to the acts of collective violence committed against the Armenians, not only to 1915, when the destruction of Ottoman Armenians commenced as a state policy, or to the 1893–96 massacres, when such violence became systematic, but even further back when the social structure became so polarized as to make such violence possible. Even though violence against particular social groups of course existed in the empire from its foundation in 1299, it had been monitored and controlled by communal leaders and the state until the eighteenth century. Only after the advent of modernity in the Ottoman Empire did social relations polarize to such a degree to make collective violence a distinct option.

Historically, the systematic modernization of the empire ensued in 1789 with the accession to the Ottoman throne of Sultan Selim III. Thus, the historical process of collective violence encompassed a very long time span of 220 years, from 1789 to 2009. Once I recovered from the shock of discovering the length of the time that I needed to analyze, the advantages of studying history through such a wide lens became evident. All too often, in countries without a strong print infrastructure, the scant historical material available confines scholars to research and analyze very limited time periods. Yet memoirs emerged as a genre in the Ottoman Empire in the second half of the nineteenth century; before then, however, imperial chronicles penned throughout imperial rule also contained ample informal and personal knowledge especially on everyday life, thereby providing information all the way back to the late eighteenth century. I therefore traced the collective violence against minorities in general and the Armenians in particular during this period through memoirs. As I did so, I became distinctly aware of how larger social, economic, and political transformations impacted both the nature of the collective violence and its denial *over time*. It was the empirical study of memoirs spanning more than two centuries that ultimately informed the theoretical framework of denial, one constituted through the interaction of structural and affective elements, and one reproduced through the layering of denial across time, in this case, almost flawlessly from the empire to the republic.

Turning now to a discussion of the spatial boundaries of memoirs, I need to articulate why I employed this particular source instead of others. In analyzing collective violence, most scholars concentrate on the official documents, since, as Charles Tilly[158] wisely pointed out, states have a monopoly over violence. Yet official documents are also socially constructed in accordance with the interests of the state as interpreted by its elites; as such, they censor information in ways that may not fully reflect the cultural repertoire of meanings that exist in the society at large. Bypassing official documents becomes even more crucial in studying official denial because the knowledge one seeks to illuminate denial is specifically the information that has often been edited, censored out, and thereby silenced. If one turns to society with the intent to find other sources of knowledge, the print media stands out as the richest and most easily accessible source, especially after the advent of mass printing. Newspapers, journals, and periodicals reveal the collective negotiations of socially significant meaning, but all too often, it can still be difficult to capture the entire spectrum of what is being discussed, especially if the print medium is censored by the state. Printed memoirs, however, tend to escape such censoring over the long term because of the state's inability to closely monitor them on the one hand and to differentiate and censor what is implied in personal recollections on the other.

Based on this reasoning, I decided to systematically read all books printed in Turkey in Turkish after the Latin script reform of 1928 that contained people's recollections of what went on around them, from the year 1789 to 2009. I did so with the intent to identify and focus on those books that contained information on collective violence, modernity, collective emotions, and significant events in general and the Armenians in particular. Most of these books were printed as individual memoirs (*hatırat* in Turkish), but I also included others that were initially printed as letters, diaries, and chronicles. Hence what guided me was not the title of the books but rather the content. After systematically reading approximately 700 books, I came up with 310 memoir writers' accounts[159] that constitute the database of this empirical study. The citations of these accounts are in Appendix A, thus presented separately from the bibliography.

It is important to understand how and why these memoirs enable me to access the process of denial in Ottoman and Turkish history. First, the main limitation of memoirs as a historical source is that it is hard to move beyond the personal idiosyncrasies of individuals in general and their political orientations in particular. Indeed, whenever I talked about my sources with colleagues, they would immediately point out this limitation. And their argument certainly stands if one focuses on individual memory; what I am doing here, however, is to move beyond individual memory to capture the *collective* memory of society through my systematic and exhaustive research of all printed memoirs. By doing so, I move beyond the individual recollections and interpretations to capture patterns of meaning that exist within society at large. Memoirs also epistemologically restore the agency of interpretation to historical actors who actually live in that society at that particular period, and who generate meaning that survives across time and space by making it to print. This is especially significant in the analysis of non-Western societies, where, as Edward Said first cautioned,[160] temporally dominant Western scholars and/or their analytical frameworks employed by others co-opt the local agency of "others."

In the case of analyzing denial, one needs to recover silences, traverse the often conscious withholding of information and selective recall, and expose the presentation of half-truths. The only way to unearth and depict what is not said is to immerse oneself in what is said by hundreds of voices present in the memoirs. As these voices are heard, they transform into pieces of a puzzle, complementing each other and thereby often illuminating what had been silenced by some. Also, these voices enable one to more beyond the hegemony of the public, formal, and institutional knowledge that tends to dominate our societies at the expense of the informal, private, and often intimate details and emotions of everyday life. And within the print medium, the affective element that constitutes denial can only be located in memoirs because it is only in the realm of informal, private, and intimate recollections that people move beyond structural constraints to reveal the affective dimension of their lives.

After pointing out the advantages of employing memoirs as the source through which to study denial, I also should delineate their limitations. The most significant drawback is their reliance on the print medium. Especially in premodern empires before the advent of mass printing and mass education, the literacy rate was around 10 percent at best, rising to about 40 percent in the nineteenth century.[161] Printed memoirs thus privilege the voices not only of the literate but of the even smaller group among them whose voices made it to the print medium. Because culture is predicated on meanings that survive, past cultures in history tend to be overdetermined by literate recollections. Sources such as songs, stories, and material artifacts would have been able to overcome the limitations of literacy, but these do not exist in as much abundance as written texts; I assume the quantitative wealth of memoirs makes up for their limitations in representation. Mass printed memoirs are also coeval with modernity and therefore also favor the urban, male representatives of the dominant majority, where the majority is defined in terms of the characteristics of those who control most of the resources deemed valuable by a particular society—in this empirical case, the Sunni Muslim male state and government officials who are ethnically Turkish.

As the ensuing discussion indicates, however, there are numerous female, Kurdish, or non-Muslim memoir writers who help to counterbalance this concentration. In addition, in the 220 years of history analyzed here, the memories of those who witnessed the transition from empire to republic from the 1900s to the 1920s stand out. This generation, born in the 1880s, not only recognized the significance of the historical transformation they were engaged in but also wrote about it and recounted it for their peers and for generations to come. One could argue that the 1880s generation distilled the imperial trauma; they were followed after the transition to the republic by the 1940s generation, which in turn negotiated what happened once the republican state repression abated toward the end of the Cold War. As such, the 1940s generation defined the republican trauma, struggling to formulate a future vision for generations to come.

I conclude this discussion by recounting two observations that surprised me the most in my analysis of these memoirs: the first concerns the practice of the public-private divide in that very few of the writers discussed their immediate family lives, privileging much more their interpretations of, reactions to, and negotiations of events and ideas circulating around them on a daily basis. The second relates to the analysis of denial in that I was pleasantly amazed by how much information was available in these memoirs to help reconstruct the past, overcoming in the process that which was censored, silenced, and made absent by the process of denial. The memoirs aptly documented not only the collective violence, the reasons that generated and sustained it, but also the ensuing justification that ultimately subverted acknowledgment, leading instead to denial.

Here I will describe the process through which I constructed my database because it is especially important to point out how technological tools made it possible for me to employ such a large number of memoirs efficiently. Once I had read and selected one or more books by particular writers, I created a computer entry for each one, first summarizing the highlights of the writer's life in terms of career, political orientation, reason for penning the memoir, and messages conveyed. Concomitantly, I researched the secondary literature to gather as much information on the writers as possible. I then took extensive notes in English and simultaneously translated significant quotations. I read through and sorted the material into four time periods structured in relation to the collective violence against Armenians, namely, the imperial (1789–1907), Young Turk (1908–18), early republican (1919–73), and late republican (1974–2009) periods, complementing the last period with my personal recollections, especially because these years corresponded to my early adulthood in Turkey. I identified patterns of collective memory in each period, constructing a narrative that was based on generalized observations supported by at least three or more sources. It was surprising to witness how many of the sources agreed on particular interpretations of meaning, regardless of the writers' political orientations, revealing to me the advantages processing such a large number of texts. The computer analysis also made it easy to reconstruct profiles of prominent imperial and republican leaders, identifying the available information on particular individuals across hundreds of accounts.

Hence, hundreds of printed memoirs of those who lived in Turkey during the period under examination, namely, from 1789 to 2009, constitute the main empirical source of this book. Because the main contention of the Turkish official narrative is that almost all of the literature on the collective violence against the Armenians in general and in 1915 in particular had been produced outside of Turkey in Western languages with the express intent to "undermine the Turkish state and society," it was crucial to rely on source material generated by those who lived in Turkey and who wrote about what they experienced for a Turkish-speaking audience. Also significant was the parameter that these had all been accessible to Turkish state and society in print because only then could the Turkish official narrative be challenged with source material generated in Turkey, mostly by ethnic Turks, that had been accessible all along to the Turkish reading audience. And, unlike the documents in the state archives, these memoirs had never been fully brought under the scrutiny and control of the Turkish state because they were haphazardly published throughout two centuries. The script in which they were printed also changed during this process.

The Arabic-scripted Ottoman in which some had initially been penned gave way, after the 1928 republican script reform, to Latin-scripted Turkish. Because the memoirs were thus produced across such a wide time span and in two disparate scripts, the Turkish state probably could not conceive that they could be systematically collected and utilized as a significant empirical resource. Indeed, there has been no systematic analysis of such memoirs in Turkish until now. This book thus employs only those memoirs printed in Turkey in Latin-scripted Turkish based on the argument that Turkish state and society had access to these memoirs but still sustained denial.

The publication of these memoirs was not altogether free and accessible as freedom of expression and thought is still legally sanctioned in Turkey today. For instance, insulting the Turkish society and state has been a legally actionable crime in republican history up to the present. All publishers that print books for the Turkish public are still required by the state to submit a copy to the Office of the Public Prosecutor to be cleared of such potential insults. In the past, many memoirs could not survive such official scrutiny. A case in point is the memoir of the Ottoman and later republican Turkish general Kazım Karabekir. This notable general of the independence struggle provided a narrative of the struggle that allegedly contradicted the one provided by his military comrade Mustafa Kemal Atatürk. Because Atatürk's account had become the official state narrative, Karabekir's memoir was initially censored and not published for almost fifty years. At present, even though many memoirs escape such censorship, those pertaining to the collective violence against the Armenians during 1915–23 still encounter special scrutiny, if not lawsuits. Yet, Turkish publishers have been able to circumvent this official control due to a built-in bureaucratic glitch. Because there often was a large backlog at the Office of the Public Prosecutor in processing these memoirs, after publishers had submitted their required copy for official examination, they immediately distributed the books without awaiting an official response, ostensibly to start recouping their cost. As a consequence, many publishers managed to avoid censorship for at least three to six months, after which their books sometimes were pulled off the market. The often small numbers in which these memoirs were initially printed also made systematic analysis of the memoirs extremely difficult. Thankfully, increased access to knowledge through the virtual sphere, as well as rich collections of such memoirs, especially outside of Turkey in Western Europe and the United States, made the job of collecting them surmountable. Initially, there was a state policy in the Turkish republic that allowed only those memoirs that supported the official state stand to be transliterated. Then, first after the end of single-party rule in the 1950s, and again at the end of the Cold War, much more contentious memoirs critical of the republican leadership were published, thereby eventually covering the spectrum of political stands.

Most of the historical actors in the memoirs turned out to be state officials who had been influential in determining the course of events during the imperial and republican periods. This was not surprising, since the production of knowledge in every society is often influenced, if not directly controlled, by the dominant social group. And the informal narrative employed led some officials to either consciously or subconsciously reveal more than they had intended. Hence, what made such memoirs unique was that they constituted, rather than the "official memory" of the Ottoman and Turkish state, the interpretations of Ottomans and Turks who lived through and observed what took place around them. By systematically reading hundreds of such memoirs, I was able to discern social patterns that ran through them all. The memoirs thus provided access to the world of meaning on the issue of denial that went beyond the one revealed in official state documents. I further supplemented this primary empirical source with substantial research I conducted on the topic through secondary sources.

Let me now provide detailed information on the memoir writers, across time and space and in relation to their gender, religion, ethnicity, profession, and the like. I employed the 356 works of 307 memoir writers (some writers had produced more than one text recounting their memories). Of these writers, the vast majority (293, or 94.8 percent) were male, and 16 (5.2 percent) were female, not an unexpected breakdown given that women were educated and also took a public stand by writing books much less often than men did. Because education often brought power along with it, it is not surprising that most of these memoir writers belonged to either the upper class or the educated upper middle class. The divide across religion favored Muslims, who penned 290 (93.8 percent) of the memoirs, with non-Muslims writing only 19 (6.1 percent) of the memoirs. This distribution is also to be expected, especially given the decreasing number of non-Muslims living in Turkey over time. In relation to ethnicity, 271 of the memoir writers were Turks (87.7 percent), with 12 Kurds (3.9 percent), 9 Armenians (2.9 percent), 7 Arabs (2.3 percent), 6 Jews (1.9 percent), 1 Greek Rum (0.3 percent), and 3 (1 percent) other, mostly Europeans living in the empire. I tried especially hard to find memoirs from those outside of the dominant Muslim Turkish majority in order to access the critical perspectives of the less powerful in relation to collective violence. As expected, especially the memoirs of Kurds and Armenians provided ample information on such collective violence. Interestingly, the distribution also reflects the many social groups that were present within the empire. Of course, there are many within the category of Turks who are of Balkan, Anatolian, or Caucasian origin, but it was hard to fully determine the subidentities, revealing that the nationally constructed Turkish identity did start to dominate throughout this period.

One major concern I had pertained to the political orientation of the memoir writers; given that the CUP had played such a significant role at the end of the empire, through the independence struggle into the republic, I was concerned that its nationalist political stands would dominate the narratives, eliminating the possibility of capturing many instances of collective violence it committed. Yet I was surprised to find out that the patriotism of CUP members led them to actually boast about the collective violence they committed against the Armenians, often considering such viciousness a necessary step in nation-building. Hence what they committed often came through in the works of 72 (23.3 percent) memoir writers who explicitly stated that they belonged to the CUP. And if these writers silenced, repressed, or subverted the violence they committed, the 24 (7.8 percent) memoir writers belonging to the Freedom and Entente Party who were their adversaries made sure to outline such violence in great detail. Part of the reason the CUP's collective violence was publicly documented in spite of the foundational role of the CUP in executing the independence struggle and founding the Turkish republic may be due to the adversarial stand Mustafa Kemal Atatürk took against the CUP with the intent to seize power for the new cadre he formed from those loyal to him. This political stand may have emboldened many to take similar stands, presenting their past violence within the context of Turkish nationalism. Still, the amount of self-censoring among CUP members was very high, with almost all of them silencing what they did during the imperial period; it was often as if they had been reborn during the independence struggle that led to the foundation of the Turkish republic. After all, this was exactly the time when they purposefully erased their imperial identities and activities, assuming instead a new, sanitized republican identity. Just as significant in determining past collective violence committed against the Armenians were the remaining 203 (65.7 percent) memoir writers who did not assert a particular political preference. I think this distribution across the political spectrum as well as the large number of memoir writers I included in the study alleviate the possibility of ideological bias.

Perhaps most significant is the distribution of memoir writers according to their professions. It was not surprising that state officials dominated, accounting for 180 (58.3 percent) of the memoir writers and reflecting the heavy role the state played in both the empire and the republic. These officials were almost evenly divided between bureaucrats and soldiers; 95 (30.7 percent) memoir writers had held significant administrative positions, and 85 (27.5 percent) held important military positions. Given that these two groups were state leaders, their writings provide as close an alternate narrative to the Turkish official narrative on the topic as possible. Among the memoir writers of military origin, 13 (4.2 percent) were also members of paramilitary organizations, thereby belonging to clandestine groups that emerged during and after Young Turk rule and continued into the republic up to the present, engaging in extralegal violence in the process. The remaining 113 (36.6 percent) writers were civilian professionals, who often made a living as journalists, academics, or public intellectuals. This distribution among state officials and civilians also generated sufficient information on the history of collective violence against non-Muslim minorities in general and Armenians in particular during the imperial and republican periods. I should also note that 7 (2.3 percent) of the memoir writers were also former perpetrators who either mentioned the collective violence they committed only briefly in passing or silenced it completely. Still, the rather large number demonstrates the success with which the perpetrators were rehabilitated during the republican era.

In summary, then, memoirs provided a very rich source that captured not only the generation of meaning in Ottoman imperial and Turkish republican societies but also the occurrence of collective violence during the same period. Ultimately, structural and affective elements intersected over time and across space to produce not acknowledgment of past collective violence but instead denial. I conclude this chapter with a discussion of denial of collective violence against the Armenians that was layered over time.

IV. Denial in Ottoman Imperial and Turkish Republican History

Why do states and societies in general and the Turkish state and society in particular deny acts of collective violence embedded in their pasts and also their present? This question informed my research here. In the Turkish case, even though the denial of the 1915–17 Armenian Genocide was my starting point, the analysis of collective violence against the Armenians, I realized, neither started nor ended there. As a consequence, I expanded my research to cover a 220-year period from 1789 to 2009. I then divided these years in accordance with the major acts of collective violence committed against the Armenians, namely, into the imperial period (1789–1907), Young Turk period (1908–18), early republican period (1919–73), and late republican period (1974–2009). The process of denial, I argue here, consists of the interaction of the structural elements of collective violence and situated modernity, and the affective elements of collective emotions and legitimating events. Methodologically, I defined memoirs as the historical source through which to study the elements of denial in each period, and I analyzed 307 memoir writers' works in depth. The following four chapters discuss, using details provided by the memoirs, the elements of collective violence, modernity, collective emotions, and legitimating events that coalesce to form a particular denial at a particular time. The narratives of denial in each period are based almost exclusively on memoirs, but I do provide extensive references to secondary literature on Ottoman and Turkish history at the beginning of each chapter; even though I did not have space to quote from the works of my colleagues, their works nevertheless informed my interpretations. I now conclude this introduction with brief synopses of each chapter.

Imperial Denial of the Origins of Violence, 1789-1907

The Ottoman social system was predicated on the rule of the sultan through the authority he delegated to his extended household of administrators. The sultan legitimated and sustained his rule through acting in accordance with the ideal of the imperial circle of justice (*daire-i adliye*). The circle was predicated on the traditional maxim that "rulers have no power without soldiers, no soldiers without money, no money without their subjects' comfort, and no comfort without justice (İnalcık 1964: 42–3)." Hence the sultan and his extended household including the military (namely *askeri*, "people of the sword and later the pen") operated alongside the judiciary (*ilmi*, "people of knowledge") to deliver comfort to the sultan's subjects. In return, the subjects, particularly peasants, artisans, and merchants, were responsible for paying mainly agricultural and commercial taxes. And in doing so, they enabled the sultan to procure the necessary economic resources to run his system of rule. This functional interdependence worked insofar as the social groups in each category worked properly, monitored their activities and the boundaries of their communities, and, if necessary, were monitored by the state. The system assumed that all recognized the legitimacy of the sultan, that the sultan had resources to distribute, that his administrators put the sultan's interests before their own, and that the merchants, artisans, and peasants among whom the non-Muslims were structurally located were content with the taxes they paid and the justice they received. During the nineteenth century, the resources upon which the system was predicated decreased as the empire started to lose land and as more of the taxes were locally retained, and as changing war technology necessitated the import of arms and armaments from the West. Hence, local conditions interacted with Western European elements to create imperial modernity.

Because the payments made to the West had to be in cash, the land tenure system based on payment in kind to the administrators gradually transformed, leading to the 1858 private property law that legally recognized the ownership of individuals over land that theoretically all belonged to the sultan who ruled the land in accordance with sharia (Islamic law). The state treasury became increasingly strapped for cash and, in turn, was unable to monitor the delivery of justice to the populace. The military institution spearheaded the reforms, receiving most of the dwindling resources. At the same time, non-Muslims in general and in the nineteenth century the Armenians in particular[162] continued to interact with Europe, becoming wealthy through engaging in trade with an expanding Europe on the one hand and adopting recent practices in secular education and political representation within their community on the other. These changes generated a divide between the secular reformists and religious clergy and the traditional elite families, one that was in turn overlaid by wealthy urban apolitical elites and their impoverished and therefore increasingly politicized rural peasant counterparts. The fragmentation within the Armenian community interacted with the diminished resources and administrative control of the sultan to generate increased anger and frustration among the administrators, most of whom were recruited from among the Sunni Muslim majority as well as within the Armenian community. Because the sultan could not monitor his subjects, and the elders within communities could not monitor their members, instances of collective violence spread throughout, taking the form of the 1894–96 massacres during which 100,000 to 300,000 Armenians lost their lives. The 1896 Ottoman Bank raid became the "legitimating event" that the sultan and many within the dominant Muslim majority seized upon to switch the blame for not only the raid but also the 1894–96 massacres on to an external actor, namely the meddling of the Great Powers. By doing so, the sultan averted taking responsibility for the failed domestic reforms that could not deliver justice to his subjects. So while the origins of the Armenian issue were domestic, it was presented by the sultan as internationally instigated. Hence the first denial of origins of the collective violence against the Armenians emerged during the imperial period.

Young Turk Denial of the Act of Violence, 1908–18

The consequences of the transformations in military education and training first became evident with the emergence of cohorts of officers trained in Western-style knowledge and skills that not only privileged acquired scientific knowledge over wisdom through experience but also created string of trust networks among officers that they drew upon to reform the empire after their vision rather than obeying or being loyal to the sultan's vision. The ensuing constitutional revolution of 1908 brought these Young Turks into power. Yet the transition from sacred to secular legitimacy was not an easy one, especially in terms of establishing rules for political representation and getting the populace to be loyal to the abstract constitution. As the political institution thus spearheaded modernity, the challenges the Young Turks faced in attaining legitimacy led them to first practice extralegal violence against their political opponents and then to execute the first military coup in 1913. It was also during this time that a series of wars started—seven years out of the ten-year Young Turk rule had wars—to not only continue the land loss but also generate feelings of animosity to difference: the Young Turks had a protonationalist agenda whereby they favored ethnically Turkish Sunni Muslims over all other subjects of the empire.

The fragmentation set in within the dominant Muslim majority as those who wanted to sustain the empire predicated on difference opposed the Young Turks to no avail. Set on monopolizing control over the political and economic spheres by any means necessary, they took on with extreme violence the one social group that posed a threat in both spheres, the Armenians, with the intent to exclude them from the nation they intended to build. Asia Minor comprised the ancestral lands of the Armenians, and they owned property and goods throughout the empire. Given the context of World War I, the Young Turk leaders assumed they could escape Western sanctions and annihilate the Armenian presence in the empire or at least reduce it to no more than 5 to 10 percent of the total population. In their stead, they would immediately locate Muslim refugees, under the assumption that they were replacing one human power with another, totally oblivious to the specialized knowledge and skills of the Armenians. The collective violence in the form of 1915–17 genocide brought the Armenians to the brink of physical and cultural extinction. The 1912–13 Balkan Wars preceding World War I had especially traumatized the Muslim populace of the imperial capital, who had never before witnessed such a large influx of desperate Muslim refugees. Blaming the Christian West for totally dismissing the Muslim loss and suffering, then facing a pincer movement by the British coming through the Dardanelles and the Russians through the Caucasus that they were sure would lead to Turk's racial extinction, and desperately looking for a homeland in Asia Minor for the Muslim Turks, rather than keeping the multiethnic population makeup, the Young Turks decided to annihilate the Armenian presence in the empire.

All memoir writers who discussed this horrid violence followed the same narrative pattern: they shifted easily from discussing the violence against the Armenians to mentioning the prior violence the Muslims had suffered in the Balkans, as if Muslims were seeking vengeance for what they had previously suffered. In the process, the memoir writers made an imagined leap not grounded in history. They overlooked the fact that the actors in the Balkans and Asia Minor were mutually exclusive; in addition, all the Armenians the Muslims attempted to eradicate were their own subjects, who had no protection and looked to their Ottoman state to provide that protection; instead, they were brutally destroyed. Yet this subversive connection to the Balkan suffering enabled the Young Turks to engage in the second denial of the act of collective violence against the Armenians: even though their intent all along had been destruction, they presented it to the public as Armenian "migration" to safe places. This constituted the most egregious Young Turk denial.

Early Republican Denial of the Actors of Violence, 1919–73

Upon establishing the new republic, the greatest challenge of former CUP leaders was to create a nation for the state they had managed to preserve. It was no accident that one of the first acts of parliament was to centralize and control all educational institutions, thereby privileging education and the control of knowledge production and distribution above all else. Educational institutions thus moved to the forefront of modernity. The first two republican generations were thus educated with a mythified version of the past cleansed of all violence committed by Turks, especially in the transition from empire to republic. The ensuing Second World War and the Cold War that followed ensured that such national knowledge production continued throughout into the 1990s. The former CUP leaders transitioned into republican heroes, with the collective violence they had committed whitewashed in the process. Because they were not held accountable for the violence they committed, violence became a normalized part of the modus operandi, now practiced to exclude others deemed not fit to be proper Turkish citizens. The decimated non-Muslim citizens no longer posed a political threat; their plundered wealth and properties were gradually exploited to boost state resources, create a Turkish bourgeoisie dependent on the state, and erase as many symbols of non-Muslim presence in the past as possible. Hence, the state expanded its control from the political to the economic sphere, making financial decisions based on state interests in general and national security concerns in particular. The ensuing economic crises were resolved by employing the legal system to try to strip the non-Muslims of the wealth they had left.

The pogroms of 6–7 September 1955 were such an attempt clandestinely organized by the military with the tacit approval of the civilian leaders. Because the state practice was to regard non-Muslims as an extension of Western powers, and because the state no longer had the international standing and power it once enjoyed, the republican leaders, military and civilian alike, tried to wield power by threatening the well-being of their own non-Muslim citizens. In this case, the idea had been to send a message to Greece: there had been tension between Turkey and Greece over the partition of Cyprus, with the local community of Greek Rum demanding additional territory. The republican state and government decided to teach Greece a lesson, by practicing violence against the local Greek Rum in the Turkish republic in particular, a violence that quickly spread to cover all non-Muslims.

In nationalist interpretations of the violence in the media and memoirs, the alleged betrayal of non-Muslim citizens collaborating with Western powers was brought up repeatedly, this time drawing a spurious connection with the 1919–22 military tribunals held at the imperial capital to try the perpetrators of the genocide. One mistrial was exploited to dismiss the veracity of Armenian claims of suffering on the one hand and to allege non-Muslim duplicity with the West on the other. Ironically, the tribunals were also employed to claim all the perpetrators had been punished, thereby whitewashing the stained pasts of republican leaders. This constituted the early republican denial of the actors of collective violence.

Late Republican Denial of the Responsibility for Violence, 1974–2009

With the gradual waning of the Cold War and the emergence of a new world economic order, the state could no longer sustain its monopoly over the economy. The economic institutions moved to the forefront of modernity as especially those formerly marginalized, religiously conservative businessmen in the provinces established direct connections with world markets, accumulating wealth in the process. Unlike their non-Muslim counterparts, these Muslim Turks were, albeit very reluctantly, allowed to transform their economic capital to political capital; they started to establish and finance religiously conservative political parties, the last one of which came to power in 2003 and is still in government today. Rather than propagating fear and anxiety over issues of national security, the new neoliberal stand of this party was to put the well-being and happiness of citizens before the interests of the state, with such happiness defined primarily in terms of consumption. The continually dwindling number of non-Muslims in Turkey further decimated their ability to have a public presence, except among liberal Turkish Muslim intellectuals there to promote democracy and rights in Turkey. And the state continued its practice of extralegal violence to suppress any criticism by singling out the weakest link, the least protected among such liberal critics, assassinating a Turkish-Armenian journalist.

Unlike what was witnessed during the aftermath of previous practices of violence, however, there was a public outcry as thousands marched in protest in İstanbul. Yet as in those instances, this protest came to naught as the new religiously conservative government followed in the footsteps of its predecessors by obfuscating the ensuing legal process, and none of those extralegal elements within the military and civilians who gave the orders to assassinate were brought to justice and punished. Instead, the media once again kept referring to a legitimating event in Turkey's recent past, namely, the 1974–85 assassinations abroad of Turkish diplomats by Armenian terrorists originating in Lebanon and the United States. Even though the Armenians of Turkey had no connections with these events, they were pressured and accused once again for collaborating with the enemy, and the violence committed against this journalist and other non-Muslims in Turkey was once again denied by constructing a faulty lineage of all Armenians as revolutionaries and terrorists always out to get Turks. This presumed reciprocity of violence was employed to officially portray not the Armenians but instead Turks as the victims, thereby engaging in the fourth and final late republican denial of responsibility of collective violence.

In summary, then, this introduction has presented the analytical framework of the book. It first discussed the complexity of denial and presented an approach to denial as a process articulated through the interaction of structural (collective violence and modernity) and affective (collective emotions and events) elements. This was followed by a discussion of these elements and their application to the empirical case of the Ottoman Empire and the Turkish republic. Finally, I emphasized that memoirs provided the most suitable empirical source through which to study the structural and affective elements. In the following chapters, I engage in a detailed analysis of imperial, Young Turk, early republican, and late republican denial through memoirs penned by 307 writers.

1

Imperial Denial of Origins of Violence, 1789–1907

> We may learn by three methods: first, by reflection, which is the noblest; second, by imitation, which is the easiest; and third, by experience, which is the bitterest.
>
> Confucius, Chinese philosopher, 551–479 B.C.E.

During March 1895, before spring thaw had even set in, Sadeddin Pasha received the imperial order of Sultan Abdülhamid II to immediately embark on a twenty-month-long mission to the eastern provinces with a large retinue. He was appointed the head of the Investigative Commission to inspect the Armenian massacres that had occurred in the provinces of Gümüşhane, Erzurum, Bitlis, and Van. Fortuitously, his handwritten partial diary covering the five-month period from 27 January to 1 June 1896 has survived to this day.[1] Unlike the official reports the pasha must have submitted upon his return, this private account provides a unique and intimate gaze into his interpretation of these violent events. Especially significant are drafts of the speeches the pasha delivered to the perpetrators (namely, the Muslim Turks and Kurds) and the victims (the Armenians). The disparate tones of these speeches highlight the distinct locations of these two social groups within Ottoman society and the escalating polarization between them.

Sadeddin Pasha's speeches are clear, concise, and pedagogically very engaging. When his audience is the Muslim Kurdish and Turkish perpetrators, the Pasha connects to them through their one mutual identity, the religion of Islam. He explains why they should be treating the non-Muslim subjects residing among them justly because that is what Islamic principles necessitate:[2]

> My coreligionists! Our exalted prophet [Muhammad] decrees "he who tortures Christians or Jews cannot find comfort in heaven." Our leader [Caliph] Ömer Efendi likewise showed mercy to non-Muslims

> in the places he conquered, protecting their honor, life, and properties. Likewise the Ottoman sultan abided by these principles and offered the same protection for six hundred years. You too got along with [the non-Muslims] as brothers of the same fatherland. Now you know this is a religious duty and the [Ottoman] state is powerful enough to punish those who make a mistake in performing this duty.... I am here to deliver the advice of the Ottoman sultan [without whose leadership] humans will be like a flock of sheep abandoned on a field; some would fall prey to wolves, others would be stolen by thieves, and still others would perish from neglect. That is why divine orders need to be obeyed.

The pasha thus states that the just treatment of non-Muslims ought to be the religious duty of all Muslim subjects; failure to do so, he is not afraid to point out, would bring punishment upon them in the future. The pasha's mention of accountability is significant here because his later remarks reveal that it was primarily the lack of accountability that led to the 1893–96 Armenians massacres: such violence occurred when the sultan's Muslim subjects took justice into their own hands. Even though there is the promise of accountability for future infractions, however, the pasha does not even mention the possibility of punishment for the violence already committed.

Instead, he elaborates on the adverse consequences of past violence, in relation to how its public visibility brings international pressure upon the sultan. His argument is based on modernity's perils: new technological elements of communication immediately diffuse knowledge of such violence everywhere:[3]

> This is the age of communication... within half an hour, we hear throughout the world what happens here today. Christian states will not permit the Muslim populace to discipline Armenians in an irregular manner.... [If you insist on doing so, then the Ottoman state] loses the chance to discipline the Armenians... and has to resort to drafting more reserves from among you. [This in turn] increases expenses coming out of you as you and your recruited men will leave all work and fields unattended.... So [in the end] you end up suffering for this action.... [In addition] as Christian states know the principles of our religion and the sayings of our prophet I mentioned, what are we to answer them if they ask us why we do not act in accordance with it?

Sadeddin Pasha's negative association with modernity highlights not the increased transparency of public action but instead the pressures such action brings upon the Ottoman state. Tools of modernity like the telegraph enable Christian states, he argues, to monitor the empire and then employ the gathered information to intervene in its domestic affairs. Interestingly, the pasha seems more worried that the Muslim subjects were actually caught by Christian states in executing violence than that they engaged in such violence in the first place. Subsequently, rather than meting out punishment for their actions, he instead addresses and assuages their emotions, particularly their fears and anxieties:[4]

> Do not presume that the [Ottoman] state has given or will give in to the Armenians. They are one-sixth or one-tenth your size [in population]. You are famous warriors [whereas] they make a mess of using arms. Do not think that they could handle you and win their principality by force.... There is no truth to the news you have heard that the Armenians have been granted a principality. In this [Van] province, there are three Muslims for every Armenian. How is it possible for one Armenian to dominate three Muslims?... [Also] Muslims benefit more from the state reforms as roads are built, ships operated, and mines worked.... Why then [in spite of all this], did you murder Armenians, rob their villages, and seize their goods?

The pasha acknowledges the rumors about the Armenian subjects' desire to have their own principality in the eastern regions, but he dismisses the actualization of such a possibility based on two factors that make Muslim subjects dominant in the empire: they monopolized the right to bear arms for centuries, and they are also more numerous in the eastern provinces. What he silences in the process is the third factor, that the Ottoman legal system based on Islam also favors Muslims over all other subjects, a factor that have in turn may shed light on the sources of Armenian discontent. The pasha's final rhetorical question acknowledges the collective violence committed against the Armenians but oddly fails to note that the Ottoman state should and would hold the Muslim perpetrators accountable for it.

The speech Sadeddin Pasha then delivers to the Armenian victims is very different in tone. He starts off by noting in general terms that "your exalted sultan's desire is to unequivocally prevent the spilling of blood."[5] There is no acknowledgment of or apology for the Armenian blood that had already been spilled. Nor is there chastisement of Muslim perpetrators who engaged in such violence. The pasha connects to the Armenian subjects not through their religion but instead through the common historical heritage they all share. After presenting a detailed history of Armenians, Kurds, and Turks in Asia Minor, he states that the Armenian subjects have to be grateful to the Ottoman sultan for preserving their community within his empire:[6]

> "Compatriots!... The... populace you see around here today [were in the past all] Meds.... But, as they were prevented from speaking their

> languages and practicing their traditions ... [they all] turned into Turks, Kurds, or Armenians.... Three hundred eighty years ago, the Ottoman state made the rest of the world tremble ... [and] it was then that you entered under Ottoman rule, [whereas] you had [previously] been under the domination of the Kurds.... [If the Ottoman state had then forced Islam onto you], after a couple of generations, there would not have been any Armenians left.

Sadeddin Pasha's use of "compatriots" reveals how he connects to the Armenians through a term brought about by modernity as well as through the land they all came to share. He also highlights the virtues of Islam in structurally separating them as a community, a separation, he argues, that enabled Armenians to survive through history as a community. Silenced in this account is the downside of the organization of non-Muslims into communities, a negative dimension that would have once again shed light into Armenian discontent. How the Armenians benefited from modernity is discussed next; they gained financially from the ascendance of a market-centered system as they enriched themselves and also benefited politically as some assumed important state posts.[7] Silenced in this account are the impoverishment faced by rural-based Armenian peasants on the one hand and the unsystematic nature through which such state appointments were executed on the other. Instead, upset that the Armenians are not grateful for what they had been given, the pasha concludes his speech with a threat:[8]

> You are traveling down a wrong path, with the danger of death awaiting you. Here, [I as the representative of the Ottoman] state, notify you. Give up, do not deviate from the path you have been following for the last four centuries; do not part from loyalty. You will regret it. And regrets after the fact would be of no use. What you hope and desire does not have [the slightest] chance [of success] because it does not fit the European political balance. Most of those with whom you share the same race are not in our country, but [located] in Iran and Russia. Take this [fact] into account. Do not plunge into any rash acts. If you do, you will find yourselves alone with the Kurds. [And] do not forget that in this [Van] province there are three Kurds for every Armenian and that [while] Kurds are warriors, Armenians [are] cowards from birth. In addition, one can guess where the Armenians' lack of familiarity with arms will lead. I think you can grasp this with the intelligence that has caused you to produce these terrible incidents.

The pasha predicts failure for the Armenian subjects based on four factors: political interests of European states do not favor Armenian independence;

Armenians are scattered across the Ottoman, Russian, and Persian empires and therefore lack the population concentration necessary for political liberation; the Ottoman state would not protect its own Armenian subjects against the Kurds if and when conflict emerges between the two; and, finally, Armenians lack the fundamental courage and skills necessary for military victory.

Once again, significant silences prevail in this prediction. That some Balkan provinces were previously able to attain their independence in spite of, at times, lesser numbers is conveniently overlooked. Also not mentioned is the reason that Armenians are "cowards from birth": their *dhimmi* status in Islamic law forbade them for centuries from bearing arms.[9] Probably the most disturbing silence is the Ottoman state's threat of withdrawing its protection over Armenians. The pasha states in no uncertain terms that if Armenians were to get into conflict with the Kurds, the Ottoman state will cease to protect its own Armenian subjects. Implied in this drastic action is the pasha's—and also the Ottoman state's—association of the violent acts of some Armenian revolutionaries that began to escalate during this time with the entire Armenian community, displaying a willingness to punish all Armenian subjects for the violence of a few. In short, the pasha's two speeches make it hard to distinguish the innocent from the guilty, the victim from the perpetrator. Even though approximately 300,000 Armenian subjects were massacred during this violence as opposed to possibly 15,000 Muslims, the pasha's speeches seem to target and threaten the Armenian subjects more than the Muslim ones, almost entirely blaming them for bringing this collective violence against themselves.

Why does an Ottoman official sent to investigate the 1893–96 Armenian massacres not acknowledge the committed collective violence? In seeking answers to this question, the chapter analyzes the larger context that eventually produced such massacres. Temporally, it traces the origins of such collective violence to the interaction of local structural divides with Ottoman situated modernity that commenced with Sultan Selim III's accession to the throne in 1789, when modernizing imperial reforms became systematic. Such interaction escalated social polarization between the Muslims and non-Muslims in the ensuing century, one that combined with emotions to eventually trigger collective violence against the Armenian subjects. Yet, rather than acknowledging this collective violence, Ottoman state and society employed a legitimating event, namely, the 1896 Ottoman Bank raid by Armenian revolutionaries, to justify the past collective violence. Western European intervention and the ensuing safe passage of these violent revolutionaries to Europe thereby enabled the first phase of denial, namely, the denial of origins. Even though the origins of the collective violence committed against Armenians were domestic, the official narrative of Ottoman state and society argued that the Armenian revolts leading to massacres were externally instigated by the Great Powers with the intent to destablize the Ottoman Empire.

Ottoman Imperial Structure of Difference

All empires are predicated on three fundamental principles. First, unlike nation-states based on an often secular contractual arrangement, empires are organized around a ruler who legitimates his position through sacred and often religious attributes. Second, unlike nation-states based on horizontal integration, with all citizens having the same relationship to the state, empires comprise many diverse communities and social groups that are vertically integrated, thereby sustaining their differences. Third, unlike nation-states that have clearly defined and monitored boundaries that are defended at all costs, empires are based on the principle of expansion where many different groups and communities are incorporated into the imperial body as human resources.

The Ottoman Empire was organized along these principles as well. It transformed into an empire around the rule of Sultan Mehmed II (r. 1444–46, 1451–81) upon the conquest of Constantinople; Sultan Selim I (r. 1512–20) then furthered the sacredness of the Ottoman dynasty by conquering Egypt and assuming the title of the caliph of Islam. This ancestry enabled Sultan Süleyman I (r. 1520–66) to develop the main legal parameters of Ottoman imperial rule. The state thus predicated on the Ottoman dynasty persisted until the rule of Sultan Vahdeddin (r. 1918–22), who lost the sovereignty of rule at the end of World War I with the advent of the Turkish independence struggle that led to the establishment of the Turkish republic in 1923; subsequently, Sultan Abdülmecid II (r. 1922–24) lost the title of caliphate that had initially survived the transition into the republic, thereby effectively ending the Ottoman Empire as a political entity.

The Ottoman sultans ruled through the delegation of their authority to officials who symbolically constituted the members of their household.[10] The sultan's officials delivered justice and provided security to the subjects in return for taxes and, mostly in the case of Muslim Turks, military conscription. At its height in the sixteenth century, the empire comprised a vast expanse of land stretching from the Caucasus, the Arabian Peninsula, and North Africa to eastern Europe. The local arrangements varied, as some provinces were directly ruled while others had local sovereignty but were nominally a part of the empire as they paid tributes.

In addition to the sultan's laws (*kanun*), imperial rule was legally based on the Islamic law of sharia. The principles of the Islamic legal system took root and reproduced over time to shape social relations within the empire. The fundamental horizontal divide was between the Muslims and the rest; while the Muslims and especially the Ottoman Turks became the dominant social group, non-Muslim subjects were initially organized into the three communities of the Greek Orthodox also known as "Rum,"[11] the Armenians, and the

Jews. These self-administering non-Muslim communities were protected by the state in return for paying a special poll tax (*cizye*), not bearing arms, and wearing special clothing that visibly differentiated them from the Muslims. Over time, however, this initial legal divide separating the Muslims and non-Muslims transformed into a structural one: non-Muslim subjects who could not serve in the military instead excelled in trade and commerce. Male non-Muslims who were not permitted to marry across the religious divide lived alongside Muslims without socially integrating into the dominant social group. The initial legal arrangement thus produced a structural divide over time as the Muslims specialized in the affairs of the empire through three professions: in administration (*mülkiye*), legal and religious affairs (*ilmiye*), and the military (*seyfiye*). The professions in the domain of trade and commerce were mostly relegated to non-Muslims.

The Ottoman Empire initially expanded until the end of the seventeenth century, when it was challenged by other empires, namely, the Habsburgs in the west, the Russians in the north, and the Persians in the east. From the eighteenth century on, such constriction had adverse effects on the Ottoman social structure. The lucrative professions in administration, jurisprudence, and the military started to lose their allure as resources began to dry up. The constant warfare that the empire engaged in did not generate new resources but instead consumed them in ever-increasing proportions.[12] In addition to the dearth of material wealth, human resources also suffered as more and more Muslim soldiers lost their lives during military service that became lengthier in duration. Concomitantly, the Industrial Revolution in Western Europe escalated the significance of trade and commerce, thereby improving the position of the non-Muslim subjects in the empire. Hence, from the eighteenth century onward and especially during the nineteenth century, the Ottoman social structure was turned almost upside down as the dominant Muslims became poorer while the non-Muslims living in urban areas were enriched through trade and commerce with the West.

Contemporaneous Ottoman memoirs give meaning to this general portrayal, revealing how Ottoman society renegotiated its imperial status during the eighteenth and nineteenth centuries. One eminent grand vizier noted that his predecessor had articulated the four principles of Ottoman imperial rule as "the Muslim nation, the Turkish state, the Ottoman dynasty, and İstanbul as the imperial capital."[13] Hence not only was the dominant group in the empire defined as Muslims, but the state belonging to the Turks ascertained Muslim Turkish dominance in governance. This imperial structure was headed by the Ottoman dynasty located at the imperial capital.[14] An Ottoman chronicler then described the origins of the Ottoman social structure and the ensuing religious divide within as follows:[15]

> [Historically], certain conditions had been issued in return for the protection of life and property and the freedom of religious practice that the Caliph Omar bestowed upon the Christian populace at the conquest of Jerusalem. These conditions then became practiced in all Muslim states. Prohibitions such as the requirement of those who were not a part of the Muslim populace to dress in attire of different colors and shapes, to not mount horses within the city limits, and to not carry arms were also in effect. These differences pertaining to local and social issues never impacted their real rights because those in power had to make judgments for both the Muslims and the non-Muslims in accordance with the same law. There were no separate judgments for separate classes as had been the practice in the European feudal system. [Non-Muslim subjects referred to as] *reaya* had fully gotten used to these conditions.

Hence Ottoman officials not only legitimated the existence of non-Muslims in their midst through Islamic practice but also naturalized this difference by assuming that the non-Muslims of the empire were as content with this arrangement as the Muslims. How this initial legal divide eventually transformed into a structural one is clear as the chronicler then noted, in the same paragraph, the gradual specialization of Muslims as opposed to non-Muslims.[16]

> As is known, those non-Muslim subjects we call "*reaya*" were not a part of the dominant nation [*hakim-i millet*] and instead [actually served] like the latter's working capital. Not only were their property, lives, and honor under the security of the sharia, but they had also acquired significant permits in agriculture, arts, industry, and commerce. As the dominant nation [of Turkish Muslims] was responsible for state administration and military service, it did not at all engage in these economic issues and left these matters to the [non-Muslim] *reaya*.... The latter were the laborers and producers of the country who made the most money through their work. Since they suffered no losses in population due to participation in wars... the *reaya* villages always appeared more prosperous than the Muslim ones. That this valuable social group was necessary for the country and that they [therefore] had to be protected had been constantly made clear through imperial orders, proclamations, and laws.

This Ottoman ethnic division of labor articulated by many contemporaneous officials demonstrates how the Muslims and non-Muslims complemented each other in theory. Yet how did this translate into practice? Contemporaneous memoirs provide ample evidence on how the Muslim Turks were steered toward certain state-related careers as opposed to other civilian ones often manned by non-Muslims. This dramatic reaction that one journalist recounted is typical:[17]

> My grandmother had showered me with affection [imagining me] as a future district governor. . . . When I told her about my choice of profession, it is impossible to describe the deep astonishment on that old woman's face. . . . She held her head with her two hands and shouted: "Lord help us! What do I hear in my last moments! Is this an indication of doomsday? My son, you will be a tradesman then! Pity all my labor!" She sobbed violently and muttered in between the sobs, "Who would give their daughter to a tradesman. And I had such dreams for you!"

How such a professional divide between the Muslims and non-Muslims also translated into their use of social space is evident in the frequent recollections of neighborhood children; it becomes virtually impossible for members of either community to venture into the social space of the other. Another journalist remembered his Balkan childhood in Usturumca near Salonica as follows:[18]

> We would go up to the hills and throw stones with our slingshots at the Christian neighborhoods. The Christian children would [then] immediately go to the opposite hills with their slingshots and war with us. This went on for hours. We would get excited as if we were in a national war and continued until we were able to chase the infidel children away. As the enemy withdrew from the war, we spread out onto the mountains with yells, gathered crocuses, and returned to town like heroes who had won wars. While we were still children, they instilled animosity in us toward the Christians. And since we did not know any better, we regarded the Christian children who were infidels as the enemy. They were not [yet] Greek and we were not [yet] Turkish. Back then, society was divided into two, as Christian and Muslim.

This recollection of spatial separation of Muslims and non-Muslims through symbolic violence in western parts of the empire was widespread, with similar recollections registered by a statesman on the Black Sea coast in Sinop, a pasha at the imperial capital, and a brigadier general in Erzurum to the east.[19] Yet this symbolic violence was often not equal in that the dominant Turkish Muslim majority often prevailed over the non-Muslims, both in childhood and later as adults.[20] Hence religious differences were negotiated in a manner that gave non-Muslim subjects less power to retaliate and fewer positions to assume in Ottoman society.[21]

What, then, were the main signifiers of social identity in the empire? Even though Abdurrahman Şeref Efendi highlighted the significance of the non-Muslim subjects of the empire as a resource-producing social group, how the latter were actually treated within Ottoman society and how they interpreted the legal arrangement are still unclear. It is evident that during the late nineteenth century, however, identities among the dominant Muslim Turks were locally defined as geographical origins prevailed both at schools and thereafter.[22] Also during this time, the concepts of Turkishness and who was a Turk were frequently discussed. In remembering the first time the concept emerged, a novelist stated:[23]

> I do not really remember when I called myself a Turk. In our childhood, Turk meant vulgar and wild [*kaba ve yabani*]. We were of the community of Islam and Ottoman. In the books explaining the principles of Islam [*ilmihal*], we learned that religion and nationality were one and the same. The word fatherland [*vatan*] was forbidden.... We had been subjects of the sultan. At the end of the school week, we lined up and shouted "long live our sultan!"... We had no knowledge about state affairs as these were not discussed in our presence lest we would talk about it in other contexts.

Still, this naturalized dominance based on the religion of Islam did contain an undercurrent of the hegemonic Turkish ethnicity. For instance, one Muslim official noted, "One night [when I was seven] my father called me to his side; he had formed the habit of giving me advice. 'Son,' he said, 'even though we are called the Ottoman state, never forget that we are Turks. Never tolerate the belittlement of Turkishness.' "[24] Given that a substantial proportion of the Ottoman Empire consisted not of Turks but of Arabs, Greeks, Armenians, Bulgarians, and Serbians, the prejudice and discrimination against the non-Muslims emerged most saliently when one delved into everyday interactions. The innate dominance of the Turks that gradually became acknowledged contained many references to non-Muslims that were at best disparaging.

Probably the instance that best revealed the naturalized dominance of the Muslim Turkish majority[25] was ironically recorded to prove the opposite, that is, the lack of prejudice. Once again, the same official recounted:

> Yet, we never held the minorities in contempt. For instance, we said "neither the candy of Damascus nor the visage of Arabs [on the assumption that both are vile]," but we intended to address not the Arabs, but blacks. As for the Arabs, we respected them for sharing the ancestry of the prophet Muhammad. We called the Greeks/Rum "*palikarya*." With

> this [terminology], we wanted to point out that they howled at the slightest provocation. Yet we did not hold an anti-Greek stand. On the contrary, the cute stories they told with their unique accents circulated continuously.

This quotation does not contain any awareness of the stereotyping employed toward minorities, that is, of reducing them to only particular attributes and in the process demeaning and dehumanizing them. Many similar examples abound in the case of the Ottoman Christian subjects in general and the Armenians in particular.[26] For instance, a chronicler narrated that in the late eighteenth century the Janissary master rebuking other Janissaries who unfairly beat up an old man said, "Why did you need to cause a public commotion by whipping [the old man] as if he were an Armenian infidel?!"[27] All these naturalized uses revealed the underlying prejudice against the non-Muslims in the empire. This also became evident when the Muslim Turks attended schools run by non-Muslims as their Muslim relatives and neighbors severely criticized such behavior.[28] Yet the main difference in this case was that the Muslims as the dominant majority often had access to networks connecting them to the state that enabled them to negotiate and not heed these criticisms; they also lived in a society based on the Islamic rule of law that ultimately favored them. The non-Muslims, however, were restricted in their social and legal recourse: not only did they lack such networks to the state, but they also had to live within a legal context that did not favor them. As a consequence, even though both the Muslims and non-Muslims often encountered violence, the recourse for non-Muslims was much more limited.

The wealth non-Muslims accumulated was often more at the mercy of the Ottoman state than that of Muslims because, unlike their Muslim counterparts, the non-Muslims could not politically activate family networks close to the sultan to have such decisions eventually reversed.[29] Hence, not only were non-Muslims unable to translate their economic wealth into political power, but even their wealth was at the mercy of the sultan long after the 1839, 1856, and 1876 reforms that theoretically protected the life and property of all non-Muslim subjects. In addition to such naturalized prejudice and discrimination, the inherent inequality embedded in everyday interactions between Muslims and non-Muslims is captured by an incident that an Ottoman official recounted in 1885; it occurred between the Muslim governor of Kastamonu and an Armenian monk paying him a visit. What is significant here is how the monk called the pasha on his prejudice and the ensuing discrimination:[30]

> The monk did not stop with the greeting, but advanced to shake the pasha's hand. [Yet] the pasha extended his left hand. The short and very likable monk smiled, stating with a grin, "pasha, when one's right hand

> is perfectly fine, one does not put forth the left one. Give me the other one. What are you guarding against? My heart is as pure as my hand. I guess you did not like my attire. Those who want to know others solely through their attire can never escape being fooled. The one who came to pay his greetings to you is not my attire but my person." The pasha replied that "it was through absentmindedness that I extended my left hand" and put forth his right one.... The monk continued: "Do not place that much value upon the rags humans produce. Try to see God's creatures as they really are."

This exchange reveals the inherent prejudice some Muslim officials had in not extending to Christians their right hand used for carrying out their Muslim religious duties, presenting instead the left one, meant to be used for "unclean things." By extending his left hand, the pasha implied the monk was unclean because he was a Christian.

Such prejudice and ensuing discrimination against non-Muslim subjects impacted and structured over time the use of space. All too often, Muslims and non-Muslims dwelled separately. Yet such differentiation was much more prevalent in urban centers and provincial towns than in rural villages. Contemporaneous memoirs provide ample information on the imperial city. One Ottoman Armenian who provided a history of the imperial capital from his own standpoint carefully delineated how, through the city's history, the Armenians came to dwell in certain quarters.[31] In the use of religious space, like all conquering imperial forces, the Ottoman state gradually transformed many churches, including Armenian ones, into mosques.[32] Cemeteries belonging to non-Muslims met a similar fate.[33] Parts of the capital where the non-Muslims formed the majority were likewise strictly separated from the Muslims.[34] In some of these spaces, it was often difficult for Muslims to purchase property as well.[35] There were also non-Muslim families living intermixed with the Muslims. Over time, however, even when the non-Muslim population became spatially diffused into the dominant Muslim Turkish majority, non-Muslim property was often co-opted by legal maneuvering, first by the Ottoman and later the Turkish state, gradually excluding such non-Muslim existence in the midst of Muslims.[36]

There is less information on the coexistence of Muslims and non-Muslims in the rest of the empire; they seem to have lived together in some places and apart in others.[37] Existing evidence on the use of space nevertheless reflects the escalating structural divide. For instance, one journalist noted that during his childhood in Urumca near Salonica, "the town dwellers had bifurcated. Christians and mostly Greeks lived on the top parts of the city. They formed most of the population.... The Turks lived in the lower part." On the other end of the empire in Aleppo, the situation was similar according to the recollections of another journalist, who stated that "the Jews, Christians, and Muslims lived as separately from one another as possible and did not at all interact with each other." In the imperial regions in between, especially in Asia Minor, there was more mixing of the populations. Notably, there was also intracommunal tension within the empire. For instance, Jews and Christians often encountered problems. Yet another journalist wrote that in Serez in the Balkans, "whenever a priest passed by, the Jews shouted that he did so 'in black with worms coming out of his mouth. In the frequent fights between the Jews and the Rum, the latter referred to as 'Grekaya' were always destined to lose. The Bulgarians were known as bullies while Albanians were trusted.... As for the Turks, they were the home-owners from whom one held off."[38]

What enabled this Ottoman social structure predicated on religious difference to sustain itself? Accountability and legal redress. Existing social relations worked properly insofar as the dominant Muslim majority was able to recognize and protect the precarious existence of non-Muslim communities in their midst. The state-backed efforts were complemented by non-Muslim communal leaders who likewise monitored the actions of their particular communities. As long as the Ottoman state was able to redress the injustices experienced by non-Muslim communities, the system worked properly. Indeed, many instances until the mid-nineteenth century reveal how peaceful social relations between Muslims and non-Muslims were sustained through redress. For instance, an Ottoman chronicler stated that at the imperial capital in 1811, an Ottoman Muslim named Bostancı Arnabud Islam plundered produce from the garden of an "infidel" (*kefere*). When the latter protested, Islam struck and killed him. When a European merchant owning the adjoining garden complained to the authorities about what transpired, the Muslim perpetrator was captured and beheaded. In early nineteenth-century chronicles, many similar instances of redress abound.[39] Still, many cases of injustice committed by Muslims against non-Muslims often did not come to the attention of Ottoman state authorities. For instance, in 1812 Veli Pasha, the tax collector of Eğin, unlawfully collected more taxes from the non-Muslim residents than what was owed, "knowing well that they would not ask for it back out of fear." The pasha was nevertheless eventually punished for his behavior. In yet another instance, the Ottoman state monitored the sale of houses to non-Muslims to ensure Muslim neighborhoods spatially remained Muslim.[40] Hence the system sustained itself because of the redress the Ottoman state undertook to protect non-Muslims, but always in accordance with legal principles that ultimately sustained Muslim dominance and insofar as the non-Muslims were willing to take the risk to bring forth their complaints under these circumstances.

Moving from the imperial capital to the provinces, there are similar attempts to redress the injustices especially the non-Muslim subjects faced.[41] As one moved away from the imperial capital, however, the effectiveness of such measures quickly declined, especially after the mid-nineteenth century. A case in point on the injustices meted upon the populace by the Kurds took place in Erzurum in 1874. The Ottoman governor and commander recounted what transpired as follows:[42]

> The Kurdish descendants of feudal lords ... attack[ed] the weak, be they Muslim or Armenian. Property is the foundation of justice, and it is the duty of [Ottoman] state officials to show care about its execution. Even though all government offices were constantly warned not to err on this matter, it was not very effective.... When the causes of this [ineffectiveness] were investigated, it was understood that this situation persisted not because of the negligence ... [of] officials, but [because] ... most of the wronged did not launch official complaints. [This was so] since those who came to complain either failed to prove their case or faced even more wrongs after the guilty party served his term and returned.... [The perpetrators] continuously escalated their injustice, causing the wronged to cease their complaints ... [giving] full rein to such [evil] guys. Most of the Christians in those areas were Armenians, and the young and dishonest ones among them had bad ideas in their heads.... I had no doubt in my mind ... that [all this] would eventually result in a big war with Russia. I acted immediately ... to exile the Kurdish lords who had made a tradition out of delivering injustice to the weak ... [and] arrested the leading thirteen people.... Even though I ... requested orders from the Porte to dispatch them ... to reside in another province, the answer [I received] from the grand vizier Mahmud Nedim Pasha was that this kind of exile would be a grave punishment ... that cannot be fulfilled.

Hence the state's failure to deliver justice mostly harmed the socially weak, in this case the poor Muslims and Armenians. When the governor attempted to redress the injustice by banishing the aggressive Kurdish leaders, however, the Ottoman government insisted on protecting the perpetrators at the expense of the victims. It is later revealed that the governor persisted, only to be removed from office. This failure foreshadows future problems as the Ottoman state increasingly failed to protect especially the properties of its Armenian subjects in the eastern provinces from Kurdish aggression. In summary, then, the Ottoman social structure predicated on difference and Islamic law only worked insofar as the state and communal leaders monitored and redressed the persistent tension and ensuing injustice. Such accountability and legal redress declined across time and space, as one moved away from the imperial capital to the provinces, and as the Ottoman state had fewer and fewer resources with which to intervene and guarantee justice.

Emergence of Ottoman Imperial Modernity

During the eighteenth century, the Ottoman sultan and officials closely watched the eighteenth-century industrial and political transformations in Western Europe, and the empire suffered from the adverse military and commercial consequences of these transformations throughout the nineteenth century. The primary concern of both the Ottoman sultan and his officials was their inability to sustain territorial expansion, which was regarded as the linchpin of imperial survival. During the course of the nineteenth century, not only was the Ottoman army defeated with increasing frequency, but the cost of preserving the imperial lands rose precipitously. Frequent lost wars, adverse commercial treaties, and escalating independence rebellions in the Balkans forced the Ottoman sultans and their officials to identify domestic weaknesses with the intent to fix them and recover former imperial strength. Crucial to this comeback was the improvement of the military, the institution upon which imperial expansion had been predicated. With the accession to the Ottoman throne of Sultan Selim III in 1789, the reform attempts became systematic for the first time; the entire system of governance was modified with the intent to raise more taxes and restructure the military after the model of its successful Western European counterparts.

Yet, like all other contemporaneous non-Western powers, the Ottoman sultans and their officials gradually became aware that the necessary change had to be much broader and deeper than earlier instances of adoption and adaptation of a specific practice that had limited impact on the Ottoman social structure. The emergent Western European modernity was, again for the first time, the consequence of a long, complex transformation of state-society relations; it entailed a new ontology predicated on human reason, a new epistemology based on formal scientific investigation, and a new ethics where human interests prevailed over all else. Unlike earlier instances of the piecemeal adoption of particular European innovations like a specific new cannon, rifle, or armored galley that often did not impact the rest of the social structure, modernity entailed the very unique intersection of military and commercial practices supported by the political practice of a mass-mobilized citizenry. Yet contemporaneous non-Western states and societies experienced this modernity not initially through an organic social transformation but through its two visible consequences: military strength and commercial capability, which set Western European powers in general and Britain and France in particular on their imperialist course. In their attempts to negotiate and contain this imperialist expansion and dominance, other states and societies resorted to what they had practiced from time immemorial: they attempted to replicate the consequences of Western European modernity, with the expectation that these would eventually enabled them to withstand Western expansion. Such mirrored adoption copied the visible consequences of modernity in form, without adequately taking into account the content that had generated the form in the first place. It was often assumed that the purchase of technologically advanced armaments and the consumption of mass-produced goods would magically reproduce modernity. Their adoption of form was not wholesale, either; those elements of modernity most in tune with the social structure were selectively prioritized over others. Once these elements entered any social system, they quickly diffused and impacted the social structure, often in its entirety. This mirrored impact of Western European modernity in the Ottoman Empire during the eighteenth, nineteenth, and early twentieth centuries is articulated next.

During this phase, covering the period from 1789 to 1907, the Ottoman sultans and their officials initially prioritized military reforms. Yet such reforms quickly necessitated concomitant changes in the land tenure system, since taxation financed the army; in the state administration, since the military reorganization necessitated bureaucratic changes; and in education, since continuous military training required the acquisition of new skills, knowledge, and expertise. Educational reforms in particular generated a new cadre of educated officers that soon engaged in political action with the intent to assume leadership instead of the sultans and their officials. It is especially significant that the Ottoman military was primarily composed of Muslims in general and Muslim Turks of Anatolia in particular; non-Muslims, who did not have the right to bear arms, concentrated in and eventually controlled Ottoman commerce. So unlike in Western Europe, where modernity was predominantly spearheaded by the same ethnic and religious group, the Ottoman structural divide between the Muslims and non-Muslims made it impossible for these two social groups to mobilize and act in unison to fully transform state and society after the Western European model. Yet, this impossibility was not evident during the adoption process; it only became clear after the two-century-long process of modernization. At the time, the Ottoman state undertook three reforms in 1839, 1856, and 1876 to overcome the structural divide, but to no avail. During this process, escalating frustration was experienced by all of the involved social groups. The Muslims observed the "civilized" West and became increasingly aggravated as they failed to achieve the same end results; they traced the failure not to the impossibility of such transformation but instead to internal obstacles. The non-Muslims interacted with Western merchants and industrialists, but they were frustrated when the Ottoman state restricted their activities to the commercial sphere alone. While they were able to accumulate economic capital, they could not invest it either to develop an Ottoman industry or to attain political power to participate in the social system on an equal footing with the Muslims. As a consequence, Ottoman communal relations did not improve but instead became more polarized as the increasingly impoverished Muslims resented the new opulent lifestyle of the non-Muslims, and the latter were frustrated as the political and legal equality promised by the reforms failed to materialize.

Contemporaneous Ottoman memoirs reveal in full the reaction not only to the military reforms but also to the economic and educational efforts. As such memoirs become available only after the first half of the nineteenth century, the Ottoman transformation from 1789 to the 1860s has to be traced through Ottoman chronicles and secondary sources. By the end of the seventeenth century, the dominant Ottoman imperial vision still emphasized the necessity of "an 'ever-victorious army' and an 'ever-expanding frontier.' "[43] The increased inability of the empire to actualize this vision raised concern among various Ottoman thinkers, who initially blamed their ruler either for his neglect of justice and religion that in turn led to the breakdown of army discipline and training, or for his inability to control the emergence of bribery and corruption. By the end of the eighteenth century, escalating Ottoman defeats at the hands of European armies put an end to any mention of an ever-expanding frontier.[44] Discussions now centered on what to do with the Ottoman army to make it victorious once again. Though many Ottoman thinkers agreed that what was being practiced did not work, it was especially difficult for the religiously devout to accept that the armies of Islam—a religion revealed after Christianity and therefore presumably containing a fuller revelation of truth—were now being defeated by forces of a "lesser" one.[45] The recommended solutions diverged significantly: some called for an immediate return to the way things were in the past, in purer form and with more passion so as to reproduce the former success; others recommended the total imitation of Western European practices. This bifurcated recommendation set the stage for a new structural divide that accompanies modernity, one between "conservatives," historically prioritizing past practice, and "modernists," ahistorically emphasizing the present and possible future practice. The 1774 military defeat against Russia in particular generated "an intense debate between the conservative and 'modernist' forces on the subject of military reform."[46] It is also significant to note that at this juncture, the initial focus of Ottoman modernity was not on human rights and the protection of property but instead on military improvement for imperial defense spearheaded by the state. Hence, not only were the agents initiating the process of modernity different, but so were their aims: the main institution that ultimately defined the parameters of Ottoman and later Turkish modernity was the state in general and the military in particular.

Systematic Westernizing Reforms of Sultan Selim III

When Sultan Selim III (r. 1789–1807) ascended the Ottoman throne, he commanded his officials to prepare proposals (*layiha*) on the causes of imperial weaknesses as well as suggestions for reform. Three views emerged; while all aimed to recover the military glories of the Ottoman golden age, what they proposed differed. The first view recommended totally reverting to earlier military methods, the second suggested merging "new Frankish training and weapons" with the existing military order, and the third argued for the radical eradication of the old military order incapable of reform, to instead establish an entirely new army equipped and trained on the Western European model. Alongside the mounted provincial cavalry that increasingly became outdated in modern warfare, the Janissary units formed the backbone of the standing army. The Janissaries opposed the reform efforts, namely, the introduction of new organizations, tactics, and weapons that would necessitate constant training and drills. Selim III therefore had to establish a separate infantry unit trained and equipped in accordance to the Western European model. Initially referred to as "the army of the New Order" (*Nizam-ı Cedid*), the term "New Order" then became synonymous with the reign of Selim III because of the many systematic changes the sultan undertook.[47] To finance this army, Selim III had to set up a special new treasury. To train his new soldiers, he also had to transform the existing School of Mathematics into the military Land Engineering School and Naval Engineering School.[48] Selim III also granted his non-Muslim subjects the right to establish their own community schools, which multiplied rapidly both at the capital and throughout the empire.[49] Modernity necessitated increased access to information, domestically on the empire and externally abroad. Selim III therefore established an advisory council of experts (*Meclis-i Meşveret*) composed mainly of retired civil and military officials.[50] To directly access systematic information from Europe, he sent permanent diplomatic representation to the European capitals of London, Paris, Vienna, and Berlin—as well as St. Petersburg once the wars with Russia abated—for three-year periods; ambassadors serving in these cities had in their retinues young, mostly Muslim men who would learn languages and subjects useful to the Ottoman state.[51] Economically, Selim III also appointed non-Muslim merchants as consuls to attend to Ottoman commercial interests abroad. The intent behind his appointment of Ottoman merchants, both Muslim and non-Muslim, termed Avrupa ve Hayriye Tüccarı, was to get them to trade within the empire with special privileges; by doing so, the sultan attempted to counteract those Ottoman non-Muslims who chose to trade under the protection of European powers due to better tariffs.[52]

Among these selected elements of Western European modernity, neither the new army nor the diplomatic and commercial corps survived Selim III's reign; the discontented segments rebelled and deposed him. Yet those trained in these two institutions nevertheless formed the seeds of the reformist officials and officers who eventually dictated the course of modernity first in the empire and later in the republic. The advisory council of experts that did continue under the succeeding sultans Mustafa IV and Mahmud II likewise formed the nucleus of a constitutional assembly. It is no accident that non-Muslim subjects were not closely involved in this process spearheaded by the state. Because most non-Muslims—with the exception of some units in the Balkans—could not bear arms, they were not initially impacted by the military reforms.[53] They could not normally join the ranks of modernist officials because of their religion; non-Muslims therefore failed to become prominent in the diplomatic corps[54] or the advisory council as a social group. While receiving the right to establish modern communal schools enabled the non-Muslims to gain access to new Western knowledge, their activities remained limited to the commercial sphere. Unlike in Western European modernity, then, Ottoman private commercial and public state enterprises could not and ultimately did not complement each other. It is telling that even though Sultan Selim III established the consulate system that had worked so successfully in furthering the commercial interests of the Great Powers, the system failed to take root in the empire. Having relegated the commercial sphere to non-Muslim subjects, the Ottoman state assigned a lower priority to the state protection of trade and commerce. The non-Muslim consuls Selim III appointed tapered off as there was neither consistent state support nor an established Ottoman practice of employing such services. Because all significant state decisions were made by Muslim officials, the Ottoman consulate system that could have potentially transformed the empire was never again revived. Still, Selim III did create privileged Ottoman merchants to match the advantageous import and export tariffs that the European powers had won for their subjects under the capitulatory treaties; many non-Muslim merchants ended up taking advantage of this opportunity instead of their Muslim counterparts.[55] Even though the adoption of this element could not counter the overwhelming Western European trade advantage, it nevertheless protected non-Muslim merchants to a certain degree in the one area in which they excelled, namely, that of trade and commerce through which many became enriched.

The Ottoman course of modernity became firmly set during the reign of the succeeding sultan, Mahmud II (r. 1808–39), as the new reformed state institutions and practices started to take root. Having ascended to the Ottoman throne in 1808, the young sultan had to first sign a "Document of Agreement" (Sened-i İttifak) that checked the power of the Janissaries while recognizing the power of provincial notables.[56] The agreement did not last, however, as the sultan eventually abolished the Janissary corps in June 1826, establishing instead a new army as well as a military college to train officers loyal to his person.[57] He also undercut the power of provincial notables by gradually transforming them into salaried state employees. Administratively, the office of the grand vizier was converted to that of the prime minister, who in turn coordinated the activities of the ministers. The Council of Ministers (Meclis-i Vükela) and a series of advisory councils not only oversaw the execution of reforms but also started to eventually share decision-making power with the sultan. With the establishment of the Translation Office (Tercüme Odası) especially in the aftermath of the 1821 Greek Revolution, young Muslim Turks gradually replaced the Greek Rum as translators. This office became the training ground of Ottoman diplomats and educated bureaucrats in general, and new top-ranking reformist officials like Sadık Rifat, Ali, Fuat, and Mithat Pashas in particular. The form was there, but the content remained problematic: the selection and decisions of these consultative bodies were not regulated. Even though an attempt was made to separate the executive, legislative, and judicial powers, the ultimate authority to appoint and dismiss all members continued to reside with the sultan alone. Hence, even though the Ottoman administrative structure transformed under the impact of modernity, officials could not function properly because the power and authority remained concentrated in the person of the sultan. Still, as a regular salary system and a penal code were established for these sultans' officials, they developed into a well-defined social group of bureaucrats: the structure of Ottoman governance known as the Sublime Porte (Bab-ı Ali) thus came into existence.

Adopting the Western Military Form

When Sultan Mahmud II died in 1839, the Ottoman Reform (*Tanzimat*) Edict that had been drafted as a consequence of all the preceding structural transformations was about to be proclaimed. His son and successor, Sultan Abdülmecid I (r. 1839–61), did indeed issue an imperial ordinance (*hatt-ı hümayun*) on 3 November 1839, one that for the first time recognized and guaranteed the right to life, property, and honor of all Ottoman subjects, promised to collect taxes according to income, and also assured military recruitment would be executed on a regular basis.[58] Even though these principles "mirrored" elements of Western European modernity, according to two contemporaneous memoirs, the Reform Edict was proclaimed as a defensive military measure to garner Western European support against the forces of the Egyptian khedive Mehmed Ali Pasha.[59] The 1838 Anglo-Ottoman trade treaty that effectively abolished trade barriers, thereby exposing Ottoman commerce to Western European penetration, preceded the Reform Edict. Once again, as the trade treaty and the edict were signed to appease the West for its continued military support, Ottoman military interests trumped commercial and political priorities.

Also during the reign of Abdülmecid I, a second Reform Order (*islahat fermanı*) was issued in 1856, once more promising equality in education, government appointments, and administration of justice to all subjects regardless of creed. The reasons for the promulgation of this order were likewise primarily militaristic.[60] In their memoirs, two Ottoman statesmen discuss the negotiations preceding the 1856 order in great detail.[61] Especially disturbing to the Ottoman state was Article 4 of the peace treaty, according to which the European powers wanted to place guarantees in relation to reforms concerning the Christian subjects. The Ottoman sultan and his officials regarded this article as a threat against state sovereignty. Once again, the 1856 Reform Order was primarily issued not as a consequence of domestic developments but rather due to the quandary the Ottoman state faced as a consequence of its weakened military state. Likewise, the 1876 Reform Edict issued by sultan Abdülhamid II—who succeeded to the throne after the violent removal of his predecessor, Sultan Abdülaziz I—was promulgated to unsuccessfully prevent Russian complaints about the integration of non-Muslims into Ottoman governance; the Ottoman state also tried to appease and garner the support of Western European states against Russia. In all, then, military concerns dictated the advent of modernity into the empire.

Such military concerns also impacted the local composition of the Ottoman army. The gradual imperial contraction necessitated the recruitment of more soldiers at a greater cost, leading to chronic shortages in paying military salaries.[62] The army's population base of Anatolian and Balkan Muslims started to be insufficient.[63] In addition, their salaries were often in arrears as military costs soared beyond state revenues. By the mid-nineteenth century, military expenses had become the largest single expense item of the Ottoman treasury. The combination of long years of service and inadequate pay led to increased corruption that one statesman was certain would eventually bring the empire down.[64] Due to these limitations, as many commanders noted, the Ottoman state had to resort to recruiting tribal regiments of the Hümavend, Kurds, Circassians, and Chechens, who were often employed with adverse effects. Not only were they not properly trained, but they often disregarded military orders to engage in plunder and rape, wreaking havoc among the local inhabitants. Non-Muslim villages that had less protection due to lack of arms were frequent targets.[65] Given such adverse conditions, because the empire's population was almost equally divided into Muslims and non-Muslims, it would have been rational for the state to start recruiting non-Muslims.[66] Yet, in spite of the many reforms guaranteeing equality to all subjects regardless of creed, this next natural step was not actualized until the very end. Sultan Abdülhamid

II (r. 1876–1909) opposed the recruitment of soldiers from non-Muslim communities (*millet askeri*) as well as the education of non-Muslims in imperial military academies. The sultan's own memoir explained his reasoning as follows:

> Requiring military service from non-Muslims is merely a pipe dream that would be akin to suicide for us. If we, the Turks, who are the dominant nation agree to do military service under equal conditions with those among our subjects from different religions and sects, we would be sure to find ourselves in a bad situation. Immediately, the leaders of these communities and especially the Great Powers that intervene in our business at every opportunity would generate problems for us. [If non-Muslims are fully integrated into the army], they would... decide to convert.... [If separate regiments are established]... it would amount to forming an army within the army.... It is certain that we would be harmed during any turmoil. We are right to be anxious about this because the Christians within our empire have always united with the Great Powers and worked against us.... If state and religion were two entirely separate administrations, then one could think of Muslims and Christians undertaking joint military service. Yet no caliph would agree to such an absurd idea.

This frank account reveals two factors that hinder the integration of non-Muslims into the Ottoman military: their potential alliance with the Great Powers against the Ottoman state, and, more important, the lack of separation between state and religion in the empire. In spite of escalating military needs, the Ottoman state was unable to overcome the structural divide to recruit non-Muslims into the army. Instead, along with escalating armament costs, the military started to rely on fewer well-trained recruits along with local militia, which increasingly undermined the security and protection of all imperial subjects in general and non-Muslims in particular.

As superior Western European technology made its way into the Ottoman Empire, the Ottoman state initially tried to produce such military equipment locally at the imperial capital.[67] The first Ottoman arms factory was founded at the capital during the reign of Selim III and then updated by Sultan Mahmut II. An iron production facility and an iron ore foundry were established in 1833 and 1837; in 1867, four industrial labor battalions were formed to work at cannon production facilities.[68] The year 1901 witnessed the foundation of a Mauser rifle cartridge factory, addressing the complexity of the parts required by new industrial armaments. At these industrial production facilities, all established in the imperial capital by the state, young Muslim Turks acquired expertise; they imitated and copied Western armaments or repaired imported ones, trying to produce industrial accessories locally at a lower cost. Yet the importation and imitation of Western military industrial production without mastering the social process that had produced it generated many problems. The trained experts tried to fix and reproduce the disparate armaments and especially cannons purchased from different companies. All too often, the ammunitions imported from one Western factory would not match the rifles purchased from another, leading much to rot away in storage. The lack of scientific knowledge about these weapons within the empire led to many abuses; many generals purchased obsolete armaments, or the sultan intervened in the decision-making process.[69] The prices paid for such purchases were often exorbitant because the Ottoman officers did not know the market prices.[70] These dire consequences were due to the Ottoman state's insistence on maintaining a monopoly over local arms production. In Western Europe and the United States, private companies and entrepreneurs participated in armament production, thereby sustaining technological innovation. Yet the Ottoman state did not trust its non-Muslim subjects to control the commercial sphere and therefore did not allow them to engage in industrial production. Such state control drained the treasury as excessive numbers of mismatched armaments were purchased without any expertise at highly inflated prices.

Military Reforms Necessitate Economic Change

Because the main source of Ottoman state revenue was agricultural taxation, additional financial resources necessary to reform the Ottoman military had to come from agriculture. The traditional tax collection was mostly done in kind as the produce generated by lifetime land grants was collected by state-appointed officials who, in turn, were responsible for sending mounted cavalry to the Ottoman army. As modern military warfare increasingly relied on a permanent standing army that needed to be constantly drilled using armaments, such cavalry became outdated. In addition, the purchase of modern armaments necessitated access to large amounts of cash. Lifetime land grants that used to be bestowed upon those who demonstrated merit during warfare (*tımar*) gradually transformed into state grants (*mukataa*). Now, tax collectors (*mültezim*) bid on the lands in cash, and then tried to raise the cash by gathering the produce. In order to prevent the overuse of the lands, the state also had the tax collectors agree to the condition that the lands they worked with would be passed onto their male heirs (*malikane*). Because the sultan symbolically owned all the imperial lands, he retained the right to confiscate the lands and properties of those who accrued what he deemed too much wealth and power. Still, the sultan's greater reliance on cash revenues increased the power of local provincial notables who controlled such sources of cash, gradually wresting power away from the sultan.[71] The 1808 Document of the Union (Sened-i İttifak) abolished the sultan's right to confiscate land and property, making private property truly hereditary for the first time. The concept of imperial law regulating all land transactions was instituted, in turn, by the imperial decree of 1839.

During the 1840s and 1895s, imperial land expansion halted while the need for modern armaments escalated as the world entered serious financial straits. As a consequence, the Ottoman state treasury experienced its first significant cash shortage.[72] In 1851, the nonpayment of state salaries for an entire week due to lack of cash in the treasury made Ottoman statesmen realize the extent of the crisis their state had fallen into. And there were very few among them who were knowledgeable in economic and financial matters because these were not only secondary to military and governance affairs but also relegated to non-Muslims. Because there was no appropriate Ottoman term to describe this dire state of affairs, the term "crisis" (*buhran*) was coined at that juncture. That the Ottoman state had to fight with Russia over the Crimea in 1856 further drained the Ottoman treasury. It was indeed during this war that the Ottoman state had to borrow money for the first time from Western Europe, France to be exact, in order to purchase modern armaments and pay the newly trained soldiers. Ottoman state debt "that had been 25 million at the end of the rule of sultan Abdülmecid I (r. 1839–1861) increased tenfold in twelve years reaching 250 million during the rule of his successor sultan Abdülaziz I (r. 1861–1876)."[73] The increased power of state officials at the expense of the sultan became evident as Sultan Abdülaziz I was deposed because of his profligate spending. The Ottoman officials were largely unaware, however, that the financial crisis was worldwide, and that the sultan expended a lot of cash to import state-of-the-art equipment to build up the Ottoman army and the navy. During this time, in order to pay back the growing debts, grand viziers with limited economic sense undertook drastic financial measures such as halving the interests paid on state bonds, which in turn destroyed the trust of the populace that had purchased the bonds.[74] Escalating state debt worsened to such a degree that the empire could not make payments on the borrowed cash and was forced to declare bankruptcy in 1875.

Suppressing Reformist Muslim Officials

Even though the Western industrial production of armaments ultimately could not be replicated within the empire, other Western technology continued to spread throughout the empire, especially at the end of the nineteenth century and the beginning of the twentieth century.[75] The one Ottoman statesman who had grasped how the elements of Western European modernity had to be negotiated—unfortunately, to no avail—was Mithat Pasha (1822–84).[76] During his service as governor in the Danube and Syrian provinces, the pasha constantly stressed the need to build a sound economic infrastructure that would enable not only the execution of the reforms but also their long-term sustenance for the benefit—rather than harm—of the entire populace. He prioritized the construction of paved roads and a carriage service for the transportation of local produce, and the building of dams for an increase in agricultural yield. In order to discipline and order state administration in the service of such economic activities, the pasha redesigned state offices in such a way that the populace could have recourse around the clock. Local administrative councils not only participated in his endeavors but had actual local power and agency in determining their own needs and assigning the resources necessary to meet them. He also founded a local police force (*zaptiye*) to provide constant security for the populace and established schools for Muslim and non-Muslim orphan boys to turn them into productive subjects with skills.[77] In his memoir, Mithat Pasha outlined a blueprint for economic reforms that, unfortunately, were not followed. Rather than executing the plan, Sultan Abülhamid II eventually executed the pasha for insubordination. Mithat Pasha's blueprint demonstrates how economically perceptive some Ottoman statesmen actually were, but to no avail:

> The first issue was the construction, with the support of the locals, of macadamized roads as well as bridges.... The second was the issue of security and public order that was secured through the reorganization of the gendarmerie.... The third was the establishment of community chests [*menafii sandıkları*] since the farmers had to borrow money at usurious rates and ended up losing their land; [instead] the peasants, Muslim and Christian alike, pooled their capital and administered it as a community chest themselves.... The fourth was the procurement of commercial vessels... [and the construction of] trade fairgrounds for produce the upkeep of which was also locally administered.... The fifth was the institution and regulation of carriage companies for transportation.... The sixth was the establishment of reformatories for Muslim and Christian boys... to teach them trades as well as a printing house the expenses of which were met by the rents of the granaries built explicitly for this purpose.... The seventh was the settlement and employment of the Muslim refugees with the intent to make them productive as they had had no services provided to them until then.... The eighth was the reorganization of the government offices and prisons, the expenses of which were procured by the local notables with great pleasure.... The ninth was the establishment of municipal offices that had until then been nonexistent; building such offices enabled the

> cleaning of the streets, construction of pavements, protection of necessary goods, control of weights, and the adjustment of prices. The functioning of all of these was regulated through new legislation as a consequence of which both the prosperity as well as the happiness of the populace increased.... Once the populace tasted this [ensuing] security, prosperity, and freedom, trade increased by leaps and bounds and... everyone became reenergized.

The most significant aspect of this blueprint was increased local control over the economy.[78] Yet, such decentralization of economic power was not tolerated by the sultan. Once again, state interests prevailed over economic foresight, leading the economic impact of modernity to be a disastrous one for the empire. For instance, when the government was notified of increased tax yields as a consequence of the pasha's economic measures, the pasha was immediately ordered to send the surplus to the capital, thereby effectively preventing him from what he had proposed, that is, investing the yield locally in other similarly productive local activities. The tenure of Mithat Pasha in office was also not determined by his merit but rather by the sultan's often politically motivated decision to remove officials at any time. As a consequence, the constructive economic changes such officials undertook could not be sustained over the long term and remained limited to the duration of their tenure, the length of which was decided by the sultan alone. And the infighting especially between the conservative and reformist officials enabled the sultan to sustain his position by successively appointing one from each camp; the first course of action each appointed official undertook was to undermine the local changes introduced by his predecessor. Indeed, in Mithat Pasha's case, the conservative officials at the imperial capital attempted—and succeeded—to undermine the many projects he had undertaken and wanted to embark on in the future; the officials either incited local forces against the pasha or intervened through the offices they controlled to undermine his constructive endeavors. In the end, Mithat Pasha not only was removed from office, with his successors undoing many of his reforms, but also was exiled from the empire and eventually strangled upon the orders of the sultan, who had begun to regard him as a challenge to his rule.

As such political infighting undermined the agency and efficacy of reformist Muslim state officials to undertake and sustain reforms, the only social actors left to undertake the necessary infrastructural investments were Western European companies. Indeed, upon the sultan's approval, many such companies competed to directly invest in developing the empire's infrastructure. For instance, imperial communication improved as ninety-three foreign postal systems and many shipping lines began to operate,[79] and railroad and telegraph construction commenced.[80] Many Ottoman Muslims objected to the introduction of railroads, arguing that increased Western intervention in imperial affairs would follow.[81] Yet the sultans' political concerns over sustaining their power undermined the possibility of either Ottoman Muslim officials or non-Muslim entrepreneurs engaging in such large-scale activities, leading Western European companies to instead penetrate Ottoman domestic economy. These large-scale Western European technological investments under state control were accompanied at a much faster pace by the importation of small-scale Western technology, one deemed to be not as significant politically and therefore not as much controlled by the Ottoman state. Newspaper production created a new space for public discussion and debate;[82] escalating orders of automobiles,[83] telephones, and the municipal lighting, gas, and garbage collection systems improved daily life. Yet once again, the importation of Western products without the mastery of the embedded technology increased reliance not only on these items but also on their Western European producers. Lack of knowledge in operating and maintaining such machines forced the new domestic consumers of the empire to either constantly buy new products when what they had broke down, or get Western European producers to establish local branches for the upkeep of such products.

It appeared as if Western European modernity, which had generated flourishing military and economic enterprises on the Continent, produced just the opposite result in the Ottoman Empire as the latter faced one military and financial crisis after another. Contemporaneous memoirs narrate some of the locally adverse consequences of the modern technologies that were introduced to the empire. For instance, when the newly built İzmit-Ankara railroad connected Ankara to the imperial city, cheap imported Western European goods flooded Ankara, gradually destroying local production that could not withstand the competition.[84] Likewise, the introduction of boat service by Western European companies along the Bosporus in the imperial city led prices of mansions along the route to skyrocket. In addition, the profits that accrued from boat ticket sales were assigned not to the state treasury but instead as income to various members of the Ottoman dynasty.[85] Another adverse factor was the government's excessively slow decision-making process in matters concerning the economy. A case in point was the piloting services provided to the ships going through the Bosporus and later the Dardanelles. Even though a non-Muslim had petitioned to operate the piloting concession, the state decided instead to execute the service itself but then took decades to implement the decision. Western European companies profited in the interim.[86] In summary, in most economic decisions that were made regarding the impact of modernity, dynastic and state interests trumped the interests of the populace, leading to increased economic havoc. And reformist Muslim officials who were engaged in the state modernizing process followed a precarious course. They were only able to successfully challenge the power of the sultan and conservative officials with the 1908 constitutional revolution. Ironically, the revolution against the sultan succeeded mainly due to the large cohorts of reformist cadres educated in the Western-style schools the sultan had established with the intent to raise future state officials loyal to the dynasty.

Restricting Non-Muslim Entrepreneurs

In negotiating and interpreting the elements of Western European modernity, the agency of Muslim reformist officials was suppressed by their competing conservative counterparts and the sultan, both of whom prioritized the traditional practices of governance and the interests of the dynasty over reform. Another social group that could have played a significant constructive role in such negotiation were non-Muslim merchants and entrepreneurs, who had dominated Ottoman trade and commerce for centuries. Because of this societal location, they were also probably the most knowledgeable Ottomans regarding recent Western European developments in trade, commerce, and technology. Yet the inherent Ottoman Muslim lack of trust in their agency emanating from the structural divide led the Ottoman sultan and his officials to initially inhibit non-Muslim involvement in military industrial production. Non-Muslims' ability to accumulate economic capital to levels necessary for such industrial production was also initially restricted by the sultan's potential to confiscate wealth. Although the latter "restriction of wealth" was legally lifted over time, the former "restriction of trust" remained unabated. As a consequence, Ottoman non-Muslim entrepreneurship was confined to the local production of Western consumer goods such as stoves, the local representation of Western companies such as ones producing sewing machines, and the local sale of Western clothing and accessories in new, fancy stores. Ottoman non-Muslims were thus able to engage only in economic activities that were not considered a threat by the Ottoman state, and did so insofar as they lived in major cities and towns, where their activities could be easily monitored, and insofar as they did not attempt to translate their newly acquired economic capital into political power.

Hence, non-Muslim economic contributions to Ottoman mirrored modernity escalated rapidly, but not under conditions of their own choosing.[87] In major Ottoman cities, they established almost all the main firms, companies, and banks that conducted business with Western Europe. They administered the state custom houses, lent cash to the government, and managed the finances of Ottoman Muslim statesmen, including the sultans. They spearheaded the first attempts at urban modernization by building modern houses in stone, establishing modern shops, and undertaking municipal services. They also often indirectly engaged in agricultural production, lending money to tax farmers; after the reforms, they started to serve in that capacity themselves. Non-Muslim peasants in the rural countryside were more restricted in engaging in modernizing activities because they were often challenged by local Muslim notables. Still, non-Muslim villages became increasingly modernized over time as new schools and farming techniques were introduced.

Even though contemporaneous Ottoman Muslim memoirs rarely acknowledged the many economic endeavors initially developed by non-Muslims, a careful reading of the offhanded remarks reveals their significant presence. At the imperial capital, the gunpowder factory at Yedikule was constructed by "an Armenian named Hacı Arakel, called Hacı Dad for short, who was originally from the Beryan family at the Gamaragab village of Eğin." Likewise, "a factory for the recently invented embroidered prints was founded at the village [of Kuzguncuk] by Serkis Kalfa of Sivas whereby the multicolored flowered print was given the name 'Serkis Kalfa Print' to honor its founder."[88] Many other non-Muslims were involved in banking, often working for the numerous Western firms established there.[89] After the Ottoman state's 1857 bankruptcy, they were also employed in the large companies such as the Ottoman Debt Administration and the Ottoman Tobacco Monopoly that Western European states founded at the capital to recover the debts the imperial state owed them.[90] Non-Muslim prominence in Ottoman economic life is best captured by the following narration of nineteenth-century everyday life at the imperial capital:[91]

> The name of our family doctor was Andonaki, pharmacist Petraki. My father's moneychanger was Artin. Our grocer was Bodosaki, our tailor Karnik, jeweler Garbis, and our barber Yani. In front of our seaside mansion, the usurer Mishon, crisp-toast seller Yanko, dried-foods seller Vasil went by daily in their rowboats selling us foodstuff. Our boatman was Dimitri, the footman was called Istepan, and the woman peddler Mannik Dudu.... None of the captains of the boats who transported us on the Bosporus were Turks. Neither were there any Turks in railroad administration, banks, the quarantine and lighthouse management.... Journalism and printing... were also in the hands of those who were not Turks. The owners of daily newspapers were called Churchill, Fillip, Mihran, Nikolaidi; Karabets, Kaspars, and Ohanneses published the journals.

The economic presence of non-Muslims became more visible especially as they started to engage in new modern professions such as banking, business administration, printing, and the like.

Non-Muslims were economically active in the provinces as well. For instance, silk production in Bursa was developed through the initiative of the Armenian translator Hoca Agop Efendi, who had accompanied Ambassador Mustafa Reshid Pasha to Paris.[92] In Çüngüş near Elazığ, Ottoman Armenians established tanneries, producing stout leather for soles "that were sold all the way to India and the United States."[93] In Sivas in 1877, Armenian silversmiths "could manufacture the European revolver, other arms and bullets. They had also learned surgery techniques from the American Dr. West."[94] Throughout the eighteenth and nineteenth centuries, almost all the modern professionals—physicians, dentists, and pharmacists—in Sivas and Tokat were Armenians, with not a single Muslim Turk among them.[95] Yet not all Ottoman Armenians were successful in the provinces, especially when they worked for the state. Just like their Muslim counterparts, all their modernizing activities came to naught when they were appointed to another post.[96]

The relationships of these non-Muslims with the dominant Muslim Turkish majority were initially symbiotic and peaceful, becoming more tense when they accumulated more wealth than their Muslim counterparts. For instance, the Armenians of Eskişehir had traditionally acted as middlemen attending to the businesses of local Muslim notables at the imperial capital. The younger generations of local Muslim Turks began to view such activities more disparagingly, claiming the non-Muslim middlemen made a lot of unearned profit, especially on the orders they took or the money they lent.[97] Yet not all non-Muslims had such tense relationships; others helped out Muslim Turks with the latter's businesses to such a degree that once such help ceased, the business failed.[98] Ultimately, non-Muslims were able to accumulate wealth in cities and towns predominantly as middlemen to both Muslims and Western European companies; they could only retain their economic capital if they did not try to convert it into political power. Even though the series of Ottoman reforms promulgated in 1839, 1856, and 1876 promised them full legal equality with their Muslim counterparts, these were not systematically exercised and sustained over the long term.

Refracted Politics of Equal Rights for All

The Ottoman negotiation of the abstract Enlightenment concept of universal rights took the visible form of three imperial decrees issued in 1839, 1856, and 1876; all three guaranteed the state protection of life and property. Especially the protection of property rights indicated that sultans could no longer confiscate the wealth of their subjects, thereby draining the sultans of another source of political and economic power. In governance, the establishment of new institutions also gradually transformed the sultan's household of officials into salaried employees of particular ministries. Discussions of these reforms in contemporary memoirs reveal that the most culturally contentious consequence of all three was that non-Muslim subjects would now have equal legal rights with their Muslim counterparts. This indeed turned out to be the hardest reform to put into practice. The impact of three reforms indicates what was accomplished: non-Muslims were gradually included in governance. With the 1839 reform, provincial councils were established, enabling the local participation of Muslims and non-Muslims alike. The 1856 reform enabled the membership of non-Muslims in the High Council of Legal Affairs (Meclis-i Ahkam-ı Adliye) and made membership in provincial councils more representative of the populace. Another significant reform was the abolition of the main structural factor that had so long separated non-Muslims from Muslims: the poll tax non-Muslims had to pay in exchange for their exclusion from military service was abolished, and non-Muslims were allowed to serve in the army for the first time. The properties of all subjects were also theoretically protected by the state with the 1858 Land Code (Arazi Kanunnamesi) that legally recognized the private ownership of land for the first time. Ensuing Ottoman regulations (*nizamname*) of 1864 and 1867 extended the practice of provincial administrative councils and the general council to every province and also tried to install the concept of representation at local courts. In the application of regulations concerning local governance through councils, Muslims and non-Muslims participated equally. The 1876 reform presented the first official Ottoman constitution that enabled the participation in the assembly of both Muslim and non-Muslim delegates, thus marking the first significant transition to constitutional rule in the empire.[99]

In spite of such constructive attempts at integrating non-Muslims and Muslims into one body politic, how and why did these reforms fail?[100] How they failed becomes evident in the discussions of the memoirs regarding implementation. The provincial councils established in 1839 could not monitor and contain local injustice and ensuing violence because they lacked the executive power to enforce their decisions. As a consequence, council members instead ended up looking after their own personal interests.[101] Especially in the eastern provinces, the appointment of officials from the imperial capital also adversely affected the local balance of power. Disaffected local Kurdish notables began to be exiled from their local bases of power to no avail due to lack of administrative continuity in governance.[102] Hence, the state's unwillingness to share power locally on the one hand and to sustain policies beyond the tenure of officials on the other impeded constructive change. Even though the 1856 edict appointed non-Muslims to the High Council of Legal Affairs, such non-Muslim members were often representatives of prominent families that already had good relations with the Ottoman state. As a consequence, the non-Muslim members of the High Council failed to address complaints originating among the non-Muslim poor at the capital and in the provinces.[103] Care was taken to make the provincial councils more representative of the populace, but the members were not elected but rather appointed, often leading, once again, to the reproduction of the status quo rather than the participation of the politically disenfranchised.

The 1856 edict also attempted to overcome the structural divide by abolishing the poll tax and enabling non-Muslims to participate in military service. Yet, many non-Muslims protested this decision, stating that they would rather pay taxes, since they did not have any military experience and would therefore be disadvantaged in the Ottoman army. As a consequence, a new tax (Bedel-i Nakdi) was promulgated for all the subjects of the empire in exchange for military service, thereby allowing the wealthy, Muslim and non-Muslim alike, to avoid such service. Hence not only did the structural divide persist, but wealthy Muslims could now avoid military service as well, transforming a previously religious divide into a class divide based on wealth.

The 1858 Land Code promulgated to recognize private property wreaked havoc in the eastern provinces, where land relations had for centuries been based on usufructuary rights. Because non-Muslims were disadvantaged by the Islamic legal system, and because they lacked the arms especially Muslim Kurdish leaders employed to enforce their landownership, local notables who were predominantly Muslim took charge and registered all lands under their own names.[104] Likewise, the 1864 and 1867 regulations that diffused local councils to every province failed to increase political participation. This was the case because the council members were not truly elected but actually appointed from among those whose taxes were above a particular threshold. In addition, their nomination also had to be approved by the governors. Given this high level of selectivity in choosing members, the decisions reached did not initiate significant change but instead sustained the status quo. Likewise, the 1876 declaration of the constitution and ensuing participation of Muslims and non-Muslims in governance worked more in theory than practice. Most significantly, the sultan retained his ultimate authority in ratifying or rejecting any decision reached. Sultan Abdülhamid II did indeed use his authority that very same year to dismiss the Ottoman assembly and to place the constitution on hold for the next three decades.

Why these three reforms failed is discussed in depth in the memoirs as well. The main significant theme that permeates all the memoirs is the official ambivalence and ambiguity in the promulgation and execution of all three reforms. First, the discussions of why all three reforms were promulgated at particular junctures of Ottoman history indicate that the driving force was not internally produced but externally driven. Two contemporaneous sources assert that Mustafa Reşid Pasha prepared the 1839 reform decree to gain Europe's support in containing the threat posed to the empire by the Egyptian khedive Mehmed Ali Pasha.[105] The 1856 Reform Edict was once again declared due to the preconditions France and England set in return for supporting the Ottoman Empire in its war with Russia over the Crimea.[106] Likewise, the 1876 reform was executed in an attempt to ward off another war with Russia, hopefully through once again garnering European support.[107] Yet European powers failed to provide any support, leading the empire to experience its first disastrous defeat by Russia. Such proximity between the reforms and the external crises the empire faced generated ambivalence in proclamation because the Ottoman state was literally forced into taking such action.

Second, such an ambivalent stand in proclaiming the reforms in turn led to official ambiguity in their execution. How the proposed equality would be put into practice was unclear; the majority of state officials took a stand against the reforms because their positive impact for their well-being and that of the empire was never explained. In addition, even the reformist Muslim officials differed in their interpretations of equality.[108] Third, even though over the course of reforms it had become evident that the integration of non-Muslims to the Ottoman body politic was the main challenge, the state officials and the sultan insisted in proclaiming the reforms for Muslims and non-Muslims alike, without specifying how the reforms benefited the Muslim populace. Hence, the state never officially addressed the non-Muslim integration problem directly. Fourth, the reforms faced staunch resistance by the Muslim populace, a stand that was reiterated by some non-Muslim leaders. The Muslims initially objected to the 1839 reform treaty due to what they interpreted as the loss of their naturalized legal dominance.[109] Non-Muslims were also unhappy with the legal reforms because they destabilized the existing hierarchy among the non-Muslim communities.[110] All non-Muslim religious leaders were discontent because such reforms would undermine the control they had over their communities by enabling the participation of lay members in communal governance. In addition, how non-Muslim communities would fare under this promised legal equality after giving up their traditional legal protection was unclear; even though such equality was promised time and again, it was not easily put into practice because the prevailing Islamic legal system did not change. After the proclamation of the 1856 edict, many Muslim Turks started to openly complain that such reforms meant losing their legal dominance, their "sacred right earned by the blood of their ancestors."[111] Non-Muslims once again brought up their discontent in the destabilization of the hierarchy among the non-Muslims communities that placed the Greek Rum at the top, followed by the Armenians and then the Jews.

Fifth, the course of reforms clearly indicated escalating intervention of the Great Powers in the affairs of the empire regarding the integration of non-Muslims into the Ottoman body politic; they actively attempted to oversee the implementation of the reforms they proposed.[112] The Great Powers also intervened through their ambassadors at the imperial capital if the reform efforts did not fit their interests or if they did not approve of particular appointed officials.[113] Their focus on individual rights instead of communal ones oddly made communal identity and difference within the empire more salient and problematic. Especially the eastern provinces where religious communities lived intermixed came under close scrutiny, where the reform proposal advocated the redivision of space according to sameness.[114] In addition, the reforms the Great Powers advocated for the empire diverged from what they promoted in Europe to their coreligionists; while they advocated constitutional rule on the Continent, they did not promote the adoption of a constitution and parliamentary government to the Ottoman sultan.[115] The reason for this selectivity became evident *sixty years later* in 1908 after the British foreign minister Edward Grey was forced to recognize the Ottoman constitutional revolution. At the time, he noted in a private correspondence that "the consequences [of the proclamation of an Ottoman constitution] will reach further than any of us can yet foresee. The effect in Egypt will be tremendous and will make itself felt in India... the demand for a Constitution in Egypt will gain great force. What the Great Powers thus encouraged in the [Ottoman] empire was not structural change in the form of a constitution, but administrative reforms." Hence the Great Powers placed their own political interests before the spread of universal human rights because such Ottoman political transformation would destabilize European colonial rule over large Muslim populations. The gradual placement of Ottoman imperial reforms under the supervision of the Great Powers did not increase their efficacy, either. On the contrary, each political actor started to exploit this state of affairs to its own advantage and the disadvantage of others.[116] Hence, realpolitik intervened to take center stage, leading all political actors to exploit the impending reforms to their own particular advantage.[117]

According to contemporaneous memoirs, the 1839, 1856, and 1876 reforms generated two new political issues, the non-Muslim "problem" accompanied by escalating political violence and repression, and the problem regarding the nature of despotic rule. The state of upheaval instigated by the reforms was evident throughout the empire. After the 1839 edict, rebellions occurred in Syria, Jiddah, and Lebanon in the east. The 1861 uprising in Lebanon led the Ottoman state to appoint to this province a Christian governor who also acquired independence in conducting its internal affairs. This set a dangerous precedence to all other local, especially non-Muslim, communities seeking political representation. In the west, rebellions emerged throughout the Balkans. The 1876 Herzegovina rebellion led to the spread of rumors in Salonica as well as the imperial capital that mutual massacres were about to occur, leading the Christian and Muslim populace to arm. The subsequent Bulgarian attacks in the Balkans on Muslim villages and the ensuing massacres reverberated at the capital, leading to the first student-led protest of the empire. As the Muslim students of theology predominantly from the Balkans were notified of the massacre suffered by their families, they staged a rebellion against Sultan Abdülaziz I that led to the removal first of the grand vizier and then of the sultan himself. The escalating violence in the eastern provinces led Sultan Abdülhamid II to establish the Kurdish paramilitary organization known as the Hamidiye regiments. These regiments wreaked havoc in the eastern provinces as their actions were not monitored by the state. As a consequence, it is no accident that they eventually played a significant role in the ensuing 1893–96 massacres of Armenian subjects.

Top-level reformist officials increasingly beame aware that the reforms necessary for the transformation of the empire could only be executed insofar as the sultans fully supported them. As long as such support wavered, the reforms also suffered. Yet the sultans approached the reforms not in relation to the well-being of all their subjects but rather in terms of the preservation of the Ottoman dynasty and state.[118] This political priority explains the sultans' unwillingness to relinquish power. Sultans Selim III and Mahmud II had primarily executed the reforms with the intent to centralize their power. Sultan Abdülaziz I had initially decided to support the reform efforts because of what he had observed in Europe when he had traveled there as the crown prince. Yet, over time, he insisted on overseeing all reform efforts personally, blamed failures on his officials, and worried that reforms would ultimately undermine dynastic rule.[119] Indeed, what is executed in all empires depends exclusively on the personal will of the rulers, a political condition Max Weber discusses under patrimonial rule in general and sultanic rule in particular. Attempts at systematic reforms in the empire gradually challenged sultanic rule, revealing especially to the reformist officials the political precariousness of such rule and leading to their increased interest in a constitution that would sustain changes over time without the sultan's intervention.[120]

In summary, then, the refracted politics of equal rights generated new problems in Ottoman governance, including the minority issue, the interconnected issue of Western intervention, and the issue of sultanic rule. Once again, just like the military and economic elements of modernity, the negotiation of the political elements also adversely affected the Ottoman Empire.

New Educational Endeavors

Western-style schools established from the middle of the nineteenth century on were crucial in negotiating the diffusion of Western science and knowledge into the empire. The Ottoman state's educational reform strategy was not carefully planned but rather haphazard, based on the particular initiatives and visions of officials.[121] For instance, when the grand vizier Mustafa Reshid Pasha took office in 1845, he systematically developed education for the dominant

Muslim Turkish majority by establishing the Education Council, the Ministry of Public Education, and a scientific association (Encümen-i Daniş) similar to the Academie Française. Yet the pasha was not able to sustain such endeavors as he was soon thereafter replaced by an official who did not look favorably upon these institutions. Disparate officials continued to reform based on their own private initiatives, yet none lasted after the tenure of the officials at their posts.[122] The officials could also not agree on the direction in which the educational system should be reformed. While some officials argued that change ought to be introduced from the top down, starting with higher education, others contended that it would be more effective to transform the system from the bottom up, by first changing elementary schools. Yet what finally occurred was neither of these. The establishment of a university, middle schools, high schools, and elementary schools occurred without any particular order, starting in this case at the middle school because the need was not determined from within society but rather imposed by the state.[123]

It is significant to note that initially there was distrust displayed toward the attempts of Muslim officials to learn Western languages and toward the educational system that accompanied such learning.[124] One memoir writer noted that her father, Ahmet Cevdet Pasha, initially had to learn French in secret because it was not "considered proper among the religious officials [*ulema*] to learn a foreign language." That those who learned the language of the infidels would "naturally" turn into infidels was the main point of contention of those who opposed such reforms.[125] The Muslim students who attended the schools of non-Muslims also faced discrimination, however.[126] Part of the reason for such Muslim Turks attending non-Muslim schools was the poor quality of the education provided in state-funded schools.[127] Still, new educational spaces became available to Muslims and non-Muslims alike outside formal education; some Ottoman subjects started to establish public libraries, where people could read books, journals, and newspapers for a very small fee. Bookstores constituted another source of Western knowledge.[128]

Toward the end of the nineteenth century, many Western-style schools were eventually established by the state. The Galatasaray Lyceum, founded in the mid-nineteenth century, continued to educate both Muslim and non-Muslim subjects of the empire.[129] Yet more significant was the modern secular education now undertaken at the military (*harbiye*), medical (*tıbbiye*), and administrative (*mülkiye*) academies where reformist officials and officers were trained. In addition, during the reign of Abdülhamid II, five war academies were established in İstanbul, Adrianople, Monastir, Erzincan, and Damascus, and many officers were also eventually sent to teach there. Among these academies, there eventually emerged a rank order, with the one at the imperial capital regarded as the most prestigious, training the top leaders of the military corps. Contemporaneous memoirs narrate vivid memories regarding this new Western-style military education; the two emerging themes center around the negotiation of the role of religion and history on the one hand and the emphasis on theoretical knowledge without adequate practice on the other.[130] Even though the military students were forced to pray, there was no adequate time set aside to do so. This lack of adequate religious practice also extended to the curriculum in that instead of receiving a moral education, students were told religious fables and folk tales.[131] They received an official censored version of history that did not include discussion of either the recent defeats or the recent attempts at political democratization.[132] Hence, instead of critical thinking skills and knowledge about the past, they received specialized technical knowledge and training on warfare, with an emphasis on theory rather than practice out in the field; the military cadets were often not issued ammunition to practice active training lest they employ the opportunity to rebel against the sultan.[133]

Still, this new modern educational context made one significant social contribution to their knowledge: they were increasingly exposed to new topics like economics and finance, and new histories like that of the French Revolution.[134] Being taught that "the strengths of countries and nations were now predicated on financial organization and the workplace," they could not help but compare their new knowledge with the fatalistic interpretations of their own imperial history. In processing what they learned regarding the French Revolution, at times, they were so "deeply influenced that out in the courtyard" they "put on stage the great revolution ourselves. One would take on the role of Danton, another Robespierre, and still another Marat, with other friends assuming the roles of other revolutionary figures, and we would almost create an open-air theater."[135] Hence, not only were they exposed to new ideas, but they started to internalize them and generate new visions for the future of their empire. This Western-style education was also employed by the sultan to expand his sphere of power and influence over the provinces. Especially significant in this context was the tribal school (Aşiret Mektebi) that Sultan Abdülhamid II established to educate and assimilate the sons of Arab, Druzi, and Kurdish notables to the empire. Yet, contemporaneous memoirs reveal that these non-Turkish social groups of the empire also faced inherent prejudice and discrimination in that the dominant Muslim Turkish majority was often reproachful in educating them.[136] Another important school established during this period was the school of fine arts (Sanayi-i Nefise). Once again, the structural divide within the empire reproduced itself because this school was attended mostly by non-Muslims; Muslim families looked down on art and on any profession other than one in governance or the military.[137] In all, Western-style education spearheaded by the state concentrated almost exclusively on Muslim students' needs. As more and more Muslim social groups of the empire came into contact with each other in this new space of learning, the ethnic and religious differences among the Muslims became more evident. The exposure to modern ways of thinking about the world and taking subsequent action triggered the issue of social identity; Muslim students of Turkish origin started to increasingly highlight their Turkish identity.

The case of the school of fine arts provides clues to how non-Muslim students were impacted by the introduction of Western-style education into the empire. Non-Muslims were granted the right to establish their own secular communal schools by the imperial reform decrees. Over time, vast qualitative and quantitative differences appeared between the education the non-Muslims received at their schools and the education the Muslims received in theirs. Non-Muslims were permitted to receive a secular education, but, unlike the education of the Muslim Turkish majority, theirs was not financed by the state.[138] Predicated on private initiative and financial support of their own community—much along the lines of what Mithat Pasha had once envisioned for the entire empire—non-Muslim education was much more extensive.[139] The decentralization of power in establishing schools enabled non-Muslims to create a much more successful educational model. Many communal schools also provided education not only for the children but also for the adults during the weekend; the pedagogy was likewise much more engaging and participatory. In relation to the population composition, non-Muslims often had many more schools and students. This educational ascendancy was also enhanced with the additional establishment of many Christian missionary schools throughout the empire as these also initially focused exclusively on educating their coreligionists. Over time, the inequities between the number and quality of Muslim and non-Muslim schools became dramatically evident to all, Muslim and non-Muslim alike.[140] The remarkable difference in the quailty is evident in the memoirs of one Ottoman official who in the late 1890s stated that, when he was in Erzurum,[141]

> I had heard then that the school was founded by a rich Armenian named Sanasaryan and that he had had the teachers educated in Germany. There was, during our time, a well-educated, smart and totally civilized man named doctor Moryan…who then served as a deputy in the Ottoman parliament. This school offered courses like biology, geology, and music that were not yet taught at our [Muslim] schools. The cultural courses were taught by very valuable instructors. Also, many sports like…ice skating…skiing…and others that are still not yet available in Turkey were offered there.

Interestingly enough, rather than being inspired by this excellent education offered in the empire, the official instead focused on the potential danger such communal schools would pose, specifically because of their excellence. "Could there be a better example [than this one] to demonstrate what a great danger the alertness of this Armenian race of the Eastern provinces had started to pose," he queried, "this race exploited by Russia and Britain in accordance with their own political ends during a period of Ottoman decline?"

In a way, the official was correct in that the excellent education non-Muslims received deepened the structural divide between the Muslims and non-Muslims of the empire. Not only did non-Muslims receive a better education, but what they then accomplished could not be fully integrated into the Ottoman social system in a manner that benefited everyone. Their activities upon graduation often remained limited to trade and finance.[142] Yet, the sultan did attempt to also incorporate non-Muslims into the secular state schools where the future imperial officials were trained. It was in general easier to integrate non-Muslims into all modern state schools except the military academies; this was the case even after the abolition of the laws preventing non-Muslims from military service. Eventually, while there were indeed some non-Muslim students at the state lyceum of Galatasaray as well as the college of public administration, the war college, and the medical school, non-Muslims nevertheless remained a small minority, neither fully integrated into the student body[143] nor promoted after graduation within Ottoman governance at the same rate as Muslims. In spite of the establishment of rules and regulations regarding non-Muslim recruitment into the state bureaucracy, even though some non-Muslims were indeed recruited, very few actually made it all the way to the top because they were not considered "trustworthy."[144] The appointment of non-Muslim officials to state administration was especially challenging, since the Ottoman state did not seem to trust the non-Muslims or, more important, attempted to preserve the dominance of the Muslims over them. Still, many non-Muslims "considered loyal and qualified" initially served in governance, especially as ambassadors to European capitals. Yet such appointments "were later abandoned as Sultan Abdülhamid started to instead appoint Muslim Turks whom he personally trusted."[145] Many non-Muslim students sent abroad by their families and community to Europe legally expected more from the state after their return, also deepening the divide.[146] The one capacity in which the non-Muslims did serve successfully was as instructors at the state schools; non-Muslim intellectuals educated the students in the new, modern topics of economy, finance, medicine, world history, and European languages.[147] In all, then, the negotiation of modern knowledge in the empire was gradually institutionalized through the establishment of Western-style schools by the Muslim state as well as non-Muslims communities. All exposed students to new knowledge and novel ways of thinking about the world, though with significant differences between Muslims and non-Muslims; the latter received a much higher quality of education, while the former increasingly noticed their separate ethnic identity. The non-Muslim integration into state schools commenced, but at much lower rates than expected. The educational replications of Western European modernity in the empire thus continued not to contain but instead to accentuate ethnic and religious differences among the imperial subjects.

Repressing Ideological Reverberations

The most significant ideological element of Western European modernity was the principle of universal human rights that not only transformed imperial subjects into citizens but also erased differences among social groups in Europe. These rights were articulated through the concepts of liberty, equality, and fraternity; humans were ideally free and equal but also were attached to each other through brotherly love. Yet how these ideas transformed into social practice varied in accordance with the boundaries set by the preexisting social structure. All three concepts were fundamentally challenging to the Ottoman imperial rules. Liberty required the participation of all in the political structure, thereby indirectly undermining the sovereignty of the sultan. Equality necessitated a transformation from communal to individual rights, inherently destabilizing the concept of difference on which the Ottoman Empire was predicated. Fraternity demanded the establishment of a new social tie among all that overrode existing loyalties and allegiances. This was the most challenging concept in that it contained an exclusionary component: usually the dominant social group decided who qualified for the fraternity, excluding those who did not fit in. In the Ottoman Empire, liberty translated into increased demands for political participation as subjects pushed for constitutional rule. Equality proved to be challenging in that the preexisting social structure predicated on difference had to transform into a system that erased communal privileges. Fraternity in turn triggered the search for unifying principles that at first generated the concept of Ottoman identity that eventually failed to overcome existing differences, leading instead to the emergence of particular political identities that eventually fractured the imperial social system. In practice, the Ottoman state attempted to censor new visions through controlling the boundaries of modern knowledge on the one hand and the activities of students on the other. Yet such censorship could not contain the emergence of secret organizations in especially Muslim state schools with the intent to transform the empire in accordance with a new vision: the Young Turks who eventually organized into the Committee of Union and Progress (CUP) to undertake the 1908 constitutional revolution originated as such a secret organization.

Contemporaneous memoirs document especially the sultans' attempts to censor the alternate visions of political rule that was emerging in the media.[148] The 1865 Print Regulation (Matbuat Nizamnamesi) stipulated that Ottoman newspapers "promised not to write against the sultanate and the state" and also provided the names of guarantors who backed this promise. There was increased censorship in printing books as drafts had to be submitted to the state before publication.[149] The punishment for failing to abide by these regulations led to the closing down of the publication, punishment by imprisonment, or exile of the authors as well as the owners. Once the censorship of ideas commenced, it became increasingly difficult to set boundaries, since the ideas and with them censored thoughts kept expanding. The reading public was quick to determine the scope of things that should not be mentioned. One Ottoman intellectual provided a detailed list of what was censored during the reign of Sultan Abdülhamid II:[150]

> In those days, it was totally forbidden to talk about emperors, foreign governments, socialism, nihilism, rebellion, anarchy, freedom, patriotism, public rights, religion and religious scholars, [the prophets] Muhammad, Jesus, and Moses, the church, atheism, the misrule of officials, misuse of resources, women, the harem, fatherland, heaven and hell, nationalism and tribalism, international law, republicanism, deputies of the Ottoman assembly, constitutionalism, dynamites and bombs, Mithat Pasha, [Namık] Kemal Bey, Sultan Murad, crescent and the cross, Macedonia, eastern provinces, and reforms. Yet one could amply discuss rain, good weather, street dogs, and the munificence of the sultan, his good qualities, and the things he built. If it became necessary to talk about domestic politics, care was taken to make sure this was not on a [controversial] topic.

Significant in this list of censored topics are Western ideas and institutions pertaining to an alternate political rule like patriotism, nationalism, constitutionalism, republicanism, freedom, and rights as well as the Ottoman assembly that had been suspended by the sultan. Also forbidden were names of the reformist official Mithat Pasha, the patriotic poet Namık Kemal, and the deposed Sultan Murad V, who was replaced by his brother Sultan Abdülhamid II. Also significant was prohibiting the mention of the eastern and western parts of the empire, where frequent rebellions had started to occur.

Such state control of the access of the emerging Ottoman public to certain ideas and knowledge critical of the current political rule also expanded to Western-style schools. Certain courses on European history were banned from the curriculum, the course syllabi of instructors were controlled, and students were frequently under surveillance to ensure they did not possess certain "dangerous" Western books, journals, and newspapers.[151] Other sites of such official scrutiny outside the empire were the Ottoman embassies, where state officials kept track of all activities related to the empire by attending meetings, maintaining informants, and preparing reports on seditious acts undertaken by Ottoman students there.[152] These embassies also tracked down and attempted to purchase both Ottoman Muslim and non-Muslim presses in an attempt to prevent their future publications.[153] Still, the Ottoman lack of sovereignty over the postal system enabled many censored materials, especially Ottoman newspapers printed abroad, to slip in.[154] In addition, at many Western-style schools, the like-minded instructors often overlooked students' possession of banned materials.

The sultan's intent in establishing such censorship was to ascertain that students trained in Western-style schools remained loyal to him and his dynasty. Yet the modern knowledge the students received instead inspired in them not an allegiance to the sultan but rather the abstract idea of "their" state in accordance with their own vision. This inspiration initially led to the formation of secret student organizations in these modern schools, ones fashioned after the European revolutionary societies of the Carbonari in Italy and Etniki Eteria in Greece. The most significant secret organization was the one founded by those who opposed the sultan with the intention to establish a constitutional regime, a social group that eventually came to be referred to as the "Young Turks,"whose organization was the Committee of Union and Progress.[155] The term "Young Turk" signified their two fundamental characteristics: they were mostly Muslim students in the early years of adulthood, and their initial identification was as Turks.[156] They were not old and wise but rather young and inexperienced, and therefore willing to try new, untested solutions.[157] In addition, even though the initial conceptualization of the category of "Turks" was theoretically all-encompassing, there was nevertheless an inherent, naturalized emphasis on Muslims in general and ethnic Turks in particular to the exclusion of others. The name Committee of Union and Progress also highlighted the group's inherent vision: the concept of progress was directly derived from the Enlightenment ideology especially articulated by Auguste Comte. The concept of union highlighted the empire's need to unite its disparate social groups and communities that until then had been located in the social structure on the basis of difference. Hence, the CUP was a fundamentally secular, modernist organization, one that originated in the empire and then solidified into an organization while in exile. Many students and intellectuals who escaped to Western Europe to avoid the sultan's censorship and punishment initially established oppositional presses, especially in France, Switzerland, and London. These then gradually united under the leadership of Ahmed Rıza, who headed the organization in Paris for more than two decades.[158] While in Paris, the CUP also closely followed the activities of secret organizations founded by the non-Muslims of the empire, especially those of Armenians, Greek Rum, and Bulgarians, drawing lessons from the latter's activities. In its own activities, the CUP prioritized money and sacrifice; while raising money from like-minded notables and especially the Egyptian khedive, it recruited not according to rank or title but "spirit."[159] The practices of swearing an oath of allegiance, using secret codes in communication, and sending CUP seals to imperial cities where members established branches followed suit. In 1895, the CUP's newspaper, *Meshveret* (Consultation), began publication in Paris, enabling the organization to more effectively communicate and network with its followers and members both outside and within the empire. These members were then able to establish CUP branches within and outside the imperial city, and especially in the western provinces. Hence an oppositional organization formed and ably used the new public space generated through Western-style institutions and the print media.

The years 1895, 1902, and 1907 signified turning points in CUP history. The year 1895 marked the year the CUP first took public action within the empire. The CUP was triggered into action because of the escalating collective violence in the empire at that particular juncture: the 1893 massacres of Armenians started in the provinces of Muş, Bitlis, and Samsun, leading to a demonstration at the imperial city on 30 September 1895. The CUP secretly distributed pamphlets throughout the city; the pamphlets, which addressed the Muslim populace, blamed the violence on the sultan's autocratic rule. This bold public move was initially contained in 1897 as seventy-eight CUP leaders were exiled to Tripoli in a boat named *Şeref* (Honor), leading the exiled group to be referred to as "*Şeref* victims." During the interrogations leading to their arrests, the CUP members' lack of loyalty to the sultan who educated them was the main point of contention; the accused were asked to declare their loyalty to the Ottoman dynasty but staunchly refused to do so.[160] The radicalization and militarization of the movement occurred in the aftermath of this 1897 exile and were quickly accompanied by the exile of others to distant imperial lands. Also during this time, the CUP secret paramilitary group known as the Special Organization (SO;Teşkilat-ı Mahsusa) was formed.[161]

In the years 1902 and 1907, the CUP held two congresses in exile, further enabling it to develop its organization and reach. During the 1902 Paris Congress, Muslim CUP members for the first time met with other non-Muslim secret organizations with the intent to unify the opposition against the autocratic regime of Sultan Abdülhamid II. Yet during the discussion, two major disagreements emerged among the participants. The first concerned the recruitment of Muslim military officers into the CUP to hasten the revolution. Physicians Bahaeddin Şakir and Nazım in particular advocated such inclusion; even though Ahmed Rıza and others objected to it, the CUP did start to actively recruit officers from within the Ottoman military in the aftermath of the congress, a move that eventually enabled them to seize power. The second disagreement concerned the role of Western governments in producing imperial change. Non-Muslim participants and especially the Armenian Droshag and Hnchak revolutionary committee members made this recommendation. While the faction led by Ahmed Rıza and İsmail Kemal objected to such Western intervention in the affairs of the empire, the majority led by Prince Sabahaddin welcomed such an intervention. This divide reflected a deeper CUP split between those like Ahmed Rıza, who garnered a more nationalistic disposition emphasizing and retaining the dominance of Muslim Turks, and Prince Sabahaddin and his followers, who demonstrated more tolerance toward including cooperation with the Western governments and Ottoman non-Muslims.[162]

After the 1905 failed assassination attempt against Sultan Abdülhamid II, the non-Muslim revolutionary committees that had undertaken the assassination attempt started to work with the CUP in earnest. Dashnak representative Malumyan proposed a second Young Turk Congress that convened in 1907.[163] In the interim, in 1906, Prince Sabahaddin had founded the Association for Individual Initiative and Decentralization and started to print the newspaper *Terakki* (Progress). Unlike the followers of Ahmed Rıza, who were certain that a revolution leading to the reestablishment of the constitution would be sufficient for the necessary change, Prince Sabahaddin argued the establishment of decentralization and individual initiative had to accompany the redeclaration of constitution. The prince regarded decentralization as a necessary administrative need, yet Ahmed Rıza and his followers considered this to be a political proposal that would tear the empire apart. What the prince proposed would have been more beneficial to all elements of the empire, but it unfortunately did not prevail over the more exclusionary and ultimately nationalist alternative. Indeed, during the Young Turk Congress in 1907, convened under the leadership of Prince Sabahaddin, Ahmed Rıza caused an uproar when he declared that the congress ought to accept the legal principles of the Islamic caliphate and the Ottoman dynasty, principles that would have reproduced the naturalized Muslim Turkish dominance. Especially the Armenian participants noted that they were in attendance not to recognize the sultanate and caliphate but instead to discuss the inherent rights of oppressed Ottomans.[164] The congress statement that all sides ultimately agreed upon identified the sultan's autocracy and his failure to undertake reforms as the causes for all imperial unrest and demanded the reproclamation of the constitution.

These three turning points in CUP history identify the process through which members of the dominant Muslim Turkish majority educated in Western-style schools initially organized the secret opposition to the sultan under their vision. Yet such organization revealed two disparate visions predicated on nationalism and liberalism: those advocating the continued salience of an innate Turkish Muslim identity based on state centralization prevailed over those who supported the development of a multiethnic, multireligious identity based on decentralization and private initiative. It should be stressed once again that even though the CUP claimed to be an organization that included all imperial subjects regardless of ethnicity and religious creed, there were in practice very few non-Muslim members.[165] During the course of the years 1907 and 1908, oppositional print materials sent from Europe infiltrated into the empire with escalating frequency, and Muslim military officers especially stationed in the western Balkan provinces—removed from the direct scrutiny of the sultan and in closer proximity to Western Europe—were recruited into the CUP in large numbers.[166] Hence, the repressed ideological reverberations of Ottoman mirrored modernity once again triggered social upheaval as the oppositional groups situated to democratize the empire fractured and fragmented.

Transformation of Ottoman Imperial Sentiments

Western Lifestyle and Escalating Feelings of Frustration

The consumption of modern lifestyle was the one unconditionally successful adoption of Western European modernity. Until the mid-nineteenth century, the Ottoman imperial capital was locally administered, with no tax collection for urban services. In the empire, the organization and upkeep of private space had always trumped any significant investment in public space. Mosques (and the stores built around them for their economic support) and bridges (the maintenance of which was assigned to local towns and villages in return for tax exemption) were probably the two most significant state investments. After the advent of Western modernity predicated on the display of public control, order, and progress, Ottoman public life appeared inadequate and in need of improvement. Especially Western attire, entertainment, and services became increasingly visible as some Ottoman subjects started to dress, consume, entertain, and, in general, live like their modern European counterparts. Such adoption of a Western European lifestyle produced and sustained the illusion of Ottoman modernity. It also led many Muslims to start comparing Ottoman modernity to its Western European counterpart. Failures in properly maintaining such Western forms, and in generating the necessary infrastructure to transform the Ottoman content quickly led to feelings of frustration, disillusion, and embarrassment toward Western Europe.

Contemporaneous memoirs map out the process through which the modern form became increasingly visible especially in the urban centers of the empire through modern public attire, entertainment, and services. People dressed in Western-style attire started to promenade on paved streets and sidewalks, shopping at large department stores stocked with Western products; at night, they rode their cars or tramways in well-lit streets, frequenting the growing number of restaurants and cafes and attending performances at theaters and concert halls. This marked a significant difference from the traditional Ottoman lifestyle, in which such entertainment often occurred within private houses. The new modern lifestyle first became visible through the diffusion of Western public attire of hats, jackets, and pants that replaced turbans, caftans, and loose trousers; initially Westerners and non-Muslims,[167] then modernizing Muslim officers and officials,[168] and finally the rest of the Muslim populace[169] adopted this change in personal appearance. The Ottoman traditional regulation of non-Muslim attire to distinguish them from Muslims became irrelevant. New spaces for public entertainment such as concert halls, theaters, restaurants, cafes, hotels, shops, and later movie houses emerged alongside the traditional coffeehouses where Muslim entertainment used to take place. The Ottoman state officials closely monitored and attempted to control the participation of Muslim Turks in such places of Western entertainment, but to no avail.[170] Social gatherings such as teas and dinner parties organized by non-Muslims started to be gradually frequented by Muslim Turks as well.[171] Western music that was initially heard only on the streets gave way to public concerts in theaters.[172] Soon municipal services such as local transportation through tramways and boats, communication through telephones, and services in the form of gas and electricity, sewage and garbage collection, and construction of sidewalks and modern stone buildings were provided by Western private companies. Such transformation of Ottoman public space was highly selective, however, in that initially only Westerners and non-Muslims adopted such uses, thereby visibly differentiating non-Muslim and Muslim neighborhoods, to the benefit of the former. This meant the Ottoman traditional order had been turned upside down as non-Muslims began to enjoy a much higher quality of life than their Muslim counterparts.

The temptations of this Western way of life and especially the conspicuous consumption associated with it then started to draw in young Muslim Turkish males. Especially those belonging to wealthy families frequently escaped to the Westernized Christian quarter of Pera. If they got too carried away in this activity, one memoir writer noted, they were said to have "fallen to the other side," where "the other side was half Europe.... The entire [Muslim] neighborhood would curse the profligacy of these youth... their squandering [their wealth] on the other side barely lasted a month or two [until they ran out of money]."[173] Such now locally available temptations of modern consumption divided the Muslim populace as some resented and rejected the Western lifestyle and others wholeheartedly embraced it. The adoption of such Western forms came to be regarded as an advantage among those Ottomans involved in trade, commerce, government, and military service yet as a liability to the religious and the conservatives who tried to disregard the change.

Yet those Ottomans adopting the Western form increasingly compared Western European modernity with the Ottoman mirrored modernity, to the detriment of the latter. For instance, a Muslim intellectual wrote about "a depression of feelings including jealousy, anger, and intimidation" upon finding out as a student that those educated in Western schools were much more advanced at a much younger age.[174] Those Ottoman officers and officials who now visited Europe with increased frequency also admired what they saw, on the one hand, yet felt distressed when they compared it to the conditions within the Ottoman Empire, on the other.[175] Perhaps the most pungent account is provided in the memoirs of Hayrullah Efendi, who, after traveling to Europe in the 1869s, articulated all those things available in Western Europe that were missing in the empire.[176] The well-kept, well-lit public face of Paris contrasted deeply with the ill-lit, ill-kept public spaces in İstanbul. He articulated his strong feelings of frustration as follows:

> Why is there not similar organization and order, this level of care and abundance available in our country? Aren't we human beings just like them?... While they do not have any outstanding characteristics different from us, we still need their manufactured goods, and all we are left with is arrogance, haughtiness, and pride. [However,] most of the clothing and goods that give us such arrogance and haughtiness are originally produced in our country, then processed and manufactured in Europe, only to then reappear before our eyes in valuable form. Why can't all this be produced in our country? Don't we have [all the necessary ingredients] in our country?

Hayrullah Efendi's questions constantly occupied many succeeding generations of Ottoman and later Turkish intellectuals. With the advent of Western European modernity, they started to constantly measure themselves against Western Europe and became increasingly frustrated at not reaching the same level of order and progress. Because they could not successfully express their frustration against the ever-triumphant West, some instead projected their negative emotions at those they associated with the West within their midst, namely, the non-Muslim subjects.

Increasingly Polarized Communal Relations

The adverse impact of Ottoman mirrored modernity was accentuated during this time period with rebellions and wars that further challenged the empire. Among these, contemporaneous memoirs commented the most on the 1821

Greek rebellion and the 1876–78 war with Russia. The Greek rebellion was the first significant domestic rebellion at the end of which the empire had to recognize the first independent country (of Greece) formed on imperial lands. Greek independence generated within the Ottoman governing elite the blueprint of what all non-Muslim demands would lead to if they remained unchecked and not suppressed by force. As expected, all non-Muslim communities in general and the remaining Greek Rum in the empire in particular were now treated with increased public distrust. The 1876–78 war with Russia marked the first instance of total Ottoman defeat as Russian forces swept through the Balkans all the way to the outskirts of the imperial capital. The defeat was devastating on two grounds: never in Ottoman history had any army directly threatened the imperial capital, and never had so many Muslim refugees poured into the empire from Russia. As a consequence, the empire's population composition changed irreversibly in favor of Muslims. The refugee stories of Christian cruelty also projected onto the non-Muslim communities of the empire that started to experience additional prejudice and discrimination. All along, the impact of situated modernity persisted as non-Muslims began to live a distinctly more modern lifestyle, making their difference from the Muslim populace more pronounced. Especially among the Armenians, another significant development was intra-communal fragmentation as modern urban and secular Armenians developed vision and behavior that differed from and often challenged their traditional rural and religious counterparts. At a time of escalating Muslim prejudice, discrimination, and distrust toward non-Muslim communities, the Armenian intra-communal fragmentation was most unfortunate in that it precluded a united stand that probably could have lessened the ensuing collective violence.

Adverse Social Impact of Rebellions and Wars

The first significant rebellions resulting in land loss originated in the Balkans, commencing with the 1821 Greek uprising that led to independence in 1830. These rebellions reverberated in the imperial capital in the form of rumors of massacre scenarios, agitating the dominant Muslim Turkish majority against non-Muslims living in their midst.[177] The Muslim Turkish populace had very little means of gathering information other than through their personal networks, and they were therefore quick to believe that the Greek Rum of the imperial capital planned a massacre against them. Only the government's intervention by having imams at mosques address the fallacy of such rumors contained potential conflict. Yet the Muslim fury and distrust against the Greek Rum continued, since many among the latter did indeed support the Greek independence movement, either financially or in spirit.[178] Similar rebellions later started to occur at the other end of the empire; in 1841, the Christian governor and local Christians in Lebanon clashed with the Druzes, and unrest continued for almost two decades as Muslims and non-Muslims attacked and plundered each other's neighborhoods. At this particular instance, the Great Powers also started to actively intervene in the affairs of the empire; the French army under the command of General Beaufort d'Haipoul entered Lebanon to restore order. In the 1870s, rebellions in the Balkans worsened as the Bulgarians followed the example of the Greeks to eventually also gain their independence.[179]

During the course of the nineteenth century, such domestic rebellions were accompanied by frequent wars in 1787–92, 1809–12, 1828–29, 1853–56, and 1876–78 that the Ottoman army fought against Russia. Among these, the last one was the most devastating in that defeat was total. Contemporaneous memoirs articulate the trauma this "'93 War"[180] produced in Ottoman society.[181] The most prominent Ottoman who commented on this war was Sultan Abdülhamid II, who had succeeded to the throne right before the declaration of the war; he stated that "the '93 War has been an ever bleeding wound in me for forty years. I tried very hard to prevent it, but did not succeed. Then I wore myself out to win it, sacrificing from my sleep at night and my comfort during the day, but I could not win." As many Muslims fled to the empire, the Ottoman state faced its first significant refugee problem.[182] In addition, accounts of the sufferings of the remaining Muslim Turks in the Balkans—who for the first time had to live under the rule of Greeks and Bulgarians—became public for the first time. One remarked that on upon the arrival of the Russian occupying forces, "the Muslim nation turned into live corpses, retiring into their houses in silence... [while] the local Bulgarians put on their holiday outfits with joy and pride, running out to greet the Russians with [food]... and flower bouquets." What upset the Muslim Turks even more was the West's inability or unwillingness to prevent the ensuing violence. "It was assumed that the Great Powers would not permit the Russians to engage in murder and plunder," the author noted. "Such a shame! In their official speeches and correspondence, the Russian tsar and his commanders named this war 'the battle for religion and the cross, instigating all Christians to take action against the Muslim world.'" He then added that even though thousands of Muslims had been massacred, the West focused almost exclusively on the massacre of 300 Bulgarians who had refused to surrender to the Ottoman forces. "The bones of those [Bulgarians] killed are still shown as proof of Muslim barbarity to all those consuls and foreign representatives arriving at Zağra... yet the deceitful Bulgarians hid all the Muslim massacres they committed and the esteemed consul did not bother to see and learn [about the latter]." The trauma of this first public rejection by the West, the inability of the Ottoman forces to withstand the attacks, and the indifference of the West to Muslim suffering generated not only feelings of fear, anxiety, and disappointment but also fury against the West.

This fury was daily sustained by the more than a million Muslim refugees who flooded the empire. The adverse impact on the Ottoman public morale was also accompanied by worsening economic conditions as the refugees were settled in mostly barren, uninhabitable areas of the empire.[183] The sufferings the refugees continued to face after their arrival, often being decimated through epidemics and malnourishment, radicalized them on the one hand and destroyed their ethics on the other, leading many to resort to local thievery and plunder for survival. Local non-Muslims who were less protected by the state became their frequent targets.[184]

Once the West started to be perceived by the Ottoman public as a vicious "Christian" force out to destroy the empire, all world events were then interpreted through such a lens. For instance, the 1904–5 Russo-Japanese War was followed by the Ottoman populace with great interest, as a war of a Western Christian civilization against an Eastern, non-Christian one. Ottoman Muslim Turks of course fervently supported Japan to such a degree that some named their sons after famous Japanese generals.[185] Hence, an Ottoman identity predicated on a divide with the Christian West came into being not only through their own local experiences but also through knowledge they started to acquire about similar cases in other parts of the world.

Escalating Publicly Expressed Emotions

Wars and personal experience of a Western lifestyle formed the two direct interactions of especially the Muslim Turks in relation to the West. Wars that increasingly resulted in Ottoman defeats against the West fostered anti-Western sentiments on the one hand and frustrated feelings of revenge on the other. For instance, one author's preface to his memoirs captures the emotional impact of the disastrous consequences of the '93 War with Russia as follows:[186]

> Oh son of Turk, during the wars with Russia, the ones who bestowed upon you the blood in your veins spilled their own blood to the last. Regardless of what you are today and will become tomorrow, never forget until eternity that you are the orphan of those martyrs.... Like this religion, this state and this fatherland, this anger, this vengeance is likewise their sacred legacy. Be respectful of this right and duty until there is not a single Russian left on earth: Son of a Turk, your right is to kill, and your duty, if necessary, to die immediately!

This public anger and vengeance, less directed against what did not work within the empire, was quickly and more easily projected against the "enemies." In this case, they were the Great Powers, with Russia as the main aggressor, and other Western European states as Russia's implicit supporters. It is no accident that this particular Ottoman generation impacted in their youth by the violence of the '93 War reached adulthood in the early 1900s, when they replicated the violence they heard about or experienced against their own non-Muslim subjects.[187]

In addition, their continued interaction with Western Europe and its modern lifestyle not only triggered but also reproduced feelings of shame accompanied by pain.[188] Especially Muslim officials who experienced Western European modernity by traveling there quickly compared what they saw to the imperial conditions, only to feel increasingly inadequate. Those who associated with Westerners within the empire started to believe that they were constantly mocked behind their backs for the inadequacies of Ottoman mirrored modernity.[189] According to one Muslim Turk, the classical music concerts given at the foreign embassies in İstanbul provided another context of inadequacy. The few Muslim Turks who sneaked into such concerts narrated that they "felt belittlement in [the Europeans'] looks that was like a slap on our faces, [making us become aware] of our backwardness.... They were additionally polite to cover this belittlement."[190] This Ottoman inferiority, felt for the first time, gradually expanded to include the Ottoman non-Muslim subjects as well because, unlike Muslim Turks, non-Muslim Ottomans were much more comfortable in the presence of Europeans and easily adopted the Western lifestyle within the empire. One Muslim Turk recounted that they "envied the [Ottoman] Christians who were all comfortable, prosperous and dressed well, whose happy women we saw behind the open doors of their stone houses...not only foreigners who were [legally] privileged, but also [Ottoman] Christians....After the cross, the major symbol of the infidel was the hat; I see in my mind's eye many chance encounters when all Muslims felt inferior in front of the hat."[191] Another added that "from the grand vizier down to the common gendarmerie, we were impaired with the largest and most terrifying infirmity: the feeling of inferiority, with ignorance added onto it."[192] Even though foreigners were legally beyond reach, most non-Muslims were still Ottoman subjects and therefore frequently became the target of such adverse emotions.

The individual encounters with the West and the Western lifestyle multiplied over time to negatively mark the experiences of entire generations with feelings of anxiety and angst at their ever-challenged and increasingly defeated empire. One Muslim official, for instance, described his father as "a member of that generation that had lived through the resentment created by the shrinking empire, and had personally agonized to stop this process of shrinking."[193] Yet the younger generations were often unaware of and therefore unprepared for the degree of imperial loss of lands because what they were taught at school still stressed past imperial glory, not at all acknowledging recent defeats. Another official thus reflected on the extraordinary transformation his generation went through as follows:[194]

> We were the last children of the Ottoman Empire. When we grew up and took notice of our surroundings, the boundaries of the country extended from the Adriatic Sea to the Persian Gulf. According to our high school geography textbook, the country was even larger: Egypt and the Sudan, the Bulgarian Princedom, Bosnia and Herzegovina all appeared within our borders; we were still the Turkey of the Danube, Nile, and Euphrates Rivers.... [In school]... our teachers were eloquent about the glories of the Ottoman dynasty. They would not discuss [the recent defeats].... We were unaware that we sat on an insecure fatherland.

This lack of knowledge made it even more difficult for the young generations to face contemporary harsh realities; as many not only refused to come to terms with the worsening conditions but were instead taught about former imperial glories, their frustration coupled with their conviction that they were powerful enough to challenge and take revenge on the West. In addition, firm in their belief that maintaining the status quo would bring back former days of glory, many opposed and resisted the reforms.[195] Also significant in their stand was the limitless trust they had in the conviction that the superiority of their religion would ultimately help them prevail over the ephemeral victories of the infidels.[196] And because they had no access to the powerful West to avenge their suffering, it was much easier and safer to direct their negative feelings toward those whom they identified with the West, namely, the non-Muslim subjects. Such a negative stand prevented the integration of non-Muslims into the social structure through reforms on the one hand and escalated the tensions of Muslim non-Muslim interaction on the other. As a consequence, Muslims were ready to attack their non-Muslim counterparts at the slightest rumor of "misbehavior," including that committed by foreigners.[197] And the Ottoman state defended such episodic violence on the grounds that it was committed for internal security.

Increasingly Polarized Use of Space

Because Muslim and non-Muslim subjects of the empire absorbed elements of Western modernity to different degrees, the non-Muslim use of space started to visibly diverge from the Muslim use, and did so to the detriment of the latter. Non-Muslim neighborhoods could thus be visibly distinguished in terms of their orderliness, cleanliness, and brightness.[198] At the imperial city, the most Westernized neighborhood was Pera, across the Golden Horn, where the foreign embassies were also located. The impressions of Muslim Turks "crossing over" to that side as well as the pain and inferiority they felt in doing so were frequently described in memoirs. One recounted "the visible slowness in Muslim neighborhoods" and the "provincialness" Muslim Turks felt in Pera, where "many stores barely 'deigned' to respond to anyone who could not speak in any language other than Turkish." As a consequence, "one did not often hear 'the Turks of the other side' speak Turkish either. . . . He . . . hid his Turkishness and was embarrassed about it."[199] Many Muslim Turks were impressed by the efficiency of foreign companies and yearned for such orderliness in their lives as well. The drama of crossing over from one (Muslim) style of life to the (non-Muslim) other was best captured by one Muslim Turk, who stated:[200]

> If a [European] theater company came to Pera and . . . if you live in [the Muslim part] in Istanbul . . . and if you did not have enough money in your purse to rent a carriage . . . then you would have to go from [Muslim] Istanbul's mud-covered streets immersed in darkness, across the . . . bridge, climb the hills, and, half penitent by this time, enter the theater. . . . You were still happy if you enjoyed art for two hours to forget all that trouble, difficulties, your hurt personal pride. As you returned home soiled [in mud], staggering in the dark, something twisted in your heart as you thought, your heart aching about the foreigners, the Greek Rum, the Armenians and Jews on the other side of the bridge leading a very pleasant life in their own magnificent mansions, while the Turk on the opposite side pulled the blanket of his deprived life . . . over his head to sleep, only to awaken the following day to see the sun turbid once again. This was the life of the Turk and the degree of the unhappiness and misery felt by the [Muslim Turkish] youth of the time.

The modern lifestyle thus segmented the imperial city into different existences and realities. It increasingly made Ottoman public space foreign to any signs of Muslim Turkishness; the signs on the shops, the street names, the building styles, and even the people promenading the streets became all foreign. "Truthfully," one Muslim Turk lamented, "there was not in all of great İstanbul a single hotel, a restaurant or a well-known national institution that could be attributed to the Turks . . . [who] were only left with military service and officialdom. All matters pertaining to industry and technology were manned by foreigners or non-Muslims, and all industrial goods down to thread and needle were imported from abroad. In exchange, we [the Turks] popularized commonness, demeaning our national identity and moral decline to such a degree that we drew pleasure from calling each other ass of a Turk."[201] The situation was no different outside the imperial city. In describing the city of Edirne (Adrianople), one Turkish

Muslim official noted that "the Muslims, that is, the Turks, and the non-Muslim Jews, Greeks, and Armenians lived in different worlds. [The latter]...led quite an advanced life in a neighborhood where the houses and streets were relatively clean and orderly."[202] This feeling of being surrounded by suffocating Western European superiority within their own empire upset and alienated the Muslim Turkish populace, making them resentful toward the new division of labor that privileged the foreigners and non-Muslim subjects.

As such polarization between the Muslim and non-Muslim lifestyles increased, so did the dissatisfaction of the non-Muslim subjects with their location in society. They now had wealth, but they still lacked any power in the Ottoman social system.[203] Interestingly, in their memoirs, very few Muslim Turkish officials went beyond their felt resentment to actually reflect on the reasons behind this non-Muslim dissatisfaction. Among the few who did, one Muslim Turkish official conjectured that "the new ideas of the time, of equal freedom to all, mobilized the non-Muslim subjects to push for these principles." He added that the practice of many non-Muslims sending their children and relatives to Europe to get an education did not help either; those who then returned to the empire started to demand more fervently the equality that was promised by the Ottoman state and government but not fully accomplished. As a consequence, the official continued, non-Muslims complained about "lacking total equality with Muslims," and "the non-Muslims no longer hid these words as they previously used to."[204] Hence, in addition to adopting the Western European lifestyle and knowledge at a faster rate, non-Muslims also began to express their discontent publicly and with increasing frequency. Interestingly, at the schools they attended, the dominant Muslim Turkish majority also became increasingly aware of how the reforms had impacted them more adversely than their non-Muslim counterparts. One Muslim Turkish official recounted his experiences at the medical academy as follows:[205]

> They taught us that the sword of freedom was going to be double-edged and upon seizing it, we could not avoid getting cut up by it. This was due to our lack of culture; our ignorance caused irreparable damage on all fronts. For instance, [our instructors] said, look at the education non-Muslims provide for their children and compare that with our population. Think of all of their developed neighborhoods throughout the empire. Their economic development is closely tied to the financial centers of foreign [Western European] countries. Our only strength drew from thoughtlessly purchasing the goods of peasants and turning these over to them. We pursued our interests at the gates of government, in jobs that are barren and narrowly conceived.

The imagery of Western European modernity as a "double-edged sword" was indeed very apt. All the while the Ottoman state fervently modernized through military and bureaucratic reforms, the dominant Muslim Turkish majority remained restricted to state jobs that did not pay nearly as well as they once did. Therefore, while experiencing escalating impoverishment, they noticed that non-Muslims, who for centuries had specialized in trade and commerce with Western Europe, were able to adapt much more quickly and positively to the ensuing transformations. As non-Muslims started to do much better in a transforming world system where the economy prevailed over politics, unlike their Western European counterparts, Ottoman non-Muslims not only failed to transfer their wealth into political power but continued to face discrimination.[206] Such escalation of prejudice and ensuing discrimination was not confined to non-Muslims, however. Gradually, all communities different from the the Muslim Turks, such as the Kurds and Arabs, also stood out and were excluded from the body politic—so much so that in the late nineteenth century, one Muslim military official recounted in his memoirs that upon his arrival at the imperial war academy at the capital, his provincial clothing caused Turkish students to make fun of him and others dressed like him, calling them "Kurds."[207] Social relations outside of the imperial capital were similarly polarized in other major cities like Izmir,[208] Eskişehir,[209] Gümüşhane,[210] Erzurum,[211] and Diyarbekir.[212] In the provinces, especially non-Muslims, and Armenians among them in particular, faced escalating prejudice and discrimination.[213] Unlike in the past, the Armenian subjects felt that they were no longer protected by the state; Muslims who aggressed upon them were no longer held accountable for their violence. They also noted that such discriminatory behavior was much more rampant in towns than in surrounding villages. The delivery of justice to non-Muslims was no longer systematically enforced by the state; it instead became contingent upon the particular personal attitudes of local Muslim Turkish officials.

Intra-Armenian Polarization

Within non-Muslim communities of the empire, not all subjects benefited equally from the changing economic conditions. Western European modernity in general and the emphasis on trade and commerce in particular privileged cities and towns at the expense of the countryside. Among all non-Muslim communities, the Greek Rum had initially topped the communal stratification system due to their connection with the Balkan provinces, where they assumed state positions and also served as translators to the court. In the aftermath of Greek independence in the early nineteenth century, however, the Ottoman state's trust in them waned, and they were gradually replaced by members of the

Armenian community. Yet the emerging benefits of modernity were not equally distributed within the Armenian community. Therefore, rather than uniting the benefits as a community to fight for equal rights, the Armenians became increasingly polarized and fragmented. There were two significant sources of such intra-Armenian polarization: the religious-secular divide on the one hand and the urban-rural divide on the other. The intersection of these divides and the increasing subsequent fragmentation enabled the newly emergent Armenian revolutionary committees to find a fertile ground on which to flourish.

The Armenians motivated by secular liberal thoughts started to challenge the rule of the traditional community leaders named *amira* exercised in conjunction with the church clergy.[214] In addition, the contemporaneous establishment of the Catholic and Protestant denominations further undermined the predominance of the Armenian Apostolic Church. The first political reaction came from the tradesmen who had sufficient accumulated economic capital through their interaction with the West; they employed this economic power to attain political power within their community. The church attempted to appease both parties by appointing members to the administrative council. The subsequent complaints of the *amira* to the sultan led to the formation of two councils, civil and spiritual, overseen by the patriarch. Ranks of the secular reformists were then supplemented by the increasing number of Armenians educated abroad who increasingly contributed to the modernization of their community in such a way that gradually, traditionalist *amira* representing the status quo lost power. It is notable that the traditional-modern divide culturally articulated itself within the Armenian community over language. In 1853, the first Armenian Teaching Commission (Usumnagan Khorhurt) was formed after the model of the French Academy, splitting the community between the progressive Lusavoryal and the conservative Khavaryal. The split was so fervent that the conservatives had Nahabed Rusinyan's book entitled *Speaking the Armenian Language Correctly (Uğğakhosutyun Arti Hay Levzin)* banned by a patriarchal decree. Yet the efforts of the modernizers continued, leading to their proposal in 1855 for a community constitution that led to the production of a text in 1857 that, even though approved by the Armenian council, was rejected by the Ottoman state. It appears that the *amira* employed their power to have this text turned down. Yet in 1858, after Serovpe Viçenyan was elected to head the High Civilian Council, he was able to form a constitutional commission (comprising 2 bishops, 2 monks, 5 priests, and 15 civilians) that put together an Armenian constitution, approved in 1860 and put into circulation without awaiting the sultan's affirmation. The Ottoman state did not directly approve the text, asking for some revisions whereby the final Armenian National Constitution was finally approved on 17 March 1863. At the councils that formed as a consequence of the constitutional principles, Armenian bureaucrats, merchants, and intellectuals further replaced the *amira*.

Still, of the Armenian administrative council comprising 140 delegates, 20 had to be religious men; of the rest, 80 were selected from the imperial capital, and the remaining 40 from the provinces. Thus, even though most of the Armenian population lived in the provinces, they were not proportionally represented on the council. Vartan Pasha strongly opposed this inequity, but to no avail. Hence, the religious-secular divide intersected with the urban-rural one. Unlike the Armenians in cities and towns who often accumulated wealth through trade and commerce, the economic condition of rural Armenians especially in the eastern provinces worsened. Here, those engaging in trade and commerce managed to survive, but those in agriculture experienced greater poverty as their lands were increasingly possessed by local Muslim notables. Seizure of Armenian property and lands escalated especially during the second half of the nineteenth century.[215] Armenians had tilled their ancestral lands over which they did not have legal ownership. With the promulgation of private property law in 1858, however, many local Muslim notables forcefully seized and claimed ownership over the Armenian lands with new, false title deeds. Two factors further triggered such unlawful behavior: the escalating number of Muslim refugees flooding the empire at a time when the state lacked the means to settle them,[216] and increased state pressure on nomadic Kurdish tribes to settle.[217] Because the Ottoman legal system favored Muslims, and because Armenians did not have access to arms, they suffered the most land loss in the provinces and became increasingly impoverished. The adverse conditions of Armenians were sometimes documented by Ottoman officials.[218] Another factor that led property to change hand in the eastern provinces was the intervention of the Russians buying land on which to settle Christians.[219]

Especially after the 1860s, the election of patriarch Mıgırdiç Hrimyan from the provinces brought the injustices suffered by rural Armenians to the forefront. Around this time, the communal divide between the urban, apolitical, wealthier Armenians and their rural, impoverished and increasingly politically radicalized counterparts became a prevalent theme in communal discussions, one that was nevertheless unresolved as the brief power takeover of Mıgırdiç Hrimyan was contained as the later patriarchs often sided with the urban segment.[220] Still, the discontent in the provinces continued unabated. During the last two decades of the nineteenth century, various secret Armenian committees became more active and successful among the impoverished and therefore radicalized rural Armenians, especially those in the eastern provinces. While recruiting members among the discontented, these revolutionary committees employed violence to undermine the communal power of wealthy and loyal Armenians. Wealthy Armenians were forced to make donations to the committees; if they refused, they were threatened and then assassinated. Those who held official posts were also forced to resign and likewise were murdered if they refused.

Contemporaneous memoirs of two Muslim officials in particular discussed this intra-Armenian violence. One Muslim official recounted what he personally encountered on two separate occasions during his investigation in the eastern provinces. Once, at an Armenian village where he stayed, he noted that whereas the village elderly hosting them were loyal to the state, the chief steward and priest were revolutionaries. The revolutionaries beat up the village elders for hosting Ottoman officials; when searches of their houses revealed many armaments, they were eventually arrested by the official and sent to the city for trial. The other encounter took place in a city, where the Armenian urban notables complained to the official that not only had the younger Armenian generation turned revolutionary, but they no longer obeyed the orders of the communal leaders.[221] Another official who served as the interior minister during the 1890s remarked that the Ottoman security forces could not capture the revolutionary assassins due to lack of cooperation from the Armenian community on the one hand and the sultan's habit of pardoning those revolutionaries who were captured on the other.[222] The Armenian community and the Ottoman sultan were complicitous in not holding the revolutionary assassins accountable for their crimes through appropriate punishment. While it is understandable that community members were unwilling to name their own members, the sultan's stand is more perplexing. Such imperial pardons effectively undermined the promised state protection over all subjects of the empire, regardless of religious creed. Instead, the sultan actually escalated these divides by adopting the policy of bestowing "lots of medals, ranks and rewards" upon the urban, loyal Armenians he deemed to be serving his dynasty and the state.[223] The remarks of these officials highlight three dimensions of intra-Armenian polarization: the inefficacy of the sultan in containing the violence, the complicity of the community in harboring assassins, and the escalating intergenerational and urban-rural divide within the Armenian community in supporting revolutionary committee members. Those wealthy urban Armenians especially in the imperial capital were amply rewarded insofar as they remained apolitical, and those opposing the sultan's rule or protesting the injustices they encountered were, upon being caught, often pardoned. The secular-religious and urban-rural divides were thus compounded by the sultan with a third divide based on loyalty, separating Armenians who were loyal to the sultan and those who opposed him.

Collective Violence against the Armenians: The 1893–96 Massacres

Escalating polarization in the Ottoman social structure with the advent of Western European modernity gradually transformed the preexisting prejudice and discrimination of Muslims against non-Muslim subjects into acts of episodic violence. Crucial in triggering this process was the dramatic defeat of the 1876–78 Russo-Ottoman War, including the first major land loss, Bulgarian independence, and a flood of Muslim Turkish refugees. The Ayastefanos and Berlin Treaties signed at the end of the war enabled the Great Powers to acquire the right intervene in the affairs of the empire to oversee modernizing reforms. Also crucial at this juncture was the advent of the thirty-three-year reign of Sultan Abdülhamid II, who suspended the constitution and the Ottoman assembly, centralizing decision-making power in his person. As the sultan prioritized the preservation of the dynasty and the state over the protection of his subjects, the rural Armenians, especially in the eastern provinces, endured escalating threats to their security as the Ottoman government increasingly failed to provide protection. The emerging local disturbances were not contained in time due to the sultan's fear that the Great Powers would exploit these conflicts to send troops into the empire, thereby effectively ending Ottoman sovereignty. During the delay in the intervention of Ottoman security forces, the local Muslim populace exercised popular justice by attacking the Armenian neighborhoods. Because the Muslim populace had the right to carry arms and the non-Muslims did not, the Armenian casualties were much larger in number, with approximately 100,000 to 300,000 losing their lives; the Muslim losses were much lower. The chronology of this first instance of collective violence against the Armenians can best be traced in two phases: the pre-1893 episodic violence and the subsequent 1893–1907 period of collective violence.

The Pre-1893 Episodic Violence

The 1876 promulgation of the Ottoman constitution and the formation of the first Ottoman assembly in which Armenian members also participated had raised hopes that were quickly dashed when Sultan Abdülhamid II used the war with Russia to suspend both efforts.[224] It is no accident that the first Armenian parties were founded during this period, with the Armenagan Party established in 1885, the Hnchakian in 1887, the Armenian Revolutionary Federation in 1890, and the Armenian Revolutionary Party in 1891. The initial unrest put down by violence was not systematic but rather episodic in nature.

The first incidents of violence occurred in 1890 "when the Ottoman state tried to shut down some Armenian schools that actively fostered rebellion by teaching about the names of old Armenian kings with the intent to keep alive the memory of the old Armenian kingdom and to foster Armenian racism."[225] The Armenian protests led to massacres in Muş and Erzurum. During the unrest that also spread to Adıyaman and Malatya, some Kurdish leaders actually saved the Armenians from the ensuing violence.[226] Then the rural Armenians brought their complaints to the imperial city, asking for justice, but the Armenian patriarch

Horen I refused to take their complaints to the sultan.[227] When the Armenian demonstrators started to march to the palace to personally deliver their complaints, the sultan attempted to contain them by ordering firemen to disperse them with water. More insight into this 1890 Kumkapı[228] incident is provided by the contemporaneous accounts of Ottoman officials.[229] All involved agreed that the rural disturbances and the demonstration in the imperial city had been organized by Russian Armenian revolutionaries, which may explain why the patriarch did not intervene on their behalf because they were not Ottoman subjects. Even though the main culprits were identified, the sultan once again pardoned them all, turning them over to the Russian ambassador. He did so because he had received an informer's report that the incident was actually instigated by his own officials in an attempt to remove him from the throne. In the end, the Armenian instigators were not held accountable for their actions and escaped without any punishment.

The sultan then came up with a local solution to contain the unrest in the eastern provinces; in 1891, he established the Hamidiye regiments, thirty regiments manned by Kurdish tribal leaders and their armed guards who acted as the sultan's paramilitary units.[230] Given the sultan's reservations about employing official forces due to his fears about subsequent Western intervention, it is no accident that he instead turned to enforcing such indirectly state-sanctioned, informal, and local violence. Yet these regiments failed to bring peace and instead aggravated the existing unrest by aggressing upon rural Armenians and poor Muslim peasants. An Ottoman official who was a governor in the region opposed the privatization of violence in the hands of such Kurdish militia because, he argued, such splintering of state authority made the ensuing violence arbitrary and much harder to control.[231]

The next rebellion occurred in 1893 in Zeytun in Cilicia. Contemporaneous accounts of Ottoman officials once again narrated the events from the vantage point of the state.[232] Only 300 regular soldiers were stationed in Zeytun; the security minister wrote to the government to increase their number and also supply them with a few cannon but to no avail. The Armenian fighters killed all of the 300 regular soldiers stationed there and then attacked and murdered Muslims in the neighboring villages. Meanwhile, fights also broke out in Urfa, Maraş, and Elbistan and then spread to Antep. The Armenian fighters' eventual clash with the Ottoman military at Köksün led to their retreat to Zeytun, leaving behind more than 800 dead and wounded. Upon the insistence of foreign ambassadors, however, the sultan once again decided "to unconditionally pardon the Armenians who had burned hundreds of Muslim villages causing the blood of thousands of Turks to be spilled, and to let the pardoned committee leaders travel to Europe." Many Armenian leaders left, but the remainder continued to cause trouble.[233] This time, the number of Armenians killed was more than three times the number of Muslims.

The pattern that emerged from this episodic violence reveals the presence of Armenian revolutionaries instigating local communities to action on the one hand and the absence of timely intervention by Ottoman government forces on the other. And the instigators escaped punishment as they were pardoned by the sultan as a consequence of foreign pressure. It is significant that the Ottoman officials narrating this episodic violence never remarked about the disparity in numbers between the large non-Muslim and much smaller Muslim casualties. In addition, their narratives gave agency to the Armenians only as the instigators or perpetrators of violence, with no discussion of or reflection upon the initial injustices that led so many Armenians to participate in such unrest in the first place. At the same time, they dismissed the violent actions of the Muslims; Muslim agency emerged only in a defensive capacity, as they resisted the attacks "in their own country, their own fatherland." The Muslim Turkish officials overlooked that the same lands were the ancestral lands of the Armenians who had been living there since before the arrival of the Turks, portrayed the Armenians as the sole instigators of violence, and legitimated the much harsher violence of the Muslims as being defensive in nature.

Incidents of Collective Violence, 1893–1907

Given this framework of action, it is not surprising that such episodic incidents of violence became more systematic over time. The next incident occurred in 1894 in Sasun; when the Armenian subjects refused to pay their taxes, the sultan's official sent to contain the resistance instead bombed the entire place flat.[234] Significantly, Dr. Mehmet Şahingiray, who was arrested in the aftermath of 1915 for perpetrating massacres against the Armenian populace, initially served as an army physician in Sasun for five months.[235] Hence some young Muslim officers exposed to such violence also were becoming radicalized. In discussing the massacre of Sasun Armenians, the sultan defended his actions by stating that "even though he said [to the appointed official] that they should be hit, he did not say they should be massacred."[236] The sultan assumed the Armenian subjects were naturally the guilty party and therefore deserved punishment; he only objected to the level of punishment delivered, blaming the official for the violent outcome. Rather than correcting the injustice against his Armenian subjects, the sultan was much more concerned about preempting European intervention because the Great Powers once again brought the reform issue to the table. Yet the sultan contained them by appointing Shakir Pasha to investigate and oversee the execution of the reforms.

The year 1895 was a crucial turning point because of the "Babıali[237] demonstration," the first significant public protest rally at the imperial capital instigated by the Armenian subjects. Many contemporaneous memoirs of Ottoman officials discussed the event in great detail, especially noting that this was the first time they had become aware of the "Armenian problem."[238] Prior to the demonstration, the Hnchak committee organizing it had sent a declaration to all the foreign embassies, stating that it intended to carry out a peaceful demonstration and would not assume any responsibility if it was prevented by a show of arms. The Armenian subjects once again convened at the patriarchate in Kumkapı and delivered speeches voicing their complaints. As they set out to march to the seat of the Ottoman government, they were asked to disperse and send a committee instead. The crowd refused, and in the ensuing skirmish an Ottoman colonel was shot. The invoved officials were afraid to take action because they were unclear as to what course of action the sultan would have approved. And the sultan was unclear about the origins of the demonstration. Certain that the Armenian subjects could not be acting on their own, he was trying to figure out who was behind the unrest: the Great Powers, his own officials and the crown prince, or the secret committee of the Young Turks.[239] Because the sultan eventually did not allow regular troops to be sent, the ensuing street fight between the demonstrating Armenians and the Muslim populace turned into a three-day bloodbath, with many Armenians hunted down in the imperial city and massacred.[240]

Those within the Muslim populace who retaliated against the Armenian demonstrators were religious students, Kurds, Turks, porters, and religious fanatics who employed sticks and guns to kill any Armenian they came across.."[241] Additional details noted in the memoirs include the following: "As there were no soldiers to keep order, the ones who put the rebellion down were those with zeal.... some privates, a group of religious school students and the [Muslim] populace appointed themselves the helpers of this weak government and joined in the fight... tearing out the rails of the Sultanahmet Park." The Muslim perpetrators initially gathered by the Kumkapı Armenian church, shouting that the Armenians' behavior was "treachery to the state and the nation... inviting foreign intervention... thus buttering the bread of the revolutionaries." Even though the accounts argued that the bloodshed spread to both sides, all narrated incidents reveal that it was almost exclusively Armenians who were indiscriminately massacred. One narrator remembered that he had been sitting in his office at the Debt Administration as the governor inspector. Upon hearing the event, he called the gendarmerie sergeant who was guarding the building, instructing him to take most of his men to help out the state forces. He stated that they should merely get hold of the Armenian protesters and deliver them to the police. Yet the sergeant returned in half an hour to note that, while he was taking the Armenians to the police, some effendis and refugees attacked them, took the Armenians away, beat them until they fell down, and then went searching for others. The narrator states that "unlike what the foreign press reported, the fanaticism which had risen was never directed against all Christians, and I had no doubt that the killings, however much they spread, would always remain restricted to the Armenian element." That evening, he heard his acquaintances discuss the day's incidents, boasting about "how the Armenians had been chopped into pieces"; one even claimed that "the Armenians never stayed still and had therefore deserved this lesson." Another narrator who was at the capital as a student likewise remarked that he was on his way to class at the Fatih mosque when he "encountered an Armenian who, in order to get rid of the police, was ritually purifying himself for ablutions by washing at the fountain. The ones around immediately noticed the mistakes he committed in doing so, and killed him there right in front of my eyes with their blows. They found the two Armenians taking the corpse away, and killed them in front of Siperciler as well."

Reverberations of the Babıali demonstration raised the consciousness of the Muslim Turks about the Armenian "threat" only when the decades-long unrest of the provinces suddenly made its way to the imperial capital. Prominent Muslim Turks started to take a stand against all Ottoman Armenians as a consequence of this incident; some fired their Armenian retainers, other stopped shopping at stores owned by Armenians, and still others remarked that their first feelings of nationalism emerged at this juncture.[242] A demonstration not contained in time had evolved into a massacre of Armenian subjects. Rather than criticizing the inadequate government measures to contain the violence and expressing compassion for the massacred Armenians and their community, the majority of Muslim Turks followed the sultan's lead in not only blaming the Great Powers for instigating the events but also distancing themselves from the Armenians at the capital, who were not the perpetrators but instead the victims of violence. Another significant reverberation produced by the demonstration was the first public appearance of the secret Committee of Union and Progress.[243] The Young Turks prepared their first public declaration, printing a thousand copies that they secretly posted on walls and sent to important government offices and the palace; they also provided a French translation for the Great Powers. The declaration addressed only "Muslims and our beloved Turkish citizens," noting that the Young Turks "regretted the insolence of the Armenians, yet it was injustice, autocracy and maladministration that created such regretful events." "We the Turks, like all Ottomans, also want freedom and reform from this autocratic government," it concluded. The public emergence of the CUP at this juncture not only points to the close connection of their activities with those of the Armenian revolutionaries but also highlights the coevalness in the emergence of Turkish and Armenian secret activities. The CUP capitalized on the increasing concern of the Muslim Turkish populace to further its own cause. Once again, the CUP also interpreted this incident not as the work of some Armenians but instead as the political action of the entire Armenian community living in the empire, thereby revealing its inherently Muslim Turkish bias at its point of origin.

The 1895 Babıali demonstration caused unrest throughout the empire as well, especially in the eastern provinces.[244] For instance, one Armenian noted that the ensuing massacre in Tokat occupied a significant place in his mother's life and memories. "After the massacre started," he explained, "my mother's father managed to escape and reach home, but my physically disabled uncle Kutlamış was caught in front of their tailor shop . . . and killed through beheading. My mother and relatives managed to get my uncle Aram who was still a baby, put up a ladder to the garden wall, and manage to find shelter at the French school. The massacre lasted four hours. After it was over, the human corpses torn apart with their heads severed from their bodies were collected from the streets, loaded on horse carts, and taken outside the city. This went on for hours." Some Armenian subjects demonstrated their disaffection with the Ottoman government in a variety of ways but to no avail; not only were they heard by the Ottoman government, but the Armenian revolutionary committees also assassinated the ones who were loyal to the state.[245] Hence, many local Armenians faced death either way. Once again, the ensuing Armenian casualties were much more severe than the Muslim ones.

The most significant unrest of 1895 took place a couple of months later, once again in Zeytun. Even though the Ottoman officials remarked that the Armenian nonpayment of taxes to the state was the reason for the unrest, they failed to acknowledge that the Armenians protested because they also had to pay additional tributes to the local Turkish and Kurdish notables.[246] The collective violence against the Armenians continued into 1896, when the most prevalent massacres committed in Van led the sultan to send Sadeddin Pasha, whose diaries were discussed at the beginning of this chapter. The pasha was ordered to advise the Armenians as well as the Kurds who had inflicted much damage through the Hamidiye regiments.[247] In recounting his findings, the pasha also placed the entire blame on the Armenians, stating that the attack of an Armenian band from Iran on the Kurds led the latter, "who were by nature rancorous and bloodthirsty," to attack "the Armenian villages to confiscate goods and animals and sometimes spill blood." Yet the pasha also substantiated the Armenian massacres when he addressed the Kurdish tribes, asking them why they "murdered the Armenians, robbed their villages, and seized their goods." The Kurds first skirted the issue by blaming other tribes to then own up to the violence, arguing that they did so "in the name of Islam," hearing that allegedly "an imperial decree had been issued that the goods of the Armenians were religiously permissible [to seize]." Also hearing a rumor that some Armenians had attacked the sultan's officials somewhere else, the Kurdish militia regiments took it upon themselves to indiscriminately punish all the local Armenians for that attack. The pasha stated that they should not do so in the future and should not even considering punishing them. Yet it is evident from the pasha's subsequent meetings with the Van governor and military commander that the Kurdish militia had not listened to the Ottoman officials in charge, turning down their invitations by stating, "We are the commanders of the Hamidiye regiments; we are soldiers. We are not under the command of governors, district governors, or subdistrict governors." When the Ottoman officials had attempted to take action against the Kurds, the latter escaped into Iran, thereby avoiding punishment. The government had then appointed a Muslim Turkish official to take back the goods of a plundered Armenian village, and the Kurdish leaders had initially been willing to acquiesce. Yet the military commander then issued an order stating that the sultan's soldiers could not be employed in retrieving plundered goods.[248] The Kurds went back on their word, realizing that they were going to get away with whatever violence they engaged in. Then, they had not only plundered other Armenian villages but massacred the inhabitants as well. Hence, the sultan's delegation of authority to the Hamidiye militia combined with some Ottoman officials' willingness to overlook the militia's violence led to the massacres. The pasha also noted that the Kurdish militia was provoked by both the Turkish and the Armenian local notables into attacking the Armenian villages. The Muslim notables of Van kept sending them messages stating, "What are you waiting for? Can't you see the wildness of these dirty Armenians? Come attack the Armenian villages and kill the Armenians." The Armenian notables of Van also agitated the Kurdish militia to attack in order to demonstrate to the local Christian missionaries and consuls residing there the violence they suffered, hoping that such reports would instigate the Great Powers to intervene in the empire on their behalf. The entire populace was so fed up with the injustice that as the pasha was leaving the city, "both the oppressed Muslim and Christian populace laid down in the middle of the marketplace to prevent my departure. I was extremely upset and saddened, cursing the district governors for this sorry state of affairs." Hence, the militia activity, official nonactivity, and the politicization of local notables kept reproducing the violence instead of containing it.

These incidents capture the scope of the first wave of violence committed against the Armenians.[249] The violence continued on a smaller scale during the rest of the nineteenth century. One Ottoman official argued that "most of the problem originated from the government's indifference and negligence: the lands vacated by the Armenians escaping sultan Abdülhamid's atrocities [*mezalim*] were given to the Kurds who settled in and tilled these places, eventually regarding them as their own."[250] The Armenian subjects were continually shortchanged, since they could not recover their lands and became, as a consequence, increasingly impoverished and also radicalized.[251] When the Great Powers contacted the sultan, he focused primarily on delaying their actions by setting up committees and bringing foreign delegations to the imperial capital with large salaries; he did not attempt to address and resolve the injustices committed against the Armenians, and he kept claiming that the casualties were suffered by Armenians and Muslims alike. Yet a tally of the figures provided by the interior minister Hüseyin Nazım Pasha in his book captures the disparity; Armenians were massacred in much larger numbers.[252] Please refer to Table 1.1 at the end of this chapter for a list of the casualties indicated in the book.

These are the only figures for the 1893–96 massacres provided by an Ottoman state official who in his narrative was more inclined to acknowledge Muslim casualties than Armenian ones. It is unclear how such data were gathered and whether these numbers included casualties in the rural countryside as well as all the casualties in cities and towns. The figures are dramatically lower than the 100,000 to 300,000 casualties claimed by the Armenians and the Western powers. Nevertheless, they reveal a pattern that indicates the Armenian casualties were about four times more numerous than the Muslim ones; likewise, 50 percent more Armenians than Muslims were wounded. The Muslim figures would have contained many Kurds alongside the Turks, but the legal system categorized all as Muslims. When the instances are analyzed separately, the Muslims had the upper hand in killing the Armenians at all locations except Kiğı. Still, the significant number of Muslims killed demonstrates that there was indeed a concerted Armenian effort to challenge the state. The fact that Sultan Abdülhamid II pardoned the Armenian leaders due to foreign pressure did not alleviate the mounting animosity of the Muslims. Nazım Pasha attempted to justify the disparity in casulties by stating that "those who attack lose more people than those who defend themselves" (thereby arguing that the Armenians were the aggressors), and that "in the eastern provinces the [Muslim] populace is naturally very skillful in the use of firearms and horseback riding" (thereby overlooking the structural divide that for centuries prevented the Armenians from developing such skills).

Significantly, in 1903, Sultan Abdülhamid actually—albeit indirectly—acknowledged the violence committed against his Armenian subjects during the 1895 massacres and paid reparations for those Armenians who had also been American citizens. One Ottoman official recounted how these negotiations took place during the purchase from the United States of a warship for the navy:[253]

> The American government had asked our government for compensation based on the claims of the losses suffered by some Armenians who had escaped [from the empire] and migrated there to then become citizens. We had not considered the demand valid since the Armenians who had become American citizens had initially escaped. This demand

Table 1.1 **Casualties of Collective Violence during the 1893–96 Massacres according to the Book by the interior minister Hüseyin Nazım Pasha**

		Muslims		***Armenians***	
	Page No.	*Dead*	*Wounded*	*Dead*	*Wounded*
Maraş	119	59	110	111	97
Bitlis	132	38	135	139	40
Van	157	324	255	456	456
Trabzon	163	21	25	203	18
Trabzon	165	2	4	8	12
Erzurum	169	21	84	264	179
Bayburt	172	17	22	544	72
Hınıs	173	6	–	32	–
Erzincan	175	10	107	111	157
Refahiye	175	1	16	18	-
Kiğı	175	56	19	20	13
Kuruçay	175	2	3	9	5
Pasinler	177	25	5	140	42
Sivas	180	145	12	444	12
Karahisar-ı Şarki	181	9	4	–	220
Gerüme	181	64	56	476	35
Merzifon	186	18	–	80	–
Niksar	190	40	15	140	12
Köprü	191	5	8	50	15
Kayseri	200	6	3	270	40
Diyarbekir	205	70	80	300	120
Siverek	205	13	–	76	–
Total		**952**	**963**	**3891**	**1545**

and refusal continued on for a number of years until 1901 when the American government, in order to strengthen its demand, sent its Dakota warship...under the command of Captain Chester. When the captain, accompanied by the American ambassador, was received by the sultan, his [positive] behavior incurred the sultan's favor, and banquets were given in his honor. The claim of the American government and ours was resolved with a solution of this captain... [thereby ending]

> the dispute between the two governments. An order was placed [by the Ottoman government] for the Mecidiye warship. The solution accepted by the sultan was that the reparations [for the Armenian losses] that amounted to a total of $96,000 would be added on to the price [to be paid to the factory] . . . and the American government would then settle with the factory so as to assure that the Ottoman government did not make a payment [directly] to the American government as Armenian reparations.

This hitherto unknown transaction demonstrates not only the strategy of Sultan Abdülhamid II to publicly cover up the Armenian reparations that the Ottoman state actually paid but also the negotiation and acceptance of the American government to receive compensation for the damages the American Armenians incurred in such an indirect manner. Whether the reparations were actually dispensed by the American government to the families of the Armenian victims is unknown.

Armenian revolutionary activities against the sultan escalated in 1905 into an assassination attempt carried out during his Friday prayer attendance at a mosque.[254] The bomb was planted in a carriage and went off before the sultan's departure from the mosque, killing many in the audience. The sultan, delayed due to his conversation with one of his officials, was unhurt. Upon taking in the mayhem, he got into his carriage by himself, riding alone all the way back to the palace.[255] Twenty to thirty innocent Armenians at the Yıldız Square where the bombing had occurred were lynched, and their surviving relatives were placed in the houses of high-ranking Ottoman officials.[256] A detailed investigation conducted both within the empire and abroad produced a thousand-page investigative report. Once again, the sultan pardoned the leader of the assassination attempt and placed him on the state payroll; the assassin then served the sultan many years as a spy. Hence the sultan kept his enemies close. In addition, in an attempt to cut off the revolutionaries' monetary supply, he decided to deliver "an economic blow to [all] the Armenians by excluding them from all transactions involving the Ottoman state." The Armenian subjects tried hard to reverse this decision, sending many prominent Armenians to the palace to plead on their behalf but to no avail. The sultan's reaction demonstrated that he held all Armenian subjects responsible for an incident that most had not directly contributed to. In summary, then, the unrest escalated throughout the nineteenth century, and none of the Muslim or Armenian perpetrators was punished. Over time, the sultan, his state, and the dominant Muslim Turkish majoriy all united in blaming the entire Ottoman Armenian community for the collective violence that had transpired.

During this period, not only the Armenian revolutionary committees but also the CUP of the Young Turks began to engage in episodic violence. In the case of the Young Turks, according to one officer's memoirs, from the moment he joined the CUP branch in Monastir, each cell of three to five people also had an accompanying paramilitary organization of guerrilla fighters or assassins (*fedai*) who reported directly to Karabekir and Enver Bey (later pasha). These fighters were "ready to risk death if necessary to assume the duty, alone if necessary, of murdering whoever prevented the proclamation of freedom." Of course, it was the CUP that informally and secretly decided who such people were. As a consequence, the CUP murdered many Bulgarians and assassinated some of sultan's officials for remaining loyal to him. Because many CUP members were also officers, they covered up the murders in their reports.[257] Such violence demonstrates the proclivity of especially the Monastir and Salonica braches of the CUP, manned mostly by officers, to engage in militia violence. Because the CUP in the Balkans often had to engage in guerrilla warfare with the Bulgarian committees, it seems to have assumed the same clandestine tactics to further its own causes. It is no accident that such clandestine militia activity persisted once the CUP came to power in the empire.

Many contemporaneous memoirs contain information on the violent activities of the Armenian revolutionary committees.[258] Two memoirs in particular provide detailed descriptions.[259] One Armenian recounted what he heard from his friend Dırtat, a Dashnak revolutionary. When Dırtat first arrived in İstanbul as a Dashnak militant, he was one of 120, and they all had lists of the Armenian traitors they were assigned to assassinate. Indeed, Dırtat had to kill two: Hımayak Aramyants, who had informed on Aram Açıkbaşyan, and an Armenian woman married to a policeman who worked as an informant. He killed them both. The other account of the security minister at the time is much more thorough.[260] The pasha recounted in great detail the seditious material Ottoman security forces recovered from the houses of Armenian revolutionary committee members throughout the empire. He took this propaganda material at face value, failing to distinguish revolutionary rhetoric from actual action. Still, the pasha did recover a lot of arms, bombs, and ammunition. He argued that the committees continued to assassinate those who did not join them and smuggled fighters into the empire dressed as Muslims, going so far as to have thirty Armenians who spoke excellent Turkish circumcised to avoid detection even though their covers were eventually blown. Probably the most significant insight into the pasha's ethical values emerges from his complaint about the Armenian religious leaders' and especially patriarch İzmirliyan's support of these committees. When the pasha was given the opportunity to assassinate the patriarch, he refused, stating that with the means available to him, he could have "not only one person shot but maybe ten, fifty, one hundred as well, and can even do so without leaving a trace.... But then what difference would there be between me and say, Baron Agasi or Hamparsum Boyacıyan? Are we paramilitary fighters or the government?...I am all for conducting business straight, through legal means. Perhaps the road will get longer if one proceeds in this manner, perhaps things will develop slowly. But mixing secret murders into clean honest governmental business would transform authority into the period of the Inquisition." The pasha's stand distinguishes his ethics not only from those of the Armenian revolutionaries but also from the Young Turks who succeeded him. Until then, all business of the empire was publicly conducted, with no secrecy on the part of the involved officials.[261] The tradition of the Ottoman state engaging in extralegal secret murders and assassinations was to emerge later in the empire, after the coming to power of the Young Turks.

Legitimating Event: The 1896 Ottoman Bank Raid by Armenian Revolutionaries

Most cases of collective violence are followed by acknowledgment enabling both the victims and the perpetrators to come to terms with the damage inflicted on the moral fabric of society. The victims then start a healing process, emotionally negotiating what happened, grieving their losses to eventually, hopefully, restore their faith in humanity. The perpetrators are held accountable through punishment, with the goal that they would not engage in such destructive behavior in the future. Yet, what marked the first phase of collective violence against the Armenians is that none of this happened. Instead, denial of the collective violence ensued. I attempted to locate the reasons for this denial instead of acknowledgment in the contemporaneous memoirs. I located the one event that enabled especially the dominant Muslim Turkish majority to legitimate the replacement of acknowledgment with denial. Indeed, I argue that certain events in a country's history contain structures of meaning that enable the state and society to legitimate past collective violence. In the case of the Ottoman Empire from 1789 to 1907, the preceding collective violence against the Armenian subjects was legitimated through the 1896 Ottoman Bank raid. This pivotal event occurred on 26 August 1896 at the Ottoman capital during the reign of Sultan Abdülhamid II. On that day, twenty-eight armed members of the Armenian Revolutionary Federation (also known as the Dashnak Party) stormed and took over the Ottoman Bank largely manned by French and British personnel. The intent was to draw the attention of Western powers to the Armenian massacres and possibly trigger their military intervention in the Ottoman Empire. The fourteen-hour-long seizure resulted in the deaths of a few soldiers as well as some revolutionaries. Upon the diplomatic—and not military—intervention of Western powers, however, the rest of the revolutionaries were given amnesty by the Ottoman sultan and then escorted out of the building into a private yacht that gave them safe passage to France.

The immediate consequence of the bank raid was another massacre, this time at the capital, of approximately 6,000 minorities—mostly, but not exclusively, Armenians. Contemporaneous accounts penned by Ottoman Turkish officials revealed other, less noted consequences. In the collective memory of the dominant Ottoman Turkish majority, this event was repeatedly mentioned as the first instance of how they became aware of the seriousness of the "Armenian issue," which until then had remained mostly confined to the provinces. They especially remarked on the fact that previously there had never been any significant challenge to the long authoritarian rule of Sultan Abdülhamid II, certainly not at his well-fortified imperial capital. Members of the then secret Young Turk political organization started to discuss how they could likewise initiate action against the sultan, a course that previously had not occurred to them as a viable possibility. Another significant impression that registered in the collective conscience of the dominant majority was the shock and astonishment at how the revolutionaries escaped "scot-free" without any punishment because of Western protection. As such, it vividly demonstrated to them the power Western states had begun to wield within the empire. Hence, for the dominant Muslim Turkish majority, the bank raid fed into and substantiated their belief that all the Armenian subjects were out to destroy the empire, and as such the collective violence against them had been legitimate. As a consequence, rather than differentiating the action of a radical few from the innocent Armenian subjects of the empire, they instead stereotyped and condemned them all.

Sultan Abdülhamid employed the event most creatively as he underlined in his own narrative the seriousness of the Armenian issue and the ensuing European intervention. He then took the additional step of drawing a causal connection between these two factors by emphasizing that the event demonstrated how the Western powers had actually created the Armenian issue in the first place. In doing so, the sultan initiated the process of officially "othering" the Armenian subjects of his empire by raising doubts about their intent and ultimate allegiance. He indirectly legitimated the past as well as possible future collective violence against the Armenians by thus symbolically removing them from his protection. Such a rhetorical move also obfuscated the origins of the Armenian issue, origins domestically located in the failure of repeated reform efforts in 1839, 1856, and 1876 to bring legal equality to all imperial subjects. An official narrative of denial thus formed as the sultan selectively acknowledged what occurred, when—minimizing and legitimating the past and present collective violence against the Armenians while maximizing and delegitimating the divisive role of both the Armenians and the European powers. Hence, the pivotal legitimating event of the 1896 bank raid ended up indelibly connecting the Armenian issue internationally to European powers. As such, the event contained the ten postulates William Sewell Jr., discussed in the Introduction, formulated in discussing the theory of historical events.

The 1896 Ottoman Bank raid rearticulated structures by redefining the connection between the Ottoman state and the Armenian subjects, symbolically removing state protection over the Armenian community. The raid originated in the Armenian frustration over failed reforms and subsequent unaccounted massacres, leading to the shock of the dominant Turkish Muslim majority over the vulnerability of their state. The emerging ritual drew upon existing practices while also attempting to alter them by resorting to cultural creativity. In the raid, the Armenian revolutionaries operated within the existing parameters of political challenge; they decided to take on the sultan at his capital after unsuccessfully attempting to execute a rebellion in the eastern provinces of the empire. Their decision, however, was also novel in that it constituted the first act of urban violence in the empire. They had initially considered sabotaging the capital's water supply or road infrastructure, or assassinating the sultan (which they attempted later, unsuccessfully, on 21 July 1905), but settled instead upon raiding the Ottoman Bank, owned primarily by Great Britain and France. The event also involved attempts to rearticulate authoritative sanction at the expense of the state, but it ultimately failed because the state and the dominant Turkish Muslim majority contained and co-opted the rearticulation.

Complex spatial and temporal processes marked the event.[262] With the raid, the Armenian issue definitively moved from the provinces, where it had emerged due to failure of reforms, to the urban imperial capital. As the Armenian revolutionaries raided a commercial space belonging to European powers, the conflict quickly expanded into the international arena. In addition, the raiders beckoned not only from among the Armenian subjects of the empire but also from Russia, where they had initially developed their alternate vision of bringing freedom to all Armenians. The raid's resolution also trespassed on multiple spaces. Even though the Armenian revolutionaries initially did challenge the sultan's authoritative space, they eventually sought amnesty and were removed from the scene to Europe, thereby escaping from the Ottoman legal space into that of the Western powers, where they were not punished for their violent act.

Temporally, the whole process was instigated because of the historical recollection of the collective violence the Armenian subjects had suffered in the empire since the advent of the nineteenth century, a process that had culminated in the 1893–96 massacres. Even though the event took place over a couple of weeks, its impact became forever embedded in the memories of both the Armenians and the Turks; to this day, the Armenians belonging to the Armenian Revolutionary Federation still sing the revolutionary songs composed in honor of the bank raid. The dominant Turkish majority still employs the event as proof of aggressive Armenian violence.

What separates the 1896 Ottoman Bank raid from Sewell's conception, however, was its impact.[263] In the case of the French Revolution that Sewell analyzed, the process eventually led to complete structural transformation—the subjects gradually became citizens with rights that enabled them to participate in the social system. Hence the end result was politically liberating. In the case studied here, however, even though various social actors attempted to transform the existing structure, what ensued was the reification of the existing structure and the legitimation of collective violence, leading to the final and ultimate form of violence, namely, denial. The Armenian revolutionaries undertook the raid first to draw Western attention to the plight of their coreligionists. Yet, not only were they not able to get Western powers to intervene in the Ottoman Empire on behalf of the Armenian subjects, but they ended up provoking a massacre at the capital that led to the murder of 6,000 non-Muslims—while they themselves were escorted out of the empire using transportation provided by the Western powers. Although their actions may have heartened some Ottoman Armenians, they also raised the awareness and contributed to the anxiety of the dominant Turkish Muslim majority, enabling the latter to legitimate not only past but also present and future collective violence against the Armenians. In all, then, an act undertaken to weaken the Ottoman state and liberate the populace ended up further reifying the power of the state and its use of collective violence. All too often, historical events are sociologically analyzed after the example of the French Revolution with the intent to articulate their liberating potential. Historical events do indeed transform, but they do so, as in this case, by leading instead to further containment and conservatism. The case under question here therefore employs the Sewellian theory of historical events to articulate not liberation but containment and repression.

Contemporaneous memoirs help substantiate this conceptualization.[264] More than twenty members of the Dashnak revolutionary party raided the Ottoman Bank, taking 120 hostages. The raiders asked for the sultan's pardon of Armenian tax debts as well as the release of those Armenians imprisoned on political charges. The Dashnak committee had initially planned five actions: "The first was to bomb the Ottoman seat of government, the second to organize a rebellion and take over in Samatya, the third was to occupy the Ottoman Bank, the fourth was to raid another bank, Credit Lyonnais, and the fifth was to bomb the Galata and Voyvoda police stations." To further undermine the sultan's authority, these actions were to occur on the anniversary of his accession to the throne. Yet, denunciation by one of the committee members on 25 August 1896 caused the Ottoman security forces to raid a school in Samatya where the bombs were manufactured, leading the committee to take action earlier than expected.

The impact on the dominant Muslim Turkish majority was significant in that all those narrating the event could specifically recall where they were at the time and what they were doing. It thus became culturally embedded in their collective memory. One intellectual vividly remembered that he was in the company of an author friend, at the headquarters of the literary journal *Servet-i Fünun*, when "the skylines of the city shook with an explosion the greatness of which had not been heard until then.... Half an hour later, a horse carriage full of killed persons accompanied by police [going] by... as well as the information we received from a friend... enabled us to understand the tragic nature of what had happened. This was the 'bank incident' of the Armenians."[265] An officer noted that he had just turned fifteen when the bank incident occurred. His family heard the gun shots from their house. "Yet rather than the gunshots, I was more interested in the things my brother and his friends secretly whispered," he continued. "We heard that with these concomitant rebellions, the Armenians wanted to have their own principality."[266]

A religious scholar had been planning a trip to Edirne when "trouble and violence broke out. The stores all shut down. The situation was like [the rebellions that occurred] at the time of the old Janissaries." "My travel to Edirne was delayed," he concluded.[267] The grand vizier at the time remarked that there was so much noise that he was sent from the sultan's palace to find out what was going on. When he got off at Beşiktaş, "two shots were fired at the grain store on the road. A person with baggy trousers and a jacket [who was the store owner] flung himself on the barley like a poor hungry chicken. For a dainty person like yours, this truly was a terribly tragic scene," he remarked.[268] Another person, then a student at the capital, recounted that large numbers of Armenians at a nearby inn refused to give themselves up, throwing bombs and firing shots. He and his friends went to watch but were told by a policeman to go back to their rooms.[269] The religious scholar corroborated the student's depiction, stating that "with many grenades and revolvers in their hands, the Armenians who gathered in one or two locations around the Galata port, Kadıköyü, Kumkapı, and at the Celal Bey Inn around Yeni Cami opened fire onto the soldiers and the populace. Their actual intention was to execute their sedition by attacking the Ottoman Bank. The heads of the rebels were saved through the protection of the foreigners and placed on a ship. It is said that they were sent to Europe."[270] A writer's account provided much more detailed information:[271]

> Both the bank and the Public Debt Administration building had suffered substantial damage from the attackers' bombs. The Armenians sheltered themselves in stone-walled inns, houses, and shops to rain fire through bombs; the soldiers used arms, [and] streams of blood flowed on the streets [as] piles of the dead and the moaning wounded

> turned the city into a battlefield.... My brother-in-law's eyes filled with suspicion turned to the neighborhoods going down the coast (back then, there was a large Armenian community living there), drawing a big question mark in the horizon of possibilities as if to say "only God knows where this will end." I had slowly gotten up in bed, listening to him.... Finally the cauldron of rebellion that had been boiling for so long had erupted, letting out waves of flame, not [only] far away in Erzurum, Sivas, Diyarbekir, Van, Zeytun... but also at the fear-filled capital of [Sultan] Abdülhamid, at the most emotional point of the crazed-up honor of the Turkish race, kindling a fire the dire end of which was hard to predict.

The suddenness with which the provincial unrest had been brought to the imperial city took especially the members of the Muslim Turkish majority with surprise. The degree of witnessed violence as well as their immediate suspicions about all Armenians reveal the ease with which public emotions were triggered. Indeed, contemporaneous memoirs reflect the range of these emotions in full detail. The primary aim of the Armenian Dashnak revolutionaries had been to draw the attention of the Great Powers; they had not taken into account or perhaps cared about the local consequences of their actions. The bank raid made an indelible impression especially on the Muslim populace, demonstrating to them what had always been claimed by the state but had never been physically proved, namely, that there really was a connection between the Armenian actions and the Great Powers. That the West intended to intervene in the affairs of the empire and did so through the Armenians was established when the Armenian revolutionaries were led way from the imperial capital under the protection of the European powers. The event also confirmed in the minds of the Muslim populace that not only the intent of the revolutionaries but the desire of *all* Armenian subjects had been to establish a principality all along.[272] The memoirs of the writer cited previously once again captured the anxiety of the Muslim Turks as he dramatically noted:[273]

> The following day, in spite of the tremble in my legs, the fog in my eyes, and the attempts of my close friends to stop me, I got outside. The city resembled the day after battle. On the road, pockets of rebels resisted the security forces. The fire continued, demonstrating a tendency to be rekindled even more strongly. I walked amid all this with a bitter twist in my heart, constantly thinking about the danger the future was to bring [upon us]. Was my poor homeland approaching its last days? Had the existence of my homeland... finally turned into ashes through the fire of eight or ten revolutionary arsonists? As I crossed the [Golden

> Horn] bridge, I craved to sit down right there, and cry with my eyes fixated on the minarets that had [once] witnessed so many splendors of eminence-superiority-pride.

This despair caused by the empire's lost "eminence-superiority-pride" unleashed the collective violence against the Armenians at the imperial capital. After the handful of Armenian revolutionaries were led out of the country unpunished, the Muslim populace turned against the innocent Armenians residing in the city, who were not at all complicit in the raid. The then security minister remarked that the Muslim populace was able to react so violently because the military was once again not deployed to contain them.[274] The sultan's fear that any military action might provoke the Great Powers to intervene in the affairs of the empire and perhaps mobilize the masses against his rule again let popular justice take its course. A Kurdish intellectual who personally participated in the violence stated that all Armenians "were like rabid dogs attacking the family that fed them." With this incident, the Muslim populace "was finally permitted to interfere with the Armenians." He and his friends found Armenians in a carpet store and killed them all. He added that during the night, all the corpses of the killed Armenians were taken in horse carriages to Saray Burnu (where the sea current is the strongest) and thrown into the sea.[275] Another account remarked that the disturbance continued for two days and two nights; it was "rumored that about a thousand Turks were martyred . . . and there was no limit to the thousands of Armenians killed by the [Muslim] populace."[276] A Greek Rum banker provided the most vivid account of the ensuing massacres of Armenians. He claimed that in every city district, "the sultan gave orders during the night to the imams of mosques and students attending religious schools to incite the populace to rebel and start murdering all Armenians without exception . . . equipped with sticks." The leaders of these religious zealots knew which houses and shops belonged to the Armenians and went after them. The banker continued:[277]

> The barbarous band would go everywhere. As soon as they recognized an Armenian from his attire or speech, they would knock him to the ground. In spite of being armed, no Armenian would have the courage to defend himself in the slightest. Each Armenian, in spite of having two or three guns in his belt, would fall onto his knees in front of the first person bearing a stick, leave his guns on the ground, plead with the murderer, crying, and accept death without any resistance. I do not remember how many thousands of armed Armenians these people with sticks actually murdered. . . . I saw in Therapia with my very own eyes the mounted police chasing four Armenians in a carriage. They

> killed two of them where they sat, and the other two who attempted to escape by swimming out to sea they executed with their bullets.

On the third day, he noted, the sultan called off the massacres and the Muslim populace returned to their houses. It is difficult to think that the sultan actually ordered the massacres; it is more likely that the Muslim populace exploited the lack of security and protection in the city, a state of affairs caused by the sultan's indecision, to indiscriminately attack and murder all the Armenians they could find.

All along, the Ottoman populace was barely aware of the scope of violence and destruction due to strict state censorship of the media.[278] Those Armenians who escaped the massacres suffered as a consequence of this incident as well. For instance, the suspicion of a connection with the bank raid forced the prominent Noradunkyan family to sell their mansion on the Bosporus "because it was considered dangerous for a [non-Muslim] family to own a residence so close to the [sultan's] Çırağan Palace."[279] The Armenian revolutionaries sent to Europe escaped a similar fate; some even returned to the empire later to serve as deputies in the Ottoman parliament.[280] The other significant reverberation was once again the spurring of the CUP members into action "handing out brochures and gluing posters on walls at night... to explain to Europe that the Armenians were not the only ones suffering from injustice, and that all Ottomans complained about the sultan's autocratic rule."[281] Yet, just as the Young Turks had feared, the massacres at the capital did indeed turn European opinion against the empire.[282] And within the empire, public opinion turned against all Armenians. The Greek Rum banker once again noted that "the foolish, panicked [Armenian] rebels passed the streets of Galata in shame, leaving Turkey forever.... Even though the Greek Rum were sympathetic to the Armenians, the entire public opinion turned against them as a consequence of this illogical rebellion."[283] In summary, the 1896 Ottoman Bank raid was an event that changed the parameters of the Armenian problem, legitimating for the dominant Muslim Turkish majority the past and present collective violence against the Armenians.

First Denial: Domestic Origins of Collective Violence against the Armenians

The denial of collective violence contains within it an unwillingness to critically reflect on one's actions. As such, it inhibits transformation for a peaceful future, instead fostering further collective violence. It also reifies existing structures of power. Contemporaneous Muslim Turkish memoirs contain very few critical reflections on collective violence; they are often defensive in nature, reiterating and prioritizing the ultimate need for the survival of one's own community at the expense of all others. What is narrated therefore becomes highly selective, almost celebrating the perpetrators of violent events while denigrating the suffering of the victims. Things become pure white or pitch black as a consequence. A sole exception to this trend is the memoir of one Muslim Turkish writer. In explaining the reasons for his decision to write his personal account of Ottoman history, this memoirist critically noted that what had often been written had always covered, depending on the era, only the good or bad things that had transpired. This way of viewing the past through such a monochromatic lens, he conjectured, was due to one's "enslavement to the mentality of servitude," of "not having had any training in the freedom of thought." To the morality of such people, he continued, "it is perfectly acceptable to practice either praise or blame, goodness or wickedness because all their lives, [they] have been only subjected to these." "What need does truth serve in history?" he pungently added. "Ottoman history has been a world of lies because of this. Lie is not a source of embarrassment in the East."[284] This skeptical and rather harsh assessment of Ottoman history leads one to the issue of ethics, to how humans judge each other and interpret events.

Yet ethics constitutes a significant dimension of history. In the case of the events that transpired in the Ottoman Empire during the era under question here, the employed ethical frameworks are important to articulate because of the shift in the ethical framework that occurred with the advent of Western European modernity. With the idea of universal human rights, the existing world order was fundamentally challenged. Instead of a social structure based on communal rights vertically integrated around the physical persons of rulers, the emergence of the concept of individual rights for all instead necessitated a horizontal integration as humans now related to each other around the abstract principles of freedom, equality, and fraternity. Such a shift undermined the legitimacy of rulers, gradually replacing them with the abstract concept of a state that drew its legitimacy from the social contract drawn up with individual citizens. The shift also impacted the Ottoman Empire as attempts to move from one ethical framework to another caused social polarization. Collective violence ensued against those whose communal rights were challenged and eliminated without the proper bestowal of individual rights.

Also significant in this context is the discrepancy between ideal and practice. Even though the ethical framework of Western modernity did indeed present an ideal model based on unconditional individual rights to all humans, the practice fell short. The states that embraced such democratic representation prioritized the "practical" preservation of the state and the nation it comprised over the fundamental ethical principle of the "ideal" preservation of human lives. Such prioritization of state interests—especially when combined with the preservation of the nation through a process of including certain social groups and excluding others—undermined the fundamental ethical principle of first preserving the lives of all humans at all costs. It is ironic that through their practice, it was specifically Western European states that first prioritized the interests of their own states and nations at the expense of others; they embarked on an imperialist civilizing mission to shape the world after their own national vision. The Ottoman Empire renegotiated its own state-society relations with the reality of such a vision.

In the Ottoman Empire, the dynasty was primarily responsible for the preservation of all its "flocks" and the communities comprising them. Yet the sultans also had to preserve their dynasty and their personal rule within. The tight and precarious balance between these two ethical principles of preservation was maintained through the delivery of justice to all. The Ottoman imperial system legitimated itself insofar as this balance was carefully maintained. Starting in the eighteenth century, however, as the resources of the empire began to dissipate due to the halt of imperial expansion and as the ensuing wars led to the gradual contraction of the imperial borders, it became increasingly difficult to deliver justice to all. The linchpin of Ottoman imperial policy should have been the delivery of justice, I would argue, not to the dominant Muslim Turkish majority that was already the main beneficiary of the system but instead to those non-Muslim communities in the minority that first experienced the adverse consequences of the imperial loss of power. But such communities had never been fully integrated within the body politic, and never fully protected by the imperial state at times of adversity. Therefore, during the course of the nineteenth century, first the ones in the Balkans took a stand against the empire, leading to their eventual sovereignty as the Greek and Bulgarian states. The other significant non-Muslim community of Armenians faced additional challenges because of their geographical location throughout the heartland of the empire in Asia Minor, a space that also constituted their ancestral lands. Especially the Armenians living in the eastern provinces suffered increasing injustice. As the reforms promised by the Ottoman state failed to alleviate such injustice, rebellions emerged. Hence the rebellions that the Ottoman state eventually referred to as "the Armenian problem" were domestic in origin. Yet both the Ottoman state and the dominant Muslim Turkish majority overlooked this local origin, projecting the causes onto the provocation of the Great Powers. How did such denial emerge?

Crucial at this juncture is the reign of Sultan Abülhamid II because the elements of the denial of domestic origins were articulated during his rule. Because the preservation of his flock through the delivery of justice was ethically the sultan's first priority, his failure would have undermined the legitimacy of his rule. Hence, the sultan could not acknowledge that the collective violence against the Armenians had been due to shortcomings in his own rule. In order to sustain his legitimacy and preserve the rule of the Ottoman dynasty in general and his own rule in particular, the sultan instead claimed that the origins of the Armenian "problem" were located in Western Europe, outside his imperial domains.

The ensuing denial of origins had three major components. The first concerned the role of the West, especially Western complicity and hypocrisy in interpreting the Armenian protests. Siding with the Armenians and acknowledging violence in the empire only when it pertained to non-Muslims, the Western powers consistently overlooked the violence committed against Muslims; they also silenced the violence they themselves engaged in throughout the world. Such an ethical stand enabled the Ottoman sultan and his officials to develop a narrative identifying the West as the main culprit of collective violence. The second pertained to the Armenian community's location within the empire. While the Armenians in the eastern provinces did indeed suffer greatly from injustice, those in the western regions and especially in the imperial capital led relatively comfortable lives. This duality of impoverished rural Armenians alongside wealthy urban ones enabled the Ottoman state to selectively highlight the conditions of the wealthy at the expense of the impoverished, arguing that all were treated justly. The third concerned the naturalized location of the dominant Muslim Turkish majority. The Ottoman official narrative never fully acknowledged that the whole social system had been geared to sustaining and reproducing the privileges of this majority. Because this majority fully received the sultan's justice, he could claim that he treated all his subjects equally and in a just manner.

These components can be documented through an analysis of Sultan Abdülhamid II's two printed memoirs, one comprising the diaries he kept during his reign and the other his recollections after his deposition.[285] In them, the sultan clearly stated that "the Armenians have been forced into rebellion by outside forces." He then identified these outside forces as follows: First, Russia incited the Armenians with promises of sovereignty, in order to generate problems for Turkey. Soon thereafter, the French and the British joined in this endeavor because they too wanted to have a say in which pieces were torn away from the Ottoman country; the United States followed suit. The sultan also traced the origins of Western involvement and subsequent Armenian unrest to the "establishment of the [Protestant] religious school in Merzifon." In both narrations, the Armenian revolutionary committees were first established "not in Turkey, but Paris," the sultan argued, "mak[ing] everything evident, that the head of the discord was outside." The intention of all these Armenian committees was to get the Western powers to intervene, thus enabling them to establish their own principality. That is why, the sultan conjectured, the Armenians then "turned around and provoked the Muslim populace to attack them," leading to the Armenian massacres of 1893–96. Even though the Ottoman Armenian subjects initially regarded these provocations unfavorably, due to the Ottoman state's inability to protect them from the assassinations of Armenian revolutionaries, they too started providing at least financial support to such seditious activities. The accounts of two Ottoman officials reiterated the sultan's official narration.[286] Yet these instead traced the origins of the Armenian problem specifically to Article 61 of the Berlin Congress, which "led the Armenians to be toyed around by Russian and British policies." They thus argued that "not maladministration or violent treatment, but rather the treaties [of the Great Powers] were behind the Armenian rebellions." This official narration not only denied the domestic origins of the Armenian issue but also reduced the agency of the Ottoman Armenian community to the singular trait of treachery, thereby silencing the domestic failures of the Ottoman state.

The still prevalent narrative about the Ottoman Muslim Turks not having a single friend, being all alone in a world surrounded by enemies, emerged at this juncture as well.[287] Sultan Abdülhamid II dramatically stated that upon succeeding to the throne, he realized that "we are alone in the world. There are enemies, but no friends! The cross can always find an ally, but the crescent always remained alone. Those who awaited benefits from the Ottomans appeared to be friends, but when they could not get what they hoped, they immediately turned into enemies. And this is what I founded my policy upon: it was imperative to attack the enemy with the arms of the enemy." He continued to note that he constantly observed the European balance of powers, exploiting the tensions within to the advantage of the Ottoman state. The sultan also took issue with the Western European criticisms "that we do not have the capacity to undertake reforms because of being Asian, that we would never be regarded as European . . . and that the Armenian massacres did not occur due to foreign instigation." While the sultan's official interpretation did indeed divert attention from domestic imperial weaknesses, he nevertheless made valid points regarding Western European duplicity. He noted that the primary interest of Britain was to secure routes to India, which it had seized, and to penetrate into Central Asia and China. He also recorded all instances of Western violence that went unaddressed, such as the "pogroms in Russia, but no one was brave enough to prevent their Christian brothers from undertaking such actions," as well as "the bloody victories of the Spanish, the French occupation of Algiers, the British suppression of the Indian uprising, the conquest of the Congo by the Belgians, and the cruelties of the Russians in Siberia." The sultan further accused Great Britain of doing all it could to sustain world attention on the Armenian issue in order to cover up the violence it committed in Egypt. His criticisms reveal that powerful states determined the public world agenda at the expense of the weak ones like the Ottoman Empire had become. Yet an Ottoman official was more astute in his observations of the Great Powers, remarking that "Europe followed and was inclined to believe that only the Christians suffered . . . that is, they were singly attuned to the condition of Christians like them."[288] This criticism captures the contemporaneous Western duplicity in acknowledging human suffering not universally but only as it pertained to Christians with a Western European heritage. This selective recognition of suffering was noted by Ottoman officials during the rule of Sultan Abdülhamid II, in the aftermath of the 1878 Russo-Ottoman War when hundreds of thousands of Muslim refugees flooded the empire, recounting the violence they suffered in the Balkans and Russia. Yet the Great Powers did not recognize this Muslim suffering. Such selectivity indirectly supported the official Ottoman narration of blaming the Great Powers for all the unrest.

The sultan also claimed that his Armenian subjects had always been and still were content with Ottoman rule.[289] He argued that contrary to what the Great Powers alleged, "everything was in place and the Christians and Muslims in the empire cohabited perfectly." The sultan objected to the European claims that the Armenians were tormented and tortured, stating instead that

> Armenians have always been very wealthy...much richer than our Muslim subjects. They have reached the highest positions in officialdom at every period, including ministries...[constituting] a third of all the [Ottoman] officials. In addition, they do not perform military service like the rest of the populace. And the tax they pay for this [exclusion] is so minimal that they more than compensate it during the time Muslims perform military service. The trade of Armenians is in excellent shape.... [They opposed the abolition of the poll tax] because they did not want to give up their precious privileges, wishing everything to remain as it had been in the past. Other than the Armenians on the Kurdish mountains who live a very poor life, the Armenians are the richest among all our subjects, including the Greek Rum.

This narration is significant through the silences it contains, through what the sultan does not articulate. The claim that Christians and Muslims cohabited perfectly in the empire is made not by the Armenian subjects but by a sultan ruling in accordance to religious principles that favor the dominant Muslim majority. The positive depiction of the Armenians fails to acknowledge not only the structural divide between the sultan's Muslim and non-Muslim subjects but its origin in the imperial legal system. The sultan also privileges the existence of wealthy Armenians and those who occupy official positions, equating wealth and selective—not systematic—access to authority with the Armenians' well-being, overlooking their lack of legal and political rights. Yet it was exactly this lack and subsequent injustice that generated Armenian unrest not only in the eastern provinces, as the sultan acknowledges, but throughout the empire.

Also absent is any discussion of the failure of state reforms in relation to the Armenian community.

Unlike the sultan, contemporaneous memoirs of some Ottoman officials discussed—albeit indirectly—the domestic origins of the collective violence against the Armenians. They pointed out that the reforms undertaken to deliver justice to all Ottoman subjects were never fully actualized, and that existing inequities escalated instead. They also noted that especially Sultan Abdülhamid II was fully cognizant of these failures but never publicly owned up to them. Some, like Mithat Pasha, tried extremely hard to reform the existing Ottoman social system to address and alleviate the injustices committed against all subjects regardless of religious creed. Others, like Mizancı Murad, noted that the imperial reforms could only succeed if they encompassed the entire country, Muslims and non-Muslims alike.[290] Yet such reforms were not fully actualized. Another Muslim official argued that the Ottoman state treated the reforms only as a diplomatic tool to take pressure off the Great Powers, never fully carrying them through:[291]

> Even though the grand vizier Said Pasha wept at the Armenian patriarch's complaints and woes and promised everything, he did nothing. Even though it was first decided, then printed and announced many times that a reform delegation was to be sent to the Eastern Anatolian provinces under the leadership of the Minister of Foundations Hayri Bey, after a while, this too ceased to be discussed. . . . Just as we forced the Albanians into the laps of the Montenegrins and Serbians, so too we obliged the Armenians to seek kindness from their sworn enemies, the Russians. . . . The Armenians had gotten tired of waiting for the Turks [to reform matters] and had lost hope. . . . In order to deny the existence of the Armenians during the Abdülhamid era, we reduced their population and also invented the formula "Armenia is only a geographical term." . . . Another cause of the Armenian problem was land disputes; there had never been a successful legal system established for land ownership, and this was where injustice reigned in the most pervasive manner.

This official thus acknowledged not only the failure of the reforms but also the domestic reasons behind the Armenian unrest. First, the Armenian subjects patiently waited for the reforms to be actualized, only to realize with time that this was a false hope. Second, the origin of the Armenian problem lay within the empire, especially in the land disputes that were not legally settled in a just manner. Another Muslim intellectual also pointed out that unlike what the Ottoman official narration claimed, he had personally read through all the documents of the Hnchak Socialist Revolutionary Committee and found "no references to separatist and independence seeking clauses."[292] Hence, the Armenians' demands for an improvement in their conditions was taken out of context by the official Ottoman narration that instead portrayed them solely as seditious actors with the intent to establish their own sovereignty.

Another factor that officials frequently discussed was their concern over how the sultans' interests in preserving their dynasty and rule started to conflict with the protection of either the state or its subjects. Even though Sultan Abdülhamid II would never acknowledge the divergence between dynastic and state interests, two Ottoman officials critically commented on it in their memoirs.[293] Right at the end of the 1878 Russo-Ottoman War, one successful Ottoman commander was asked to comment on what had to be done militarily to defend the imperial capital against the advancing Russian forces. The commander noted that although the gathered officials had argued in favor of bringing additional forces for the defense, the sultan would neither decrease the substantive forces he had around the imperial palace nor assign additional forces to the military for the defense of the capital because he feared these would then turn against him and remove him from his throne. So the discussions continued until midnight to no avail. The sultan's concerns regarding the preservation of his throne took precedence over even the defense of the imperial capital.

In the other instance in 1898, an Ottoman governor penning a petition to the sultan noted that the former wrote a couple of lines concluding with the sentence "And I declare that I will not ever depart from my loyalty to your imperial being [*zat-ı şahane*] and the sublime state [*devlet-i aliye*]."[294] A friend who read the petition commented: "Okay, it is fine, but it would have been better if you had not mixed in the state." The governor then explained the significance of their exchange as follows: "In [Ottoman] government positions, one pledges an oath of loyalty to both the person [of the sultan] and the state. I realized from my friend's words the contradiction of pledging loyalty to both the sultan and the state. I had never thought that under some conditions, it would not be possible to be loyal to both, and one would be required to assign the loyalty exclusively to one." Indeed, until the end of the period analyzed here, in the eyes of officials, the sultan's demands for loyalty to his rule took precedence over the declaration of loyalty to the state. Yet that was soon to change.

In summary, then, during this phase of Ottoman rule, the Ottoman ethical framework gave precedence to the preservation of the sultan's dynasty. Because the sultan's rule was legitimated through the delivery of justice to all his subjects, rather than acknowledge the failure in such delivery to his Armenian subjects through the reforms of 1839, 1856, and 1876, the sultan instead blamed the intervention of the Great Powers in the affairs of the empire, thereby claiming that the Armenian unrest and ensuing massacres had foreign origins. The denial of the domestic origins of the violence against the Armenians thus constituted the first stage of denial.

2

Young Turk Denial of the Act of Violence, 1908–1918

Violence, even well intentioned, always rebounds upon oneself.
Lao Tzu, Chinese philosopher, 600–531 B.C.E.

A year after the entry of the Ottoman Empire into World War I on the side of the Axis powers, in 1915, the director of dispatches, Ahmed Refik (Altınay), arrived in Eskişehir. Because the British attack on the Dardanelles had recently put the imperial capital under the danger of occupation, his task was to coordinate the possible relocation of the seat of the Ottoman government there, away from the imperial capital. The imperial treasury had already been transported, and "the elegant Armenian houses around the train station [were] evacuated and set apart for members of government."[1] While in Eskişehir, Ahmed Refik also witnessed the deportation of Ottoman Armenians from and through this city and provided one of the most frank and forthright descriptions of the tragic process:[2]

> One morning, something out of the ordinary happened at the Eskişehir train station... a caravan of [Armenian] children, women, girls, and the elderly [emerged from the trains]. This small caravan was so sad and heartrending; the condition of babies grasping their mothers with their chubby arms, sleeping sorrowfully hungry and sweaty under the heat of the summer sun, tore one's heart out. Was this all of them? "They'll go to Konya," it was said, but they did not have a cent in their pockets for train fare. All were poor, unlucky peasants. At the station, in front of the railing, an old woman sat destitute with a five- or six-year-old blond, blue-eyed girl in her lap and a boy by her side. I asked: they were a soldier's family; their father was drafted, and their mother had died. [The old woman] was bringing up these two unfortunate orphans; I asked the girl's name: "Siranuş!" The poor innocent had a piece of bread in her hand which she ate dipping it into water. I had people bring her food

> and showed her affection; a friendship formed between us from that day on. Yet Siranuş never smiled; there was sadness, dejection in her looks, eyes, and face. It was as if her spirit was crushed by this deportation, this cruelty, this unlawful action; her innocent heart was broken, and her heart filled with a deep grudge against the [Armenian] community she belonged to; she took the fruit I gave her without a smile and without looking at me, as if she was cross, and put it with her thin fingers into her tiny mouth.

The Armenian deportations witnessed with the arrival of this train were soon followed by many others as the forcefully deported Armenians kept arriving. "There was no lantern, no light, no guide, nothing," Ahmed Refik continued. "Thousands of poor, rich, hungry, and miserable families, women with children weeping in their arms, priests with unkempt beards collecting their long robes and hauling their loads onto their shoulders, and mothers in full sweat trying to get out of the freight cars while carrying their invalids, struggling hard not to lose their children, mothers, and belongings."[3] These train passengers were soon joined by others who arrived by land, "their feet covered with blood, accompanied by a few poor gendarmes."[4] Numbers at the train station soon reached 10,000 to 20,000, and no one knew where they were headed, so makeshift tents emerged next; the Armenian families purchased wood and poles from the marketplace, covering them with rags. Even though the townspeople initially tried to help, the enormity of the scale overwhelmed them. Soon, the local Armenians were also ordered to be deported, even though "they were not at all involved in the Armenian problem; they were occupied with trade and agriculture, and had no business with rifles and bombs."[5] Weeks went by, yet the forcefully deported Armenians were still not transported. Hunger started among these thousands of families as "they had no food, money, nothing. They finally decided to sell their goods... the lacework, satin bed sheets, wedding gowns that girls had prepared for their dowry with such sweet hopes... sold on the streets for nothing." This was soon followed by an escalating number of deaths because, Ahmed Refik remarked, "even those invalids sick in bed with consumption, those at the brink of death, the insane, and the beggars who could not walk had been expelled."[6]

When the city evacuated all of its Armenian residents, a night curfew was issued, and "a deathly silence commenced in the houses, lit only the night before in peace and tranquility. Guards waited at every street corner while hammering sounds emanated from the houses.... all those innocent women, young girls, the elderly, unfortunate children... they too were to join this flood of disaster and death."[7] Even though Ahmed Refik tried hard to save this innocent populace and prevented the deportation of Catholic Armenians, the families of soldiers, and workers at the train companies, others had to go. Many Muslims between Adapazarı and Eskişehir attempted to save their Armenian neighbors by petitioning the government but to no avail. As for the property and goods the Eskişehir Armenians left behind, what transpired was similar to evacuations of Izmit and Adapazarı in that "the government was incapable of protecting these, and everything was stolen at night."[8] In many cases, after the theft and plunder, the houses were burned down to cover the illegal acts. Though many Armenians were at the train station, Ahmed Refik further explained: [9]

> No one wanted to move for all [the Armenians] believed that a fearsome force awaited them there: death. Forests around the mountains were filled with the armed bands the CUP government had sent from İstanbul. In order to stay alive, the people were willing to remain in Eskişehir.... Rivers are filled with human torsos and heads of children. This view tears one's heart to pieces. But won't people one day be called to account for this?... One had to be diseased with the mentality of armed bandits not to damn this cruelty.... massacres [of Armenians] in the villages of the Anatolian provinces varied, depending on the abilities and murderous inclinations of governors at particular locations.... It was said that the gravest [Armenian] calamities had occurred in Bursa and Ankara. The ones who had arrived from Ankara narrate sorrowfully how the houses had been blockaded, and hundreds of Armenian families loaded onto carriages and dumped in streams. Many women witnessing these atrocities had lost their minds. The houses of the wealthy Armenians were purchased and, as soon as the official document for the transfer of property was issued, the monies were forcefully and cruelly taken back.... it was certain that one day these atrocities had to be accounted for; this was murder against humanity. No government at any historical period has committed murders with such cruelty. The bloodied deportation of Armenians meant the deprivation of the country from one of its most important organs.... My eyes turned toward the train tracks and... I thought of the families who had cried, slept, and had nightmares in the cold darkness of the night. Who knows where, at which mountain, in the claws of which cruel armed band the [Armenians] had now been sacrificed. Poor, beautiful, innocent Siranuş, where are you now?

Ahmed Refik thus fully disclosed how forced Armenian deportations were turned into massacres by the Committee of Union and Progress government that had legally ordered them in the first place. The CUP responsible clerks at every town and city oversaw the execution, and the secret militia formed and led by the CUP Special Organization (SO) was secretly ordered to massacre the Armenians.

Ahmed Refik made a number of significant observations relating to the forced Armenian deportations. He stated that "if Germany had to do so officially, it could have prevented this massacre," since the CUP leaders "did not do anything against the word of the Germans." Yet Germany, "intoxicated with the interests it was going to acquire in Anatolia, remained an indifferent observer of these murders."[10] Ahmed Refik also attempted to introduce some humane measures in the execution of the deportations. The allocated trains were not even covered freight cars but open ones used for the transport of animals; he asked the official from the Refugee Administration who had arrived to at least transport the Armenians in covered rail cars. Yet the latter "did not budge when he said in a nonchalant manner: 'So much the better, they'll get some fresh air.' "[11] This cruel mode of transportation contrasted, Ahmed Refik commented, with the manner in which the commander in chief, Enver Pasha, passed by one morning in another special train in full splendor and pomp; "he stepped to the front section of the train, his hands in his pockets, head uncovered, his eyes on lofty horizons, going by with lightning speed. He did not stoop to turn his head and look at the unfortunate [Armenian] subjects sprawled on the ground dying of hunger." The lack of knowledge about the extent of these Armenian massacres could be partially explained, Ahmet Refik further conjectured, by the strict censorship the CUP government applied at the capital; "no one in İstanbul knew anything [about these Armenian deportations and massacres]. The terrible censorship of Enver Pasha tried to hide these calamities from the populace, as if the lands lost could be recovered in this manner."[12] The majority of CUP leaders were fully cognizant of the cruel destiny of the deported Armenians, but they censored the knowledge to the best of their abilities.

Ahmed Refik recorded his memoirs of the Armenian deportations in his book *Two Committees Two Massacres* (*İki Komite İki Kıtal*) in the aftermath of World War I, during that brief period in 1919 when the Ottoman state and society attempted to come to terms with this collective violence. As the book's title indicates, he also included accounts of the massacres the Armenian revolutionary committee Dashnak committed against the Muslims in 1918 from Erzurum all the way to Trabzon. Ahmed Refik specifically criticized the Armenian committee's choice "to be bound by the hateful influence of ambitions gnawing their hearts for years as they also committed atrocities upon the withdrawal of the Russians [due to the 1917 revolution]... looking for an opportunity to take the revenge of the Van and Bitlis massacres and the Anatolian deportations."[13] He then described this ferocious second wave of Armenian revolutionary violence against the Muslims in full detail.[14] Even though this second wave of violence triggered by the Armenian revolutionary committees was nowhere close to the ferocity of the violence committed by the CUP, why did Ahmed Refik discussed both in his book? This is a significant question because such a discussion inadvertently equated the two massacres, thereby enabling an inherent denial of the enormity of the massacres committed by the CUP. In order to fully comprehend such denial, this chapter once again traces the context within which such an equation emerged.

Young Turk Social Structure of Similarity

This phase, covering the decade of 1908 to 1918, commences with the reinstitution by the Committee of Union and Progress of the Ottoman constitution and assembly, an event also referred to as the "constitutional revolution." The secret CUP opposition against the sultan turned into a political force after the committee started to actively recruit members from among army officers. Especially those CUP branches in Salonica and Monastir, manned mostly by soldiers, spearheaded the rebellion against the sultan's authority, initially by taking to the mountains as the Greek and Bulgarian guerrillas they fought had done.[15] Interestingly, CUP members were a product of the Western-style schools the sultan had established, yet the students trained there formed their political allegiance not to the sultan but instead to the abstract concept of the Ottoman state and nation they thought they could reform better than the sultans before them. These protomodern CUP members were young and had acquired modern scientific knowledge through education, but they lacked experience, especially in governance. They replaced the sultan's authority with the legal parameters of a constitution but did not have the legitimacy to have it enforced. As a consequence, to sustain their rule, they concentrated power within the CUP central committee and resorted to violence. The episodic violence was first exercised against the sultan's loyal officials, then spread to those who joined the political opposition to CUP; the assassinations of journalists who criticized the CUP followed suit.

The continuous wars the Ottoman Empire engaged in during this period—in Tripoli against the Italians in 1911–12; in the Balkans against Bulgaria, Greece, Montenegro, and Serbia in 1912–13; and on the side of the Axis powers during World War I—further polarized the structural divide within society. In addition to the divide between the Muslims and non-Muslims, a new structural divide sharpened and became institutionalized within the dominant Muslim Turkish majority: some, led by the Freedom and Entente Party (FEP), aspired to sustain the empire's multiethnic structure, while others, spearheaded by the CUP, eventually advocated an ethnically homogeneous Turkish nation-state. Hence the social structure predicated on difference was effectively challenged and violently replaced by one predicated on similarity. Now, those social groups judged by the dominant Muslim Turkish majority to be different were repressed, excluded from the body politic, and even destroyed. The most significant destruction the CUP undertook within this vision was directed against its Armenian subjects, more than a million of whom were forcibly deported and many massacred. The CUP escaped punishment and accountability because all its violence was clandestine, secretly executed by paramilitary groups. As a consequence, the empire based on difference was forcefully transformed into a nation predicated on similarity at the expense of hundreds of thousands of lives, destroying the social and ethical fabric of the central lands of the empire in Asia Minor.

During this era, similarity also started to prevail over difference as both Muslim and non-Muslim subjects actively engaged in separatist movements. Yet the ultimate form of social structure was determined by the aspirations and subsequent violent acts of those in power, namely, the CUP. Just like the inherent hegemonic identity of the previous era, the initial dominant CUP identity was Sunni Muslim. The initial secret CUP committees that challenged the sultan's rule contained many Albanians, Arabs, and Circassians alongside the Turks. There were even a few non-Muslims sprinkled in, although the majority of non-Muslims opposing the sultan's rule had formed separate organizations, like the Armenian revolutionary committees. The CUP interacted with these non-Muslim committees but never formed equal partnerships with them. The CUP identity started to transform after its successful constitutional revolution. The majority of the officers actualizing the revolution through military force were Muslim Turks; civilian CUP members were also predominantly Muslim Turkish. Yet this Muslim Turkish identity initially remained subsumed as CUP leaders aspired to first save the Ottoman state by equally including all the subjects in the body politic. Escalating opposition, rebellions, and wars gradually forced the ethnic Turkish identity to prevail over all others. The CUP increasingly marginalized and oppressed the non-Muslim and non-Turkish communities. During World War I, this exclusion turned into collective violence as the CUP systematically destroyed the Ottoman Armenian community through forced deportations and ensuing massacres. The end of World War I signaled the end of the Ottoman Empire; the ensuing independence struggle instigated by the CUP eventually led to the establishment of the Turkish republic along the same premises of similarity rather than difference.

Emergence of Young Turk Modernity

The fundamental reason behind the secret opposition of the Western-style-educated officers and officials to the sultan was their belief that a constitutional monarchy and a parliament would magically solve all the problems of the empire. They actualized their fundamental aim of political change through the 1908 revolution. Yet this move that had democratized Western Europe instead exacerbated the empire's problems to the point of destruction. It was especially hard to get the populace to abide by the constitution and to have the parliament engage in peaceful opposition. The CUP could only hold onto power by ruling the empire autocratically through its central committee, engaging in propaganda and populism, and carrying out systemic violence against the opposition. Lacking a reform agenda, the CUP was effective in carrying out changes in two spheres, the military and the economy. It retired senior army officers, replacing them with its own CUP members who had knowledge and training but lacked experience; it replicated the same strategy for the state bureaucracy as well. As a consequence, the state became increasingly politicized and polarized, leading to dramatic losses in the ensuing wars. The CUP decided that the economy could only be improved by generating a Turkish bourgeoisie; it therefore channeled funds away from the existing non-Muslim bourgeoisie and provided economic capital to the Turks. Yet, because the Turks lacked economic knowledge and skills, many of the companies they formed ended in bankruptcy. Hence, the two main measures the CUP undertook to what it believed was democratizing the social structure led to further disarray. As such, this phase was marked by the most dramatic difference between the form and content of modernity; the CUP mirrored modernity replicated the form, but the content that developed completely contradicted what the form was supposed to have led to, that is, to the democratization of the empire. Instead, increased autocracy and collective violence ensued.

First the Political Refractions

With the constitutional revolution, the CUP eliminated the sultan's mediation and filter, as well as dynastic vision and experience of rule, replacing them with the parameters, based on the French Revolution, of freedom, equality, and fraternity politically institutionalized as constitutional monarchy and the parliament. Yet contemporaneous memoirs discuss in detail the ensuing chaos. Military officers came to the forefront, employing the technologies and elements of modernity not to liberate but to control, dominate, and violently eliminate all political opposition. The CUP employed telegraph technology to centralize power, crowd manipulation through propaganda to exercise power, and the censorship of the media and the educational system not to teach the populace but to discipline obedience to the CUP. Political governance was ensured through the placement of the CUP's own young, inexperienced men into both the army and the bureaucracy, and through the use of the parliament to merely rubber-stamp

CUP decisions. Hence, Western European modernity leading to liberation and democratization instead produced repression and autocratic populism.

After the constitutional revolution, the Ottoman dynasty irreversibly lost power to the CUP central committee. And the secret CUP branches in predominantly western Balkan provinces initially decided to take action in the aftermath of the 9 June 1908 "Reval meeting"[16] of the British king with the Russian tsar. The CUP members were certain that the meeting was held to determine how to apportion the Ottoman Empire among the Great Powers. Deciding to preserve the Ottoman state at all costs, they mobilized to force the Ottoman sultan into action by rebelling against him. Ottoman army officers, with leaders such as Enver and Niyazi Bey, took to the mountains, while others assassinated the Ottoman officials sent by the sultan to contain them. In the end, the CUP executed a revolution as the sultan reinstated the constitution on 24 July 1908.[17] The course of the constitutional revolution demonstrates how the violent elements of CUP rule came to being.

Actualization of the Revolution

The new technology of telegraph communication had initially become the primary channel through which the sultan received information from all the provinces. Yet the same technology also brought the sultan down because the CUP members trained to man the telegraph system employed it to get the sultan to believe the rebellion was much more widespread than it actually was. They sent separate telegrams to the sultan from Salonica, Tikveş, Skopje, Monastir, Resne, and Ohri to create such an illusion. The telegrams stated that all members of the military, the security forces, as well as top-level administrative officials had joined the revolution.[18] Likewise, CUP member Talat Bey (later Pasha), a telegraph clerk himself, let all those wanting to join the CUP ranks send similar telegrams from their own locales.[19] Many officials noted in their memoirs that even when there was no CUP activity at their locale, they received telegrams from CUP members as if they were local CUP leaders and then forwarded these to other provinces to magnify the extent of the movement.[20] The CUP branch in the Balkans that had successfully masterminded this mobilization then telegraphed the CUP branch at the capital, notifying it that a group had departed for the capital to negotiate with the government and oversee the election of the deputies.[21]

Although news of the reestablishment of the constitution was printed in the newspapers, initially very few knew what happened, why, and to what ends. At the capital, the dozen or so CUP members tried to mobilize the urban populace on the one hand and contain them on the other. Their spontaneous course of action mostly consisted of forcing the sultan's officials to swear allegiance to the new constitution. This chaotic course of action was due to the fact that the CUP did not have any plan in place in case of success.[22] The temporary leadership of the local CUP branch at the capital was quickly eclipsed upon the arrival of CUP members from the Balkans. The arriving members were first upset that there was no greeting ceremony.[23] Then, infighting ensued as everyone began to vie for power.[24] While discussing what course of action to take next, the CUP decided to keep its membership secret, to hide either its small size or its lack of preparation.[25] This decision was crucial in that it quickly expanded the boundaries of the CUP as an organization; literally everyone could claim to be a CUP member without any burden of proof—so much so that when Ahmed Rıza Bey, the CUP leader in Paris, arrived at the capital two months later, he was shocked to encounter at the CUP headquarters "some strange men I did not know and whose names I had not even heard. Each and every one of them swaggered with pride and dictated matters as if they had all worked and sacrificed for the Constitution more than I had."[26] While this decision did quickly multiply CUP membership and power, it also destabilized and diluted the movement, turning the revolution into an amorphous populist movement.

The initial course of CUP political action again reveals the unpreparedness of the CUP to assume a role in governance. Some civilian members wanted the CUP to merely observe and not intervene in governance, but to no avail.[27] Other military members forced the CUP to issue a public declaration regarding what it intended to do. And the CUP did indeed issue declarations stating that "we have no political program; until now, we worked to destroy. Now, we shall try to protect the constitution to the letter. The CUP will not cease to exist; we shall start to work . . . with the government for the future of the country, for its development. And if the government does not work properly, then the CUP will force it to be rightful. . . . We want those who defended the rights of Greeks, Armenians, and Bulgarians with their pens to also think of us, the Turks. For we, too, have suffered a lot."[28] The message is noteworthy on two counts. First, the CUP assumed that once the constitution was reinstituted, everything would magically fall into place. And it had focused so much on opposing the sultan that it had not developed any plans of action lest they succeeded. That was why the CUP initially could not directly engage in politics but instead assumed a supervisory role over governance. This decision eventually created an informal shadow government consisting of the CUP central committee that, unlike the formal government, could act with impunity. Second, the CUP claimed to have come to power to act on behalf of the Turks rather than all imperial subjects. And while governance continued as usual, the CUP spread its organization throughout the empire by establishing many local branches. For the first time in Ottoman history, a political organization employed modern methods to deeply penetrate into society. These local CUP branches then started to actively engage in politics by recruiting mostly local Muslim notables, forcing the CUP to appoint inspectors for oversight and responsible secretaries at every branch for local representation.[29] Still, many local CUP clubs immediately intervened in local governance by ordering government officials to do as they were told.[30] Rather than transforming the existing power structure, the CUP thus managed to create an informal shadow power structure, one that paralleled the existing one.

Another first was the modern use of public space. Crowds mobilized by the CUP took to the streets in its support; the term *miting*—derived from the British word "meeting"—was introduced into the Ottoman language as "demonstration." People "mostly gathered somewhere and shouted."[31] CUP members' speeches at public squares created the impression among the populace that they were participating in a great change; many bookstores were adorned with flags, and newspaper distributors did a brisk business, frequently running out of issues. Some thought this was how the French Revolution must have felt.[32] Yet, what such feeling would lead to next was still undetermined.[33] The populace celebrated freedom but had no idea what freedom actually was.[34] The most prominent public practice was that of popular justice, namely, forcibly removing from office those officials regarded poorly by the crowd and freeing all the prisoners.[35]

Gradual Loss of the Sultan's Power

One significant outcome was immediately evident to all, however: the Ottoman dynasty and its current sultan had irrevocably lost power to the CUP.[36] Discussions of the 1908 revolution figure heavily in all contemporaneous memoirs; the writers discuss in depth where they were when the revolution occurred, and what they thought it meant for them and for the empire. The thirty-three-year-long palace oligarchy and its government were replaced, one noted, by "an association of patriotic guerrilla fighters with weird accents, primitive manners, and the temperament of mountain people."[37] Another stated that "the Abdülhamid period was filled with a stagnation that depressed the country's air . . . filled with the spell of an ancient cemetery where one did not hear even an owl. . . . On this dead crowd, the revolution's scream produced the effect of the angel of death's blow of the last trumpet. We seriously saw a day of judgment confronting us, one where the greatest disease among the people present was the lack of distinguished men."[38] Still another contrasted CUP members with the Ottoman elite, noting that "we the Ottoman elite are sober, serious-minded people with foresight. We do not like adventures the way they do because a state's destiny cannot be tossed like a backgammon dice. . . . do not let their outward appearance fool you; they talk sweetly, appear charming, but their dreams are vast and their demands infinite."[39] The CUP's public intent of adhering to the constitution to the letter was much harder to put into practice as well. One official discussed the encountered difficulties as follows:[40]

> If one were to pick up a few Eskimos from the North Pole and from Australia half a dozen...men, blindfold them, put them on a plane, and dump them on a street in London, what would happen to those poor wretched men? Well, that was the way we were [at the advent of] the constitutional era. We suddenly found ourselves in front of a huge machine which we had never once witnessed in operation. And we were authorized to make it work. As we were never used to operating it, all the procedures in the machine necessary to operate it with ease turned into a source of torture and pain for us. And we could not get it to work, so we preferred to break it [instead]!

This official continued his analogy by noting that "the governor pasha [*sic*] who during the reign of Sultan Abdülhamid II was used to riding the administrative horse like a calm, neutered cart horse, suddenly found himself on top of a rearing, irritable colt that would accept neither the whip nor the stirrup. And the animal soon started to run away in full gallop."

Meanwhile, the CUP officers became increasingly radicalized when it was clear that obedience and loyalty to the sultan—the former source of legitimacy and promotion—no longer worked.[41] Constitutional rule was different from the sultanic one in that it required the populace to believe in, support, respect, and obey the abstract concept of freedom embodied in the constitution. Until then, the populace was used to display obedience to the sultan because of the sacredness enveloping the post; the sultan physically embodied both the historical might of the Ottoman dynasty and the religious legitimacy of the caliphate. Because the abstract constitution did not have such sacred legitimacy, the CUP struggled to determine what to do in its stead.

New Political Visions

What exactly was the CUP's political vision, and how did it translate into action? The CUP firmly believed in the greatness of its mission, defined as "saving the country in every which way possible."[42] One official argued that the CUP "had nothing to do with domestic and ideological reform; it was at best a secret organization...one that was born out of the political problems in Macedonia, that aimed to bring back the constitution."[43] The CUP's insistence on remaining a secret organization also prevented it from achieving the revolution it had initially envisioned. Another official claimed that the committee was too small and too inexperienced to assume the governance of an empire; it also had not planned ahead, assuming that the sultan's removal would naturally end the empire's problems.[44] Still another contended that within the CUP decision-making process, the only shared principles were "equality among them as brothers" and "their love of the fatherland."[45] All these accounts alluded to abstract political principles of an earlier form of nationalism, a protonationalism predicated on a particular type of brotherhood the parameters of which were still naturalized or unclear.

In late 1908, the CUP convened a congress in Salonica with the explicit intent to discuss its mission, but it ended up focusing instead on issues of internal organization. It was decided that the CUP central committee would "administer the organization and the government, while the army would protect the constitution."[46] This division of labor squarely placed political power in the hands of the military that defined, decided, and acted on what formed a threat to the new system.[47] One official skeptically pointed out that these young officers "had a lot of rhetoric about change, but no clue about what constitutionalism meant.... They were only capable of considering it patriotic to declare all those who did not join the CUP the enemy, vowing to destroy them."[48] Such a political vision did not unite but further divided the empire through exclusion. The civilian CUP officials initially attempted to unite all the elements of the empire as brothers. Yet this proved challenging, as indicated by the account of two CUP members' visit to the then grand vizier, Kamil Pasha. When the two described their vision, explaining how they were going to accomplish this task and asking the grand vizier's opinion, they received the following skeptical response:[49]

> Kamil Pasha listened, and listened for a long time and then asked his famous question: "Are you done, effendis?" When they answered in the affirmative, he... said: "It is not possible, effendis, it cannot be done... because this country has its own particular dynamics. So do the people who live in it. You groundlessly imagine these conditions in your mind's eye by likening us to others or others to us, you get yourselves to believe in what you have created, and then you reject the real truth.... If a magical precaution cannot be found in our empire to contain these diverse masses of various nationalities, religions, races around a single thought, then each of these disparate elements will perceive and consider the Constitutional Monarchy, Freedom, Justice, and Equality [*sic*] in accordance to their own conditions, and that is when the immense danger shall confront us.

The grand vizier pointed out the endemic problem encountered by all empires based on difference when challenged by the vision of sameness inherent in the conceptions of equality and fraternity. How could difference be brought in without segmenting the empire's structure? One could do so around the dominant Muslim Turkish majority, but that would not "encompass the Christian citizens."[50] Indeed, the eventual failure of this civilian CUP vision turned the CUP into "the mortal enemy of all nationalist and independence-seeking elements... against all minorities, Albanians, Armenians, the Greek Rum, and Arabs." The future course could be glimpsed from the first political action of the Muslim Turkish students upon hearing about the constitution's reestablishment. They went "to Pera! To scream and shout in front of foreign and Christian stores as if we had beaten, run their countries to the ground! We did not yet have either a march or a freedom song. Both we and the entire populace constantly screamed 'long live our sultan!' causing the stores to close down in fright."[51] The new political vision thus started to publicly identify the non-Muslim elements as the other.[52]

Still, the CUP initially attempted to appease the previous injustices committed against non-Muslim subjects. In January 1909, it formed a commission with two Armenian and two Turkish members to inspect the land disputes between the Armenians and the Kurds in the eastern provinces. Yet due to the strong opposition of the Kurds, none of the recommendations were carried out.[53] The CUP efforts to bring the Greek Rum into the Ottoman fold also failed because rather than first delivering the Greek Rum benefits in return for their participation in this new political unity, the CUP instead attempted to first abolish all of their privileges "on the premise that the equal rights brought by constitutional law would be beneficial to them."[54] Also significant was increased public awareness of the dominant Muslim Turkish majority's naturalized privileges. One liberal thinker noted that the "only obstacle to achieving such [full] equality [with the non-Muslim subjects] was our national pride and grandeur. [This equality] had always been kept away from the imagination of the [Muslim] populace because of the grandness of our past and our limitless esteem and trust in our religion." He added that the country did indeed belong to the Muslim Turks "who conquered it by their swords," but the non-Muslim subjects could not be excluded because they had "tilled this soil and regarded it as their homeland while we were still nomads in the Asian deserts."[55] Yet such critical approaches were to remain in opposition as the CUP instead began to redefine Ottoman identity along Turkish nationalism.

Emergence of Proto-Turkish Nationalism

Rather than critically reflecting on the rule of the dominant Turkish Muslim majority with the intent to expand it to include other elements within a liberal framework, the CUP instead renaturalized such domination by violently repressing any attempts at imperial self-definition that did not center on a Muslim

Turkish identity. Two prominent CUP intellectuals, Ziya Gökalp and Yahya Kemal Beyatlı, played a decisive role in articulating this new protonationalist identity. Gökalp scientifically shaped the CUP ideology in a protonationalist manner that initially defined the new nation not in ethnic but rather in cultural terms.[56] His conceptualization included all those who shared the Turkish culture and spoke the Turkish language.[57] Beyatlı provided the rhetoric of this new protonationalist direction by bringing in and glorifying the past history of the Turks. Rather than taking the cultural elements of nationalism from the West, he proposed that Turks look toward their own history to generate their own definition.[58] Yet Beyatlı's interpretation reproduced the dominance of the Muslim Turkish majority in the empire, conveniently overlooking the contribution of non-Muslims, who constituted almost half of the imperial populace. Such discussions among the Turks led all non-Turkish elements in the empire to become wary of any CUP action. When the constitution declared Turkish as the official language of the empire, non-Turkish elements immediately interpreted it as "both a domination of Turkishness and as a tool to 'Turkify' them."[59] Another contemporaneous intellectual blamed the CUP, claiming that it did not prioritize the two elements of science and justice that would have truly awakened the nation and helped develop an inclusive identity; the CUP engaged instead in rhetoric and oppression.[60] Eventually, the CUP definition of a true patriot became "those members who blindly followed CUP orders."[61] Hence, for the CUP, unity remained a rhetorical ideal, translating into practice as an exclusionary stand promoting Turkishness. One writer aptly captured what the CUP had turned into upon assuming power as follows:[62]

> [The CUP] was not a political party but a faith. Political parties generally represent and defend the interests of a particular class. A political committee, however, often emerges out of the union of people with character who are ready to sacrifice their lives for a higher moral order and political ideal.... [As the CUP was initially formed in secret opposition to the sultan], the slightest ideal talk, the smallest treason could bring about their imprisonment, exile, and perhaps death.... What connected [the CUP members] was not personal gain, base and despicable thought, but instead a commitment to high ideals. And this ideal consisted of the love of the fatherland. They were all like believers prostrating themselves in front of the stand of the fatherland. All their hearts beat for martyrdom in defense of their faith. There was nothing they would not have sacrificed for this ideal.

According to this writer, the CUP was not even aware of what it formulated. First, it had believed that the proclamation of freedom through the restoration of the constitution alone would dissipate all the tensions of the empire; it thus had no idea what such a restoration would lead to. Second, its members were not experienced statesmen but instead all young, low-level officials, officers, and clerks. They therefore did not have much of an education or experience regarding how a government should be administered. They were unaware of the complexity, greatness, and certainty of the dangers awaiting them. They had never seen a political program and could not even fathom the mechanisms and difficulties of parliamentarian life and constitutional rule. Yet they fully embraced governance, willing to sacrifice their lives to save their country at all costs.

Role of Political Propaganda

The CUP quickly became aware that it needed to gain and sustain the support of the populace to legitimate its rule. It is therefore no accident that the CUP also introduced into the Ottoman vocabulary the word "propaganda" and then started to systematically practice it.[63] The CUP not only mobilized all its members to penetrate and garner public support by any means necessary but also strictly controlled and shaped the print media to diffuse its propaganda. In his memoirs, one foreign journalist complained that those newspapers "forthright in their reporting have been shut down. As for the rest, they are connected to the present government and generally write things that have nothing to do with what is really taking place. They do not say 'let us write the truth even if the populace may not happy about it.' "[64] A general remarked that the newspaper announcements of the Ottoman military campaigns contained a "corrected" version of the truth. The Ottoman populace "was not told the truth as is; [our] victories were portrayed more gloriously, [those] of the enemies lightly, and their defeats as routings... one traipsed around 'truth' and skipped over 'reality.' Bitter truths were thus hidden, and the populace was nurtured through [false] hopes and dreams."[65] The CUP was able to engage in such propaganda because CUP member and officer Enver Pasha, who had become a general and eventually the chief commander of the Ottoman military, bought intellectuals off by giving them vast amounts of money "for works he commissioned from them."[66] The CUP also bought its own newspaper and recruited all the best pens to write for it.[67]

How the CUP carefully shaped the knowledge and information disseminated through the media is most evident in three disparate accounts. In one, a journalist noted that he and his colleague had to go to Talat Pasha's house to "get the topics on which they could write" and that the pasha had "an Oriental morality." "This morality," he stated, "accepts righteousness and merit in a very narrow sense: it is intolerant of private, personal shames and improprieties... but considers neither lies nor cruelty immoral."[68] Hence the CUP leaders cared about personal ethics, but when it came to public morality, they could easily lie and bend the truth. In the second account, a journalist wrote a three-column article as if he had interviewed Enver Pasha; the pasha liked the printed article so much that he asked the journalist to join him as a correspondent on his trip to Germany.[69] The third account by yet another journalist explained how he was sent to Enver Pasha when the latter called and requested an "obedient" journalist. After giving some news, the pasha stated that "it should appear as if the *Tanin* newspaper heard this news and came to interview me." The pasha then told the journalist what the main message of the interview should be, asking him "to pen an interview along these lines and print it tomorrow." Enver Pasha then ended the meeting by making the journalist once again repeat what he was to do.[70] The same CUP approach to the media not as a source of information and knowledge but rather as a propaganda tool is also apparent in the publications that began to emerge in the provinces.[71]

Reversed Military Content

Officers educated at Western-style military schools of the empire in general, and those rebellious officers of the Third Army stationed in the Balkans in particular claimed that they had actualized the 1908 constitutional revolution.[72] The young reformist officers were not satisfied with the mastery of modern military knowledge and skills alone; they also wanted to politically save the Ottoman state from the sultan. In doing so, they were inspired by the Prussian military model that did not separate state and military interests but instead placed both above the interests and rights of citizens—one that was identified as the "closest to Ottoman culture."[73] The empire's deteriorating economic conditions increased their resolve; the escalating cost of modern armaments produced through Western industrial technology alongside diminishing, irregularly paid military salaries radicalized them.

Right after the 1908 revolution, privates at the capital who had temporally fulfilled their military service did not want to go out to train; they instead left their barracks shouting, "We want to be discharged."[74] Officers reacted differently; many actively engaged in forcing pashas in positions of power to take oaths of allegiance to the CUP and the revolution.[75] The oath taken was as follows:[76]

> With my hand placed upon the exalted Qur'an, I swear in the name of Allah that I will obey every letter of the exalted decrees of the Constitution bestowed upon his loyal subjects by our beloved sultan. If it so happens that in the future the Constitution—may God's protection be upon it—is abolished upon the treason of some disgraceful people the way it had been for thirty-two years, then, in order to protect

> the freedom of the fatherland, I promise to help the CUP until the last drop of my blood, personally killing with my own hands whoever has the audacity to engage in sedition against the CUP. I promise to provide loyalty and servitude to our beloved sultan who bestowed this favor upon us as well as to our religion, nation, and fatherland.

The oath forced the Muslim audience to swear to serve the CUP "until the last drop of blood" and, if necessary, to commit violence on its behalf. CUP members visited the Western-style military, medical, and naval schools, schools of engineering and cannonry, the Selimiye military barracks, and the officers and laborers at the Tophane armament complex, making them all swear allegiance not only to the constitution but also to the CUP. This crucial coupling enabled the CUP to equate the protection of the constitution and state sovereignty with CUP membership. It caused some dissent, however, as some wanted to swear allegiance only to the constitution but not to the CUP because they did not want to effectively become CUP members by doing so.[77] Yet such dissent was rare and often led to imprisonment. The identities of the majority of students, officers, and state officials became politicized as all were forced to take this political oath. The forcefully recruited CUP members then engaged in politics, eventually considering themselves above the law.[78]

This dramatic entrance of the military into the political sphere was a double-edged sword: it had enabled the CUP to assume power, but it also began to sap military discipline and strength, generating much political discord within the ranks. The CUP central committee recognized this danger and therefore accepted the principle that soldiers should not engage in politics or join political parties and organizations. Yet, it did not enforce this decision and did not hold the soldiers who did join accountable, thereby indirectly promoting CUP membership within the military as well as the bureaucracy.[79] In the end, the entire army, all the way up to the general staff, fell under the influence of the CUP.[80] Thus emerged a bizarre historical connection whereby young, educated military officers were accepted as the only viable force that would establish and sustain liberty and democracy on Ottoman lands.[81]

The CUP-influenced bureaucracy and the military then collaborated to execute dramatic reforms. The CUP member and military officer Enver Bey was promoted first to major general and then became the war minister; once at that post, he ordered the retirement of hundreds of high-ranking officers, claiming they had been promoted not on merit but due to their loyalty to the sultan. This was soon followed by similar retirements of many officials and clerks at the War Ministry.[82] These too were replaced by young, like-minded officers who naturally developed loyalty to the CUP.[83] Among the younger officers, promotions also occurred at a much faster pace, to the detriment of those already in the ranks.[84] Facing criticism, the CUP promised to investigate unjust retirements, reinstating some officers, yet a year went by and nothing was done.[85] Because all those who resisted the new modern pace were immediately retired, no one had courage left to protest.[86]

Such appointments of commanders proved difficult, however, because there were insufficient numbers of reserve officers. In addition, Enver Pasha and his friends often did not trust, respect, and appoint any commanders they did not personally know. In the Ottoman army, competent command and management of troops required at least five to ten years of serious active duty, but the top CUP officers had at most only two to three years of such experience. As a consequence, "when we were called to command [entire] divisions with such junior ranks," one officer remarked, "most of us adopted the easiest route possible from time immemorial that is to hit, break, hang, and chop up and then declare 'It [just] happened!' "How many before us had either directly killed with their own hands or had murdered through aides their own officers and soldiers," he wondered, "without any trial [whatsoever]? We did not find the need to think about this even for a moment."[87] Hence, this rapid turnover quickly eliminated accountability for committed violence. The only advantage of such drastic military reforms was that the young officers the CUP had recruited and promoted were able to remain in service for a very long time. The empire engaged in nonstop wars for a decade, from 1912 to 1922; during this entire time, the same group of officers kept fighting, thereby gaining experience. When they won the independence struggle, they continued on to establish and govern the Turkish republic. Indeed, the military was the only institution that made the transformation from the empire to the republic intact; this explains the inordinate power the military still has in Turkey today.

The other significant CUP reform concerned the issue of non-Muslim recruitment for military service. After all, the constitution promised equal rights to non-Muslims, introducing in return equal responsibility in service. The CUP passed a law enabling non-Muslims to also serve in the military, but given the lack of trust many Muslim officers felt toward non-Muslims, such a transformation was fraught with problems, with many commanders wary of the negative reaction of the Muslim soldiers.[88] And the source of such problems was traced not to the Muslims who had excluded the non-Muslims from military service on grounds of religion for centuries but instead to the unwillingness of the non-Muslims. As a consequence, even though non-Muslims did start to serve in the Ottoman military at the 1912–13 Balkan Wars, they were never accepted and rewarded equally. During CUP rule, the prejudice and discrimination against non-Muslims not only persisted but became further institutionalized in the military.

Inverted Education

The members of the CUP central committee were cognizant of the significance of education, since they had come to power through the acquisition of Western-style knowledge and skills at schools. The committee therefore established many schools just as Sultan Abdülhamid II had done, but now with the intent to raise Muslim citizens loyal to the CUP. The instructors and curricula of both the civilian and the military schools were also transformed, specifically lauding the CUP's triumph over autocratic sultans.[89] In a similar populist move, the CUP lifted the quota and the examination system that had limited the number of students attending the schools of law and public administration, instead admitting all literate applicants.[90] Schools also became increasingly politicized as CUP members went to schools, delivering provocative speeches to recruit students into CUP ranks.[91] Students then began to participate in their schools' governance informally, protesting and booing some instructors out of the classroom not because of inadequacies in their teaching but rather for their political stand and possible connections with and loyalty to the sultan instead of the CUP. Unlike in the time of Sultan Abdülhamid II, the school administration tolerated such behavior, and no one was punished. CUP members or CUP sympathizers were duly appointed instead of the ousted instructors. Political factions began to form among the students as well.[92] When graduates were then appointed to their first official posts, in addition to carrying out their official duties, they also taught courses at local high schools, thereby further spreading their political influence throughout the empire.[93]

The most significant CUP intervention was the public, informal one offered within and outside the empire. Courses and lectures at CUP clubs and at the cultural association of the Turkish Hearths (Türk Ocakları) instigated nationalist and patriotic sentiments especially among Muslim Turkish students.[94] Such newly created public spaces for education did not tolerate dissent; those Muslim Turks found to be unpatriotic were quickly excluded. Turkish identity eventually prevailed above and beyond all others, including religion. Outside the empire, the CUP central committee sent young Muslim Turkish students and apprentices especially to Germany to improve their training, as well as to reward and sustain their loyalty to the CUP.[95] Because the selection criteria were not based on merit, those who did get trained abroad ended up supporting primarily not science and objective knowledge but CUP interests.[96] They also started to compare the conditions in their empire with what they had seen on the Continent, furthering both their resolve toward pursuing progress at all costs and their resentment of the West.[97] Still, this CUP project exposed many middle- and lower-class Muslim Turks to Western Europe.

The politicization of identity was not restricted to Muslim education alone. Non-Muslims often educated at separate schools also tried to define and identify their role and location within the rapidly transforming system. One Ottoman official and CUP member recounted his surprise visit to an Armenian school as follows:[98]

> [In this particular village], they greeted my unexpected visit with bewilderment and surprise. They explained their [middle school] curriculum, trying to point out that they taught Turkish language as well. I asked them which book they used for Turkish. They showed a primer written in Turkish and Armenian. In one class, only three children had this primer, but the pages had not yet been cut open... there was not a single student who could read Turkish properly. In order to change the ensuing cold atmosphere, the teacher tried to get the students to sing a song. They started to sing a song in Armenian. "Don't they know [one] in Turkish?" I asked. The instructor separated a group among the more senior students. They sang, shouting out one of the popular freedom songs of the time. [Yet] in the verses, they kept substituting the word "Armenian" for "Ottoman," singing "we are the bravest of the brave; we are Armenians." The children had no idea what they were singing, and the instructor kept changing color [from embarrassment]. In those days, there was not much that could be done other than leaving the Armenians alone, only preventing them when they openly took offensive action.

This narration contradicts the common perception that most non-Muslims in Anatolia spoke Turkish as their first language. The exception may be generational in that the new generations, just like those of the dominant Muslim Turkish majority, were becoming cognizant of their separate social identity. Just as significant was the increased surveillance by new CUP officials of the non-Muslim educational system, with the intent to interrogate, monitor, and find fault. And still many others openly resented the excellence of the large number of non-Muslim schools, noting that the Muslim ones were greatly inferior in comparison.[99]

Reversed Economic Practices

The economic policy of Sultan Abdülhamid II had replicated the traditional imperial one of allowing non-Muslim subjects to dominate in trade and commerce insofar as their economic capital did not translate into political power. Yet the CUP was not bound by such past principles and practices. When it became politically and socially dominant, it also faced an almost empty state treasury and therefore had to focus on raising funds. Until then, the economic sphere was indeed dominated by non-Muslims, who constituted the initial Ottoman bourgeoisie. The CUP's attention immediately turned to challenging this domination, on the premise that the non-Muslim subjects had intentionally controlled and taken economic resources away from the dominant Muslim Turkish majority. It therefore pursued a two-pronged economic policy: it employed the remaining state funds as well as loans from the West to create a Turkish Muslim bourgeoisie on the one hand, and it undermined non-Muslim economic activities on the other. Hence, just as it had underestimated the significance of experience in the military sphere, the CUP downplayed the significance of economic skills and commercial experience. The severe and often violent measures it subsequently took to transfer economic wealth from non-Muslims to Muslim Turks certainly impoverished the non-Muslim bourgeoisie, but they failed to create a Muslim Turkish one largely due to the latter's lack of economic acumen. In addition, once again, the CUP appointed Muslim Turks to economic enterprises based not on merit but instead on their loyalty to the CUP.[100] And the majority of Muslim Turks who thus failed blamed not their own lack of economic skills but instead the competition they faced from the non-Muslim bourgeoisie.

During CUP rule, non-Muslims were still economically dominant especially in the empire's urban centers.[101] Due to their lack of integration into Ottoman society on equal terms, the majority had become increasingly dependent in their interaction with Western European companies, often engaging in brokering and marketing Western products. The ones with less capital and expertise worked as tailors and grocers.[102] A contemporaneous account of this non-Muslim economic dominance is depicted in one memoir as follows:[103]

> All of trade, artisanal, and economic jobs are in the hands of minorities and foreigners. It is very surprising to see how minimal the Turkish role in economic life is.... The Turkish urban populace comprises three groups, officials, soldiers, and religious men. The small group of intellectuals comprising lawyers, physicians, journalists, poets, and literary men are of course removed from trade and artisanal activities.... Some among the Turkish lower classes engage in trade, [but] they are too few and insignificant to impact the country's economic life. For instance... street peddlers, cart drivers, oarsmen, porters are mostly Turkish Muslims. It is not that there are not some merchants engaged in the trade of sundries, dry goods, grocery, and in owning businesses, but these too are few and insignificant in the general trade of the country. All of the advantageous and fundamental businesses conducted in accordance with the new trade rules of the century are in

> the hands of foreigners and Christians.... They control, for instance, all the banks and banking... railroad companies... [and] the largest trade item of Turkey, namely, the tobacco trade... all transportation facilities like tramways, telephone and other public utility companies.... All the largest arcades and shops belong to the Christians. The most orderly neighborhoods are those of the Christians.

Such non-Muslim dominance was noticed at a time when one-third of the entire Ottoman budget went to paying external debts, largely accrued for military procurements. The financial crisis was initially so severe that in an attempt to raise money, the CUP government auctioned off the sultan's jewelry in Paris.[104] With the establishment of the Public Debt Administration to recover the foreign debts of the Ottoman state, all profitable revenue resources went to this organization that was run mainly by foreigners and non-Muslims.

The CUP initiatives to "correct" this inequity penetrated the entire economic sphere. At the bottom, the CUP formed close connections with Muslim tradesmen's organizations like bread makers, food sellers, porters, and the like.[105] Leading this effort was CUP member Kara Kemal, who argued that there had not been a rich class of Turks until then because economic capital had always been concentrated in the hands of non-Muslims. He therefore intended to "raise a rich Turkish class and by doing so, procure a superior role for the Turks." The same contemporaneous account stated that Kara Kemal "had created a kind of commando force out of the porters whom he had organized, placed his men to organize and control all the tradesmen and artisans. He was like a sheikh and all the organized tradesmen acted as his disciples, blindly following his orders. This had created the impression that if what he wanted was not done, he could turn everything upside down with his rabble. Everyone, including... the cabinet and the central committee, treated Kara Kemal as a force that could not be messed with and tried to be on good terms with him."[106] The CUP also employed this "rabble" to stage demonstrations against the non-Muslim establishments at the capital, storming, stoning, and at times setting fire to them. Protests at the 1916 CUP Congress led to Kara Kemal's removal, but he continued to wield power indirectly. As Turkish trade organizations and unions were established through CUP oversight, an independent Turkish working class also failed to emerge.

At the middle level, the CUP gave many recently retired state officials and officers lump-sum severance payments with which to establish businesses. Yet one memoir stated that "most consumed this capital without establishing a business. Some attempted to open stores, but many could not make it work and had to shut their stores down within six months, for they could not compete with the Greek Rum who had been engaged in trade for generations. Today, very few of these [former] officials engage in trade."[107] The CUP also created another source of revenue at this level by issuing domestic debt vouchers (istikraz-ı dahili) to the members of the populace who had some income. All investors were promised they would receive monthly interest, but they were given interest only during the first month. After that, payment was discontinued, since the state lacked the resources to pay any of this domestic debt, plunging many into poverty.[108] The situation was no different in the provinces of the empire. CUP members and officials intervened in trade and commerce with the intent to benefit the Muslim Turks at the expense of the non-Muslims.[109] Like the Turkish working class, the burgeoning Turkish bourgeoisie also formed not independently but through state support. And many failed.

At the top, the CUP established a national export company (Milli İthalat Şirketi), a level scales company (Kantariye Şirketi), and a bank called the National Credit Bank (İtibar-ı Milli Bankası). These were not financially successful either, often surviving through state support alone. The analysis of the financial acumen of top CUP leaders, specifically Enver, Talat, and Cemal Pashas, provides insight into why such economic measures failed. All three had been state employees; Talat was a low-level bureaucrat, and Enver and Cemal were military officers. None had ever made a living from scratch; all received monthly salaries for engaging in noneconomic activities. As a consequence, they could not grasp how money was made. For instance, during the Ottoman war with Tripoli, Talat Pasha handed over a suitcase full of Crédit Foncier bonds for military expenses without even counting them or asking for a receipt.[110] During the same war, when Enver Bey ran out of cash, "he had pieces of cardboard cut out, had them stamped with his commander's seal, and used them instead of cash." Likewise, when Enver Bey became a pasha later on, he tried to solve all economic problems by personally creating state-sanctioned practices with the argument that "if there is no law, make the law yourself, and there will be law."[111] It is therefore not surprising that during World War I, Enver Pasha merely sent orders commanding the procurement of certain items throughout the empire, without considering how his demands impacted the economy. In the process, he created starvation and disease throughout imperial lands, in spite of the 1914 produce yield having been at record levels.[112] The economic measures Cemal Pasha took were likewise totally uninformed. When serving in Syria with full powers in military and civilian affairs, Cemal Pasha was unhappy about the huge differential between the value of gold and money, that is, monetary devaluation. He attempted to resolve this economic crisis by deporting, based on a lottery system, one-tenth of those people who were influential in the economic life of Adana, Aleppo, Syria, Beirut, Jerusalem, and Lebanon to distant Anatolian provinces and the Balkans.[113] It is not surprising that even though some were indeed deported, the devaluation could not be stopped.

In assessing CUP economic policy, one of the few successful Turkish businessmen recounted that "not a single rich person remained from among the [CUP] profiteers of the Unionists. One had hoped that capital accumulation could have accrued from such robbery! [After all], the foundation of accumulation in the West was also to a certain degree [such] robbery, yet there, the robbery occurred outside [the countries], providing the [necessary] sources for industrialization."[114] In addition, in the Ottoman case, the criteria the CUP employed in creating a Turkish bourgeoisie were predominantly political. The Turkification of the bourgeoisie "was not done in a systematic manner according to the needs of the country with a well thought out plan, but carried out rather haphazardly. Hence rather than founding a national economy, instead a protection system was established where the interests of the Turkish elements were protected. Even though this had started with good intentions, it devolved into people looking out for their own interests."[115] The CUP basically employed economic resources to reward its members. One CUP member defended such actions by stating:[116]

> The CUP could not have relied on the non-Muslim minority who controlled all the economic institutions of the country; it was necessary for some segment of the economic power to be transferred into the hands of the Turks. How could this be accomplished? ... Until then, the CUP had always been administered through its members' dues. When the government was in their hands [however], it could not directly or even secretly help its members.... So rather than legally or illegally enriching the CUP, it seemed imperative to form companies with those Turks who believed in them, and to establish banks with their mediation. This issue, brought up by [Kara] Kemal Bey, had been one of the main items at the CUP Congress, and a couple of positive decisions had been reached. Kemal Bey carried out the decisions ... and some companies and a bank were established.

As political decisions dictated economic ones, generating failure, the dire outcome was blamed on the financially skilled non-Muslims. Contemporaneous memoirs offer glimpses of the increased economic discrimination non-Muslims began to experience as a consequence. In one, the governor of Aleppo recounted the sufferings of an Armenian from Bab named Cib Nizipliyan whose land was illegally taken away from him through the collaboration of the local kadi with the local Muslim officials and officers. The governor intervened and restored Nizipliyan's lands, but the CUP government did not punish the perpetrators, but instead sent them to serve at other provinces.[117] In another instance in Anatolia, a state official and CUP member recounted establishing local Muslim companies, in what he termed "a battle in the economic realm against the non-Muslims."[118] In this case, the collusion of the local official with the local Muslim notables destroyed not only non-Muslim economic activities but also the local economy. The rhetoric the CUP employed in describing non-Muslim economic endeavors and wealth also changed. One account literally celebrated the escalating economic troubles and confiscations that non-Muslims faced.[119]

The most significant wealth transfer from non-Muslims to Muslim Turks before the 1915–17 Armenian collective violence occurred under CUP rule in the Smyrna region in 1912–13, with Enver Pasha's support. He decided with the SO director to secretly send its member Celal Bayar—who was to later become a minister, prime minister, and president in the Turkish republic—to scare away the local Greek Rum, confiscating their goods and properties in the process. The Greek Rum metropolite complained about the violence to Enver Pasha, who was visiting the region, stating:

> My dear son... for centuries this nation has distributed the professions among its members. Trade has been left to us upon your decision and desire. To upset this centuries-old style of life will only bring grief. And there is no need for it. It is dangerous to upset the order. The CUP responsible secretary [Celal Bayar] has started to take away from our hands the transport of goods by train wagons and the entire trade. When those who have been used to doing these jobs become unemployed and turn to sedition, would they not have an excuse?

The SO director at the meeting recounted that "there was a fleeting smile on Enver's lips."[120] And in spite of the wise words of the Greek Rum metropolite, the CUP continued to destroy the local economy through the harassment of the local non-Muslim subjects. All these CUP economic endeavors were undertaken without any knowledge of or consideration for entrepreneurship, a lack that literally destroyed the Ottoman economy instead of improving it. Financial resources that were forcefully taken away from non-Muslims and bestowed upon Muslim Turks with the backing of the state did not generate and sustain an economic base through which to modernize the empire.

In summary, CUP members, filled with an idealism to restore the empire to its former grandeur through political, economic, and educational modernization inspired by the successful Western European model, reintroduced a constitution and a parliament, reformulated the military now led by Western-educated officers, established more Western-style schools, and founded an economy that provided capital to future entrepreneurs. Unlike the Western European experience, however, this mirrored modernity created havoc, destroying what had already existed without adequately replacing it with. A crucial aspect of this failure was the escalating social polarization as the CUP followed a protonationalist vision based on Muslim Turkish dominance, a polarization that not only exacerbated the preexisting one between Muslims and non-Muslims but also institutionalized another between reformist and traditionalist Muslim Turks.

Elements of Young Turk Sentiments

Distorted Social Practices

Educated at Western-style schools, many CUP members were able to practice elements of the modern lifestyle in their everyday lives. They learned Western etiquette at military schools, attended new places of entertainment like theaters, concert halls, and cafes, and lived in newly built apartments. The entertainment of the dominant Muslim Turkish majority had initially been private in character; public entertainment predominantly consisted of going to coffeehouses to listen to traveling bards, visiting fairgrounds during religious holidays, taking excursions to the countryside, and, most important, visiting each other at their residences. From the eighteenth century on, however, new public spaces like theaters began to develop, first within Western embassies and then among the non-Muslims, who introduced the stage to the Ottoman populace. Theater companies manned and directed by especially the Armenians dominated the stage. Among contemporaneous actors, Vahram Papazyan was the most gifted one, playing every part to perfection with impeccable Turkish.[121] Yet the CUP gradually penetrated this public space as well by establishing the conservatory (Dar-ül-bedayi) and a school for fine arts. Not surprisingly, the majority of the students were initially non-Muslim; Muslim Turks eventually started to participate in producing Western-style music and theater. The CUP also began to send art exhibits and musical groups to Europe, thus portraying abroad the public face of the new "civilized" Ottoman Empire.[122]

The cultural creation of a "modern" lifestyle for officers was actively practiced at military schools, where they were systemically taught Western etiquette. A case in point was the imperial naval academy: first British and later German training officers sat down with Muslim cadets at their meals, showing them how to eat with a knife and a fork (instead of the traditional spoon). More specifically, "a banquet adorned with flowers visible from every corner would be prepared in the dining hall, and cadet students to be rewarded for their behavior at school or their grades would be seated there . . . eating, depending on the level of their accomplishment, with the officer on duty, the teacher, or the commander. The wives of the British teachers sometimes joined these tables as well, thereby increasing the cadets' experience of how to behave at tables where [unlike in

Muslim households] women were present."[123] The cadets also learned good manners, practicing saying phrases such as "good morning to each other upon waking up and good night before going to bed." All this training was undertaken with the intent that "one day [when] they dined with queens, they would have learned the necessary etiquette such as not to mix beans with rice, to always shave every morning and also in the afternoon if they were to go out in the evening, to act very politely to the elderly, the disabled, and especially women, to never carry when in uniform anything other than a small package and certainly not any children, and to never shake someone's hand with their gloves on."[124] Through such training, the reformed military gradually developed a new, modern public face, one also matched by state officials as they too started to publicly live and portray a modern lifestyle.

Such a transition was not without problems, however. Many memoirs noted the great difficulty in wearing a hat, for instance, since among the Muslim Turks hats had always been associated with the enemy infidel.[125] The adjustment to modern attire occurred in stages. First, they started to wear Western-style attire while abroad. Then the practice moved into the empire itself, spreading first among Muslim state officials and military cadets, then among the rest of the urban populace in the western provinces, and from there to the rest of the urban areas of the empire. This spread was enhanced through the increased mobility of state officers and officials, who now traveled to Western Europe much more frequently than their predecessors had.[126] And religious practices often continued alongside the modern ones. For instance, public officials did not work during the call to prayer or on days of fasting during e Ramadan; at some public schools, both civilian and military, all students were forced to perform ablutions during their noon break.[127] People on the streets who did not observe the fast during Ramadan would also be arrested.

Intra-Muslim Turkish Polarization

In the aftermath of the 1908 revolution, all those who had wanted reform initially joined the CUP. Yet, because the CUP remained a secret organization for four years, many initially joined the various political parties that were being quickly formed. The pattern that emerged as a consequence of this political mobilization revealed a significant bifurcation in relation to political vision: while some wanted to sustain the imperial structure of difference by keeping multiple identities while striving to provide equal rights for all social groups, others, thinking along the lines advocated by the CUP, instead proposed a new structure of similarity whereby the already dominant Muslim Turkish identity would be promoted at the expense of all others. Interestingly, even though the CUP did not form a public political party until 1912, it nevertheless did not allow any other political parties advocating their own stand to form. In addition, it employed systematic violence against all the political parties that promoted an alternate, multiethnic, multireligious vision. Had this alternate vision managed to prevail, it would have entirely altered the course of Ottoman and later Turkish history. Yet the secret and destructive CUP presence in Ottoman political life inhibited and eventually eliminated the development of such a vision. Still, the political polarization during this era among the Muslim Turks transformed the previous reformist-conservative divide into a protonationalist-liberal one, where the latter lost during the course of CUP rule. This significant political battle is discussed in detail by contemporaneous memoirs, pointing out how the Ottoman body politic formed and transformed.

Even though many joined the newly formed political parties, they did so, many argued, less out of political conviction than to seek shelter within a new organization. In doing so, many remembered the traditional household structure in which people joined the households of powerful officials for protection. Similarly, as one memoir writer remarked, they were replicating the traditional Ottoman custom of "joining a household...for the abundance of favors rather than the need felt for wisdom and insight."[128] Unlike in Western Europe, where such parties formed from the ground up, in the Ottoman case, the process was reversed: first the political organizations were established that then created their political identity. As a consequence, what such organizations could materially offer to their members was prioritized. One account noted that "the feelings and interests of 'the party and partisanship' ceaselessly drowned 'intellectual struggles' in bloodshed."[129] Unnecessary and untimely demonstrations of strength and dreams of suddenly regaining the old imperial power and grandeur in turn mobilized many to act with impunity. Hence Ottoman political party formation fostered partisanship on the one hand and violence on the other. The manner in which such political parties were formed further articulates this process.

Formation of Political Parties

Initially, the political opposition to the CUP was diverse, yet all were motivated by a decentralized imperial vision rather than a nationalist, centralized one. The first major opposition party formed was the Party of Freedoms (Ahrar Fırkası) established after the vision of Prince Sabahaddin, who advocated personalized initiative and decentralized government.[130] While in exile, the prince had been a significant player along with the CUP in opposing the sultan's autocratic rule. After the revolution, he arrived at the capital with the intent to join the CUP central committee, but many in his retinue were arrested instead. The CUP legitimated its action by arguing that such decentralization with the intent to include all the social elements of the empire would instead lead to its fragmentation and eventual demise.[131] Because Prince Sabahaddin could not join forces with the CUP, he instead met with Armenian and Kurdish leaders, starting his own political party supplemented by its print organ, the *Serbesti* newspaper.[132] The media became increasingly abrasive as a consequence, with the "decentralist" and "protonationalist" newspapers attacking the opposition.[133] The ensuing political campaigns were not at all fair due to the CUP's stand on violence; Prince Sabahaddin's supporters were beaten up, arrested, and even murdered; opposition presses were attacked and burned down.[134]

The elections of December 1908 took place in such an environment. Because voting was a new experience for the Muslim populace, very few actually turned up to elect the representatives who would in turn elect the deputies.[135] This lack of organization within the Muslim Turks sharply contrasted with the already existent organization among the traditionally self-governing non-Muslim communities. After all, they been electing their communal representatives since the middle of the nineteenth century. The first-held municipal elections, in which many non-Muslims were elected, alerted all parties to the possibility that the Muslim Turks might end up without a single deputy.[136] It did not help that every Ottoman who wanted to become a candidate had to get a petition with at least 150 signatures from those eligible to vote, then submit it to the election committee. While non-Muslims quickly gathered signatures, the first question Muslims asked before signing in one case was "what the orders of the committee headquarters were."[137] Still, the political elections helped the Muslim Turkish majority to solidify into a social group and acquire political consciousness over time. In the 1908 elections, the CUP gained only 60 of the 275 seats, with the liberal parties winning the rest.

After the 1908 elections, political opposition to the CUP continued. In November 1909, the CUP opponents founded within the parliament the Party of Moderate Freedom Lovers (Mutedil Hürriyetperveran Fırkası) with fifty to sixty deputies who were mostly supported by non-Muslims. In February 1910, a second party named the Populace Party (Ahali Fırkası) was formed; in May 1910 the democrats also started to publish the *Türkiye* newspaper. Yet the CUP continued to portray the political opposition as the enemy, doing everything in its power to quench all such political activities. One account bitterly complained about the current state of affairs:[138]

> The CUP never wanted to understand our thoughts and purpose. They had learned politics from Balkan guerrilla fighters. They wanted to rule the country through a single party without letting other parties develop, destroying and breaking down all who were not one of them. They did so in order to carry out whatever they wanted without any criticism and responsibility, using any means necessary to accomplish this.

> This was the regime they followed. . . . [They] either court-martialed, imprisoned, or exiled all the democrats they considered to be their opponents. This is what happened to the Samsun and Aleppo democrat clubs as their founders were all imprisoned; the Monastir club faced the same end. . . . [Meanwhile,] the charlatan CUP newspapers printed in the Balkans with names like "Cannon," "Bullet," "Bayonet" and "Rifle" shouted that all democrats had to be hanged from the poles of a bridge.

Many others also noted not only that the CUP presence in the political sphere was fraught with violence but that no one could be held accountable and punished for it.[139] This violence eventually culminated in the assassination of the opposition journalist Ahmet Samim by the CUP Special Organization. Samim had been receiving threats from the CUP for a long time. Yet none of the assassins were brought to justice, since these acts of violence, sanctioned by the CUP, were committed in secrecy. The Turkish-language media did not even adequately cover Ahmet Samim's assassination, while the German, English, French, Greek, and Armenian-language newspapers all did so, also inviting the government to do its duty in finding the assassins.[140]

31 March 1909 Counterrevolution

The assassination of a prominent opposition journalist and the ensuing funeral attended by thousands triggered the 31 March 1909 counterrevolution. The primary instigation was discontent with CUP violence, but the rebellion quickly transformed in character. Defining its agenda as punishing those who rebelled against the sultan and also brought modern secular practices to the empire, the counterrevolution took on a religious disguise; some discontented religious scholars and students also wanted to bring back sharia. It is telling that the reactionaries tried to hunt down as their target those clean-shaven men who attended Western-style schools, who were termed the *mektepli*, that is, "the schooled ones."[141] A populist reaction at best, the counterrevolution lacked the organization necessary to succeed. Once the CUP got over the initial shock, it quickly mobilized the Ottoman army in the Balkans, suppressing the counterrevolution. After the CUP was back in power, the central committee realized that Sultan Abdülhamid II served as a rallying point against the CUP and therefore decided to depose him, falsely alleging that he was behind the counterrevolution.[142] In the aftermath of the counterrevolution, many memoirs noted that the CUP became even more violent and repressive.[143] Rather than attempting to understand the reasons behind such a political reaction, the CUP instead hanged the leaders, defining all who reacted as enemies of the state. Under direct orders from the CUP central committee, many such perceived opponents were exiled from the capital, just as the CUP members had once been exiled by the sultan.[144]

The 1911 occupation of Tripoli by the Italians, the specter of the 1912 Balkan Wars, and continuing CUP violence led the political opposition to unite under the newly formed FEP (Hürriyet ve İtilaf Fırkası). Once again advocating the imperial vision of Ottomanism, this party nevertheless lacked the CUP's organizational skills as well as a united political vision, containing within its ranks all the disparate elements that opposed the CUP. Another Ottoman political problem was that opposition parties were established not in accordance with thoughts, ideas, and visions but rather in connection with personages around whom people coalesced, personages who often wanted vengeance.[145] Şerif Pasha, who attempted to lead the LEP, was initially a CUP member who had become disillusioned with the CUP because of its nationalist direction and participation in assassinations and violence. He instead proposed "a constitutional system based on a liberal economy where all religious and ethnic groups have equal representation." Şerif Pasha especially criticized the CUP's reliance on the military, "employment of illegal means to offend all Ottoman nations from the Greek Rum to the Armenian, the Arab to the Albanian, alleging separatist revolutionary intentions to all of them, and monopolization public-spiritedness and patriotism."[146] Due to the lack of leadership and unity, however, the LEP was not able to counter and contain CUP violence. Instead, the Ottoman body politic now became polarized into two political factions, the "CUP Unionists" versus the "LEP Ententists." This polarization diffused into the entire Ottoman state and society, including the military.[147] Soon thereafter, the LEP started to engage in the same political violence that it had opposed.[148]

The general elections of 1912 took place in this polarized political context. The CUP engaged in ruthless propaganda to discredit all political opposition.[149] According to one account, the elections "were rigged with the stick of the guard and the butt of a gendarmerie's rifle." Especially recruiting Muslim Turkish youth to their cause through nationalism, the CUP discredited the "union of the communities" that the political opposition supported. "As it did everything else," the same account continued, "the CUP had also taken nationalism under its monopoly. Yet the spirit it displayed was not at all national.... For these men, everything was political."[150] With the 1912 elections, the CUP increased its parliamentary representation to 184 seats. The CUP political repression continued unabated.[151] In the aftermath of the 1912 assassination of the grand vizier Mahmud Şevket Pasha, the CUP exploited the assassination as a cover to once again decimate the political opposition, exiling about 500 political opponents to Sinop.[152] It was in this context that Ottoman patriot Tevfik Fikret wrote his scathing poem "The Inn of Plunder" ("Han-ı Yağma"), chastising the CUP for its violence against and exploitation of the populace. Fikret referred to the

CUP, termed İttihat Terakki (Union and Progress) in Turkish, as the *'İrtikap ve Tedenni Çetesi,'* namely 'the armed band of dirty deeds and regression', as a political organization "that was nothing more than a group of bandits who managed to cause the country more material and spiritual damage in three years than Sultan Abdülhamid II could not manage in thirty."[153]

When the LEP briefly assumed power in 1912, one of its first measures was to appoint many non-Muslim officials to positions throughout the empire, only to be later fired by the CUP.[154] While the LEP was still in power, the Balkan Wars commenced, leading to a great Ottoman defeat, mostly due to the politicization within the military between the CUP Unionists and the LEP Ententists; some among the former insisted that eliminating the LEP as a consequence of a military defeat was more important than winning the war. Meanwhile, the CUP, now out of the government and in opposition, actively provoked local CUP clubs throughout the empire to rebel against LEP rule as well.[155] Such political polarization ended with the 1913 military coup d'état led by the CUP leader Enver Pasha, who then took over the government. This was the first time that the CUP, which established its own party only in 1912, fully assumed power as a political party, immediately passing laws that made political opposition impossible. It sustained its autocratic rule until after the Great War, when it disbanded after losing the empire. The saga of these political parties demonstrates the manner in which the CUP oppressed and eventually eliminated any opposition by systematically harassing members, assassinating some and exiling others. And it could not be held publicly accountable because it employed extralegal violence through the SO. In the end, it emerged triumphant as the sole powerful party; the LEP continued to exist but in much weaker form. This course of events necessitates a more in-depth analysis of what transpired within the CUP during this period.

The CUP Phenomenon

When the CUP arrived at the capital, its members had not yet reached full agreement about their future political vision; Ottomanism, advocating the unity of all social groups, coexisted with Turkism, which promoted the dominance of the Turks. Hence, the first CUP divide was between Ottomanism and Turkism. Among CUP ideologues, Ziya Gökalp supported somehow joining the two, Cemal Bey was an Ottomanist to the core, and Bahaeddin Shakir strongly advocated Turkism. Talat Bey attempted to get the CUP to embrace both visions, yet Gökalp pointed out that Ottomanism was an artificial construct, since it was impossible for all the elements within the empire to unite. Bahaeddin Shakir concurred, arguing that "sooner or later they were going to witness a bloody conflict over such unity."[156] This anti-CUP interpretation is counterbalanced by another account arguing that in reality the CUP had very limited control over its branches, leading CUP members with personal ambitions to prevail at every branch. As the CUP branches became increasingly autocratic, the military and civilian members started to challenge each other over political administration, with both vying for power within the organization.[157] The CUP military officers were loosely headed by Enver Pasha, while the civilian members preferred the guidance of Talat Pasha.[158] This second CUP "civilian-military" divide led a third, much more radical group to wield inordinate power as both sides tried to get them on their side. This group of "fifteen to twenty men" had purposefully not assumed any official government positions or positions within the CUP. One account insinuates that this third group eventually formed the backbone of the paramilitary Special Organization.[159]

These initial divides within the CUP may thus explain why it ended up engaging in so much clandestine violence executed by the SO: both CUP civilian and military members accepted such violence with the intent to draw this third faction to their camp.[160] The embedded secrecy eventually led the CUP central committee, which contained both civilian and military members under the informal leadership of Talat Pasha, to take over the decision-making process, with Talat Pasha thereafter systematically suppressing any opposition, both within and outside.[161] The initial extraofficial CUP participation in the 1908 and 1912 elections accompanied by centralized decision making that was then executed by the paramilitary SO set in place the CUP mode of operation: centrally decide what is best for the CUP (and presumably for the empire), and then execute the decision by any means necessary (including the use of SO extralegal violence). An account documented that rather than following a democratic course of letting the votes determine a political outcome, the CUP instead decided ahead of time on the outcome it wanted, then worked behind the scenes to actualize it.[162] Likewise, when the CUP central committee decided on the necessity of having some non-Muslim deputies to support its rhetoric of respecting difference, it first determined who these deputies ought to be and then ensured their election.[163] All such elected CUP deputies were chosen not by the populace but according to their loyalty or at least subservience to the CUP.[164] This CUP mode of operation that diverted democratization to autocracy in turn subverted the parliamentary process.

The Ottoman Parliament and the CUP Cabinet

The duly created Ottoman parliament faced a major obstacle from the start: it had to establish a common unifying language for all the deputies hailing from different parts of the empire. Yet, as one account described, "It was unclear how…Bosho Efendi, the Serviçe deputy who constantly declared: 'My father is Turkey, my mother Greece' would agree on anything with a Sabri

Efendi advocating a 'Muslim community' as the only way forward and... how Shefikulmueyyed who spoke half in French and half in Arabic would come to an agreement with the Draç deputy Esat Pasha who only knew Albanian."[165] In addition, in the deputy selection process, influence trumped knowledge, and so many had no understanding of politics; professional standards often maintained in fields such as medicine and law were entirely abandoned in the much more societally significant political sphere.[166]

In the parliament, the CUP stand on the principle of full centralization, giving "the entire sovereignty to the Turkish element which already controlled the sultanate," upset the deputies in opposition; the CUP claimed only the Turks among them had adequately performed their duties for the sultanate and therefore should be the only ones ruling the empire.[167] Hence, rather than turning the Ottoman parliament into a public space to discuss and negotiate critical issues in imperial governance, the CUP deputies acted as a united group, strictly executing the orders of the central committee, and all the opposition deputies could do was protest. [168] The CUP deputies "would slap opponents... in the name of patriotism and some [opposition] deputies could not even deliver their speeches due to protests."[169] As a consequence, the parliament ended up rubber-stamping all the decisions of the CUP central committee without much discussion.[170] One account referred to the CUP central committee, which was silently active behind all this political maneuvering, as "absentee dignitaries" (*rical-i gayb*).[171] As the CUP thus assumed full parliamentary control, the opposition could not prevent the promulgation of temporary laws (*kanun-u muvakkat*) through which the CUP established martial law, thereby tightening its rule throughout the empire.[172] Prominent CUP member Hüseyin Cahit Yalçın defended this course of action, arguing that the CUP deputies were "clean men who loved their country, aware of the dangers Turkishness faced. Yet they were simple men with limited knowledge, unaware of international political issues at large.... Talat kept the communication and the unity with them." He then dismissed all political opposition as committing "treasonous assassinations all undertaken to destroy the Ottoman Empire and to crush the Turk."[173]

Political troubles in Bosnia, Herzegovina, Bulgaria, and Crete that eventually led to the Balkan Wars further polarized the already tense relationship.[174] During that time, the CUP central committee became so concerned with the actions of the opposition that it ordered the SO to investigate and compile files on all the non-Muslim deputies.[175] Hence, in addition to fostering an inherent distrust of non-Muslims, rather than alleviating the ensuing polarization through dialogue, the CUP instead institutionalized it by gathering information through illegal means.[176] In doing so, it blatantly overlooked the activities of non-Muslim deputies who did indeed work for the benefit of the entire Ottoman populace. A case in point was the public works minister Bedros Hallacyan Efendi, who tried hard to build a road infrastructure in Anatolia but to no avail.[177]

Details of how the CUP's governance of the empire was also executed in accordance with partisan decision-making emerge from various contemporaneous accounts. First, many officers and officials refused to give up their CUP affiliation even after becoming state employees.[178] Gradually, through such appointments as well as the political activities of the local CUP clubs, many central and local positions of leadership, including governors, commanders, and teachers, were taken over by CUP members. Such appointees naturally placed CUP interests before all else, and if they did not, they were quickly punished.[179] How much the CUP inserted power and intervened in local affairs was narrated by Hüseyin Kazım Kadri, initially appointed by Talat Pasha as the district governor of Serres (Siroz) island to fight the bandits there. Upon his arrival, two local CUP delegates promptly visited his office, telling him that "on all matters, he had to work jointly with the CUP center there." "It seems," Kadri noted, "I was to work there not as a government official, as a district governor, but as a functionary of the CUP headquarters." Even though he strongly opposed the advance of these two local CUP delegates, he nevertheless noted:[180]

> I thought: if these men find the courage to make such a proposition to someone like me who had a prominent position in the CUP, what sorts of pressures did they bring upon government officials who did not have such connections, and how could those poor officials respond to them? In such a situation, where would the government, its integrity, the responsibility of one's duty, the laws ... end up? I thought about all these and was scared of what the future held. The government had been transferred into hidden hands.... The ones who directed matters were men without any [official] responsibility.

Upon his return to the capital, Kadri also protested the fact that even though he had been appointed to the central committee by the CUP Congress, he was not notified of the decisions reached by the committee. After Kadri had words with Talat Bey pertaining to this matter, Said Halim Pasha came up to him and said: "I had great trust and high regard about you before today, but after today's argument, I have to admit I now think otherwise. You forget who the people you are dealing with are; you talk as if you are in front of state elites who have been in state administration for long years, therefore acquiring experience and understanding matters. The men you address are nothing more than revolutionaries. What good is there in talking to these people about the ways of state governance, political wisdom, and the like? I cannot imagine anything more astounding than your inability to recognize this!"

This exchange reveals that the necessary distinction between the state and the government that is crucial to democratic governance could not be set. Instead, the dictates of sultanic governance prevailed in content: the Ottoman sultans had traditionally appointed members of their household as their representatives. Because sultans headed both the state and the government, there did not have to be a distinction between the two. With the advent of the constitution, however, such a distinction and with it the accompanying separation of the (state) professional and the (government) political had to be established both for the delivery of justice to all and for the sustenance of democratic rule. Instead, the CUP regarded all state positions as political as well, co-opting the state into its government. Some officials tried to challenge this major obstacle to democratization but to no avail.[181] In the end, the despotic nature of CUP rule became so prominent that Süleyman Nazif narrated the following joke: "A father asked his son how many [Sultan] Selims there were in Ottoman history to receive the answer three. When he asked how many [Sultan] Abdülhamids there were and upon the answer of two, the father protested: 'You did not get that one right. However many members there are at the CUP central committee, so too are that many Abdülhamids.' "[182]

Given that Talat, Enver, and Cemal Pashas emerged as the three top leaders in shaping the CUP decision-making process, contemporaneous memoirs need to be analyzed to further highlight their thoughts, ideas, and actions. Eight memoirs that mentioned Talat remarked about his charisma, fervent patriotism, and ability as an organizer to network; he was also noted for his ability to contain all dissent within the CUP by staying well informed about everything that occurred within the committee. The memoirs added that Talat was a revolutionary at heart, not heeding any rules and regulations to accomplish what he had defined as best for the CUP and the Turks. And he did so with very limited knowledge, experience, and education, often producing catastrophic results. He only became remorseful about his course of action after their downfall.[183] Enver Pasha was often portrayed as a shy, conservative, stubborn, narrow-minded, yet very ambitious man, one who could become easily angered or excited and who sometimes took rash action without thinking things through. His role in the unexpected success of the 1908 constitutional revolution was conjectured to have given Enver the idea that he was destined for greatness, and that everything he touched would immediately thrive.[184] He was also a religious man, praying even while at the war front. His vision was to unite all the Muslim Turks, including the ones in Central Asia, under the banner of the Ottoman Empire. It is therefore no accident that Enver Pasha explicitly kept files on the ethnic origins of all Ottoman officers; he appointed them accordingly and criticized the appointment of Kurds, Arabs, and Circassians to top positions.[185] Cemal Pasha was a soldier like Enver and was very competitive with the latter in terms of received military promotions. Having spent some time in Germany, Enver and Cemal were also ardent believers in the Prussian spirit, especially in terms of the discipline, obedience, and loyalty it advocated.[186] Unlike Enver, who often prioritized the Muslim element, however, Cemal was more supportive of the Turkish element, envisioning an empire uniting all the Turks with a dominant Turkish majority ruling over it. It should also be mentioned in this context that both Enver and Cemal were wary of the future Turkish leader Mustafa Kemal (Atatürk) because of his ambitions and military acumen and therefore made sure he remained at the margins of all significant military action.[187] Hence, the three men, Talat, Enver, and Cemal, were oddly complementary; Talat was a civilian and a pragmatist, and Cemal and Enver were soldiers who believed solely in the Muslim and Turkish elements of the empire. The division of labor among the three was such that while Cemal and Enver administered the military and the actual use of force, with Enver also overseeing the SO, Talat took care of all civilian affairs and also dissipated the tension between the other two. Such a division of labor enabled Talat to single-handedly rule the CUP and, through it, the empire, all the while privileging the interests of Muslim Turks at the expense of all others.

One needs to delve further into the factors that radicalized the CUP over time. Ahmed Rıza, pivotal in the CUP opposition to the sultan but then marginalized within the CUP over time, reflected on this matter specifically. After remarking that the Tripoli incident, the Kosovo revolution, the Havran rebellion, the Balkan Wars and in the end the Great War had broken the CUP's 'arms and wings' [*sic*], he stated that because he had been living abroad for twenty years, he did not know the mental state of the Ottoman populace. To his surprise, however, his CUP friends, mostly of Balkan origin, did not know the populace either. They thought people were "delicate like a respectable woman and therefore treated her with utmost delicacy, executing the reforms very slowly in order not to offend her." Yet the slow pace of reforms irritated many people; they also had no conception of the sovereignty that was bestowed upon them. In addition, Ahmed Rıza had observed a certain pride among some youths. "I had initially been very pleased, attributing this thinking to their bravery and honor and to the fact that they had grasped the freedom of conscience. Yet," he bitterly continued, "I later understood that this merely comprised egotism, disapproval of everyone else, disrespect toward the elders, and sycophancy and vileness for their own interests."[188] His account highlighted the CUP's lack of experience in governance and the democratic process. This lack was compounded by the lack of knowledge about the empire's external affairs. During especially the preceding rule of Sultan Abdülhamid II, all imperial decision-making had been centralized in his person, sharing only limited information with his officials on a need-to-know basis. When the CUP took over, it did not have many policy guidelines to follow.

Since the CUP members excluded many of the sultan's officials from governance because of the latter's imputed allegiance to the sultan, they were left with very few resources to rule the empire.[189] Subsequent limited CUP foreign policy was exacerbated by the adverse stand of the Great Powers that promoted constitutional rule for European states but not for the Ottoman Empire, given their colonies in Africa and Asia with large Muslim populations. They therefore advocated sultanic reforms instead; upon the 1908 revolution, they initially appeared to support such an action, but European public opinion quickly turned against the CUP as well. One account conjectured that "no European power would accept the Ottoman Empire as an ally because it demanded not its survival, but rather its fragmentation and eventual destruction."[190]

In summary, among all the political parties established in the aftermath of the 1908 constitutional revolution, the CUP ultimately prevailed over all others because of its strategic location. During the first four years of constitutional rule, the CUP formally remained a secret organization, nevertheless fully engaging in politics informally and with violence. While all other political parties had to publicly account for their activities, the CUP did not, and it exploited this advantage to systematically eliminate any viable opposition. Yet no one could publicly or legally confront the violence because the CUP remained a secret organization. This little-noted fact explains why the Ottoman political system could not initially challenge, control, and contain CUP violence, and also why the CUP gradually marginalized all other parties. And all this political transformation occurred during a period of massive land loss, generating despair among the Ottoman populace.

Escalating Emotions of Despair

During the decade-long CUP rule, the empire lost 35 percent of its land mass. Frequent rebellions and defeats at war, accompanied by continuous criticism by the Great Powers, led many Muslim Turks to feel despair that their empire was not going to survive, and especially that the Turks would be erased from the earth through the collaboration of the Christian West with non-Muslim communities. Many contemporaneous accounts reveal the extent of this public despair felt by Muslim Turks. One account aptly described this despair as follows:[191]

> My childhood and the early years of my youth passed by in great historical upheavals and countercurrents such as the proclamation of the constitution, the occupation of Tripoli by the Italians, our loss of Crete, the Balkan war, and finally World War I. I watched the fall of a vast empire like the collapse of an old mansion, without comprehending a thing, moaning with great suffering as if I had been caught under its wreck.

> A nation was disintegrating, sinking into the darkness of history.... All we could do was... protest [to no avail]... sing bitter marches and shout "vengeance, vengeance."... But what was going to happen to the Turkish nation? For it had tied all it ever had, its entire being, to this state. As the state withdrew from those places we had been in for centuries, the [Turkish] nation also ceased to exist. The sun set, night took over, and for the Turkish nation, darkness commenced and everything ended.... Our only salvation was to attach ourselves and actualize in the fatherland the ideal of a new Turkish state and a new Turkish nation we still could hang onto, where the majority of the populace was Turkish.... If we the Turks did not save ourselves by escaping this collapsing building, we would have remained under its wreckage. That would have been the end of our life as a nation.

This sense of impending extinction led the Turks to search for a fatherland where they could continue to exist: the central lands of the empire in Anatolia where the empire had originated emerged as the only possible space the Turks could hold onto. Süleyman Şefik Pasha reflected on this dire state of affairs in his memoirs, pointing out the way to salvation by giving the example of the British. "Some of us love the British," he stated, "yet unfortunately that British person regards not only us, but all nations other than his own including his most civilized neighbor the Europeans as beneath him. He does not deem us worthy of anything he thinks is appropriate for him. He does not accept us as his equal. So, it does not at all matter as to how civilized, how knowledgeable, and how virtuous we are. Then, we too have to preserve our traditions to in turn preserve our existence."[192] In relation to who the culprits were in leading to this state of Turkish demise, Süleyman Nazif blamed the West and political modernity emanating from it. "For the last forty years, whenever the word 'rights' came out of the mouths of Europe," Nazif argued, "the East suffering injustice was once again oppressed and trodden over. When its selfish intentions reveal an ugliness that can no longer be covered, Europe tries to hide its inherent insolence with the grace of this word." Europe then attacked the empire with no cause, not expressing "even with a single word the pure anger of clear conscience as it silently covered the incidents that demonstrated how the right to fight prevailed over the right to live." Words like "peace, rights and reaching agreements have no meaning" to the Europeans, leading the Turks to decide that the only way to save themselves was through constantly remembering who among them betrayed the fatherland. Hence, gradually Western Europe and the non-Muslims of the empire as their representatives within emerged as the culprits upon whom Turks blamed all their misfortune and defeat.

CUP and Non-Muslim Communities

Political polarization among the Muslim Turks was also accompanied by an escalating divide between the Turkish elements and the rest, especially the non-Muslims. The structural divide between Muslims and non-Muslims had become part and parcel of the empire.[193] With the advent of modernity, the perceived divide escalated as especially the urban economic resources and subsequently non-Muslim lifestyles improved dramatically.[194] The ever-present prejudice and discrimination assumed a new form under CUP rule: instead of merely noting the divide, increasing number of Turks started to compare their lives to those of non-Muslims, stating time and again their belief that non-Muslims attained such conditions not through hard work but through the exploitation of the Turks. They added that they deserved to live under better conditions because they had been the ones fighting and dying for the empire, so they should be compensated for their sacrifices.[195] As a consequence, there "was an incredible degree of insecurity between the Muslim and Christian populace, with each side having armed itself against the possible attack of the other." [196] Until then, the many instances of prejudice and discrimination had been monitored and contained by both the non-Muslim communities themselves and the Ottoman state that protected them. With the advent of the constitutional revolution, all presumably became equal as individual citizens, so the communal boundaries that had separated, monitored, and sustained the non-Muslim communities were no longer there. In addition, the state and government were now controlled by the CUP, which openly privileged the Muslim Turks over all other imperial elements. The Turks had initially survived with the solace of their old dominance, a solace that was quickly wiped away during CUP rule, generating first anger and then vengeance; when they could not avenge their anger from the West, they instead turned it against what they perceived as symbols of the West within, the non-Muslims.[197]

Contemporaneous memoirs document the process through which unrest among the religious communities escalated in the aftermath of the revolution.[198] It reached a new high with the advent of the Balkan Wars; many protonationalist newspapers did not carefully distinguish European and Balkan Christians from their own non-Muslim subjects, damning them all and penning incendiary articles against the non-Muslims. Greek Rum stores were boycotted.[199] The Armenians were accused of sedition, and the Turks transformed into eternal victims who were aggressed upon, oppressed, and exploited by everyone, both outside and within.[200] Such negative portrayals especially of the Armenians, the most active community in trade and commerce, totally overlooked and naturalized the injustices they suffered; worse still, such negative stereotyping gradually diffused into the rest of society.[201] Given the escalation in public feelings of despair many Turks expressed about losing their empire and being extinguished as a race, the ideas the CUP radicals advocated to save Turks at all costs could not be contained. During this political transformation, the single element uniting the CUP turned into an inherent "grudge and malice against the non-Muslim subjects of the empire."[202]

Ultimate CUP Collective Violence: Armenian Deportations and Massacres, 1915–17

The most destructive action the CUP undertook during its rule was the 1915–17 forced deportations and ensuing massacres of the Ottoman Armenians. Entire Armenian families and neighborhoods were emptied out throughout the empire and often destroyed to ensure that no more than a minute fraction remained, small enough not to be a viable political presence; this CUP collective violence effectively annihilated the Armenians on what for millennia had been their ancestral lands. Desperate to hang onto a homeland in a swiftly shrinking empire, rather than choosing to live in peace, the Muslim Turkish populace hegemonized by a CUP radical faction destroyed what they perceived to be a threat and challenge to their existence. This faction exploited wartime conditions to forcefully remove, deport, and extinguish innocent Armenian subjects the Ottoman state had been duty-bound to protect. How was such a ruthless and destructive act possible? Contemporaneous memoirs reveal what is often not captured in official narratives: the CUP rule was predicated on a culture of violence, one that gradually escalated to finally destroy the millennia-long Armenian existence in Asia Minor.

The CUP culture of violence commenced in stages: it was first directed against officials and officers loyal to the sultan, then, after the revolution, against all political opponents, followed by the deportations from Anatolia of those "different" imperial communities like the Arabs, Assyrians, Kurds, and the Greek Rum, culminating in the mass deportations and ensuing massacres of the Armenian community. Among these imperial communities, the Armenians were considered the most dangerous because of their ancestral claims to Asia Minor that the CUP now regarded as the last refuge of the Turkish race and therefore faced the most collective violence. This section maps a historical genealogy of CUP violence through contemporaneous memoirs.

Prelude to CUP Violence: The Formative Years

When the CUP was initially established as a secret organization, it did not condone violence. Especially the initial CUP headquarters in Paris headed by Ahmed

Rıza was in principle against the employment of violence to reach the political aim of restoring the constitution and bringing back parliamentary rule. Such violence was first introduced as a tool in the Balkan branches, Monastir and Salonica in particular, when the CUP decided to actively recruit military officers as members in 1907. These CUP officers rebelled against the sultan, assassinating his officials to bring about the 1908 constitutional revolution. Hence CUP success was coeval with acts of violence that were then sustained throughout its rule. The presence of a culture of violence and the use of force in the Balkan branches were evident from the very start.[203] Such violence escalated in the aftermath of the Reval meeting on 9 June 1907, since many CUP officers were certain the meeting was about apportioning the Ottoman Empire and therefore decided to take direct public action by assassinating officers and officials loyal to the sultan.[204] The ranks of the targeted gradually escalated to include pashas and muftis.[205]

The violence first became public when military officer Resneli Niyazi and later Enver Bey took to the mountains with soldiers, attempting to organize a rebellion against the sultan. Şemsi Pasha was sent from the palace to investigate and put down the rebellion. Yet on 24 June 1908, he was assassinated by the Monastir CUP member officer Atıf Kamçıl, who later became a deputy to the Ottoman parliament. After the succesful assassination, Kamçıl, who was wounded, escaped and was sheltered in the house of Lieutenant Mahmud, who later also served as an Ottoman parliament deputy from Siirt.[206] This cycle of violence continued with the assassination of İsmail Mahir Pasha, who was a relative of Şemsi Pasha. Even though the former had not committed any crimes, the CUP decided that he too should be eliminated, and he was. None of these military assassins were punished by the CUP; on the contrary, they were hailed as patriotic heroes and later rewarded with important state posts. Right after the 1908 revolution, the CUP carried out additional assassinations in Salonica, claiming that the victims had been the sultan's spies.[207] The CUP justified these murders by stating that they had not been specifically ordered by the committee but resulted from the individual initiative of particular members. This mode, the CUP argued, absolved the organization of any responsibility. This justification and the secrecy of the committee—no one knew the members of the other branches except the very few at the top— reveal the manner in which the CUP cloaked the violence it committed, never taking responsibility for any of the crimes committed in its name. As the CUP was about to move from the Balkans to the capital in 1908, one of the first actions its leaders took was to send ten assassins to the capital.[208]

CUP Violence after Arrival at the Capital

After the success of the constitutional revolution, the CUP initially remained a secret organization, intervening behind the scenes. Its inability to establish order and security quickly led the organization to resort to violence. The CUP especially took issue with the fact that group identities in the empire had started to quickly become politicized.[209] It conjectured that "if the elements comprising the empire were given the rights to have representatives in the Ottoman parliament in proportion with their population ratios, the Turks would have remained a minority."[210] The CUP thus decided on behalf of the Ottoman Turks that they should not lose their dominance in the empire to become one of the equal elements of the empire. It also imputed seditious aims to all the other elements to justify its reproduction of Muslim Turkish dominance.[211] While it had been decided that the exclusive right to determine the empire's destiny had to remain in the hands of the Turks, many Turks as well as non-Muslims initially opposed the CUP, forming political parties and establishing newspapers. Elections had to be held for the parliament, and non-Muslim and non-Turkish elements that constituted about half of the empire's total population had to be given political voice. The CUP's Turkish vision clashed with the political course of action, generating episodic violence in the process.

The elected parliament and the government started to operate with this initial tension between the CUP's vision of Turkish dominance and all others, intent on including in the Ottoman body politic all elements on equal terms. Yet the CUP's public rhetoric presented an entirely different political stand: it continually claimed to include and accomodate all non-Muslims.[212] Memoirs document that what took place in practice was exactly the opposite. The CUP paramilitary assassins decimated and silenced any political opposition to the committee through threats of violence and possible blackmail.[213] The CUP governments were not any better, since they included many CUP members who had previously employed violence on behalf of the committee with impunity. As one account remarked:[214]

> What should one term the cabinet of Talat Pasha? Many who had committed murders had entered this cabinet... so one could term it the cabinet of assassins and murderers of the CUP armed band. All the patriots in opposition who had not been hanged were cleansed and unbelievable acts of injustice and murders were conducted. The government had no qualms about murdering the populace, with the intent not to free the country, but instead to silence the opposition. They then had their murderers plunder the properties of the populace who were either murdered or deported and did so in order to replenish the treasury of the committee.... They also engaged in commerce, accumulating great wealth through profiteering.

Another account similarly summed up the CUP era by stating that "a pasha and a few journalists were murdered at night; the murderers of some were not even searched for and those found were protected with the influence of the [CUP] central committee."[215] Through such violence combined with the lack of accountability, CUP violence soon expanded throughout the entire social structure.

This expansion was facilitated through the establishment of CUP clubs all over the empire on the one hand and the frequent appointment of CUP members to key administrative positions on the other.[216] The appointment of relatively young and totally inexperienced members to such positions further escalated the unrest, leading CUP officers to step into politics to establish security and order.[217] While some of these officers enjoyed engaging in politics, others were irked that such engagement took them away from what they had been professionally trained to do.[218] Also challenging were the assassinations of the few appointed non-Muslim officials by Armenian revolutionary organizations like the Dashnak.[219] Also unsavory was the fact that some Armenians initially appointed to inferior positions had to resort to extralegal means to have their appointments changed.[220] Crucial in executing the CUP's orders and establishing the semblance of security in the empire was the secret paramilitary CUP Special Organization.

Primary Tool of CUP Violence: The Special Organization

Unlike official accounts, that are almost entirely silent on the subject, many contemporaneous memoirs frequently discuss the secret paramilitary Special Organization that undertook almost all the violent acts attributed to the CUP. The history of the SO during the CUP era can be divided into four stages: the pre-1908 stage; the post-1908 stage at the capital, North Africa, and the Balkans; the first stage of World War I in the east and the Arabian Peninsula; and the second stage of World War I against the Armenians. The seeds of SO were initially sown in the Balkans, where Bulgarian guerrilla activities against the Ottoman army probably provided the initial model. When the CUP recruited army officers, many were initially signed on as assassins, swearing an oath to obey the committee orders to the death if necessary. After the constitutional revolution, many of these assassins remained active at the capital, then participating in the 1911 clandestine war against the Italians who had occupied Tripoli, and also in the 1912–13 Balkan Wars. After the 1913 CUP military coup, the SO transformed from being a specifically CUP organization to becoming a paramilitary force within the Ottoman state and government. It acquired significant material and human resources during World War I, engaging in clandestine activities alongside the Ottoman army. These activities initially occurred outside Ottoman lands, as the SO incited unrest in Iran, the Caucasus, and Russia. After the 1914–15 Ottoman defeat by the Russians at Sarıkamış, however, the SO regrouped to eliminate what it now defined as the "internal enemy," namely, the Armenians, actively engaging in the Armenian deportations and especially in the ensuing massacres.

Pre-1908 Stage

The assassins who later constituted the SO initially emerged among the young military officers recruited into the CUP in the Balkans; they considered their violence to be patriotic acts of bravery and were lauded by many within the CUP and criticized by others. Talat Bey (later Pasha) and Enver Bey (later Pasha) emerged as the two CUP leaders organizing and directing the actions of this group of assassins. The CUP referred to the assassins as *fedai*, which originated from *feda*, deriving from the first letters of *filiyas elenikis desmos anton* meaning "this is the tie of Greek friendship." The term thus originally derived from Greek and Bulgarian guerrilla activities in the Balkans and then also employed by Ottoman militia fighters. In the context of the CUP, it came to signify "men who have sworn allegiance to the committee, and have joined other sworn friends."[221] The Salonica and Monastir CUP branches where such assassins were most active led the two most prevalent bands, which were named after these locations. The Salonica assassins, effective in eliminating with brute force the spies of Sultan Abdülhamid and CUP opponents, were gradually referred to as the "Serez band." Their most significant member was Çerkez (Circassian) Ahmed Bey; the band later executed the assassinations of opposition journalists as well as the murders of the Ottoman deputies Vartkes Serengülyan, Krikor Zohrab, and Dikran Kelekyan during the Armenian deportations.[222] Only Talat Pasha could contain these assassins because he was the only one they respected and obeyed.[223] The memoir of one such assassin provided a glorified definition of what such men actually engaged in and to which particular ends:[224]

> Being such a man was not, as some think, committing acts of robbery and plunder. Just the opposite, [it] is the most extreme form of patriotism!... a person who sacrifices everything, even his life, for the cause of the fatherland, who does not forsake anything, and who has renounced his whole being from head to toe. When it is necessary for the interests of his country and nation, he abandons compassion; if it is necessary to burn something, he burns; if there is a need to destroy, he destroys it all! He does not leave standing one stone on top of another or a head on top of a torso!! We were left in such situations so many times, and we always did what had to be done! Now that I look back, if we had not acted so radically in this or that business, who knows under whose feet

> the country would have remained, and under whose enslavement this honorable nation would have been doomed!

Such men claimed that the 1908 revolution had been actualized through their violent acts, and they therefore clandestinely continued to participate in the ensuing CUP rule. According to CUP regulations, there could be three degrees of villainy committed against the CUP: wrongdoing, crime, and murder. The punishment of wrongdoing would be reprimand, of crime a monetary punishment, and of murder, death by hanging. The assassins were given the responsibility of executing all these regulations throughout CUP rule.[225]

Post-1908 Stage at the Capital, North Africa, and the Balkans

As CUP leaders set out to the capital, they first sent these assassins in order to provide for their security against the sultan in case he decided to eliminate them. The assassins were also assigned the task of getting the populace at the capital to recognize the strength and influence of the CUP; as they did so, their own strength and influence within the CUP increased. At the capital, they murdered political opponents and organized public demonstrations. Yet they were never visible, and their names were never uttered in public. Even though most were of military origin, they resigned their posts to remain active solely within the committee, assuming no public positions. Significant members at this stage were Süleyman Askeri, Yakup Cemil, Sapancalı Hakkı, Hüsrev Sami, Eyüp Sabri, İzmitli Mümtaz, Topçu İhsan, and Mülazım Atıf.[226] Enver and Cemal Beys were the natural leaders of this group, with Talat, the only civilian, often intervening to contain their constantly combative tendencies.[227] They became very active with the advent of the wars in North Africa in Tripoli and the rebellions and ensuing war in the Balkans. As their influence grew, they came to define themselves as the real founders of the CUP. They in turn formed and armed their own retinues, thereby turning into a significant force when necessary.[228]

With the approval of especially the CUP leaders Talat, Enver, Cemal, and Bahaeddin Şakir Beys, the assassins were initially organized under the leadership of Süleyman Askeri.[229] Until 1910, their activities had remained confined to the capital as well as the Balkans from where they had originated.[230] One such assassin recounted the murders they undertook at the capital to establish control over the populace.[231] They thought they could change the course of history with a single bullet, also believing that the moral responsibility for such violent acts belonged to those who made the decision rather than the assassins who executed them. Because they did not think the CUP central committee could ever make a wrong decision, they had no qualms about executing all the orders they were given. The three major assassinations they carried out during this stage at the imperial capital were those of three prominent opposition journalists. *Serbesti* newspaper journalist Hasan Fehmi Bey was killed on top of the Galata bridge on 5 April 1909, *Seda-yı Millet* newspaper journalist Ahnet Samim Bey at Bahçekapı on 9 June 1910, and the Public Debt Administration director Zeki Bey at Huban Street in Bakırköy on 11 July 1911.[232] Hasan Fehmi had written editorials criticizing the CUP. Ahmet Samim had drawn the ire of the government by documenting the secret tortures employed by the military tribunals as well as the bribes the CUP had taken during the Soma-Bandırma railroad construction. He had received threatening letters that contained, instead of a proper signature, depictions of either a revolver or a sword, which were known to be the symbols of the SO. He had also written about these letters in his editorials. One memoir writer who narrated Ahmet Samim's assassination was literally walking next to Ahmet Samim the night the latter was shot in the back of the head.[233] Zeki Bey had been collecting documents of illegal CUP activities when he was assassinated. Only the assassin of Zeki Bey was later caught, by chance: he was the CUP member Şükrü Bey, who then became the minister of education. Even though he was put on trial, the CUP saved him by shutting down the trial due to lack of evidence. As a consequence, one memoir writer remarked that "not only has he not been cleared from the crime, but he acquired an inordinate amount of [illegal] force as a consequence of such an [illegal] acquittal."[234] The suspected CUP assassin in the other two cases was Çerkes Ahmed, with one account claiming that the CUP assassins Çerkes Ahmed, Halil, and Nazım had murdered Zeki Bey.[235] Many others recounted being threatened by the CUP.[236]

The SO continued to execute such violent acts because no one was held accountable and punished for their actions. Often, the police at the murder location would be sent somewhere else, with the CUP members in government covering any evidence that surfaced. And many assassins could be appointed to positions of power if they so desired.[237] This explains the great allure the SO held for those within the CUP and outside; here were men who could do anything with no accountability, and in return for their service, they would be rewarded with anything they wanted. The assassins would also punish those CUP members who were considered to be straying from the principles set by the committee—of total loyalty and obedience—by criticizing its actions. One person, Mustafa Kemal (Atatürk), who criticized the CUP was almost assassinated by Captain Abdülkadir Bey, barely saving his life by drawing his revolver before the assassin.[238] Others escaped such assassinations with the help and intervention of other CUP members.[239] SO members who did not obey the guidelines to the letter were murdered as well.[240] It is fascinating that even though there is so much information in contemporaneous memoirs naming and implicating many SO members for the murders they committed, no legal action was ever taken based on this information, either then or at present. This failure to hold individuals accountable for violence demonstrates how much such violence was becoming naturalized and embedded in Ottoman state and society.

In 1910, upon the orders of Sultan Reşad V, the SO was attached to the office of general chief of staff, with Eşref Sencer Kuşçubaşı designated as their leader from 1910 to 1918.[241] The first major SO engagement was in the 1911 Tripoli war, where they acquired additional experienced in guerrilla warfare against the Italian army. Among their duties was the gathering of information within and outside the country that was of significance to the state, establishing organizations with this intent, and accomplishing by personal initiative incidents that a state could not officially undertake but that nevertheless imperative to execute. Many distinguished SO officers often held ordinary, minor posts assigned to them in the Ottoman military. They then actively participated in the Balkan Wars of 1912 and 1913, primarily inciting rebellions against the Greeks and Bulgarians, and forming militia bands by recruiting local Muslim Turks. After the Balkan Wars, the SO was reorganized into independent cells, with each cell having a leader, a physician, two or three executors, and a valet. The physician treated the cell members when they were wounded or got sick; the valet cooked for them and took care of their needs. The cells were known by the name of the cell leader or the physicians, who were often members of the military medical school belonging to the Turkish Hearth.[242] One of the significant duties the SO undertook toward the end of this period was the collection of information about the local populations throughout the empire, indicating on colored maps the specific ethnic and religious composition in each region. State security at the capital was also reorganized; Talat Pasha appointed SO members to lead this endeavor.[243] During this period, the SO gained experience and expertise, eventually turning into a state organization. This institutionalization may explain why no legal action has ever been taken against it to date.

First Stage of World War I in the East, the Arabian Peninsula, and the Capital

Right after the entrance of the empire into the war, the CUP decided to unilaterally abolish the trade capitulations. At the capital, Talat orchestrated the public demonstrations supporting the abolition of the capitulations with SO help as well, and he did so while publicly condemning such demonstrations. The SO members who raided and destroyed those foreign and non-Muslim establishments presumably benefiting from the capitulations were caught, tried, and sentenced. Yet Talat once again made sure that on the way to imprisonment, they were kidnapped by local CUP responsible secretaries and informally released to then continue on with their seditious activities.[244] It was also during World War I that the SO transformed into a paramilitary organization to fight alongside the

Ottoman army, undertaking illegal activities the army could not publicly carry out. Right after the assassination of Archduke Ferdinand on 28 June 1914, select members of the CUP central committee started to have meetings at the War Ministry led by Enver Pasha and the Interior Ministry headed by Talat Pasha. The memoirs contain detailed information only about the secret meetings held at the War Ministry.[245] CUP commanding officers serving at strategic locations were invited to the capital for various, unrelated reasons. The main topic of discussion was the liquidation of non-Muslim masses clustered at strategic locations in order to prevent their possible collaboration with the enemy. That only a few within the CUP were aware of these meetings reveals the already very small size of the actual CUP decision-makers at this juncture. Once the empire joined the war, another significant meeting was held in early August 1914 by Talat with the intent to reorganize and assign specific tasks to the SO behind enemy lines.[246] Talat assigned Bahaeddin Shakir, one of the most radically nationalist CUP members, to head the operations in the east on the grounds that the latter had acquired ample experience during the Balkan Wars.[247]

Enver and Talat jointly determined the CUP and SO course of action. The tension between the CUP civilians headed by Talat and the military officers spearheaded by Enver ended by World War I, when they started to work together, "even though each wanted to have full control."[248] The SO members leading the armed militia bands were appointed by Talat, yet the activities as well as where such activities were to take place were determined and organized by the personal directives of Enver. So Talat appointed the cadres and oversaw the SO administration while the official and unofficial military officers headed by Enver determined what was to be done. The CUP decided to employ the SO during the war because of its success in employing guerrilla warfare against the Italians in North Africa and during the Balkan Wars. The SO was once again reorganized at this juncture. At the War Ministry, the deputy commander of the Ottoman forces established a special department to deal with SO affairs. Now, SO was divided into internal and external branches; while the external branch continued its activities in tsarist Russia, India, and Iran, the internal one was appointed "to secure safety and public order, direct local resistance movements on those Ottoman lands brought under enemy occupation, and conduct guerrilla warfare." Ottoman governors of the border provinces, especially those in Musul, Van, Erzurum, and Trabzon, were also recruited to assist the SO in this task.[249] Ömer Naci was appointed to the northern Caucasus; Bahaeddin Shakir and Ruşeni to Erzurum; Süleyman Şefik Pasha, Rauf Orbay, and Ubeydullah Efendi to Afghanistan; Hüsrev Sami to Trabzon; Dr. Reşit Şahingiray to eastern Anatolia; Süleyman Askeri to the Iraqi front; and İbrahim, İskeçeli Ali Rıza, Eyüp Sabri, and the Bulgarian deputy Celal to the Balkans.[250] The largest detachment was sent to the Caucasus under the command of Yakup Cemil. Now, the newly reorganized SO also had the support of select governors and military commanders who were CUP members. This collaboration of an extralegal organization with state and government officials and officers explains the high degree of collective violence the SO was ultimately able to commit.

Additional SO leaders and fighters were also secretly recruited; among these were bandits and prisoners explicitly released to serve in the SO.[251] Contemporaneous memoirs vividly describe this recruitment process in the case of the Kastamonu prison convicts.[252] One day, they received the news

> that the prison was being evacuated and the prisoners transferred to Kastamonu. This was truly something to be seen. The CUP remembered the prisoners on the occasion of World War I; they planned to release and use them during the war.... After half an hour we heard the clangs of chains: "They're coming!" A couple of whips cracked: "Make way!"... then a row of six people showed up. All six had been tied to each other with iron rings. The prisoner at one end was an Albanian from Kayseri. He had had a shave that day and curled his moustaches. His eyes were bloodshot; he looked around. Next to him was another with a swarthy face and a stark white beard. The local next to me... explained he was consecutively sentenced to 201 years... for murdering two people while still in prison.... We could not at first at all understand why this evacuation occurred.... With time we learned the reason... these prisoners were going to be registered into armed bands.

CUP governors and local CUP responsible clerks worked actively during this recruitment process. One account estimated that in the end, the total SO number "was around 8000 to 10,000 people organized in small units of at least 10 and at most 50 with leaders willing to commit... all atrocities without blinking an eye.... Not only did they not have any fear of prosecution, legal action, and imprisonment, but murder and savagery were regarded as a service to the fatherland."[253] Hence in SO organization and execution, there was now full cooperation among the state administration, government, and military.

The SO activities in the east first coalesced in Trabzon and Artvin under the command of Rıza and Nail Beys; they were later joined by CUP responsible clerks. They attempted to gather information from the Russians and Georgians and also "form armed bands from the prisoners under the command of officers, especially employing those prisoners who had excelled in banditry as band leaders.... In addition, in Rize, the Black Sea pirates and those who had murdered the gendarmerie were likewise given amnesty on the grounds that they knew the area well and could help."[254] This SO band was then joined by three Germans sent from the capital. Yet the SO had no idea of how to successfully administer the forces it had created. These bands were formed to attack the enemy rear lines, but all they wanted was to capture places and be known as conquerors. The only SO success was delivered by an SO band under the command of Rıza Bey, who briefly occupied Artvin. Yet the sudden retaliatory attack of the regular Russian forces caught everyone off guard, and the SO band retreated in disarray, leaving behind all their armaments.The SO activities in the Arab provinces and the Arabian Peninsula were initially overseen by Eşref Kuşçubaşı.[255] In 1916, Cemal and Enver Pashas ordered him to collect information on the Arab nationalists who were in touch with the French. He illegally broke into the French consulate in Beirut; the consulate that had been shut down during the war was officially off limits due to diplomatic immunity. It was based on the information gathered from these illegally stolen documents that Cemal Pasha sent many Arab leaders to the courts to be tried and then quickly hanged. Farther south, during a confrontation with the British regular forces, the SO band including some Arab tribes under Süleyman Askeri Bey's command again ran away in disarray. Askeri immediately committed suicide because he could not fulfill the duty the SO had given him.[256] These two incidents reveal the fervor with which committed SO members undertook their assignments; they were willing to engage in illegal activities and also to sacrifice their lives upon failure, all in the name of serving the fatherland. As Enver became increasingly immersed in fighting the war, all authority eventually gravitated to Talat, who even had to look after the War Ministry while Enver ran from one war front to the other.

Second Stage of World War I against the Armenians

SO armed bands that proved unsuccessful in fighting the Russians then merged with the bands in Erzurum under the command of Bahaeddin Shakir, Hilmi, and the Erzurum governor, Tahsin Bey.[257] Bahaeddin Shakir and Yakup Cemil initially captured Ardahan, but they had no means of defending the city and therefore had to quickly withdraw.[258] Bahaeddin Shakir then engaged in assassination attempts against prominent local non-Muslims. Perhaps his most significant attempted violence at this stage was his decision to murder all the Armenian Dashnaks holding a congress in Erzurum with the Ottoman and Russian Armenian deputies.[259] In carrying out SO activities, Shakir ended up in conflict with some Ottoman officers who wanted the military to have the sole control in maintaining order the region. These military units could not reach an agreement with the SO because many had not been officially notified of the latter's existence and activities; some of those who were informed were extremely critical of Shakir and SO activities.[260] Some military commanders, upon seeing SO bands going around in arms to raid and plunder local villages, escalated their patrols to secure order in their regions. Although the military units were eventually notified, the relations between the SO and the military remained tense. It was only in January 1915 that the SO armed bands officially joined the ranks of the Ottoman military.

What had transpired in January 1915? The Ottoman Third Army under the command of Enver fighting the Russians at Sarıkamış was literally wiped out in December 1914 and January 1915. This dramatic defeat prevented the Otoman army from traveling to Van to put down the Armenian rebellion there.[261] Instead, the Ottoman army had to hastily withdraw toward Bitlis while armed Armenian bands accompanying the Russian forces attacked them. The disastrous Ottoman military defeat at Sarıkamış as well as the poor performance of SO armed bands when confronted by regular forces caused Bahaeddin Shakir to return to the capital in January 1915. It was then that Shakir gave up fighting the external enemies, deciding to focus instead on the "enemies within." "After witnessing the collaboration of Armenians with the Russians, he had been convinced that one needed to fear the internal enemy as much as the external one," one account noted.[262] Another account conjectured that the CUP decision to liquidate the Ottoman Armenian community was taken at this juncture, at a secret CUP meeting attended by Talat, Enver, Kara Kemal, Cavid, and doctors Nazım and Bahaeddin Shakir. Nazım was said to have argued that the CUP needed to seize the opportunity created by the war, to attack "blameless Armenian women, children and populace"; even though this would be savagery, "wasn't war itself savagery?" Nazım queried rhetorically. And they all agreed upon having "only the Turks live on this land."[263] As a consequence, it appears that the CUP decision to deport and destroy the Armenians was duly taken in January 1915 by select members. It should be noted that neither the Ottoman parliament nor the government was notified. After this secret meeting, according to the same account, the course of events unfolded as follows:[264]

> Government officials in the provinces sprung into action upon receiving this order from the [CUP] center. While some... enacted the order in moderation with composure without crossing the boundary of governance, others turned into hell's angels putting secret committee work before governance.... SO bands waited for the deported Armenians like vultures.... upon arriving at the locations where SO bands were located, [the Armenians] were turned over to them by the gendarmerie who had received orders to do so.... These caravans were dispatched like herds of sheep to the slaughterhouse of ferocious SO monsters.... the pen is embarrassed to write the huge sin and murder conducted by this herd of bandits and murderers... including severing with an ax the head of an innocent baby wrested from the mother amid laughter and applause, forcing all other refugees to applaud as well... attacking and

> beating up seven- to eight-year-old innocents...seeking bestial pleasure in that moment of pain.... In spite of very strong CUP censorship, all these were documented by photographs that made it to the world media, leading to many protests.

Armenian deportations thus commenced in January 1915, with the deported Armenians being massacred through the collaboration of local CUP members, the gendarmerie, and the SO bands. The bands made sure to undertake such violence after the deported Armenians had left cities, towns, and villages so as to minimize witnesses.

Many contemporaneous memoirs document the SO role in the Armenian deportations and massacres at various locations. One account witnessed the SO massacre of Armenians at the Kemah pass; SO members involved in the massacres were Kara Kemal, Nail of Yenibahçe, artillery major Trabzonlu Rıza, Trabzon governor Cemal, Erzurum governor Tahsin, Dr, Bahaeddin Shakir, and Dr. Fuat Sabit. The same account pointed out that "the fundamental SO purpose [at this point] was the project of the total annihilation of the non-Turkish elements within Turkey."[265] Another account reported the Armenian massacres in Diyarbekir. Again an SO commander, Dr. Reşit Şahingiray who was also the Diyarbekir governor at the time, headed the Circassian gendarmerie and the Kurdish militia in executing the violence against Armenians. Some local Ottoman state officials who protested the Armenian massacre were also assassinated by Dr. Şahingiray's force.[266] Yet another account chronicled the SO role in the massacre of Armenians at Pürk and Şebinkarahisar. In this case, the Zara SO under the command of Nuri Efendi alighted at the Armenian village that had been armed by the Dashnak, and provoked the Armenian villagers by ordering them to provide beasts of burden to the SO. When the villagers refused, confrontation ensued, eventually leading to the massacres there.[267] The SO's collaboration with the Ottoman government and the state in destroying the Ottoman Armenian communities probably explains the fervor with which contemporary Turkish military and state so actively attempt to refute the assertions of Armenian genocide.

Yet the capability of these SO armed bands to execute such violence against Ottoman Armenian communities in the central imperial lands needs to be viewed in a larger context. Such contextualization is necessary to explain how and why so many Turks, civilian and military alike, not only did not protest against such violence but actually participated in them. After all, as Hannah Arendt has aptly noted in the case of the Holocaust, scholars need to analyze the larger societal and especially the political context, focusing on the roles not only of the active participants, like the SO bands discussed here, but also those of the bystanders and the enablers. I would argue that the gradual radicalization of CUP violence climaxed in the destruction of the Ottoma Armenian communities. I now turn to chronicling the gradual radicalization of CUP violence through cotemporaneous memoirs.

Gradual Radicalization of CUP Violence

A brief survey of the main events during CUP rule reveals the gradual radicalization of the violence that had been inherent in the organization. Even though genocide scholar Donald Bloxham has argued that the collective violence leading to the destruction of the Armenians occurred as a consequence of the CUP's gradual radicalization, this process has not yet been documented by any empirical accounts.[268] In this section, I undertake a sociological analysis of CUP radicalization, defining in the process nine significant stages, the last of which was the destruction of Armenians.

Stage I. The 1909 Counterrevolution

The CUP wanted to portray and delegitimate the 31 March 1909 counterrevolution as a conservative religious reaction, thereby silencing the initial CUP violence that had triggered it.[269] It could do so because the opposition to the CUP remained unorganized. Given that the only organization outside of the state belonged to the religious establishment, it was not surprising that religious scholars soon headed the rebelling low-ranked soldiers and civilian CUP opponents.[270] When the outcome became uncertain, Prince Sabahaddin, the most prominent leader of the political opposition, disappeared to Europe on his yacht.[271] The CUP quickly put down the counterrevolution with the aid of an army contingent arriving from the Balkans, commanded by Mahmud Şevket Pasha. With this military intervention, the officers increased their influence within the CUP, turning it into a more forceful and autocratic organization.[272] The CUP also took this opportunity to round up, hang, or exile all political opponents with the claim they had participated in the counterrevolution; ten of the sixty-four instigators were publicly hanged.[273]

Stage II. 1909 Massacres of the Adana Armenians

The Adana massacres started on 19 April 1909, approximately three weeks after the counterrevolution, resulting in the deaths of 17,000 Armenians and 1,850 Muslims. While the disproportionately large number of Armenian casualties (about 10 to 1) documents that they were the true victims of this violence, the number Muslim casualties reveals the presence of some armed Armenian opposition. In the memoirs, all contemporaneous eyewitness accounts emphasized the inadequacy of the Ottoman administration in handling the initial unrest that turned into violence.[274] What instigated the violence? One account argued that the CUP sent groups of armed Muslim peasants to Adana, frightening the local Armenians.[275] Another blamed the mass demonstration organized by the CUP journalist İhsan Fikri for escalating the tensions.[276] On 13 April 1909, an Armenian carpenter named Latfik was murdered, with his body left at a public space. When the local Armenians did not open their shops the following day, Governor Cevat Bey and Commander Remzi Pasha sent two notables, (Muslim) Bağdadizade Abdülkadir and (Armenian) Urfalıyan Davut Efendis to counsel the Muslim and Armenian populace. Yet Urfalıyan Davut Efendi was torn to pieces in front of Bağdadizade Abdülkadir, and factory owner Şardikyan Artin Agha was likewise murdered. Because the three initial murders were of Armenians, it is most likely that the Muslim populace initiated the violence.

Armed conflict ensued. All non-Muslims including Armenians had gained the right to purchase arms in the aftermath of the 1908 revolution, leading especially Armenian revolutionary committees to arm some Armenians. The Muslims attacked the Armenian neighborhood, but the fierce defense they encountered led them to plunder the marketplace instead; they nevertheless also set the Armenian neighborhood on fire that night. The fighting continued for three days until an American missionary, Jim Pears, established an armistice. The Dedeağaç battalion arrived from the capital and was placed at strategic posts within the Armenian neighborhood. Yet the battalion then started firing upon the neighborhood; the massacre and accompanying arson and plunder continued until the following morning. With the joint efforts of Jim Pears and "Perjov" [*sic*] who was the director of the Jesuit schools, all surviving Armenians were collected at the garden in front of the government building and cordoned off by the military; they eventually returned to their homes. This account summarizes the main course of events of the 1909 Adana massacres.

Meanwhile, the Ottoman parliament sent Deputies Tengirşenk and Babikyan to investigate and prepare a report. Yet upon their return, Babikyan did not want to sign the report Tengirşenk had prepared; Babikyan died mysteriously that very night from a heart attack. When Tengirşenk's report blaming the Armenians for the massacres was read by the commission formed at the parliament, the Armenian deputies objected, and no decision could be reached. Deputy Zohrab was asked by the commission to examine Babikyan's notes and report back a week later. He did so, placing full responsibility for the incidents on the Turks, yet once again a decision proved impossible to reach. Cemal Pasha, the former Adana governor, was sent there by the CUP to hold trials.[277] Cemal Pasha declared the lack of state authority had produced the ensuing anarchy, blaming the establishment of the Armenian Dashnak and Hnchak political committees against the Turkish committees for polarizing the situation.[278] Yet, Cemal Pasha had forty-seven Muslims and one Armenian hanged for their role in the massacres—the large number of hanged Muslims inadvertently pointed out the main culprits. The reaction of the Muslim Turks to the hanging of so many Muslims, including a mufti, was one of total shock: they had never before been held accountable at such a high level for conducting violence against non-Muslims.[279] The Adana massacres also reverberated throughout the empire; contemporaneous accounts of Ottoman officials reveal that incidents occurred at Antioch, Lazkiye, Aleppo, and Kayseri.[280] In all such instances, the Armenians suffered from the ensuing violence, being massacred in large numbers. The Adana massacres revealed how polarized the relations had become between the Muslims and non-Muslims in the aftermath of the 1908 constitutional revolution. It is no accident that such violence first occurred in Adana, where the primary official who instigated the massacres by distributing arms to Muslims was a CUP member. Had there been officials who acted in the interest of all imperial elements instead of the Turks, such violence would probably not have occurred.

Stage III. 1913 CUP Coup d'État

The CUP military coup against the government known as the "Bab-ı Ali raid" occurred on 23 January 1913 during the Balkan Wars. The CUP was in opposition and was actively seeking an opportunity to take over the government. At the time, the CUP was being investigated for inciting rebellion against the ruling party. Yet the CUP leaders had given their personal assurance and word of honor to the war minister, Nazım Pasha, never to engage in political sedition. Blaming the ruling party for the disastrous defeats of the Balkan Wars, Enver had suddenly decided to attempt the coup d'état, thereby undertaking the first modern political intervention in government.[281] The SO assassins led by Enver and Talat Beys stormed the government, murdering Nazım Pasha and forcing the grand vizier Kamil Pasha to resign at gunpoint.[282] During the coup, Enver Bey claimed he was acting on behalf of the nation, telling the grand vizier, "The nation does not want you; write your resignation!"[283] Hence, at this point, the CUP started to publicly legitimate its violent acts by taking upon itself the goal of acting on behalf of the nation. After the raid, Talat, who appointed himself the interior minister, boasted that "they had conquered the government with only 17 people [who had carried out the raid]."[284] Upon the CUP's request, Mahmud Şevket Pasha, who had commanded the Balkan army in suppressing the counterrevolution, was appointed the grand vizier.

Once again, SO member Yakup Cemil, who had murdered Nazım Pasha during the coup, not punished. The other SO member İsmail Canbolat (later Turkish republican deputy) who had killed the military security official was kept in court for more than a month; during the period, he managed to escape from military prison. In addition to such lack of accountability, Enver Bey was actually rewarded for his violence; he assumed the position of war minister a year later, thus becoming a pasha. Unbeknownst to most CUP members, in case there was a coup attempt against the CUP similar to the one he had led, Enver Pasha also started to keep a reserve force of 10,000 soldiers on both shores of the imperial capital.[285] Now solidly in control of the state and the government, the CUP engaged in its Turkification policy of the empire, leading to increased tension among the non-Muslim and non-Turkish communities.[286] Some CUP members actively removed the non-Muslim officials appointed by the former ruling party, the LEP.[287] The CUP's exclusionary stand against its own non-Muslim subjects continued despite the declarations of some Armenians to the contrary; editorials by CUP members in newspapers criticizing and blaming the Armenians started to appear with increased frequency.[288] Armenian revolutionaries also escalated their activities at the capital.[289]

Stage IV. 1913 Assassination of Mahmud Şevket Pasha

The next violence the CUP participated in in the aftermath of the 1913 coup was the assassination of the grand vizier Mahmud Şevket Pasha in the spring of the same year. The pasha's diaries reveal that he was becoming increasingly disappointed with and critical of the CUP government. Even though the assassins were never caught, many contemporaneous memoirs concur that the CUP either undertook the assassination to eliminate this last obstacle on the path to full governance or had at least knowingly turned a blind eye by not only failing to take security measures but actually removing the existing guards.[290] The assassination once again enabled the CUP to round up, hang, or exile its opponents.[291] One account stated that interior minister Talat Pasha met Cemal Pasha, now the commander of the imperial capital, in Bahaeddin Shakir's room at the CUP headquarters, thanking Cemal "for cleaning İstanbul up."[292]

The CUP's relations with non-Muslims continued to deteriorate as well. During the summer of 1913, the Ottoman parliament leader and CUP member Halil Menteşe and the interior minister Talat Pasha had numerous meetings in the houses of Hallaçyan and Zohrab Efendi with the Dashnak leadership, namely, Malumyan Aknumi, Sahirikian, Vartkes, Vahan the deputy of Van, and Pastırmacıyan Efendi, the deputy from Erzurum. The CUP's intent was "to turn them around from the dangerous road they had set upon [and engage in reforms together]...yet it was not possible to convince these dreamers."[293] Given the CUP's increasingly nationalist stand, it is not surprising that the Armenian leaders did not believe that the CUP was intent on executing reforms; all its activities pointed in the opposite direction.

Stage V. 1913–14 Pogroms against the Greek Rum

Once firmly in rule, the CUP leaders started to survey and take action against non-Muslim populations concentrated at strategic locations. In this respect, the Ottoman Greek Rum residing along the western coast of Asia Minor were identified as being the most dangerous to Muslim Turkish interests. The SO member Kuşçubaşı was initially appointed to travel in the region in cognito; he reported that approximately 760,000 Greek Rum were concentrated in this area. Because these local communities did not often engage in violence, the CUP could not take public action against them. Instead, the SO was mobilized to secretly collaborate with the local CUP branches to engage in violence with the intent to get the Greek Rum to migrate to Greece.[294] Three sets of precautions taken to that end involved the state, the military, and the CUP working in conjunction with each other. Contemporaneous accounts reveal the mode as well scope of these pogroms.[295] The SO member—and later Turkish president—Celal Bayar was appointed the local CUP responsible clerk; he collaborated with Kuşçubaşı in plunder, arson, and murder to scare the Greek Rum into fleeing from the region. Other CUP members also participated in these illicit, violent activities.[296] In Karesi, the district governor was personally engaged in getting the Greek Rum "to migrate without any problems."[297] The Muslim Turkish refugees from the Balkans recently settled in the area also became active in the violence, thereby starting "to slowly show the Greek Rum the torture they themselves had suffered in the Balkans."[298] One CUP member who was also the Çeşme district governor speeded up the migration by burning down Greek Rum monasteries and churches and then blaming the local Greek Rum for these violent acts.[299] Whenever complaints emerged, the CUP covered its tracks by officially appointing other CUP members who prepared official reports stating that there was no evidence of violence.[300]

In his memoirs, Celal Bayar described these violent activities as "the business of the Greek deportation in the Smyrna hinterland," conducted in the aftermath of "the cheap victory the Greeks had attained at the Balkan Wars, instigating them to mobilize the [Ottoman] Greek Rum to their side. . . . Also, the wretched state of the Muslim Turkish refugees from the Balkans who sought shelter in their motherland whipped up national feelings. A counternational movement had started under this effect to result in, if my memory serves me right, about 130,000 Greeks migrating to Greece from the various districts of Smyrna."[301] Hence, the flood of Muslim Turkish refugees into the empire in the aftermath of the Balkan Wars gave the CUP both the idea and the means of replacing local Greek Rum with these refugees. The CUP conjectured that such violent replacement of populations would guarantee that local activities continued unabated, yet this time with a significant increase in the Muslim Turkish population.

Prioritizing Muslim Turkish interests trumped all other considerations; this violence was "courageously" undertaken "to Turkify infidel Smyrna... to rescue the economy of Smyrna from nonnational, treacherous, deliberate hands and sources."[302] In doing so, the CUP once again revealed its ignorance and inexperience, not at all taking into consideration that these Turkish refugees who were mostly simple peasants lacked the agricultural and commercial skills the Greek Rum had developed over centuries.

The region suffered gravely as a consequence of CUP pogroms against the Greek Rum. Once the refugees were settled in the former Greek Rum neighborhoods, life did not continue unabated. Instead, the quality of life in all the towns and villages declined significantly:[303]

> The whole composition of the town altered with the arrival of Muslim Turkish refugees especially since most of them were peasants who knew nothing about the region's agriculture. For instance, there were some who had seen anise for the first time, trying to feed it to their animals. There were many goods left behind by the Greek Rum; people entered these residences, taking all these unclaimed goods without realizing that it was thievery—because such goods were considered permissible by the sharia [for belonging to infidels]. So our greatest occupation became the patrolling of all the houses and stores, gathering all the items necessary for the Treasury and stocking them.... It was also difficult to get the refugees to decide upon a home; they constantly changed residences and the unoccupied ones were destroyed. At the same time, the vineyards and fields in every village were distributed to the refugees yet many had no idea about how to keep a vineyard.... that these refugees could live under such adverse circumstances was due to the fact that their standards of life had been low to start with.... One of the reasons the settlement of refugees has been so unsuccessful is because these refugees were not classified in accordance with the agricultural requirements of the regions.... The seeds they were given to plant were often used for their consumption because they lacked provisions.

Another account took issue with such Greek Rum removal, noting that "we were trying by force to remove these Greek Rum elements that had been almost completely Turkified."[304] As 40,000 of the 45,000 Greek Rum residents left for the Greek islands "in peace," often in the same boats that had brought the Muslim Turkish refugees, CUP officials made sure that the "tons of goods and trade material left behind were gathered, classified, and either distributed to the refugees or sent to the center to the Treasury or the Red Crescent."[305] With the Greek Rum pogrom, the CUP also started the practice of not only removing non-Muslims but also confiscating for the state the goods and properties that non-Muslims had toiled to create over many generations.

With the advent of World War I, such violent activities against the Greek Rum gained speed. Through August 1914, the main topic of the meetings held at CUP headquarters and the War Ministry was "the elimination of the non-Turkish masses tied to negative foreign influences that had accumulated at strategic points."[306] During the war, Bayar's actions became so destructive that the Smyrna governor, Rahmi Bey—himself a prominent CUP member—told Enver that he was going to expel Bayar if Enver failed to remove him immediately. Yet once again, no action was taken against Bayar. Instead, also upon the suggestions of the German general Liman von Sanders, the CUP government forcefully moved the remaining Greek Rum settled along the Aegean coast in general and Gallipoli in particular elsewhere in the empire.[307] The dire conditions such deported Greek Rum faced were described in one account as follows:[308]

> With the sad events brought about by the [Great] war, the daughters of the minority population had all fallen into the dead end of extreme poverty, easily giving themselves to strangers.... these were mostly girls from good families. They had been removed by the military for security reasons from the Marmara coastal areas and the Dardanelles. These families faced extreme wretchedness as their finances worsened. The poor creatures had to prostitute themselves in order to help their families and provide their sustenance.

The CUP ideologically justified the pogrom against the Greek Rum on grounds of security and Turkish national interests, declaring them "foreign elements" even though they had been living in the Aegean region for centuries, if not millennia. The CUP then employed the many CUP members engaged in this forced removal and who had "acquired the necessary experience and skills" in the forced deportation of Armenians from 1915 to 1917. Also, once again, no one who engaged in this violence was ever held accountable for their actions; instead, they were rewarded by the CUP.

Stage VI. CUP Entrance into World War I

The Ottoman Empire entered World War I on the side of Germans when two warships under the command of Admiral Suchon that the Ottoman state purchased from the Germans bombed the Russian ports in the Black Sea after entering the Ottoman waters.[309] It appears that some of the CUP leaders knew of the attack even though they all claimed surprise. Many accounts agreed that Enver

Pasha was the main force advocating entry into the war on the German side; he did so to regain all the imperial lands that had been lost, thereby restoring the empire to its former grandeur. Enver's aspiration and dream were also supported by many other Turks who thought that victory was a distinct possibility.[310] That the financial state of the empire was not at all prepared for war was not taken into account.[311] And some had the foresight to realize that not entering the war was the only way to preserve the empire, and entering on the side of Germany "would at best turn the empire into a German colony."[312]

Perhaps the ease with which the CUP had started to dictate Ottoman domestic and foreign policy led it to pursue increasingly ambitious dreams and aspirations. The entry into the war took so many by surprise because there had been little public discussion of such a possibility. Had the CUP allowed such public discussion at the Ottoman parliament and in the print media, and, more important, had the CUP then heeded opposing views that were expressed, it might not have entered this organized violence termed war that ultimately brought the Ottoman Empire to an end, in the process destroying the lives of 2 million Ottomans, mostly Turkish Muslim soldiers who died during the war.

Stage VII. CUP Challenges during World War I

During World War I, the CUP faced three significant in 1915: the battle in the east headed by Enver Pasha against the Russians during the winter of 1915 that ended disastrously with the defeat at Sarıkamış; the siege of the Dardanelles in the west during the winter and early spring of 1915, where the Ottoman army was miraculously able to resist the British; and the war in the southeast against the British headed by Cemal Pasha, again in the spring of 1915, that ended with a disastrous defeat.

In the east, the CUP leaders were initially excited about getting the Muslim Turkish populace in Russia to rebel against the Russian empire, joining them in fighting the Russians. But this did not materialize.[313] The Ottoman army sent to fight the Russians was extremely ill-provisioned, with no winter clothing, supply services, transportation, or medical corps for wounded soldiers.[314] Accounts of the fighting reveal three recurrent themes. During the skirmishes with the Russians, the Ottoman army often ended up fighting its own soldiers because no adequate information and communication were relayed about troop movements.[315] Politics adversely impacted the Ottoman army as experienced commanders criticizing CUP officers were quickly removed.[316] After the disastrous defeat at Sarıkamış and the subsequent advance of the Russian army, the Ottoman officers increasingly mentioned the Armenians' attacks against the local Muslim populace.[317] Forced Armenian deportations undertaken by the

CUP ensued on account of such violence. Subsequently, as the Russian army retreated in 1917, Muslims were massacred by the Armenians who had remained behind from the Russian army.[318] In the aftermath of the battle in the east, many Ottoman officers were captured by the Russians and sent to Siberia while the Muslim refugees from the east moved to central Anatolia, destroying all in their path.[319] Hence the unsuccessful wars in the east were pivotal in triggering the forced Armenian deportations; the reciprocating violence by the Armenians in 1917 was employed by the CUP and later the Turkish state to retroactively justify the initial 1915 violence committed against them.

The war at the Dardanelles took a great toll on the Ottoman army, with 251,309 soldiers lost over the course of a few weeks.[320] The siege at the Dardanelles brought about the possibility of the conquest of the imperial capital by enemy forces. Turkish families at the capital tried to decide when to move to which Anatolian city in order to escape the invading forces. The Ottoman government likewise started to move the sultan, the ministries, and the state treasury to Eskişehir, and the sacred belongings of the prophet Muhammad and other relics to Konya.[321] The torrent of refugees from the capital to the Anatolian cities reached a high level. It was only in March 1915 that it became evident that the Allied Forces would have a difficult time breaking through the Dardanelles. Interestingly, one memoir writer remarked that he first heard that the country faced a significant Armenian problem from Enver when he was accompanying the latter to the Dardanelles:[322]

> When he talked about the events at the Caucasian front, [Enver] recounted the difficulties the army faced, the damage it suffered, and the danger it fell into. In their attempt to hit the Turkish army from the rear, the rebelling Armenian committees attacked supply lines, killed the wounded, spied for the enemy, in short created a catastrophe for the Turkish army. In order to prevent this danger, Enver said he believed in the necessity to uproot all the Armenians in the eastern provinces, sending them elsewhere. When he saw me hesitate in front of the scope and difficulty of this endeavor, he explicated as if to respond to a question I had in my mind, but could not express.... Nothing will happen to these Armenians, and provisions will be made to settle them in places where they will not produce any harm.

Rather than blaming the disastrous defeat at Sarıkamış in the east on his deficient command, Enver chose to blame the defeat on the Armenians—and not only on the few who did engage in seditious activities but on all Armenian communities. Even though Enver claimed that no harm would be brought upon the

Armenians, the memoir writer stated that he found out about the devastation Enver had started to wreak upon returning to the capital.

It was also during the spring of 1915 that the Ottoman army in the southeast commanded by Cemal Pasha faced a disastrous defeat against the British during what was known as the "Canal expedition."[323] Enver Pasha had told Cemal that the Arab and Egyptian leaders had indicated that if the Ottoman army could appear in front of the Suez Canal before the British had a chance to mobilize, they could be certain that the Egyptian populace would stab the British in the back, and the subsequent liberation of Egypt would greatly impress the rest of the Muslim world, mobilizing many colonies against the British. The SO members accompanying the Ottoman army likewise made boastful claims about how they would expel the British. Yet none of this was actualized. The Arab contingents in the Ottoman army escaped in disarray, and Cemal Pasha had to retreat with heavy casualties. It was estimated that 130,000 Turkish soldiers had died in Yemen and the Arabian Peninsula. Cemal also contacted Enver and Talat at the time, asking for the removal of non-Muslim populations in the rear of the withdrawing Ottoman army, who mostly happened to be Armenians, into the central regions of Asia Minor, like Konya. According to his memoirs, Cemal initially thought this was being done, only to be later find out that entire Armenian communities instead were being deported to the Syrian deserts. Cemal protested that such an action would undermine the security of his army but to no avail. Hence the three war challenges the CUP faced coalesced in 1915, leading to the commencement of the Armenian forced deportations during the same year.

When the Ottoman Empire entered World War I, it had a population of 22 million and lands of 1.7 million square kilometers. At the end of the war, it had lost 12 million of its population and about 1 million square kilometers of land.[324] In addition to this massive population loss, Anatolia was devastated especially in the east, where the retreating Russian and Ottoman armies wreaked havoc. The defeats during the war reveal the dynamics that led to the Armenian deportations and massacres, but just as significant is the trajectory of CUP violence that culminated in this violent act. The 1909 Adana massacres, the 1913 Greek Rum pogroms and subsequent deportations, and the deportations of Ottoman Jews and Arabs during World War I enabled the CUP to develop the modus operandi for the 1915–17 Armenian deportations and massacres.

Stage VIII. 1914–15 Forced Deportations of Ottoman Jews and Arabs

During World War I, two non-Turkish communities deemed untrustworthy by the CUP, namely. Ottoman Jews and Arabs. were also deported. In order to procure provisions for the Fourth Army, Cemal Pasha decided to deport the Jews out of Jaffa. Yet given the degree of international outcry over such an action, he had to make a deal with the local Jews and, calling their leaders, made the following proposal: "[You have] one of two choices. I either forcefully deport you like the Armenians whereby you would leave your houses, gardens and vineyards, going toward places that produce wheat. Or I assign guards to delegations from among you to protect all your houses, gardens and vineyards, hanging anyone who touches even a single orange. I will send you in trains. Yet for this second choice to actualize, all the press in Vienna and Berlin has to quiet down by tomorrow." The Jews suppressed not only these centers but also the ones in Paris and London, and they were indeed deported to Hama and Humus without any harm.[325] Still, it should be noted that the Jews of Jaffa were a much smaller non-Muslim community than the Armenians. That the CUP was careful about maintaining a positive public image in the media is evident in Cemal's comments. It is also evident that forced deportations were increasingly considered by the CUP as a "natural" wartime measure.

Forced Arab deportations were documented by Emir Şekip Arslan, who was a CUP member and a deputy at the Ottoman parliament.[326] Arslan noted that he was sent by the CUP to Damascus, where one of the first things the Ottoman regional commander Zeki Pasha wanted him to do was collect all the arms of the Christians in Lebanon "for they could be provoked by the Allied Powers to rebel against the state, thus bringing danger upon the Ottoman state." Yet Arslan refused to do so, stating that he had not observed any preparation among the Christians, and all they wanted was to please the Ottoman state. The other issue concerned the searches of the consulates of the Allied Powers in Lebanon to identify Arab informants. Even though Arslan opposed such an action because it would create animosity among the Arabs, and the Beirut governor Bekir Sami Bey concurred, the latter was then removed and replaced by Azmi Bey, who procured the necessary material for Cemal Pasha with the aid of the SO, leading the Arab collaborators to be either hanged or exiled to Jerusalem. Arslan intervened to get some of the exiled Arabs back, succeeding in a few instances. Arslan then recounted another Arab deportation that occurred about the same time as the Armenian one. Discussing the reasons for such a forced deportation, he explained that the Ottoman success at the Dardanelles "very much toughened the decisions the CUP had taken upon the advent of the war." Ending the Arab domination in Syria had been one such CUP decision, one that was now put into practice. At the advent of the war, Cemal Pasha had exiled some Arabs to Jerusalem and others to Anatolia but shortly thereafter had forgiven them, allowing them to return to their homeland.

A year later, in 1915, Cemal Pasha "returned to the starting point and not only did he have those he had forgiven recaptured, but he also had other Arabs caught as well, sending hundreds of people to exile." Arslan estimated that about 2,000

Arabs were deported to Anatolia during this period. Yet this time, they were sent with their families, and their properties were carefully scrutinized. They were exiled to Izmir, Manisa, Izmit, Bursa, Eskişehir, Yenişehir, Akşehir, Tokat, Sivas, Konya, and Edirne. It was rumored that the Ottoman commission established to register the properties and goods of the exiled Arabs did so in order to give them comparable property in Anatolia, settling Turks in their stead. Arslan thought this initial 2,000 would eventually escalate to the forced settlement in Anatolia of tens of thousands of Syrians, especially noble families. Arslan returned to the capital in 1917 and again in 1918 to intervene on behalf of the exiled Syrian Arabs, making sure that their allowances were increased, that they could be exiled to a place other than what the CUP had determined like the capital, and that women and men older than sixty could go back. His aim was to constantly pressure everyone for the deported Arabs' eventual return to their place of origin. Arslan went to Talat Pasha, stating that he would be the first to object and get other Arab deputies in the Ottoman parliament to join him if a motion was introduced to give land to the exiled Arabs in Anatolia. Talat convinced him, however, that "this matter will never make its way to the Parliament." What eventually happened to these 2,000 Arab families is not known, but many probably did make it back to their places of origin at the end of the war. Still, whether they were then able to recover their original goods and properties is unclear. Unlike what later happened to the Armenians, the Jewish and Arab communities that were forcefully deported were not physically harmed. Such deportations nevertheless demonstrate the ease with which the CUP moved its own subjects, subjects the CUP as the representative of the Ottoman government was responsible to protect.

Stage IX. 1915–17 Forced Armenian Deportations and Ensuing Massacres

Contemporaneous memoirs contain ample information on the inherent violence of the Armenian deportations.[327] In discussing why such deportations happened, the most significant observation was made by Sultan Abdülhamid II. It was alarming to the sultan that "the CUP separated the state from the military; they spoke as if the military was a state within the state! The meaning of this was as follows: today CUP is the state and the government.... So the dynasty had merely become an adornment.... For the first time in Ottoman history, an irresponsible committee had fully seized the Ottoman state."[328] As the CUP seized power, its inherent violence spread to the entire empire. In describing the course of events leading to the Armenian massacres, one account stated that "we ourselves are the ones that created this problem! The Armenians' conditions were very poor before constitutional rule, but they were able to transform from a governed community to a dominant position through their intelligence and hard work. Yet the Turks failed to comprehend where this superiority originated, [instead] only lamenting that [the Turks] had to continually withdraw from all they had conquered by their swords." "Armenians too were hopeful that they could achieve their independence," the account continued, "and the words of constitution and reform could not withstand in front of such an ambition."[329] Many recount the role of Russia in aiding the Armenians, with one account stating, however, that the Russians had never intended to grant the Armenians their independence in the east because of the large number of Muslims residing there.[330] Still, those Armenians who did collaborate with the Russians provided the opportunity for the CUP to execute its goal, a goal that ultimately enabled, one account admitted, the establishment of the Turkish republic in Asia Minor.[331] Another pointed out that the 1915 massacres the Armenians committed in Van and their hindrance of the Ottoman military maneuvers provided the CUP with the opportunity to actualize its goal. It should be noted that while the CUP destroyed 800,000 to 1.5 million Armenian lives, Armenians massacred at most 40,000 to 60,000 Muslims. Still, the account continued to explain why such collective violence occurred as follows:[332]

> What would a government confident in its justice and power have done under such conditions? It would have punished those who had rebelled against the government. But the Unionists wanted to destroy the Armenians, thereby doing away with the problem of the Six [Armenian] Provinces. The hasty uprising of the Armenians at the eastern borders of Anatolia, thinking their day of liberation had arrived, constituted the beginning of the massacres. Thousands of children of the homeland, Armenian and Turk, were trampled under the feet of the committees. Many armed bands were sent to Anatolia from Istanbul at the beginning of the war; these bands comprised the thieves and murderers that had been released from prisons. They underwent a week of training at the War Ministry, and then were sent by the SO to the Caucasian border. These bands conducted the most heinous murders of the Armenian atrocities. There was however a general chaos in East Anatolia; the bands and the populace destroyed each other and much blood was shed. The Armenians had joined the Russians and were attacking Van.... But the most innocent and sinless were those Armenians living in the provinces of Bursa, Ankara, Eskişehir, and Konya who were inflicted with the calamity of deportation even though they had committed no crimes.

According to contemporaneous memoirs, the CUP exploited the crisis in the east to eliminate the Armenian "problem," unjustly deporting and massacring all Armenian subjects, most of whom were innocent and not involved in the violence.

How was it that the CUP could actually execute and get away with such an expansive act of collective violence? One account portrayed the CUP mentality at the time, noting that "they had realized that the time had come for them to focus on with all they possessed the salvation of the Turk, to mold and liberate what had been left of the country as the national fatherland.... In the old days... Anatolia did not give us the feeling of a 'whole.'... Yet that had now become the last homeland of the Turk."[333] The CUP took drastic and radical action to eliminate all other contenders for the same land, and most prominent among such contenders were, according to the CUP interpretation, the Armenians. Many accounts confirm that Talat was prominent in making the decision to remove and destroy the Armenians; he was the only one within the CUP with the necessary skills to execute such a plan.[334] Talat at the capital oversaw the forced Armenian deportations and ensuing massacres, yet most contemporaneous accounts concur that Bahaeddin Shakir was the CUP representative on the ground who actually executed this violent decision. One account reflected on Shakir's role as follows:[335]

> What was Bahaeddin Shakir's role in the [Armenian] deportation business? This issue was not dissected or illuminated even at our most intimate [CUP] meetings. I do not have a clear, absolute opinion, but from a word used when other issues were being discussed, a thought that leaked out, jests that could not be contained, in summary, from all such fine and slight clues, according to the guess that strongly manifested itself in me, he was the greatest motivator and creator of the deportation business. I strongly suspect that he created the groundwork by traveling in the eastern provinces alone, determining the fundamental principles, and as he attempted to put into practice his personal decisions, his orders were [carried out] because of the position he held, the orders of the government and the general headquarters, and finally because he dragged along with him some of his influential friends in government.

Yet what is stated next is most telling. Rather than condemning Shakir for his violent acts that ultimately destroyed and maimed the lives of hundreds of thousands of human beings, the memoir concluded by stating that "because of [these actions], when there comes one day the need to rejuvenate Shakir's memory, the eastern provinces would bare their chests to his statute in gratitude." While the CUP was in government with the full force of the state and the military behind it, most of the Armenians were unarmed civilian subjects of the empire who should have been protected by the very same government and state.

With the Ottoman parliament containing many non-Muslim deputies, the sultan and/or the Ottoman populace should have been able to intervene to prevent such collective violence. Yet one account[336] dismissed that possibility by stating that

> the sultan was not capable of differentiating good from evil, the senate did not include the intellectually distinguished people of the empire, and the majority at the parliament was "the faithful and loyal CUP servants, their duties consisting of trade, flattery, wealth accumulation and debauchery." Within the parliament, not only did the Turkish deputies act irresponsibly, but "the Greek Rum and Armenian deputies were also lazy in defending the rights of their constituencies... so much so that neither the deportation nor the massacre of their coreligionists caused the non-Muslim deputies to protest." As for the Ottoman [Muslim Turkish] populace, it was difficult for them to protest because 'there were no masses assembled around [certain] ideas; few made a living through trade and agriculture as almost everyone tried to gain their livelihood through the government.

Hence the weakness of the sultan, the inability of the populace to generate ideas strong enough to counter the CUP's radical nationalism, and the deputies' prioritization of their personal interests before all else stopped these groups from protesting, intervening, and preventing this destructive process. Yet, just as crucial in the execution of collective violence of such magnitude was the participation of the military, which had already been politicized by the CUP. Thus, no sites of resistance remained, with all directly or indirectly complying with destructive CUP actions. This compliance had reached such a degree that the same account queried:[337]

> Who had raised their voices when Enver Pasha sacrificed 150,000 Turks to his ignorance at the Sarıkamış [battle]? When had the perpetrator of any murder, any calamity ever been punished? Didn't the CUP mentality and the perseverance of its political body forgive all murders anyhow? In [the CUP's] regard, murder was the most brilliant virtue demonstrating courage and fortitude. There were murderers even among those who occupied ministerial positions. The populace had become used to living under such an administration. The heroes who had brought freedom from Salonica to Istanbul were all tough armed youth; even the names of the newspapers they printed had names like *Weapon*, and *Cannon*.... They even titled their newspapers *Dagger*,

> adding onto the margin the following threat "to those who deserve it." According to [the CUP] way of thinking, the ones who deserved this dagger were those who had enlightened themselves and others through science and knowledge, who employed the European strategy of fearlessly stating the dangers inflicted on the fatherland, and who did not accept the Ottoman homeland to be disgraced in the hands of [such] roughnecks. The wicked ones who should have had their heads blown by canons, and their chests thrust with daggers should [instead] have been [the CUP members].

Such an account places the responsibility for the violence against the Armenians squarely on the shoulders of the CUP, aptly summarizing the manner in which it paralyzed the entire social structure.

Contemporaneous accounts also provide abundant information on how the CUP y deported and massacred Armenians throughout the empire. Six accounts recount what occurred in the vicinity of Trabzon, Artvin, Erzurum, and Van where the most devastation occurred.[338] In Trabzon, the CUP responsible secretary first accepted the jewelry rich Armenian bankers kept as collateral for safekeeping to then murder them in cold blood.[339] The wife of the Antep subdistrict governor witnessed the abject conditions of the Armenian caravans deported from Artvin as many perished.[340] Another state official remarked on the emptied-out Armenian village in Artvin that he passed on his way to his post.[341] Still another interviewed the SO members who had routed the Armenians of Artvin, Van, and Ardahan.[342] An officer noted the desperate state of Armenians deported from Erzurum and Sivas, especially the Armenian women and girls who were left destitute on the streets.[343] These regions were additionally devastated in 1918 when the withdrawing Armenians cruelly massacred Kurds and Turks.[344]

Four contemporaneous accounts described the CUP violence against the Armenians in Ordu, Samsun, Sinop, and Kastamonu. One noted that the family of an official posted to Samsun in 1915 and to Ordu in 1916 was settled in both cases in houses left behind by the forcefully deported local Armenians.[345] The other three described the SO armed bands recruited from the Sivas prisons.[346] What began to occur around this time at the imperial city as well as in Adapazarı, Çankırı, and Ankara in its vicinity was captured by five accounts.[347] One woman memoir writer described the forced removal and massacre of approximately 250 prominent Armenian intellectuals of the imperial capital on 24 April 1915, a day still commemorated by world Armenians as "Armenian Genocide Day."[348] Another Ottoman official personally witnessed the "trainloads of Armenian intellectuals and artisans" who had been forcefully deported from the imperial city.[349] That some of these intellectuals were immediately killed in İstanbul and others at their destinations was noted in another account.[350] Still another described how the property left behind in İstanbul was confiscated by the Ottoman state.[351] The forced Armenian deportations from Adapazarı were mentioned in passing in the memoirs of an Ottoman official.[352] In addition to most of the Armenians of the capital who were not deported, the only other exception took place in the city of Smyrna (İzmir), and three memoirs commented on this exception to the rule.[353] All noted the role played by the prominent CUP member and Smyrna governor Rahmi Bey, who prevented the Christians in his province from being deported. One could surmise that Smyrna's being a major commercial port of the empire inhabited by many foreigners also enabled Rahmi Bey to stand his ground.

The accounts of the Armenian deportations from Eskişehir, Tokat, and Konya are much more detailed due to the personal engagement of five memoir writers in the process, three Muslim Turks and two Armenian deportees.[354] One official had been stationed at Eskişehir as an inspector.[355] After noting that at the advent of 1915 the CUP İstanbul deputy delivered a speech there, likening "the Christian elements among the Turks [of the empire] to snakes and scorpions," the account specified that "some officials, the gendarmerie and the police" exercised the most cruelty against the Armenians. The account then stated:

> It was said that the gravest calamities had occurred in Bursa and Ankara. The ones who had arrived [in Eskişehir, which was on the deportation route] from Ankara narrated sorrowfully how the houses had been blockaded, hundreds of Armenian families were loaded onto carriages, and [many] dumped in streams. Many women witnessing these atrocities had lost their mind. The houses of the wealthy Armenians were purchased and, as soon as the official document for the transfer of property was issued, the monies were forcefully and cruelly taken back.

The account of an actual Armenian deportee provided more detail on the other deportation routes. According to this writer,[356] the CUP removed the Armenian population

> living in the towns and villages starting from Tekirdağ in Thrace, from İzmit-Adapazarı-Bahçecik-Afyonkarahisar-Kütahya, in short from all the provinces along the Baghdad railroad and in convoys accompanied by the gendarmerie, deporting them all the way to the Arabian deserts. Most of the men were killed en masse before setting out on the road. The [remaining] masses comprising mostly women, elderly, and the children lost their lives on the roads due to starvation, epidemics such as typhoid and typhus fever, and attacks with knives and axes. Some of those who succeeded in reaching Aleppo were killed in Aleppo, in

places such as Deyrzor, Meskene, Resül Ayn... due to starvation and dehydration as well as with axes and guns.... Among these people were also members of my family who got the chance to return.

As a consequence of these deportations, Central Anatolia "that had been a grain depot before the deportation of the Armenians was now struggling with hunger."[357] One local notable at Eskişehir who benefited from the Armenian deportations described what happened, somewhat uncertain about the destructive role he personally played, namely, overseeing the process, plundering the goods, and then cheaply purchasing all the shops the Armenians left behind.[358] Another memoir writer remembered that when the deportation order for Tokat came in July 1915, many Armenian girls were converted to Islam and married off to local Muslims; the rest went on the deportation, never to be heard from again.[359] The memoir of the other Armenian deportee chronicled his family's deportation from Karaman, Konya.[360]

The memoirs of three Ottoman officials and one Armenian deportee provided details of the Armenian deportations from Kayseri and Adana.[361] The Kayseri mayor and CUP member noted how he took it upon himself to organize the local Armenian deportations, recruiting men with whom to execute the deportations as follows:[362]

> Zekai Bey requested that I choose a particular town, taking along with me the men I wanted to oversee the deportation proceedings there; he addressed my [nationalist?] feelings [to get me to accept]. I then organized a committee comprising the CUP responsible secretary Cemil Bey, the municipal assembly member Feyzizade Osman Bey, and the policeman (and my relative) Sami Efendi. The military division commander gave... fifteen privates... and ordered the Bünyan district governor to place the security forces of the town under the authority of the [deportation] committee.

After first systematically removing everyone from the villages, the committee then moved to the district center and towns. During this process, some Armenians were protected by their Muslim neighbors who hid them away. At this juncture, the deportation committee took care to ensure no one profited from this deportation except the military and the state; the perishable goods left behind were utilized to feed the army and the populace. The committee also ordered that a register be kept of the inventories of all abandoned goods, including the estimated value of each item within a house and its description and quantity, as well as all the produce that was sold, including who purchased it and for what price. The account also recorded with great care the abuses committed by the local Muslim populace who plundered what the Armenians had to leave behind, also detailing the violence committed against the Armenians during the deportation process. Because such detailed information on what actually happened to the Armenians is rarely found, this formal list is presented here in its entirety:

> Zeki, the district governor of Develi; gendarmerie sergeant Muharrem; gendarmerie privates Dursun, Hacı Tahir, Melek Gazi, Küçük Süleyman, Ömer, Osman, İbrahim: For torturing and causing bodily harm while questioning those Armenians whose names are written in the investigation documents—need to try for murder according to articles 45 and 103. District governor Zeki: (In addition to the abovementioned), the extortion and rape of a woman. Subdistrict governor Zekai; Sezai, the judge of Develi; police officers Rükni, Halil; ranking police officer Asım; Halil, the Bünyan district governor; Kevkep, the subdistrict administrative director: For murdering and causing to have murdered many Armenians—need to try for murder according to articles 45 and 103. Celal, the subdistrict administrative director; gendarmerie corporal Hüseyin; corporal Abdurrahman; Ömer; Şükrü; Mehmet: Need to try for torture according to article 103. [Local] notable Katipzade Nuh Naci; merchant Hacı Kamil; merchant Bıçakçıoğlu Mehmet; policeman Ahmet: For opening Yazıcıyan's shop and taking his commercial goods—need to try in accordance with article 220. Secretary general Sabri; chief clerk of the provincial subdivision council Nurullah; notable İmamzade Reşid; notable Hayrullah; notable Taşçızade Ömer; his brother Mehmet; his brother Hüseyin; notable Karabeyzade Mustafa; notable Kürkçüzade Ömer; notable Germirli Ali Efendi: For conspiring through devious means to reduce the price of the abandoned properties and goods below the market value and for purchasing them with such lowered prices—even though this fits article 239, no need for public trial due to the expiration of the time period within which to file a suit [against them]. Public prosecutor Ziya; Tevfik, president of the war council; Halim, president of the commission for abandoned properties and goods: For abusing their office by purchasing the goods they were given for safeguarding—even though this fits the first section of article 82, no need for public trial due to the expiration of the time period within which to file a suit [against them]. Osman, the subdistrict administrative director: For beating up some Armenians—even though it fits article 179, no need for public trial due to the expiration of the time period within which to file a suit [against him]. Mihran Yazıcıyan: Undertake action according to article 65.

The list details the complicity of many Muslim Turks, including local notables, officials, and officers, in not only inflicting harm on the deported Armenians but also plundering what was left behind. In many cases, no legal action was taken due to time limits on prosecuting those who committed such violence. There are probably many such lists in the Ottoman and republican archives, and detailed documentation of the Armenian properties at the Directorate of Title Deeds and Cadasters (*Tapu ve Kadastro Müdürlüğü*), but the refusal of the Turkish state to make these sources fully available to scholars prevents the determination of the entire scope of the collective violence.

In Adana, an Ottoman official recounted meeting with the local Muslim notables who had prepared a list of all Armenians they wanted deported even though the deportation order of Adana Armenians had not yet been issued.[363] Another account criticized the state measures taken during the deportations of the Adana and Aleppo Armenians.[364] The most poignant and extensive account of the Adana Armenians was provided by the account of an Armenian deportee, describing how his mother and father died in front of his eyes when he was only nine years old. He also witnessed the massacre of entire convoys, noting the role of the Germans in the process. Also significant was the destruction of the Assyrian villages he personally witnessed.[365]

The Armenian deportations from Mamuretülaziz (Elazığ), Dersim, Muş, and Bingöl were discussed in the accounts of two Ottoman officers and three Kurdish intellectuals.[366] While one Kurd who at the time was working as a veterinarian for the Ottoman army witnessed "the massacre of the Armenian convoys of Erzurum-Erzincan-Trabzon at the Kemah gorge,"[367] another narrated how a famous Armenian bard in the region had survived the massacres as a child by begging for food.[368] Still another Kurdish intellectual claimed that in Muş, the Turkish commander ordered the Kurds to murder the Armenians, also stating that at times the Turkish soldiers burned down Kurdish villages and then blamed the Armenians.[369] One Ottoman officer narrated the destruction of deported Armenians as his division retreated toward Damascus; especially between Meskene and Deyr Zor, he saw "on the two sides of the road unburied corpses of those among the refugee convoys who had fallen sick and died."[370] Another Ottoman officer recounted as follows an abandoned Armenian village named Temran near Kiğı that his unit passed by:[371]

> During the rest stop, I toured the village. There is no mosque here, only a largish Armenian church. I guess the village must have been entirely Armenian. I walked through the church very thoroughly. There was quite a large library inside. I quickly looked through some of the books written entirely in the Armenian script. The beautifully bound books with the pictures of Jesus, Mary, and the Apostles in them have been

> torn to pieces and thrown on the ground. The bookshelves have been destroyed. The pews in the church were also missing. It is like an empty warehouse.

The Armenian villagers were undoubtedly deported before the officer's unit had arrived there. The same officer then noted how the region suffered economically because the Armenian artisans were no longer there to produce basic amenities.

The Armenian deportations from Diyarbekir are described in full detail by eight accounts by four Ottoman Turkish officials, three Kurds, and one Armenian.[372] Two themes run across these accounts; the Ottoman officials comment on the violent acts of Dr. Mehmet Şahingiray, a CUP and SO member as well as the Diyarbekir governor during the massacres, and the others provide eyewitness accounts of Kurdish notables and an Armenian deportee of the massacres. How Şahingiray was able to decimate the Armenian strongholds in Diyarbekir is narrated by one Kurdish intellectual.[373] His horrific account of Governor Şahingiray's machinations to get rid of the Armenians at all costs was also confirmed by the account of another Ottoman Turk whose father and other officials were murdered by Şahingiray for protesting the violent Armenian deportations.[374] The dire consequences of the governor's violence were detailed in other accounts. Two Kurdish intellectuals documented how many local Kurds personally witnessed the atrocities.[375] The narration of the Armenian deportee revealed how the Armenians who had once been wealthy were reduced, if they survived the massacres, to mere servants as a consequence of the deportations.[376]

Why did Dr. Mehmet Reşid Şahingiray engage in such atrocious violence that earned him the nickname "Butcher"? Clues are provided by the accounts of Şahingiray himself and also the CUP general secretary who specifically asked the doctor that question.[377] Şahingiray's account dismissed the murders of the officials attributed to him, stating that instead either the Armenian bands or the Kurdish brigands in the region were responsible. He then argued that "the precautions taken in relation to the Armenian issue were a matter of life or death to the Turkish populace and undertaken as legitimate defense.... Ottoman history is replete with the murders and calamaties committed during the many massacres and rebellions of non-Muslim communities." When the CUP general secretary wondered how Reşid Bey, a physician charged with saving lives, could throw so many into the lap of death, "he looked at my face and, after a long silence, answered me as sternly as I had addressed him: 'Being a physician could not make me forget my nationality,... My nationality comes before all else,... It was going to be either them or us,... Put another way, they are the ones who provoked us to act for the legitimate defense of ourselves.' " When the general secretary then queried: "Doctor, doesn't such behavior bother your conscience?" the latter responded, "Of course it does. But I did not act as such for my personal pride or gain. I saw that the fatherland was going to be lost, closed my eyes for the good of the country, and I fearlessly stepped forward." Yet the general secretary did not stop there. "What about historical responsibility?" he asked next. The response he received was "If I am held responsible by history for my deeds, so be it. I do not care about what the other nations write about me now or in the future." This exchange reveals the jaundiced view of a radical nationalist who, like another doctor, Bahaeddin Shakir, perceived the world only in black and white, and without any moral anchor whatsoever in humanity at large. National interests came before all else, and anyone who was perceived as threatening these interests became fair game. Nationalist radicalism trumped even the ethical stand necessary for a physician, that is, placing the saving of human lives before all else.

The deportations of the Armenians in Urfa, Maraş, and Antep are documented by three accounts.[378] The account on Urfa is noteworthy in that the Ottoman commander described the resistance the local Armenian initially put up in September 1915 to no avail; the commander concluded his narration by noting the Turks who perished, not remarking at all on the thousands of Armenians who died as well.[379] The other two accounts reveal the inherent Turkish nationalism that percolates through many recollections of the Muslim Turks, whitewashing the crimes of the perpetrators.[380] Indeed, one writer actually thanked and lauded the vile actions of Talat and Bahaeddin Shakir, praying for their souls and stating that he constantly heard such prayers from the local Muslim populace.

The Armenian deportations and massacres in Aleppo, Damascus, and Syria were discussed in great detail by ten contemporaneous accounts.[381] In all, Cemal Pasha, the CUP leader and commander of the Fourth Army in Syria, emerged as a significant figure negotiating the safety of the deported Armenians, since most who survived ended up in his province. Three incidents in particular reveal Cemal's interpretation. The first pertained to his treatment of the deported Armenians, the second to the vast number of Armenian orphans, and the third to the perpetrators of the violence against the Armenians. First, Cemal Pasha initially reacted to the Zeytoun rebellion of March 1915 by asking the Ottoman state to remove these Armenians to central Anatolia; instead, Talat sent them to the southeast of Aleppo and the vicinity of Zor and Urfa.[382] In his attempt to secure Turkish rule in the region, Cemal was concerned at the time to reduce Arab dominance, often by resorting to violence against the Arabs.[383] He therefore saw the deported Armenians as an element that could counterbalance the Arab dominance. Unlike the prevalent CUP practice, he therefore provided them with food, shelter, and clothing.[384] Still, many Armenians suffered from illness and epidemics due to the adverse conditions in which they traveled, and these threatened the health of the Ottoman army. This might be still another reason for Cemal's care of the Armenians.[385] All along, the Ottoman military commanders had ultimate authority to decide on which Armenians to remove for "being harmful"; one of Cemal Pasha's aides argued that many such orders were sent for the removal of such Armenians, explicitly leaving blank the space on the document specifying where they were to be deported.[386] Still, Cemal did open a hospital in Aleppo to take care of the sick.[387]

Second, the forced deportations and deaths of hundreds of thousands of Armenians generated a vast number of Armenian orphans, so much so that three orphanages had to be opened. Many prominent Turks like Lütfi Kırdar and Halide Edip Adıvar worked at these orphanages. Yet tensions arose when Cemal wanted to convert the Armenian orphans to Islam.[388] It is evident that he wanted to further Turkify the orphans and viewed their acceptance of Islam as well as new Muslim names as an inherent part of that Turkification.

Third, Cemal had to personally negotiate the cases of prominent Armenians sent to his region because he was also the top local political and military authority. The Ottoman deputies Krikor Zohrab and (Ohannes) Vartkes (Serengülyan) who had been sent from the capital on trumped-up charges to be court-martialed in Van arrived in Damascus. They asked for Cemal's intervention on their behalf, and Cemal telegraphed Talat, requesting their settlement in Lebanon. Talat replied to let them continue as they would not be harmed. Yet two SO members murdered the deputies en route. Cemal was furious and ultimately had the two tried and hanged within a day.[389] These men had not only massacred thousands of Armenians but had also personally murdered the Ottoman deputies Zohrab and Vartkes with their bare hands. Still, their execution was an exception rather than the rule. They got into trouble for disobeying Cemal Pasha's orders. Interestingly enough, the bloodstained gold coins and jewelry they had plundered from their Armenian victims were used against them not because of the crimes they committed to get the coins in the first place but because they had not turned them into the Ottoman state treasury as had been decided by the CUP. It is evident that at some level Cemal was indeed aware of the violence he committed against the non-Turkish and non-Muslim elements of the empire.[390] Still, in his memoirs, he selectively reiterated the suffering not of the Armenians but instead of the Turks. Cemal queried: "How is it that the Turks are responsible for the Armenian massacres, but Armenians are not responsible for the general wretchedness and massacres of the Turks and the Kurds? Or is it that the value of a Turk and a Kurd is, as it is in the eyes of [Western] politicians such as Morgenthau and Mandelstam, at par with that of a fly?" Once again, the CUP's nationalism reared its ugly head to legitimate the collective violence committed against the Armenians by referring to the wretched conditions and suffering of the Turks.

"Just Turks" Resisting the Armenian Deportations and Massacres

Throughout the execution of the Armenian deportations, there were also many "just Turks" who fervently opposed such CUP violence, often at the cost of their own lives. Six memoirs noted the actions of such just Turks.[391] Probably the most detailed account of such protest by the Bursa governor Ali Osman Bey to the CUP deportation order revealed the speed with which the CUP removed dissenting officials, and it could do so because Talat was the interior minister and the grand vizier.[392] Another official who opposed the CUP actions was the Kütahya governor Faik Ali Bey; an Armenian deportee lauded him as the only man who tried to save the Armenians by personally acting as a guarantor to them.[393] Of course, İzmir governor Rahmi Bey needs to be recognized for single-handedly protecting the Armenians of his province, using his influence within the CUP to do so.[394] Another official mentioned in the memoirs is the Lice district governor who protected the Armenians, saving many from being massacred.[395] Also, the Ottoman general Vehip Pasha was known for protecting the Armenians and especially the Greek Rum during the forced deportations; the account conjectured that he did so because he was originally from Yanya in the Balkans.[396] Of course, the best-known instance of Ottoman officials who protected the Armenians, paying for their actions with their lives, are the Basra governor Ferit, the Müntefek district governor Bedii Nuri, the deputy district governor of Beşiri, and the Lice district governor Hüseyin Nesimi. They were all murdered upon the orders of the Diyarbekir governor Dr. Mehmet Reşid Şahingiray.[397]

There probably are countless others, Turk and non-Turk alike, who attempted to help, successfully or not, but they are not recorded in the surveyed contemporaneous memoirs. Oral histories conducted with the Armenian survivors may enable this modest list to grow over time. In all, this detailed discussion of contemporaneous memoirs reveals the extent of CUP collective violence as narrated by Muslim Turkish officers and officials. The careful documentation of such violence will hopefully enable the contemporary Turks to recognize what happened in their past as narrated by their own ancestors. At this juncture it is essential to understand why there was—and still is—such staunch resistance to acknowledging this collective violence. The next section identifies the events that enabled contemporaneous Muslim Turks to rationalize the collective violence committed against the Armenians.

1912–13 Balkan Wars as the Legitimating Event of CUP Collective Violence

Certain events in a country's history become pivotal in redefining the cultural framework of both state and society, and eventually legitimating future courses of action, including collective violence. In the case of CUP rule from 1908 to 1918, the tragedy and devastation of the Balkan Wars, I argue, legitimated the subsequent collective violence against the non-Muslims of the empire in general, and the Armenians in particular. This legitimation was the consequence of a long process of failed expectations. At first, the Ottoman government engaged in a war against the Balkan states in 1912–13, certain that the swift and final victory would offset and reverse the decades-long land loss and rebellions in the western provinces of the empire. The newly reformed military was likewise certain of victory in spite of the reservations of a few wise statesmen. The Great Powers were also so sure of an Ottoman victory that they initially insisted that the land status quo in the Balkans would be sustained after the war regardless. Yet the war was disastrous for the empire; it lost 146,100 square kilometers of land, and approximately a million Balkan Turks were either massacred or escaped to the empire with nothing except the clothes on their backs.[398] In the end, the population of the empire decreased by 5 million, corresponding to a loss of about a quarter of all land mass. It was tragic that most of those provinces considered to be the most technologically and industrially advanced due to their proximity to Western Europe were lost; these had also been the provinces that generated the most resources for the empire. The Ottoman administration not only had to heal and settle the flooding refugees but also found out that the Great Powers "betrayed" the Ottoman empire by changing their argument about maintaining the prewar status quo. "Once the cross replaced the crescent," the argument went, "reversal was impossible."[399]

This disastrous state of affairs led the CUP that had been in opposition to stage the first successful military coup in Ottoman history in January 1913. The CUP thus assumed full control of the government and the state. And the conflict among the Balkan states over dividing the spoils of war enabled the CUP to recover the former imperial city of Adrianople that had been initially conquered by the Bulgarians. Thus, somewhat enabling the Ottoman Empire to regain the gravely injured Ottoman pride and self-esteem, the Balkan Wars nevertheless indelibly and irretrievably altered relations between the Turks and the rest of the Ottoman populace, especially the non-Muslims, for the worse. All contemporaneous memoirs consistently identify the Balkan Wars as the trigger that legitimated Turkish nationalism and the ensuing Turkish prioritization of securing a fatherland at the expense of all the rest. These emotions of devastation, betrayal, and escalating vengeance to remove the stained Ottoman pride in turn helped rationalize the ensuing and much more devastating collective violence committed against the Armenians during World War I. The denial of the intent to cause such devastation quickly ensued.

Politics of the Disastrous Balkan Wars

The Balkan Wars emerged as a consequence of the interaction of contentious domestic policies with foreign policy blunders. Contemporaneous memoirs fully articulate these dynamics.[400] All were disappointed in the inability of the Ottoman parliament, established with the hope of resolving all the imperial problems, to be effective. While the CUP members blamed the criticisms of non-Turkish deputies, others instead pointed to the CUP political practice of determining its domestic policy by putting its own interests before all else. "When the Unionists started to lose their majority in the Ottoman Parliament in 1911," one account stated, "[they determined] the only way out was dissolving the parliament."[401] Yet this cost the CUP because the new parliament elected in 1912 could not contain the CUP opposition. Another account conjectured that the CUP actually mishandled the escalating crisis in the Balkans, thereby not being able to prevent the advent of war; not only did the CUP lack knowledge and inexperience in responding to crises in the region, but it often intervened to late and without adequate preparation. "The Balkan states keep holding military and political agreement deliberations right under your nose, finalizing their war preparations while you squander the haphazardly put together forces at a civil war against a handful of rebels on the mountains of Albania and, not even managing to take care of this, [have to] leave the government," one account complained.[402] The ultimate CUP fault was the way in which the CUP then blamed the opposition government of Kamil Pasha for all the ensuing failures.

Another account emphasized the CUP's inability to formulate a proper foreign policy for dealing with the emerging problems in the Balkans. The CUP, the account argued, always preferred advocating the use of force instead of peaceful solutions. Specifically, the Albanians rebelled "because CUP had decided to eliminate the political opposition, therefore intervening [politically] to ensure that none of the Albanian candidates were elected." The CUP employment of political force in the elections to get their predominantly Muslim Turkish candidates elected caused the Albania rebellions, thereby conveniently eliminating the obstacles the Albanians would have presented to the union of all Balkan countries. The CUP likewise failed to establish an effective administration in the province of Macedonia. The account noted:[403]

> It was the war in Tripoli... that in turn triggered the Balkan Wars: the European powers instigated the Balkan countries to war to draw attention away from Tripoli.... In Crete, even though the Muslims formed only 20 percent of the population, the CUP followed a very aggressive and noncompromising policy that alienated the Greek Rum.... Under the influence of the [aforementioned] calamities, a hand drew the

> [Ottoman] state into this maelstrom. This time, those who had become used to organizing demonstrations with shouts of "Crete or death!," "Tripoli or death!" made the populace wear hats with the words "Sofia or death!" and shout [in protest]. Yet [in the end], there was neither Crete nor Tripoli left in the empire. Let alone entering Ṣofia, the entire Balkans slipped off our hands. As for those [CUP instigators], nothing happened to them.

The CUP started advocating such a policy due to its inherent vision, which placed the interests of the dominant Muslim Turkish majority above all other elements of the empire. By not giving any agency to these elements, and by not being willing to listen to their complaints and act upon them, the CUP's only recourse was violence and suppression, a recourse that was bound to unite all the Balkan states against the empire. This inherent vision first became public with the 1908 constitutional revolution as the CUP promised the recovery of all imperial lands that had been lost over the course of previous centuries.

Escalating Publicly Expressed Frustration

Such a promise made the utter devastation the Ottoman army suffered in the Balkan Wars all the more dramatic and distressing. One account captured the ensuing Ottoman public disappointment well:[404]

> [With the advent of the 1908 constitutional revolution], according to what we children and the populace gathered from the newspapers and the speeches, we [the Ottoman Empire] were about to reconquer all that was lost by the last few sultans. We even sang the songs of [conquering] Buda[pest]. Given these lofty dreams, the reality that they had to confront in relation to the Balkans was even harsher to absorb: after Bosnia and Hercegovina, the independence of Bulgaria, followed by Crete! In reality, none of these were novel developments: for quite some time, they had been a part of the empire [only] nominally. But... it felt as if all was happening because of the constitution.

Such failed expectations along with the CUP violence in dealing with all the expressed criticism led the populace to take a stand against the CUP. Rather than addressing these concerns, however, the CUP reacted by escalating its violence. One account pointed out the negative consequence of the union of all imperial elements that the constitutional revolution advocated in theory but could not execute in practice. As a consequence, rather than uniting with the Turks, the

Balkan elements, namely, the Greeks, Serbians, and Bulgarians, instead united to get the Turks out of the Balkans.[405]

Also significant in these dire developments was the pro-war rhetoric the CUP advocated at all costs. Five memoirs discuss the various dimensions of this rhetoric.[406] The CUP considered the war as an opportunity to regain lands. It assumed that the Balkan states—that had been imperial subjects prior to gaining sovereignty in the course of the nineteenth century—would not constitute a true threat. The CUP was therefore certain that victory would be swift and that all the previously lost Balkan lands would be quickly recovered. As a consequence, the CUP not only mobilized the populace of the capital, and especially the students in pro-war demonstrations, but actually participated in them. One account described this process well:[407]

> We, the İstanbul youth, wanted war and took to the streets led by the spokesmen of the [CUP] Unionist clubs whose voices were hoarse by giving one to two dozen public speeches a day. Flags in our hands, we shouted in unison the march "Crete is our heart and soul!" ... We cared neither about the government proclamations nor the police. "War, war!" We were going to take back the eastern Balkans from Bulgaria, Thesselia from Greece, Nissa [*Niş*] from Serbia. Okay, we were merely [CUP] clubs; we had bought many arms in the last couple of years. It was said that we should actually be glad about the rumors of impending war since we were going to defeat [the Balkan states] anyhow. Other than the Western civilized world, no one could withstand this flow of the people's will for war.... So everyone was for war.

Another account concurred that the CUP adamantly supported such a war, recounting that prominent CUP members like Talat Bey and the Ottoman deputy Hallaçyan Efendi were among the people demonstrating at the palace gardens.[408] Many similar demonstrations ensued.[409] The war enabled the CUP to act as the savior of the empire, thereby giving it the opportunity to regain influence. In particular, "the feelings of animosity of the Balkan states ... their war preparations and actions such as forming a 'sacred war alliance' against Turkey had deeply hurt our national feelings and the arousal of emotions reached its utmost level," the memoir concluded. The CUP benefited from this general sorrow to exploit the first gunshots at the Bulgarian war front to mobilize national feelings. The Smyrna CUP came alive with exuberance at the declaration of war. Such feelings were accompanied with incendiary articles mostly written by CUP members.[410] For instance, one such poem written on occasion of the war claimed: "From every bit of soil I tread upon, blood will spurt / From under the claw I extend, spring will turn into autumn / If

I leave stone upon stone, may the hearth I leave behind be extinguished / With my bayonet, I shall turn rose gardens into cemeteries / Leaving to history an utterly leveled ruin, upon which civilization will not bloom for ten centuries."[411] The same fervor had even penetrated into the schools.[412] Students sang patriotic songs and recited poems at the top of their voices, insisting that "honor can only be cleaned by blood, and they were going to spill blood in the Balkans in the name of Turkishness to acquire fame." The ensuing war is in turn summarized by all contemporaneous accounts as being totally disastrous.[413] Russian secret documents later revealed not only that the Russians had gotten all Balkan countries to sign a joint pact, but that the Ottoman state was also aware of this pact but entered the war regardless.[414] In addition, the Russians also raised money for the Balkan state armies from the Caucasus and Kars down to the remotest villages.[415]

Once the war was declared, the Ottoman army experienced a disastrous defeat for a number of reasons. Contemporaneous accounts identify five factors that led to the defeat: (1) the recent military discharge of large contingents of soldiers from the Balkans; (2) the military reforms that decimated the experienced officer cadres, replacing them with young, inexperienced officers; (3) the ensuing unpreparedness of the reformed army; (4) the lack of armaments, provisions, and communication; and (5) a politicized military that prioritized political loyalty over making the right military decisions. About 75,000 to 80,000 soldiers of Balkan origin in the Third Army, born in 1888 or earlier, had been decommissioned two weeks before the war. When the war started, only a third of this number could be recruited, and all lacked their predecessors' experience. As a consequence, the Ottoman army had 250,000 soldiers on the battlefield to face the 510,000 of the other side.[416] The recent CUP reform of the Ottoman officer corps had retired almost 285 former commanders.[417] The lower ranks had also been transformed. Enver Bey, who had been quickly promoted through two ranks to achieve a senior position at a very young age, made these decisions. Although the former commander in chief had proposed decommissioning only 300 former officers, Enver ended up retiring almost 1,500 and did so not solely on the basis of age but lack of loyalty to the CUP.[418] The ensuing lack of communication among the remaining officers and the absence of effective vertical command due to the youth of the appointed officers were significant factors that contributed to the defeat.

The hastily put together Ottoman army had almost no training prior to the war. One memoir writer stated that his older brother who was an officer had said that the soldiers under his command "were so unprepared that they were going to learn how to use arms at the front.... They set on the road that night, got off the train at the front, and all, including my brother who commanded them, died right away."[419] Of the recruited reserves, "more than a third in each battalion had never fired a rifle in their lives and had not at all been trained in military discipline, leading them to immediately dissolve."[420] Not only was there a lack of reserves but also an absence of reconnaissance patrols.[421] Yet, the high command was so certain of victory that it did not summon the reserve forces in Syria, Iraq, and East Anatolia. And the recruited went to war in great spirits, certain of their victory; at the capital, "day and night, wagons full of battalions of army reserves from various parts of Anatolia came, marching in front of us shouting in unison with the entire strength of their larynxes cries of hatred and vengeance that left long echoes in our ears."[422] Indeed, the Ottoman state was so sure that it would eradicate all the Balkan states within a month that the war minister, Nazım Pasha, "had instructed all the Ottoman officers to have their official uniforms on the battlefield and to not take them off until entering Sofia, Belgrade, and Athens. When the war commenced, they had [thus] donned their official uniforms as if victory was theirs for certain."[423]

Those few who did fight lacked armaments. During the first two weeks of the general mobilization, the Anatolian recruits joined the Vardar army to fight the Greeks at only 10 percent capacity and with missing arms and clothing; the Western Army thus had only half the numbers it should have had.[424] The Ottoman lack of armaments, which had to be purchased from the West, was palpable. When the Ottoman military command applied to Western European states to purchase especially cannon and howitzer shells, all, including Germany, refused to sell them; in addition, the Balkan armies quickly seized the Ottoman armaments of the retiring army to then employ these weapons against them.[425] It was especially difficult to make use of the remaining field guns around which battles were fought because these would quickly get stuck in the mud due to the lack of the necessary infrastructure.[426]

The lack of provisions and supplies was another major obstacle. Until then, each Ottoman battalion used to carry its provisions, and each soldier had enough food to sustain him for three days. The modernizing reforms after the German model led to the abandonment of such precautions, not taking into account that the new model had assumed a steady food supply. Here was another example of adopting the form without negotiating the necessary content. As a consequence, there was widespread hunger among the soldiers. The army starved, dying from hunger and illness; the retreating soldiers had not had "anything to eat for weeks or even months other than a handful of corn, devoid of any medicine that could have saved them from illness, totally severed from the rest of the world, devoid of even an iota of that famous morale, losing not only his identity but his entire existence."[427] The provisioning of the army was so poorly planned that, after the war, "four train wagons filled to the brim with shovels and pickaxes necessary for building trenches were discovered in an abandoned lot at the Sirkeci train station in İstanbul; they had never been sent."[428]

Political infighting that had entered the Ottoman military with the CUP also caused havoc. Some CUP officers refused to work for the victory of the opposition government; as a consequence, the officers did not coordinate their maneuvers among themselves, often ending up attacking unsuccessfully without each other's support.[429] Some accounts take this contention further. One alleged that because the CUP cared more about deposing the opposition party through a defeat than winning the war, it sent representatives who infiltrated the ranks of the Anatolian soldiers, telling them, "What should you care about the Balkans, your fatherland is in Anatolia. Oh, do not sacrifice your life for nothing! The government is traitorous and wants to destroy you intentionally."[430] Another claimed that the strategic plans for a possible war initially prepared by the CUP cadre were not followed.[431] It also did not help that an experienced commander like Mahmud Şevket Pasha had informed Talat and the education minister, Şükrü Bey, about the poor state of the Ottoman military, thereby trying to stop them from making the decision to enter the war. Yet "the behavior of these men who did not at all heed what they had been told was almost insane."[432]

Experiencing the First Full-Scale Public Trauma

The ensuing massacres of the Balkan Muslim Turks are told in detail by many accounts, revealing the extent of the trauma of the Ottoman populace that had been readying itself for a very quick victory.[433] The Ottoman newspapers initially did not reveal the battles the Ottoman army had lost, stating instead that the Bulgarians were expected at any minute to withdraw to their borders, when they were in fact winning the battles. Likewise, the Serbian conquest of Monastir was not reported; the newspapers instead claimed that the Ottoman commanders had decided to move the army to another location for strategic reasons, leading many to believe that Monastir was not lost, and that Salonica had been reconquered when it was not. They also failed to mention that many Ottoman soldiers had become prisoners of war, losing their arms and ammunitions.[434] Yet the dire situation was evident to those in the battlefield. One officer recounted losing all his belongings and barely escaping slaughter; he then witnessed the Greeks burning all the Muslim inhabitants of Suruvich near Monastir "with tears in his eyes."[435] As their towns and villages were demolished and burned down, the Turks in Macedonia and Thrace watched thousands of their relatives being massacred by the Bulgarians and other local Christians. "My mind was constantly preoccupied by my parents and my sisters. They must have been raided [by the Bulgarians] at Dedeağaç. What were their fates?" another officer in the battlefield wondered, the thought bringing tears to his eyes and plunging him into deep anxiety.[436] Two others recounted that the Bulgarians and Greeks "attacked civilians, murdering women and children in mosques."[437]

After declaring that the Balkan Wars constituted one of the most catastrophic events of Turkish history, one official recounted the manner in which the Ottoman army experienced a terrifying defeat and a total rout. As the soldiers withdrew in complete disarray without establishing any defense, they responded to queries regarding where they were headed with "To Anatolia, to our villages!" Talat Bey, a volunteer soldier in this army, recounted the calamity by stating that he was "so exhausted from fatigue and hopelessness that [he] could no longer think of the fatherland, the nation, or the state; all his ideals and desires were focused on one thing: Ah! I wish a village appears ahead of me so I could sprawl out on a hayloft and lie down! Sleep and sleep!"[438] One Ottoman journalist, in Salonica at the time, described the ultimate disappointment he experienced. Having been falsely told that 50,000 prisoners of war were being transported there by train the following morning, and that the Turkish populace should go to the train station to greet the victorious Ottoman soldiers, he continued:

> The populace had been thirsting for such news.... We were at the station early the following morning.... Then the train appeared and an applause exploded as it entered the station amid yells of joy. All our eyes are affixed on the windows, but they had Greek caps and Greek bayonets. Instead of the 50,000 prisoners of war we expected, 50,000 Greek soldiers had arrived.... We returned in tears. As the Greek soldiers marched into the city in rows, we did not even have the courage to look at them. We were so unhappy; our eyes wet. The populace was hit hard emotionally.... We had lost Salonica. We had lost Thrace. This part of the Ottoman Empire that had turned gangrenous was torn off and taken away from us.

The end result of the Balkan Wars was an immense feeling of shame. As the Bulgarians marched victoriously all the way to the outskirts of the Ottoman imperial capital, the Ottoman army withdrew in total disarray. What made the Ottoman defeat especially difficult and poignant was that the Turks "were fleeing in front of those who a half century ago had been their shepherds."[439]

Worse still, hundreds of thousands of refugees flooded the empire ahead of the Bulgarian army. Just like the 1878 flood of Muslim Turkish refugees in the aftermath of the '93 War with Russia, the 1912 Balkan War ended with another flood. For the second time in its history, the settlement of refugees became a significant state issue.[440] The Directorate of Refugees kept sending the refugees "to Anatolia in droves," while at least 40,000 to 50,000 ill and neglected ones remained behind at the capital.[441] With this flood, the populace of the imperial capital also witnessed the trauma of the Balkan Wars.[442] The impact of this trauma is evident in contemporaneous memoirs through the accounts of those who were refugees, who lost family members to the war, or who observed the refugees in their city, in some cases listening to the refugees' harrowing accounts. After noting that he belonged to a Balkan refugee family settled in Balikesir in the aftermath of the 1878 war with Russia, one memoir writer remembered that his father was martyred during the Balkan War. His father's body was never recovered, but the writer eventually found out that his father had been killed by the Bulgarians during the defense of Adrianople. His father's death was followed by the death of his mother out of grief, causing the family to relocate to the capital.[443] One journalist remarked that he was a Balkan refugee who had barely escaped, along with many others, with only their lives, losing everything they once owned. Most of his relatives "died during the Balkan war either under the bayonets of the Bulgarians or during the migration [to the empire]."[444] The family of another memoir writer remained in the Balkans. Their properties included a large office building, about twenty shops, and a large, lucrative fruit garden, but it became increasingly difficult for them to preserve their properties as the Greek state confiscated, for instance, their fruit garden based on the claims of two Greek priests that a holy person had been buried there.[445]

More telling were the imperial city dwellers' reactions to the despair and destitution of the Balkan refugees they suddenly found in their midst. One writer stated that "İstanbul and especially the Sirkeci area [where the train station was located] transformed into the Day of Judgment with miserable crowds of soldiers and civilians mixed into each other, swelling, overflowing streets and cramming up all the public squares and mosque courtyards. What was this? It could not be called a portrayal of military defeat. This was the tragic display of masses of people with their skinny children, pale-faced women, and disheveled men who had barely escaped a *geological* calamity. And who were these people? Our children, our mothers, fathers and brothers.... I passed by them shedding tears of blood."[446] Two others commented on the vast numbers of refugees swamping the city; every space was filled to the brim with the sick and the wounded, where "soldiers walked supporting themselves against the walls on deserted and muddy streets among trembling [civilian] refugees. Never will I cease seeing in my mind's eye the temporary hospitals at Sirkeci and the side streets around it."[447] While the Muslim and non-Muslim families of the city helped the refugees, they could not help prevent the "4,000 to 5000 who perished daily... and the people had to trample the corpses lying on the streets."[448]

While the Balkan refugees settled in the empire, they shared their harrowing tragedies with the rest of the populace.[449] Because of the frequent hair-raising variations of rapes and massacres the refugees narrated, one account noted that "the deadly news delivered by the convoys of migrants on a daily basis poisoned us."[450] Families often welcomed refugees into their homes; one writer stated that "we had done so as well, taking in and feeding with his children a Turkish notable from Zağra and... these refugees [eventually] became like brothers, relatives to us."[451] Two concomitant characteristics made these Balkan subjects very close to the Muslim Turks. Like them, the refugees were also Muslim and Turkish, thereby leading to the emergence of a new visceral connection that did not exist, for instance, with either the non-Muslim or the non-Turkish subjects. So unlike the latter, these Balkan refugees were quickly integrated into both Ottoman society and the imperial body politic.[452] Simultaneously, the Muslim Turks, who possessed a newfound awareness, especially resented the non-Muslim subjects, easily othering them alongside the Christians who had defeated them in the Balkans.

In settling the refugees, local finance chests in the provinces were ordered to absorb the entire expense of this settlement process; the state promised to reimburse them according to the number of refugees settled at a particular location. This process altered relations between Muslims and non-Muslims in the provinces as local population compositions changed in favor of the Muslim Turks. Quickly, the Ottoman officials overseeing the settlement as well as the local populace became agitated by the increased impoverishment in the provinces. The challenge, one noted, was "to see if the 3 million Turks in the Balkans could be settled in Anatolia or not. One needed at least 3 million gold coins for this process that could only be done gradually and over a very long time period."[453] Yet the state did not have either the financial means or the time with which to execute this project.

There was one reprieve during this disastrous period. After the initial victory, the Balkan states commenced to fight among themselves over apportioning the Ottoman spoils of war. The CUP seized this opportunity to first assume the government through a military coup and then seize the former imperial capital of Adrianople back from the Bulgarians. This reconquest enabled the CUP to legitimate its political violence, further fostering Turkish nationalism through this relatively puny victory against the Balkan states. The impact of first the fall and then the CUP recapture of Adrianople is articulated in great detail in many contemporaneous memoirs.[454] The initial fall, one account conjectured, resulted from the inability of Enver and Fethi (Okyar) Pashas to coordinate their attacks, an incompetence that was swept under the rug with the reconquest.[455] Two other memoir writers were officials in Adrianople during the fall of the city to the Bulgarians. It was especially tragic that the city had to "let through the trains filled with provisions and ammunition for the Bulgarian army that had advanced as far as Çatalca to lay siege on the capital."[456] Some Ottoman officers had wanted to blow up a bridge to stop this process, but the cabinet instructed the commander to prevent them from doing so and then decided to give the city up in order to secure peace. As the Ottoman Turks retreated, they witnessed the immediate plunder of all the residences they left behind.

It is significant that many prominent CUP leaders were especially traumatized by the Balkan Wars. Three significant leaders, Talat, Enver, and Bahaeddin Shakir, personally participated in the war. Shakir was in Adrianople heading the Red Crescent when the city was under siege. A contemporaneous account narrated how disraught Shakir was:[457]

> At the hospital, I encountered Bahaeddin Shakir's face darkened by grief and sleeplessness. He asked me about what went on outside. I told him what I had seen. Shakir could not contain himself and cried. Now we all cried for the lost pieces of the fatherland, for the army that lost its honor, for the [Muslim Turkish] populace trodden over by the enemy, and for our stained virtues. A few days later, a new disaster struck as some [Bulgarian] bandit soldiers came to the hospital in the middle of the night. One of the Austrian priests went down, asking them what they wanted. They stated they were there to take Shakir away, and threw him in prison. The poor patriot spent many difficult days in captivity until he was finally exchanged with some Bulgarian captives in Anatolia. As this saddened patriot was leaving Adrianople by train, the Bulgarians entered shrieking victory songs.

Just as Dr. Bahaeddin Shakir was traumatized by the loss of Adrianople, so was Talat, whose family, originally from Adrianople, settled there after the '93 War had turned them into refugees. Enver was likewise born in Macedonia that was now lost as well. Enver never came to terms with the Balkan Wars and was extremely sad about the loss of Thrace, stating:[458]

> How could one forget those plains and plateaus irrigated by the blood of our ancestors; to leave to yesterday's servants those open spaces where the Turkish frontier warriors once rode their horses; to depart from our mosques, tombs, religious lodges, bridges, and castles. To be expelled from the Balkans into Anatolia is something a person cannot bear. I am willing to give the rest of my life to get vengeance from the Greeks, Bulgarians, and Montenegrins.

Enver's emotions were matched by those of Talat. According to Talat's wife, the saddest day in her husband's life "was during the Balkan Wars when Adrianople fell to the enemy.... Talat cried.... That day, for the first time [in my life], I saw him cry."[459] When the CUP general secretary, also originally from the Balkans, remarked that it would be impossible to take Adrianople back with such an exhausted army, Talat insisted, stating that it had to be reconquered at all costs: "If we get Adrianople back, no one will ever be able to remove us from there again!"[460]

Origins of the Ottoman Turkish Public Rage at the West

One prominent theme that runs through many memoirs discussing this unexpected defeat at great length was the Western betrayal of the Ottoman Empire through hypocrisy and duplicity.[461] In reacting to the Balkan Wars, Western Europe had utterly disregarded the traumatic massacres and suffering of the Balkan Muslims, focusing instead on the much lesser Christian suffering. Such hypocrisy in interpreting human suffering was constantly pointed out. At the advent of the Balkan Wars, in order to preserve land integrity after the probable Ottoman victory, the Great Powers had declared that the status quo in the Balkans would be preserved regardless of the outcome of the war.[462] Yet the Great Powers went back on their word when the war ended with the victory of the Balkan states, letting these states keep the conquered lands and properties; many memoirs commented on this as indestructible proof of duplicity.

Western Hypocrisy

During the war, one officer noted that the British and French soldiers in the warships anchored at Dedeağaç witnessed the murders of a thousand Muslim villagers by the Bulgarians right in front of their eyes but did not intervene. Even though "a British and French regiment of a hundred could have landed on shore to prevent the massacre, when the ones killed were Muslims and the ones killing Christians, no one objected to it."[463] A Muslim journalist took a broader view, criticizing Europe's alleged civilized humanitarian values that only had apathy to Turkish suffering and stating that "all those socialists and humanitarians in Europe who mobilized the entire continent in protest when the socialist Ferrer was murdered in Spain did not make a peep when thousands of Muslims were strangled by the Balkan barbarians.... My God, this is so unjust!"[464] "The world civilization exploiting the smallest incidents to intervene in our affairs, acting treacherously toward us was now silenced, reacting with [undue] tolerance. Where was that passionate, intellectual, poetic, philosophical Europe that adored humanity?!... We would have wanted to see the Europe that through the pens of her historians sent floods of curse to past adventures of savagery.... Human rights, agreement among states, national honor, ethical principles, laws of justice, all of them, all had gone bankrupt," another observed.[465] Likewise, an Ottoman intellectual complained that "not a sound was raised from the civilized (!) world protesting 'enough already with this brutality, they too are humans!' On the contrary, in the eyes of the civilized world, these [massacres] remained a worthless film that just kept winding on."[466] Another reiterated the European apathy by stating that "when we suffered the vilest brutality and massacre in the hands of the Bulgarians, Europe did not feel in its heart the slightest stirring to take pity on us."[467] Even though 150,000 Muslim refugees fleeing from the Balkans with nothing was a disgrace of humanity, the European states "that claim to be the protectors of human rights, supposing themselves to be the teachers of the principles of civilization to humanity, did nothing. Had a tenth of the ugly and awful behavior that occurred against the Balkan Muslims had happened to the Christians, all of Europe would have been up in arms, their screams reaching the skies, and all their fleets filling [our] coasts to inform people about this situation day and night," another noted.[468]

It was thus evident to many that Europe refused to recognize collective violence when the Muslim Turks were the victims, not the perpetrators. The Christian-Muslim divide started to appear frequently in the memoirs as a consequence. "What about those unjust massacres in Macedonia, Epyr, and Serbia that cost the lives of 300,000 Muslims!...Why haven't these murders stirred even the slightest degree of compassion among those [Europeans] who raise hell at the slightest false news about an attack on Christians?" one asked.[469] An Ottoman official attempted to explain this unfair Western hypocrisy by arguing that "we are the poor Muslims...the gifts [are instead] bestowed upon the Christian children.... Oh how great you are, the civilization of the twentieth century!"[470] The next inevitable connection was then made between the Christian powers and the non-Muslims serving as soldiers in the Balkan Wars for the first time in recent Ottoman history. Even though many had died fighting for the empire, some had joined the Balkan armies instead. Focusing exclusively on such defecting non-Muslim recruits, one account claimed that "those [non-Muslim soldiers] who were Ottoman subjects...joined the Greek army at [either] the advent of the war...or later to help destroy the Turkish element with the bullets supplied by the Ottomans." Hence, the structural divide between Muslims and non-Muslims once again unfairly brought the betrayal back home.

Yet what seems to have hurt the Ottoman Muslim public the most as a consequence of this hypocrisy was the feeling of total abandonment, the realization that not a single Western European state supported them:[471]

> At the inauspicious [Balkan] wars, almost all the Europeans could not even bother to hide the disgusting joy they felt at the collapse of the Turks....Austria and Italy protected the Albanians; while Albania was occupied by the Serbians and Greeks, these two countries insisted on the independence of Albania and succeeded. The French in Syria, the British in Iraq, and the Russians at the eastern provinces [of the Ottoman Empire] pursued the same policy. It was [only] the Turks and Turks alone who did not have a friend and a protector. While the populace of Adrianople was two-thirds Turkish and at most one-third Greek Rum, some of the Great Powers insisted so much to turn it over to the

> Bulgarians, that [it became evident that] not only did the Turks not have any friends, that words such as justice and humanity did not have any meaning in the Europeans' opinion concerning the Turks.

It could be conjectured that the Ottoman Turks' observation that the rhetoric of European civilization and compassion did not apply to all humans led them to take a much more cynical view of human rights and of Western European civilization. When such skepticism was combined with the observation that they had no friends in the world, the Ottoman Turks probably abandoned the principles of universal moral accountability in their subsequent actions with greater ease.

Western Duplicity

Empires at the height of their power have the luxury to not take notice of other states' reactions. As their power starts to wane, however, political stands of other states gain more significance and influence. In this case, at the advent of the Balkan War, the Ottoman public might not have emphasized Western European declarations regarding the preservation of the status quo in the Balkans regardless of the outcome. Yet at the end of the war, many Ottoman intellectuals certainly took notice, mentioning this promise. Two accounts pointed out the failure of the Great Powers [comprising England, France, Germany, Russia, and Italy] to even mention this diplomatic note.[472] What added insult to injury was the declaration of the French statesman Raymond Poincaré that "the Turks, not the Balkan people, were the savage ones; wherever the cross enters, the crescent can never again prevail."[473] One traced the loss of Ottoman Turkish tolerance toward the non-Turks and non-Muslims of the empire to this particular juncture. After citing the exact declaration, another account also drew a connection to the emergence of Turkish nationalism: "That the West had so blatantly discriminated against the Muslim Turks . . . was one of the major reasons for the eruption of the excessive nationalist feelings among the Turks. . . . It was almost as if this [Western] act subconsciously instilled in some of the Turks that they could only survive through the destruction of those among them who were not Muslim or Turkish."[474]

Origins of Turkish Protonationalism

After the successful military coup, the CUP move to retake Adrianople began with a media campaign. Talat ordered Yunus Nadi of the *Tasvir-i Efkar* newspaper to prepare the Ottoman public opinion. With this campaign, "the foreign states were going to be given the impression that the CUP government was forced into such an action because it could not withstand the public pressure.

So a fierce campaign started in the Unionist press about the need to take the city."[475] Three accounts concur that the CUP employed the Special Organization to reconquer the city.[476] Particularly the SO forces in the eastern provinces were quickly mobilized to liberate the city; Mutki tribe leader Hacı Musa Bey, militia forces commanded by Said Nur, and the Karakeçili tribe leader Durağı Bey led the attack. This could all be actualized because the War Ministry now headed by Enver gave the SO wide-ranging powers to establish a special militia force with this aim in mind. Many were thrilled when the SO forces succeeded in seizing Adrianople from the Bulgarians.[477] One recounted Talat's joy upon running into him two days after the conquest: "Talat's eyes were shining with happiness akin to that of a child.... One of course loves one's fatherland in its totality. Yet there is a particular corner regardless that one is especially attached to with childish feelings. For Talat, Adrianople was that corner."[478] Talat fondly reminisced about his childhood days in a village near the city, about the excitement he felt at seeing the Selimiye mosque for the first time when his father took him there. One account best captured the consequence of the city's reconquest by the CUP, conjecturing it was at that particular juncture that the CUP "started to follow a policy of strong Turkish nationalism.... The sole aim of the CUP then became to either irrevocably Turkify or totally liquidate all the non-Turkish elements."[479]

Many contemporaneous memoirs chronicle this surge of broad nationalist emotions.[480] The initial reaction to the disastrous defeat was one of depression, grief, and self-sacrifice to preserve the empire. This was quickly accompanied by feelings of shame, revenge, and vengeance. Perhaps the most significant emotional consequence was, however, increased polarization among the Ottoman subjects as especially the dominant Muslim Turkish majority lost all trust not only in the West but, by haphazard association, also in all their non-Muslim subjects. This sustained suspicion toward non-Muslim minorities was also accompanied by self-reflection as Muslim Turks became increasingly convinced that Anatolia now remained the last refuge of the Turkish race.

While one account noted that losing the Balkan Wars caused everyone "to fall into total moral depression,"[481] another instead stressed the "great grief that enveloped the entire youth who suddenly started to volunteer in great numbers to join the military."[482] Still another argued that the youth, including him, felt "the pain of this undigested defeat" much more than the elderly, "who had somehow learned to give in to things inescapable."[483] This young man then captured the transformation in the Turkish state of mind as it slipped more and more into nationalism:

> In all the schools, marches of revenge with compositions weirder than the lyrics, and lyrics more quaint than the compositions were being sung.... [A friend said,] "This is bad, because first of all, what is being

> sung is not [actually] music.... Such things [would] then transform within the lives of nations into bottomless wells! We need to abolish an education based on emotions! This is more dangerous for us than other nations because we lose our freedom of thought and action, and get dragged into unnecessary adventures. For two hundred years, we have lived by stating 'let us retake these places from the enemy' and we constantly lost."... The awful development of the Balkan Wars had destroyed many barriers within [Ottoman] society, throwing every problem into the [public sphere for discussion]. Though often receiving laughable and incompetent responses, these issues... like Turkishness, women, individualism, internal development... decentralization and personal initiative... were nevertheless discussed everywhere by everyone. Yet the most important [consequence] was the doubt and dissatisfaction that started to occupy every mind.

Specifically, the ensuing doubt and dissatisfaction might have emotionally set the groundwork for later domestic violence as segments of Muslim Turks acted upon such feelings, commencing not only to exclude and marginalize but also to destroy. Many accounts articulated this process. The CUP leader Cemal Pasha immediately delivered a speech in Fatih, stating that the revenge of the Balkan War was going to be taken sooner or later.[484] One account remarked that "not a few days had passed [after the defeat] when we, who once used to sing 'Crete is our heart and soul,' [instead] started chanting another very solemn, heaving tune like a funeral march 'on [the Islamic calendar year] one thousand... twenty eight... the honor of the Turk... was stained... Oh... Revenge!' "[485] Particulary shameful was the Ottoman army's defeat by their "former shepherds and barkeepers," whom most of the Ottoman public did not even deign to consider proper nation-states. Yet, the latter not only were able to defeat the Turks but did so very thoroughly. It was as if "a stain had been placed upon the nation's forehead with the Balkan War.... at this particular juncture, [one writer] coined the term 'my religion is my rancor' to specify the course the Muslims had decided to take."[486] Other than ideally uniting all Muslims against all Christians, what this course actually consisted of was—as in the case of all such nationalist visions—extremely and purposefully vague. This vision combined Islam with Turkish ethnic identity, producing Turanism, which was especially advocated by Enver Pasha. What Turanism meant in practice was unclear, however. One account queried: "Where was Turan? Was it at the skirts of the Tanrı Mountains or beyond the Maveraünnehir River? Was it beyond the Caucasus? The banks of the Volga River or the Crimea? Was it the homeland of the Uzbeks?" The visceral emotional reaction to the Balkan Wars whitewashed and annulled any serious rational reflection. In addition, such emotions were strong among a significant segment of top CUP members, since "they were either from the Balkans or had held official posts, breathing its air. [The cities of] Salonica, Monastir, Skopje, İşkodra, Yanya, and Kosovo created an ardent desire in them, and causing them to feel the bewilderment and fury of one who had lost everything down to their last penny at the gambling table."[487] Another account articulated what this emotional reaction produced as follows:[488]

> So this soil, this sacred soil molded by our ancestors' glorious history was leaving our possession, gliding away from our hand? Oh my god, this is such terrible, bitter, irreversible decline! Yet no.... No! Sometimes decline brings about an even more glorious birth.... At this moment, fire and sparks sprout from my veins with the agitation of the most fanatical, most fierce nationalist.... My whole spirit, my entire being screams vengeance! vengeance!... If in this century, as in others, humanity is still so far removed from the thoughts of civilization in spite of all the pomp... if there is still no sign of justice among states... if there is not an iota of affection in the heart of the century to be moved and saddened by blood and cruelty.... Yes, so this is how things are.... Then pity upon us as Turks, as Ottomans if we do not scream Vengeance! Vengeance!... From now on, let us rock our children's cradles not with dark supine refrains, but with fiery orations of radiant, vengeful poems.... We should raise in the laps of mothers and the bosoms of schools such a new race, such a new generation that it should not love anything in the world except its fatherland and not feel any emotion other than vengeance.

This ardent surge of radical emotions was indeed going to shape the future course of events during World War I, which commenced only a year later.

Especially significant among these emotions was the feeling of despair as all started to ponder how their particular community could survive and continue to exist under such an interminable onslaught of adversity, in the process irrevocably losing the trust and tolerance they once had, Muslim and non-Muslim alike. Yet, one could argue that this was much harder for the Muslims Turks who had for centuries had such naturalized dominance and such security regarding their empire that was now on the brink of extinction. According to contemporaneous accounts, a visceral survival instinct emerged among the Muslim Turks, one that took the form of abstract fury against the West and the Balkan states, and hatred against non-Muslim elements living in their midst. That the Ottoman non-Muslims had less power and protection than their Western European counterparts made them a much easier, though utterly unfair target. Many memoirs remarked on the escalating distrust toward non-Muslims.[489] One stated that after this terrible calamity, they all started to doubt the future of the empire in general and the future and survival of the Turks in particular, and, as a consequence, "everyone started to look out for themselves."[490] Another commented on the loss of the Turks' trust toward the Ottoman minorities.[491] This was so, a Turkish Muslim journalist conjectured, because during the Balkan War, "many Christians in the Ottoman army had betrayed the Turks."[492] Prominent CUP members started to lecture that what had been defeated in the Balkan Wars was not Turkishness but instead Ottomanism; the war demonstrated that this political vision advocated since the advent of Ottoman mirrored modernity was not a viable ideology. "Turks are a noble nation; they have not been spoiled. If they had administered the government alone by themselves, of course the state would not have faced such calamities.... Experience shows that only the Turks can protect the country's interests," one conjectured.[493] This sentiment was also reflected at the schools, "as one day those non-Muslim, non-Turkish students from the Balkans disappeared" from their school, only to be replaced by Balkan refugees "whose hearts were filled with hatred. They inoculated us with this hatred and we started to lose our traditional feeling of tolerance."[494] Two CUP and SO members remarked that many non-Muslim subjects had financed the military expenses of the victorious Balkan states.[495] One pointed out in particular that such non-Muslims "who had earned those monies on our soil weighed very heavily on our hearts." Yet the immediate reaction to non-Muslims was not physical violence at first but populist economic embargo. Some Turks mobilized to prevent trade and commerce with non-Muslim shop owners, merchants, and tradesmen. Indeed, one CUP and SO member even penned a popular book advocating such a stand, a book that went through many reprints.[496]

It was perhaps unavoidable that such despair would next lead some Turks to conjecture that after the Balkan defeat, they were taking their last stand before their total annihilation as a race.[497] One writer remarked that all the Turks were now left with was "the lands of Anatolia."[498] A prominent Muslim Turkish official shared the same sentiment, stating that "the entire Balkans has been lost; now, we can only rely on Anatolia. The Arab soldier in Syria will never fight; until now, the empire has been defended everywhere by the Turkish soldier."[499] "All the rest are merely words," he concluded. A prominent CUP member recounted the departure from the Turkish Homeland Association of the Albanians and Circassians "as they too had started to perceive that they no longer belonged to the empire now fully dominated by the Turks."[500] The particular betrayal of the empire by Western powers led another CUP member to also take an emotional stand against Europe" "An amazing fire of rebellion was kindled in my heart against political ambitions, European politics and imperialists, and imperialism. I have never been able to put this fire out; it still burns!"[501] After the Balkan Wars, it became almost impossible for some Turks to identify and align with any single social group within the empire or a Western European state outside. "My personal opinion starting with the Balkan war," an Ottoman naval officer declared, "is that the Turk should not expect any friendship from either the Muslim or the Christian states, and trust himself only to his God."[502] In summary, then, the totally unexpected disastrous defeat in the Balkan Wars generated heightened emotions of despair that the extinction of the Turkish race was near. The Turkish rage against the Christians in Europe and the Balkans was projected onto the readily accessible and unprotected ones in their midst, the non-Muslim subjects. The beginning of the Great War the following year destroyed the possibility to rationally reflect on this emotional course toward additional violence. Not only did the CUP commit collective violence against its own unprotected Armenian subjects, but it then kept legitimating such violence by constantly referring to their suffering during the Balkan Wars and by claiming that this was the only way the Turkish nation could have survived. This violently destructive nationalist stand, which is still dominant in contemporary Turkey today, thus originated in the aftermath of the disastrous Balkan Wars.

Second Denial: The Major Act of Violence Commited against the Armenians

The violent and systematic elimination of the Ottoman Armenians by the CUP, the government, and state forces was carried out under the legal cover of "temporary deportations." This, I argue, constituted the denial of the act, namely, an act that was intent on destruction but was presented to the public as an innocuous wartime measure. With this act, the CUP unfortunately removed the alleged "threat" posed by the Armenians, destroying the lives of hundreds of thousands of innocent Armenian civilians, including the women, children, and the elderly, to ensure Anatolia was the ethnic Turks' homeland alone.

Accumulation of Denial

The denial of the destructive intent of the Armenian deportations also built upon the previous denial of the domestic origins of the Armenian unrest. While in opposition, the CUP had initially taken a stand against all of the sultan's policies; once in power, however, it also built upon the previous denial, arguing that the Great Powers had instigated the Armenian "problem." The adverse stand of the Great Powers against the empire during and in the aftermath of the Balkan Wars probably contributed to such a move. Rather than take responsibility for its ultimate collective violence, it was much easier for the CUP to blame it on others. As Sultan Abdülhamid II had already blamed the origins of the Armenian problem on the Great Powers, the CUP then built on this stand to justify its much more massive and systematic collective violence against its own Armenian citizens. It is significant that both denials emerged in the aftermath of disastrous Ottoman defeats: the initial denial of the domestic origins of the Armenian unrest originated in the devastating 1878 Ottoman defeat by the Russians; the denial of the act occurred two years after the catastrophic Ottoman defeat during the 1912–13 Balkan Wars.

Twin Strategies of Young Turk Denial: Selective Silences and Selective Subversions

Both the manner in which the CUP officially denied the intent and extent of Armenian destruction and the memoir of Talat Pasha that discusses the Armenian massacres reveal the twin strategies of CUP denial. On the one hand, the past is remembered through intentionally silencing the events and actors that contradict the official narration. On the other hand, the remembered past knowingly subverts what transpired only including only the events and actors that are publicly known, while excluding the events and actors involved in secret and informal execution of the collective violence. Hence, first the past is whitewashed by selecting only those events and actors that contribute to the official narration; all else is silenced. Then these events and actors are employed to recreate what happened in the past, a (sub)version presenting a plausible explanation of what transpired because the audience does not know all that has been left out in the first place. And the CUP was able to engage in such denial because it committed all its violence secretly and informally, making sure that what was publicly known did not include any of these events or the actors involved. It could then generate a plausible script based on this public knowledge alone. This public-private distinction in relation to violence was first introduced into the Ottoman state and society by the CUP. All CUP members made sure to appear innocent and honorable in public, and they executed their violence in private through extralegal means. As a consequence, they were able to sustain their violence for a decade without being held publicly accountable for their extensive destruction. Yet contemporaneous memoirs destabilize this carefully kept public representation, documenting in detail what went on behind the scenes in private, and thereby also documenting the strategies of denial.

In the official CUP denial, the CUP silenced its own destructive intent by covering the lawlessness of its decision-making process, secretly working behind the scenes privately and informally to eliminate any viable opposition. The lawlessness of the CUP decision-making process is captured by contemporaneous memoirs.[503] An Ottoman official recounted the manner in which the CUP undermined any public opposition to its hegemony through private measures. It confiscated the informers' reports uncovered at Sultan Abdülhamid II's palace "to blackmail the experts, managing to put ringers on the noses of old elites... making them dance [like bears] to the tune they wanted... and [likewise] forcing some deputies at the Ottoman parliament not to criticize the Unionist government."[504] Another contemporaneous writer noted that CUP leaders like Talat "bore grudges. That [they] had no problem in talking, even complimenting men [they] did not like... was due to [their] being rather informal, and playing the politics of the assassins [behind the scenes]."[505] Such a duplicitous approach also extended to the CUP's public rhetoric. It publicly claimed to abide by the laws, but the CUP members "did not obey any laws, generating a provisional law every day [through their deputies in the parliament] whenever they were in trouble."[506] This was the case in relation to the Armenian deportations as well. Although Talat "did not deny the tragic events that followed the Armenian deportations, he still pointed to the Armenians as the instigators of the aforementioned events and, after comparing the harm Armenians inflicted on the Turkish nation, reached the conclusion that the Armenians did not have any rights to appear in front of any court as plaintiffs."[507] Insight into this warped and immoral mentality is provided by one Ottoman officer who first noted that the Dreyfus affair had demonstrated that the reason of state should not supersede the rights of the individual. "Yet," he continued, "the CUP did not even justify its collective violence by reason of the state [*hikmet-i devlet*]," employing instead "the reason of governance [*hikmet-i idare*] secretly defined by a few members within the CUP central committee."[508]

Given the CUP's extensive control of the state, government, and the media, Talat had no problem altering the public discourse, claiming that the rumors about massacres of Armenians in 1915 were "lies and slander the Armenians had started to contrive and fabricate about [some] Turkish and Kurdish massacres."[509] And Talat did so when he had full knowledge that such massacres were occurring, executed mainly by the SO armed bands he had personally helped organize and fortify. In 1915, the CUP also published propaganda material to allegedly demonstrate the destructive intent of all Armenians, material originally confiscated by the Ottoman state during the 1893–96 rebellions. Yet, with the advent of the 1908 constitutional revolution, the Armenian community largely gave up opposing the state, instead starting to work with the CUP for a more equitable empire. In the aftermath of the Armenian deportations and massacres, the CUP once again published propaganda as early as 1917 and 1918, perhaps due to the limited Armenian massacres of the Turks and Kurds in the east after the withdrawal of the Russian empire from the Great War, leading "those who had been ashamed by the Armenian deportations to change their views as a consequence of this propaganda, to instead start feeling animosity toward the Armenians."[510]

The CUP propaganda and subversion of the alleged aims of all the Armenian subjects of the empire commenced with a protonationalist narration, based on a false portrayal of the past.[511] All Armenian suffering in the past was categorically whitewashed to argue that from time immemorial, there had never been any tension between the Muslim and non-Muslim communities, and that everyone had always lived in perfect peace. Such a portrayal overlooked the inherent structural divide between Muslims and non-Muslims, a divide that had become increasingly problematic with the advent of Ottoman mirrored modernity. It also enabled the CUP to claim that its current problem with the Armenians was an anomaly instigated from the outside by the Great Powers. Also silenced was the reason that the Ottoman non-Muslims did not serve in the military, that the state's interpretation of Islamic law explicitly excluded them from this service. Yet, the erasure of this past practice led one memoir writer to complain that "not a single Armenian suffered during all the wars we fought until now... our Armenian compatriots enrich themselves by purchasing for almost nothing the houses and gardens of our Turks who lost their lives fighting in the deserts of Yemen and the Balkans."[512] Another writer boldy argued that "the Armenians were not satisfied with [the constitutional revolution]... [and therefore], unit[ing] with the enemies of this nation, tried to stab our army in the back."[513] Still another official drew on the complicity of all Armenians with foreign (Western) powers to justify their destruction; "given that the Armenians formed a threat through their alliance with the Russians, this threat needed to be removed through deportations during which there may have been some misuse, but no one was killed unjustly," he reasoned.[514]

How all the Armenian subjects of the empire were first marginalized by the CUP and then targeted for destruction is best captured by the memoir of Dr. Mehmet Şahingiray, a CUP and SO member accused of deporting and massacring thousands of Armenians.[515] He argued that "the caves in the mountains and the houses in the Armenian neighborhoods had been turned into arms depots," conveniently overlooking the fact that after the 1908 revolution, all Ottoman subjects were given the right to purchase arms. Some may have done so in self-defense, as many other Ottoman subjects did, but Şahingiray was certain that the intent of every Armenian was to take action against the Ottoman army. Just like other CUP leaders, Şahingiray presented a completely false public account, blatantly claiming that "no orders were issued to anyone for the destruction of the Armenians; on the contrary, [during] the deportation taken out of political necessity, [the orders] stated that they be sent as comfortably as possible," then claiming that he had followed the order to the letter. Şahingiray also alleged that all Armenians "intended to drive the Turks from [the latter's] beloved ancestral homelands of eight to ten centuries," thereby also conveniently silencing the fact that the Armenians had been living in the same homeland long before the Turks. He then identified the Armenians as the instigators of all violence in the east to then rhetorically ask:

> [Why should] the Armenians not be punished? Which "civilized government" would have remained just an onlooker? Which government would expose its political survival to such danger? Just as the government is obliged to undertake precautionary measures, it is also natural for there to be a danger for the Muslim populace to get carried away by their emotions, reacting in kind to the rapacious and terrible murders of the [Armenian] element with which they had lived for so many centuries, considering them [fellow] citizens and brethren.

Şahingiray made two arguments here, first that the government took "precautionary" measures, without articulating what these were and on what grounds, and second that the Armenians initiated the violence, which justified the popular justice and collective violence the Muslims then executed in response.

This false equation of the Armenian violence with the Turkish one whitewashed the disparity between two sufferings, conveniently overlooking two factors. The two sufferings were much different in scale; the violence the Muslims suffered in the east led to the deaths of at most 60,000 Muslims, yet the collective violence the CUP perpetrated led to the deaths of at least 800,000 Armenians. Also, the two instances of suffering occurred under disparate conditions. The Muslim suffering in the east at the hands of the Russians and Armenians was, and remained, regional. About 2 million Muslims perished during the course of World War I, but they did so throughout the empire, primarily at battlefields fighting the Allied soldiers, and thereby without any contact with the Armenians. Yet the Armenian suffering was empire-wide, with the Ottoman state, government, and military forcibly and systematically removing and subsequently destroying civilian Armenian communities of mostly women, children, and the elderly that had nothing to do with either the war or the sedition against the Muslim populace.

Yet many contemporaneous memoirs penned by CUP members conveniently overlooked these crucial differences, drawing instead on the limited Muslim suffering in the eastern provinces to argue that "both sides equally suffered." Indeed, an Ottoman officer, upon encountering "on the two sides of the road [between Meskene and Deyr Zor] unburied corpses of those among the [Armenian] refugee convoys who had fallen sick and died," continued to state that he could not[516]

> help feeling sorrow for the Armenians who had perished during the migration due to illness. Throughout history, Russian imperialism has made the Turks and Armenians throttle one another.... The CUP government was forced to remove these Armenians from the regions near military conflict due to the inevitability of [the conditions of] war. But during this migration executed without any organization or transportation, some among the Armenian refugees died due to exhaustion and disease. Yet according to our calculations at the time, THE LOSS OF THE TURKISH POPULACE WAS MUCH MORE THAN THAT OF THE ARMENIANS.

The official then tried to dismiss his feelings of sorrow by immediately recollecting "the scene of drowned Turkish men, women, and children floating on Lake Van [he had witnessed] eight months ago." By establishing that Muslims and Armenians suffered equally, he was able to marginalize the Armenian calamity that he personally witnessed. The last sentence in the preceding long quotation was printed in capital letters with the intent to influence the Turkish audience. Some Turks such as this officer took it upon themselves to judge and determine what should be defined as suffering, maximizing their own suffering while marginalizing the suffering of the Armenians in the process.[517] Another factor that such memoirs conveniently overlooked was that most of the Muslim populace murdered by the Armenians were not actually Turks alone, but Kurds.[518]

The CUP denial of the destructive intent of the Armenian deportations is best documented by the memoir of Talat Pasha himself, complemented by two other memoirs.[519] Talat Pasha's work, penned after World War I while he was in exile in Europe, was more of his and CUP's defense for committing the collective violence against the Armenians than a proper memoir. Before being printed, it was scrutinized by quite a number of CUP leaders in exile. In his account, Talat mostly explained in great detail the reasons for the execution of the Armenian deportations, with the ensuing violence comprising only about 10 percent of the total text. In the explanation, Talat spent an inordinate amount of time printing the documents seized from the Armenian Dashnak Party to argue that all the Armenians of the empire had always been seditious. He conveniently flattened time to make an ahistorical argument and blamed the Armenians for sedition from time immemorial. His memoir was just as striking for what it silenced. In this carefully written, monochromatic narrative, the CUP always appeared as the victimized innocent, and Armenians as the perpetrators. In the text, the fact that this defensive narrative was constructed to explain the crimes the CUP perpetrated conveniently disappeared.

At the start of the narrative, Talat explained that he had to write his memoirs now because he could not bear "the unjust accusations made today by the centuries-old sly politics [of the Great Powers] against the Ottoman state . . . spewing hatred, and securing [their own] interests." He conveniently cited the European injustices committed against the Turks, especially during the Balkan Wars, to identify next the ultimate hidden enemy of all Turks. Then, he took on the Armenians, claimed that the CUP administration was determined to carry out reforms in the east, only to be turned down by the Armenians. He silenced the facts that the CUP contacted the Armenian deputies in 1914, and that none of the CUP attempts at reform during the previous six years bore any fruit. Finally, in addition to the Great Powers and the Armenians, the third legitimating factor emerged as the worsening context of the empire and the subsequent dangers the Turks faced. After arguing that "the constant Ottoman defeats and especially the ensuing Turkish migrations into Anatolia alongside a great famine and abuses in rule that worsened the state of affairs," Talat alleged that "the Turkish lands would have been destroyed, and the Turkish populace, that is, *the real population of the country* would have been subjected to disastrous deprivations, thereby evoking a terrifying impact [on the Turks] [emphasis mine]."

It is in this context that the CUP was mentioned first as assuming a "pure and honorable stand" in defending the Turks, and second as "not at all getting involved in the affairs of government." The only part of Talat's claim supported by contemporaneous memoirs is that the CUP defended the Turks, and the Turks alone. Talat then criticized such slanderous accusations consciously made by "foreign hands," staining the Ottoman state with the accusation that it sought revenge from its enemies. "Let us conjecture that some members of the CUP central committee did indeed engage in the massacres [of the Armenians]," Talat Pasha simply conjectured. "If they have done so, they did it as individuals, and therefore their actions cannot be generalized to other members who would reject such violent acts." This political stand actually employed the same tactics that the CUP utilized in dismissing all prior violence initially committed against their opponents as individual acts. Such violence was secretly executed by the SO, an organization whose existence Talat took pains to totally silence in the text, making it legally difficult for the victims to prove CUP involvement back then. And Talat, trying to absolve the CUP from any responsibility, hoped the same would happen now.

Talat then commenced to analyze the Armenian issue in the empire. He alleged that the Armenians always sought autonomy in the eastern provinces and therefore spread lies about the Turkish and Kurdish massacres committed against them. He silenced the fierce Kurdish opposition to the CUP reforms in the east and the subsequent CUP complicity in supporting the Kurds; instead, the blame fell squarely on the Armenians. Talat then supported his allegation with two documents penned by the Dashnak and Hnchak committees to demonstrate the Armenians' intentions to join Russia with the intent to establish independence. Talat silenced the fact that the two documents belonging to particular Armenian revolutionary groups could not be generalized to represent the views of all Armenian subjects living in the empire. He then proceeded to marginalize and delegitimate the false claim of independence by arguing:

> The Ottomans did not conquer the eastern provinces from the Armenians. And the Armenians did not engage in any effort or service to the Ottoman state, defending its borders and maintaining its security. This [Armenian] populace that had joined the Ottoman was always treated with tolerance and as Ottoman citizens.... [Yet] they constantly exploited both the happiness and the suffering of the country; they never engaged in a war to spill even a drop of blood for the fatherland.... They now attempt to tear away a part of the Ottoman fatherland by expelling the [Muslim] populace and declaring their independence.

In this explanation, all the statements are half-truths, conveniently subverting the past by selectively silencing some facts. The Ottomans did not conquer the east from the Armenians; the Seljuks did so before them. The Armenians served the Ottoman state not by choice but due to the legal imposition on their community by the Ottoman state. The Armenians were generally treated with tolerance in the distant past but certainly not in the immediate past. Some Armenians had recently become enriched but only due to changes in the world economic structure. Some Armenians did communicate with Russia, and some wanted additional representation in local governance, they but did so initially only after the Ottoman reforms for equality failed for forty years, from 1839 until 1878.

In relation to the temporary law passed by the parliament sanctioning the Armenian deportations, Talat stated that he was personally against it, since he "knew that its execution by the militia instead of the local gendarmerie and police would create very ugly results." It was, he claimed, the Russian occupation of Van on 20 May 1915 that led the Ottoman army (read Enver Pasha and Bahaeddin Shakir) to insist upon such a deportation, conveniently postponing the initial January 1915 CUP decision to deport to the aftermath of the parliament's promulgation of the law rubber-stamping the Armenian deportations that had already commenced. Talat then defined the framework within which such violence occurred, arguing that "many sad incidents had demonstrated to [him] that even though Europe treated the injustices the Christians committed against the Muslims with great tolerance and silence, the slightest action of the Muslims was immediately taken out of proportion." He thus simultaneously underscored Western hypocrisy and duplicity, highlighted Turkish suffering, and downplayed Armenian suffering to strategically delegitimate the Armenian suffering and place the entire blame on the West in one strategic move. Talat then described the execution of the deportations: "First enacted in Erzurum," they then spread "to Van, İzmit and Adapazarı, Bursa, Adana, Samsun, İzmir, Urfa, Şarkikarahisar, and Yozgat on the grounds that many arms and ammunition belonging to the Armenians were recovered at all these locations." That the Armenians who were deported were not merely those who may have possessed such arms but entire communities, including women, children, and the elderly, was conveniently silenced once again. After arguing that he personally did all he could to punish the individual acts of those ill-mannered people who abused the situation, Talat noted that "it is a known fact that the Muslims in the eastern provinces accrued just as much loss as our Armenian citizens." The CUP did indeed punish the abusers, but it defined such abuse not as perpetrating crimes against the Armenians but instead as keeping what was plundered for themselves instead of properly overturning all Armenian wealth to the CUP as intended. The Muslims in the east did accrue losses, but not as many and not under the conditions the Armenians did. Talat then attempted to demonstrate that the perpetrators were actually innocent, since "no one in government with the exception of a few former officials and officers engaged in such ignoble accusations that stain the national honor," once again reducing the scope of collective violence to a few individuals. He concluded by stating:

> Just as the allegations present the ultimate proof of my innocence, so too all investigations into my life as a statesman and a politician would witness that I merely served my fatherland. During my political life, I never gave in to my emotions and never thought of my person or my relatives. Many have accused me of going soft on my old friends; this is utterly wrong! I only acknowledged the sacrifice [I undertook] in all contexts, [those] necessitated by the well-being of the populace and the fatherland. According to my opinion, there is no other person who has occupied a post for the good of the fatherland. Those who know me well would confirm this. And those who do not will be able to confirm given the incidents of the day.

This was probably the only instance in his memoirs in which Talat was completely honest: he indeed did serve his fatherland, did not employ emotions or enrich his family, and did not go soft on his friends. Yet he conveniently silenced the details that would have revealed his intent, that Talat served a fatherland that was to be populated only by the Turks, that his actions were dictated by Turkish nationalism, and that his sacrifice involved placing the interests of the Turkish nation before his own. And he did so while governing an empire with substantive non-Muslim, non-Turkish populations that he intended to eliminate.

Some contemporaneous memoirs point out the fallacies in Talat's propagandistic defense discussed earlier.[520] One Ottoman analyzed in detail the SO activities he primarily blamed for executing the destructive CUP intent:[521]

> The armed bands formed under the SO stained the [reputation of] the entire Turkish nation in the view of the world, causing the inclusion of bloody and barbarous pages in her history. It is not within the purview of justice and fairness to have the responsibility and consequences of these events placed squarely upon the shoulders of Anatolian Turks. Instead, the CUP leaders and especially... [Drs.] Bahaeddin Shakir, Nazım and [education minister] Şükrü who invented and administered this SO must be mentioned.

The official defined the SO as "a group of bandits consisting of the CUP's bloody murderers and plunderers exempt from legal procedure, acting independently only in accordance with the orders of the committee of three [Shakir, Nazım, and Şükrü]" that had, "become very dangerous with its own independent and irresponsible executive council, secretary, investigators... like a government within a government, a committee within a committee." The SO then went on "to wreak fury in Anatolia." The official ended by dismissing the official denial of the allegations of an Armenian massacre as a "propagandist falsehood."

A Kurdish intellectual presented the most damning account directly contradicting Talat's denial of the Armenian massacres, one he heard from the prominent CUP member Şükrü Baban:[522]

> [Baban's] father Zihni Pasha who had retired as the Beirut governor was a close friend of Talat Pasha. Every Friday [which was the Muslim holiday], the latter would come to our mansion in Süleymaniye to drink *rakı* [a traditional alcoholic drink] and play chess with my father. About that time, in 1915, I had graduated from the Faculty of Political Science in France and came back [to the capital]. I had wanted to stay in France a while longer, but the outbreak of the [Great] war forced me to return. One Friday, the servants informed me that my father was calling for me. I went to the part of the house reserved for males [*selamlık*], kissing the hands of my father and Talat Pasha. The pasha said: "Oh Şükrü, may God's grace be upon you, you have grown and become a man.... And you have graduated as well, is that so?" "Yes, my Pasha," I replied. "Then, my son, from this day on, I appoint you the General Director of Settlements." Bewildered, I asked, "Uncle Pasha, who am I going to settle?" to which he laughed, replying, "My son, you are going to settle the Armenians." When I responded, "Okay, but aren't the Armenians

> [already] settled; are they to become nomads instead? How can I do this job, I do not know," he laughed out loud, saying: "Şükrü, you went to Paris, but are still a child.... My son, it is easy; you are going to give the command. When the Armenians in Erzurum come to Muş, they will be settled on the road; those of Van will be settled in Bitlis, the ones of Bitlis in Siirt, those of Diyarbekir in Urfa, the ones of Urfa in Mardin, and those in Mardin can be settled on the way to Musul." When I understood [the scope of] this pretend settlement on the road and the [ensuing] calamity, I turned white and could not utter a word. They immediately ordered me to leave.

Baban then went through to the part of the house reserved for females (*haremlik*), where his mother asked what was wrong, but Baban could not speak. With that anxiety over what was expected of him, he could neither eat nor sleep in peace until the next Friday. When they again called him the following Friday, Baban was shaking from head to toe. "If they force me to take on this duty, I would either escape to Paris or commit suicide," he thought. But that was not what happened. When Baban entered, Talat Pasha saw the poor condition he was in, telling him "Do not be afraid, come forward. So you think there are no other Şükrü's. We found a better Şükrü [for the job of Armenian destruction]." What he called "the better Şükrü" was Şükrü Kaya, who did indeed assume the directorship of the Armenian "settlement" then and later the Kurdish deportations and destruction during the republican period.

In summary, once the CUP defined the preservation of the state and the establishment of a Turkish fatherland as its sole aim, these national interests trumped all else, especially the interests of all non-Muslim and non-Turkish subjects. The Armenians in particular were targeted for destruction because the same lands had been their fatherland for centuries, before the arrival of the Turks. Yet this CUP destruction was covered by denial based on the twin strategy of selective silences and subversions. The CUP first identified Western European interventions in the domestic affairs of the empire and Armenian sedition as the instigators of the violence. The ensuing CUP collective violence against the Armenians was first dismissed as punishment and then reduced to the same level as Muslim suffering in the east. Talat Pasha in particular developed the narrative of the denial of destructive intent. Claiming that the Armenians once living in peace were provoked by the Great Powers—thereby building upon the initial denial of origins—he then articulated the elements of the second CUP denial: he generalized the destructive ideas and activities of some Armenian revolutionary parties to the entire Armenian populace and then absolved the CUP of all blame by arguing the collective violence was in fact the particular violence of a few individuals. Yet contemporaneous memoirs document the silences and subversions of the official CUP narrative. Especially Talat had written his memoirs with the intent to publicly falsify the Armenian massacres; in private, however, he and many CUP members actively tried to destroy the Armenian presence in Anatolia through deportations, counting on and receiving the support of the state, military, and local populace during the process. It is no accident that Talat's memoirs have gone through many recent printings in contemporary Turkey, indicating that the Turkish nationalism he helped construct continued unabated into the Turkish republic.

3

Early Republican Denial of Actors of Violence, 1919–1973

There is only one good, knowledge, and one evil, ignorance.
Socrates, Greek philosopher, 470–399 B.C.E.

In his memoirs, Burhan Oğuz, a bureaucrat, amateur historian, and the stepson of prominent CUP leader Yenibahçeli Şükrü Bey, recounted the significant events of Turkish republican history that he personally witnessed.[1] Among these, the most prominent one was the collective violence committed against Turkish non-Muslims on 6–7 September 1955. The incidents began on 6 September after the Democrat Party's evening newspaper, the *İstanbul Ekspres*, printed and distributed for free 290,000 copies of its most recent issue.[2] The striking news item warranting such distribution was the bombing in Salonica, Greece, of the birth house of Mustafa Kemal Atatürk, the founder of the Turkish republic. The bombing was later proved to have been executed by Oktay Engin, a member of the Turkish National Intelligence Organization (Milli İstihbarat Teşkilatı; MIT). Not only was Engin never arrested, but he later served as the republican governor of Nevşehir from 1992 to 1993. The bombing followed on the footsteps of the unrest in Cyprus between the Cypriot Greeks and Turks, in which some Turks were massacred by Greek Cypriot guerrillas. Sedat Simavi, the owner and editor in chief of the widely circulated *Hürriyet* newspaper, had already written many editorials stating that Cyprus was a national cause that should never be given up, that "Cyprus was and had to remain Turkish."

On that particular day, the "Cyprus Is Turkish" Association put on a public demonstration at the Taksim Square in İstanbul. Even though the administrative capital of the new republic had been moved inland to Ankara, the former imperial city remained the economic capital. İstanbul also served as the relatively safe haven remaining in the republic for the rapidly dwindling non-Muslim Turkish citizens. At this public event at Taksim Square on 6 September 1955, the tens of thousands of exclusively Muslim Turkish demonstrators in attendance turned violent, flooding the wealthy neighborhoods of the city, plundering and setting fire specifically to the non-Muslim shops, residences, churches, schools, and cemeteries. During the violence, which lasted for two days, about 10 to 15 non-Muslims were killed and 35 wounded; 73 churches, 8 holy springs, 1 synagogue, 2 monasteries, 4,340 shops, 110 hotels and restaurants, 27 pharmacies, 21 factories, 3 Greek Rum newspapers, 5 Greek Rum clubs, 2,600 houses, and 52 Greek Rum and 8 Armenian schools were destroyed. Of the total destruction, 59 percent was suffered by the Greek Rum, 17 percent by the Armenians, and 12 percent by the Jews. The Greek Rum were the apparent target, but the demonstrators quickly turned into perpetrators of collective violence, not differentiating among the non-Muslims and attacking everyone alike. The total financial damage reached $300 million.

All the arrested perpetrators were eventually acquitted in court. Turkish security forces and the military were present during the violence, but neither intervened to protect the non-Muslims. Instead, they actively aided the perpetrators, only securing the Muslim Turkish properties in the process. At the time, former CUP and Special Organization member Celal Bayar was the president of the republic; the Democrat Party he had founded was in government. The leader of the main opposition party was the former CUP and SO member İsmet İnönü. The government initially attempted to blame the pogroms on the fifty-two leftist intellectuals they immediately arrested, but it soon became evident that the state and government were complicit in organizing the collective violence. The death toll was low because the demonstrators bused in from all over Turkey were explicitly instructed not to kill but instead to destroy. Fifty years later, in an interview, the National Security Council general secretary and officer Sabri Yirmibeşoğlu, who back then had been a member of the military's Mobilization Investigative Commission, stated that the events of 6–7 September were "the work of the military Special Operations unit executed with magnificent precision, reaching its intended aim."[3]

Burhan Oğuz provided ample detail on this republican incident of collective violence against its non-Muslim citizens, first describing what had transpired:

> Churches were burned down, priests attacked, people raped, minority cemeteries desecrated, the elderly thrown off their beds, and houses and stores [of the non-Muslim minorities] utterly destroyed.... The scenery... in İstanbul... certainly sent a chill down one's spine.... Everyone narrated the events in accordance with their own perceptions, emotions, and desires. Yet the conclusion they all reached was that the incident was totally set up.

Oğuz then explained how he personally had realized that the violent incident was set up:

> Everywhere, the procedure followed was the same. First, a group identified and marked the spots to be destroyed, the group following them with iron rods in their hands broke down the doors and roll-down shutters, and the ones after them smashed the furniture and goods inside, throwing them out on the street. Everything was cut into small pieces so that they could not be salvaged. And the police and soldiers with bayonets in hand remained total spectators to all this [destruction], [only intervening to] prevent attacks at Turkish [Muslim] houses and businesses by mistake as well as to point out to the perpetrators the minority stores they had overlooked.

He also stated that some people knew about the impending violence ahead of time; at a "meeting at İstanbul University with the finance minister in attendance, waiters about to serve the late luncheon were told that soon some disturbance was to ensue . . . but that [the place they were at] was going to be protected so no one could enter." Oğuz also added what he personally witnessed as additional proof of prior planning:

> The populace could not plan something on this scale without the knowledge of the government . . . and there is ample evidence that the military and the police supported the destruction. . . . [For instance,] my friend the Armenian jeweler Saran recounted . . . that the group first went by his store and then, upon a policeman pointing it out, came back and destroyed it. . . . When [Saran] asked the soldiers to intervene, they refused, stating they had received orders not to intervene.

In addition to the nonintervention of the Turkish government and military, the Muslim Turkish populace of İstanbul also went along with the destruction, only intervening in a few cases to protect their non-Muslim friends.[4] The discriminatory stand of the Muslim Turkish populace toward the non-Muslim citizens had not changed. Oğuz recounted that upon arriving at the bank where he worked, he found his coworkers "immersed in newspapers, reading on the one side, looking at the pictures on the other, saying things like 'it is a good thing this happened; it was necessary; these rotten bastards had gotten too big for their britches; it was time to teach them a lesson.' " Later during the same week, Oğuz traveled to Eskişehir on business, where a friend narrated to him during lunch what the latter had witnessed in that city. While the X-ray machine of his non-Muslim physician friend was being thrown out of the window, his doctor friend feared for a moment that he was going to accompany the machine. At that moment, one of the people from the next table overheard their conversation and commented: "Never mind the physician, pity on the X-ray machine." The value of a machine trumped the value of a human life. Many Muslim Turks also exploited this calamity by not paying their debts to non-Muslim businessman because "along with the destroyed safes, the documentation of the Turks' debts to non-Muslim minorities had also disappeared.... There were not too many Turks who renewed their promissory notes or paid them."

How and why did such wanton destruction occur in a republic that had guaranteed the rights of its non-Muslim citizens with the Lausanne Treaty, the international foundational document of the Turkish state? Oğuz stated that "this [incident] had been planned among a few people like [President] Celal Bayar, [Prime Minister] Adnan Menderes, [Governor] Fahrettin Kerim Gökay, and others [in the military]." "One immediately remembers at this juncture," he added, "that Celal Bey was trained by the Unionists who had become famous for their violent behavior." This is an important commentary because it highlights the continuity between the CUP leaders of the empire and the political leaders of the ensuing Turkish republic, a continuity that has been officially and ardently denied by all republican leaders. In order to fully understand this denial, this chapter once again traces the context within which it emerged.

Early Republican Social Structure of Sameness

The 1919–73 period analyzed here commences with the Turkish independence struggle in 1919, continues with the establishment of the Turkish republic on 29 October 1923, and concludes at the end of its first fifty years of existence in 1973. Particularly spotlighting the republican aftermath of the collective violence committed against the Armenians, it argues that the perpetrators largely remained unpunished because these men joined the top ranks of the republican state, becoming its leaders and heroes. This continuity in governing officers and officials from empire to republic normalized and routinized the collective violence against the non-Muslims in republican practices. In addition, such violence was also applied to the new enemies identified by the republican leaders. Republican mirrored modernity in politics and education sustained this violence. While the new political structure did not punish but instead rewarded the former perpetrators by appointing them to significant official posts, the unified educational system in turn mythified the past by exclusively lauding Turkish bravery during the independence struggle, conveniently silencing the preceding collective violence that also continued during the independence struggle.

The same educational system instigated further polarization. In addition to non-Muslim citizens, all those like the Kurds, leftist intellectuals, and Islamists criticizing and opposing the republican agenda were declared internal enemies. A steady progression of collective violence ensued; while not reaching preRepublican levels, it once again curbed all opposition to the new republican state. Cases in point are the 1925–26 and 1937–38 Kurdish rebellions and the 1926 assassination attempt against Mustafa Kemal, all forcefully put down by many hangings. Likewise, the 1934 events in Thrace led to the forced deportation of local Jews; the 1941–42 forced conscription of three generations of non-Muslim citizens into labor battalions was followed by the 1942–43 wealth tax placed upon them at rates that were three to four times those of Muslim Turkish citizens. The Tan printing press in İstanbul was stormed and destroyed on 4 December 1945 on the grounds that the intellectuals running the publications were communists who had to be punished and destroyed. Later in 1964, Greek Rum citizens who held Greek passports were given two days to leave Turkey with nothing more than a suitcase and $100 in cash. Leftist Muslim Turkish student leaders who opposed the government were captured and executed by the state in May 1972.

Significant in all these continuing acts of collective violence is that none of the perpetrators have ever been punished. The search for the event legitimating the ensuing republican violence against non-Muslim citizens points to the 1919–22 military tribunals conducted against the perpetrators of the 1915–17 collective violence against the Armenians. The tribunals ended with the hanging of only a handful of perpetrators as CUP officials in state administration either destroyed or withheld evidence. Many of the perpetrators were removed by the British occupying forces to the island of Malta, only to be later exchanged, without trial, for British prisoners held by the Turkish nationalist forces. Many perpetrators avoided the military tribunals by escaping and throwing in their lot with the Turkish nationalist forces carrying out an independence struggle. During the military tribunals, while some of the accused, like the Boğazlıyan district governor Kemal Bey, were found guilty and duly hanged, others like the Urfa subdistrict governor Nusret Bey appeared to be innocent. Still, after being illegally tried for the same crime thrice, Nusret Bey was also hanged. This latter injustice enabled Turkish nationalists to argue that the military tribunals were a "kangaroo court," serving the interests of Allied powers intent on destroying the Turks by any means necessary. The Turkish nationalists further exploited the few injustices committed at court to delegitimate the 1915–17 collective violence committed against the Armenians. Dissolving the tribunals in 1922 and releasing all the accused perpetrators, the nationalists stated all the perpetrators had already been punished and the "Armenian problem" thus resolved. The next denial emerged out of this context. The official republican stand was that all the actors who had perpetrated the collective violence against the Armenians were punished, thereby denying that the majority of the perpetrators had actually escaped without any punishment, assuming instead significant state and government posts in the ensuing Turkish republic.

At the end of World War I, as the Ottoman Empire disintegrated, the Young Turks mobilized to start an independence struggle under the leadership of Mustafa Kemal Atatürk that led in 1923 to the establishment of the Turkish republic. At this particular juncture, the population of Turkey became predominantly Muslim and Turkish. The 1915–17 destruction of Armenians was followed by the 1924 Turkish-Greek population exchange, turning the Greek Rum into a small minority. Many Jews immigrated to Europe or Palestine. Of the Muslim communities that were ethnically different from the Turks, Albanians in the Balkans and Arabs in the Arabian Peninsula were no longer a majority within republican borders. The only remaining substantive community consisted of Kurds who lived within the three nation-states of Turkey, Syria, and Iraq.

The republic assumed the secular principles first advocated by the Young Turks in determining the parameters of the Turkish nation. Turkishness was proposed as an overarching identity all citizens could assume regardless of their ethnicity, religion, or geographical or cultural location. In practice, however, Turkish ethnicity eventually trumped all other identities as urban, secularized, Sunni Turks emerged as the dominant majority at the expense of non-Muslims, Kurds, and Alewites. Hence the historical religious divide layered with secularism once again reproduced itself as Muslim Turks became the dominant majority. The Turkish nation came to comprise secular ethnic Turks; all others became marginalized to different degrees. Those ethnic Turks insistent on keeping their Islamic identity were moved to the periphery of the power structure. Those Kurds insistent on retaining their Kurdish identity were violently repressed with state force. Those secular ethnic Turks who attempted to advocate a political system alternative to the state-dominated structure were likewise suppressed. In all, the republic advocated a social structure based on sameness in that it assumed and also intervened to actualize a nation composed entirely of secular Turkish citizens.

Even though political rule was secular, with legal institutions that presumably treated all citizens of Turkey equally, non-Turkish and non-Muslim communities were once again discriminated against in practice. After all, as Andreas Wimmer astutely remarks,[5] "The dynamics of ethnic conflict, exclusions along national lines, and institutionalized forms of xenophobia accompanied the formation of modern nation-states." In spite of the secular, universal principles of equality espoused by all nation-states, the ethnic divide prevailed in the Turkish case as well. Non-Muslims were promised and given equal citizenship rights in theory, yet they were excluded from the body politic in practice. Their wealth and property were not legally protected by the Turkish state and society as well as those of their ethnic Turkish Sunni counterparts.

Elements of Early Republican Modernity

With the adoption of a republican system of governance, the leaders of the independence struggle furthered the systematic political modernization process initiated by the CUP. The republican form diverged from its Western counterparts in content, however. First, rather than including the nation in governance, the system was actually employed by the republican leaders to systematically exclude all social groups deemed different from the national body politic. Hence, rather than the nation determining and participating in the political system, the republican leaders decided on the boundaries of what constituted the nation.

First the Political Inversions

The most significant element of the republican mirrored modernity was the political establishment of a republic on 29 October 1923. Turkish Muslim soldiers finally ended their decade-long fighting, which had started with the Balkan Wars (1912–13) and was followed by World War I (1914–18) and the ensuing independence struggle (1919–22). During this decade, more than 2 million Muslim Turks perished, and Anatolia, the newly designated Turkish fatherland, was devastated due to the decade-long wars on the one hand and the violent deportations of the Armenians as well as the Greek Rum, Kurds, Arabs, and Assyrians on the other. Given its violent recent past, the newly founded republic emphasized the collective theme of a "birth," with the Turkish nation created anew from scratch. Such a move is common to all projects of state and nation formation; nations highlight their unique bravery and courage, downplay the inherent difference and divisions within, and accordingly mythify the past by whitewashing all former acts of violence committed by the nation. Yet such nation-building processes have often been followed by a critical reflexive phase in the aftermath of fascism and Nazism that revealed the collective violence inherent in nationalism. Yet, the Turkish republic did not engage in such critical reflection, instead sustaining willfull amnesia regarding past collective violence due to a string of national and international events. The republic did not participate in World War II (1938–45) but legitimated the violence it nevertheless exercised against the populace in the name of national defense. Then, during the following Cold War (1946–91), the republic was a staunch Western ally. Because the United States, leading the western bloc, was more concerned with political stability in allied countries than with democratic governance, the Turkish state and its governments continued to violate human rights and democracy with impunity. As a consequence, exclusionary Turkish nationalism constructed by the new republican, former CUP leaders managed to persist for seven decades at the expense of minorities.

Politics of Past Collective Violence against Armenians

Building a nation-state out of an empire necessitated delegitimating the former rule of the sultans, particularly with the intent to prevent the return of such imperial rule. In 1924, all members of the Ottoman dynasty were permanently exiled from Turkey.[6] Yet expunging the immediate past, namely, the decade of CUP rule, proved more problematic because most former CUP members had remained active, joining the ranks of the republican state elite. Mustafa Kemal prevented the return to the republic of the three most prominent CUP leaders, namely, Talat, Enver, and Cemal Pashas. He publicly distanced himself from the CUP but remained close friends with many prominent members, like Celal Bayar, İsmet İnönü, Mazhar Müfit Kansu, and Tevfik Rüştü Aras, and continued to employ the skills, financial resources, and organizational network of the CUP. Some maintained that "the Turkish nation had to gather strength from its past."[7] Thus, how the immediate CUP past ought to be remembered remained unclear.

It is significant in this context that the CUP members did not publish their memoirs until decades into the republic.[8] One needs to further analyze why they did not do so for such a long time, and why, when they finally did, they severely censored their activities. One memoir addressed this issue, stating that Turks did not write their memoirs for three reasons: "laziness" (or rather, I would argue, lack of such a habit), "wrongful doings of the times that may also implicate them," and "fear that they may be legally investigated by the state."[9] The latter two reasons reveal that former CUP members knew many of their actions were violent and illegal and therefore did not want to publicly reveal or own up to them. Memoirs thus came to be regarded by the republican elite as a dangerous source of knowledge that could potentially bring the republic down. The problems the CUP member and republican general Kazım Karabekir faced in 1933 upon publishing his memoirs critical of Mustafa Kemal and his cadre provide a case in point. The publishing house that printed his memoirs was raided, and copies were burned; his house was also raided, and his documents were taken away.[10] What ensued, another account argued, was an "intergenerational break in historical memory" regarding past collective violence due to the hesitance of many former CUP members to reflect on the past collective violence they had personally participated in.[11] Indeed, the statement of one memoir writer supported this possibility:[12]

> We have been a generation that until 1918 paid for the memories of the past without avail, without becoming well-behaved until the last moment, and without ever sobering up. We suffered the heavy and bitter torments of sins we had not committed. We passed through tests of survival that could yield significant lessons for the present and future.

> There may be many people who may want to relive their lives. Yet I do not think that there will be many among our generation who would dare to do so. A Turk with any emotions would not want to remember, let alone live those dark days from the end of the nineteenth century to the first decades of the twentieth. I am still amazed we survived without being buried into the cemetery of history.

The gravity of the emotional trauma Turks faced during the demise of the empire and the subsequent emergence of the republic may indeed be the main reason for the lack of memoirs specifically articulating past collective violence. People simply did not want to remember the suffering they went through or the suffering they caused. This initial lack made the Mustafa Kemal Atatürk's personal recollections of the history of the independence struggle all the more significant, literally providing the republic with its own official memory and narrative.[13] The account celebrating the victory of the struggle emphasized Mustafa Kemal's role at the expense of all others to such a degree that, to this day, many Turks think he singlehandedly won the independence struggle. In and through the *Speech* Mustafa Kemal delivered in 1927, he emerged as the sole political symbol of Turkish nationalism. Many attempts to criticize it were suppressed in a manner similar to the CUP's censorship of the previous era.[14]

Once the national narrative presenting all opponents in a negative light became hegemonic, Turkish public national knowledge was also structured along the same lines. A case in point is the memoirs of Ali Kemal, a fierce opponent of the nationalist movement, who was kidnapped and assassinated by nationalists as a consequence.[15] Once again, none of the perpetrators were punished. His grandson, penning the preface to the memoirs, noted that Ali Kemal "died about sixty years ago, but then, the people pretended that he did not exist because of the conditions of the time. There was no mention of him in the press; his name was erased from the literature. Then pieces started to appear about him, mostly written by his enemies. These of course recounted Ali Kemal's character and actions from their own viewpoint. They did not always respect his deeds either." The republican memory of the CUP leaders Talat, Enver, and Cemal Pashas followed another trajectory.[16] All three initially remained active outside of the empire, working with the hope to eventually return.[17] Yet, they were to return to Turkey only after a long period and after having been killed.[18] They were all targeted to be murdered by Armenian assassins as a part of Operation Nemesis, based on a seven-person list drawn up by Manuk Hambardzumian, financed by the Dashnaksutiun Boston Central Committee, and organized by Armen Garo.[19] Talat was killed by the Armenian assassin Simon Tehlirian; Enver was killed during a skirmish with the Russian army; Cemal was assassinated by Russian agents, including Stepan Dzaghigian. Among the CUP leaders who had escaped, only Dr. Nazım made it back alive, to then become a deputy. In 1926, he was tried and hanged for sedition.[20]

Once the physical threat of the three CUP leaders was removed, they were included in the official national rhetoric as heroes. First, in Talat's case, the Turkish national assembly protested in 1921 that the assassin Tehlirian was acquitted after a two-month trial, largely as a consequence of the efforts of the German ambassador.[21] After the death of Mustafa Kemal and the ascendance to power of former CUP and SO member İsmet İnönü, who had now become the president of the republic, Talat's remains were brought to Turkey in 1943 and buried with a state ceremony.[22] In Cemal's case, his coffin arrived in Erzurum in 1922, and he was duly given a proper burial as a martyr. In 1996, Enver's remains were likewise brought back to Turkey, and the bodies of all three CUP leaders were then transported to a special monument in İstanbul constructed for "the martyrs of the Turkish nation-state." Hence, the three CUP leaders who had engaged in past collective violence against the Armenians were celebrated after their deaths as national heroes. The sentiments of the Turkish state and populace toward these CUP leaders are best captured in one memoir that noted:[23]

> There were no Armenians left in east, central Anatolia and to a certain degree in the western regions. If this cleaning had not been carried out, getting the independence struggle to succeed could have been much more difficult and could have cost us much more. May God be merciful and compassionate toward Enver and Talat Pashas who actualized this [cleaning]. Their foresight has saved the Turkish nation. As for the ones in the southern regions, the commander of that region Cemal Pasha for some reason did not clean them out. That commander too was a patriot; perhaps he did not undertake such a task due to the conditions of the times and his personal political thoughts.

These remarks demonstrate the prioritization of Turkish interests under the vestige of nationalism over the interests of humanity that would have necessitated the acknowledgment of especially the hundreds of thousands of Armenian deaths by Talat, and Turkish and Armenian deaths by Enver.

The most significant yet least publicly discussed issue of the republican era concerned the politics of the properties and wealth abandoned by the massacred Armenians as well as those of Greek Rum who were either massacred or deported to Greece as a consequence of the 1923 Turkish-Greek population exchange, when 1,250,000 Greek Rum left for Greece and 500,000 Muslim Turks of Greece "returned" to Turkey. The issue of abandoned properties and wealth of the Armenians has not been studied in depth because contemporaneous Turkish cadastral surveys are still closed to scholars by the military on grounds of possible threats such an examination might pose to "national security." Recently, however, studies have nevertheless started to emerge built on information that escaped such censorship.[24] Contemporaneous memoirs of especially Turkish Muslim officials and officers also provide ample evidence regarding the devastation and ensuing plunder

Many memoirs note the social and economic devastation of Anatolia as a consequence of the collective violence.[25] For instance, in Ankara before 1915, "the rich neighborhoods and well-tended summer residences belonged to Armenians"; one memoir writer recalled that he "ate at Armenian restaurants and stayed at an Armenian hotel named 'Central' which had a good restaurant and clean comfortable beds." When he arrived in Ankara later in 1923, there was "no sign left of the Christian neighborhood except the vineyard houses.... We had burned down everything of the Ankara I had first seen that had been created in the name of civilization, life with Greek Rum, Armenians, and all that could be termed 'prosperous' had been torn away to disappear."[26] The same writer also commented on the state western Anatolia was in, as "the Greek Rum populace was thrown away from its roots. With that, we also tore and threw away the economy of Smyrna and the entire western Anatolia.... Turks were therefore doomed to start from ground zero at places destroyed by fire, and at empty, closed-down stores."[27] In the case of southern Anatolia and specifically Adana, another memoir writer commented that "the transfer of Armenians to Syria turned our Adana province into a totally empty state. Not a single market, bazaar, artisan remained. All the stores and businesses were shut down. The absence of even tinners and solderers became our most serious problem.... The country had turned into a very wretched state.... The streets had become home to the hungry and the impoverished."[28] Another account from Kozan near Adana stated that "there were once Greeks and Armenians there, every place was cultivated... the best grapes once grew on the vines and the rarest flowers in the gardens... there were mansions, houses, roads, masterpieces of stonework. Now, it is covered with thistles."[29] Upon talking to local residents, the writer also found out that these properties had been turned over to the treasury, which settled Muslim Turkish refugees on them. "These [refugees] have withdrawn into the basement of the ruins, sleeping together with their goats," he commented. The writer also chatted with the Kozan mayor, Mehmet Akçalı, a very wealthy man largely because of "the large citrus gardens and rice fields left behind by the Armenians." During their conversation, he tried to convince the mayor to build upon what he had acquired through no work by establishing "a small electric plant and a factory for canning juice extract, preserves, jams, and the like." Yet the mayor did not bother, assuring the writer that "a family member served at the Turkish national assembly every term," and further commenting that "if we had not thrown those Armenians out from here, all of us would have been their laborers today."

Yet the ensuing devastation reveals the fallacy of the CUP and later republican decision to violently replace the local Christian population with Muslim Turkish refugees, on the premise that the latter would successfully sustain the local social system and economy without disruption. Such nationalist decision-making failed to take into account human capital; the skills and expertise of the local Christian population could not be replaced either by Muslim Turkish refugees, most of whom were peasants, or by local notables, who did not have the skills, work ethic, and vision to sustain what they had confiscated. The adverse impact of nationalist decision-making was most evident in Çamardı near Niğde. The same writer recounted:

> At the district center of Çamardı, there are two neighborhoods [called Maden and Bereket] a couple of hundred meters away from one another. Maden is orderly, filled with lush green gardens and vineyards, and beautiful spacious houses. Yet there is not a single tree at Bereket.... [Unkept] houses are like stables. "Why is [the latter] barren?" I asked; "because there is no water," they replied. Yet in Maden, water was not spurting out of the earth either. Maden residents had utilized the stream that flowed in between the two neighborhoods with extensive and patient labor, constructing arc after arc to transform the place into heaven. I got thinking as to why the others had not done the same thing. Then things cleared up: Maden was an old Armenian neighborhood. And Muslims lived at Bereket. While [Armenians] sweated, moving huge rocks, opening arcs, digging wells, [Muslims] preferred to take their cattle and shoot the breeze up at the mountain. Now the agha of Bereket lives in Maden, sells the God-given apple Armenians had planted, and his laborers stay in their old place putting the agha's goats onto pasture at the mountain.

Hence the Muslim Turkish notables who had confiscated what Armenians had once created were able to improve their standard of living without any work, while the rest of their lands still remained in poverty because they did not take the initiative to improve them but instead relied on keeping family members at the national assembly to ensure the continuation of their privileges. The same state of affairs prevailed in Dörtyol, where a large Armenian population once resided and engaged in citrus production. One memoir writer noted that "the population has decreased to a third of what it used to be. The [Muslim Turkish] refugees who have been settled in this region since the exodus of the Armenians are unfortunately not qualified in this art.... Dörtyol that once used to have beautiful mansions and wealthy residents is today a ruin."[30] Conditions in southeastern Anatolia were not any different. One memoir writer recounted what he observed in Çüngüş near Diyarbekir. Mustafa Bey showed them around town, especially pointing to the remains of a large and impressive Armenian church. "Then there were large and run-down tanneries left from the Armenian times," he continued. "According to what Mustafa Bey said, the various leathers and stout leather for soles worked there were sold all the way to India and the United States."[31] Çüngüş, which once a prosperous town with an Armenian majority, had now been reduced to poverty as the remaining town dwellers were unable to sustain previous production.[32]

Names of Rewarded Perpetrators

The hegemonic nationalist narrative ensured no public discussion took place regarding those perpetrators who continued to live in Turkey unpunished. A few memoirs nevertheless contain information on them. I should note that local oral histories contain much more detailed knowledge; during my five-year-long travels to the eastern regions where Armenians once lived, I often talked to elderly Muslim Turkish residents of villages, towns, and cities who did not have any trouble providing detailed accounts of which lands and properties had been initially owned by which massacred Armenian families. Yet, until such oral histories are conducted systematically, one has to rely on the sporadic information provided in contemporaneous memoirs. In the case of Nusaybin in the Mardin province, the Pirinççioğlu family not only massacred and usurped the lands and properties of Armenians but continued their influence and abuse of the system during the republican era.[33] Crucial in this continuation of violence was the election of Feyzi Pirinççizade as deputy to the Turkish national assembly after his return from Malta.

Two memoirs recounted those local Muslim Turkish notables who had amassed wealth at the expense of the Armenians.[34] Avni Pasha, the first public works minister to then become the naval minister, was, according to the claims and documentation of CUP members, "one of the ringleaders who had personally participated in the Trabzon deportation and had gained personal benefits from it."[35] Hence, many former Ottoman and later republican officials informally knew about the crimes committed by members of their cohort, but such crimes did not prevent the perpetrators from being appointed to significant republican posts. Another memoir identified Hacı Musa Bey, Haydaranlı Hüseyin Pasha, Hayranlı Selahattin Bey, and İzzet Bey, the son of Hastanlı Halit Bey, as having been "involved in the massacres of Armenians during the Great War through which they amassed great wealth." "These men," the memoir continued, then "went to Erzurum during Mustafa Kemal's visit there [for the congress], receiving additional funds from him."[36] Two additional memoirs noted other perpetrators.[37] Prominent CUP member and Kayseri district governor Zekai Bey "was sought in relation to the Armenian massacres but managed to escape to Europe to evade prosecution."[38] The Trabzon governor and perpetrator of the Armenian massacres "moved to Ordu," where he was referred to as the "black governor"; upon his departure from the city, he personally carried a "bulky briefcase filled to the brim."[39]

Confiscated Armenian Gold, Monies, and Goods

The problem was somewhat different regarding the valuable goods such as jewelry and gold coins that deported Armenians were forced to give up, hid, or entrusted to their Muslim Turkish neighbors, never to recover. Four incidents described in separate memoirs discuss these distinct possibilities in turn.[40] One civilian writer commented on what he encountered upon the 1921 repossession by the nationalist forces of İzmit and Adapazarı near İstanbul. One of the first acts of the Geyve district governor Sadettin, appointed and sent there as the subdistrict governor, was to in turn appoint a director to the Abandoned Properties Commission. This director took it upon himself to unseal a jewelry shop "filled to the brim with jewelry" left behind by forcefully deported Armenians. The writer, who was responsible for the protection of all abandoned properties, objected to this turn of events, only to be arrested. Even though he then escaped imprisonment, the same district governor, who then became the republican chief of security, had the writer falsely arrested on the grounds that he had conspired to assassinate Mustafa Kemal. The writer was eventually acquitted by the independence court and released. There is no mention of what happened to the abandoned properties in general and the jewelry shop in particular.[41] Such valuable goods and properties were supposed to be turned over to the treasury, but one can surmise that local notables probably divided up movable wealth like jewelry in collusion with state officials. It is poignant to note that the republican political system favored not those who attempted to protect the Armenian properties but instead those who plundered them.

Another writer, this time a military officer, recounted escaping to Samsun to join forces with Mustafa Kemal. The first task he was assigned was "to find the suitcase with about 6,000 lira inside that was going to be used for national affairs." Tufan traveled to Amasya, locating the suitcase "in the house of an Armenian soldier who had not yet been discharged."[42] There is no information on how they came to know about this suitcase, what the money was then used for, who the Armenian soldier was from whom the suitcase was taken, and what subsequently happened to him. In spite of the sketchy description, however, it is clear that this money was illegally confiscated by the nationalist forces. The sketchiness of this narration necessitates further comment. In many of the 356 texts analyzed here, a pattern emerges whereby first the acts of violence are described, but then the once detailed narratives suddenly turn vague and imprecise, probably in attempts to avoid providing self-incriminating information.

The third writer chronicled how some people became wealthy upon discovering the buried gold and valuables Armenians had been forced to leave behind. In this case, Şeyhmus Paketçi, originally from the Şexan village of Mardin, moved to Diyarbekir, working first as an itinerant peddler and then as a contraband tobacco dealer. "As he lived in run-down Armenian houses in Diyarbekir," the writer continued, "he came across a large earthenware jar full of gold and jewelry. The man was able to put this to good use, becoming one of the richest men of Diyarbekir today."[43] Ironically, Paketçi employed an Armenian architect, "the son of the [wealthy] Sarrafyan family of Maden, having then escaped to Vienna during the Armenian Genocide," to draw an excellent plan. Paketçi then used the plan to build a great tourist hotel in Diyarbekir. I should also note that during my five-year-long travels in former Armenian provinces, I constantly encountered the theme of finding buried Armenian gold. The Armenians traveling with me were often asked if they came with maps of buried treasures. We saw many churches, monasteries, and houses destroyed, dynamited by treasure hunters. Our conversations with the locals also revealed that some had indeed found buried gold. Unlike Paketçi, however, they had wasted it on entertainment.

The final account articulates the disputes between the local Muslim populace and state representatives over confiscated Armenian goods. A military officer provided a rare glimpse into what transpired in Erzurum:[44]

> The real source [of conflict]...was the unclaimed [Armenian] goods stored in the big church. Especially after Armenians left the city during the war years, goods from their houses and stores were placed in the Great Church, with an armed guard posted in front of its sealed door. Neither the Russians during the invasion nor ours after recovering the city from them had touched the depot. Yet, when taxes collected from the impoverished people did not suffice, it was thought that revenues from the sale of these goods should be turned over to the military. And this was where the problem emerged. A part of the populace complained about the improprieties of officials evaluating the goods in the church, especially by the fact these officials were not local, but had instead arrived from other regions. The sickness [called] regionalism emerged.... Some commanders also sided with such people. Kazım Karabekir Pasha and others tried to get rid of this polarization....And perhaps [with the same intent]...two national assembly deputies had also arrived in Erzurum during those days.

The narration is marked just as much by what it leaves out. Armenian goods and properties were unclaimed in Erzurum because the SO bands had almost completely massacred the departing Armenians. The military then decided to liquidate these protected goods and properties, using the proceeds for their own mounting expenses. Local Muslims probably opposed having "outside" people engage in this process because they could not use their local influence to co-opt some of these for their own use.

Failed Armenian Attempts to Recover "Abandoned" Properties

At the end of World War I, the occupying Allied powers immediately set upon bringing back surviving Armenians to their places of origin, intending to restore their residences, properties, and lands. The independence struggle that commenced one year later wreaked havoc on this plan, however, as the nationalist forces expelled the returning Armenians alongside the occupying forces. Contemporaneous memoirs once again detail this complex process.[45]

As early as 1918, the Greek deputies of the Ottoman assembly had submitted a motion to investigate the collective violence committed against the Armenians, punish the perpetrators, and account for the property and goods of deported Armenians. In the interim, however, the CUP had worked diligently to ensure all such property and goods were quickly confiscated by the Ottoman state and government.[46] Many Muslim local notables ended up keeping Armenian goods and property for their own use, however. One account contained a detailed list of such people, "including some of the prominent [Muslim Turkish] businessmen of Kayseri."[47] Even though legal investigations ensued, the outcome is not discussed; the lack of court records from this period as well as the ensuing silence lead one to conjecture that local notables ended up keeping everything, thereby continuing their immorally enriched lives with impunity.

Such plunder followed by the passage of time made the restoration of properties to returning Armenians problematic. CUP member and finance minister Cavid Bey, penning his memoirs during the armistice period, recounted two particular difficulties, noting that "1. Most of the [Armenian] real estate is occupied by [Muslim Turkish] refugees and government officials. Some of it has been demolished. Hence if [Armenians] return right away, there could possibly be a large housing crisis; the emergence of many conflicts is also natural; 2. It is necessary to determine the Muslim population in the eastern provinces and compare it with the population of returning…Armenians…said to be about 400,000."[48] Armenians were prevented from reclaiming their lands and properties to ensure that Muslim Turks remained a dominant majority throughout what eventually became the Turkish nation-state.

The anxiety returning Armenians produced among former CUP officials was palpable. One former CUP member and district governor complained about "the problem of the Armenians who had remained here and there to return to Kayseri after the war to reclaim their houses." In the interim, some of these houses were distributed by the state to local Muslim residents who did not want to move out because the government had built a prison where their houses had once been. Yet they were forced to do so, upsetting the district governor.[49] The inherent nationalism in this case is noteworthy. While the district governor complained about the victimization of Turks, he did not acknowledge or address the double victimization of Armenians, first forcefully being deported from their homes to survive atrocities, and then returning to find their homes occupied. Also noteworthy is the nationalist silencing of those responsible for making these decisions, in this case, the CUP government in general and its member and Kayseri governor Muharrem Bey in particular. Similar problems were encountered in Edirne and Kırklareli at the end of the independence struggle. In this case, one memoir writer narrated how he had asked İsmet İnönü, returning from Lausanne Treaty negotiations in 1923, that "the three hundred private soldiers [who had initially been] recruited as militia be given, by the special order of the Council of Ministers, houses and shops in Edirne and Kırklareli from among the abandoned properties so that [these soldiers] received a material reward for the hardships they had suffered."[50] This case demonstrates the possible complicity of the newly emerging republican state in giving out Armenian residences to former militia. The decision of republican ministers is not known, but the fact that such action was considered legal and appropriate in the first place points to the prevalent thinking of the time.

A similar process occurred in Antep. One account noted that during the British occupation of the city, "deported Armenians came back alongside the British. It would have been one thing if the arriving Armenians had only been those who had initially been deported, but seizing the opportunity, all Armenians deported from the eastern provinces filled Antep up like a vengeful army. The [Muslim Turkish] populace referred to them as *'illik ermenisi* (Armenian of the provinces?).' These [Armenians] did everything possible to take revenge from the Antep Muslims, raiding our houses, even seizing our daughters' dowries that they themselves had knit, claiming them to be the goods they had left behind." Some even took away their children, claiming them to be theirs.[51] Once again, the Armenian suffering and ensuing violence that had placed them in this situation was completely overlooked; the memoir writer solely portrayed the local Muslim Turks as victims. The memoir also pointed to another problem, however. Some returning Armenians tried to take back what they could, even goods that were not theirs in the first place. It also indicates how difficult it must have been to prove who owned what residence, especially if local Muslims colluded in challenging the claims. In some cases, such as in the Adana region, returning Armenians employed local armed bands to get their land and properties back, often opposed by the military commanders of the independence struggle.[52]

There are only two accounts of returning Armenians.[53] Deportee Sarkis Çerkezyan, whose family was originally from Adana provides, the longest narration. During the armistice, when Adana was under French rule, his wealthy father, Sarkis Agha, was initially able to recover his numerous shops in Karaman. Yet things worsened when the family decided to stay after the departure of the French, when "a memorandum was issued to the effect that 'those who want to can leave within a month. Otherwise, we assume no responsibility for what might happen to them.'" As a consequence, most Adana Armenians returned to Syria, Lebanon, and Aleppo. One day, Sarkis Agha, who chose to stay, was suddenly deported along with all the Armenian adult males. He escaped to the mountains, where his Muslim friend Büyük Mustafa Agha protected him and sent him food. After hiding there for two years, he secretly came to the city to see his son; the Greek Rum neighbors informed the Turkish authorities, who first imprisoned him and forced him to sell everything by threatening to hang him, and then exiled him. After moving to İstanbul, Sarkis Agha tried three times to legally recover his substantial properties. In response to his 1935 lawsuit, the Turkish state acknowledged the properties were his but refused to return, them citing an order issued by the Interior Ministry. When Sarkis Agha tried to file another lawsuit, three assassins were sent from Adana, probably hired by the current "owners," so he stopped. In 1946, Sarkis Agha tried once again, this time hiring a Muslim Turkish lawyer, who not only kept the title deeds but tried to blackmail him, asking him for money in return for the title deeds.[54] In the end, the once-rich Armenian family could only live in Turkey in poverty.

The second memoir belongs to Vartan İhmalyan, whose family was from Konya. When the Italians left Konya and the Turkish national forces entered the city a week later, İhmalyan's father decided to settle in İstanbul. His mother suggested that they sell the farm before their departure, since they had already received an offer of 2,000 gold coins. Yet his father did not want to sell; after their departure from Konya, national forces confiscated the farm, illegally registering it as abandoned property. In the end, the İhmalyan family, too, was legally unable to recover their farm in Konya.[55] These two memoirs display the persistence with which the Turkish state authorities and local Turkish lawyers who were also party members acted in unison to ensure that no non-Muslim minorities continued to hold properties in the Turkish republic. Many republican leaders were fully aware of abandoned Armenian properties, including Mustafa Kemal, who, unlike others, took care to avoid them, probably on ethical grounds.[56]

Some local Muslims also acted in good faith as legal representatives of Armenians. Among one memoir writer's jobs was to sell the houses and property of Armenians living outside Turkey. Thus acting as an informal real estate agent, he probably kept part of the proceeds himself, sending the rest to the Armenian owners in exile.[57] In addition, one of the biggest scandals of the early republican era was the Armenian smuggling operation. Many of the forcefully deported Armenians had left without any belongings, including their passports. Even if they did have passports, the Turkish state legally considered those Armenians living abroad to have given up their Ottoman and later Turkish citizenship. As a consequence, wealthy Armenians who wanted to reclaim their properties had to be smuggled into İstanbul. One account revealed that a few of Mustafa Kemal's friends were among those involved in the smuggling operation, but their names were never publicly revealed. "The Armenians had been whisked out of the country when the scandal surfaced," the account noted, continuing to state that some national assembly deputies "longed for those CUP days of profiteering or for the pleasure of plunder during the days of banditry of the National Forces."[58] About 11,000 of these uprooted Armenians ended up settling in present-day Armenia.[59]

Fate of the Confiscated Armenian Properties

Many returning Armenians were thus unable to reclaim their properties, and still others had been massacred and failed to return. What happened to these properties? This is a rarely discussed issue in contemporary Turkey, where the closed republican archives and cadastral surveys make it impossible to carry out a systematic study. Contemporaneous memoirs nevertheless provide ample details that, when put together, reveal the general contours of what happened.[60] The majority of the Armenian properties were confiscated by the Turkish military; many properties confiscated by the Turkish state were turned into schools, theaters, or other public buildings such as prisons or government mansions. The rest became the private property of Muslim Turks.

In relation to military confiscations, six memoirs penned mostly by Turkish officers provide details. In two cases, Turkish army regiments occupied abandoned Armenian villages.[61] In another, the Turkish national government confiscated all the properties of a man named Apranonyan throughout the fatherland where "mixed commissions comprising the finance department and the military accounted for all his property, sealing everything and placing armed guards to protect it. . . . The goods were [later] all brought to the large shop in Kastamonu, and the Turkish army was provisioned with cloth, attires, shoes, and tents."[62] In still another, an officer recounted that in Antalya, the Turkish government rewarded Armenian abandoned properties to reserve officers and soldiers.[63] This military practice continued into the 1950s. Turkish military commanders posted throughout Anatolia were likewise immediately allocated the largest houses, ones often previously belonging to Armenians.[64] In İstanbul, a Turkish officer recounted renting from the pertinent military commission a flat that formerly belonged to the *Sabah* newspaper owner, Mihran Kelekyan Efendi.[65] This military practice was not confined to Armenian properties but also extended to Greek Rum residences.[66]

Five memoirs provide information on the Armenian properties confiscated by the Turkish state. Tokat Girls' Institute and Mardin Village Boarding School were both housed in abandoned Armenian properties.[67] In Erzurum, the famous Erzurum Congress that launched the independence struggle was held at the Armenian Sanasaryan School that had then been transformed into a Turkish high school.[68] In Gaziantep, the Turkish state confiscated two Armenian churches, turning one into the Turkish state prison,[69] and the other into the official government mansion.[70] Oddly, memoirs also contain many instances of Armenian churches that were turned into Turkish state theaters.[71] Churches in Smyrna, specifically at Karşıyaka, Akhisar and Kırkağaç, in Eskişehir, in Ayancık near Giresun, in Ordu,[72] and in Diyarbekir were all transformed into theaters. Some churches, like those in Bursa and Antlay, were also given by the state to nationalist organizations like the Turkish Hearth.[73] Perhaps this outcome is not surprising given that the Muslim Turks did not previously have such large secular public spaces, which they now needed for national state functions.

Many Muslim local notables were also able to wrest away confiscated Armenian properties, keeping them for their own use. In Adana, the family of Judge Özbey, who had originally migrated from the Balkans, "suddenly became rich, owning many vineyards, farms, and houses."[74] Also in Adana, a local Muslim notable had turned an Armenian church into the Turnan movie theater; the toilets were now located where the church pulpit had once been.[75] The pattern in Gaziantep was one where the Turkish state took over the abandoned properties and then sold them to local notables.[76] For instance, the Armenian Girls School first became the model girls school, to be then sold to Kamil Samlı. The Atinikan School and Church first became a Muslim orphanage and then a thread factory owned by Cemil Alevli. The property of the Armenian Kabakyan first became the local Trade High School and then belonged to descendants of Kabakoğlu Arif Efendi. As expected, there were many instances of such confiscation in İstanbul as well. The Lale movie theater and the Amasya apartment were built on two properties belonging to Gabriel Noradunkyan; another Noradunkyan house became the winter headquarters of the Turkish Yacht Club. Many of the old buildings around the Taksim Square once belonged to the Dadians.[77] It is interesting to note that some properties of members of the Ottoman dynasty expelled from the republic were also gradually bought by individuals. Unlike the case of the Armenians, however, the dynasty members were able to sell their properties, even if at low prices.

Persistent Republican Exploitation

The Lausanne Treaty theoretically guaranteed the legal rights of non-Muslim minorities remaining in Turkey. Militant Turkish ethnic nationalism practiced by state authorities, as well as the local Muslims, ensured, however, that they did not have much, if any, legal protection. In addition, the inability of these non-Muslims to recover their properties left them in reduced circumstances; they were not only forced to give up their education but often ended up working as servants in Turkish households. Any transaction with the Turks carried the danger of nonpayment, forcing the withering communities to interact only with their own. Contemporaneous memoirs once again provide several instances of this republican exploitation.[78] Vartan İhmalyan, whose father's farm in Konya was confiscated by the Turkish state, had to leave his university education and start working instead. İhmalyan's brother also had to leave his education at the French school and transfer to a public school due to lack of funds.[79] One Turkish memoir writer remarked gleefully on how the Armenian and Greek Rum female servants at their house provided him with sexual experience.[80] A socialist intellectual recounted proudly that he rented a house from an Armenian, Boghos Agha, and did not pay rent for years. Even though Boghos Agha went to the police chief to recover his rents, they remained unpaid. The intellectual's father eventually paid all the arrears years later upon becoming a public prosecutor. "Boghos Agha was very grateful," the intellectual concluded, not at all acknowledging the years of hardship and loss of money due to inflation he had cost the agha.[81] In all, then, neither the non-Muslims forced to leave Turkey nor those who stayed behind could recover their "abandoned" properties due to the intentional collusion of the local Turks with the Turkish state authorities. Though the non-Muslims theoretically had equal legal rights with the Turks, they could not practice these rights, leading many to live in reduced circumstances, constantly anxious about possible future exploitation.

Another Turkish state measure accompanying the unlawful confiscation of non-Muslim properties throughout the country was the systematic replacement of place names of Armenian and Greek Rum origin with Turkish ones. This measure gradually erased all traces of the Armenians and Greek Rum from their ancestral lands. Generations of Turks were then brought up with these new Turkified place names, thereby having no memory that peoples other than the Turks once lived on these lands. Especially crucial was the establishment in 1957 of a state organization, the Special Commission to Change Place Names. One Turkish state bureaucrat mentioned in his memoirs that he served on this commission, but he failed to explain how and why the need for such a commission emerged.[82] The bureaucrat never questioned or reflected on any of his duties, other than the minimal corrections he made for the system to work more efficiently. He also attempted to revive local history writing in all the places he served, once again without addressing the existence of any local actors other than the Turks. Such totalizing ethnic Turkish nationalism eventually diffused into every pore of state and society, not only erasing past violence but also eradicating all symbolic references to non-Muslim minorities from national space.

Distorted Economic Practices

Economic elements of modernity are often generated and sustained by an independent bourgeoisie supported but not controlled by the state. Yet in the case of republican Turkey, the previous CUP practice of permitting only a state-dependent Turkish ethnic bourgeoisie to emerge continued. The Turkish state and governments systematically attempted to control and eliminate remnants of the non-Muslim bourgeoisie, often through violence. The same control and violence were also applied to the emerging Turkish bourgeoisie, if and when they did not act in accordance with the principles and boundaries set by the state. In all economic decision-making, the republican cadres were taught to place the material interests of the state before all else, including the interests of the populace. In addition, those heading the subsequently established state economic enterprises were selected based not on merit and entrepreneurship skills but instead on their loyalty and obedience to the state. As a consequence, the decisions made did not maximize profits, and people did not work with utmost efficiency. Rather, all performed their tasks in accordance with the maxims and priorities set by the state. This prioritization caused Turkey's state-led industrialization to develop slowly and ineffectively.

According to contemporaneous memoirs, the republican era was marked by a prominent tension between the state and businessmen. State and government officials attempted to either control all economic endeavors or allocate economic privileges to private individuals selected not on grounds of economic merit but of party loyalty. Entrepreneurs and businessmen observed and often informally wrote, to no avail, about the inefficient manner in which the Turkish state ran the country's economy, making decisions based not on profit maximization, efficiency, productivity but on party loyalty, national security, or personal bribery. The economic outcome was understandably disappointing to all. In one of the very few civilian memoirs chronicling the development of the republican economy, the memoir writer stated that the Ottoman industrial infrastructure as well as Ottoman bureaucratic organization formed the initial backbone of republican economic production; the main challenge once again was the inability to locally produce goods and arms due to lack of local technology, experience, and knowledge.[83]

During 1919–22, the economic concerns of the dominant Muslim Turkish majority in parts of the empire controlled by the sultan and the occupying Allied forces revolved around their inability to take any independent economic action; those living in parts controlled by the nationalist forces instead complained about the extremely heavy payments they had to make to finance the independence struggle.[84] A case in point was the establishment of a pilot tugboat organization to service the Bosphorus. The process took decades as different state organizations fought over the concession, not providing the funds or the legal permits in the process. The memoir writer argued that this behavior was akin to "commanding a man missing both legs to march." Meanwhile, private tugboats belonging to foreigners and non-Muslims kept operating with great profits. Frustrated by this course of events, the officer in charge was eventually able to control this resource not through market competition but through political means; he passed a legal stipulation that "only the Turks among the private tugboat companies would be issued licenses."[85] This points to how the state, crippled in its economic decision-making process, eliminated private competition by resorting to legal means, making it impossible for private foreign and non-Muslim competition to survive.

The economic struggle was entirely different in the parts of the empire controlled by the Turkish national forces. There, the Law of National Proposal (Tekalif-i Milliye), issued in 1921, stipulated that everyone had to give 20 to 40 percent of what they possessed to the national government.[86] In addition, the local populace had to contribute funds to the irregular defense forces called the Mobile Units (Kuvva-i Seyyare), headed by Çerkes Ethem.[87] If they did not, funds were forcefully taken from them, often through armed threats or kidnappings.[88] Because funds and resources thus collected did not have to be accounted for, many abuses occurred; those involved in the collection enriched themselves, often at the expense of the populace.[89] Another economic source for the independence struggle came from the gold and armaments provided by Soviet Russia, intent on funding another revolution it regarded to be similar to its own. Five separate contemporaneous memoirs note that the Soviet state annually sent millions of gold rubles and substantive shipments of armaments to the Turkish national forces.[90] One conjectured that the source of the gold was "the hundred million rubles in the Buhara treasury."[91]

Hence, during the independence struggle, military leaders kept receiving funds from a variety of sources—the local Muslim populace, the Soviet state, and "abandoned" Armenian and Greek Rum wealth—without having any notion about the labor and skills that were needed to produce these economic resources in the first place. They also could not understand, appreciate, or act upon the economic advice provided by experts. A case in point is what transpired during the Lausanne Treaty negotiations that effectively established Turkey as a nation-state; the republican delegates had to ask former CUP finance minister Cavid Bey to accompany them, specifically to help with the economic negotiation of the Ottoman debt. Yet Cavid's sound advice was not appreciated by the delegation's leader, İsmet İnönü, who, being a soldier, had limited knowledge on economic issues.[92] At Lausanne, the new Turkish state was settled with the very large Ottoman foreign debt of 107,528,461 gold coins. And it was to pay such a large amount in a country that had effectively liquidated the driving force of the local economy, namely, the non-Muslims.

Given that there was yet no significant capital accumulation among the Muslim Turkish populace, the republican state stepped in to oversee the economy.[93] Yet the manner in which it stepped in was not amenable to capital accumulation outside the state-owned enterprises. The state did not exercise selective economic intervention by interceding only in instances when the resources of the private sector were insufficient, to then withdraw once the private sector was strengthened. Instead, the republican state practiced total intervention, turning into a capitalist, but a bad one that made economic decisions based not on profit but on political priorities. It was therefore impossible to avoid the tension that developed between İstanbul, where almost all the existing private sector was located, and Ankara, which became the center of the public sector, now heavily involved in the economy. Business enterprises in İstanbul were wary of Ankara, which began to intervene in their affairs, taking over anything that was profitable. One memoir writer narrated this tension at the 1923 İzmir Economy Congress, where the finance minister and lawyer Mahmut Esat (Bozkurt) Bey did not at all welcome the Turkish delegates from İstanbul, referring to them as "those who had committed treason to the national struggle."[94] As such political priorities took over the settlement of economic issues, Turkish businessmen and experts from İstanbul who could have contributed to economic development were marginalized. The ensuing haphazard rogue state industrialization of the country was bound to lead to price inflation, and it did. Turkish businessmen were especially disheartened by the political appointments of finance ministers who knew next to nothing about matters of finance. One such businessman complained that the economic decision-making at the national assembly, where almost all the members were state officials, was impaired because they "approve[d] everything as if they were under the influence of hashish," putting their personal interests and state interests before the interests of the Turkish economy.[95]

This particular economic stand of the Turkish state only produced prominent Turkish businessmen who took on large state projects as either entrepreneurs or building contractors. [96] Another venue to republican economic success was representing European companies, yet such representation once again often went to those businessmen in Ankara who had close connections with the government.[97] Those who succeeded in business thus did so through their state and government connections; they did not have to rely on their own economic skills but instead on their political connections. This distorted approach undermined the independent economic entrepreneurs in İstanbul who not only did not receive any state support but were often harassed with the threat of a takeover. One memoir writer who was also an economist best summarized the weaknesses of the economic decision-making process in the 1920s as follows:[98]

> Due to their origins and professions, these idealist fighters [of the independence struggle] ultimately did not belong to the class of economists and business administrators. Their greatest mistake has been not to organize the state in accordance with the economic conditions of the day [and not to do so] by hiring experts. Time has demonstrated to us that it is not possible to improve a country with victory songs. It took our officials twenty-five years to comprehend this reality! One of the major mistakes committed after the independence struggle has been animosity toward foreign capital. This was probably due to the effect of the [imperial] regime of capitulations.... Another mistake they committed was [the adoption of the policy of] statism... in state manufacturing, where the cost is much higher and abuses rampant; the directors do not make businesses their own like the owners would have.

This pattern continued through the 1930s, when the three major economic activities of the Turkish state were the establishment of model farms, the purchase of foreign partnerships, and the foundation of a state industry. In establishing model farms, the state appointed as directors state officials like governors who were not knowledgable in agriculture.[99] In relation to foreign partnerships, all foreign utility and railroad companies were purchased by the republican state, which then made it mandatory for all those working at such companies to speak and conduct business in Turkish. This legal measure advantaged the recruitment of ethnic Turks over non-Muslim minorities and foreigners.[100] Founding a state industry proved to be the most problematic economic endeavor because the industry was established with short- and long-term treasury credits that increased Turkish currency two- or threefold in value, quickly leading to inflation. Also, in determining the location of factories, military necessities were prioritized over existing economic infrastructure. In deciding what industries to select, the state did not consider if the industry fit the country's needs. Finally, all these decisions were taken without following a planned, long-term economic program.[101] Probably the most drastic mistake was the lack of accountability of those officials appointed to head the farms, partnerships, and industries; none had to answer for their economic failures. In the private sector, many Turks were aware that the economy was a significant venue to accumulate wealth but assumed they could be successful merely through political connections, without any economic expertise. As a consequence, contemporaneous memoirs are replete with instances of Turks who acquired employment, businesses, and capital only to fail.[102]

Also during the 1930s, escalating state intervention in the economy caused the remaining non-Muslims who were prominent in trade and commerce to suffer significant setbacks. Five contemporaneous memoirs highlight this process. In one, the father of a non-Muslim lost his job at a foreign company that extracted coal because after its nationalization, as in similar instances, "non-Muslims working at such companies were fired." He was reduced to working as a clerk at his own father's textile shop.[103] In another, a Turk described gleefully how he got the local Muslim agha, who was also a gendarmerie corporal and the batallion's meat procurer, to threaten and take over a non-Muslim's plant bulb trade.[104] The discriminatory stand of the Turks entering economic endeavors was evident in the advice a prominent Turkish businessman gave to the Turkish youth that "under equal conditions, it is sufficient to prefer the artisans of our own [ethnic Turkish] nation; animosity to the [non-Muslim] others is both excessive and unnecessary; it is useless. Just the opposite, I like using them when necessary."[105] This Turkish attitude probably explains why the sound economic advice provided by the few non-Muslims in the national assembly fell on deaf ears. During the 1935 budget discussions, for instance, when the finance minister had proudly announced that both taxes and tax penalties had risen precipitously, one non-Muslim deputy commented that one ought not to be proud of tax penalty increases but instead should "be saddened, investigate the reasons behind it, and then attempt to save their own responsibility as well as that of their government from it."[106]

The non-Muslims were even more adversely impacted by the economy during the 1940s, when World War II destabilized the both the Turkish and the world economy. Turkey had not entered the war, but it had nevertheless mobilized a large army of half a million soldiers for defensive purposes, thereby placing a significant strain on the economy.[107] In 1944, a budget deficit emerged for the first time, reaching 40 million lira in an economy of about 900 million lira; much more dramatic was the escalation in defense spending, which quadrupled between 1939 and 1943 to reach 542 million lira. Balance of trade also ran a deficit.[108] Military expenditures started to account for more than half of the annual national budget. Domestic food provisioning also became problematic because the government waited two years before rationing food, leading to hoarding in the interim.[109] Hence poor economic planning and lack of foresight by the Turkish state and government were once again at the root of the financial crisis. As a solution, the republican leaders considered the promulgation of an extraordinary tax. Tax collection had always been problematic for the Turkish state as many, especially those in the business sector, avoided taxation.[110] Even though the propertied in Turkey included the large agricultural sector as well, the government specifically targeted businessmen because they included non-Muslims, who lacked the political power to resist such a drastic state measure.[111] This republican approach to non-Muslim minorities at times of crisis was eerily similar to that of the CUP; both regarded non-Muslims, intentionally kept out of political power, as a financial source to plunder in times of distress.

In 1942–43, the primary burden of the extraordinary tax termed the "wealth tax"—unanimously ratified by the assembly in record time—was placed almost exclusively on the shoulders of non-Muslims. At the national assembly discussions of the tax law, President İsmet İnönü and Prime Minister Şükrü Saracoğlu gave incendiary speeches, identifying and targeting non-Muslim minorities as the culprits of the current economic crisis, thereby successfully silencing the state's responsibility in producing such a crisis in the first place.[112] The lack of sound financial information on wealth and income led state officials to "guess" the wealth of non-Muslims based on hearsay. Then, the ratified tax law did not give the non-Muslims the legal right to object or appeal.[113] As a consequence, a wealth transfer occurred from the non-Muslim minorities to the dominant Turkish majority as many non-Muslims had to quickly and cheaply liquidate their properties and assets to pay the assessed exorbitant taxes within the stipulated three- to four-week period; those who could not pay were sent to labor camps.

In the late 1940s, the disastrous wealth tax combined with the pro-German stand of the Republican People's Party (RPP) gradually led to the rise of the Democrat Party (DP). Initially hailed as the "democracy heroes," it was as politically and socially conservative as the RPP.[114] Still, during the decade-long DP rule from 1950 to 1960, foreign capital started to enter Turkey at an escalating rate. How this capital was put to use was once again fraught with problems, however. The Turkish state did not properly monitor those Turkish businessmen engaging in unsafe and illegal business practices because of the businessmen's political influence.[115] Many Turkish businessmen refused to adhere to the decisions reached at economic congresses, using politics to ensure no such decisions were ever executed by the state.[116] Still others who represented American companies prioritized the cultivation of state officials and officers in Ankara with bribes.[117] After the 1960 military coup, many new companies established by Turkish businessmen started to appoint retired generals as general managers.[118] It is not surprising that many of these businesses failed in the long term because all one needed to receive a large amount of capital from the state was a personal connection to the state, government, industry, or a bank.[119]

During this time, Turkey also became more integrated to the new Cold War order by sending a Turkish brigade to fight in the Korean War (1950–53).[120] The economy worsened once again as the DP government's attempt to distribute land to the peasants backfired, generating increased unemployment. The DP's financial policy of holding the dollar exchange value at 250 kuruş when it was actually worth 1,200 kuruş "ended up benefiting not the peasants who were the producers, not the officials or the workers," but instead "the handful at the top who had access to the dollar in their transactions."[121] The monies flowing into Turkey from the United States and the newly joined NATO therefore benefited only a few Turks who employed political influence rather than solid economic and financial experience to access these sources.[122] The escalating financial crisis again necessitated the state and government to search for culprits: once again, non-Muslim minorities were targeted on 6–7 September 1955 as their businesses in major cities were raided by the Turkish populace upon the instigation of the government, the state, and the military. The continuing complaints of the military, state officials, and the RPP now in opposition, all of whom felt that they had not prospered sufficiently through this inflow of foreign capital into the country, produced the first 1960 military coup. Elections were held a couple of years later, but unaccounted economic corruption prevailed.[123] Journalists who attempted to write about the economic scandals were faced with violence as they were fired upon, their cars burned, and their newspapers impounded.[124]

In summary, republican economic modernity developed in twists and turns, continually burdened by state and government officials intervening to control the economy and entrepreneurship. The cost of all faulty economic decision-making was continually blamed on and paid by non-Muslim minorities who lacked state and government protection. Most Turkish businessmen who emerged did so through political connections, rarely learning the skills and discipline necessary to establish and successfully sustain an economic enterprise.

Rearticulated Education

Given the previously discussed problems of republican political and economic modernity, the most significant question that remains is why the Turkish populace was unable to activate their rights as citizens to alter the flow of events. The answer is embedded in the manner in which state-centralized education shaped public knowledge, thereby limiting the available options of the populace. Specifically, the state's strong control over the centralized educational system led to the indoctrination of the populace with a nationalist rhetoric on the one hand and the violent repression of any attempts at criticism on the other. This rhetoric often blamed not state and government policies but instead a continually widening array of "enemies of the Turks" for all the suffering. Non-Muslim minorities once again figured prominently as the only domestically accessible group weak enough to be aggressed upon as the enemy. Yet over time, the enemies of state and society multiplied as social groups that did not fit the Turkish ethnic nationalist mold became better educated and able to oppose the status quo. One would have expected especially the institutions of higher education to join such opposition, but they were public, not private, and therefore under strict state control. Almost all ended up siding with state and government, and duly expelled all the faculty daring to publicly oppose state and government practices. The one other possible venue of resistance and change would have been institutions of civic education like the Village Institutes (Köy Enstitüleri), but they too were closed down when the students became too empowered by the knowledge they received. Hence once again modern educational institutions that often spearheaded change in Western modernity were present in republican Turkey in form, but they assumed a conservative content, instead thereby inhibiting change. The student movement of the late 1960s was once again violently repressed through the executions of prominent student leaders.

Centralization of Education and Knowledge Production

One of the earliest decisions of the republic was to centralize all educational institutions in the country under the control of the Education Ministry. Institutions of higher learning were theoretically exempted from this process, but they too were regarded by the state and government as their agents and tools. Seven contemporaneous memoirs articulate the impact of such centralization of education and knowledge production.[125] The three outcomes the memoirs discuss pertain to the politicization of school building, the centralization of knowledge production, and the gradual demise of non-Muslim minority schools.

The politicization of school building was the first outcome as all deputies employed their connections to have the largest number of state-funded schools built in their particular regions.[126] The ensuing decisions were therefore once again predominantly undertaken according to political pressure rather than regional need. Educational inequality throughout the country escalated as deputies from the more prosperous and influential western regions could have more schools built, at the expense of those from the increasingly impoverished eastern regions.

The second outcome was the excessive centralization of knowledge production as the Education Ministry controlled the entire system from textbooks, teacher training, and course content to the questions asked at graduation examinations. All textbooks had to be reviewed and approved by the ministry; most textbooks were penned by retired officers and officials because they were able to successfully employ their political connections to have their books approved at the expense of other scholars who lacked such connections. As a consequence, rather than promoting critical thinking, the information contained in the textbooks ended up reproducing the official Turkish nationalist rhetoric.

All teachers were trained and given certificates at similarly controlled colleges and then taught the same curriculum in their own classes. At the schools, at one juncture, all graduation examinations were centrally held as well; one memoir writer noted that "the questions... all came from the ministry, to be opened at exactly the same time all over the country and the evaluation was blind as each student is assigned a number.... So all students evaluated on a particular topic had exactly the same knowledge as every other one in the country."[127] This was probably one of the most successful pedagogic exercises in the history of nation-states in standardizing knowledge. Looking back, I still remember what I was taught as I was going through this system, and how long it took me to overcome what I normalized in the process. The inherent pedagogy instigated discipline and obedience rather than creativity and self-confidence.

The third outcome was the gradual withering of non-Muslim minority schools that were all theoretically protected by the Lausanne Treaty. Given that the standards of educational and eventual life success in the republic were set at state schools, it gradually became difficult for non-Muslim parents to justify sending their children to minority schools instead. This obstacle also emerged for the few remaining foreign schools for the same reasons. This general demise in private educational institutions due to decreased demand was also enhanced by reduced state funding and increased state monitoring of non-Muslim and foreign schools.[128] The decision-making process of parents is best demonstrated in one account in which a Turkish father deciding to send his son to high school at either the state-owned Galatasaray Lyceum or the private American Robert College chose the former because "Robert College was established to educate non-Muslim minorities and especially their intelligentsia, and they had their doors closed to Turks for a long time. Regardless of its level of education, the school was 'foreign' to us in one respect. Yet Galatasaray was 'ours,' with everything it entailed. It was, in addition, oriented to the West, modern and open to innovations."[129] Such an explanation once again contained half-truths generated by official public knowledge. Foreign colleges established during the imperial era had not been allowed by the Ottoman state to educate Muslim students due to the danger of religious conversion. And many were eventually permitted by the state to accept Muslim Turkish students, still graduating some of the most fervent patriots as well as opponents of the country to this day. The Galatasaray Lyceum had initially been founded by the Ottoman state to compensate for and overcome the increasing educational inequity in the empire in favor of foreign schools. Rather than learning this history, however, many parents sought refuge in the nationalist rhetoric, once again blaming foreign and minority schools for the outcomes of the decisions of their own state.[130] Such nationalism nicely dovetailed with the increased state monitoring of minority and foreign schools as well.[131] This escalated control was especially strong in the Armenian minority schools where the almost exclusively Armenian student population was not permitted to learn Armenian history. When a principal tried to have Armenian history taught, another teacher informed on him, leading to the removal by the ministry of both the principal and the history teacher, and the state appointment of the informer as the principal.[132]

Teaching Turkish Nationalism

The teaching of Turkish nationalism pedagogically united the centralized republican educational system, highlighting not only Turkish civilizational achievements but also the bravery and righteousness of the Muslim Turks at the expense of all other religions and ethnicities.[133] Especially noteworthy was the teaching of Turkish history where the Turks were identified as the oldest inhabitants of Anatolia, thereby predating and delegitimating the existence on the same lands of the Armenians, Kurds, and Greek Rum.

Such rewriting of Turkish history along nationalist lines started early on when Mustafa Kemal took a personal interest in the historical origins of the Turks, advocating archaeological research that ended up claiming that the ancient Sumerians were actually of Turkish descent. Mustafa Kemal then visited not only elementary, middle, and high schools but also universities with the intent to investigate whether this nonacademic reformulation of history was put into practice. One memoir writer recounted that upon examining one university class, Mustafa Kemal asked a student: "Do your foreign professors tell you that Sumerians were of Turkish origin?" When the student replied after some hesitation, "No, they do not; I arrived at this conclusion based on what I learned at my Turkish high school," Mustafa Kemal was furious and responded: "So they do not say so. Where is that ass Saffet Arıkan (the minister of education)? Did we bring these professors to poison such innocent Turkish children? If this does not work out, we can send them back." He then continued quizzing the student in accordance with the newly developed "Sun Language Theory" (Güneş Dil Teorisi), which claimed that all languages and civilizations descended from the Turks and their Turkish language. When his protégé Afet İnan, accompanying him, explained that the theory was taught only in the Turcology departments, Mustafa Kemal ordered it to be taught as a mandatory course at all university departments.[134] This exchange reveals not only the strict monitoring of what was taught at all levels of education but also the control over what the university professors, who should have been free in determining the content of their courses, were subjected to. That Mustafa Kemal was willing to fire all those who did not adhere to the nationalist theories concocted by the republican leaders also demonstrates the precariousness of employment in the educational system; even university faculty had to determine their course content in accordance with the parameters of Turkish nationalism or could be subject to losing their jobs.

Such nationalist history teaching also occurred at the military academies. Turkish history was nationally constructed not to describe and explain historical events but instead to mythify and narrate them in accordance with the official nationalist rhetoric. The Turkish revolutionary history courses mandated at all schools of the republic, one memoir writer stated, "were not fulfilling. Regardless of who showed up as the instructor, rather than talking about the meaning, essence, and principles of the revolution, they narrated a series of tales... of heroism and self-sacrifice that exhilarated us.... But that should not have been the purpose of the course."[135] Over the course of eight decades, the entire Turkish populace learned the same mythified version of their history, one that glorified all actions of the Turks at the expense of all others. Because the Turkish nationalist rhetoric taught at all schools was so marginizaling of other religions and ethnicities, this historical prejudice often translated into discrimination against all students of non-Muslim and non-Turkish origin.[136] The official intent of state education was therefore not to develop each child to his or her potential regardless of creed and ethnicity but instead to segregate and discriminate against the non-Turkish and the non-Muslim.

In all schools, the Turkish Muslim teachers often ended up discriminating against their non-Muslim students. One non-Muslim recounted in his memoir that when the students made too much noise in the classroom, his third-class teacher, Selma Hanım, shouted, "Be quiet! You've turned the classroom into a synagogue!" When a student wanted to know what stingy meant, she replied: "Like the Jews; forty Jews get together to eat one fish head." In fourth grade, his teacher, Saime Hanım, gathered all the students' identity cards, but when she could not settle who was Muslim and who was non-Muslim, asked the non-Muslim student: "What is the name of your prophet?" Upon receiving the response "Moses," because this was the only prophet's name the non-Muslim student had heard, she asked another student, who responded, "Muhammad." The non-Muslim student continued: "Saime Hanım smiled like a commander who had achieved a great victory. That was that. She had outed 'the black one in the card deck.'" Then she went on for five minutes, delivering a pretentious speech about how the two students had different prophets. He recalled, "While lauding the greatness and wisdom of Muhammad [however, she] did not utter a word about Moses." Such discrimination naturally impacted the students as they too started to discriminate on the same grounds.[137]

Other sources of knowledge that impacted the students were the daily newspapers and journals they read; these too often portrayed non-Muslims in a negative light, leading Turkish students to replicate the same prejudicial stand.[138] Another non-Muslim memoir writer recounted how, at another school, one male non-Muslim student was ordered to leave the military service class in case he "learned all the Turkish military secrets and sold them to the enemy."[139] The situation was no different in the non-Muslim minority schools, since the Turkish history teachers were appointed by the ministry and almost always were chosen from among the most fervently patriotic Turks. Such was the case in the school attended by an Armenian student who remembered that "bald Emin Bey kept saying 'there is nothing called Armenian; you are all Turks,' also telling them he had named his son 'Vural,' literally 'hit and take it,' because he wanted his son to grow up thinking why was given this name, to then understand and hit the [Aegean] islands, getting them back from the Greeks." The Armenian student ended by commenting that "the entire anxiety of those governing the [Turkish] state was not to recognize any other national identity on this geography."[140]

The incidents recounted so far demonstrate explicit prejudice and discrimination in schools; at times, however, this took a more complex form as the teachers singled out the non-Muslim students to then chastise the Turkish ones for not managing to be as good as them. For instance, one Armenian student recounted that at the Turkish state school he attended, the physics teacher, Kenan Bey, "had gathered all those who had failed the literature exam the previous day, telling them by pointing me out: 'look here, the guy's mother tongue is not even Turkish and even he passed and you all failed.'" "Yet," the Armenian student noted, "the teacher was mistaken as I had two mother tongues, Armenian and Turkish. My grandmother and grandfather did not know Armenian, [so] Turkish was spoken in our house quite frequently."[141] Not all Turkish teachers were so prejudiced, however, with some treating the non-Muslims equally and also often taking on their colleagues for uttering inappropriate remarks. The same non-Muslim who so carefully articulated the prejudicial stands of his teachers stated that his best year in elementary school was fifth grade because his teacher, Mensure Öğretmen, "did not at all make anti-Semitic remarks or refer to Jews in any way." When one girl and one boy were to be chosen from their class to represent Turkish civilization, the teacher chose a non-Muslim boy. "I had not at all expected this," the chosen memoir writer continued, "it was as if I had finally been successful and accepted as a real Turk! I was so proud because of this kindness." That non-Muslim students expected to be excluded from any representation once again reveals, however, their degree of marginalization within the Turkish educational system.

Turkish students also often intervened to protect their non-Muslim classmates. While attending the Göztepe American College, one Armenian student remembered that "one day a chauvinistic student named İlhan who was a year younger than us had called me 'the Armenian infidel.' My classmate Naim Karaosmanoğlu . . . was standing next to me just then. He slapped İlhan, stating 'look here, this is a school! We are all friends regardless of whichever nation;

don't let me ever hear the word "infidel" from your mouth again.' This was the kind of international environment within which we had been raised at Göztepe American College." The last remark of course raises the question of whether the Turkish student could have taken such a stand in a state school instead of a private one, surrounded by teachers who engaged in discriminatory behavior. Having attended the American Robert College myself, I distinctly remember how we were all treated equally as students to such a degree that I had to later think back to identify who among my classmates had belonged to which religion or ethnicity. I do not recount any instances of such prejudice and discrimination in my precollege years either, but that was partly because there were no non-Muslims in my elementary school classes. Looking back, however, I remember listening to racist jokes without at all registering or challenging the naturalized prejudice.

Early Republican Institutes of Higher Education and Research

State institutions of higher education should have been relatively free of such nationalism given their assumed focus on the practice of independent research and thinking. According to many contemporaneous memoirs, however, often this was not the case.[142] The RPP government's opposition to Turkish critical thinking commenced with the 1945 storming and burning of the leftist Tan Press that primarily published critical journals and newspapers by university students. Universities quickly became politicized a year later in the aftermath of the 1946 election that had for the first time destabilized RPP's single-party hegemony. Some university students taking issue with the change attacked particular faculty who held political views opposite to theirs.[143] Such political intolerance by the students reflected the escalating Turkish state intolerance of opposing political stands. In 1948, the state first shut down the leftist Turkish Workers' Party headed by Mehmet Ali Aybar and then removed from state universities many internationally prominent scholars such as the sociologists Behice Boran, Niyazi Berkes, social psychologist Muzaffer Sherif, and Pertev Naili Boratav for being leftists. In his memoirs, Niyazi Berkes analyzed the course of events leading to their expulsion as follows:[144]

> The attack of the universities spearheaded by [radical nationalist] Şemsettin Sirer first started with trumped-up allegations against [the liberal education minister] Hasan Ali Yücel; the intent was to remove him from his post [in which they succeeded, as he resigned in 1946].... These nationalist republican leaders later opposed a conference organized at the university on the grounds that they considered it against Turkish

> nationalism.... The possible unrest the conference might have created led... the university president... not interested in ensuring that it took place... to close it down.... The "leftist" professors who opposed this action were marked and eventually removed from their posts on the grounds that they advocated communism at their lectures.

When two law professors opposed the university senate decision, stating that it was against the laws governing the universities and that before such removal the professors had the right to defend themselves, the university senate decided to stand by its decision. The media did not support but instead immediately took a stand against these two professors, leading to their subsequent expulsion for "committing crimes that destroyed the university's honor."

Interestingly enough, rather than rallying in support of their colleagues, many Turkish university professors sided with the government and the state, arguing that state interests should precede scientific priorities. In explaining this twisted turn of events, Berkes noted that the social sciences had not been introduced to the republic through a gradual grounds-up social movement, as had been the case in Western Europe, but instead had been adopted "as an adornment, posturing, and imitation." They therefore had no potential influence on the state or the populace. "The main reason for this was the lack of the freedom to think and research," Berkes continued, as well as the fact that "those frightened by research results had more power in their hands than [those advocating] scientific research." Hence at the universities, proving allegiance to the state trumped scientific research and knowledge. Such politicization also impacted the foreign Western European professors teaching at Turkish state universities, who had mostly arrived in Turkey as a consequence of the witch-hunt in Germany against Jewish faculty. Yet they were accused by many Turks of being spies and therefore eventually left Turkey, never to return.

The situation at the universities worsened after the 1960 military coup as it was now the turn of Turkish military officers to decide what constituted proper academic research. They targeted and expelled 147 valuable academics whose names still read like a "who's who" in Turkish academia.[145] One memoir writer queried:[146]

> How was the incident of the [expulsion of] 147 [faculty members] actualized? Which committee consisting of whom, based on what criteria, according to what causes... decided upon these [particular] 147 faculty members...? We do not know even today! The education minister then was Bedreddin Tuncel whom I personally knew and he was unaware of the "147 incident"... like everyone else, he too had learned of the incident from the radio.

Once again some faculty actually approved the expulsions, demonstrating how naturalized and pervasive the state and government hegemony had become. Another university reform during this period was the addition of tuition to the formerly fully state-subsidized university education. "As the access of the universities to the [Muslim Turkish populace] was restricted," one memoir writer recounted, "the proportion of non-Muslim minorities at the universities increased. Thus emerged yet another opportunity to gnash one's teeth against [such minorities], as statements like 'It is a shame [Sultan Mehmed] the Conqueror [of İstanbul] did not totally eradicate the [minorities]'...or 'I am especially mad at those Armenians' started to be heard with increased frequency."[147]

The situation was not any better at the research institutes, also tightly controlled by the state and government. These too had been created not through grass-roots societal demand but by top-down state initiative. One memoir writer identified the origins of Turkish research institutes as follows:[148]

> One day in 1928 they showed Mustafa Kemal Atatürk a French geography book where people had been ranked according to their color with the Turks placed second after whites as a part of the yellow race. Atatürk could not accept this and started to work on history...and established the Turkish Historical and Turkish Language Societies as well as the [university] Faculty of Language, History and Geography...due to his belief that the Turkish nation whose great role in world history and whose exalted civilizational abilities he knew and appreciated [so much] could not be regarded a second-class race.

Such nationalist intent in the production of knowledge naturally colored and affected all subsequent research. The proofs of Turkish history textbooks were also continually reviewed with a similar intent, one memoir writer noted, "to correct the mistakes...of many of the history books published in our country...[that] had either consciously or unknowingly minimized the role of Turks in world history."[149] Public intellectuals and the populace participated in the construction of this nationalist presentation alongside scholars. The state's inclusion of such nonacademic groups into discussions on how to write history textbooks further popularized and mythified Turkish history. The appointments at these institutes were initially also political. For instance, Hasan Cemil Çambel, who became the director of the Turkish Historical Society in 1941, was initially trained as a military officer and then became a deputy from Bolu. It is no accident that the Historical Society failed to carry out independent research of Turkish history, remaining instead the voice of the official ideology. The same Historical Society has since then systematically published all the books that deny the collective violence committed against the Armenians.

Civic Education and Its Consequences

The republic initially invested extensive resources in civic education with the intent to produce the proper Turkish citizen. From 1932 to 1940, the People's Houses (Halk Evleri) and later the People's Rooms (Halk Odaları) were established as the urban and village centers of civic education, especially with the intent to generate support for state reforms. Yet just like the earlier CUP clubs, initially established to educate, organize, and mobilize the Turkish populace within a protonationalist vision, they too were quickly politicized, starting to promote the views of the RPP. The more significant initiative was undertaken in 1940: Village Institutes, initially inspired by the Soviet educational model, were founded specifically to train the rural populace, especially young, bright peasants boys and girls, who were to then go back to their villages to educate others and improve agricultural practices.[150] These institutes combined acquiring knowledge with learning practical skills. Contemporaneous memoirs articulate the social meanings these organizations acquired while in existence.[151] Upon the arrival of multiparty system, however, republican leaders in the RPP and then also the DP "became afraid of the business of building schools for villages and educating teachers. Even though [such institutes] would have been beneficial to the nation, it could nevertheless be harmful to [the republican leaders]."[152] The Village Institutes, which were more effective than the People's Rooms and People's Houses, were shut down because they had begun to empower Turkish village children, who then desired to participate in the republican political system. Because such an orientation upset the status quo sustaining the rule of republican leaders, the two parties were able to collaborate in this destructive action, thereby removing a significant tool that had given agency to the Turkish peasants.

In all, then, the state's centralization and control of the educational system restricted the agency of the members of Turkish society in determining their own destiny by mobilizing their rights. The ensuing system produced public knowledge that instituted, diffused, and reproduced Turkish ethnic nationalism, distorting the past and erasing the presence in and contributions of non-Muslims and non-Turks to Turkish history. Two contemporaneous memoirs demonstrate the adverse impact of this nationalist approach.[153] One of the memoir writers, who penned many books on Anatolian folklore, especially mysticism and other folk beliefs, never referred to Asia Minor's multireligious and multiethnic past, solely highlighting Turkish practices instead. The other writer was an Islamist intellectual. Once again, in the chronicle of his life, it is striking to observe the ethnically and religiously homogeneous life the new generation of republican religious leaders had started to lead; they interacted only with other Muslims, focusing solely on visiting other Muslim countries or criticizing the state politicization of religion in Turkey.

Many other local studies likewise contain totally monochromatic accounts of the country's past as well its present, unconsciously yet systematically obliterating its multicultural character in the process. In fact, I have recently started to collect such local studies with the intent to analyze the patterns of this cultural exclusion. In summary, early republican modernity, undertaken with the intent to democratize the country and successfully transform former Ottoman subjects into Turkish citizens, instead produced a society hegemonized by the Turkish state and government in particular and the dominant Turkish majority in general.

Elements of Early Republican Sentiments

Early Republican Intrasocietal Polarization

The divide between the reformist CUP and the conservative Freedom and Entente Party within the dominant Turkish Muslim majority persisted throughout the armistice period and the ensuing independence struggle. While the Allied occupation made all Muslim Turks increasingly patriotic, many disagreed on what this patriotism should entail. The Ententists continued their allegiance to the sultan and the imperial structure; the Unionists, who had lost the war, formally dissolved the CUP and then witnessed the subsequent escape of their top leaders to Europe. Yet many CUP members remained in the empire; their resistance to Allied occupation formed the bases on which the independence struggle was built. As they actively participated in the independence struggle, they shed their Unionist identity, transforming into nationalists or, as they were referred to locally, into Kemalists, that is, the followers of Mustafa Kemal. With their foundation of a republic on 29 October 1923, the nature of the political regime was determined, but who constituted the nation remained unclear.

Ensuing polarizations within the Turkish majority shaped the boundaries of the nation in four stages. The first stage occurred during the course of the independence struggle where only Muslim elements in Anatolia, namely, the Turks and the Kurds, were allowed to fight in the struggle; non-Muslim elements were specifically excluded. This religious polarization was then followed by an ethnic one. During the second stage, which commenced right after the advent of the republic, the largest remaining non-Turkish group, the Kurds, were also excluded from the body politic as only those Kurds who were willing to give up their ethnic identity managed to be included in the new political system as Turks. This ethnic polarization was followed by yet another religious one, this time among the Muslim Turks. The third stage of polarization emerged as a consequence of the republican decision to adopt a secular legal system instead of the sharia-based system in which only those Turks who were willing to adopt a secular identity could publicly participate in the body politic. The fourth and final stage of polarization took place during the ensuing three decades of the republic as all regime opponents were systematically repressed and excluded from leadership positions. In all, then, non-Muslims were excluded from the struggle; non-Turkish ethnicities like Kurds from the republic; the Islamic element from the secular system; and the secular yet opposing Turks from the ensuing body politic.

This pattern of polarization thus charted the course of the Turkish nation formation. Non-Muslims were the easiest to exclude from the nation, since they had never been fully included in the body politic; the Kurds were also easy to leave out because their inclusion in the body politic had never been fully acknowledged. It was much harder to negotiate the fragmentation and ensuing exclusion within the dominant Muslim Turkish majority, since the republican leaders also belonged to this category. The adoption of secularism as a republican principle killed two birds with one stone. On the one hand, it undermined all those who had been formerly legitimated in the Ottoman system through the centrality of religion; religious scholars, foundations, schools, and other institutions no longer had any political power. On the other hand, the privatization of religion removed all these people and institutions from the public sphere, leaving only secular Turks within the new republican power structure. Among the secular Turks, however, many aspired to participate in state and government. The adoption of the single-party rule during the first three decades kept the republican leadership intact; those in state and government united and solidified into one group that systematically defined the priorities of the nation in accordance with the needs of state and government.[154] This lack of separation among the executive, legislative, and administrative functions of governance was to haunt the republic for years to come; even after the advent of the multiparty system, all political parties had trouble negotiating this separation. In addition to the initial adoption of single-party rule, the other political practice through which the republican leadership solidified and legitimated itself was the creation of "enemies of the nation." The first "enemies" of the republic were "naturally" identified as non-Muslim minorities. The other defined "enemies" emerging as threats to the republic were Kurds, leftist communists, and, in the 1970s, the Islamists.[155] In all, this era not only reinforced the continuing social polarization between the Muslims and the non-Muslims but also brought in new fragmentation as the Turks began to split along ethnic (Kurd), ideological (leftist), and religious (Islamist) lines. This is exactly what differentiated CUP protonationalism from republican nationalism: during the CUP era, the Islamic religious and Turkish ethnic identities had not yet fully separated. Only with the republic did Turkish nationalism publicly shed its religious component. I have been able to identify this process of polarization and ensuing fragmentation once again through the information contained in contemporaneous memoirs.

Feeling Turkish Nationalism

Exclusionary Turkish nationalism became the most significant horizontal tie defining republican political mirrored modernity. The boundaries of the nation as an imagined community were initially constructed geographically, including all those living in Turkey and sharing the Turkish culture; the minority groups of non-Muslims as well as Alewites, Arabs, and Kurds were by definition part of this new body politic. With the 1923 Lausanne Treaty, the non-Muslims in Turkey were formally defined as "minorities" with special privileges, the state thus promising to treat them as equal citizens under these terms. The republic soon thereafter adopted a secular legal system, privatizing religion and removing it from the public sphere controlled by the state. Theoretically, such secularization would have been more inclusionary. Over time, however, the empire's dominant Muslim Turkish majority once again emerged as an ethnic "majority" controlling all political, economic, and social resources. This transformation from geographical to ethnic nationalism occurred in three phases: (1) from the advent of the independence struggle, including the Erzurum, Amasya, and Sivas Congresses, to the formation of the first national assembly in Ankara (1919–22); (2) the period of republican rule under the presidency of Mustafa Kemal Atatürk (1923–38); and (3) World War II, the transition to a multiparty system, and the 1960 and 1971 military coups (1939–73). This new periodization merits a detailed discussion because it presents an alternate history of the republic, one that counters the still-dominant official version.

Patriotic Fervor (1919–22)

Contemporaneous memoirs highlight the significant parameters of this initial phase.[156] Many regarded the Sèvres Treaty signed at the end of World War I as too harsh, almost guaranteeing that, "under its stipulations, it would be impossible for the country to be independent."[157] Therefore, during the ensuing Allied occupation, former CUP officials and officers gathered at the capital to discuss how the country could be saved. In one significant meeting, the first question discussed was whether an independence struggle ought to originate in İstanbul or Anatolia; many agreed that Anatolia, removed from direct Allied control, would be the better political choice. The next question concerned who should lead such a struggle; Ahmed İzzet Pasha emerged as the prominent CUP leaders' top candidate, but he turned down the invitation, causing the CUP leaders to turn to their second choice, the Ottoman general Mustafa Kemal. All former

CUP members then started to work on getting Mustafa Kemal to Anatolia and making sure he succeeded.[158] On 19 May 1919, Mustafa Kemal alighted in Samsun with a large retinue of seventy-four former CUP officials and officers to commence the independence struggle.

Crucial in Mustafa Kemal's selection had been his national vision, one that could unite all the nationalist local congresses and disparate independence movements. Prior to Mustafa Kemal's arrival, various local defensive fronts had already been established in the west, specifically in Ayvalık, Soma, Aydın, Nazilli, and Salihli, and the east, especially in Erzurum. Yet the Erzurum Congress Mustafa Kemal attended was politically recognized as the first official national meeting of the independence movement, thereby delegitimating all previous attempts. Mustafa Kemal quickly and methodically organized the various local actors into the seeds of a body politic. Ten days after disembarking in Samsun, he issued directives detailing the resistance organization, including the duties of all military and civilian officials. The imperatives were to resist the Armenian armed bands, defend the Mediterranean and Black Sea shores in the event of an enemy attack, transport all the arms and ammunitions out of the regions under Allied control, increase the number of soldiers in the battalions through recruitment, establish guerrilla units for emergencies, and prepare large buildings for destruction if necessary.[159] These details demonstrate, on the one hand, the attention with which Mustafa Kemal organized the initial national space and, on the other, the coevalness of the perceived Armenian threat to the emerging Turkish nation.

Two practices were especially significant in this initial nation formation process: the employment of modern communication technology and the exclusion of non-Muslims. Access to and control of especially the modern telegraph system enabled the leaders to organize politically in Anatolia, away from the imperial capital, which was still under the sultan's rule and the occupying Allied forces. Ottoman imperial and Turkish national spaces thus diverged, leading to the formation of two political structures from 1918 to 1923, with an imperial İstanbul government headed by the sultan and a national Ankara government led by Mustafa Kemal. While the İstanbul government aimed to sustain the imperial structure, the Ankara government gradually moved away from it to a republican one. This political separation occurred as follows: When Mustafa Kemal and his large retinue initially moved to Samsun, they were still sultan's officials. Eventually, as national congresses were held and governors, commanders, and some of the local Muslim Turkish populace joined the independence struggle, these social groups declared their allegiance to the Ankara government. Mustafa Kemal resigned his military post, eventually becoming the leader of the movement, first as the civilian president of the national assembly and then as the commander of the nationalist forces. The İstanbul government attempted to control the telegraph system, thereby attempting to leave the burgeoning Ankara government without a communication network. Yet most local communication personnel had already joined the national movement and therefore shut İstanbul out of Anatolia instead. Mustafa Kemal sent telegraphs to all army corps commanders, stating that the next necessary step was to form an assembly that was to meet in Ankara in fifteen days; elections had to be held immediately. Republican mirrored modernity thus inverted the nation-formation process in two significant ways: rather than the nation forming a new state, the former CUP state mobilized to create the Turkish nation; rather than employing modern methods of communication and organization such as use of the telegraph for communication and of bureaucratic structure for efficiency with the intent to include more individuals in the body politic, the independence movement utilized these modern tools to exclude those deemed loyal to the İstanbul government.

Especially significant in the formation of the national body politic was Mustafa Kemal's specific stipulation that "non-Muslim subjects were not to participate in these elections." Hence, non-Muslims in general and the Armenians in particular were excluded from the national body politic from the start, largely due to the possible establishment of an Armenia and Kurdistan in the eastern provinces. The Allied forces were not willing to commit the large forces necessary to establish such Armenian and Kurdistan states, however. This lack of commitment eventually left the Turkish national movement as the only viable political option for independence. This initial counterposition of Turkish and Armenian visions partially explains the difficulty that contemporary Turkish state and society have in confronting the collective violence against the Armenians. At the time, this counterposition also prevented the proper investigation of the perpetrators of the collective violence; in addition, many perpetrators joined the independence struggle in order to avoid being tried at the capital.[160] One memoir writer specifically stated that "upon the end of the war, when the British and their allies decided to get those who had been Unionists and especially those who had killed Armenians [to be held accountable], everyone who took offense armed themselves and joined an armed band.... In the West, the[se] bands are the first heroes of the nationalist forces."[161] As the perpetrators joined the nationalist forces, formal inquiries by the İstanbul government into the Armenian massacres in Anatolia remained mostly ineffective. The Turkish character of the national movement also emerged during the course of the independence struggle, with the Turks, the nation, and Mustafa Kemal gradually coalescing into one body.[162]

Escalating Patriotism during the Allied Occupation

The trauma experienced by many Muslim Turks at witnessing the Allied occupation of the Ottoman imperial capital, which had escaped such an experience for almost half a millennium (470 years, to be exact), is evident in contemporary memoirs. Upon seeing all Allied warships docked at the imperial capital, one memoir writer stated: "Our eyes are wide open. Something within bitterly urges to look at them, yet not see them. An unseen hand tries to squeeze and strangle our inner being, yet we angrily look [at the warships] and cannot take our eyes away from them." Another noted that "they had pointed their cannons at İstanbul...the sadness of the poor [city] settled within me, making me burn up....My blood caused me to take an oath to save Turkishness from the wickedness of both the owners of these weapons and our bad government that had turned into their instrument....I promised my God and my Turkish blood. I still burned up inside, but my soul had quieted down." Still another interpreted the initial shock and reticence as "cowardice [which is] our chronic disease," then indignantly remarked that "even though [the sultan's officials] are going to be fired in three days, the [populace] still live in the terror and groundless fear for an officialdom that would only last three days. The country is going [down]. With the country, the nation and even [our] livelihood is in danger. Yet cowardice and callousness still rule...[we are] at each other's throats, insulting each other, shouting 'you were able to steal, yet I was not,' assisting the enemy in applauding the friend and crushing the opponent." Such escalated feelings of patriotism further alienated the populace from the sultan, who had to associate with the Allied forces out of necessity.

The entitled behavior of the Allied forces occupying the imperial city, treating the Turkish Muslim populace as if they were colonial subjects, caused the most consternation. The Muslim Turkish populace could be physically easily identified because the men were wearing fezzes and the women were covered; these two social groups felt especially targeted. At the same time, being the target of such physical violence also fostered feelings of patriotism. One memoir recounted the acts of resistance that slowly emerged as a consequence:

> In Kadıköy, two Senegalese soldiers were taking one of our sailors, pushing and shoving [him]....Smiling at them, he tried to free himself....Yet the power [he struggled against] was not willing to accept even that much friendship and equal behavior. The material superiority of its victory was not sufficient [as] it also spiritually exploited this victory, belittling the city and the peoples over which it ruled. The impossibility of preserving values! Because of all this, people at the dock were startled by the sound of the slap, followed by yet another and another one. Then whistles were heard, filling the dock with the officers and soldiers of the occupying forces. I will never forget the face of that child still trying to be freed from those holding him, with blood spilling from his lip and nose, under the cruel and harsh glimmer of the eyes of those beating him. It was exactly the slap of the master. One doubts if those who executed it could one day recover the humanity [they had lost].

> Then the second incident occurred. A tall, thin, elderly woman, fingers filled with diamond rings, moved forward exclaiming "you swine!" and twice brought down her thick umbrella smack on the face of the [colonial soldier] beating [the sailor]. All these transpired in an instance. "You swine, what do you want from the poor child!" We, the people on the dock, all saw the handle of the umbrella break into two on the face of this foreigner. The populace, struggling until then in nervousness and desperation, suddenly mobilized. Things again became confused. When everything calmed down, we could see neither the sailor nor the old woman. The populace had helped them both escape.

It was especially difficult for Muslim Turkish officers to accept the occupation because it constantly reminded them of their inability to perform their duty of protecting the populace. To avoid having to salute the officers of the occupation, many changed their routes.

As the Muslim Turkish populace was increasingly aggravated by the occupation, the political arena was marked by greater polarization between the Unionists and the Ententists. Closely cooperating with the occupying forces, the Ententists attempted to punish the Unionists for losing the war and the empire in general and for committing massacres against the Armenians in particular. The Unionists instead took a patriotic stand, exploiting ethnic nationalism to deligitimate their past violence with the argument that they had done so for the sake of the fatherland. In attempting to punish the Unionists, the Ententists often went to extremes, taking action not only against Unionists but also against Unionist sympathizers, soon replicating previous exclusionary CUP violence themselves. A case in point can be seen in the attempts first by the Ententist interior minister and then by the grand vizier to deport from the capital all the*dönmes*—seventeenth-century converts from Judaism to Islam—on the grounds that many among them had been Unionists. Such excessive Ententist violence and zeal enabled the Unionists to assume the role of victims on the one hand and claim all past violence they committed had been falsely attributed to them by the Ententists to curry favors with the occupying forces on the other. In summary, during the armistice period, the Unionists started to gradually undermine and remove the stigma of past collective violence through resorting to patriotism.

Violent Sentiments during the Independence Struggle

During the armistice period, the decision of the British to allow the Greek forces to invaded Smyrna on 15 May 1919 proved to be a turning point, mobilizing many former CUP members to form spontaneous defense committees throughout Anatolia. While the Ententist stand became increasingly delegitimated, nationalist Unionist sentiments were now sanctioned. With the advent of the struggle, then, the Unionists transformed into patriots now defending their fatherland, eventually choosing Mustafa Kemal to lead the struggle. On 18 May 1919, a few days after the Greek occupation, Mustafa Kemal and his Unionist retinue left for Anatolia and quickly united the local resistances with disparate agendas into one movement. Yet it took some time for the leadership and the populace to connect due to class, Balkan-Anatolia cultural, and urban-rural divides. As the independence struggle took shape, those involved selected and let into their ranks only those Unionists who were willing to give up their previous identity for the new one of patriotic nationalists who declared full allegiance to the struggle.

During the course of the independence struggle, these new "nationalists" commenced to take violent action against those who did not support the struggle. Perhaps the most significant single act committed against the opposition was the 1922 kidnapping and subsequent staged lynching of the Ententist opponent Ali Kemal by the nationalist forces led by Nurettin Pasha. Yet the nationalists at the assembly in Ankara also began to fragment over Mustafa Kemal's leadership, dividing into the supporters and opponents of Mustafa Kemal. While some deputies objected to Mustafa Kemal assuming both the presidency of the assembly and the command of the national forces, others argued that the success of the struggle necessitated such an action. Halide Edip, who was among the few Muslim Turkish women who had joined the struggle, commented on Mustafa Kemal's regard of such opposition. In her memoirs, she narrated her conversation with the commander right after the Turkish army's victorious final battle at Sakarya:

> I said to Mustafa Kemal Pasha: "You will rest after the conquest of İzmir, my pasha, as you have become extremely tired." "Rest? After the Greeks, we will fight each other; we will go after one another." "Why? There is so much to be done!" "Still what about all those men who opposed me?" "Isn't it natural [for that to occur] at a national assembly?" At this point, his eyes flared dangerously and he mentioned two names from among the opposition group, stating they deserved to be lynched by the people. I did not take these words seriously.... [Yet] a little later, while having dinner, he continued: "After this struggle is over, things are going to be distressing. We have to find another exciting task, my lady." These words provide the key to the nature of Mustafa Kemal. All those who achieve great power possess this trait.

Also during this time, Halide Edip began to have doubts about the government that was going to be established after the struggle. Like many others, she was worried that there would not be adequate space for any political opposition to Mustafa Kemal. Halide Edip recounted another conversation she had with Mustafa Kemal:

> [During a long conversation we had], I did not understand much of what he said and told him so. Asking me to come and sit by him, he very clearly explained what he meant as follows: "What I mean is this: everyone has to execute the order I give." "Haven't they done so until now for the safety and security of Turkey?" "I do not want any thoughts or criticism; I only want the execution of my orders." "Even from me, my pasha?" "Yes, from you as well." I responded very frankly: "I will obey you as long as you serve the national cause." "You shall always obey my orders [regardless]!" I again answered frankly: "Is this a threat, my pasha?" He suddenly changed his attitude, stating, "I am sorry; I would never threaten you." Although I knew Mustafa Kemal accomplished what he wanted through threats, I was sure he had not said so to threaten me. Then we started to talk normally. Now this is the only interaction I had with Mustafa Kemal Pasha that was akin to a dispute. I was immersed in thoughts that night. I constantly remembered Mustafa Kemal's words pertaining to how power cannot be divided. Yet as I knew what a significant and necessary place he occupied [in the struggle], I decided to put this feeling aside. I believed that Mustafa Kemal Pasha was going to save the country. Even though I was sure that [he] would not forget this small incident, I nevertheless decided to write about it one day in English.

With such doubts, after the success of the independence struggle, the Turkish republic was formally established on 29 October 1923.

Monopolizing Sentimentalities (1923–38)

During the early years of the republic, Mustafa Kemal initially stated that every person who regarded himself as a Turk should be considered one. Yet such an inclusionary stand in theory did not translate into practice, especially because the same leader declared that "the noble blood in the veins of Turks" was the reason for the existence of the nation.[163] Another component that accompanied this ethnic stand was the increased role of the military, with one officer stating:[164]

> No nation in the universe other than the Turkish nation has placed as much value and significance on its weapon. The weapon is the honor and chastity of the Turk, his everything. For the Turk knows that he will protect his religion, beliefs, honor, chastity, all his holy things, children,

> wife, fatherland, everything he possesses only with his weapon; he knows he would not survive even a single day if he does not hold onto his weapon so well.

Within this context, Mustafa Kemal, heading the state, the nation, and the military as both a civilian and a military leader, gradually established full control over the country. Such control enabled him to engage in decade-long sweeping reforms. Mustafa Kemal had explained much earlier why such modernizing reforms were necessary, stating in a letter:[165]

> If I have great power and responsibility one day, I think I would actualize the revolution desired in our domestic lives all at once with a coup . . . because I do not accept the argument that this should be actualized gradually by [first] getting the thoughts of the populace . . . my soul rebels against such an approach. Why should I, after having received an education for so many years and after having spent so long to analyze civilized and domestic life, lower myself to the level of the populace? I should instead elevate the populace to my level so they become like me, rather than I like them.

This "civilized and domestic life" was the one Western-style-educated officials and officers like Mustafa Kemal had been trained to follow, especially during the Young Turk period. Given their political victory and their authoritarian way of thinking, they transformed the imagined nation from the top down after the modern form in their mind's eye. The 1922 abrogation of the sultanate and the 1923 promulgation of the Turkish republic with Ankara as its official capital were followed by the most significant political change of secularism as religion was privatized and separated from politics. The 1924 dissolution of the caliphate was followed by the 1925 closing down of religious institutions and the 1928 declaration of Turkey as a secular republic, to this day the only one of its kind in a predominantly Muslim society. The legal system was secularized with the 1924–37 adoption of an amalgam of laws from Western European countries that "befit Turkish culture." In addition, women were given political rights between 1930 and 1934. There were also two attempts to establish opposition parties in 1924 (Progressive Republican Party) and 1930 (Free Republican Party), but both had to be quickly shut down because of the rapid mobilization of the populace around religion and against the reigning Republican People's Party established and headed by Mustafa Kemal.

The most sociologically significant reforms determining the countours of national knowledge and social practice pertained to education and everyday life. In 1924, all educational institutions were centralized under state control. Then, in 1928, the Arabic script was replaced by the Latin one, dramatically restricting the new nation's access to its past. The state then carefully monitored the creation of national knowledge: only those historical documents sanctioned by the official narrative were transliterated into the Latin script, excluding and silencing political opposition on the one hand and past collective violence against the minorities on the other. The accompanying establishment of the national Turkish History Association and national Language Association further shaped this new knowledge; the nationalist rhetoric on mythified accounts of the past generated at these institutions then diffused into the centralized educational system. In terms of everyday life, the hat and clothing reform of 1925 especially advocated all Turkish males to dress and to wear hats as in the "civilized West."[166] Many other Western European practices were adopted between 1925 and 1931 as well. Specifically, the national holiday was changed from Friday (holy day in Islam) to Sunday; timekeeping from the Arabic (in accordance to natural cycles corresponding to Muslim prayer times) to the Western one, and all weights and measurements to European standards. The 1934 surname law touched the lives of all citizens. Until then, people had been identified with patronymics, places of origin, or particular titles indicating their position in society, indicators that emphasized difference. Now all citizens legally had to take surnames, registering these names with state authorities. Thus, in a Foucauldian move, sameness replaced difference within a decade.

Yet such total transformation was not easy. Contemporaneous memoirs articulate the trials and tribulations of change.[167] For instance, during Mustafa Kemal's morning visit to a provincial town, the district governor donned an evening jacket and white bow tie, unaware that such form of Western dress could only be worn at a particular appropriate context.[168] Secularism also meant the removal from public space of any religious symbols and rituals, Muslim and Christian alike, that used to bring communities together.[169] Another significant change was the exclusion from the public spaces of any signs of lack of progress. The Ankara governor forbade peasants in poor outfits to walk on the modern Çankaya Street where the foreign ambassadors lived and Atatürk passed by.[170] This republican attempt to constantly monitor the public space with the intent to present a public "civilized" face became a permanent theme; while the civilized form was made public, the content that failed to quickly transform was either censored or silenced.

Such censorship and silencing were especially significant in the case of non-Muslim minorities who were forced to assimilate into the newly generated republican sameness. The "Citizen, Speak Turkish!" campaign commencing in the late 1920s and continuing through the 1930s generated the most significant pressure on the non-Muslim minorities within urban space. All were forbidden to speak any language other than Turkish in public spaces. Self-appointed Turks took it upon themselves to apply the law; once, in a streetcar, one such Turk handed a non-Muslim woman who was speaking French a yellow card as a warning, but he did so after first slapping her hard. No one said or did anything.[171] The dialects, customs, and habits of minorities were also constantly mocked in newspapers and theater performances.[172] Such social control and ridicule in public spaces transformed into official discrimination as newspaper advertisements for state and government positions specifically indicated that the applicant "had to be a Turk." Likewise, when non-Muslims had to perform military service, the ads specifically mentioned that "minorities have to come to [a separate] recruitment office." Regardless of their level of education, none of the non-Muslim males could serve as officers but were instead placed in separate labor battalions to work on road construction. In the 1934 adoption of last names, non-Muslims could not keep their ancestral last names because the law specifically prohibited the use of "foreign" names. At times, state officials at the registration bureaus did not like any of the proposed surnames, forcing people to come up with new ones at the last minute.[173] As a consequence of such forced assimilation, some non-Muslims converted to Islam to better fit in with the dominant Turkish majority.[174] Even when many such minorities gave up their identities in order to assimilate, however, as evinced in the next phase, they were still not fully accepted into the public space of the Turkish nation.

Exclusionary Positions (1939–73)

Turkish nationalism became more exclusionary after the 1938 death of Mustafa Kemal (Atatürk) as forced assimilation transformed into systemic violence. During World War II, Turkey managed to remain neutral, but it was nevertheless adversely impacted by the rise of fascism in Europe as most Republican leaders quickly became its fierce advocates.[175] National Socialism's political influence on Turkey took two forms. Ideologically, Turkish nationalism started to be widely interpreted first as pan-Turkism and then as pan-Turanism, aspiring to unite all the Turks of the world all the way to Central Asia under the Turkish flag. Administratively, Turkey was ruled by a hegemonic political party that aspired to control the country through National Socialist practices. İsmet İnönü, the political leader during much of this phase, tried to promote himself as the "national leader," complementing Mustafa Kemal's official depiction as the "eternal leader." The transition to a multiparty system after the end of war enabled the opposition Democrat Party to win the 1950 elections with a landslide victory. Although the DP also won the elections of 1954 and 1957, the RPP in opposition allied with the armed forces to actualize the first military coup of the republic in 1960. This was followed by another coup in 1971, with the military solidly establishing itself as the main political force in Turkish state and society.

In spite of the transition to a multiparty system, Turkish nationalism persisted as all parties across the spectrum were infused with the same nationalistic values. The Turkish military took this nationalism to new heights. What did this militant nationalism comprise? Its most significant prerogative was the protection of the state-defined interests of the Turkish nation at all costs. Such protection was legitimated by two additional components. First, the Turkish nation was constantly portrayed as brave, courageous, and deserving of everything, a self-inflated imagery that in turn was supported by the educational system. As a consequence, generations of insulated Turkish citizens became certain that Turkey occupied a very significant place in the world. Second, the country's central significance in the world also made Turkey the target of many secretly developed sinister designs by its neighbors, with their potential allies of minorities within, all initially instigated by the West. The populace had to remain in a state of constant alertness for such evil designs against the Turkish fatherland, leading them to develop a sense of potential victimization on the one hand and to approve vast military spending reaching more than half the annual budget on the other. Such a stand also legitimated the systemic violence against the minorities, who were deemed to be different and outside the national body politic.

Four instances demonstrate how non-Muslim exclusion was practiced by the state and government without any opposition from the populace: During 1941–42, three generations of non-Muslim males were taken under arms for almost two years, followed right afterward by the 1942 imposition of a wealth tax that specifically targeted non-Muslims with the intent to transfer their wealth to the dominant Turkish majority. The next aggression occurred a decade later in the form of the 6–7 September 1955 pogroms in major cities as Turkish mobs instigated by the state and government destroyed the remaining non-Muslim material and symbolic wealth. Then again, almost a decade later in 1964, the Greek Rum of Turkey holding Greek passports were given two days within which to leave the country with only one suitcase and $100 in cash. Because none of the aggressors involved in these incidents were ever punished, these acts of aggression helped normalize and naturalize militant Turkish ethnic nationalism at the expense of all others who were not ethnically Turkish. Likewise, the republic did not acknowledge but instead suppressed past collective violence committed against the minorities.

Practicing Exclusionary Nationalism

Republican leadership consolidated its ranks and established its legitimacy through a series of exclusions. First, the national assembly guiding the country through the struggle was dissolved and replaced by party-appointed—not democratically elected—deputies, thereby effectively eliminating all opposition to Mustafa Kemal and his RPP. Then, 150 opponents of the regime were expelled from the country and stripped of their citizenship, including some Circassians who had allied with the sultan; all members of the Ottoman dynasty were exiled as well.[176] Those who had fought alongside Mustafa Kemal but did not agree with the recent political developments also left eventually, with Halide Edip and her husband among them.[177] Finally, those perceived political opponents of the regime were systematically eliminated through independence courts operating with total impunity.[178] As the republican leadership consolidated its ranks, the Muslim Turks started to negotiate the meaning of the struggle, locating themselves on top of the newly emerging nation. The first polarization among them occurred around geographical origin: those who came from Anatolia considered the struggle theirs, starting to look down upon the Turks arriving from the Balkans and elsewhere.[179] The second polarization concerned where specific people had been during the course of the struggle: those who had moved to Ankara started to denigrate the ones who had stayed behind in İstanbul, accusing the latter of being decadent and cosmopolitan.[180] The third polarization centered on one's stand regarding the connection between Mustafa Kemal and the struggle: while some argued the struggle had been won by him alone, others pointed out that many officers, officials, and locals had also participated.[181] The most significant consequence of these tensions was the emergence of a totalizing conception of "the Turk" that became symbolically equated with participation in the independence struggle and the republic.[182]

From the 1930s through the 1960s, another social polarization formed along party lines. Although the RPP had been established as the official party of the republic under the leadership of Mustafa Kemal, there were two attempts to further democratize the country by founding opposition parties, once in 1924 and again in 1930. Both were quickly shut down after some months, however, when political opposition quickly mobilized around them. One memoir writer explained that the failure of these two attempts was mainly "due to Mustafa Kemal's insistence in staying both the president of the republic as well as the leader of the Republican People's Party," that is, as both the head of state and the head of government.[183] The third attempt at establishing an opposition party succeeded in the late 1940s, and the new Democrat Party came to power in 1950 with a landslide. One memoir writer remembered the ensuing polarization of the populace into RPP or DP members by stating that "the supporters of the two parties were like enemies of one another. We too felt the tension within our circle of friends and family, divided into RPP versus DP. We had many upsetting and hurtful discussions."[184] During the single-party era, the RPP had been criticized for "controlling the entire state with some deputies and local representatives who considered themselves 'above the law.' "[185] Though the DP had criticized that stand, once it was in power, its representatives and deputies acted in exactly the same way, with no impunity. The DP was just as partisan as the RPP;

one memoir writer noted that "it immediately wanted all local administrative spots to be filled by its party members, attempted to use the state's machinery for their private ends, and kept tabs on which officials greeted which party representatives."[186] Such increased political polarization resulted in the RPP supporting the first military coup of the republic.

In the aftermath of the 1960 coup, DP members were sought out, arrested, and imprisoned by the military with great fervor.[187] Almost all the memoirs dating from this decade note the violence the DP members faced.[188] With the gradual return to civilian rule, the RPP once again came to power, starting to exercise the same repression and lack of accountability and transparency of which it had accused the DP. Although new parties emerged, they could not produce new visions, remaining confined within the parameters set by the republican leadership supported by the military. During the Cold War, increased interactions with the United States and the Marshall Plan once again polarized the country, dividing it into those who wanted and accepted the plan, and those who objected to it on the grounds that it produced a dependent relationship. Meanwhile, a new generation emerged, educated and with the intent to participate in both the government and the public sphere. University students became active; forty faculty members issued a declaration in November 1965 criticizing the United States' policies in Cyprus and Vietnam. Yet the republican leadership once again tried to control both through violence and repression.[189] In addition, the RPP got conservative academics to react, leading them to issue a counterdeclaration in January 1966, warning the first group to stay out of politics. The 1970s commenced with yet another military coup in 1971, as many student leaders were tried and executed by the military.[190]

Reproducing Exclusionary Nationalism

How was the republican leadership able to successfully practice and sustain such exclusionary nationalism? The triangulation of particular political, military, and legal practices—undemocratic elections, threat of military force, and state-controlled judiciary—produced hegemonic rule. This rule was then reproduced through two practices, the exercise of censorship and repression, and the creation of "internal enemies." The evolution of the political practice of undemocratic elections is amply documented by contemporaneous memoirs.[191] In holding the initial elections for the national assembly, military and civil authorities wanted "strong and patriotic people."[192] Still, the first 1920 national assembly, guiding the country through the independence struggle, was the most democratic because the deputies had been locally selected and appointed. The elections for the second 1923 national assembly were much more closely controlled by the new republican leaders, however, eliminating all opposition through the direct appointment of selected deputies.[193] Such appointed officials of course once again developed loyalty not to the populace but instead to the state, looking after their personal interests in the meantime.[194] In the 1934 elections, the republican leaders continued to minimize popular participation; before the elections, "the list of deputies to be elected was given its final form at the Dolmabahçe palace by the [RPP] party council."[195] One memoir writer who was nominated first expressed his surprise, then noted that "fifteen days later, he was elected the Samsun deputy," even though he had never been to Samsun in his entire life.[196] Only with the 1946 elections, with the emergence of a viable opposition party (the DP), did the deputies visit their electoral districts for the first time.[197] The RPP managed to hold onto the government in these elections, but it did so through election fraud, similar to what the CUP had put into practice.[198] When the DP won the 1950 elections by a landslide, the former CUP and SO member Celal Bayar became the president, revealing how the RPP and the DP were actually cut from the same cloth. Indeed, one of the first DP acts was to declare that RPP members would not be held accountable for the injustices committed during their twenty-seven-year single-party rule.[199] Given this lack of accountability, it is not surprising that soon thereafter, DP members also engaged in practices similar to the RPP; their city and town organizations "would create files on those state officials they deemed necessary [for actualizing their business] and send these to the party leadership. The state appointments were then made in accordance to this information."[200]

In terms of the legal system, this carefully appointed national assembly first formed "independence courts" from among its members with the intent to "legally" try and punish all those who either criticized or objected to the independence struggle. The court judges did not necessarily have any legal training. For instance, among the members of these courts, deputy Kılıç Ali was a mere high school graduate; deputy Ali Çetinkaya had shot and killed Halit Pasha during a session at the national assembly, escaping any punishment for the murder. The verdicts the judges reached were drastic, and no one could appeal their decisions.[201] Blatant disregard of the legal system continued with the establishment of two additional independence courts in 1925 and 1926. The 1925 court was presumably formed to suppress the Sheikh Said Rebellion in the east. Yet the main conflict such severe and illegal measures reflected was the larger fight within the national assembly over adopting either the liberal or the authoritarian parameters of political rule. While the hawks advocated martial law, independence courts, and severe military repression, including illegal practices, the doves proposed finding mutual solutions through dialogue within the legal framework and without martial law. The hawks won, determining the course of republican history for the next seven decades. One judge who served on the 1925 independence court noted in his memoirs that his every attempt to stay within the parameters of law was objected to on the grounds that "they had a particular national aim. In order to reach it, we would certainly go beyond the boundaries set by law." Not only did this court decide on what constituted a crime, but it had the right to summarily execute its decisions, with the accused having no recourse.[202] The 1926 independence court was constituted to try those who had unsuccessfully attempted to assassinate Mustafa Kemal. Once again, the accused had no legal recourse. Actually, this court too was the outcome of the power struggle within the assembly, effectively eliminating all those who had opposed the hawks as well as those who could potentially oust the republican leaders, that is, former CUP leaders like Cavid Bey, Dr. Nazım, Kara Kemal, and others. All these political opponents were tried on trumped-up charges and executed.[203] This harsh legal course quickly eliminated any remaining opposition. During this era, from that point on, the judiciary came to be regarded not as an independent institution but rather as the state's legal arm, legitimating the state's decisions.

The third leg of the hegemony was the strong influence of the military in the national assembly and also in state administration.[204] Even though Mustafa Kemal stated time and again that the military and politics ought to be kept apart, the military always ended up meddling in politics.[205] The members of the Turkish military considered themselves "above the law," always intervening to protect their own even when events clearly demonstrated them to be guilty.[206] They also made extremely expensive and inappropriate armament purchases, but not only were they not held accountable for their actions, but one such purchaser then became the defense minister.[207] The children of the military also had privileged status and often abused their privileges.[208]

The strong involvement of the military in politics continued during two-party rule as well, this time in repressing civilian opposition.[209] Especially telling are the memoirs of the constitutional law professor Ali İhsan Başgil. As military officers joined the RPP in opposing the DP government, Başgil, who legally challenged and criticized such an involvement, was questioned and investigated by the military. Then, the military carried out the 1960 coup, abolishing the DP, hanging three of its leaders, including the prime minister, and imprisoning and trying many other members and deputies. After the coup, with the return to civilian rule, Başgil decided to engage in politics and was elected senator in 1965. He then became a candidate for the presidency, a candidacy that had garnered him much popular support. Başgil recounted how he was then invited to the prime ministry, where he knew he would be pressured to withdraw his candidacy. He nevertheless went, stating that becoming a candidate was a political right, that no one could prevent him from doing so because such prevention would be illegal, and that he did not think the government would resort to such a measure.[210] The generals who were at the meeting were not at all interested in Başgil's thoughts; they told him point-blank that he "had to withdraw his candidacy because we cannot ever allow any candidate to emerge other than [the military's candidate, General] Cemal Gürsel Pasha." Başgil was so unnerved by this exchange that he not only immediately withdrew his candidacy but left the country, going into exile in Switzerland.

In the 1961 elections, the RPP had a slight lead over the newly founded Justice Party (JP), which was in fact a continuation of the abolished DP. The JP then won the 1965 and 1969 elections with a clear majority, only to face another military coup in 1971. The subsequent 1973 elections once again gave the RPP, now under the leadership of the young Bülent Ecevit, a slight lead over the JP. This period was also marked by increased unrest in the country, as well as student movements aiming to liberate the country from the hegemony of this select group of republican leaders. These student intellectuals were violently suppressed as well. One publisher was arrested and imprisoned in 1971; in his memoirs, he stated that the main document that led to his arrest was the wrapping paper of his publishing house, which had quotations from famous political leaders like Lenin, Mao Tse-tung and Mustafa Kemal "on freedom, brotherhood, independence, democracy, and socialism."[211]

As domestic political unrest continued, Turkey's foreign policy was brought increasingly under the control of the United States, the country that supplied the Turkish military with a significant portion of its arms and armaments. The UN representative of Turkey during this period recounted in his memoirs the manner in which the Turkish republic executed its foreign policy, totally dependent on the United States:[212]

> In those days, the UN was like a club of the rich; only 55 governments were represented.... The task of the Turkish representative was very easy.... One point that was fastidiously attended to was to make sure the [Turkish] representative comfortably saw the American ambassador from where he sat. During the general council, it was necessary that he followed whether the American representative voted for or against an action. We adjusted our vote accordingly.

In the republic, a very unstable political start with almost no political participation by the populace for almost three decades, transformed, upon increased political participation through the multiparty system, into a series of military interventions. The authoritarian rule was supported by the United States, which prioritized political stability in all allied countries over increased democratization. In his memoirs, one writer best summed up this era when he complained about all Turkish state and government officials constantly making things difficult, "as if they were not of this world, but came from another planet to make life difficult for us."[213]

THROUGH CENSORSHIP AND REPRESSION The civic sphere outside the Turkish state was also tightly controlled to produce obedient subjects of the state rather than expressive citizens of the republic. Contemporaneous memoirs point to three significant ways in which such state control over society was actualized: curbing civic expression through repression, surveillance of potential suspects, and, most significantly, close censoring of the national media.[214] They specifically comment on the adverse political shift with the death of Mustafa Kemal in 1938 and the coming to power of the former CUP and SO member İsmet İnönü. The larger international context, especially the rise of fascism in Europe and continued economic depression, also fostered such authoritarian tendencies. State control over society escalated as the state monitored the boundaries of public decency by censoring the naked paintings at a private gallery and deeming books pornographic in an attempt "to preserve the morality of Turkish people."[215] In 1946–48, when the Soviet repatriation program commenced and all Armenians were invited to settle in Armenia, Armenians of Turkey were not permitted to leave.[216] In addition, the state had those individuals it had identified as potential dangers to the current regime kept under constant surveillance.[217] Such practices continued into the 1970s.[218]

The most significant state and government control was established over the main source of knowledge of the Turkish populace at large, namely, the print media, in a manner very similar to prior CUP practice. Such control started from the inception of the republic as Mustafa Kemal often had his views printed under the signatures of prevalent journalists, thereby curbing their freedom of expression.[219] The same control escalated under İsmet İnönü.[220] This time, however, in order to maintain the appearance of the freedom of expression, state and government authorities also attempted to socialize journalists into self-censorship. Another method employed was to have the Press Directorate in Ankara send specific directives on how significant current events should be interpreted by the newspapers.[221] At times, the prime minister had press conferences where he cautioned newspaper owners or representatives as if he were issuing orders. One journalist recalled the nature of this interaction as follows:[222]

> At one such occasion, [Prime Minister] Refik Saydam explained in great detail what we had to write the following day in relation to a foreign policy matter. He then looked at me and asked rather mockingly: "Do you get it?" When I halfheartedly replied, "I do," he then asked as if he were quizzing me, "OK then, tell us, what are you are going to write tomorrow?" As this second question was akin to having an inexperienced orderly repeat a given order, one [embarrassingly] asked in front of my colleagues, it upset me immensely, and I responded in a cross manner. I still remember how shocked my older colleagues were at my

reaction, looking at me with pity, and how Saydam defused the ensuing frigid air in the room with a joke.

According to the press law at the time, under no circumstances could state officials have their articles published in newspapers and journals, thereby curbing their freedom of expression as well. Any attempts to establish intellectual journals discussing world events from the Turkish perspective were also shut down, like the *Kadro* journal was, since the state wanted to sustain its monopoly over the interpretation of public meaning.[223] Likewise, when republican leaders like İsmet İnönü engaged in improper behavior by publicly chastising senior journalists, media attempts to write about such incidents were immediately censored with threats of newspaper closure.[224]

Official censorship of the media escalated during World War II. Newspapers were not free to write about certain events or to write about other events at a length the state did not approve. Every afternoon, a courier on a motorcycle would arrive from the Press Directorate in Ankara, distributing orders on "what could or could not be written about, which news items should be expanded upon and others minimized."[225] Those newspapers that did not toe the official line were shut down.[226] Individual journalists who did not adhere to state orders were continually harassed by public prosecutors filing lawsuits against them, effectively curbing the journalists' freedom of expression. Not only did such official actions waste the time and resources of the accused journalists, causing them emotional anguish in the process, but the lawsuits were then decided by judges who considered themselves to be state officials before all else. Rather than reaching legal decisions independently, the judges too were forced by the state to ensure that the legal outcome was the one the officials wanted. Such tight control over the media curbed the ability of Turkish journalists to practice their calling as professionals. Rather than researching news stories, they instead started to write imaginary accounts in accordance with the official line.[227] Because the state controlled what they could write and research, and because the state held them accountable only when they criticized the state, Turkish journalists were not able to develop the necessary ethical standards. Outside the parameters set by the state, they could write any imaginary thing and not be held accountable. This increased the power of journalists, but it did so negatively: only those among them who could generate or act upon mere rumors with impunity stood out and became successful.

State control over the media continued unabated throughout the 1950s, 1960s, and 1970s. Even though multiparty rule had been then established, upon coming to power, the DP as well as ensuing political parties continued the same restrictive practices.[228] Newspaper owners were also complicit in sustaining the official control over knowledge; this was partly because they knew their failure to comply would lead to the closing down of their own newspapers.[229] In addition, another power the state held over the media was its monopoly over bulk paper sales; it could reduce the amount of bulk paper allocated to particular newspapers, thereby once again forcing them to toe the official line.[230] Because major civilian actors like prominent journalists and newspaper owners who could have objected never did so, the circulated knowledge gradually socialized the entire populace to think along the official line, in the process limiting their ability to develop into independent, constructively critical citizens: the standpoints of the state and society became one and the same. The Turkish print media became a mouthpiece of the state, and those who wanted to attain official posts or receive promotions did so by writing newspaper articles promoting the official narrative.[231] It is befitting to end this section with the reflections of one memoir writer on the freedom of expression and print in Turkey:[232]

> At school, we teach our children that criticism is the first vitamin of a civilized person; [though] it does not satiate the stomach, it is [nevertheless] the primary need of the intellect. It is the soap with which the spirit is cleansed.... But let us be honest, friends. If you ask any sane person, "are you really sure we have freedom of print and criticism [in Turkey]?" the answer would be in the negative.... It is there only in name... our journalists and intellectuals know that one could rise in our [Turkish] society not through criticizing the government administration, but by toadying up to it.

THROUGH THE CREATION OF INTERNAL ENEMIES In order to consolidate, legitimate, and reproduce the republican leadership, it became even more crucial to strictly define the boundaries of the nation, identifying those social groups within that posed a threat to the unity of the country. Such exclusionary practices solidified the hegemony of republican leadership. Over time, the first officially defined internal enemies were the non-Muslims. Initially, the polarization between the dominant Muslim Turkish majority and the non-Muslims intensified during the armistice period due to several factors. First, the non-Muslim enthusiasm and support for the occupation drew the ire of Muslim Turks.[233] Second, the occupying forces employed non-Muslims in administering the imperial city, further upsetting the Turks, who had no authority left in their interactions with non-Muslims.[234] Third, as the non-Muslims thus increasingly interacted with the Muslim Turks on an everyday basis, they often became overzealous in exercising their authority.[235] The situation had reversed from the earlier imperial order. Now, while the Turks did not carry arms, the Christians were armed by the occupying forces. Given the increased agitation of the Muslim

Turkish populace in relation to recent non-Muslim social superiority, appointments of non-Muslims to government positions became increasingly difficult as some tried to continue the previous practice of appointing a few non-Muslims, while others began to object, "seeing drawbacks to having Christian members among them."[236]

Non-Muslims Relations between Armenians and Turks became especially strained due to the collective violence committed against Armenians from 1915 to 1917.[237] The strain centered around three issues: the recovery of Armenian children and women in Muslim households; [238] the return of Armenian properties and goods confiscated by the state, government, and locals; and the legal investigation and punishment of perpetrators of Armenian massacres at the military tribunal established in İstanbul and elsewhere in Anatolia. While the Ottoman loss in World War I enabled the occupying Allied forces to initially place these issues on the agenda of the Ottoman government in 1919, the advent of the independence struggle the same year derailed the process. The recovery of Armenian women and children as well as Armenian properties and goods could only occur in locations under the jurisdiction of the occupying forces, a space that became increasingly confined as the nationalists began to win the independence struggle. In these newly created national spaces, the returning Armenians not only were unable to recover anything but also had to leave or were forcefully deported by the nationalist forces. The ongoing trials in Anatolia were likewise stunted and did not produce any positive outcome for the Armenians, since the judges were state officials who employed the legal system to stall the process and, worse still, to rule against Armenian claims. The passage of time since the collective violence and the destruction of evidence and documentation in the process also contributed to, or were intentionally utilized in reaching, verdicts against Armenian claims. Even though the most active trials occurred at the imperial capital with the support of the Entente government, the independence struggle undermined the legal process, attempting to hold the perpetrators accountable for their violent crimes. Old Unionists and new "patriotic" nationalists increasingly destroyed incriminating official evidence, pressured witnesses to withdraw their testimony and legal officials to resign their posts, and actively helped the perpetrators to escape into Anatolia to either hide or join the independence struggle. These developments ended up with almost all the perpetrators, including those who committed the massacres against the Armenians and those who had plundered Armenian properties, goods, and especially lands, getting away. According to contemporaneous memoirs, perhaps the one exception to this pattern was the recovery of Armenian women and children from Muslim households as this practice was quite successful but also rather contentious. The homes of many prominent Turks were raided and searched on the basis of tips that they housed hidden Armenian children; the accused rarely had any recourse to prove otherwise. Although some undoubtedly did house Armenian children and women, many had also taken in women and children of Muslim refugees from the Balkans and the Caucasus. And they had often done so informally, without any proper documentation. As a consequence, it became hard to prove the identities of those who were sheltered in Turkish households, further polarizing Armenian-Turkish relations.[239]

Outside the imperial capital, relations with the Armenians became especially tense in the aftermath of the 20 November 1919 agreement Bogos Nubar Pasha and Sherif Pasha signed to establish Armenian and Kurdish states. The Armenian soldiers then started to accompany the Allied occupation forces to the Ottoman provinces. Contemporaneous memoirs reveal how this process occurred in five cities, namely, Kars, Adana, Maraş, Alaşehir, and Antep.[240] The occupation soldiers were a visible presence at the İzmit, Eskişehir, and Konya train stations and were accompanied at Pozantı by the Legion Armenienne. In Kars, the Muslim populace objected more to the arrival by train of ten railway cars of Armenians than to the occupying forces; an American organization, Near East Relief, also arrived to collect 12,000 orphaned Armenian children. In Adana, the occupying forces armed the Armenian youth and appointed Armenians to key administrative positions; they then started to go around, trying to recover Armenian properties, an act that upset the local Muslim populace, which in turn took precautions and mobilized to save their lives and properties. The same happened in Antep as the occupying forces ordered the evacuation of Armenian houses that had been settled by Muslim refugees. In Maraş, the Muslim populace protested the appointment of "Armenian Vahan" as governor and, storming the mansion, gave him a beating; they also marched and hoisted the Ottoman flag. The situation in Alaşehir was different, since it was not under occupation and thus the governor was a Muslim Turk. His actions were exclusionary in that he thought non-Muslims should not live, let alone get appointed to official positions. He also acted illegally to protect Turkish interests at the expense of the non-Muslims. These interactions reveal the extreme polarization that set in as the local Muslim populace protested the arrival of Armenians more than the occupying forces and started to take action against the occupying forces and join the independence struggle only after realizing that they would have to return what they had plundered from the Armenians and also possibly account for the crimes they had committed.

Memoirs once again reveal what happened in Adana, Ankara, Giresun, and İzmir.[241] At schools in İzmir, local non-Muslim students harassed the Muslim ones, tearing away their fezzes. In Ankara, the Turkish police chief was upset by the celebrating non-Muslims but could not prevent them, since they would then complain to the British and the French. In Giresun, local Turkish militia were already harassing the non-Muslim population, plundering their properties, stealing their wealth, and blowing up their churches to ensure that they would not return. In Adana, the French occupation had led to the emergence of Turkish guerrilla activity and a rebellion because the Armenians who had joined the French forces were trying to recover their confiscated property and goods. The Turkish resistance was already active in Adana, an occupied city, and in Giresun, which was not occupied.

It is interesting that although the Sèvres Treaty supported the establishment of both an Armenian and a Kurdish state, the memoirs do not display any fear of or anxiety about a possible Kurdish state. This difference in the Turkish reaction is probably due to two factors. First, as Christians, the Armenians had the support of the Allied forces much more than the Kurds; the Armenian Diaspora was also mobilized, helping out. Second, the Turks had much more to lose by the establishment of an Armenian state than a Kurdish one, and the Kurds were often complicit in the violence against the Armenians, which in turn may explain their support of the independence struggle.

According to the memoirs, resistance to the possible establishment of an Armenian state was the main instigator of the Turkish independence struggle. This causal connection also explains in part the continuing denial of the collective violence against the Armenians because admitting to it would undermine the dominant myth that the independence struggle emerged to liberate the Turks from Allied occupation. Indeed, during the Balıkesir, Erzurum, Alaşehir, and Sivas Congresses that took place during the summer and early fall of 1919, the organizers continuously cited the threat of an Armenian state as the main factor to get the Muslim populace to mobilize and participate in the independence struggle.[242] The Balıkesir Congress in June and July 1919 declared that "Anatolia ought to belong to the Turks." The Erzurum Congress in late July 1919 stated that "the Christian populace will not be issued new privileges that would upset the social balance and [Turkish] political dominance"; the letters Mustafa Kemal sent to the Kurdish leaders at the end of the congress likewise noted that "our nation that has [until now] willingly shed its blood for the Islamic world is about to be enslaved through the establishment of an Armenian state in our fatherland." At the Alaşehir Congress in August 1919, the main topic was "the rumors that eastern cities were to be given to the Armenians." Mustafa Kemal gave a speech at the Sivas Congress in September 1919, stating that "in the east, the Armenians drew plans to expand all the way to the Kızılırmak River [in central Anatolia] and have already approached Turkish borders with preparations for a massacre"' the Turks decided to take up arms "rather than yield any part of the lands to Armenia." Also at the Sivas Congress, the decision was made to not start any animosity toward Armenians at the moment, "given how the Armenian incident [of 1915] mobilized the entire Christian world against Turks." Hence such a cautionary stand was strategic, determined by the historical conjuncture. Also, American general James G. Harbord had traveled to Anatolia in August 1919 with the intent to assess the possibility of sustaining American interests in the region and establishing an Armenian state. [243] Mustafa Kemal met with Harbord, assuring the American general that non-Muslims were not going to be harmed by the national forces and even issuing a statement to that effect. Yet the nationalist forces under his command were biding their time. During the course of 1920 and 1921, they became stronger and started to conquer the Allied-occupied cities.[244]

The nationalist forces' course of action against the Armenians upon entering such cities is discussed in the case of Adapazarı, Ankara, Antep, Maraş, Kadirli, Haçin, Kozan, Zeytun, and Kars.[245] In Adapazarı, the locals were relieved with the arrival of the nationalist forces, since the British had been trying to take the wife of a gendarme, claiming she was Armenian. In Ankara, the police chief flexed his muscles to demonstrate to the non-Muslims who was really in power now by harassing them. In Antep, Muslim notables wanted to reach an agreement with the local Armenians to expel the French, but the nationalist commander objected, stating he could not trust the Armenians. In Maraş, the nationalist commander tried to understand the reason for Armenian rancor and fury; two Armenian priests blamed the Russian Armenians. In the end, however, the nationalist forces entered the city and violently massacred the Armenians. In Kadirli, nationalist forces easily defeated the Armenians as the latter were mostly artisans and therefore did not know how to fight. The situation was different in Haçin and Kozan, where they had a hard time defeating the Armenians. In Haçin, the Armenians hid in caves and used sniper fire, to which the nationalists responded by pouring gasoline into the caves to bring them out. The nationalist general constantly referred to the Armenians in Zeytun, Şar, Haçin, and Antep attacking to procure food as "boils behind our front lines." Only in Kars did the Turkish commander provide some protection to the Armenians he had previously known. In İstanbul, two non-Muslims helped the independence struggle, and another two who were active within the SO lived in poverty afterward because "they were not give pensions like the Turks."[246] In all, the Turkish nationalist forces regarded the Armenians as the enemy, trying to get them all to leave their ancestral lands for good.

And in 1922, most Armenians did leave. Contemporaneous memoirs contain information on Kayseri, İstanbul, and İzmir.[247] In İstanbul, many Armenians left after the 1922 lynching of Ali Kemal by the nationalist forces, thinking they would be next. In Kayseri, the local Armenians stated that many decided to leave rather than face the ire of the nationalist forces. In İzmir, all the Armenians were rounded up, and after all their belongings and money were taken away, they were imprisoned, beaten, and raped. Especially in Akhisar, even though the local Muslims had sworn on the Quran that they would protect the local Armenians upon the arrival of the nationalist forces, they instead allied with the forces, plundering and massacring the Armenians. After all such forced departures of Armenians from Anatolia, what they had created was also often destroyed by arson, thereby eliminating incriminating evidence and any sign of their existence in the first place. A memoir writer stated that this destruction was due to the feeling of inferiority:[248]

> The plunderers caused the fire to expand.... Why did we burn Izmir? Were we afraid that if mansions, hotels, outdoor cafes of Konak remained, we would not be rid of the minorities? When the Armenians had been deported during World War I, because of this fear, we had also burned down all the habitable neighborhoods and quarters of Anatolian cities and towns. This does not solely emerge from the emotion to destroy. There is also the influence of the feeling of inferiority. It was as if each corner that looked like a piece of Europe had the destiny to be Christian and foreign, and for sure not ours. If we had been defeated at another war, would it have been sufficient to protect the Turkishness of the city solely by turning it into vacant lots?

In 1923, the nationalists slowly established control over Anatolia. Yet the vengeance and distrust toward the remaining Armenians are evident in a speech Mustafa Kemal gave in Mersin stating that "there ought to be the feeling of vengeance in the hearts of nations. This will be no common vengeance, but one aimed at wiping off the injury inflicted by those hostile to the nation's life, future, and prosperity.... compassion to the enemy [demonstrates] weakness and shortcomings." He then noted that he felt the non-Muslim houses reflecting wealth "are not ours. Though the money that went into building these... houses came out of our pockets, we do not own the deed!" Mistrusting the crying non-Muslims for having sentiments other than his own, Mustafa Kemal ended by specifically addressing the Muslims, declaring, "You do not own your lands; you should become the true owner of your country."[249] Likewise, during the Lausanne negotiations taking place the same year, one of the discussions centered on whether non-Muslims remaining in Turkey would have special status, exempting them military service. The Turkish negotiators supported the non-Muslims' full participation in the military because the latter might then leave the country in order not to serve, thereby "getting rid of Christians we were not able to expel through population exchange."[250] Gradually, a nationalist narrative emerged, with views that ranged from declaring that "the Armenians are the eternal enemy of the Turk in the past and the future" to being "saddened that the

Armenians had to be gotten rid of." Yet they all concurred on one point: the collective violence against the Armenians was the main reason behind the success of the independence struggle.[251]

After the establishment of the republic, sustained prejudice and discrimination against non-Muslim citizens briefly turned to forced assimilation in the 1930s. Non-Muslims were given a chance to integrate into the Turkish body politic, but on terms set by the Turkish state, shedding their "foreign" names, speaking Turkish in public, and "totally destroying the community spirit," in order to fully belong to the nation.[252] "Sarkis" became "Niyazi," "Beki" turned into "Bedia," and all non-Muslims abided by the "Citizen, Speak Turkish!" campaign.[253] And many non-Muslims did indeed take all the necessary measures, only to experience continued prejudice and discrimination. Remaining non-Muslims with jobs in foreign companies, state, and government were systematically replaced by ethnic Turks; those non-Muslims in Anatolia gradually migrated to İstanbul, where they could live in relative peace. Turkish professionals like lawyers, who the non-Muslims turned to for justice, ended up further abusing them with the help of the legal system.[254] Social relations with the non-Muslims quickly declined as well; marrying them was now legally permissible but mostly interpreted as "a loss to the Turk undertaking it and to all Turkishness."[255] Non-Muslim cultural properties like churches, monasteries, and especially cemeteries were systematically destroyed as well.[256] Needless to say, there was no accountability for engaging in such destructive behavior. The communal protection the Ottoman Empire had once offered to its non-Muslim communities was replaced by a modern legal system and a state that gave all equal rights as citizens, but in practice ended up discriminating against them with impunity. Interestingly, non-Muslims instead fought each other, blaming themselves and each other for not being able to assimilate.[257] They were unaware that their failure at forced assimilation was mostly due to continued Turkish prejudice and discrimination.[258] A case in point is the manner in which the Turks chose last names in 1934 when the state dictated it; one memoir writer declared, "As for the search for a last name, I personally established many principles. The name should not be similar to a European one as if imitating them . . . [and] not resemble an Armenian or Greek name."[259]

Such prejudice and discrimination was most evident and persistent in the military, where non-Muslim males were now obligated to do mandatory service. They had to report to a military office separate from that for the Turks. Then, even though college-educated Turks served as officers, their non-Muslim counterparts could only be privates, who were assigned to menial tasks, under constant scrutiny to prevent them from stealing military secrets or bringing in bombs in their lunch baskets.[260] One who had changed his name to a Muslim one was nevertheless not permitted to work at the military headquarters and kept witnessing discrimination in the military and in everyday life.[261]

The situation was no different in non-Muslims' relations with the Turkish state and the RPP. Non-Muslims could not hold any state or government jobs; the wealthy ones were also informally forced to make large contributions to the RPP.[262] In 1934, such somewhat subtle but institutionalized prejudice and discrimination became public as the Turkish military forcibly deported the Jewish citizens in Adrianople and its environs on the grounds that they posed a threat to national security.[263] Yet other military commanders took precautions to ensure the Jews of Smyrna were not removed in a similar manner.[264] And non-Muslims often noted their surprise when some Turks did not discriminate against them, treating them first as human beings.[265]

The rising fascist movement in Europe and the advent of World War II escalated the portrayal of non-Muslims as enemies of the country. Turks increasingly employed "non-Muslim" as a pejorative word in everyday life, some claiming that non-Muslims brought "nothing but harm to state and society," while others intentionally aggressed upon non-Muslims.[266] The fascist ideology also diffused into the Turkish school system, from elementary school all the way to the universities.[267] Worse still was the active state and government discrimination at two separate yet consecutive junctures: in 1941–42, three generations of non-Muslim males were forcibly drafted into the military, all serving in labor battalions engaged in road construction; in 1942–43, non-Muslims were forced to pay an extraordinary wealth tax that ensured a wealth transfer from non-Muslims to Turks while also raising money for the Turkish state and government. Contemporaneous memoirs reveal the non-Muslim trauma that resulted from such violent acts. During the 1941–42 forced conscription, many non-Muslims worried that the state and government intended to massacre them as they had previously done during World War I. While in service, they were issued castoff garbage collector uniforms, were not issued half boots, and were kept apart from the rest of the army.[268] Many of the same non-Muslims ended up in labor camps in 1942–43 when they failed to pay the excessive wealth tax forced on them by the Turkish state and government. The detailed memoirs of a state official who worked in collecting this tax reveal the extent of discrimination in assessment and collection:[269]

> The scale was straightforward; the M [Muslim] group would pay a tax that was 1–3 times what they had declared in their taxes as profit; as for [non-Muslim] minorities, it would be minimally twice and maximally thrice those of Muslims.... We estimated that about 200 million would

> be collected from İstanbul alone.... Even though this is what we had [initially] proposed, Ankara objected to it. Instead, the taxes of minorities were increased at least to 5–10 times. I was told time and time again by the [finance] minister [Şükrü Saracoğlu] that it was the prime minister [İsmet İnönü] who had determined these rates.

It also became difficult for foreigners, especially Jews, to get residency permits during this period, since the Turkish state and government seemed intent on getting rid of all "foreign elements."[270]

It is best to end the discussion of the difficult 1940s with an account that captures the increased marginalization and exclusion that non-Muslims felt:[271]

> No matter what a non-Muslim Turk does, he will never be regarded as a Turk. Whatever the reason may be, the truth is evident.... There is always a difference.... It is either the state that provides and determines this difference and inequality with a law, or the still very ignorant populace and officials who interpret and apply the laws according to their narrow understanding.... Even my most educated and civilized friend, one day when I least expect it, feels no reluctance to throw at my face that I am not really a Turk. He does not feel reluctant because he considers this a principle of machoism and nationalism. When my best friend praises me, he says, "this one is not like the Jews you know." He never accepts my Turkishness.... [When you are] about to win an argument, someone yells, "shut up, you Jew!" immediately deflating your sails. You stop the argument, losing the bet because you have been shot from your weakest point. Yes, you are Jewish or Armenian. You will not be considered Turkish. Actually the greatest force Turks, that is Muslims, have in their offense is their reminding you that you are not Turkish, that you should not be too big for your britches, and that, consequently, it is necessary for you to [always] remain silent.

Such blatant prejudice and discrimination against non-Muslims continued in the 1950s, ranging, according to the memoirs, from playing practical jokes on them to blaming them for things over which they had no control.[272] In terms of state policy, Black Sea Turks were settled on the Aegean Islands populated by the Greek Rum, once again on grounds that the latter posed a national security threat.[273] Destroying non-Muslim cultural property such as churches also persisted.[274] The Turkish military continued to maintain high discriminatory standards. In this context, the exchange between a non-Muslim recruit and his Turkish senior officers is revealing. When the officers argued there was no discrimination against non-Muslims in Turkey, the recruit replied as follows:[275]

> My lieutenant colonel, I said, can you find a [single] minority clerk or worker in a Turkish, that is, a Muslim bank? Are minorities in the Turkish army [ever] handed even the simplest arms of rifles? Is there a [single] minority policeman, gendarmerie, or guard? Do they accept minorities into the military academy, school of civil administration, [or] school of foreign service? Every year, hundreds of students are sent [by the state] to Europe for education. Have you ever researched to find out, just as an example, if there had ever been at least one minority member among them? Have you ever encountered a minority government official? Are there ever minority personnel in a Turkish company? Was a minority member ever [permitted] to take the [state] examination allocating free room, board and tuition to students? Have you ever seen an Armenian postman? Even among the customs porters, can one ever encounter a minority porter? In Turkey, is there a Greek Rum district governor or a Jewish governor? Is there even a minority tramway conductor? I had gotten carried away; I do not remember what else I said.

The officers' response was all the more telling. "Yes," they said, "you are correct, but before World War I, the situation was exactly the reverse. Now, it is your turn to suffer and be treated unjustly." The most significant act of violence such vengeance produced was the 6–7 September 1955 pogroms committed against the non-Muslims through the complicity of Turkish state, government, and the military, which will be discussed in detail later.

In the 1960s and 1970s, non-Muslims kept dwindling in number, on the one hand, and fewer and fewer Turks personally knew non-Muslims, on the other. As a consequence, non-Muslims receded into that gray area of jokes and pejorative remarks. Contemporaneous memoirs are replete with jokes told at the expense of Armenians, for instance, mimicking non-Muslim accents.[276] References to non-Muslims also entered the everyday language to indicate denigration.[277] Though non-Muslims were no longer even a significant minority in terms of population, when officials wanted to criticize the actions of the West by employing nationalist rhetoric, non-Muslims kept appearing in the media as the proxy, the enemies who could be aggressed upon with impunity. Such an official stand publicly erased the religious complexity of the republic; many Turkish Muslim households initially contained both Muslim and Christian lineage, but the transformation of non-Muslims into enemies led many families to silence this lineage, emphatically advocating their Muslim side alone. One memoir narrates such an intersection.[278] The head of the Department of Islamic Religious Opinion in Turkey, Lütfi Doğan, and the Armenian patriarch Sinork Kalustyan were brothers. The memoir explains this connection, which had become increasingly difficult to acknowledge publicly:

> Patriarch Sinork had lost his father at a very young age and his mother had married a Turk; they had children together one of whom was Lütfi Doğan. For this reason, the mother-son relationship [with Kalustyan] was severed. At an advanced age, the mother came here to Kumkapı [where the Armenian Patriarchate is located] and said to her other [Muslim] children: "I long for him [her first son, the patriarch Kalustyan], please let me go and stay with him." The mother died while in Kumkapı. Lütfi Doğan and the other [Muslim] children came to her [Christian] funeral. Then everyone said: "she is such a blessed woman; she has two sons and one son is the patriarch of the Armenians and the other of the Muslims." Patriarch Sinork was also a child of deportation, he grew up in orphanages; he knew what that meant very well.

During the violent 1915 deportations, while the orphaned Armenian son grew up in orphanages to become the patriarch, his Armenian mother was married off to a Muslim Turk, only to produce another son who rose to assume the highest Muslim position in the republic. After the creation of internal enemies, it became increasingly difficult to publicly discuss such complexities, leading Turkish state and society to become more and more intolerant of difference. The initial non-Muslim "enemies of the republic" were soon accompanied by three other groups, namely, the Kurds, communists, and Islamists. Such new internalized enemies were created, I argue, as the unaccounted collective violence committed against the Armenians became normalized into republican state practice.

Kurds The geographical location of the Kurds in between the Russian, Persian, and Ottoman Empires on the one hand and their nomadic structure on the other had initially gave them certain advantages and disadvantages. Their location amid the three empires enabled Kurds to retain local sovereignty by paying annual tributes. Their nomadic lifestyle also gave them the mobility to negotiate their interests by moving from one empire to another, maximizing their own interests in the process. In the Ottoman Empire, Kurdish rebellions escalated with the advent of Ottoman modernity, which prioritized settled populations over nomadic ones and regular, centralized tax collection instead of annual tributes. Sultan Abdülhamid II attempted to incorporate the Kurds into the empire by establishing the paramilitary Hamidiye regiments that wrought havoc on local Armenians. During CUP rule, although the CUP was prejudiced against

Kurds, this prejudice did not fully transform into discrimination because the Turkish protonationalism the CUP practiced had not yet fully differentiated the Turkish component from the Muslim one. Aggression against the Armenians took precedence as a consequence.

Yet the Ottoman defeat in World War I and the ensuing Sèvres Treaty brought up new possibilities, among them the establishment of a Kurdish state in the eastern provinces.[279] Rather than focusing on the possible foundation of a Kurdish state, however, the independence struggle mobilized around the establishment of an Armenian state. A prominent Kurdish leader specifically pointed out that the Kurds joined the independence struggle upon the promise of equal rights and local sovereignty.[280] In order to garner Kurdish support, the Turkish leadership of the independence struggle in turn first went along with this promise, by appointing Kurds to positions of command to appease them on the one hand and by trying to contain their actions on the other.[281] Yet, once the Turkish republic was established, the republican leaders not only renege on their promise to the Kurds but also adopted secularism, thereby destroying the religious connection with the Kurds that had once made the two communities equal as believers. Then Turkish ethnicity became the main centralizing identity of the republic, marginalizing the Kurds even more. Turkish nationalists now declared that "their" fatherland was one indivisible whole, thereby effectively removing the possibility of Kurdish local sovereignty. With the articulation of such exclusionary republican priorities, the Kurds started to rebel right after the establishment of the Turkish republic and kept rebelling throughout this period until the 1940s.[282]

The first Kurdish rebellion, the Sheikh Said Rebellion, occurred in 1925.[283] Fierce debates in the national assembly over the course of action to take against the Kurds led to the adoption of violent repression exercised through 'independence' courts, that is courts established with the intent to solidify the political status quo attained at the end of the Turkish independence struggle.[284] Contemporaneous memoirs comment on the violence, brutality, and illegality with which these courts operated, with the explicit intent to summarily arrest, try, and hang many Kurdish leaders with impunity.[285] It was no accident that the interior minister appointed to "settle" the Kurdish question was Şükrü Kaya, the former CUP and SO member who had also directed the Armenian "settlement" in 1915–17.[286] Violence against the Kurds as well as Kurdish rebellions continued throughout the 1930s. The rebellions were finally brutally repressed in 1938, as the Turkish military razed many Kurdish towns and villages, massacring thousands in the process.

Contemporaneous memoirs covering the 1940s through the 1970s reveal a pattern of action against the Kurds similar to that against the non-Muslims: prejudice and discrimination on the one hand and forced assimilation on the other.

Among such memoirs, one that provides the most information on the treatment of the Kurds was penned by Sıdıka Avar, the director of a girls' institute in Elazığ from 1943 to 1959.[287]

Upon arriving at the institute, Avar first noted the belittlement of the boarding Kurdish village children by the Turkish teachers and staff; Kurdish children were used in all menial jobs, including cleaning and cooking, and were forced to cater to the personal needs of the teachers as well. The justification for such punishing treatment was that "these were the descendants of the Kurds who had rebelled against the Turkish state." Kurdish children were also frequently punished by not being fed; in addition, they were not permitted to apologize and be forgiven for their mistakes. That the punishments given were too severe was indicated by the large number of Kurdish girls who attempted to commit suicide.

Avar treated the Kurdish children compassionately and was therefore well liked by them, yet she too participated in the attempt to assimilate them: Kurdish children were forbidden to speak Kurdish and were taught to speak Turkish instead, a process that gradually led the children to view Kurdish as inferior to Turkish. Another factor that escalated feelings of inferiority among the Kurdish students was the manner in which they were treated by visiting Turkish officials. For instance, when the Bingöl governor Şahinbaş visited the classroom, Avar described his behavior as follows:

> He entered the classroom of seniors, and the girls got up with respect and love in their eyes. The governor asked: "Are these the Kurdish girls?" The love in the girls' eyes changed immediately, now increasingly treacherous [instead]. The governor continued: "You witnessed the mistakes your fathers and grandfathers committed with their rebellion; they paid for them with their lives." I interrupted: "Oh, not the fathers of these children, they were honorable..." "How could they not be? Aren't they all Kurdish? If you act in this way..." Even though I tried to stop him by intervening once or twice, he continued: "The [Turkish] government is very strong; it would annihilate you all!"... [Afterward] I went to the third grade, they all cried, asking the following questions in between: "Why do they consider us so guilty? Why do they constantly insult us by calling us Kurds? Why do they regard the Kurds even beneath the wretched? Why did you keep telling us that we were all Turks?" There was no end to such painful questions.

Such a punitive official attitude treated the Kurds as a monolithic group of traitors to the Turkish nation, one that had to be constantly punished for rebelling against the state. Significant here is the collapse of the categories of nation and state, with Turkish officials acting punitively and legitimating their violence in the name of both. In all their interactions with the state or government, unlike the Turks, the Kurds were explicitly and intentionally not provided any support.

Even the humane Avar affirmed in her annual reports that her main aim was to "civilize" the Kurds. History lessons taught at the institute declared that the Turkish nation was "the most courageous, brave, upright, and ancient in the world." What they learned at the institute eventually led the Kurdish girls to look down upon their traditional lifestyle, deciding that they had previously lived "as animals." It is interesting that Avar faced much resistance during recruitment; because she needed the approval of both parents to enroll a Kurdish girl at her institute, she was mostly able to take in orphaned children. Avar did try hard to especially lure children of Kurdish leaders in towns and villages, knowing well that their higher status meant that the returning assimilated girls would have a greater impact in their communities. Yet these assimilated Kurdish girls were not fully accepted either by the Turks or by their Kurdish family and community; what they had been taught clashed with what existed there, leading many girls to be forced into marriages and to suffer assaults and beatings, if not death. Orphaned Kurdish girls were often adopted by Turkish families only to be treated poorly, forced to perform menial tasks. Indeed, Avar often complained about visiting Turkish officials who wanted to take away the Kurdish girls with such an explicit intent. Given the inherent injustice in this mode of action, and also given the continued prejudice and discrimination against Kurds, it is not surprising that few Turkish memoirs actually recount or comment on this adoption strategy, and most instead carefully silence it.[288]

The forced assimilation of Kurdish males instead took place in the Turkish army, since all male citizens were and still are mandated to perform a two-year military service. Incoming Kurdish recruits were taught to read, write, and speak the Turkish language.[289] The Turkish officers also made sure that the Kurds knew the Turks were superior to them in every way. As many Kurds were forced into silencing their ethnic identity, the Turkish official stand began to promote the idea that Kurds were actually mere "mountain Turks," thereby attempting to fully co-opt any remaining Kurdish cultural space.[290] Once again, contemporaneous Turkish memoirs mostly silence such inherent prejudice and discrimination. Only some note the virulence with which some nationalist Turks wanted the Kurds to be either "destroyed or deported elsewhere" and replaced instead by ethnic Turks.[291] In another account, an ethnically Turkish official complained about the discrimination he encountered for having been born in a Kurdish area during his father's military service there. The mere fact that his original birthplace was in Kurdish geographical space came up as a significant obstacle during his bureaucratic career.[292] Given such official prejudice and discrimination, many Kurds who did succeed in the republic did so in the private sector.

Communists The now normalized violence within the republic employed against the Kurds was also utilized against those who did not oppose the Turkish state and government politically but merely criticized them. This official prejudice and discrimination created another internal enemy, the communists. Communism as an ideology had initially emerged during the last years of the Ottoman Empire in the aftermath of the 1917 Soviet revolution. The leaders of the independence struggle then appeared to tolerate communism as an ideology in order to receive substantial funds and armaments from the Soviet state, but they did not tolerate communism in practice. Mustafa Suphi was the first communist leader to be persecuted and murdered along with fifteen of his friends after their arrival in Anatolia to join the struggle. Suphi had initially escaped to Russia in 1914, joining the Bolshevik Party there and later getting elected the president of the First Congress of the Communist Party of Turkey, held in Baku in 1920. Upon his arrival in Erzurum with his retinue, the hostility they encountered led them to decide to return to Baku. According to one memoir, on their return trip, while setting sail from Trabzon on the night of 28 January 1921, all were murdered by the Trabzon boat steward and former CUP member Yahya Kaptan and his armed band.[293]

During the early republican period, the leadership initially tolerated the initiative of other communists establishing a communist party, once again probably to appease the Soviet Republic. Yet, such political opposition was not tolerated for long; the members, and later members of the subsequently founded Workers' Party, faced repression and imprisonment.[294] Many who openly advocated communism ended up serving long prison sentences on trumped-up charges. A case in point was the poet Nazım Hikmet, who eventually escaped to Soviet Russia, dying there in exile. The few contemporaneous memoirs by Armenians indicate that communist parties of Turkey were among the few organizations that actually accepted non-Muslims as members; Vartan İhmalyan and Sarkis Çerkezyan both joined the Turkish Communist Party, facing official adversity as a consequence.[295] The violent official stand toward communists persisted throughout the 1940s, mostly as a consequence of the rise and spread of fascism within the Turkish state and society.

In 1945, such state and government harassment turned into collective violence, one articulated in the contemporaneous memoir of a Turkish intellectual and writer.[296] An intellectual couple had established the Tan printing press, which published newspapers, journals, and articles in which many intellectuals discussed domestic and international developments. Yet the raised criticisms challenged the lack of accountability of Turkish state and government officials. An incendiary newspaper editorial of the former CUP member Hüseyin Cahit Yalçın, entitled "Rise, Oh Possessors of the Country," also provoked the populace. On 4 December 1945, the offices of the *Tan* newspaper and the press were raided and destroyed by a group of students instigated by the RPP government of İsmet İnönü. The students were given red paint to carry with them, to thus publicly demonstrate that they considered the press and newspaper a "red threat" that could not be tolerated in the republic. According to the memoir writer, Zekeriya Sertel narrated what occurred as follows:

> The crowd that appeared in front of the newspaper had plainclothes policemen among them. They carried sledgehammers, destructive tools, and red paint. They raided the press, but the police did nothing except to watch as everything was destroyed. They looked for my wife Sabiha Sertel, but could not find her. . . . They destroyed the newspaper published by Sabahattin Ali and Cami Baykurt as well as two other bookstores, while the police stood by and did nothing.

Similar state violence was also practiced against others who were not targeted so publicly. Many were harassed by constant police surveillance, others were imprisoned on false charges, and still others were not issued passports. For instance, the intellectual, novelist, and poet Sabahattin Ali, who had realized he was going to be arrested and imprisoned for being a communist, attempted to escape, only to be caught and murdered by a member of the National Intelligence Organization (Milli İstihbarat Teşkilatı) at the Turkish border with Bulgaria. The famous folk singer and composer Ruhi Su, who had initially studied at the Ankara conservatory and then worked at the opera as one of its leading stars, was expelled from the opera and imprisoned for many years for having been labeled a communist. The adverse association of Turkish Communist Party members with the Soviet Union was similar to the former negative association of non-Muslim citizens with Western Europe. In both cases, the Turkish state and government prevented sharing the countries' resources and thus democratizing the country by declaring non-Muslims and later communists as enemies of the nation.

In the aftermath of World War II, after Turkey joined the West in the emerging Cold War between the United States and the Soviet Union, not only did official repression against Turkish communists escalate, but any political movement to democratize the country was immediately labeled communist and persecuted. One memoir noted that the Socialist Workers' Party, the Labor Party, as well as a human rights organization, all established in 1946, were shut down because of the "red threat" they posed.[297] President İsmet İnönü explicitly exploited the rising Soviet threat to Turkey to suppress all democratic moves, dismissing all those who opposed and criticized his rule as communists.[298] During the 1950s, the republican state increasingly blamed the newly identified enemies for the collective violence they themselves had committed. This is exactly what transpired with the pogroms of 6–7 September 1955 against the non-Muslims; although the state, government, and military had conspired in organizing and instigating the pogroms, they initially arrested fifty-two leftists with the intent to blame the violence on these innocent men.[299] One journalist who interviewed the martial law commander Nurettin Aknoz Pasha asked the latter what they intended to do with the fifty-two leftists under arrest at the military academy and received the following response: "They are the ones that brought İstanbul down; I will make sure they all get the punishment they deserve. I will hang about 10 to 15 of them and have the rest rot in jail for 20 to 30 years each." Such blatantly false allegations did not stick, however, on two grounds. In what the eyewitnesses told the newspapers, the violence was organized at a level of competence that the "leftists" sorely lacked. There had also been no public symbols demonstrating leftist participation. Eventually, the official blame against the leftists was replaced by the declaration that the spontaneous, uncontrolled rabble was the ultimate culprit. Still, many leftists like the famous author Kemal Tahir "completed an unjust imprisonment of thirteen years."

Similar state and government persecution of political opposition continued into the 1960s and 1970s. Joining particular political parties and participating in student demonstrations led to imprisonment. Fethi Naci, for instance, was first arrested in 1951 and then again in 1963 after joining the Turkish Workers' Party.[300] The police and security forces would photograph the attenders, create files, and then take action by arresting them.[301] The state and government also pitted political groups against each other, actively recruiting students with opposing political views and employing them to then assassinate or beat up their political counterparts. Evidence for this strategy comes from a memoir penned by a nationalist student activist who was involved in the murder of seven leftist students.[302] While in prison, this nationalist activist became the idol of the parties of the radical right like the National Action Party. Many of these assassins who committed extralegal violence against the targeted enemies of the state in a manner very similar to the SO of the CUP were then legally protected and quickly released to participate in the covert operations of the National Intelligence Organization.

Islamists Also at this juncture, yet another internal enemy, the Islamists, became a viable political force, partly as a consequence of the elimination of the three targeted enemies of non-Muslims, Kurds, and communists, all of whom had been secular in their orientation. Such targeted elimination gradually left behind only two social groups, those prioritizing either their ethnicity as Turks or their religion as Islamists. The former group naturally fit in with the state and government priorities in general and exclusionary nationalism in particular, therefore not constituting a political challenge during this era. Yet the latter group defied the republican principle of secularism. Especially during the Cold War years, such religious behavior was initially tolerated, since it was assumed to counterbalance the communists. With the decimation of the leftist movement, however, the Islamists emerged as the next internal enemy of the Turkish state, government, and military. Predicated on the assumption that the Islamists posed a political threat to the secular foundations of the republic, the Turkish state and government started to arrest and imprison them in increasing numbers during the 1970s and the 1980s. This group would ultimately prove much harder to contain, however, because their identity was closely shared by the dominant majority. After all, with the non-Muslims rapidly dwindling in numbers, the republic was becoming almost entirely Muslim in its population composition, with the official stand refusing to recognize Islam as a political force.

In summary, in the aftermath of World War I, former CUP members joined the independence struggle to avoid punishment for the collective violence they had committed against the Armenians, transforming into patriotic nationalists with the success of the independence struggle, and into republican leaders with the establishment of the Turkish nation-state. Sustaining and normalizing collective violence within state and government, they practiced exclusionary nationalism, systematically excluding from the body politic of the nation first the non-Muslims and then the Kurds, communists, and Islamists. In doing so, they drew upon and replicated former CUP practices. First a nonexistent association with a larger, sinister plan to "destroy Turkey" was fabricated to turn them into internal enemies, non-Muslims with the West, Kurds with the persistent interest to establish their own state, by also insinuating the duplicity of Western Europe and/or the Soviet Union; all political opposition with communists and Soviet interests; and Islamists with the United States and/or Iran and Saudi Arabia. These internal enemies were then publicly vilified, illegally aggressed upon, or imprisoned on trumped-up charges, thereby eliminating any viable political opposition to the republican leadership.

Patterns of Early Republican Collective Violence and the 6–7 September 1955 Pogroms

The republican collective violence ensued as a consequence of the exclusionary Turkish nationalism that was eventually adopted as the official stand of the state and its governments. According to contemporaneous memoirs, the pattern of violence originated during the armistice period and independence struggle, and was institutionalized during the first five decades of republican rule, after the violent settlement of scores within the republican leadership.

During the armistice period, contemporaneous memoirs signal that the main conflict occurred between the Allied actors, insistent on bringing the perpetrators to trial, and the Turkish actors, attempting dismiss such a possibility by either taking a public stand against it or escaping to hide in order not to be tried. Five contemporaneous memoirs discussed the Allied stand. According to one, the most upsetting statement was made by Prime Minister Georges Clemenceau of France, who in his letter dated 19 June 1919 criticized the Turks, accusing them of contributing nothing to civilization other than destruction. The letter was so strong that it could only be published in the local newspapers after being heavily censored.[303] Another Allied statesman in İstanbul refused to shake the hand of a Turkish official on the grounds that the hands of all Turks were covered in blood, and still another in Russia pointed out that the injustices and massacres Turks had committed opened wounds in their hearts.[304] If the intent of such statements was to get the Turks to acknowledge what had happened, the reverse occurred, with many Turks instead taking a much more defensive stand. Other Allied statesmen were more careful, stating that they insisted on putting an article about the Armenians into the armistice treaty to appease American and British public opinion. They also wanted another clause put in, stating that Haçin, Sis, Zeytun, and Antep (all regions where Armenians once dominated) would be occupied, but they then agreed with the Turkish opposition that the cities would not be occupied unless there was unrest, and that this article would be kept secret.[305] Another Allied statesman, General James G. Harbord who traveled through Anatolia to assess the possibility of an Armenian state, also commented at length about the extent of Turkish destruction against the Armenians.[306]

According to four memoirs, the Turkish reaction was already couched in rhetoric of resistance and denial. One simply noted the great animosity of the West toward the Turks because of the past violence.[307] Another claimed that the subsequent acceptance of this past violence by the ruling Entente Party was merely political, as a way to get back at the CUP with the intent to demolish the latter.[308] In the ensuing Unionist-Entente debates, the Ententists accused the Unionists of not only slaughtering the Armenians but also sending 3 million Muslim soldiers to their deaths, thereby coupling the Armenian and Muslim deaths and destruction.[309] A Turkish journalist started to survey Western accounts with the intent to identify those that alleviated the degree of Turkish destruction.[310] After debates in the Ottoman public sphere initially politicized the past violence in this manner, three memoirs revealed the unease many Turks felt. One memorist was a war prisoner in Russia who defended the Turkish violence; the two others took issue with the ensuing Allied arrests of many local Turkish notables as alleged perpetrators. Indeed, one such accused notable bribed the judge to have his court case moved to the local court, to then have the charges against him dismissed.[311]

This local negotiation of past violence took a European turn in 1921 when Talat Pasha was assassinated for the crimes he had committed against the Armenians.[312] The CUP members in exile discussed the list of perpetrators the Armenian revolutionaries had prepared, trying to figure out who would be on the list and why. Many CUP members either left the empire or continued to worry that they would be next on the list.[313] In Berlin, a Turkish club tried to get the CUP exiles deported to the empire to be tried not for the Armenian violence but for the death of millions of Turkish soldiers. Once again, the memoirs revealed the ease with which the Turkish memoir writers subverted the past Armenian violence to instead focus on and draw public attention to the Turkish deaths that occurred during the war.

All such debates were sidelined with the military successes of the independence struggle, a time of political instability and chaos within the empire. According to six contemporaneous memoirs, the armed bands loyal to the sultan, the armed bands loyal to the nationalist forces, and the armed bands of Greek Rum and Armenians all fought each other to establish their disparate visions.[314] No one was certain about the future, let alone their own lives.[315] The 1917 issuance of a Russian statement giving eastern Anatolia to Armenians was followed by the Russian withdrawal from the region due to the Soviet revolution. In 1919, the Georgians, Armenians, and Azeris united, establishing the Transcaucasian Federation, which was dissolved by the British six months later. In 1920, an Armenian state was founded to the east of Erzurum, while the land to the east of Trabzon was left to Georgia. Six months later, Turkish national forces attacked Armenia, taking back Kars. The subsequent Soviet insistence on giving lands from the Van and Bitlis provinces to the Armenian state led Mustafa Kemal to declare that "the sole reason of the fight the Turks had engaged in during the last year and a half was not to give any land to the Greeks and Armenians."[316] When accused of the Armenian massacres, Mustafa Kemal not only pointed out the homicides and murders in the United States, Great Britain, and France but also brought up the issue of Allied nonintervention when the invading Greek forces murdered the local Muslim populace.[317] The execution of either personal or collective violence was thus accompanied by attempts to justify it.

Again according to contemporaneous memoirs, the collective violence of the national forces during the independence struggle could be grouped into those committed against the non-Muslims, Kurds, the political opposition, and the Turkish populace. During this period, all non-Muslim subjects of the empire were under threat, especially the Armenians for the possible intent to establish a state and for attempting to recover their plundered goods and property, and the Greek Rum for their possible support of the invading Greek army. Twenty-seven contemporaneous memoirs capture the scope of collective violence; almost all depict how the local non-Muslims were destroyed by the local Muslim inhabitants and the nationalist forces. While one Armenian memoir writer described the manner in which the returning Armenians were once again deported by the nationalist forces, two other Turkish accounts justified the decimation of Armenians for collaborating with the Allied forces.[318] In Erzurum, while atrocities were committed by the Armenian bands as well as the Turkish forces, entire areas were eventually cleansed of Armenians.[319] It is evident that the nationalist forces rarely took any prisoners, killing both Allied soldiers and non-Muslims.[320] Collective violence committed in the vicinity of İzmir is described in great detail by numerous accounts, pointing out not only the violence of withdrawing Greek forces but also the ensuing greater violence of nationalist forces, and especially the burning of the city of Smyrna by the nationalist commander Nurettin Pasha; rapes of non-Muslim women also emerged as a prominent theme.[321] The extraordinary violence committed against local non-Muslims occurred as a result of two factors: unprotected non-Muslims provided a much easier target than the regular Greek army; in addition, the nationalist forces consisted of both local armed bands and a regular army, therefore wreaking destruction on a greater scale. In the Turkish memoirs, all such violence was justified in the name of Turkish nationalism.

The collective violence committed against the Greek Rum living along the Black Sea coast, referred to in the memoirs as the Pontus Rum, is rarely discussed in the scholarly literature and therefore deserves special mention. Four memoirs by Turks document the extent of Pontus Rum destruction, through a combination of savagery by local Turkish bands and forced deportations. One memoirist recounted how two local Pontus Rum were knifed in front of his eyes, but he did nothing, dismissing the violence by claiming that the two were probably leaders of the Pontus independence movement.[322] Another three commented on the specific violence wrought by the local militia leader, Topal Osman Agha, who cruelly murdered all the local Pontus Rum population and then boasted about his exploits; never held accountable for his violence, he was instead rewarded by the republic with a commandership.[323] The most tragic account of what happened to the Pontus Rum was provided by a Turkish woman who remembered traveling through the area in a carriage as a child with her family. As they came upon a Pontus Rum caravan consisting mostly of women, children, and the elderly, her father refused to help, stating that he did not want to intervene in the Turkish nation punishing them for being enemies of the Turks.[324]

The violence committed against the Kurds with the successful conclusion of the independence struggle was initially more symbolic than physical. One contemporaneous memoir by a Kurdish intellectual described in detail what transpired.[325] Right after the signing of the Lausanne Treaty, the elections held for the second Turkish national assembly "eliminated all the Kurdish deputies who could have caused a problem [to the republican leaders]." This was followed by the declaration of the republican constitution that accepted Turkish as the official language. As a consequence, the first national assembly that had served during the independence struggle with Kurdish deputies working alongside the Turkish deputies now became the sole domain of the Turks, marginalizing and excluding the Kurds. Unlike the non-Muslims, who had been marginalized and excluded from the independence struggle from the beginning, the Kurds were initially kept as allies, only to be excluded once the struggle successfully led to the establishment of the republic. How this exclusion became publicly evident concerned the manner in which one Kurdish deputy was treated. In the formal celebration in Ankara held on the occasion of the signing of the Lausanne Treaty, even though Mustafa Kemal had asked the Kurdish to attend the national assembly dressed in his local costume, the deputy was later tried and hanged for having attended assembly sessions in that outfit. It is thus evident that even though the rhetoric of the independence struggle claimed fair treatment toward all the non-Turks, namely, the non-Muslims and the Kurds, once the struggle was victorious, the non-Turkish elements began to be violently eliminated from the national body politic. Just as the Muslim Turks had been the dominant majority during the Ottoman Empire, the independence struggle that claimed to replace the former political system with a democratic one with all citizens participating equally in the body politic ultimately ended up reproducing the same Turkish domination.

Eight contemporaneous memoirs document the manner in which all significant political opponents of the independence struggle, including the ones at large as well as those in the national assembly, were threatened and at times assassinated. For instance, the Eskişehir subdistrict governor Hilmi Bey, who opposed the independence struggle, was assassinated;[326] commander Nureddin Pasha lynched the Greek metropolite Meletyos in İzmir and the political opponent Ali Kemal in Adapazarı.[327] Some deputies at the national assembly were likewise assassinated; Ali Çetinkaya shot and killed Deli Halit Paşa, and Topal Osman Agha, the commander of the presidential forces, murdered the Trabzon deputy Ali Şükrü Bey. Çetinkaya was never held accountable for the murder; Osman Agha was killed while resisting arrest, claiming all the while that he had acted on Mustafa Kemal's orders. Nureddin Pasha was given special amnesty by Mustafa Kemal. Interestingly, Mustafa Kemal also forgave some of those who had committed violence against the nation, such as the leader of the Konya rebellion against the nationalist forces.[328] These cases reveal the manner in which political opposition was negotiated during the independence struggle; while those who opposed the struggle were eliminated with impunity, those who either sought amnesty or were among the republican leadership remained unpunished. Such selective delivery of justice outside the court of law further normalized the exercise of collective violence.

Five contemporaneous memoirs reveal that during the independence struggle, the collective violence against the Turkish populace took one of two forms. On the one hand, the Turkish armed bands acting as the local nationalist forces robbed the populace, collecting money, food supplies, and arms by force, often murdering those who did not comply or did not provide as much as what the band leaders demanded.[329] Hence these were local acts of popular violence committed with impunity in the name of Turkish nationalism, ones for which the perpetrators were never held accountable. On the other hand, the national assembly also established independence courts during the struggle with the explicit intent to try and punish all those who resisted the struggle. These courts punished and executed hundreds if not thousands of Turks who did not participate in the independence struggle.[330] This was an act of organized extralegal violence practiced under the rubric of a court. In the memoirs, all such collective violence was dismissed through the rhetoric of Turkish nationalism.

Process of Early Republican Collective Violence

Once the republic was successfully established, almost none of the perpetrators of the collective violence were held accountable; instead, they were rewarded in the name of nationalism while those who defended the victims were punished. This lack of accountability damaged the moral fabric of the republic as the personal judgments of republican leaders often substituted for public ethics and morality based on law. Three contemporaneous memoirs by Turkish officials concur on this lack of public morality. One argued that such a lack originated in the personal histories of republican leaders; almost all came out of national resistance committees whose members had executed violence with impunity. Then, rather than holding them accountable for their actions, Mustafa Kemal transformed them all into RPP members and deputies, thereby allowing them to singlehandedly rule the country for the next three decades.[331] During such rule, it is no accident that these former perpetrators let political power rather than the legal system determine what was considered legal and illegal, not only in terms of the actions committed but for merely thinking of the possibility of such actions.[332]

Within the Leadership

It is not surprising that such a group of republican leaders experienced in violence took each other on as well, vying for positions within the emerging power structure. Divisions ensued as some who had been very active in the independence struggle, like Kazım Karabekir, were marginalized, others, like Rauf Orbay and Halide Edip Adıvar, left the country, and still others competed to instead join the personal entourage of Mustafa Kemal. Contemporaneous memoirs indicate the close tabs everyone in this circle kept on each other, deciding who was a true republican and who was not. In the process, they closely monitored each other's activities, often employing the state and security forces for surveillance.[333] As a consequence of this inner fight, all became extremely cautious in their public activities; in writing their memoirs, for instance, they carefully self-censored to exclude any possible incriminating evidence their opponents might later use against them. Those who did not, like Kazım Karabekir, faced censorship.

Karabekir was prevented from publishing his memoirs due to his criticisms of Mustafa Kemal because of the latter's faulty military strategy during the independence struggle, engaging in fighting in the eastern front while also moving troops to the western front and thereby increasing casualties, and of İsmet İnönü because of his terrible performance during the battles he conducted during the same struggle, almost losing them, only to succeed through the personal intervention of Mustafa Kemal. One memoir writer stated that when word got out that Karabekir was publishing his memoirs, Mustafa Kemal sent the writer to İstanbul to look into the matter. Rather than meeting Karabekir, however, the memoir writer went to the RPP branch director, ordering him to stop the publication:[334]

> [I told him] Very easy. Call the owner of the press. State that "the publication of this book is problematic today, so let us reimburse you for all your expenses and you decide not to publish it." If he accepts, you will purchase all the books.... I then got the approval of Mustafa Kemal and İsmet İnönü and negotiated the cost of this purchase.... I think the books were burned because there was no place to store them.... I also took a book each to Mustafa Kemal and İnönü. Especially İnönü was still worried that Karabekir could rewrite the book with the documents in his possession, so he had the public prosecutor raid Karabekir's mansion and the houses of those in his close circle.... All the [confiscated] documents were brought to the general chief of staff and examined. [Upon learning the contents of Karabekir's documents], Mustafa Kemal ordered that there was no need whatsoever for these documents to have been taken away from Karabekir, stating "Let them be immediately returned to him and let the general chief of staff determine the status of those having to do with the military.... Had I known that these were the contents of the documents and the book, I would not have permitted either the purchase of the books or the confiscation of the documents."

In spite of Mustafa Kemal's intervention, however, the documents were never returned to Karabekir. Such informal handling of issues without any recourse to the legal system set a significant precedent as the republican leaders settled scores with each other informally.

The republican leadership utilized the legal system when those they wanted to contain and censor were not particular individuals but possibly members of a larger social group. Such use, however, meant that the judges and public prosecutors also had to be carefully appointed, guaranteeing that they placed the interests of the state before all else, and did so in accordance with the parameters determined by the republican leadership. Hence, not only did the Turkish judiciary never attain the independence necessary in a democratic system, but most judges and public prosecutors instead started to regard themselves as and act as state officials. Amid claims that there was unrest in the country that needed to be forcefully put down, a law was passed enabling the death sentences issued by the independence courts to be executed without first sending them to the national assembly. The independence courts established in 1926 after the discovery of an assassination plot against Mustafa Kemal explicitly worked to decimate any remaining opposition to the republican leadership. One memoir writer in particular, a Turkish state official, noted the political destruction the independence court wrought in destroying any possible political opposition as follows:

> With this law, the lives of some of our valuable people were destroyed for no reason... many newspapers including the newly formed opposition party were shut down... the number of newspapers in circulation declined from 14 to 6... major columnists of prominent newspapers were all sent to the Diyarbekir independence court to be tried. These journalists underwent so much torture and pressure on the way there that they appealed to Mustafa Kemal twice, promising him that they would not write about İnönü and his government. Even though Mustafa Kemal did indeed intervene to save them, the İnönü government nevertheless managed to suppress the entire opposition.

Republican governance thus increasingly resembled the former CUP governance from which the new leaders had claimed to have totally distanced themselves. Public deaths by hanging followed. The most significant hangings occurred in 1926 when prominent former CUP members were all hanged for their alleged role in the conspiracy to assassinate Mustafa Kemal.

Contemporaneous memoirs often commented on these hangings.[335] According to one memoir writer who was also a judge at the 1926 trials, their intent was to protect the young republic against all possible conspiracies, dissuading new attempts with the strongest precautions.[336] Rather than a codified legal system, a group of people with power first decided what constituted a crime against the republic, and then what the pertinent punishment ought to be. This informal yet legal decision-making process meant that there were no set limits on who would be included among the accused; the slightest accusations and rumors immediately expanded the number of accused into the thousands, including many innocent people. Also, many leaders personally intervened in the process to save their friends, again by employing extralegal means. Over time, the national assembly became increasingly involved in the legal process, taking upon itself to adjudicate instead of leaving it to the judiciary.[337] Many such alleged opponents were frequently imprisoned, some dying while under arrest or in prison.[338] Imprisonment or threat of imprisonment on trumped-up charges thus turned into a strategy employed by the republican leadership with the complicity of the judiciary.[339] In interpreting the law, first the republican leaders and then the judiciary did not differentiate between thoughts, ideas (theory), and social action (praxis). As thinking about change or revolution, or merely critically commenting on governance was criminalized, the democratization process in Turkey became truly stunted. Serially, the non-Muslims, Kurds, and leftist intellectuals started to be subjected to the collective violence of the republican leadership.

Against Non-Muslims

During the 1930s and 1940s, the non-Muslims continued to be the primary targets of collective violence as they were forcefully deported in the 1930s, unfairly drafted into military service in 1941–42, unjustly taxed in 1942–43, subjected to pogroms in large cities in 1955, and forcefully extradited from the republic in 1964.[340] It is therefore no accident that their numbers quickly dwindled, as many left the country and the rest gradually migrated to İstanbul.[341] Three contemporaneous memoirs comment on the forced deportation of non-Muslims in the 1930s. While one commented on the 1934 deportation of Jews from Thrace on the grounds that they could not be trusted in the case of a possible war,[342] the other referred to a similar forced deportation of non-Muslims from Van, an incident not discussed in the literature until now.[343] The memoir writer, who was there to attend his own trial, witnessed the trial of the Van governor Hamdi Bey, who argued that he had deported the Van non-Muslims in accordance with an administrative order. Even though the interior minister argued such an order had not been given, the defendant's lawyer submitted a copy of the ciphered order to court, leading to the dismissal of the case against the governor. The ciphered order was probably sent by the military after it reached an informal decision that was obviously not conveyed to the state officials involved in the case, including the interior minister.

With the advent of World War II, republican violence against the non-Muslims further escalated as the Turkish state and government assumed a pro-German stand.[344] One immediate violent consequence of this stand was the official Turkish refusal of entry to the *Struma* boat carrying 769 Jewish refugees from Romania who were seeking asylum; the boat sank, drowning all the refugees except one. The pro-German stand was also reflected in the Turkish newspapers as an increasing number of caricatures demeaning minorities began to appear.[345] Still, the first significant violence publicly targeting non-Muslim citizens was the 1941–42 forced draft of twenty classes of non-Muslims, with fathers and sons often serving together. Three contemporaneous non-Muslim memoirs, two belonging to Armenian draftees, capture the violence the non-Muslims subsequently experienced at the hands of the Turkish military. Both draftees mentioned that many among them either died of malaria or drowned. One Armenian draftee recounted his initial anxiety as his Turkish friends worried that the military was going to kill them all, uselessly suggesting to him to stay with groups of people at all times to avoid such an end. Once the draftees had arrived at the special camps set up for them, the barracks were so crowded that many slept outside, only to be awakened by corporals with sticks. One corporal lectured them, stating that they had always lived in luxury but now had to "work like dogs." They were constantly beaten up during work, often severely enough to be hospitalized, and the letters they wrote to their families were never sent. After digging holes, they were transported to another location, walking ten hours in the snow, and then dug foundations for casemates. Upon being caught playing cards in their spare time, their hands were beaten so badly they could not hold pencils for days. The Armenian draftee then noted how they were transferred to yet another location, away from the city:[346]

> When they separated us into Jews, Greeks, and Armenians, it dawned on me that what my Turkish friends said was right, their intention was to annihilate us. [Yet] after about two weeks, they again put us on freight trains and took us to Denizli. There, local elderly men who surrounded us pitied us, saying, "Oh dear, what a shame! Why did you have to write letters to Hitler stating 'we are on you side' which caused you to be sent here?" Where this came from, we could not understand. After staying there for another two weeks, they separated us into two groups. While one group was sent to a village which had malaria, leading many to perish due to lack of quinine, I survived because our village was malaria free.... The officer said the following morning: "look here, you dishonorable people, there is no return to your homes, forget İstanbul, you will work here until you die, you will get stones out to build roads; if you die, there is the cemetery across [from us], you will disappear into it, they did not give you to us by count, no slacking, you will work like dogs...." All were horrid except one Laz corporal and the food was inedible.

The other Armenian draftee had a similar experience. Noting that many among them were highly skilled, educated professionals, they all nevertheless worked as laborers breaking stones, with many dying in the process. He also pointed out that Armenian converts from the city of Malatya also joined them, demonstrating that the Turkish state targeted all non-Muslims, including the converted.[347] Their treatment was strikingly similar to what the non-Muslim labor battalions had endured during World War I under CUP orders. Unlike that experience, however, when Germany began to lose the war, these non-Muslim draftees were not massacred but instead released. One Armenian draftee argued that had Germany defeated the Soviet Union, all of them would have been massacred.[348]

The second republican collective violence ensued soon thereafter as the Turkish state and government issued an extraordinary wealth tax, forcing non-Muslims to pay five to ten times more than the Muslims. Twenty-one memoirs, fourteen by Turkish and seven by non-Muslim writers, comment on this tax. For the first time, all fourteen Turkish memoir writers united in criticizing the tax for unfairly targeting non-Muslims, expressing their embarrassment upon seeing non-Muslims who could not pay being forced to work at labor camps. However, none of these Turkish memoir writers took any action, either to help the unjustly victimized non-Muslims or to protest against this forced wealth transfer from the non-Muslims to the Turks. All seven non-Muslim memoirs commented on the emotional trauma this tax caused, destroying families, leading some to commit suicide. Although the tax was initially introduced as a reform, it once again plundered the wealth and lives of non-Muslims, imitating Nazi measures to crush minorities.[349] Indeed, the nationalist speeches delivered by President İsmet İnönü and Prime Minister Şükrü Saracoğlu equated non-Muslims with exploitative foreigners, stating it was time for them to prove their devotion to the country.[350]

During the long national assembly discussions on the wealth tax, many Turkish deputies were fully aware that what was being proposed was illegal, but they did nothing; others justified the tax by claiming wealth was going to be distributed from the rich to the poor, thereby unfairly equating the rich with the non-Muslims.[351] This unjust exploitation of non-Muslims led to the collection of 300 million lira within six months. Many non-Muslims were traumatized as they scrambled to pay taxes that were often higher than the value of their capital, selling their properties and goods and their wives' jewelry. Some committed suicide, while others were ridiculed at schools by their Turkish friends.[352] Those non-Muslims who could not pay the tax in full during the alloted time saw their goods and property auctioned off as they were sent to labor camps, never fully recovering from the experience.[353] As the Turkish state and government had intended, the most significant consequence of the wealth tax was the transfer of wealth from the non-Muslims to the Turks. Many companies jointly owned by non-Muslims and Turks ended up in the possession of the Turks alone; many seaside mansions, large houses, and office buildings were likewise purchased by Turks at reduced prices.[354]

The third republican violence against the non-Muslims took place a little more than a decade later on 6–7 September 1955 as their houses and shops in major cities were raided and destroyed by the Turkish mobs mobilized, organized, and instigated by the Turkish state, government, and military. Twelve contemporaneous memoirs, eight Turkish and four non-Muslim, discussed the violence in detail. Once again, all the writers noted their horror at what had taken place. One prominent Turk who happened to be at Taksim Square described the violence as follows:[355]

> When one looked toward the Hilton Hotel and the Şişli neighborhood, the burning torches and the sound of destruction generated intense howls, almost like the day of reckoning. The day after, İstanbul was in total disarray. The goods in stores that had their windows broken were scattered on the streets and plundered... all the precious and valuable goods laid broken on the streets.

Many Turks exploited the chaos to destroy and rob the properties of their non-Muslim neighbors. One Armenian who experienced the destruction noted that the local Turks incited the gangs, pointing out the non-Muslim shops and houses. He saved his own house by hanging a Turkish flag around his neck and pretending to be a Turk. His two Turkish friends helped rescue his other shop by staying in it overnight. Because he was a carpenter, he later went to fix up a destroyed non-Muslim house; not only was it devastated, with the rugs cut up and everything made of glass smashed, but the perpetrators had also gathered everything in the middle of the living room and defecated on top of it. The non-Muslim owner recognized one of the perpetrators the following day; the latter not only had stolen all her jewelry but also was wearing her husband's pants. The perpetrator's son could not believe that his pious, mosque-attending father could engage in such destruction.[356]

The total cost of the damage was estimated at around 60 to 300 million lira. Stores, houses, cemeteries, schools, and churches were attacked and plundered, priests murdered, and women raped; in all, several people were killed and thirty-five wounded.[357] The violence had two significant consequences. Internationally, the slogan of the barbarous Turk once again spread throughout the world. The United Nations decided with US support not to put the Cyprus issue on its agenda, thereby turning down the Turkish request to discuss it. In addition, Europe grew distant, not investing financially in Turkey for years to come.[358] Domestically, many non-Muslims rapidly left Turkey, the Greek Rum for Greece, the Armenians for the United States, and the Jews for Israel.[359]

During this time, not only did the discussion of the 1915–17 violence against the Armenians become an ever-distant memory to the Turks, but the top CUP leaders who had perpetrated the crimes were brought back to Turkey. Only two contemporaneous memoirs referred to this past violence. One noted that upon the initiation of former CUP and SO member Celal Bayar, Talat Pasha's remains in Germany were transported in February 1943 to the republic. Talat was treated by the Turkish press of the time as a hero, ceremonially given all the highest honors, and buried at a special mausoleum built for the heroes of the republic.[360] The other memoir pointed out that in 1955, references to the Armenian massacres were carefully monitored and censored in all the publications. Upon editing a memoir of a prominent CUP member who had also been accused of perpetrating collective violence against the Armenians, the editor who wrote this memoir mentioned that he took out some pertinent paragraphs from the memoir upon the suggestion of a military captain with a law degree.[361] These two accounts indicate the gradual public silencing of the violence committed against the Armenians through censorship on the one hand and the laudatory public stand taken for the most significant perpetrator of the violence on the other.

Still, during the 1930s, some Turks had to continue negotiating this past violence during their travels overseas, especially when they visited the United States. There, they encountered the Diaspora Armenians for the first time and had to account for what had happened in their past to the local Americans who continually asked about it. One Turkish student noted that the American populace was very anti-Turkish. The moment they found out his identity, they turned their heads away, pretending not to see him and regarding all Turks as cruel, wild, savage, and barbarous.[362] Another Turk who was on his way to the United States for his education was forced to discuss what had happened to the Armenians during his travel on an American boat, but he subverted the issue by defensively pointing out the suffering of African Americans in the United States on the one hand and of Jews in Germany on the other; he failed to recognize the inherent connection of collective violence in all three cases.[363] The third memoir was written by the daughter a perpetrator who had settled in Argentina in 1930 to do business there. Not only was the daughter harassed in school for being a Turk, but her father was explicitly not invited to the Armenian Massacre Commemoration Day that the Diaspora Armenians had organized.[364] In 1939, a Turkish official who took an exhibit to the New York World's Fair was warned by American authorities to hire some bodyguards in case the exhibit was attacked by Armenians. Yet the official was pleasantly surprised when the Armenians instead came and enjoyed the Turkish exhibit, telling him time and again how much they yearned for their country.[365]

Such overseas interactions of the Turkish memoir writers continued in the 1940s, as indicated by four memoirs, three written by Turkish diplomats and one by a student. In one, a now rich Armenian businessman in Spain wanted to acquire Turkish citizenship only to be told by the then Turkish foreign minister that he could, but only in return for building a factory in Turkey. The Turkish diplomat, not feeling right about this official response, refused to pursue the matter.[366] When another Turkish diplomat serving in France asked an Armenian couple in Paris who owned a restaurant frequented by Turks why they had left Turkey, they evaded giving straight answers. The couple was very supportive of Turkish students, often helping them out with donations.[367] The same diplomat also narrated his encounters with two other Armenians in great detail. One Armenian inquired to find out if the Turkish Education Ministry would be interested in buying the books of a wealthy Armenian; even though the diplomat passed on the message, nothing came of it. The other Armenian narrated the story of his escape from the 1915 collective violence; a Turkish neighbor had secretly told his parents what was going to happen, so they sneaked their son onto a cargo train to İstanbul, from where he then escaped to Marseilles. Starting from scratch, he became a rich industrialist but still yearned for his homeland. He often sat close to Turks he ran into at cafes in order to hear them speak in Turkish.[368] The other diplomat who was stationed in New York ran into an Armenian childhood friend from İstanbul. His Armenian friend yearned to visit Turkey but could not because the Turkish state did not issue visas to the Diaspora Armenians; his request was for the Turkish state to at least consider issuing short-term visas. Upon returning to Turkey, the diplomat met with the then president, prime minister, and interior minister; they agreed to propose legislation for a short-term visa, but only on the condition that the traveling Armenians did not settle in Turkey. After returning to the United States, the diplomat did not hear from his Armenian friend for a long time. When he phoned the latter, he found out that the Armenian community had not approved the private initiative his Armenian friend had taken, stating that the matter should have been first discussed at the General Armenian Congress in Boston.[369] The final memoir, by a student, noted that he was asked to give talks on the Armenian issue at his American university. He narrated that his main arguments were that what had happened was a black page in Turkish history, that one cannot attribute such violence to the Turks' shortcomings as a race, and that every nation had such occurrences in their histories.[370] That the Turkish student admitted the past collective violence was a welcome development, yet his subsequent rationalization that all nations had such collective violence in their past did not take into account the fact that unlike Turkey, many nations acknowledge their past violence. In all, these three memoirs point to the persistent Turkish official stand of exclusion, indicated by their refusal to allow Armenians to settle in Turkey and to purchase Armenian books that are, after all, part of the cultural heritage of their country. The memoirs also reveal that the public stand of the Armenian Diaspora was now more organized in the United States, where all communal decisions were now run through a central committee.

While these overseas encounters were taking place, the fourth and final republican collective violence occurred in Turkey in 1964 when 12,562 Greek Rum who also held Greek passports were forcefully deported to Greece. Because many were married to Greek Rum women who held only Turkish passports, their spouses also had to leave, bringing the total deported up to approximately 30,000 non-Muslims, thereby literally decimating the Greek Rum community in Turkey. All the bank accounts of these deported Greek Rum were frozen by the Turkish state overnight, and their properties confiscated. They were permitted to take only one suitcase and 200 lira with them, an amount that at the time was the equivalent of approximately $100. To justify this violence, the Turkish state and government alleged that they had all been involved in the conflict between the Rum and the Turkish communities in Cyprus. One Armenian memoir writer described this event as follows:[371]

> No destruction occurred [this time], but they called everyone to the Chief of Police, taking signatures from them stating, "I am leaving of my own volition." This was of course merely a formality since they took those signatures by force. Many of the people went crying. [They had been declared] "potential enemies!" The woman goes on a stretcher because she does not have the strength to walk and she is regarded an "enemy." These too were the little pieces of work concocted by İsmet Agha [İnönü]. The [Turkish Muslim] populace, being ignorant, said "good riddance of the infidels" and was done with it. It is easy to understand them, but our [Turkish] intellectuals, I still cannot fathom... why no intellectual reacted to these policies.... [Instead] their ears were all tuned to Ankara. They did whatever the officials mouthed, whatever the deep state ordered, and were afraid to step outside those [set official] boundaries.

This description and ensuing commentary once again bring up the issue of the passivity of the Turkish populace in general, and the Turkish intellectuals in particular. It could be conjectured that the continuous state violence practiced against them prevented them from taking action; constant media exposure to the Turkish nationalist rhetoric could have also inured them to violence against the non-Muslims. In all, chronicling the republican violence against Turkey's own non-Muslim citizens during this period demonstrates the persistence of the Turkish state and government to get rid of them all on the one hand and the passivity of the Turkish populace and intellectuals in reacting to such violence on the other. These stands by the Turkish state and society indicate, I would argue, the degree to which collective violence had diffused into the Turkish republic. Indeed, in addition to non-Muslims, many others suffered from violence as well.

The mention of Armenians in the memoirs started to dwindle in the 1960s and 1970s as the non-Muslim population had become insignificant. Yet two memoirs written during this period recount the past violence committed against the Armenians. One was narrated by a Turkish journalist who attended the funeral of a former SO member, Hasan Amça, who had then turned against CUP to become a fervent critic. Amça then went on to rescue many Armenians from the Syrian Desert upon the orders of Cemal Pasha. The presence of a large crowd of Armenians at the funeral, including the patriarch, reveals that the violent past was certainly on the minds of many Armenians of Turkey, although not many Turks.[372] The other memoir was written by a novelist, recounting his happy memories at the Armenian neighborhood in İstanbul where his father worked as a janitor. His interactions with Armenian neighbors as a young child reveal that the departing non-Muslims took with them parts of those who remained behind, making it increasingly difficult for the ones left behind to reconstruct their once intact world of meaning.[373]

Against the Kurds

During this period, the Kurds also experienced escalating republican violence in three forms: massacre, exile, and assassination. Eight contemporaneous memoirs, five by Kurds and three by Turks, document the violent destruction that the Kurds experienced.[374] Although the initial Kurdish revolt in 1925 had emerged spontaneously without a clear organization, the Turkish national assembly retaliated with violence, claiming that the Kurds had been intentionally organized by antisecular Kurdish religious scholars.[375] Many Kurds, including their religious scholars, were quickly tried and hanged by the independence courts formed explicitly for this purpose. Those who survived the massacres committed by the military and the independence court trials were exiled to the western provinces, where they were often settled in the houses left behind by the forcefully deported Armenians and the Greek Rum.[376] Former CUP and SO member, now interior minister, Şükrü Kaya, stated that the intent of the Turkish republic in the eastern provinces was to "ensure that Kurds were reduced to a population that would be only half of the local Turks."[377]

In spite of such violent republican measures, however, Kurdish rebellions persisted. They were finally put down with extreme force in conjunction with the 1937–38 Dersim rebellions as Turkish warplanes bombed many Kurdish settlements while the Turkish military massacred the population. In order not to waste ammunition, the soldiers sometimes first bound the hands and feet of the Kurds and then slaughtered them.[378] To set an example for the rest, the Kurdish deserters from the military were likewise killed, tied to horses' tails and dragged through the streets. Once again, many were exiled to the western provinces. One Turkish memoir writer witnessed the eventual return of these exiled Kurds as follows:[379]

> After the Tunceli [the name Dersim was replaced by the Turkish state with Tunceli] rebellion, the mountain villages without roads were evacuated and the [Kurdish] populace settled in our western provinces, and the region was declared forbidden [to enter]. Eventually, the prohibition over the villages that had remained vacant for years was lifted and the [Kurdish] people returned to what they called their "father's hearth." . . . I saw them return to the mountain paths leading to their villages, kissing the soil and touching it to their faces. One could not help but feel respect for this great [Kurdish] love of the land. They climbed up the extremely steep mountain slopes with the greatest excitement and agility . . . and they returned, even though they had made a lot more money in the western provinces where they had also learned Turkish.

Many Kurds thus persisted in returning to their ancestral lands, while others did indeed get dispersed into the major cities, often continuing to live there, however, in their own confined neighborhoods.

The republican violence against the Kurds continued into the 1950s as well. According to the memoir of one Kurdish intellectual and journalist, this time around, the republican leadership decided to engage in extralegal covert action with the intent to massacre the entire Kurdish intelligentsia.[380] The Turkish foreign minister opposed such proposed violence but to no avail, stating:

> We cannot have such a thing [done]. I [shall] resign right now. Internationally, [the Turkish state] already cannot face anyone because of the Armenian Genocide, the Greek Rum Genocide, and the Kurdish Genocide. While the wounds [of these genocides] have just started to heal, we would not be able to defend this genocide to anyone.

According to the same memoir writer, the government instead decided to hang fifty Kurdish intellectuals. The writer escaped such massacre only by being imprisoned, which was fortunate because he had two identities that the republic leadership took issue with: he was an ethnic Kurd and also an intellectual. Also during this time, Turkish intellectuals who dared think and challenge republican practices faced collective violence as well.

Against the Turkish Populace

Contemporaneous memoirs reveal two patterns of violence against the Turks: the harassment and imprisonment of all actual or potential political opposition, be it in practice or in thought, and the actualization of two military coups in 1960 and 1971. The new republican constitution existed as a text, but once again, as with the Ottoman constitution that the CUP reinstituted but did not follow, the republican leadership continued to act not in accordance with the law but instead through the employment of personal political power. Such use inadvertently increased the significance of personal networks and cronyism instead of meritocracy. The central nodes of political power were concentrated in Ankara, in part at the national assembly, and in part around the person of Mustafa Kemal Atatürk. This informal political power structure also monitored the society at large, often employing violence to destroy any actual or potential opposition to the leadership emanating from among the Turkish populace. The intellectuals, namely, the better educated who not only read but also generated ideas, formed the greatest threat to the republican leadership because they had the potential to change the status quo. As a consequence, this segment of the Turkish populace was closely monitored with the aid of the police and security forces, censored, harassed with lawsuits, and occasionally imprisoned. Over the decades, such a course of incipient violence caused many to become increasingly obedient and servile to either the state, government, or the military.

Contemporaneous memoirs once again comment on the culmination of such harassment during this period, namely, the 1945 destruction of the *Tan* newspaper and press critical of the government, owned by two Columbia University–educated journalists, Zekeriya and Sabiha Sertel.[381] Initially, because of their newspaper and journal articles, Sabiha Sertel was arrested in 1929, and her husband exiled to Sinop for three years during which their publications were also closed down. Yet the worst was their witnessing the burning down of their press in 1945 upon the instigation of the RPP, which mobilized university students to execute this act. Neither the instigators nor the actual perpetrators were ever tried for their crimes. Instead, Sabiha and Zekeriya Sertel were arrested and tried for three months on the charge of burning down their own newspaper, being told that "this is the destiny awaiting those who take a stand against the government." The Sertels decided to leave the country and had to remain abroad because their repeated requests to return to Turkey were turned down.

The other acts of collective violence against the Turkish populace during this period were the two military coups in 1960 and 1971. In both cases, the Turkish military seized power, arrested and imprisoned those they judged were threatening the republic, and then held elections to return political power to those they deemed fit to rule. Contemporaneous memoirs by military officers and civilians capture the social meaning of the 1960 coup, when a group from within the army forcibly removed, imprisoned, and in some instances hanged members of the ruling Democrat Party.[382] Most memoirs belonged to those persecuted and eventually prosecuted by the Turkish military. Although many condemned the military violence, others blamed the DP for also having resorted to the extralegal practices they had once criticized. One memoir writer argued that what led to the coup was the DP's attempt to form a fifteen-member investigative commission that would, like the previous independence courts, assume all legal power, acting as both public prosecutors and judges and trying many people without recourse.[383] Two memoir writers argued instead that the increasing politicization of the Turkish army had led them to assume power whenever they depicted a threat to the state.[384]

The military legitimated its self-designation as the protector of the republic on a particular speech Mustafa Kemal Atatürk had once delivered, entrusting his republic to the military but also to the Turkish youth. Yet the military was organized, but the youth were not. Therefore, the Turkish military was able to capitalize on this entrustment, hegemonizing their role as republican protectors while silencing the youth. The political ascendance of the Turkish military was based on three factors. First, as the oldest institution in the republic and the only one that had survived the transition from the empire to the republic almost intact, the Turkish military had the earliest organizational structure within which to operate. All other republican institutions had to be constructed instead over time, through combining old imperial practices with new republican ones. Second, the military acquired inordinate political and social power over civilians by constantly highlighting the role soldiers played in winning the independence struggle. The official nationalist narration of the Turkish past helped this process as well, turning all soldiers into pure, brave, sacrificing heroes. Third, the first two civilian presidents of the republic, Mustafa Kemal Atatürk and İsmet İnönü, had both been military generals who had later turned into civilian leaders, first guiding the populace through war as military officers, then once again guiding them through peace as civilian officials. This symbolic, social, and political overlap of the military and civilian republican spheres led many Turkish officers to constantly develop intricate plans, strategies, and proposals to better the country, ones within which they of course played a significant role.

The memoir by one such officer described the many military meetings that preceded the 1960 coup, where a group of young officers met to eventually arrive at the twenty principles they would apply upon assuming power. These were as follows:[385]

> First, the guilty ones would be tried at a special court; second, the national assembly would be dissolved; third, all political parties would

> be closed down; fourth, a military administration would be established; fifth, a revolutionary council would be formed to administer the country along with the military junta; sixth, a new constitution would be prepared; seventh, the politicization and exploitation of religion would be prevented; eighth, a planning organization would be formed; ninth, the Atatürk reforms would be executed without any lenience, turning Kemalism into a scientific doctrine; and tenth, all institutions like the armed forces, university, the media, and state organizations would be reorganized. The other ten principles emphasized the building of national unity, giving precedence to statism, independent policy in foreign affairs, containing radical movements, and finally when the time came, holding free elections, and turning political rule over to the party that won the elections.

Such a plan articulated what was to be done in practice, totally silencing how the ideas leading to the practice had come about, what such ideas implied at whose expense, and, most significantly, who would be doing the interpreting. Specifically, who would decide upon what constituted guilt, how would the reforms be executed, and how would the universities, media, and state be reorganized? These questions reveal that the practice of personalized political governance had also penetrated the military in that they too had no interest in abiding by the legal system, instead wanting to reorganize the republic in accordance with their own vision. That there were many factions within the Turkish military became evident in 1962 when a segment unsuccessfully attempted to stage yet another coup, leading to the immediate hanging of two coup leaders. Military leadership also attempted to exploit this attempted coup to persecute and prosecute the leftists, who were once again rounded up in an attempt to tie their activities to those of the second coup leaders but to no avail.[386]

Contemporaneous memoirs capture the brutality of the Turkish military's treatment of the arrested DP deputies, members, and sympathizers. Once again, a very large number were taken into military custody, since the military did not abide by what legally constituted a crime either. Many, beaten on the way, were taken to the off-limits Yassıada Island on the Marmara Sea; no one was told what was in store for them, leading to anxiety, fatal heart attacks, and suicides, all exacerbated by frequent beatings. The ensuing military trials were also unjust, as the decisions on sentences were reached not in court but within the military leadership. It did not help that General Cemal Gürsel, the appointed coup leader and the next civilian president of the republic after the coup, stated in a speech to the nation that "at the slightest stir, we will turn Yassıada [where the arrested were taken] into a pile of meat and bones."[387] A new pattern of "Turkish military strategy of civilian governance" emerged at this juncture. Through the coups, the military would eventually reform things as they saw fit, then turning the state and government to civilian rule, but in each case preserving the republican presidency for the army by forcing the election to the post of a high-ranking military officer turned civilian. The origins of such a strategy can be traced to the 1913 coup of Enver Pasha. After 1923, Mustafa Kemal was able to establish control over the military by being a former general, over the state administration by becoming the president, and over the government by assuming the leadership of the RPP. After the transition to a multiparty system in the 1950s, the government leadership became more civilian. Yet the military then turned to sustaining its political power by still ruling over the executive and administrative branches of the state through military officers turned into civilians. It was therefore no accident that the 1960 and 1971 coups were followed by the election to the presidency of former military officers. In addition, in executing their post-coup reforms, the military complained about the messiness of civilian life, often resorting to violence to have things executed as they saw fit.[388]

During this period, the military's political control was challenged only once, when a civilian presidential candidate emerged to legally challenge the military's candidate, only to be forced to withdraw his candidacy. Contemporaneous memoirs discussed in detail the political journey of the constitutional law professor Ali Fuat Başgil, who mistakenly thought that he could be a presidential candidate after the 1960 coup.[389] After the military officers arrested Başgil, they desperately searched for any law with which to incriminate him but could not find anything and therefore released him, keeping him under constant surveillance instead. Başgil was then invited to a meeting with two top-level military officers, who warned him to withdraw his candidacy by stating they could not guarantee his life and, some contend, by pointing a gun at him to prove their point. Right after the meeting, Başgil not only withdrew his presidency but also left the country, fearing for his life.

Such state and government violence against political thought impacted not only the victims but also their families. On the one hand, they suffered financially, losing their livelihood; on the other, they turned into social pariahs as many around them stopped interacting with them, pretending they did not exist. Such a negative societal attitude enhanced and indirectly supported the initial state and government violence, making it nearly impossible for Turkish intellectuals to break out of this circle of formal state-executed and informal society-supported violence. After the 1971 coup, one memoir writer arrested for his leftist views recounted the sudden house raid leading to his arrest when his pharmacist wife was not at home and his four-year-old daughter was asleep in the other room:[390]

> They entered the room in which [my daughter] slept by kicking down the door so she was startled out of her sleep, [fearfully] watching them

> search the room.... Then they took me out of the house. As I left, I shouted to the neighbors: "Please tell her mother! My wife is working at the pharmacy and my daughter is at home alone!"... The neighbors did not inform [my pharmacist wife], so my daughter remained at home alone until midnight when my wife returned. During all that time, my daughter had stayed in the house alone in constant fear. [After that incident], she started stuttering and also suffered some psychological distress.

Having been raised in Turkey during the 1970s, I remember parents' anxiety over their children's possible involvement in politics. As the Turkish populace tried to make sense of what was happening around them and as the lack of state and government transparency prevented them from gaining any significant public knowledge, rumors and conspiracy theories on who was being watched, taped, and listened to abounded. By reading the newspapers, one only gleaned what was going on from various editorial columns; the rest of the news stories across all the newspapers were exact replicas of each other.

Such early republican violence had two major consequences. Within the Turkish state, corruption and mismanagement reigned due to lack of accountability; within Turkish society, such corruption combined with repression to tear the moral fabric, turning the populace into passive citizens bereft of democracy. Contemporaneous memoirs document these dire consequences as well. [391] Four accounts by Turkish state officials revealed the manner in which republican leaders exploited their positions to amass wealth as rampant corruption reigned in currency devaluations, naval purchases, and appointments to state posts.[392] More worrisome was the manner in which some republican leaders kept themselves and their families above the law by intervening in the legal system to have charges against their families, some as significant as murder, dismissed.[393] The blatant lack of accountability also penetrated into Turkish society at large. One memoir noted the corruption in the provinces, where many state and government officials exploited their positions for personal gain. The few who tried to challenge such corruption remained helpless.[394] For some, resorting to violence in everyday practices became a naturalized course of action.[395] In summary, then, collective violence during the independence struggle and the ensuing republic generated a republican leadership composed of state and government officials and military officers that regarded itself as above the law. These leaders' lack of accountability in execution expanded from the state to society as they violently repressed any opposition. I argue that the origins of this lack of accountability can be traced to the initial collective violence committed against the Armenians from 1915 to 1917. In negotiating the past, the republican leaders did not acknowledge this foundational violence in their past but instead denied it. The main reason behind their denial, I next argue, was due to the manner in which the 1919–22 military tribunals trying the perpetrators of the foundational violence were conducted. Some illegal procedures during the military tribunals enabled the emerging nationalist leaders to delegitimate not only the trials but also the just Armenian claims for punishment.

Legitimating Event of Early Republican Collective Violence: 1919–22 Military Tribunals

Ironically, the inherent violence of this period was legitimated by the military tribunals that were established to punish the perpetrators who had committed the Armenian massacres. This ironic turn was due to the intersection of these Ottoman trials with the Turkish independence struggle; both took place during the same period, that is, from 1919 to 1922. The surge of Turkish nationalism during the Allied occupation and the ensuing independence struggle enabled many CUP perpetrators sought by the Allied forces for punishment to escape to Anatolia to throw in their lot with the independence struggle. With the victory of the struggle, the former perpetrators transformed into new republican heroes, undoing a transformation that enabled them to whitewash their former acts of violence. The origins of such lack of differentiation between the perpetrators and the patriots can be traced to the manner in which the Allied forces initially arrested, imprisoned, and processed the guilty parties. Because this was the first case in history in which the perpetrators were tried for crimes against humanity, the Allied forces in general and the British in particular did not separate the arrested in accordance with their particular crimes. Instead, they imprisoned all top-ranking officials, officers, and civilians in one undifferentiated mass. Those patriots who wrote articles and took stands against the Allied occupation were imprisoned together with the perpetrators, making it increasingly difficult to distinguish the patriot from the perpetrator over time.

In all, only some of the perpetrators ended up getting arrested, and only a handful were then tried and hanged. The hangings of two CUP members, the Boğazlıyan district governor Kemal and the Urfa subdistrict governor Nusret, emerged as the significant events in mobilizing the Turkish Muslim populace against the military tribunals.[396] The perpetrators who were exiled by the British to Malta as well as those who escaped to Anatolia or elsewhere were never tried. In the end, although hundreds if not thousands of Turkish Muslim perpetrators participated in the collective violence against the Armenians, very few were actually punished. Over the course of republican history, those tried and hanged during the military tribunals instigated by the Allied forces then reemerged not as perpetrators, as they should have been, but instead as "the martyrs of the republic." The Turkish national assembly duly granted their families lifelong annuities, ones accruing specifically from abandoned Armenian properties. An understanding of how and why the attempt to hold the perpetrators accountable for the violence they had committed led to the state and government denial of the same violence necessitates the in-depth analysis of the events surrounding the military tribunal.

Forming Military Tribunals

The military tribunal to try the perpetrators was established at the end of World War I.[397] Four contemporaneous memoirs of Ottoman officials discussed the issues that emerged even before the tribunal was formed. The first issue concerned sovereignty. The Allied forces wanted to set up the trials, but the Ottoman leaders did not want Westerners to try what had taken place domestically in their empire.[398] Yet the Ottoman leaders also knew that their failure to punish the perpetrators might lead the Allied forces to impose much harsher terms on the empire at the onging peace talks. This possibility enabled the Allied forces to influence the ensuing course of action to such a degree that some nationalist Turks argued that the West employed the trials to beat the empire into submission. In the appointment of judges, there was some talk of bringing in judges from neutral Western European countries, but neither the Allied forces nor the Ottoman leaders entertained such a proposition and so it came to naught.[399] The extensive discussions within the Ottoman circles indicate that the first social reaction was a defensive one: many immediately brought up the subsequent 1917 Muslim massacres by the Armenians in the east, arguing that these Armenian perpetrators had to be tried as well.[400] Such legal inclusion would have effectively equated the two sets of massacres that were different not only in scale but also in intent. Still, it should be noted that the Armenian perpetrators of these massacres were never held accountable for their violent actions either.

The second issue concerned the legal boundaries of responsibility. The first debate was on who should be punished first, those who actually committed the violence or those who gave the orders. This discussion was complicated by the fact that the majority of the CUP decision-making body had successfully escaped to Europe, leaving behind mostly those who had carried out their orders. Another problem related to the manner in which the CUP decided on and executed collective violence, not publicly and formally but privately and informally through mostly orally given secret orders. Given the informal CUP connection to the Ottoman state and government, and given the accompanying extralegal SO activities, it was difficult to publicly and legally document who gave the orders and who executed them. This legal ambiguity also enabled some Turks to later argue that with the subsequent assassinations of most top-level CUP members abroad by Armenian revolutionaries, justice had been served as the decision-makers had been duly punished. They forgot to mention, however, that their punishment was delivered not in a court of law but instead through popular justice as some Armenians took the matter into their own hands.

With these two issues still unsettled,[401] the Ottoman military tribunal was finally established on 16 December 1918 to try those responsible for the Armenian deportations and massacres. The tribunal decided to first focus on the Yozgat, Trabzon, and Diyarbekir deportation cases.[402] During the trials, the lack of formal evidence on the Armenian massacres made the oral testimonies and official documentation all the more important to the court cases. The interruption of telegraph communication between the imperial capital and Anatolia after March 1920 also prevented the military tribunal from gathering information and inviting local witnesses. In addition, those CUP members remaining behind in the empire tried constantly to obstruct the delivery of justice.

Obstructing Justice

The CUP had had ten years during which to systematically appoint as many of its members to Ottoman state and government positions as possible. Six contemporaneous memoirs document that many former CUP members in the state and government did everything possible to prevent the military tribunals from operating with speed; some intentionally slowed down all pertinent correspondence, and others destroyed crucial documents that would have led to severe sentences.[403] And, of course, many others warned their friends about the upcoming Allied arrests, thereby allowing the perpetrators to escape. The ideology the CUP members employed in justifying the obstruction of justice was ethnic nationalism; all believed that the violent destruction of Armenians was a necessary measure for the Turks to establish their fatherland.

One CUP and SO member who later served as a republican minister, prime minister, and president noted in his memoirs that the CUP systematically eliminated incriminating documents in three waves. First, the CUP leaders who escaped abroad took a large chest of documents along with them. Second, the CUP members who were left behind went through the remaining documents, destroying the incriminating ones in the process. Third, they entrusted some documents to friends who would not be suspected of holding them.[404] Another memoir writer stated that the documents of the SO members who executed many of the violent crimes against the Armenians were destroyed in a similar manner: the incriminating secret files at the War Ministry and those of the general chief of staff were first moved during the night to the depot of the military publishing house and then systematically destroyed.[405] Still another memoir writer skillfully recounted this destruction of incriminating documents as follows:[406]

> The pasha and I were burning everything. It was as if the two of us were out to singlehandedly clean the entire world. In our sleepless eyes half drowned by the smoke and dripping with tears, the flames of the things we burned started to take on the color of blood. And we constantly burned that strange thing we call the past! But burning it was of no use. Everything we burned weirdly became attached to our minds, one name recalled another, lives became separated, and the memories attached themselves onto one another. Emptiness had opened its mouth wide, spewing onto us in multitude what it had just taken away.

This description aptly captures that such physical destruction of the documentation of collective violence never managed to fully destroy the violence itself, the acts of the perpetrators, or the horrendous memories of the witnesses. Nevertheless, it did prevent the collection at this juncture of the necessary legal documentation to successfully try and convict many of the perpetrators.

The memoir of still another CUP and SO member revealed that members of these organizations were fully aware that many among them would have been tried and punished if the trials were successfully held. Another strategy of destruction the SO members employed was to infiltrate the offices of the Allied forces with the intent to undermine all the latter's actions pertaining to this issue. The memoir writer proudly described their actions as follows:[407]

> For every CUP member held responsible for the Armenian deportations and massacres, either arrest or execution at any time was preordained. [So] basically, whoever got organized first and succeeded was going to win this business.... With the [help of] agents, we had infiltrated into the İstanbul offices of the Allied powers, [thereby] succeeding in obtaining all types of correspondence. We [therefore] managed to disrupt their measures and sabotaged their precautions, always placing them in a difficult position. And we upset all their actions through such precautions as well as through propaganda. During the armistice years, this was the most significant function of our SO and the armed national defense forces.

The propaganda they engaged in was evident in contemporaneous newspapers as many wrote articles delegitimating the trials by constantly connecting them to the Allied occupation of their empire and fatherland. The memoir by an

Ottoman official who served in the cabinet during this time corroborated that the CUP had been ousted from power and formally dissolved, but it nevertheless continued to be influential throughout the country and especially at the imperial capital:[408]

> In spite of its many malicious acts and defeats, the CUP was still a considerable force in the country and especially in İstanbul. Not only were all bureaucrats and members of the police force their men, but it was rumored that the officers of three battalions at the imperial capital had also sworn an oath of loyalty to Enver. The guiltier one is, the more cowardly they will become, and the more cowardly they are, the more dangerous they will be. The worry of protecting one's property and life drives one to the utmost state of recklessness and wickedness. Consequently, it would have been necessary to impel and satisfy the CUP leaders with the strength of law, justice, and love of the fatherland, and to have bound and silenced their rabble and scoundrels through these means.... I undertook many initiatives to catch them after they had escaped. I could not have done more. Even though the heads of military and civil police forces had been replaced by those who were either [politically] neutral or closer to [their] opponents, all the police, all our land forces, and all German establishments acted as [the CUP's] men and aides.

Such CUP obstruction of justice was not limited to the imperial capital. Another Ottoman official in government discussed the difficulties the state bureaucracy encountered in 1921 upon sending, under the leadership of Said Pasha, a military investigative commission to the six provinces where the Armenians had once resided as well as to Trabzon. Its mission was to look into the Armenian massacres as well as the violence executed by the Turkish National Defense Committee (Müdafaa-i Hukuk Cemiyeti). There was so much local resistance that this attempt was later abandoned. Still, the investigation of the local CUP accounts the commission managed to undertake revealed vast financial discrepancies.[409] The memoir of a CUP member and Ottoman official serving in Konya demonstrated the manner in which the CUP officials also obfuscated what had violently transpired by making sure to provide as little information as possible. Upon being asked by the governor to prepare a report on how many Armenians had lived in the district before the deportation, how many had then been transported through which means, and the names of those who had performed the massacres, this official curtly stated that they were all arrested in accordance with the deportation law, placed on trains, and sent south.[410]

Politicizing Legal Procedures

Another significant obstacle was the manner in which the Unionists and Ententists both employed the military tribunals politically to settle scores and bring each other down. According to contemporaneous memoirs, all Ententist governments in general and the Damad Ferid Pasha government in particular suffered from the stigma of having to work with the occupying Allied forces.[411] These Ententist governments were further delegitimated when they tried to punish their Unionist opponents by claiming that not only all the Unionists but also all Unionist sympathizers were guilty of crimes against the Armenians.[412] Such blanket accusations convinced many that all laws and legal procedures were being trampled in the military tribunals.[413] The Ententists tried to argue, to no avail, that their approach would lessen the severity of the Sèvres Treaty terms.[414]

When the list of perpetrators arrested and still sought appeared in the Ottoman newspapers on 31 January 1919, one memoir writer stated that he was convinced the intent was not to punish only the perpetrators but all CUP members. He had seen the original list of perpetrators that the British had prepared; when he compared the British list to the published one, he realized that many staunch Entente opponents who had nothing to do with the Armenian violence had been added on, almost doubling the size of the list.[415] Another memoir writer published the entire list of those perpetrators who had been arrested and those who were still being pursued by the Ottoman state and Allied Forces.[416] The list does indeed include many journalists and former CUP ministers who probably were not directly involved in deciding upon or executing the Armenian massacres. The preparation of such inexact, politicized lists of perpetrators was also complicated by Armenians who made false accusations against Turks for financial profit, further undermining and delegitimating the process.[417] One indication that things were not going well at the trials and investigations was the very low attendance level; even committee members were not all present during the sessions.[418]

Delegitimating the Military Tribunal and Rehabilitating the Perpetrators

The tribunal was initially headed by Lieutenant General Mahmut Hayret Pasha. Yet he was immediately accused of being overly meticulous and therefore not up to the speed the Europeans had expected. The pasha resigned as a consequence, and was replaced by Kürt Mustafa Pasha of Süleymaniye, who made it a priority to deliver speedy high-profile sentences, sometimes without following the necessary legal procedures. Mustafa Pasha quickly acquired the epithet "grim" among the Turkish populace, probably for the grim decisions he reached.

Eight contemporaneous memoirs revealed the manner in which prominent Unionists who had now become ardent patriotic nationalists gradually delegitimated the military tribunal.[419] Two memoir writers criticized head judge Mustafa Pasha's moral character; while one accused him of being unjust, the other recounted that during his own interrogation by the tribunal, the pasha and his panel of judges did not refrain from anything to prove his guilt, even arresting his assistants and telling them they would be released if they testified against the memoir writer.[420] Two others argued that the judge was "an enemy of the Turks" who was actually controlled by the Armenian patriarch.[421] Another one oddly recounted that later, when he had an opportunity to study the Armenian deportation process, he was most upset by the fact that the perpetrators had personally benefited from the plunder, not turning the proceeds over to the state as they should have. He did not at all comment on or condemn the violence the perpetrators had committed.[422]

Yet the most significant factor that ultimately enabled the nationalists to totally delegitimate the military tribunal was that the tribunal also delivered a decision against the leaders of the independence struggle, sentencing them in absentia to death by hanging.[423] Just as the British had obfuscated the separation between the perpetrators and the patriots by arresting and imprisoning them all together, the head judge of the military tribunal also reached a legal decision against the patriots while trying the perpetrators. Once again, this connection between the perpetrators and the patriots caused the nationalists and the Turkish populace to rally around the patriots, thereby taking a stand against the military tribunal and, in the process, also claiming the perpetrators as "patriots." One writer argued in particular that when the tribunal was unable to catch Mustafa Kemal (the patriot), it instead hanged Kemal and Nusret (the perpetrators).[424] Another articulated the connection between the perpetrators and the patriots more carefully:[425]

> The one gathering, readying, and transporting the witnesses [to the tribunal] is the (Armenian) Patriarchate. The Armenians are after Greater Armenia, some... after a Kurdistan next to this Armenia, the Greeks after Smyrna, Thrace, and a Pontus Kingdom on the Black Sea shores. Anatolian notables are being pursued by the denunciations of Christians, and Union and Entente members. Of course, no one would present to passersby either their honor or their life as if it were a cup of coffee. Those who have not been caught have either hidden away, or armed themselves and escaped up to the mountains, or retired to their farms. [This was how] the first source of [manpower] for the nationalist forces came into being.

It is significant that the memoir writer traces the origins of the independence struggle to the military tribunals, once again highlighting the close connection between the collective violence committed against the Armenians and the Turkish independence movement. Such persistent attempts to delegitimate and whitewash past violence become even more evident when one studies in detail the fate of the perpetrators in four categories: (1) those who were arrested, tried, and acquitted; (2) those who were exiled to Malta or Egypt by the British; (3) those who were hanged or killed; and finally (4) those who escaped trial.

Perpetrators Arrested, Tried, and Acquitted

Eleven contemporaneous memoirs contained information on perpetrators arrested for committing violence against the Armenians, all of whom were eventually acquitted.[426] While three of these were actual perpetrators,[427] six others knew perpetrators as friends, relatives, or acquaintances.[428] Interestingly, two memoir writers stated that their relatives accused of being perpetrators were saved by the personal intervention of local Armenians who provided information to the contrary, indicating that some officials might have been wrongly accused.[429]

Of the three perpetrators, the first stated that he felt at ease in prison because all his friends had gathered there, turning the prison into a CUP club. The second noted that he had been accused of conducting the Armenian massacres in Ankara but had merely been the director of Muslim refugees there, conveniently failing to discuss what had happened to the former inhabitants of the houses where he settled the refugees. The third remarked that he was tried in relation to the deportation of some Armenians from Smyrna and then argued that he did not do so because the Armenians in Smyrna did not form a dangerous quantity there. He too carefully forgot to mention the thousands of Greek Rum he had violently forced to leave.[430] These three accounts demonstrate how the perpetrators self-censored and selectively narrated their past violence, providing irrelevant information while silencing their actual acts of destruction.

Of the six who knew perpetrators, the first narrated that his brother, who had been the director of refugee settlement, had been arrested for deporting Armenians. The second pointed out that his father was accused of protecting the official charged for deporting the Armenians of Sığırköy; his father's intervention ultimately led to the acquittal of the accused official. The third had been charged with causing the forced migrations of Greek Rum. He narrated in great detail that on the boat ride to the trial and back, many Turkish nationalists expressed great warmth and adulation toward him, spontaneously offering to help him escape. This positive attitude of the Turks he encountered substantiates once again the complicity of the Turkish populace in aiding the perpetrators. The fourth mentioned that he knew of a Cezmi who had harmed Armenians during the deportations in the vicinity of Adana, but the same Cezmi had then worked for the French occupying forces and later became a republican military commander. The final two were in prison at the capital, commenting on the great time they had with their imprisoned CUP friends. The last one explained that the reason for this celebratory mood in prison was their certainty that they were all going to be acquitted.[431] Of the two whose relatives had been accused of being perpetrators, one explained that his relative had been charged with mistreating the Armenians of Smyrna while serving there as the police chief, but was acquitted when he submitted a letter that had been written by an Armenian, thanking him for his protection. The other stated that his father, who had been the Lice district governor, was about to be arrested in Adana by the French when he ran into an Armenian friend of his from Diyarbekir who testified on his behalf.[432]

Perpetrators Exiled to Malta and Egypt

Eleven contemporaneous memoirs provided information on the perpetrators who were arrested by the British and exiled to Malta and Egypt, only to be released later. Ten discussed the Malta exiles, while only one narrated the Egypt exiles in detail.[433] The memoirs reveal for the first time that the Allied forces had two different arrest procedures: while the top CUP members were arrested and brought to the capital to then be exiled to Malta, the local CUP perpetrators in the east were instead exiled to prison camps in Egypt. The scholarly literature on the topic covers the Malta exiles, but none mention the local notables who were sent to Egypt.[434]

The British decided to exile the perpetrators to Malta along with the rest of the imprisoned when the first hanging, of the perpetrator Kemal Bey, led to large protests at his funeral. They worried that subsequent hangings might lead protesters to storm the prison with the intent to release all the imprisoned Turks. The British decision was not supported by the other Allies, however; in retaliation, the French subsequently permitted some of the perpetrators to escape to Ankara.[435] When all the CUP leaders were imprisoned at the capital, the initial reaction of the populace was supportive of the arrests, as rumors spread that many had not been "pure Turks" to start with.[436] Yet subsequent systematic CUP propaganda in the media rallied the populace to then support all the imprisoned on the grounds that they were true patriots. The British decision to exile them all, that is, patriots resisting the Allied occupation along with the perpetrators, enabled the exiled perpetrators to claim that they had been imprisoned and exiled not because of the violence they perpetrated but instead for having been patriots. A case in point is Ahmed Erner, arrested for the murder of 30,000 Urfa

Armenians, who insisted that they had all been imprisoned and exiled to Malta for two reasons: to provide a bargaining chip to Lord Curzon during the Sèvres Treaty signing, and to get the Ottoman leaders away from the capital to prevent them from forming a government.[437] The British might have indeed taken such possibilities into account, but these certainly did not apply to the perpetrators.

Another Malta exile had been arrested for enabling the escape of the top CUP cadre to Germany. He stated that he had aided their escapes because he did not think they would get a fair trial at the occupied capital, failing to mention that many among them not only had made the violent decision to eliminate the Armenians but also had actively administered the deportations and massacres. He also claimed that another Malta exile, the *sheikul islam* and minister of foundations Hayri Efendi, was there with them because of the pressure of the Greek Rum and Armenian church leadership, in compensation for the murders of the Greek Rum and Armenian priests.[438] This explanation raises another issue: it is unclear whether the sixty-seven former CUP officials were exiled to Malta because of their personal involvement in the violence against the Armenians, or because of the posts they had held during the Armenian deportations and massacres, thereby making them responsible by proxy.

The memoirs of two other Malta exiles provided clues on the actual perpetrators.[439] While the Malta exiles remained there for approximately nineteen months from March 1919 to October 1920, at some point, the British wanted to negotiate the release of twenty of them in exchange for the British war prisoners in the empire, on the condition that none of the released could be actual perpetrators. At this point, thinking that the perpetrators were going to be tried and hanged, the exiles started to plan the escape of such perpetrators to Italy with the help of local fishermen. The two memoirs noted that sixteen among them were perpetrators, and they did indeed manage to escape. Among these were "Cevdet Bey, Kırzade Mustafa Bey of Trabzon, Yunus Nadi Bey, Ali İhsan Pasha, Kemal Bey, Yakup Şevki Pasha, and many governors." The exiles were especially worried about General Ali İhsan Pasha, since his "condition" was "more dangerous than the others." The names of five other perpetrators emerge from other Malta exile memoirs:[440] they were Şükrü Kaya, Fethi Okyar, Diyarbekir deputies (Pirinçcizade) Fevzi and Zülfi Beys, and Yusuf Nuri Efendi, a sergeant major of the gendarmerie.

One Malta exile, who was also a perpetrator, stood out in the information he provided in his memoirs regarding his attempts to avert his role in the Armenian violence. He openly admitted that he had initially sent a telegram to then interior minister Talat Pasha, asking the latter to also deport the Adana Armenians. He did so, he claimed, because the deportation "business" commenced according to a plan, starting in Erzurum and eventually reaching Adana. Worried that there would be bloodshed in Adana in the interim, he sent the telegram, also adding a list of the particular Armenians who should be deported first; his request was immediately granted. Then, during the armistice period, when his friends alerted him that his house was going to be searched by the Allied forces, he moved all the incriminating documents to a safe place, destroying some in the process. Yet he inadvertently left drafts of the telegram in the pocket of his briefcase, and these were found when his Armenian nanny informed the Allied authorities about it. During the ensuing questioning, he insisted to no avail on being tried not by the Allied forces but instead by the Turkish judges to ensure a more lenient sentence. When asked about the incriminating telegram, he lied, claiming that the list was of those Armenians who had been asked to make donations to some philanthropic activities in Adana.[441]

It is noteworthy that although many Malta exiles later became prominent republican statesmen and wrote their memoirs, they never mentioned the specific crimes that had landed them there, especially the ones they had committed against the Armenians, thereby effectively silencing their past violence through self-censorship.[442] While at Malta, the British did indeed attempt to try the perpetrators, asking the US State Department for incriminating documents only to be told that there were none that could be legally used in court. With the success of the independence struggle, the British then brokered a deal with Mustafa Kemal, letting all the Malta exiles to return to Ankara in exchange for the same number of British citizens sequestered in the empire. Most of the freed Malta exiles returned to Ankara, with Mustafa Kemal affectionately greeting them there in person. Yet Mustafa Kemal also seemed to have been wary of those who had committed crimes against the Armenians because he appointed them to lesser government posts than they had expected, leading some to return to İstanbul or to their places of origin.[443] In the end, however, none of the Malta exiles ever accounted for the violence they had committed.

One memoir of a possible perpetrator provided information on the local perpetrators exiled to Egypt, including the names of twenty-six.[444] Needless to say, although many were accused of committing violence against the Armenians, none admitted to their crimes. Yet what they encountered on the exile route certainly proved their guilt. As they left Antep, the local Armenians surrounded and insulted them, "laughing at us and throwing rocks." While in Aleppo, the arrested complained that every day thousands of Armenians gathered outside the inn they were staying at, making them anxious. The Armenians would get together three times a day at morning, noon, and night, protesting in shifts. After arriving at the British prison camp in Egypt, there probably were a few casualties among them due to sickness, but none of these perpetrators were ever tried for what they were accused of committing either. They were eventually released by the British, returning to their towns and cities to resume their lives.

Perpetrators Hanged or Killed

Even though only a handful of perpetrators were punished by the military tribunal, the fervor with which these "national martyrs" were written about in the contemporaneous memoirs indicated the impact such punishment had on the Turkish national psyche.[445] Among those hanged, two especially stood out in the memoirs. The first was the former Boğazlıyan district governor and Yozgat subdistrict governor Kemal Bey, the first prominent Ottoman official to be hanged. His hanging sent shock waves among the arrested CUP members, who until then were sure that since they were bring tried by an Ottoman court, they naturally would be acquitted. The second was the former Urfa subdistrict governor Nusret Bey, who seems to have been unjustly tried thrice for the same crime and then hanged through the machinations of the head judge Kürt Mustafa Pasha. The fact that the military tribunal tried the suspects in secret and without any lawyers present led them to reach swift but at times faulty decisions. Also significant in the memoirs was the discussion of a third person, the former Diyarbekir governor and physician Mehmed Reşid (Şahingiray) Bey, who escaped from prison and then committed suicide just before he could be caught. The crimes of the two (Kemal and Mehmed Reşid Beys) against the Armenians are well documented. Yet the injustice committed by the tribunal against the third (Nusret Bey) enabled the nationalists to declare all of them as "martyrs," thereby further delegitimating not only the tribunal but also the collective violence committed against the Armenians.

Two memoirs revealed two additional, lower-ranking perpetrators who were also hanged. One perpetrator was Aptullah Avni from Erzincan, also known as Hayran Baba. He was the brother of Gani Bey, CUP responsible secretary of Edirne, who was also tried and sentenced because of his involvement in the Armenian deportations and murders. Avni openly admitted to massacring Armenians, stating that he did so in revenge for the earlier murder of his family by the Armenian perpetrators, who threw his family into a well and then threw in a match, burning them.[446] The other perpetrator was former governor Nevzat Bey. He never spoke to anyone, always looking sad and offended, sitting at a table playing solitaire for hours. He did make the memoir writer who befriended him promise to write that he had been innocent.[447]

The cases of the three perpetrators who died, namely, Kemal, Nusret, and Mehmed Reşid Beys, need to be discussed in depth because they reveal the manner in which the nationalists were able to renarrate their deaths, delegitimating in the process the entire legal procedure followed by the military tribunal and, by doing so, all Armenian claims for justice as well.

Legal Case of Kemal Bey

Fourteen memoirs mentioned Kemal Bey, articulating the process through which this perpetrator was transformed into a martyr of the nationalist struggle.[448] He was the first to be hanged because the Yozgat deportation trial was the first one taken up on 5 February 1919 by the military tribunal; his trial ended two months later on 8 April 1919 with a death warrant. This first hanging became a turning point on two counts. First, it upset some Muslim Turks by confirming that such violent destruction had been committed against the Armenians, an allegation they had constantly tried so hard to refute.[449] As a consequence, the hanging acted like a litmus test, dividing the Turkish populace into two: those who sanctioned it, and those who condemned it. This was the first time the Turkish populace had been so polarized, with both sides becoming fervent in their stands.[450] Yet the invasion of Smyrna by the Greek army right around that time led the nationalists to gradually dominate the public sphere. Second, it shocked the imprisoned CUP officials, who until then were certain that the Ottoman judges were going to deliver light sentences. Indeed, they had been so certain about Kemal Bey's acquittal that when some CUP members on the outside prepared escape plans for Kemal Bey with the intent to smuggle him to Anatolia to join the independence struggle, they refused.[451]

The discussion in the memoirs of Kemal Bey's trial and subsequent hanging also revealed the manner in which he was portrayed as a victim, losing his life because of the avaricious stand of the occupying powers, the Armenians and the Entente Party.[452] As the trial commenced, Kemal Bey was transformed from being a victim into a patriot on the grounds that his sole crime had been obeying the orders he had been given. One memoir writer who was present at the trial narrated in detail the exchange between Kemal Bey and the judge:[453]

> Kemal Bey stated: "I received an order. An official is charged with obeying the order he has received. I acted in the most humane manner possible toward those expelled from the town. And I do not have any pangs of conscience now!" Yet the head judge Mustafa Pasha got up from his seat, shouting: "Were you not at all afraid of God while deporting all those people with their families and children in the middle of the winter to mountains and high plateaus? Did you never think you would one day be asked to account for these? And you also ordered the gendarmerie to bayonet them, what do you say to that?" "No, I would never accept that [charge]. I have never given an order for anyone's death." "Is making tens of thousands of helpless people including women and children march onto mountaintops in the winter, in the cold, any better than bayoneting them? To top it all, you are an administrative official; these [people] were placed under your protection. (Raising his voice) Do you know what the punishment is for instigating aggression against life and property by sending citizens living in our country against one another?" "It is death by hanging, my pasha!" "You gave your judgment

by your own mouth, Kemal Bey; and that is what we had decided for you as well."

As the initial shock at the sentence subsided, another memoir writer narrated the last moments of Kemal Bey as if he were a hero, overlooking the crimes the latter had committed. When some people placed placards around Kemal Bey's children's necks, stating that they were the children of a traitor to the motherland, those around Kemal Bey consoled him by stating that he was the true ideal fighter and patriot, and the former were the real traitors.[454] Kemal Bey was hanged at five in the afternoon rather than the usual time of five in the morning to serve as a lesson to the Turkish populace. He drew upon this nationalist rhetoric in delivering his last words to his compatriots, stating that "he had merely performed his duty by executing the orders he had received, and that he entrusted his children to the noble Turkish nation that would of course take care of them." He concluded by noting that "just like those who had died for the fatherland at the war front, he too departed as a martyr." In his last words, he prayed to God that "no harm would come to his fatherland and his nation." Kemal Bey's will, subsequently published in the newspapers, stated that he had also said that "the Turkish nation will live forever and Islam will never decline."[455] His funeral was organized by military cadets, with those in attendance chanting in unison that he had been a great patriot.[456]

Legal Case of Mehmed Reşid Bey

Dr. Mehmed Reşid Şahingiray was the murderer of not only thousands of Armenians but also the two district governors of Beşiri (Sabit Bey) and Lice (Nesimi Bey), who had opposed the Armenian massacres the former had committed. Two memoirs provided information about this perpetrator turned patriot; one was written by an opponent, and the other by Mehmed Reşid himself in the form of a diary he kept after his escape from prison.[457] Added to the diary, which was recently republished in Turkey with nationalist fanfare, is an interview he gave while in prison, providing additional insight into his violent actions. Mehmed Reşid escaped from prison on 25 January 1919, just as the military tribunal was discussing which Armenian deportation to try first. He feared that he might be hanged, especially given that he was also accused of murdering Ottoman Muslim officials. His escape occurred just as Kemal Bey's had been planned by CUP members, that is, while he was being taken from prison to the bathhouse for his weekly bath.

One memoir writer recounted that Talat Pasha had been extremely upset by Mehmed Reşid because when the latter had complained he was short on funds, he asked and was given money from the secret CUP funds. Yet then rumors circulated that Mehmed Reşid was about to buy an expensive İstanbul mansion, one he could not have purchased with the CUP funds, indicating that he had somehow gained access to substantive wealth.[458] The true nature of Mehmed Reşid is best described in the interview he gave to the *Hadisat* newspaper on 7 November 1918 in which the interviewer described him as "a haughty, derisive man answering all questions with a despising smile, as if he were someone whose might and genius had not been truly understood." The interviewer then asked the following questions:

> "It is said that you murdered more than 50,000 [Armenian] men, women, and children, innocent populace, and also three district governors, and that you usurped 300,000 lira gold cash and just as valuable jewelry from them. How much exaggeration is there in these accounts?" "It is all entirely lies…" "You have had these wretched people murdered by including in your retinue a murderer army major Rüşdü Bey as the commander of the gendarmerie and then by employing about 30 Circassians that this Rüşdü Bey had recruited from his own tribe." "I do not know." "They say that you have had Giridi Ahmed Nesimi Bey, the district governor of Lice who was also a distinguished writer known in the publishing and literary worlds, and Süveydizade Sabit Bey, the deputy *kaymakam* (provincial governor) of Beşiri who was one of the Baghdad notables and a graduate of the School of Public Administration, murdered for not obeying your order for massacre. [What is] your defense?" "All are wrongful accusations. After all, aren't newspapers the source of [all] anarchy and slander?" "It is said that by reappointing Hamid Bey, the former police chief of Diyarbekir who was fired from that post due to his immorality [to Mardin], you had [all] the wretched [people] in Mardin murdered irrespective of their religion or sect.… Those who worked to accomplish this aim were once again your gendarmerie?…" "I have no information about such things."

Mehmed Reşid effectively stonewalled all questions and accusations by refusing to engage in any discussion or defense. It appeared as if he did indeed have a noble cause, namely, placing the interests of the Turkish nation as defined by the CUP above the preservation of human lives. In interpreting this interview, the journalist stated that "the civilized world regards us as 'the murderers of the oppressed' because of people like Reşid Bey, who have executed abominable acts unacceptable to any religion, sect, or profession. This stain [placed upon us by such acts of violence] will forever remain a souvenir from our ancestors' tombstones to our children's cradles."[459]

Mehmed Reşid provided more information in his diary regarding what he had done and why, but still with great caution and self-censorship. He first mentioned on 15 January 1919 that, in addition to him, eight other people had been brought in to be tried in relation to their role in the Armenian deportations and ensuing massacres; these were the former Harput governor Sabit Bey, Trabzon agent Mustafa, director of charges Mehmed Ali, Niyazi from Trabzon, the Yozgat gendarmerie commander Tevfik Bey, Ankara police commissioner İbrahim, deputy Ali, and the court of appeals clerk İzzet Efendi. Duly noting his fury that the prisons were being emptied of all non-Muslims, with only Muslims remaining behind, Mehmed Reşid then addressed the Armenian issue:

> In relation to the Armenian issue, even though it has been so evident that I executed my patriotic duty, they insulted my honor with nonsensical talk like "he stole hundreds of thousands of lira and such."[460] My family is dependent on me, and if a catastrophe befell upon me, they will suffer extreme poverty, having no recourse to assistance from anyone. Yet I neglected my family and dedicated my body and life to this country. Damn these ingrates.

Like Kemal before him, Mehmed Reşid too claimed that he had merely performed his duty, qualifying that what he committed was a patriotic act, thereby drawing on Turkish nationalism to justify his violence. And he was more upset about the allegations of personal profit than the violence he was accused of. Mehmed Reşid concluded his diary by stating, "I am sure I have always carried out my duty in conformity with the orders I received.... If the destruction of my body is going to get rid of the crimes falsely imputed upon this nation, do not doubt that I would not hesitate for a moment to commit suicide!"[461]

Legal Case of Nusret Bey

Three memoirs discussed the trial of Nusret Bey.[462] He was accused of perpetrating massacres during the deportation of 7,000 Bayburt Armenians while serving as the Bayburt district governor and during the deportation of Ergani Madeni Armenians, where he had subsequently been appointed the district governor. Nusret Bey was initially arrested on 6 April 1919 and then released on 21 May 1919. His second arrest occurred on 6 November 1919; after being tried, he was delivered a sentence of fifteen years of hard labor on 4 July 1920. Yet he was then retried once again and received a sentence of death by hanging a month later on 3 August 1920.[463]

One memoir writer who was a commander and a perpetrator stated in his memoir that he first met Nusret Bey when the former had personally "started to annihilate, without mercy, all the enemies [namely, local Armenians] to the south of the Aras River in order to prevent a British occupation of the six Armenian provinces in Anatolia." Then, Nusret Bey had been one of the first to organize the local militia.[464] Another perpetrator and SO member commented that the populace had not believed Nusret Bey's guilt, thereby viewing his sentence not as the manifestation of justice but rather as cruelty. They damned the military tribunal for delivering such a faulty decision.[465] The third memoir belonged to a fellow prisoner who spent four to five months in the company of Nusret Bey. He described in detail the faulty procedure he personally witnessed:[466]

> The military tribunal actually reached two decisions on [Nusret Bey]. The first sentenced him to fifteen years in prison and the second to death by hanging! ... During the first trial, one of the members, Ferhat Bey, ... asked for a three-year sentence while the other two, [head judge] Mustafa Paşa and Fettah Bey, asked for his death by hanging. After a long discussion, the two additional members Recep Paşa and Recep Bey joined Ferhat Bey in reaching a majority decision of fifteen years of hard labor. On 4 July, the official report of the verdict was thus written and signed by the head judge and the members. Two days later [however], when Ferhat Bey asked if the verdict had been issued, he was told that ... it would be out in a couple of days. Meanwhile, ... the head judge brought in another witness [without consulting the other members], stating that this witness would provide testimony against the accused. Yet such a move was against judicial procedure [because a verdict had already been reached]. In spite of the head judge's insistence, the opposing members abstained from hearing the witness. When the head judge failed in his attempts, he delayed issuing the legal verdict. Ferhat Bey insisted on releasing the accused as there had been no proven criminal intent. Yet the head judge accused him of hindering the legal process, and a few days later, Ferhat Bey had to withdraw from the court upon receiving an imperial order dismissing him. He was then replaced by Niyazi Bey, leading to the issuance of a second majority decision for death by hanging and the sentence was [immediately] carried out.

In the nationalist newspapers, the injustice occurring during the trial as well as Nusret's insistence on his innocence led to an outcry. I further investigated and read the pertinent court proceedings, including Nusret's defense.[467] In summary, his defense in the case of the Bayburt Armenians was that they had been transported outside Bayburt without any casualties but were then massacred at Kelkit upon the orders of the former Erzincan subdistrict governor Memduh Bey. In the case of the Ergani Madeni Armenians, their deportations had been undertaken by his predecessor, Nazmi Bey, that is, before Nusret had been appointed there. In addition, Nusret did not employ the overly patriotic argument that he had merely obeyed orders; instead, he constantly tried to point out what I summarized earlier, but to no avail. The verdict was delivered in the evening, and Nusret was hanged very early the following morning.

After the fall of the Damad Ferid Pasha cabinet during whose governance Nusret had been hanged, one of the first actions of the succeeding government was to start a legal investigation into not only Nusret's particular case but all the decisions of the military tribunal. The legal investigation led in turn to the trial of the head judge Kürt Mustafa Pasha; he was then exiled from the empire as an "enemy of the nation." Two months later, on 7 October 1920, the national assembly in Ankara proposed and passed into law a decision to pay a monthly stipend to Nusret's widow.[468] Nusret's mistrial thus delegitimated not only his death verdict but also all the verdicts that had been reached by the tribunal, including the ones on the Armenian deportations and massacres. It also instigated the national assembly in Ankara to protect and incorporate into the body of the emerging nation not only Nusret but later the other two perpetrators as patriotic martyrs. In 1922, when the nationalist forces won all their battles, the military tribunal was dissolved, and all the prisoners were released. With this dissolution, the rising republican leaders considered the Armenian issue tried and settled. Subsequent republican discussions of the military tribunal emphasized the injustices that the tribunal had committed, thereby whitewashing the crimes of all the perpetrators who had been tried and adroitly turning them all into martyrs of the republic. Still, the perpetrators who had been arrested and tried at the military tribunal were only a small segment; many others who had escaped to join the national forces in Anatolia were never tried and punished.

Perpetrators Who Escaped to Ankara

Eleven contemporaneous memoirs contained ample information on those perpetrators who escaped trial by joining the independence struggle in Ankara that was out of the Allied forces' reach.[469] A total of seventeen perpetrators were mentioned in the memoirs; nine, that is slightly over half, of these perpetrators were memoir writers themselves.[470] Their narrations documented the complicity of many local Turkish officials in their escapes on the one hand and the support of the local Turkish notables on the other. These local officials and notables not only hid them but actively supported and guided their escapes. They were all very well received in Ankara because the leaders of the independence struggle needed educated CUP officials, officers, and civilians and therefore did not hold the perpetrators' crimes against them. After the independence struggle, many then served the republic, often as deputies. One memoir concisely captured the direct route from being a perpetrator to becoming a patriot:[471]

> Upon the end of the [Great] war when the British and their allies decided to hold those who were Unionists and especially those who had killed Armenians accountable for their crimes, everyone who took

> offense armed themselves, joining an armed band [in Anatolia]....In the west, these bands were the first heroes of the nationalist forces.

The other memoirs recounted the perpetrators, but none articulated what the crimes of the memoir writers had been. Only one perpetrator/memoir writer stated that after his escape, he ran into a British agent who told him that if he had not escaped, he certainly would have been arrested and sent to Malta.[472] Another perpetrator/memoir writer remarked that he had escaped with the help of the SO members as soon as he found out his name was on the arrest list, taking along with him two other perpetrators he had helped break out from prison.[473] Still another narrated that the military commander of another town alerted him and two other perpetrators sought for the Armenian massacres at the Kemah Pass; the military commander hid all three for a while before their escape to Ankara.[474] The duplicity of the local officials in guiding the escapes was evident in the case of the perpetrator/memoir writer who was the Bitlis governor. He described his escape in detail:[475]

> There was a decision to arrest and send me to İstanbul under guard; the governors along the way had been notified of this as well. The Ferid Pasha government was scared of the CUP organization causing trouble, so did not communicate my dismissal and arrest to Bitlis....I sent a telegram liberating myself from the governorship [nevertheless] and rather than going to İstanbul, left for Erzurum [to join Mustafa Kemal]. Meanwhile, I learned the real story from the telegram I received in code from Ali Seydi Bey, the Elazığ governor who was my classmate from the School of Public Administration. This is what Ali Seydi said in his telegram: "An order arrived for your arrest and delivery to İstanbul under guard to the military tribunal due to the issue of Armenian deportations. If you pass by Elazığ, this order will naturally not be carried out; you can stay here and hide if you want. If you want to go anywhere else, my brother, I can make sure within my province that you continue on your way securely and comfortably."

This correspondence demonstrates the strength of school ties many Turkish officials and officers had previously developed; these ties then intersected with their CUP-turned-nationalist political views, leading them to help each other escape, and thereby choosing what they perceived as national interests over the interests of humanity. Other actors became duplicitous out of material interests. One perpetrator/memoir writer pointed out that in addition to the local military commander and public prosecutor, the local Near East Relief representative let him use the organization's truck in return for "material favors."[476] Also complicitous were arresting Allied officers, helping those they had previously known by giving them time to destroy incriminating documents.[477] The perpetrators also received support and encouragement from the local notables; one perpetrator/memoir writer who went to another city for his questioning mentioned in name every local notable who came to visit him while there, including the chief secretary, public prosecutor, and financial inspector. The same person was then elected to the Ottoman assembly but escaped to Ankara when he realized he was being followed.[478] Another perpetrator/memoir writer was a local notable who first described how he had purchased properties and goods left behind by the Armenians and then explained that he did not permit the returning Armenians to recover them on the grounds that there was no such law, paying them meager amounts instead. When he was called to give a statement, he claimed that he was a rich man who did not need "rotten Armenian property that was worth nothing," also not failing to add that he had been "performing a duty for the fatherland."[479]

Three memoirs contained information that had been provided in passing. In one case, a memoir writer traveling to Anatolia by boat recounted talking to a fellow passenger only to find out that the latter had a district governor brother who was accused of committing crimes against the Armenians; when the gendarmerie were sent to arrest the brother, the Kurds intervened, whisking him to the mountains. The one at the boat was the other brother, a deputy, who first changed his identity to escape arrest, successfully getting on the boat.[480] In another case, a perpetrator/memoir writer pointed out that the former gendarmerie regiment commander colonel accused of the Armenian deportation later became the republican deputy of Cebeli Bereket.[481] The final memoir pointed out in passing that a district governor who had to escape to Europe to avoid prosecution later became a deputy at the first national assembly.[482]

In summary, the rationalizing event comprising the few injustices committed at the 1919–22 military tribunals coincided with the independence struggle, enabling the nationalists to gradually transform the former perpetrators into patriots, thereby leading only a few to be held accountable for the crimes they committed against the Armenians. The majority not only avoided prosecution but escaped to Anatolia to join the independence struggle, and with the victory of the struggle, they reemerged as republican patriots and served the newly established nation-state in high positions. This transformation effectively produced the republican denial of the perpetrators of the collective violence against the Armenians.

Third Denial: Actors of Collective Violence Committed against the Armenians

During the republican period, it is no accident that the republican leadership denied that the perpetrators of the Armenian violence had transformed into the republic with impunity, arguing instead that the Armenian issue was closed and all the perpetrators had been duly punished. This denial emerged during the transition from the Ottoman Empire to the Turkish nation-state through the independence struggle. It occurred in two stages: during the first stage, the connection between the independence struggle and the CUP was denied; this led to the second stage, when the presence of any perpetrators among the ranks of the nationalists was denied. Each stage built upon the other. As the independence struggle commenced, it was necessary for the leaders of the struggle to deny the CUP connection to prevent the Allied forces from taking action against them.[483] As the struggle grew stronger, however, the leaders consolidated their ranks, denying both their old CUP identities and the violence they had committed against the Armenians. Contemporaneous memoirs reveal, however, that there was always a strong connection between the CUP and the nationalists in that they were literally the one and the same, including many perpetrators among them. After the establishment of the republic, although the rehabilitated leaders tried to put the Armenian violence behind them, it continued to play a significant role in their private memory. These republican leaders were not ever held accountable for their past violence; their lack of accountability led them to internalize the violence and then apply it within the republic, once again with impunity.

Stage I: Denial of the CUP Connection

The first stage of the republican denial of the CUP connection emerged gradually. First, the CUP decision that its members should not write their individual memoirs but instead let the central committee construct their narrative meant that initially there was little public knowledge of the CUP's activities in general and its secret, extralegal activities in particular. The CUP members kept their memories of the past fiercely private. This scarcity enabled many to hide their CUP origins. Second, during the independence struggle, many former CUP and especially SO members who were actively involved in the struggle eagerly gave up their former stigmatized identities, assuming instead a new constructed identity emanating from the struggle. Third, the decision of the struggle leaders to prevent the return of the CUP leaders in exile to Anatolia symbolically enabled the former to publicly claim there indeed was no connection, in spite of the presence among them of many lower-ranking CUP and SO members. Fourth, not only the presence of the CUP in Ankara but the possibility of their eventually taking over the republic propelled the new republican leaders to take drastic action. Employing the 1926 assassination attempt against Mustafa Kemal as a cover, they further silenced the CUP connection by publicly trying and hanging the former CUP members who could have taken action against them.

Absence of CUP Memories

The CUP was initially a secret organization that retained its secrecy until the 1913 military coup, after which it became a political party. Still, it never became a fully public, transparent political party, sustaining its covert operations and violence throughout. In addition, its members adhered to the oaths of loyalty, including obeying the CUP central committee's decision that no members would write their individual memoirs chronicling their CUP activities. This CUP silencing of history and memory enabled the perpetrators to obfuscate their CUP origins. One such former CUP member who later became a republican leader addressed this transformation and the obfuscation of CUP origins in a section of his memoirs entitled "How is the History of the CUP That Constituted the First Stage of the Turkish Revolution to Be Written?"[484] He noted that many of them had kept their CUP memories private; when they finally wrote their memoirs, they did so not as CUP members but as the future republican leaders of the independence struggle. In doing so, they carefully silenced both their CUP activities and their own personal histories, everything that had given meaning to their world before the independence struggle. This silencing sacralized and mythified the role of the independence struggle both in their lives and in republican history.

What they had dismissed, suppressed, and silenced about their former lives, what they allowed themselves to remember only in private is captured by another memoir writer's observations of Mustafa Kemal:[485]

> The loss of the Balkans had left upon all of us a great pain of history, opening a wound in our hearts filled with national pride. I understood what a different, incurable pain and wound this had been years later, [when I witnessed] the tears of [Mustafa Kemal] Atatürk who was originally from Macedonia. When Atatürk sang Balkan songs along with his friends from the same region, the looks of [that man] who never cried [in public] would glaze over, and he would start to cry. The homelands of all the Turks from the Adriatic coast to the Maritza River had been lost. İstanbul and Anatolia had been their diaspora.

Indeed, almost all the prominent CUP members were initially from the Balkans, but they never emphasized this common geographical origin, instead mourning their lost Balkan lands in private. Yet they had also formed their political identity there, first by joining the CUP and then by successfully undertaking the 1908 constitutional revolution. Given that the Balkans had been forever lost and the CUP had emerged from the Great War defeated, these Balkan refugees had to define a new Turkish national identity, one that did not emphasize their former ethnic and political identities. Because nationalism is often predicated on an origin, however, instead of acknowledging their true origins, they constructed a new one during the independence struggle. They adopted Anatolia as their exclusive homeland, the independence struggle as their life story, and the republic as their exclusive institution. To do so, however, they needed to silence their political identity as former CUP members.

Obfuscating CUP Identities

The official Turkish narrative of the founding of the republic has been almost exclusively based on the famous 1927 *Speech* delivered by Mustafa Kemal Atatürk, in which he carefully silenced and delegitimated the CUP origins of the independence struggle, highlighting instead the activities he engaged in as the only indisputable leader of the republic. Yet, the history of the independence struggle constructed from contemporaneous memoirs tells an alternate story.[486] During the Great War, the CUP government first realized that it might lose the war in January 1915, specifically after the Ottoman battle against the British to conquer Egypt. The CUP leader Cemal Pasha, commanding these forces in the east, started to instead concentrate on mapping out and securing an Ottoman military retreat. He alerted the interior minister and the grand vizier Talat Pasha to the presence of concentrated Armenian populations, especially in Dörtyol, that could potentially pose a threat to the successful retreat of the army. Cemal Pasha requested these Dörtyol Armenians to be deported to the interior, to Konya, where they would be contained among the larger Muslim Turkish population. Even though the initial orders were indeed given for Konya, Talat Pasha then changed this order, having the Dörtyol Armenians deported instead to Deyr Zor in the Syrian Desert. It was also then, on 25 April 1915, that the Armenian intellectuals at the imperial capital were arrested en masse—and eventually massacred—in an effort to contain any public protest against the deportation of the Dörtyol Armenians. Then the forced deportation and massacres of all the Armenians in Anatolia ensued because the CUP leaders decided that an ethnically cleansed Anatolia would enable them to actualize their last opportunity to establish a Turkish state.

Another measure the CUP leaders took to establish and defend a future Turkish state was to preserve the fourth army in the east as a fresh reserve force; they planned to then employ this force to fight a resistance struggle if the empire was occupied by the Allied forces. As World War I continued, the CUP leaders also kept a similar secret reserve force at the imperial capital.[487] In addition, they mobilized the SO to hide arms and armaments for a possible future resistance that would ensue after the war. When the Allies did indeed win the war, the top CUP leadership decided to leave the empire to escape getting arrested by the occupying Allied forces. Yet, the CUP leaders in exile and those CUP members in the empire commenced, as planned, to resist the Allied occupation.[488] The crucial decision at this juncture was where, when, and especially under whose command to start the Turkish resistance.[489] According to the initial CUP plan, Enver Pasha was going to travel to the east through Russia, assume the command of the reserve forces kept in the east, and then organize and lead the Turkish resistance.[490] Enver indeed did try to travel to the east through Russia three times, yet he failed to pass through Russian lands each time because the 1917 Revolution had destabilized the region. He was caught and imprisoned when he attempted to go by land, his plane crashed when he tried to travel by air, and his boat almost capsized when he traveled by sea. As a consequence, another CUP member, Kazım Karabekir, eventually assumed the command of these fresh eastern reserve forces.

The repeated failure of Enver to reach the eastern provinces of the empire led the CUP leadership to search for another leader in the empire who could head the Turkish struggle against the occupying Allied forces, and especially against the possible establishment of an independent Armenia and Kurdistan in the east. The CUP's first and second choices were Ahmed İzzet Pasha and Hüseyin Rauf Orbay. Yet Ahmed İzzet declined the offer, finding it morally difficult to work with the CUP.[491] Rauf Orbay did not want to eliminate the option of working with especially the British occupying the empire. He was sure he could get their support in forming a Turkish state, one that would be established with much less struggle. Orbay's attempts to keep this option alive initially led him to defy Mustafa Kemal's suggestion that the former should not travel to the capital. Yet Orbay did, and he not only failed to get any British support but instead was arrested and exiled to Malta in March 1919. Hence, he too was removed him from contention. The CUP's third choice was another successful and astute general, Mustafa Kemal, who had stated time and again that he was willing to take on all the seemingly insurmountable risks to lead the empire out of occupation. Upon being offered the position by the CUP, he immediately accepted and alighted in Samsun on 19 May 1919 with a large retinue of CUP and SO members to commence the Turkish independence struggle that he conducted with great success, ingenuity, and acuity.[492]

During this time, the CUP organizations and followers were in place at the capital in perfect order, holding the entire security organization in their hands.[493] The CUP members Kara Kemal and Kara Vasıf had already started to organize and overtake existing national resistance units at the capital, and then met with Mustafa Kemal in İzmit as the sole representatives of the Turkish resistance.[494] Also, in spite of creating a new political space in Anatolia, the national government initially took over the empire's entire structure in that in Anatolia, all the Ottoman laws, regulations, and statutes were still in effect. Even the Turkish national assembly in Ankara was housed in the former CUP headquarters.[495]

This account of the origins of the Turkish independence struggle is at great variance with Mustafa Kemal's subsequent narration. The first sentence of Mustafa Kemal's speech stated that he had alighted in Samsun on 19 May 1919, thereby indirectly silencing the CUP decision-making process that got him there in the first place. Also silenced was the significant role the CUP played throughout the independence struggle by providing funds, arms, soldiers, and local support. The silencing of the CUP role in the struggle ultimately enabled the republican leaders to claim that they had executed the struggle solely with their own blood, sweat, and tears rather than the CUP organization, supplies, and infrastructure.[496] Such silencing also enforced the national myth that the independence struggle had succeeded through the efforts of Mustafa Kemal alone. This alternate narration in no way attempts to minimize or trivialize the brilliance with which Mustafa Kemal organized, conducted, and successfully concluded the independence struggle. He was undoubtedly one of the brightest minds in the empire, taking over a defeated country and creating a nation-state against incredible odds. His conduct during the struggle amply demonstrates his strategic thinking, carefully studying all details, charting out all short- and long-term possibilities, and then almost intuitively producing the most successful outcome. Yet, I argue here, he did so by presenting a version of the independence struggle that also silenced all the acts, actors, and conditions that could have taken away from the narration of an ultimate success story. Because the Turkish republic is now securely on its way to celebrating its centennial, I think it is time to place the success back on the shoulders of all those who participated in creating it, former friend and foe alike. Doing so would enable Turkey to come to terms with its past, an act that will ultimately make it stronger and more secure.

Excluding Top CUP Leaders

The most significant act that Mustafa Kemal undertook was to block the return of top CUP leaders to the country. The fact that many of these leaders were then assassinated by Armenian revolutionary committees in exile also helped Mustafa Kemal establish his unquestioned leadership over the Turkish independence struggle. Yet many CUP members kept accusing Mustafa Kemal of causing the deaths of these assassinated CUP leaders by preventing them from returning to Anatolia. The private correspondence among the top CUP leaders cited in the memoirs reveals their thoughts on this adverse course of action.[497] Even though they publicly supported Mustafa Kemal's decision, in private they were furious.[498] They also discussed why there had not been more protests among the CUP members in the empire over Mustafa Kemal's decision to keep them out, conjecturing that the Unionists who already held influential positions within the independence struggle turned their backs on their former leaders.[499] Hence Mustafa Kemal was able to sever the top CUP leadership while co-opting the rest of the CUP into his struggle under his leadership; because he divested them of their CUP identity in the process many former CUP members who had joined the new republican elite had no interest in reinstituting their old identities or actively aiding the return of the former CUP leadership to the country. Only those CUP members who opposed Mustafa Kemal's leadership continued to claim their CUP identity. It is interesting to note at this juncture that Mustafa Kemal had started to destabilize the CUP identity the moment he assumed leadership of the independence struggle, proposing an alternate one instead.[500]

Obscuring the Continuing CUP Presence

Still, the CUP opposition to Mustafa Kemal continued during the early years of the republic.[501] The CUP leaders who eventually managed to return from exile started to criticize Mustafa Kemal's republic, aligning instead with the political opposition both in İstanbul and in Ankara.[502] There were still many former CUP members in the country who considered violent CUP actions patriotic and necessary for the subsequent success of the independence struggle.[503] Those CUP leaders who had joined the independence struggle and later become prominent republic officials, officers, and deputies also did not fully support Mustafa Kemal, often criticizing him instead.[504] Ultimately, the prominent CUP members who opposed Mustafa Kemal's wresting of the independence struggle away from the CUP to instead make it his own were liquidated with trumped-up charges during the 1926 independence court proceedings.[505] Hence, once Mustafa Kemal was appointed to lead the independence struggle by the CUP, he gradually eliminated the CUP influence on the struggle by co-opting many members into his newly formed group of patriotic nationalists.

Stage II: Denial of Perpetrators within Republican Cadres

Two memoir writers commented on how the injustices of the imperial era continued into the republican period, without explaining the reasons behind this sad continuity.[506] One ironically asked: "Why was our family that suffered through long periods in exile during the imperial era as their wives and children underwent material and emotional grief and distress, then rewarded by injustices during the republican period that followed?" The other likewise pointed out that "the Turkish nation does not know how to forgive.... Their grudges do not decrease, but instead increase." Both failed to note that the initial denial of the CUP origins of the independence struggle, coupled with the eventual elimination of former CUP members who took a public stand against Mustafa Kemal, helped sustain the national myth that the CUP had been eliminated from the Turkish body politic. In reality, however, the CUP members actively organized the independence struggle and were then rehabilitated to serve as deputies in the national assembly, on the condition that they did so by forgoing all their former allegiances and instead fully placing their loyalty and trust in Mustafa Kemal.

The details provided in nineteen contemporaneous memoirs confirmed that many former CUP members continued to serve in the Turkish state and its governments, thereby reproducing the cycle of collective violence during the republican era.[507] Two memoirists noted that many Unionists had accompanied them in their escape not only from the imperial city to Anatolia to fight in the independence struggle but then to Ankara as well.[508] Had many of these escapees remained behind, another memoir writer noted, they would have been sentenced and imprisoned because of their role in the Armenian deportations and massacres.[509] Indeed, many perpetrators in Anatolia, local notables as well as CUP members wanted by the military tribunal, put aside their differences, swearing an oath not to inform on one another.[510] One argued that November 1920 was a turning point, for that was when all the former perpetrators joined the independence struggle, on the condition that they would then be honored with amnesty.[511] Indeed, many forgotten CUP assassins reemerged with the republic, turning into "heroes applauded by the Turkish nation."[512]

Former CUP members were personally rehabilitated by Mustafa Kemal to serve as deputies in the national assembly upon writing an affidavit stating that they were acting based on Mustafa Kemal's trust in them.[513] One of the two CUP assassins of Şemsi Pasha first served as Mustafa Kemal's adjutant and later became a deputy.[514] The other CUP assassin first became the director of the Ottoman State Tobacco Monopoly in a city, and was then appointed as a deputy to the national assembly; upon his death, he was buried at the Hill of Eternal Freedom as a republican hero.[515] Many former perpetrators also became deputies. One served in the assembly from 1920 to 1923, also serving as minister of justice from 1922 to 1923.[516] Another became a deputy in 1924 and then rose to the ministry posts of finance, defense, and public works. Assuming the presidency of the national assembly in 1935, he again served as the minister of defense and state minister. Two former Malta exiles served as prime ministers, and three other Malta exiles became ministers.[517] Three perpetrators served as deputies in the national assembly.[518] Other former CUP members continued to play active public roles in the republic by becoming members of political parties. Many initially joined the RPP. In such roles, they continued to exercise collective violence against non-Muslims.[519]

In addition to such former CUP members, contemporaneous memoirs indicated that the SO members also played an active role in both the independence struggle and the republic.[520] SO members organized the smuggling of arms and ammunitions from the imperial capital to Anatolia and also fought to support the nationalist forces throughout Anatolia.[521] Two CUP assassins who had perpetrated the Armenian massacres in Diyarbekir and who had also murdered two Ottoman officials then worked with a prominent nationalist general as part of the western Anatolian defense force.[522] In funding the struggle, they did not refrain from robbing banks.[523] The former SO commander served as the head of the volunteer bands formed during the independence struggle.[524] The leadership of the struggle distributed the secret irregular SO units fighting in eastern provinces into the regular army. When one SO leader could not become the head of a rifle regiment because it never formed, he was instead elected to the national assembly, thereby serving as a deputy.[525] Another SO leader and perpetrator was appointed as the republic's ambassador to three posts, serving twice as deputy and also as the RPP secretary.[526] Still another perpetrator was recruited by Mustafa Kemal to mobilize the nationalist forces in his region; this perpetrator then served as a deputy.[527] A former SO member and Enver's aide-de-camp headed the republican army as its first general chief of staff.[528] The two most important SO members in charge of SO secret funds at the end of the Great War then became, in one case, the prime minister, political party leader, and the second president of Turkey; the other became the prime minister, leader of the opposition party during the transition to the multiparty system, and also the third president of Turkey.[529]

The only ones who did not accept this transformation of perpetrators into patriots were the Allied forces and the departing Greek Rum and Armenians. The British considered Mustafa Kemal and those with him to be the "committee of murderers . . . of Christians."[530] An Armenian leaving from İzmir in 1922 noted in his memoirs that the departing Greek Rum and Armenians were forced by the nationalist forces to shout before their release "Long live Mustafa Kemal Pasha!" He then added: "Yes, long live Mustafa Pasha. We will always feel gratitude toward him for what he has done: after slaughtering thousands of Christians, and after plundering this rich city [of İzmir] into ruins, he drowned hundreds of thousands of people in indescribable pain. Yes, he can live long; we shout and we move on."[531] The Allied forces and the destroyed non-Muslims had indeed noted and protested the Unionists amid the national forces, but this did not change the future course of events because in the end, they were forced to leave, and the national movement ultimately succeeded. The subsequent national history of Turkey was penned by these winners who whitewashed the past violence against the Armenians as well as the violence they committed in achieving their victory.

As collective violence against the Armenians was thus silenced or transformed into "patriotic acts" committed for the sake of the republic, former CUP leaders and members were then acknowledged as republican heroes. Talat Pasha's wife was assigned the highest stipend from official republican funds for her husband's services to the fatherland. Talat's violence against the Armenians also became increasingly regarded as a necessary step for the successful establishment of the republic.[532] The national assembly also assigned similar stipends to those who had been tried by the military tribunal and lost their lives: the Urfa subdistrict governor Nusret Bey, the former Diyarbekir governor Mehmed Reşid Şahingiray, and the Boğazlıyan district governor Kemal Bey. The families of these "national martyrs" received pensions for "service to the fatherland." The state also provided education for their children free of charge, allocating abandoned Armenian properties to them so that they could use the rent accruing from these for their expenses. These women and children then married the offspring of other prominent CUP members.[533]

Tracing the Republic's Violent CUP/SO Legacy

To demonstrate the continuity of the CUP/SO legacy and, with it, the continuity of the perpetrators of the Armenian violence into the republican era, I undertook a detailed analysis of the backgrounds of the deputies who had served in the first Turkish national assembly. I systematically analyzed these deputies with the intent to find out three facts about them: (1) whether their place of origin was located in the Balkans or Anatolia, hypothesizing that those originating in the Balkans would still be affected by the trauma of the Balkan Wars that had not only displaced them but also made them more susceptible to either commit violence against non-Muslims or legitimate such violence; (2) whether they formerly belonged to the CUP or the SO, hypothesizing that such membership would increase their approval of past collective violence; and (3) where they were during the 1915–17 period, conjecturing that if they had been involved with the Armenians, their chances of legitimating the past violence against the Armenians would increase. I hypothesized that there would be a substantial number of deputies in the national assembly who originated in the Balkans, who were former CUP/SO members, and who engaged with the Armenians between 1915 and 1917, and that their presence not only would demonstrate the silenced continuity from the empire to the republic but also would explain the republican denial of the perpetrators of the collective violence against the Armenians. I documented this information mainly through what was written about them in *The Turkish Parliamentary History*, the official publication of the Turkish national assembly. I then complemented this information with other sources that I cite at the end of the table in Appendix B.

When I analyzed the origins of the deputies of the first national assembly, it emerged that among the 392 deputies, 54 were not from Anatolia, 12 were not of Anatolian origin in that their parents were recent immigrants to Anatolia or İstanbul, and 30 were from İstanbul. Hence, about a quarter of the deputies were of non-Anatolian origin, and most were originally refugees from the Balkans. In relation to the origins of the official Turkish denial of the Armenian massacres of 1915, I hypothesized that the continuation of CUP elements into the republic would have further strengthened the Turkish republican resolve at denial. To test this hypothesis, I analyzed whether any of the deputies had former connections with the CUP and the SO: of the 392 deputies, 69, that is, about 18 percent, had explicit connections with the CUP. In addition, these were often members who then assumed significant state and government posts in the republic, serving as governors, ministers, prime ministers, and even as presidents of the republic. And these were only the ones I could determine from the print literature in general, and the 297 memoirs I studied in particular.

I also investigated how much and what type of contact the deputies had had with the Armenians, especially from 1915 to 1917 when the majority of the Armenians were forcibly removed from Anatolia. The list of the posts the deputies held during this period suggested that all had ample knowledge about the Armenian deportations and massacres, and some also profited from the movable and immovable goods that the Armenians had left behind. A conservative focus on only those deputies who were actively involved in fighting the Armenians in the east revealed that sixteen deputies engaged in such activity, fighting mostly with their own militia or as SO members. Most telling in this context was the official information provided in *The Turkish Parliamentary History* narrating the life course of each deputy in detail. According to this official source, among the deputies, seven were accused, arrested, and in some instances actually tried for perpetrating the Armenian massacres. These seven perpetrators were Fevzi Pirinççioğlu and Zülfi Tiğrel of Diyarbekir, Mehmet Ali Cenani of Gaziantep, Rıza Silsüpür of Kırşehir, İlyas Sami Muş of Muş, Hüseyin Avni Zaimler of Saruhan, and Mehmet Feyyaz Ali Üst of Yozgat. These are only the deputies who can be identified as perpetrators based on the information provided in their official biographies in the publication cited earlier.

When I supplemented this information with other sources, four additional deputies were also implicated. In a recent book, the author referred to an oral history he conducted whereby a Kurd stated that most of the recent wealth in the region was founded on confiscated and plundered Armenian wealth. He then cited as an example that "Hacı Hüseyin Efendi acquired 417 villages that were originally Armenian villages whose people have either been murdered or deported.... He had two sons one of whom, Bedir Agha, even became a prominent deputy in the first national assembly."[534] This implicated deputy Bedir Fırat of Malatya. Deputy Kazım Özalp of Karesi, a former general of the Turkish army, also participated in the Armenian massacres. Two Turkish sources cited that Özalp, upon being appointed to the command of Muş after the loss of Van to the Armenians, was so frustrated that "he burned the Armenian neighborhood and the entire Muş valley with its Armenian population."[535] Deputy Yusuf Kemal Tengirşenk of Kastamonu, a former CUP member, was one of the two observers appointed by the Ottoman assembly to report on the 1909 Armenian massacres. According to an Ottoman newspaper, when Tengirşenk served as the legal counsel of the Ottoman Justice Ministry, he approved the recruitment of released prisoners into the SO who eventually executed most of the Armenian massacres.[536] The same newspaper also noted that Tengirşenk's brother Abdülahat Nuri was personally sent by Talat Pasha to Deyr Zor to massacre the Armenians who remained behind from the deportations.[537] Physician and deputy Ahmed Tevfik Rüştü Aras of Menteşe was the brother-in-law of the prominent CUP/SO member Dr. Nazım and also, according to one source, a partisan Unionist himself.[538] The Armenian Patriarchate Archives noted that Aras was appointed by the CUP to process the dead bodies of massacred Armenians with lime so as to minimize the possible spread of disease.[539] Needless to say, none of these eleven deputies were ever punished for the crimes committed against the Armenians. According to the Palestinian Patriarchate Archives, there was also one righteous deputy at the national assembly who protected the deported Armenians. Deputy Hasan Tahsin Uzer of İzmir was the governor of Erzurum in 1915; upon receiving the deportation order, he replied that "the complicity of the Armenians was untrue and they were actually destitute themselves."[540]

All these results supported the argument that there indeed was, as Erik Jan Zürcher had initially pointed out, a strong CUP presence within the ranks of the Turkish national assembly members. Most of them had witnessed the forcible removal of Armenians from Anatolia, and some had actually participated in the process. This analysis of course did not take into account the hundreds of other perpetrators who did not make it to the national assembly. The lengths of the terms these deputies served also demonstrated the longevity of their impact on the Turkish republic. In summary, then, this empirical analysis demonstrated how and why the republican denial of the perpetrators of the collective violence against the Armenians emerged during the 1919–73 phase.

4

Late Republican Denial of Responsibility for Violence, 1974–2009

What you do not want done to yourself, do not do to others.
Confucius, Chinese philosopher, 551–479 B.C.E.

On 19 January 2007, fifty-two-year-old journalist Hrant Dink, the editor in chief of the bilingual Armenian Turkish *Agos* newspaper, was assassinated in broad daylight. A seventeen-year-old ultranationalist assassin shot him with a bullet behind his head. Dink was a humanist who advocated human and minority rights in Turkey alongside Turkish-Armenian reconciliation. In relation to the collective violence committed against the Armenians, he criticized both the official Turkish denial of the Armenian Genocide and the Armenian Diaspora's campaign for its international recognition. As a consequence of his stand, Dink was prosecuted by the Turkish legal system three times for "denigrating Turkishness" in his newspaper editorials, receiving many death threats from the ultranationalists in the process. He had also been threatened by the İstanbul governor and two agents of the National Intelligence Organization (Milli İstihbarat Teşkilatı; MIT) for writing in his newspaper about the Armenian origins of Sabiha Gökçen, the first female pilot of Turkey as well as the adopted daughter of Mustafa Kemal Atatürk. Dink had asked for but did not receive police protection. He was about to take his legal case to the European Court of Human Rights when he was assassinated. Hrant was also my personal friend and colleague.

At this point in the book, given the currency of the covered time period, the narrative transforms from memoirs of others to my personal recollections, since I too witnessed this period, first as a college student and later as a scholar. I received the news of Dink's murder in Ann Arbor through a phone call made by a mutual friend and colleague of ours, a call I still vividly remember to this day. For the first time in my life, I experienced the brutal murder of a peer and personal friend. I had first gotten to know Hrant personally when he attended the second Workshop on Armenian Turkish Scholarship (WATS) that my colleague Ronald Grigor Suny and I organized in Ann Arbor in 2002. The first WATS had taken place at the University of Chicago in 2000. For the second one held at the University of Michigan, we had decided to invite journalists from Turkey, comprising Cengiz Çandar, Baskın Oran, and Hrant Dink. Hrant also added an element to the second workshop that was absent in the first one: until then, we had no one representing the standpoint of the Armenians of Turkey, a perspective I thought had to be included in addition to the already existing perspectives of the Armenian Diaspora, the Armenian republic, and the Turkish republic.

Until our 2002 workshop, Hrant Dink had never been outside Turkey because the Turkish state had persistently refused to issue him a passport. It therefore surprised us all when he was able to attain a passport to travel to our workshop. I later found out that some Turkish journalists had convinced the officials they personally knew to issue Dink a passport. After all, they had argued, there was no particular reason for this official restriction, indirectly affirming that Dink's being a member of a non-Muslim minority group in Turkey was the only reason behind such official action. I still recall his exclamation: "Müge, this is a miracle! What did you do to get them to give me a passport?!" I had not done anything special except writing him a formal letter of invitation. We concluded that this official reversal was perhaps yet another democratic measure taken by the Turkish state readying itself for possible European Union membership. At the workshop, Hrant provided the sorely needed Turkish Armenian standpoint, stating that the Armenians of Turkey continued to live on their ancestral lands, even though their everyday experiences often placed them on a sword's edge as they negotiated constant prejudice and discrimination. In doing so, however, Hrant did not focus solely on the collective violence committed against the Armenians. He instead approached the Armenian issue within the larger framework of Turkey's democratization process. For him, the realization of the human rights and freedom of expression for all Turkish citizens was just as significant as the public recognition of the past Armenian massacres. Hrant was also unique in this endeavor because he was not a "white Turk" like we all were. That is, he did not belong to the dominant ethnic Turkish majority that aspired to democratize Turkish state and society by acknowledging the collective violence embedded in the country's past. Hrant was often the only non-Muslim in our amorphous group, the only one whose family had lived through the violent 1915–17 decimation of almost their entire community. In addition, unlike many of us who were protected by our ethnic Turkish identity, he alone continued to face prejudice and discrimination on an everyday basis. Through his presence among us in spite of all the obstacles he faced, Hrant endowed upon us a rare, enduring gift: he made it possible for us to envision a future tolerant Turkey, one where everyone regardless of their religious, ethnic, and cultural identity lived as equals.

After attending the 2002 workshop, Dink enthusiastically participated in the succeeding WATS workshops at the University of Minnesota in 2003 and the Salzburg Institute in 2005. In addition to seeing Hrant at various scholarly conferences and keeping in touch with him through e-mail, I also got to know him better during my annual summer visits to Turkey from 2002 to 2007 when I conducted research for this book. I visited eastern Turkey, which had once been Armenian ancestral lands. I wanted to see what physically remained from the historic Armenian presence and to hear how the locals now residing there remembered the past. Hrant could not accompany me on these trips, but he made sure that I had a terrific companion, Baron Sarkis Seropyan, the owner of *Agos* newspaper and the editor of its Armenian section. Seropyan's immense knowledge of Armenian history and the local Armenian sites enabled me to explore the ruined Armenian villages, churches, monasteries, and cemeteries; to identify the former Armenian dwellings by their metalwork and stonework; and to interview the local Muslim elders, who recalled in vivid detail not only the Armenians who had once lived there but also their brutal massacre. Our interviews revealed two patterns. First, the Turkish military had often confiscated the Armenian properties for their own use; they turned former residences into official buildings and restricted access to old Armenian churches that they then often used for target practice, thereby destroying them beyond recognition. Second, in the old Armenian villages, the Turkish state had intentionally settled either Turkish Muslim refugees from the Balkans who had suffered extensive non-Muslim violence or Kurds who had endured prior Armenian violence in the east. As a consequence, the majority of the younger generations of residents had no memory of the collective violence that had once transpired at these locations; they often regarded the Armenians just as the official narrative wanted them to, as traitors.

These trips and the civilization that used to exist there, to be then so wantonly destroyed, enabled me to develop an alternate narrative to the official one advocated by the Turkish state. As an ethnic Turk, I was personally shocked to witness not only such destruction of the Armenian presence in Anatolia but also the continued prejudice and discrimination against the Kurds who had now become the dominant social group in the region. Many Kurdish leaders we talked to stated, assuming that I too was an Armenian, "What happened to you in 1915 keeps happening to us since then, and we are sorry we did not protect you back then." Also significant were the "hidden Armenians" we met, that is, the Armenians who had somehow survived the massacres by converting to Islam or by being taken in by local Muslim families, Armenians who had nevertheless not forgotten their actual origins or had found out about them as their dying elderly grandparents confessed to their Armenian origins, often on their deathbeds.

Hrant was happiest during the seminal 2005 Bilgi University conference, the first scholarly gathering held on the Armenian issue in general and the state of the Armenians at the end of the Ottoman Empire in particular. As a member of the organizing committee alongside many local Turkish colleagues, I personally witnessed the difficulties and obstacles set by the Turkish state and government in general and the ultranationalists in particular to ensure that the conference did not take place. Organized by three Turkish universities—Bosporus, Sabancı, and Bilgi—in İstanbul, the conference was initially going to take place in May at Bosporus University, right after our 2005 WATS meeting in Salzburg, but obstacles quickly emerged. First, some deputies presented a motion to the national assembly, arguing that such a "seditious" conference should not occur on Turkish soil. This was followed by the declaration of the then justice minister (and now state minister) Cemil Çiçek, claiming that our actions were akin to those of "traitors stabbing the nation in the back." Such unfortunate remarks coupled with the ultranationalist threat to storm the conference and place a bomb led the İstanbul governor to notify the university that because it could not provide the necessary security for the conference, it should be canceled. Meanwhile, my Turkish colleagues struggled with, and successfully resisted, the constant demands of the "official" historians who insisted on participating, with the intent to deliver papers. Such "official" historians denied all past collective violence against the Armenians, often presenting nationalist manifestos rather than academic research papers. They were shocked to be turned down and then claimed that the conference was obviously not "balanced," since the official view on the topic had not been included. In doing so, they did not take into account academic freedom, that is, the freedom to choose the academic participants.[1]

I still remember a meeting at a restaurant, as Hrant, my Turkish colleagues, and I lamented not being able to hold this significant conference in May 2005. Yet everyone persevered, and my Turkish colleagues decided to postpone it until November 2005, a date they specifically chose to postdate the EU discussion of Turkey's membership application in October 2005. They did so in order not to be perceived as putting additional political pressure on the EU negotiations. Yet the Justice and Development Party (Adalet ve Kalkınma Partisi; JDP) government insisted that we hold the conference in September 2005, prior to the EU negotiations, with the official intent to demonstrate to Europe that such an academic conference could actually be held in Turkey. The JDP government thus indirectly supported the conference but also made sure that we as scholars expended all our social and political capital in withstanding the ultranationalist attacks and the anticonference fury in the Turkish media. The conference was still to be held at Bosporus University. The day before, however, while in a meeting reviewing the final details, we received news that the ultranationalist lawyer Kemal Kerinçsiz, also one of the major legal harassers of Dink alongside ultranationalist retired general Veli Küçük, had filed a legal motion in a local court at 4:45 p.m. He contested the financing of the conference, wrongfully alleging that we had received conference funds from seditious Western sources intent on destroying Turkey. Had it not been for a legal oversight Kerinçsiz committed, such legal action would have necessitated the postponement of the conference once again. Yet, Kerinçsiz had filed the legal motion against the Bosporus and Sabancı universities, forgetting the third partner, Bilgi University, in the process.[2] Collapsing a three-day conference into two days, we finally managed to hold the conference at Bilgi University, although we had to be bused to the site with a police escort while a hundred or so ultranationalists standing outside protested by throwing rotten tomatoes and eggs at us. In addition, a couple of ultranationalist Turks managed to get into the auditorium where the conference was held, trying to lecture us on what had actually happened in the past. At this conference, for the first time, all those working on the Armenian issue communicated with each other in Turkish, in the process transforming into a small but significant community of like-minded thinkers. It was also there that Hrant gave an eloquent talk on the perspective of the Armenians of Turkey, stating that they wanted to live in a peaceful democratic society, one where their only demand regarding land return was to be given "a human's length of soil to lie under upon death." It is extremely poignant that this was indeed where Hrant ended only eighteen months after this historic conference.

During the unfortunately short time I knew Hrant, he was especially excited about the online listserv we at WATS had established with the intent to further Turkish Armenian dialogue among scholars and public intellectuals. It was unfortunate, however, that the listserv actually transformed into a significant international public forum due to the legal harassment Hrant was subjected to in Turkey: we undertook three signature and letter-writing campaigns in support of Hrant and against the legal charges filed against him under Article 301 of the Turkish legal code that explicitly punished the freedom of thought and expression in Turkey. The first lawsuit against him was filed in 2002, when Hrant had recounted in his column the feelings of exclusion that singing the Turkish national anthem generated in him; he was eventually acquitted in 2006. The second lawsuit, in 2004, took issue with the column Hrant wrote criticizing the Diaspora Armenians, one that was willfully and intentionally misread and misinterpreted as denigrating Turkishness, in spite of a legal expert's report to the contrary. Hrant rigorously defended what he had written, arguing to no avail that his intent had never been to insult Turkish citizens; he was convicted in 2005.

This false conviction led us to undertake yet another signature campaign on Hrant's behalf, this time in support of his appeal. Many international scholars and public intellectuals signed on to protest the Turkish legal decision, and we once again duly sent letters to the Turkish president, prime minister, and justice minister. Hrant's appeal was rejected in May 2006. Soon thereafter, in September 2006, another similar lawsuit was filed against him, leading us to undertake yet another signature campaign. "Dear Hrant, we have started to carry out signature and letter-writing campaigns with alarming frequency," I e-mailed him, "please take care of yourself." I did so because I was fully aware of the continual death threats Hrant received, threats that had led me numerous times to invite him and his family to reside in the United States until things subsided. "Müge, I am like a fish out of water when I leave Turkey for extended periods of time; I yearn to return to my soil as soon as possible. So I cannot leave my country, and my family agrees with me," he told me. My last invitation and our subsequent conversation took place in İstanbul on a beautiful August day in 2007. That was the last time I saw Hrant alive.

The collective violence committed against Hrant Dink leads into the fourth and final phase of Turkish denial, namely, the denial of responsibility for committing collective violence againt the Armenians. Hrant's assassination aptly demonstrates the continuing support of such denial within Turkish state and society; in July 2012, when I last revised this chapter, the Hrant Dink trial was still continuing, and in May 2014 when I copyedited this chapter, the main culprits have not yet been brought to justice. So far, the legal investigation has revealed that the Turkish state and especially the military were complicitious in the Dink assassination. For almost three years prior, they had known about the threats against Dink's life but did nothing to contain them. On the contrary, it appears that the young assassins were actually coerced by segments within the Turkish state and military into committing such public assassinations with the ultimate intent to violently repress and contain the Turkish democratization process. Such a poignant setting thus provides the introduction to the last phase of denial from 1974 to 2009. This period is bifurcated in terms of violence and denial: from 1974 to 2000, the violence and denial continue unabated, and from 2000 to 2009, not only does violence gradually abate but a public counterdenial narrative also emerges.

This chapter commences with the 1974 Turkish military invasion of northern Cyprus, an act that was opposed by the international community. As a consequence of this invasion, Turkey faced an internationally imposed military and economic embargo for almost two decades. The resulting political instability that brought the country to the brink of a civil war culminated in 1980 in the third Turkish military coup. In the coup's aftermath, the military abolished all political parties, arrested dissidents, drafted a new constitution bolstering the power of the military, and started to vigilantly impose Kemalist principles onto society. The social polarization initiated by this process of change not only led to the initial political repression of Turkish leftists, Islamists, Kurds, Alevis, and Armenians but also brought conservative elements into governance, thereby generating polarization within the state. Segments of staunch republican secularists challenged the Islamists' participation in "their" republic. This state polarization initially produced a high level of collective violence, one displayed through military repression and unaccounted assassinations of intellectuals, political activists, Kurds, and liberal military officers. The decade-long assassinations abroad of Turkish diplomats by the Armenian revolutionary organizations of the Armenian Secret Army for the Liberation of Armenia (ASALA) and the Justice Commandos of the Armenian Genocide (JCOAG) from 1975 to 1985 provided the "rationalizing event" for Turkish state and society that justified additional collective violence. The paramilitary organizations established within the Turkish state with the explicit intent to punish the Armenian perpetrators then moved on to execute many of these unaccounted assassinations, probably also including Dink's. The emerging Turkish official narrative that attempted to explain this recent Armenian violence against Turkish diplomats was mostly penned by retired Turkish officials. In their work, these officials further destabilized the historical investigation into past collective violence through unsystematically exploiting historical incidents and actors to deny any responsibility for the past violence committed against the Armenians. They did so by transforming past perpetrators into victims, and past victims into present perpetrators. First, they equated all past Turkish violence with past Armenian violence. Then, they argued that current Armenian violence against the Turkish diplomats was a continuation of the past Armenian violence.

There was a gradual shift and increased democratization in the late 1990s, however. With the end of the Cold War, the Turkish state that had been a staunch US ally had to redefine its location in the ensuing world economic and political order. Waning state control over the economy and communication enabled an independent Turkish public sphere to emerge for the first time. Another first was the gradual inclusion in the body politic of the religiously conservative elements that had been marginalized by the republican leadership until then. Significant in this process was the emergence of Turkey's possible membership in the EU in 2000. As a consequence, alongside this increased democratization at the beginning of the twenty-first century, the official Turkish denial has been recently challenged by many Turkish nongovernmental organizations (NGOs), scholars, and intellectuals. This is where things stood when I wrote this book, with the Turkish official stand of denial being increasingly pressured through newly emergent civilian attempts to acknowledge and account for the past collective violence embedded in Ottoman and Turkish history in general and committed against the Armenians in particular.

Late Republican Structure of Similarity in Tension with Difference

Throughout the Second World War and the Cold War years in Turkey, the prevalent ethnic divide between the Turks and the rest intersected with the divide introduced by the republican leadership between the secular and religious Muslims. However, at the end of the Cold War and the emergence of a new world order, as well as the emergence of new transnational identities suggested by the European Union, destabilized the prevailing republican social structure predicated on sameness. The world political order changed to acknowledge difference, and the world economic order necessitated the participation of all countries in world markets, thereby challenging the boundaries of the carefully confined nation composed of secular Turks alone. Because the EU was predicated on the principle of universal, equal rights for all citizens, the non-Muslim, religiously conservative, Kurdish and Alewite communities in Turkey all started to aspire to become a part of the body politic as well, thereby envisioning instead a republican social structure based on difference. Among these communities, the religiously conservative Turks residing in the countryside were especially empowered by their access to world economic markets, and the Kurds mostly located in eastern regions of the republic were emboldened by their recognition by Western Europe. Still, the urban and Sunni yet secularized Turks continued to be the dominant social majority; among these communities, only the religiously conservative rural Turks could successfully challenge the status quo, gradually and democratically taking over the government through their increased political participation.

It is significant that among all those communities initially excluded from the body politic, the republican leadership was eventually forced to allow only the religiously conservative ethnic Turks into the publicly sanctioned social structure. In doing so, the secular republican elites compromised first on secularism, but not ethnicity, thereby sustaining the dominance of ethnic Turks. The greatest contemporary challenge Turkey faces at the moment is whether the religiously conservative JDP in power is willing to transform the social structure of sameness to one based on difference by deciding to include the other marginalized communities in the body politic. On the one hand, their prior exclusion should make the religiously conservative morally more prone to get rid of such exclusions. On the other hand, however, the naturalized exclusionary nationalism within Turkish state and society, their ethnic unity with the republican leadership, and their exercise of power in governance could force the JDP to sustain the status quo. Whether non-Muslim, Kurdish, and Alewite communities would eventually be included in the body politic, thereby transforming the social structure predicated on sameness to one based on difference, remains to be seen. The integration of the Kurds poses a challenge, given the inherent prevalence of ethnic Turks in the power structure. The inclusion of the Shiite Alewites is also problematic, given the inherent domination of the Sunni Turks in state, government, and society. Also difficult is the incorporation of the non-Muslims, given the inherent prevalence of Muslims within the social structure, both secular and religious. Ultimately, the only way to peacefully accommodate all these groups on their own terms is through envisioning a social structure based on the acknowledgment and respect of difference. Especially after the reelection of the JDP into governance, its initial accommodationist stand has been compromised, most notably in the way the JDP approached the Kurds: rather than including them on their own terms, the JDP still seems set on forcefully assimilating the Kurds just as the republican leadership tried—and failed—to do before them. That is why at the moment the social structures of sameness and difference are in inherent tension.

Elements of Late Republican Modernity

The economic, social, political, and legal elements of Turkish situated modernity reveal that once again Turkish state and society in general and the republican leadership in particular adopted the form, employing many of the elements that should have, in content, led to increased democratization and inclusion. Instead, the republican leaders utilized these forms to suppress and exclude. In the end, however, their actions started to produce the expected results of inclusion and democratization but at the cost of their own exclusion from the body politic. At the moment, it is still unclear to whether the religiously conservative in power would continue to adopt the forms of modernity while altering and subverting the content, or whether they would be willing to accept the liberalizing content along with the form.

First the Convoluted Economic Institutions

This period commenced with three decades of economic instability, with the economy beginning to settle down only with the advent of the twenty-first century. The initial economic instability was created through the intersection of two events, one domestic and one international: the 1973–74 world oil crisis, when oil prices quadrupled due to the decisions of the Organization of Petroleum Exporting Countries (OPEC), leading Turkey to increase financing of its energy imports through foreign borrowing; and the 1974 invasion of Cyprus by the Turkish military that led, due to the military's refusal to reduce reinforcements, to the 1975 US arms embargo. The coupling of such a costly military intervention with quadrupled oil prices brought income-generating commercial activities within Turkey to an almost immediate halt. Tax revenues dropped precipitously, making it impossible for the Turkish state to continue paying its foreign debts. The end result was the devaluation of the Turkish currency, eight times within twenty months. The currency lost 38 percent of its value in March 1978 and went through a second devaluation in September of the same year. There was yet another devaluation in June 1979, followed by the famous "24 January decisions" in 1980 when the International Monetary Fund recommended—and the Turkish state duly executed—another devaluation; this was followed by yet another adjustment in April 1980. The Turkish foreign currency crisis continued through 1988 all the way into 1994 as the currency had to be devaluated an additional two times.

Having no significant oil reserves, Turkey was almost entirely dependent on oil imports that were hard to procure, especially given the impoverished state of the Turkish economy. In an effort to control the draining of foreign currency, foreign travel was banned in 1977; the possesson of foreign currency was criminalized as well. Foreign exports were also brought under strict state control. Such dramatic adjustments and subsequent devaluation produced significant inflation, reaching 78 percent in September 1980 and 106 percent in the December of the same year. In an effort to contain the adverse impact of the inflation on their livelihoods, the Turkish populace started to invest in banks and bankers promising high interest rates. These barely regulated financial actors failed to deliver, causing a domestic economic crisis in 1982. Eventually, in 1984, the bans on carrying foreign currency and on foreign exports were lifted in an attempt to generate more revenues for the state. Yet the state's regulated release of foreign currency initially generated many financial scandals; some businessmen engaged in "imaginary"[3] exports caused yet another domestic economic crisis. Meanwhile, the state continued to regulate the economy, refining the taxation system and introducing the value-added tax obligation. These dire economic measures led to the emergence of a Ponzi scheme in 2000, with companies now attempting to shortchange thousands of investors.[4]

During this period, one measure in particular demonstrated the persistence of Turkish nationalism in the economic decision-making of the state and government: foreigners were banned from investing in Turkey through the purchase of property. The measure was outlawed in 1985 and then again in 1986. Yet the Turkish economy continued to miraculously grow, mosly because almost half of the Turkish economy was underground, thereby escaping state control and taxation. Some infrastructural investments eventually boosted the Turkish economy. In 1983, a vast southeastern water project, which built a dam over the Euphrates River originating in Turkey, commenced. Another significant infrastructural project was the building in İstanbul of a second bridge over the Bosporus. The year 1993 witnessed the emergence of credit cards in Turkey for the domestic market, followed in 1995 with the establishment of natural gas and oil pipelines. Yet Turkey's energy policy also necessisated increased reliance on Russia; the natural gas needs of the country started to be met almost completely through Russian pipelines.

Turkey's weak economic condition produced significant financial compromises in the international sphere. In 1984, the Soviet Union expanded its economic territory over the Black Sea to 200 miles, thereby adversely impacting Turkish trade and fishing. The political instability in the country led NATO to reject Turkey's 1985 request to have Pershing cruise missiles located in Turkey, a decision that brought down the country's credit rating, making it more difficult for Turkey to borrow money. Likewise, in 1985, the European Council rejected Turkey's bid for term presidency, followed by the 1986 rejection of Turkey's application to have its workers labor freely in the EU countries, a measure that would have enabled Turkey to increase its employment rates and its foreign currency reserve through remissions. The 1986 Chernobyl nuclear explosion shrunk Turkey's Black Sea exports, especially its main crop of tea production. As the First Gulf War (1990) gravely undercut Turkey's strong trade relations with the Middle East, the country could not escape yet another domestic crisis, leading many small-scale businesses to shut down. Only with the 1995 common customs treaty with the EU did things begin to change for the better.

Also significant was the brief 1999 "suitcase trade" with Russia, when many merchants from former Soviet countries traveled to Turkey to procure all the manufactured products they could get, including many consumer goods they could not find in their own country. Yet Turkey was once again adversely impacted by the Second Gulf War (2003) as the country's Middle East trade declined, although the impact was not as adverse as during the First Gulf War. In all, however, these first three decades of this phase were marked by Turkey's increased interaction with the world economy, an interaction that adversely impacted both the state and society that had until then been mostly self-contained.

Contemporaneous memoirs supplement this general economic narrative by drawing attention to how particular economic measures impacted society. Still, the paucity of memoirs commenting on the economy reveals the continuing disinterest of many Turks in things economic;[5] many memoir writers were much more interested in politics.[6] Three contemporaneous memoirs, two by Turkish officials and the other by a businessman, nevertheless capture three tensions over the state and government economic decision-making process. One diplomat recalled his conversations with a French CEO who identified Turkey's two major economic weaknesses as always taking the cheapest bid and always being inclined to take bribes.[7] What the CEO did not articulate was the fact that such economic decisions in Turkey were made by state officials and military officers, not by businesspeople. In the 1970s, the state's and government's continuing control of the economy is best demonstrated by the remarks of the other memoir writer, who was a businessman. In 1974, Turkey had been invited, along with Greece, to enter the European Common Market. Yet the then prime minister, Bülent Ecevit, turned down the invitation on strictly political nationalist grounds, stating that the Turks did not want to be the gardeners of Europe, opening their market to foreign exploitation. The same businessman also commented on the 1980s' domestic financial scandal of "imaginary exports" abusing the state's foreign currency allocation for export by keeping it for personal use. Upon complaining to the prime minister about the abuse, he was told that he should do the same, that is, abuse the system.[8]

Behind this flippant remark was another, deeper truth. As the first republican prime minister with financial expertise, Turgut Özal was much more interested in promoting commerce than the usual republican practice of disciplining the disobedient. He was able to release the state's control over the economy that curbed entrepreneurship, but he did not address the subsequent fraudulent behavior many businesspeople engaged in by drawing funds not based on the economic merit of their projects but instead on their personal political networks. As long as the state gave funds based on political connections, rather than in accordance with sound business plans, many state resources continued to be squandered. Still, at this particular juncture in the 1980s, Turkey's economy started to move from state-controlled economic decision-making and execution to economic liberalization through decentralization. One official captured the positive economic decentralization as municipalities were given the authority to collect property taxes, using some of the local tax revenues for urban improvement. Such decentralization improved economic efficiency. It was also this measure that enabled local businesspeople to engage more in local politics, thereby slowly destabilizing the republican state monopoly over the political system.[9]

After the end of the Cold War in the late 1980s, Turkey was forced to open to world markets, enabling those religiously conservative businessmen in the provinces who had been marginalized by the secular republican establishment to participate directly in the world economy. The capital they accumulated formed the political origins of the JDP, through which they then managed to participate in domestic politics in spite of the objection of the state and the military. Also significant in this process was the empowerment of local municipalities at the expense of the center; these municipalities were allowed to keep a portion of local taxes for their own expenses, thus becoming another route through which once-marginalized religiously conservative politicians could participate in the political system. In all, then, the economic situated modernity of this period enabled the emergence and eventual triumph of the religiously conservative JDP that is in power today; this was due to the republican leadership's initial prioritization of political and military interests over economic ones. Not properly schooled in the economy and therefore not heeding the adverse impact of the combination of the 1974 Cyprus invasion and the 1974–75 world oil crisis on the economy, the leadership plunged Turkey into economic and political instability during the 1970s and the 1980s. After the 1980 military coup, as it became evident that economic concerns needed to be prioritized instead, the political end result of such prioritization was the gradual destabilization of the republican hegemony: the marginalized religiously conservative businesspeople in the provinces started to accumulate economic capital, which they then successfully invested in political capital, eventually bringing the JDP to power in 2002. Hence, situated economic modernity, undertaken by the republic leaders to salvage and sustain their hegemony, instead destabilized their hold onto power.

Then the Distorted Social Institutions

Modernity's focus on identity politics emerged with the coming to power of the first cohort of the post–World War II population. Wary of the dangers of excluded religion and ethnicity, the EU advocated the respect of cultural identity on the one hand and the increased political participation of the younger generations in governance on the other. While the 1968 student protests also resonated in Turkey in the early 1970s, such movements were quickly and violently repressed by the Turkish state and military. Many of the student leaders were either hanged, imprisoned, or murdered. Throughout the 1980s and 1990s, the Islamic, Alewite, and Kurdish identities emerging alongside the left-right political divide were periodically repressed by the Turkish state and its various governments. The inability of these segments of the population to express themselves politically led to domestic social unrest. Due to the Cold War and the support of the United States, the leftist student movements were much more violently suppressed than their counterparts because they were not interpreted as signs of increased democratization and political participation but instead as virulent symbols of "communism." As a consequence, Turkish governments and the military initially favored and supported the rightist nationalist religious movements both as a way to counterbalance the communists and also because such movements resonated more with the dominant culture. Once again, Turkish social situated modernity undertaken to democratically include more groups in the body politic initially ended up violently excluding them. Such official cultural policy initially led to the decimation of the political left and to the strengthening of religiously and nationalistically inclined parties, movements, and organizations that soon successfully challenged the control of the Turkish state. This was the unintended social consequence of social situated modernity in that the religiously conservative eventually brought down the republican leadership. And they were able to do so by successfully employing another element of modernity: the technology of communication.

Until the late 1970s, the Turkish state and military had total control over all domestic communication channels, including radios and television. The 1974 Cyprus invasion, the 1980 military coup, and the 1997 "postmodern" coup initially curbed the free flow of information and knowledge within society. During the 1980s, many newspapers were closed down.[10] Also significant was the banning of the books and novels of prominent Turkish and foreign intellectuals.[11] The waning of the Cold War and the opening to the world markets gradually undermined the state monopoly over communication, leading to the emergence of 16 national, 15 regional, and 230 local television stations, as well as 1,200 radio stations, in 1998.

Such an explosion in communication quickly expanded the weak public sphere; Turkish citizens started to be immediately informed about all the incidents taking place in their country. Hours-long public forum marathons on television enabled the Turkish populace to not only witness but also participate in the current events impacting Turkey. This emergence of the public sphere through communication was accompanied by the networks established by NGOs that speedily undermined the lack of transparency in state affairs. Suddenly, for the first time in history, the republican leadership began to be held accountable for its actions. Such close monitoring of state activities unearthed many political and financial scandals. Also significant was the gradual emergence of Islamist and Kurdish radio and television stations, thereby publicly establishing their previously banned identities and communities. After the first half of the decade of the 2000s, the possibility of Turkey's EU membership further empowered such civil organizations, which led protests against state practices such as torture and poor prison conditions. Another significant diffusion of knowledge and information also occurred through the establishment of private universities, high schools, and elementary schools, as well as their provincial counterparts. State universities also diffused throughout the country, albeit with escalated unequal resources between those established at major western cities versus their eastern provincial counterparts.

Even though censorship over the contents of newspapers thereby lessened, Turkish journalists still had difficulty in overcoming the practice of self-censorship they had practiced and had been socialized into since the advent of the republic. Also missing was any accountability over false information that often made its way into the news media, a significant weakness that continues to this day. Contemporaneous memoirs illuminate this state of affairs. One memoir writer commented that upon returning to Turkey and starting to write at a newspaper, he was told not to write on certain topics.[12] He also criticized the continued inequities in the Turkish formal education system, especially noting the small per capita spending on education.[13] During this period, the memoirs rarely discussed the domestic conditions of non-Muslim minorities because they had been effectively removed from the nationalist vision. One diplomat noted in his memoirs that Turkey was very far behind in the conception and debates surrounding minorities in Western Europe.[14] It could be conjectured that such lack of discussion regarding minorities was due to Turkey's nonentry into World War II. After all, Western Europe was forced to reexamine its policies toward the minorities due to the horror of the Holocaust. During this period, Turkey therefore sustained its prejudicial and discriminatory stand toward its minorities. A case in point is presented by a memoir writer who described the manner in which the overture toward the Turkish state and government by a very wealthy Armenian intending to live in Turkey was turned down because his request to have diplomatic status was objectionable.[15] The adverserial stand of the Turkish state and its governments toward those who did not belong to the dominant Turkish Muslim majority led the country to be deprived of the cultural richness it could have acquired over time. Because minorities were still not given the rights to fully participate in Turkish state and society, Turkey's attempts at modernization were stumped. Still, the escalating exchange of information within society enabled many participants in the newly emerging public sphere to become aware of their differences. The prior republican structure predicated on sameness started to be destabilized as a consequence.

And Then the Pressured Political Institutions

During the first three decades of this period, Turkey's strides toward political modernity in the form of increased democratization and protected civil liberties were likewise stunted. The increased military presence in Turkey in the aftermath of the 1974 Cyprus invasion went hand in hand with political repression and escalating political unrest, resulting in the declaration of martial law in 1979. Such measures culminated in the 1980 military coup, once again predicated on the premise that increased public religious expression was a threat to the republic's secular principles.[16] The military strategy was to demolish the existing political system on the one hand and redraw the constitution with increased military control on the other. Initially, military leaders singled out the activities of a minority partner in the coalition government, the National Salvation Party (Milli Selamet Partisi; MSP) and its leader, Necmettin Erbakan, as being publicly nonsecular. As a consequence, Erbakan was tried for antisecular activities and his party shut down.

Yet the coup officers did not stop there. Because they had no accountability except to each other, they took it upon themselves to engage in social engineering. They decided to rebuild the political system from scratch, presumably on the assumption that they could then oversee the rebuilding, excluding all unwanted elements in the process. They abolished all existing political parties and began to investigate and imprison all former party leaders. The military did not take into account the fact that political institution-building is a centuries-long, arduous process; that destroying political traditions led to political fragmentation, not preventing but actually fostering the emergence of religious and ethnic forces. The political situated modernity of the military was thus predicated on the assumption that the closing down of all existing political parties would eliminate the threat of religious and ethnic identities in Turkey; instead, their decision fostered the development of such identities, eventually bringing to power a party like the JDP that publicly prioritized its religious identity.

The 1982 constitution, forcefully redrawn under the influence of the military, was unlike the one that had been put together in the aftermath of the 1960 coup in that the latter was much more politically conservative. The legal changes included the reinstitution of State Security Courts—akin to former independence courts—that operated above the legal system and under the influence of the military. National security concerns determined by the military were also prioritized over civil liberties. The presidency was likewise more closely controlled by the military. After the ratification of the 1982 constitution, the military symbolically withdrew from the political arena, yet it left behind the coup-leader-turned-civilian, Kenan Evren, as the next Turkish president. As new political parties were established from scratch, the previously closed-down religiously conservative MSP mutated and reappeared as the Welfare Party (Refah Partisi). After the 1983 general elections, the center-right parties dominated Turkish political life for the next decade and a half, an outcome the military had carefully crafted. In spite of the military's open support of the Nationalist Democracy Party (Milliyetçi Demokrasi Partisi) and its leader, the retired general Turgut Sunalp, however, two other parties formed the first government coalition.[17] Because none of the newly formed parties initially received enough votes to form a government by themselves, small parties like the religious Islamist Welfare Party and the ultranationalist National Action Party (Milli Hareket Partisi) gained undue political influence in coalitions as minority partners.[18] Once again, much to the distress of the military, its situated political modernity ended up not weakening but instead strengthening the religiously conservative parties on the one hand and ethnically Turkish parties on the other.

This period of coalition governments among new political parties, none of which had initially been able to garner enough political support to govern alone, escalated political unrest. In 1997, the military executed yet another coup, yet this time it was termed "postmodern" coup because the military did not take direct political control but instead issued a manifesto articulating its anxieties regarding the increased public religious presence. The military then employed the legal system to close down the Welfare Party in 1998, which once again transmutated to emerge as the Virtue Party (Fazilet Partisi; VP). The liberals within the VP attempted to gain power over the conservatives, with Abdullah Gül running unsuccessfully against leader Erbakan's candidate. Meanwhile, Turkey had a center-left minority government headed by Bülent Ecevit, whose incapacity to rule due to old age became a significant point of contention. The republican leadership was continually marked during this period by aging political leaders refusing to retire, in the process undermining both the republican political system and their own parties. The liberals within the VP who were stonewalled by the aging leadership there established their own political party named the JDP in 2001. The main positive political transformation during this period was the JDP's election to government in 2002. In all prior Turkish general elections, the state-supported political candidates of centrist parties had all been appointed, not popularly elected. Yet the JDP had no such state support; instead, it had to engage in grass-roots political mobilization by getting citizens to vote for its candidates. To do so, the JDP imitated American electorate mobilization tactics: it surveyed neighborhoods and entered data into computers, conducted frequent surveys to pinpoint local and domestic issues people cared about, and developed policies based on these issues identified by the populace. The JDP also took a novel stand on Turkey's possible EU membership. All state-supported political parties in Turkey had initially objected to EU membership to various degrees because it would have destabilized the republican leadership's hold over Turkish state and society. Yet the JDP was not fettered by such a concern because it did not have the support of the republican leadership to start with, and its surveys clearly pointed out that the majority of the Turkish electorate was in favor of EU membership. It was probably the JDP's positive stand on the EU, coupled with its prioritization of economic concerns, that enabled it to transform into a mainstream party traversing the religious-secular divide and to subsequently win the 2002 elections. As the history of the emergence of the JDP makes clear, the political situated modernity undertaken by the military in the aftermath of its 1980 coup thus did not curb but actually fostered the political reemergence of religion into the public sphere.

Yet it was not the military alone that literally generated this adverse outcome; all previous state-supported political parties that had until then ruled due to their close connection with the republican leadership also facilitated this twisted process in that they failed to engage in mobilizing the electorate the way the JDP had. Yet the republican leadership was not willing to take the next step, that is, also allowing into the body politic not only the religiously conservative but also ethnic parties like the Kurdish-supported Democratic Turkey Party (Demokratik Türkiye Partisi; DTP) that had for the first time, in 2007, enabled the Kurds to democratically participate in the political system. The DTP was shut down in 2009 due to its alleged tie with "terrorist organizations like the PKK and activities against the unity of the Turkish state." Thirty-seven of its politicians, including those deputies who had been democratically elected, were terminated; their political immunity was removed, and they were tried in court for alleged antistate activities.

From 1971 to 2009, a total of eight political parties were systematically banned by the legal establishment.[19] Such legal bans severely curtailed the ability of the Turkish populace to express its views along the full political spectrum as only center-right and center-left parties were allowed. The year 2009 also witnessed the death of Muhsin Yazıcıoğlu, the leader of the ultranationalist and religious Great Unity Party (Büyük Birlik Partisi) in a suspicious helicopter crash. Hence, this period saw relative political liberalization and democratization as the JDP came to power as a consequence of grass-roots mobilization, but those parties like the DTP, representing ethnic interests other than those belonging to the dominant ethnic Turkish Muslim majority, were still severely repressed. In a way, the dominant Muslim Turkish majority of the Ottoman Empire ended up reestablishing itself; the republic had first prioritized Turkish ethnicity, excluding Islamic religion through secularism, but later was forced to include Islam once again.

Significant external events during this period, namely, the Iranian Revolution in 1979, the ensuing Iran-Iraq War from 1980 to 1988, the end of the Cold War in the 1990s, and the First and Second Gulf Wars in 1991 and 2003, destabilized Turkey politically and economically. In the east, thousands of refugees poured into Turkey, first from Iran and then Iraq; international trade embargoes against Iran and Iraq hurt the substantive trade Turkey had with these two countries. In the west, similar migrations occurred in the aftermath of the 1974 Cyprus invasion as well as in 1989, as more than 100,000 refugees fled the communist regime in Bulgaria to arrive in Turkey.[20] Due to the coming to power of the JDP, which advocated a "zero-problem" policy with all neighboring states, however, 2008 and 2009 also witnessed a gradual peaceful transformation in Turkey's foreign policy. Most significant among these were, in addition to developing relations with Syria and Iran, the development of relations with the Republic of Armenia. Turkey's President Abdullah Gül employed Turkey's World Cup soccer game to pay the first high-level official visit to Armenia; Armenia's President Serj Sarkisyan returned the visit a year later when he came to Turkey to watch the second soccer game.

In 2009, US president Barack Obama also visited Turkey, his first foreign visit as president. Giving a speech at the Turkish national assembly, Obama emphasized the significance of Turkey not only as a Western ally but also as a predominantly Muslim country with a strong and viable democracy. It was also in this context that he stressed Turkey's democratic need "to deal with its past."[21] Yet the "soccer diplomacy" and Turkish-Armenian accords signed on 22 April 2009 to normalize relations without any preconditions were insufficient to transform the relations between the two countries. Both Turkish and Armenian intellectuals argued that too much had been conceded politically, and they also criticized the lack of societal input and subsequent participation. The signature campaign initiated by Turkish intellectuals apologizing for the "Great Catastrophe [*Medz Yeghern*] the Armenians were subjected to in 1915" attempted to draw in and mobilize Turkish society. Yet the strong nationalist reaction once again demonstrated the need for further liberalization.[22] The situated political modernity whereby the attempts of the republican leaders to sustain their hegemony instead led to their replacement by the religiously conservative JDP pinpointed to a significant continuing absence: that of increased political participation of the populace not only in elections alone but also in governance through civil society organizations. Like the state-supported parties before it, the JDP too prioritized state interests over democratic ones, attempting to create and sustain a "zero-problem" foreign policy by state actions alone. Civil society was once again marginalized in governance.

Contemporaneous memoirs are obviously few because of the recency of the time, referring to the earlier decades of the period rather than the most current ones. The common theme running through them all is the unbearable weight of the Turkish military in politics. In relation to the 1974 Cyprus invasion, for instance, one memoir writer noted that the West had reacted negatively not to the Turkish military invasion but rather to its subsequent occupation of 38 percent of the island. This militaristic move, the writer continued, had also escalated European criticisms of Turkey on the grounds of lack of democracy and human rights.[23] Two memoir writers likewise criticized the 1980 military coup, the closing down of all political parties as a "totally emotional" reaction, and the subsequent decisions taken by the military as "lacking in reason, wisdom, and insight."[24] Yet such politically liberal stands were also accompanied by nationalist ones; one memoir writer claimed that Europe was bringing up the issues of democratization and human rights "merely as a cover for promoting its own interests at the expense of Turkey."[25] In summary, political situated modernity continued to produce results that had not been expected by the political leaders undertaking them, gradually eliminating the hold of first the military and then the state-supported parties from the Turkish body politic. Democratization and the protection of human rights remained elusive during the first three decades of this period. With the 2002 elections, the citizens of Turkey elected, for the first time, those they wanted rather than those the state forced them to elect. Yet the JDP's subsequent inclusion in the body politic still left out other political constituencies like the Kurds on the one hand and led the now resentful republican leadership to employ the legal system to bring the JDP down on the other. Both the exclusion of the Kurds and the inclusion of the Islamists gradually moved the political infighting from the political to the legal sphere that was still controlled by the republican leadership, especially due to the impact of the 1982 constitution.

Finally the Legal Refractions

Interpreting and applying the law in the name of the state, the judicial system defines its mission as guaranteeing equal justice to all under law. Hence, the delivery of justice is the first and most significant duty of the judiciary. A 2007 research report prepared in Turkey revealed, however, that the majority of Turkish judges and public prosecutors defined their mission not as such delivery of justice but instead first and foremost as the preservation of the Turkish state.[26] The in-depth interviews further articulated that for most, executing state priorities prevailed in their decision-making process. This strong connection between the judiciary and the state may explain the results of another survey conducted the following year; only 48 percent of the populace trusted the legal system, indicating that the slight majority of 52 percent did not trust the Turkish judiciary.[27] This strong state and government influence on judges and public prosecutors still constitutes the primary problem of the Turkish legal system today.

Given the legal history of the republic, where the interests of the republican leadership and the military were placed above the law, and given that the legal system was therefore often employed as a political tool to execute the measures and policies promoted by the state, government, and military, such an outcome is not surprising. I would argue that the origins of such a strong connection between the judiciary and the state were located in the origins of Turkish legal modernity. With the establishment of the republic, rather than formulating an organic legal system predicated on the Turkish social structure, the republican leaders instead adopted an amalgam of European legal systems "that fit Turkey best," resulting, for instance, in the adoption of civil codes from Switzerland and commercial laws from Italy. The subsequent lack of correspondence between such laws and the social structure ended in making the Turkish legal system not—as it should have been—independent of the political system but rather subservient to the state and its governments. Hence Turkish situated legal modernity was once again similar to the Western legal systems in form, but its content was negotiated by local actors and events that ended up not delivering justice but instead reproducing injustice.

The ensuing lack of correspondence between the Turkish social practices and the legal system produced systemic disjunctures. One memoir writer noted, for instance, that even Turkey's bar associations were not self-governed by the majority, as only a handful of members reached all the decisions. This was also the case in almost all civil society organizations, revealing a strong lack of democratic participation.[28] Ironcially, the only reforms to the constitution were carried out not by governments but instead by the military, which systematically prioritized national security concerns over civil liberties. As a consequence, judges and public prosecutors transformed into state officials.

The only different, civilian path taken to reforming the judiciary occurred in the context of possible EU membership, leading the JDP to start making legal adjustments to the Turkish system in accordance with EU parameters. The year 2000 witnessed the promulgation of a new civil code followed by general amnesty. In 2001 and 2002, the pro-military constitution also started to be liberalized. Yet, in a news article reporting on the recent developments in reformulating the Turkish constitution, one reporter noted that "in preparing the first civilian constitution in Turkey's history, the JDP was modeling the draft on the Spanish constitution."[29] Such modeling replicated the Turkish legal practice of borrowing legal practices from Western Europe. Yet, unlike with prior Turkish constitutions, those within the JDP active in its preparation were at least legal experts.

During this period, the frequent decisions of the constitutional court banning political parties revealed that the Turkish judiciary still had a long way to go before reaching legal autonomy. After all, such legal decisions demonstrated that the judiciary placed the preservation of the state over the protection of civil liberties. In addition, the judiciary interpreted secularism exactly as the republican state and the military had done. In an attempt to reestablish the dominance of republican leadership over the political system and the presidency, the constitutional court intervened in the political system twice. In 2007, it tried to prevent the democratic election of the former JDP member Abdullah Gül to the presidency. In 2008, the court likewise attempted to close down the democratically elected JDP that was at the time in government as the ruling party.[30] The possible legal crisis that would have ensued was nevertheless prevented by a close vote in favor of not closing down the ruling party. Such legal decisions point to the need of the judiciary to reform, with the intent to separate its decision-making from the influence of the Turkish state and government.

Elements of Late Republican Sentiments

Late Republican Intrastate Polarization

During this period, the most public polarization was ideological, occurring among university students, who not only became sharply divided between the political right and the political left but actually engaged in physical violence against each other. Having been a university student in Turkey at the time, I still remember the political confrontations at our campus, the gunning down of students on the streets, and the many funeral processions of murdered students we were forced to attend. Escalating military interventions did not contain but actually further escalated violence and politically polarized the populace. At the time, while some welcomed such increased military intervention on the grounds that it stabilized the country by force, others objected that the military never allowed democratic struggles to take place, which could gradually lead to stability through peaceful means.

Alongside the ideological polarization of the students, ethnic and religious polarization also escalated as the Islamists, Alewites, and Kurds formed many organizations defending their rights for political participation in the system on their own terms, attempts that were violently suppressed especially through the declaration of martial law to contain the violence by closing down such organizations and imprisoning their members. Among the small remaining population of non-Muslims, a mere 100,000 in a country of 72 million (.01 percent), the Armenian community experienced the most religious polarization due to the escalating violent attacks of Armenian terrorists abroad against Turkish diplomats. The dominant Turkish Muslim majority, once again unable to distinguish and differentiate the Armenians of Turkey from such terrorists, repeatedly pressured the Armenians of Turkey to publicly declare their undying allegiance to the Turkish nation-state by issuing apologies, writing to their coreligionists abroad, and holding public religious ceremonies mourning the murdered Turkish diplomats. Many of the Turkish Armenians I have spoken to describe this time as one of the most difficult they experienced in Turkey; many left the country during this period.

Contesting Political Ideologies

After the 1974 Cyprus invasion, as the country plunged into economic and political crisis, the student movements throughout the world for increased political participation also impacted Turkey. Many of the politically active students initially wanted to merely participate in the system by expressing their ideas. Yet their inability to do so due to state repression that summarily labeled and stigmatized them all as communists led many student groups to first polarize into leftists and rightists camps to then fight each other.[31] Such student activism, which escalated in the late 1970s, was violently suppressed by the 1980 military coup: academics holding leftist political views that the military did not approve were summarily expelled from the universities, and the university campuses that were supposed to be democratic spaces were also brought under scrutiny as hundreds of students were imprisoned. Replicating an earlier pattern, many students sought by the military, especially the leftists, escaped to Europe to become active abroad. As for the rightists, while some were imprisoned, others became recruited into the secret paramilitary state organizations to engage in violence on behalf of the state. Hence the ideological polarization resulted in the decimation of the left and the extralegal incorporation of the right into the state apparatus, preparing the groundwork for the eventual rise of the religiously conservative.

Professing Religion

During this period, religious polarization affected two disparate social groups: the religiously conservative Islamists suffered from the secular sanctions of the republican leadership, while the Armenians endured the harassment of the same leadership due to the ASALA and JCOAG murders of Turkish diplomats. During the Cold War years, the Turkish state and its governments initially tolerated and even unofficially supported the Islamic movements in Turkey as an antidote to the leftist and "communist" movements. Yet their quick spread throughout the country, and especially their subsequent mobilization into political parties, led to an official policy change: the republican leadership now took a stand against the public expression of religion with the intent to contain it. Especially after the 1980 coup, the Turkish military established and advocated a staunch position against the Islamists, yet it was too little too late. Especially the political vacuum created by the abolition of all political parties enabled the religiously conservative to mobilize the electorate and attain increased political power. With such power came the public discussion of the boundaries of republican secularism, with the exclusion of headscarved women from the state-controlled public spaces emerging as the most significant topic. Because all educational institutions in the country were under state control, the exclusion of headscarved women from getting an education led to frequent confrontations.[32] The women's movement in Turkey also became sharply divided over this issue: some feminists supported the wearing of the headscarf, while others fervently opposed it for being antimodern and antisecular. With its 2007 electoral victory, the JDP decided to take the headscarf issue public with the support of the National Action Party, promoting a constitutional change that would allow the headscarf to be worn at all state-controlled public spaces. Yet this public political act almost led to the closing down of the governing JDP by the constitutional court on the allegation that the party had acted against the secular principles of the republic; the JDP stepped back from such an initiative.[33]

During this time, not only did the republican leadership closely monitor all public spaces with the intent to keep them strictly secular, but the Turkish media joined the witch-hunt by issuing scandalized reports on any infraction, real, imagined, or staged by the radical fringes, to aggravate the populace.[34] The Turkish military was the most significant state institution to take a staunch secular stand against the public presence of religion within its ranks, often expelling cadets and officers for engaging in any religious activity.[35] The office of the presidency soon turned into another contested public space within the state. After the 1980 coup and with the 1982 constitution, the military had strengthened its hold over the presidency. Yet the solid majority with which the JDP won the 2002 and 2006 elections enabled it to contest the military control over the presidency. Because the president was elected by the national assembly, and because the JDP now held the majority in the assembly, the members of the national assembly decided to elect as the next president of the republic Abdullah Gül, a JDP member, deputy, and former foreign minister. In 2007, the military fervently opposed Gül's election because as president would assume command over the military. The constitutional court tried to intervene on a legal technicality but to no avail. Gül was elected president, and the secularist influence of the military was curbed, effectively reducing such influence to the legal sphere alone.

Contemporary memoirs rarely addressed this secular-religious polarization, since most of the memoir writers were members of the dominant secular majority. The one exception is the memoir of a religious scholar who lived in an insular world that did not intersect with the secular one in everyday activities except during military service and the attainment of children's birth certificates.[36] Once he started to participate in the secular world in his professional capacity as a religious scholar, however, his presence was immediately challenged on the grounds of republican secular principles. He was pressured to resign from his position as a faculty member in a religion department; he then decided to go into exile in Holland, where he still lives.

The other religious polarization occurred along the Muslim-Christian axis and was triggered by the ASALA and JCOAG assassinations of Turkish diplomats abroad. Although the Armenians of Turkey were not in any way involved in these violent acts, the increased prejudice and discrimination they faced, especially from 1975 to 1985, led many to leave Turkey, further decimating the Armenian population to about 60,000. Contemporaneous memoirs of two Armenians of Turkey and a Kurd who resided in an Armenian neighborhood during his childhood reveal the dynamics of this polarization.[37] The memoir of an Armenian film actor is noteworthy for its silences in relation to the author's ethnic and religious identity, revealing the immense pressure within Turkish society for sameness that led the actor to hide his difference.[38] In his memoir, published in Turkish, he did not mention that he was Armenian or that he had attended Armenian schools. Anecdotes demonstrating the prejudice and discrimination non-Muslims often experienced in Turkey were likewise entirely missing, except in one instance: during his mandatory military service, he stated that he "had a dispute with his captain" but did not specify what the dispute was about. Likewise, he narrated that he had "dreamt about and very much desired to become a policeman," to then merely note that he "chased after that possibility a lot, but it did not actualize," once again not discussing the official state discrimination against employing non-Muslims. He continually highlighted his profession, silencing his ethnic origin in the process.[39]

The memoir of the other Armenian differs in this respect, as he openly discusses his Armenian identity, even commenting on some of the Armenian assassins involved in the ASALA and JCOAG murders. Narrating an anecdote pertaining to the Lebanese Armenian Levon Ekmekçiyan, who was involved in a bombing in Turkey only to be caught and eventually hanged, he stated:[40]

> [Ekmekçiyan] was from Lebanon and a [radical] Dashnak [revolutionary].... [I feel] both pity and anger toward this man.... [Ekmekçiyan's] family was from Anatolia. They lived through all the pains of the [1915] deportation. They could not return to their lands, remaining in Arab countries [instead]. They were the remnants of families who had once been well off in Anatolia, [but now] grew up in an Arab neighborhood under the most wretched conditions... doing everything possible just to survive. But when they came home at night, they always listened at the dinner table to the stories of the massacres the Turks committed against them.... Then they came here, killed a few Turks, and [thought they thus] contributed to the solution of the problem: this is what is pitiful.... What else could [Ekmekçiyan] have done, he is ignorant; his father was a drug addict. This man is only capable of [such violent action]. You can either pity him or get angry at him. He of course was not going to have a bouquet of flowers made, bringing that [to the Turks]; [he] instead argued, "you have done such and such to us all these years."... [As an Armenian in Lebanon], you could either become a communist or a nationalist. He became a nationalist. He was wounded here. The [Turkish] state first healed [Ekmekçiyan] then had him deliver talks of penitence on [Turkish] television to finally hang him. Very befitting, the [Turkish] state would do that.

Unlike most nationalist Turkish narratives, this memoir attempted to understand the actual conditions that led to the creation of such an Armenian militant. Having lived in Turkey during this period, I can attest that no such voices were ever publicly present in the Turkish media. Yet this narration reveals how much the Turkish public would have benefited from having had such voices in their midst.

The Kurdish memoir writer discussed the reasons for the departure of Armenians from Turkey, pointing out their everyday experiences of prejudice and discrimination. The Turkish Muslim populace referred to non-Muslims as "the dirty Greek Rum, the backstabbing Armenian, and the cowardly Jew even though in reality they were as cowardly or courageous as everyone else." This prejudicial stand resonated with the official one that legally treated them as if they were "strangers" and "foreigners" on their own ancestral lands.[41] The writer also described how the increasingly tense atmosphere after the 1974 Cyprus invasion and the advent of the 1975–85 ASALA and JCOAG murders poisoned the neighborhoods. Many Turks started to circulate unfounded rumors that the non-Muslims of Turkey were up to no good:

> The ones who constantly talked about these rumors were the [Turkish] regulars of the coffeehouses. Most were [uneducated] people who frequently changed jobs, and in whose words and actions the neighborhood residents did not put much value and trust. It took us years to understand what type of people, those whom we once called "older brother," were actually like [in moral character]. . . . In that environment, we were not at all aware of the troubles of our neighbors. Only when one learns years later the things that had been experienced at Kurtuluş, it is only then that one realizes events could be approached from a variety of perspectives. It turns out there were some [Armenians] who left Kurtuluş without touching any of their goods, [merely] leaving a note behind stating "[thank goodness] I am being set free from this torment."

Another anecdote regarding the prejudice and discrimination non-Muslims encountered was provided by a Turkish memoir writer.[42] He noted that during this period, he as a lawyer witnessed many instances "which did not at all befit either the ethics of the profession or the honor of humanity." After this very general self-censored statement, the writer went on to describe the legal case of an elderly Armenian couple who had given power of attorney to two young Turkish lawyers. When the Armenian husband died, these lawyers came the day after the funeral, making the grieving widow sign some papers, arguing that the documents pertained to the funeral and inheritance procedures. Yet the elderly Armenian woman then found out that she had been stripped of most of her wealth. Hence, such polarization also brought with it violence as those like the non-Muslims, who were less powerful, were shamelessly exploited with impunity by the ethnic Turks in power. It is significant that even though the memoir writer described this injustice, he did not take any action against it. Another legal problem non-Muslims continually faced was retaining their properties out of the confiscating reach of the Turkish state.[43] Interestingly, it was only after the possible EU candidacy of Turkey that such injustices have started to be domestically investigated, leading the authors of the report to file lawsuits with the European Court of Human Rights after exhausting avenues within the Turkish legal system. In 2008, even though the JDP introduced several amendments to the Law of Foundations (Vakıflar Kanunu) monitoring the operations of all the foundations in Turkey from a directorate under the Prime Ministry, to resolve this discriminatory state practice, they were challenged by the nationalist opposition parties, which objected to the amendments by appealing them to the Turkish constitutional court.

Such legal injustice currently continues not only against "othered" individuals but also against any cultural and religious symbols of difference. Rather than acknowledging the tensions and working to decrease them by protecting all communities equally, for instance, the Turkish state instead actively changed Armenian and Kurdish village names, replacing them with Turkish ones. Since 1940, officials replaced the names of 12,211 villages (38 percent of all the villages in Turkey) in this manner.[44] Prime Minister Erdoğan stated that a positive symbolic step regarding the Kurdish question would be to give back Kurdish place names, but no such consideration was shown toward the censored Armenian names. Also significant in this context was the official changing of the names of animals that were of Armenian or Kurdish origin as these too were changed into Turkish.[45] The Turkish minister of the environment justified these changes by arguing that "the old names were contrary to Turkish unity . . . and the names were being used to argue that Armenians or Kurds had lived in the areas where the animals were found."

Asserting Ethnicity

During this period, ethnic polarization emerged in the context of two rather disparate social groups, the Kurds on the one hand and the ethnically Turkish refugees from Bulgaria on the other. In the 1970s, the Kurdish Workers' Party (Parti Kerkeren Kurdistan; PKK) was initially established to empower the Kurdish community. Especially after the 1980 military coup, increased military repression such as banning the Kurds from speaking their own language in all state-controlled public spaces also radicalized the PKK, which started to engage in armed resistance against the state in 1984. The state in turn fragmented the Kurdish community by officially appointing and arming some Kurds as village guards to monitor and control the rest, a practice similar to Sultan Abdülhamid II's establishment of the Hamidiye regiments. As PKK attacks continued, the military took action against them, forcing the PKK leader, Abdullah Öcalan, to escape to Syria in the mid-1980s. Continuing the practice of monitoring of its public spaces, the Turkish state also outlawed public praise of the PKK or even interviewing PKK members.[46]

The official ban against speaking and singing in Kurdish was only lifted in 1991. Still, during the same year, when the deputies of the People's Labor Party (Halkın Emek Partisi; HEP) decided to exercise their right by speaking Kurdish in the national assembly, other Turkish deputies protested and subsequently excluded the HEP from the assembly. In 1994, when the party reemerged as the Democracy Party (Demokrasi Partisi; DEP), the political immunity of the Kurdish deputies was removed, leading to their trial and imprisonment with fifteen-year sentences. Kurdish intellectuals who voiced their concerns by criticizing the Turkish state were imprisoned as well.[47] Meanwhile, many Kurds who had left Turkey for Western Europe in the aftermath of the 1980 military coup started organizing there. In 1995, the Kurds held a conference in Holland, and the Kurdish parliament met for the first time in Europe, in exile. The Kurds in Turkey continued to organize politically, this time around the newly founded People's Democracy Party (Halkın Demokrasi Partisi; HADEP). At a HADEP party congress, when the Turkish flag was replaced by the PKK flag by a group of Kurdish activists, the congress was shut down. The Turkish state sustained its oppositional stand against the PKK, issuing an official protest against Greece in 1995 and Italy in 1998 for their support of the PKK in general and their invitation to host the PKK leader Abdullah Öcalan in particular. The state also forced Syria to expel Öcalan, who went into exile in Nairobi, Kenya, only to be captured with the help of the US Secret Service; as he was brought to Turkey, his trial and subsequent imprisonment generated a media debate, with most Turkish newspapers advocating that he should face death by hanging. He was instead imprisoned and remains in solitary confinement at this time. At the time I copy-edited the book in May 2014, Öcalan still remains in solitary confinement but is no longer referred to as 'the terrorist' since the Prime Minister Tayyip Erdoğan announced his decision to include Öcalan in his negotiations with the Kurdish community in Turkey.

In the first half of the decade of the 2000s, the possibility of EU membership led to the gradual liberalization in the legal system, leading to the release of the imprisoned Kurds in 2004, followed by the permission to establish private Kurdish-language courses in the east in 2005. The "Kurdish opening," indicating a peaceful approach to the Kurdish question, gained speed during this period as well; for the first time, Kurds were permitted to legally register their Kurdish names with the Turkish authorities. Until then, they had not been permitted to have such "ethnic" names. Yet such positive developments were accompanied by political repression when, in 2009, another Kurdish party, the Democratic Turkey Party (Demokratık Türkiye Partisi; DTP), was closed down. As a consequence of this negative development, the political immunity of the democratically elected Kurdish deputies was once again removed, and lawsuits were filed against them. Interestingly, 2009 also witnessed the state declaration of a general amnesty to PKK members, with thirty-four members returning to Turkey. The ebullient reception they received led to yet another legal investigation.

This chronological discussion of the Kurds' location in Turkey during this time reveals that the Turkish state and its governments, including the JDP, still only allow the Kurds to participate in the state-controlled public sphere under conditions determined not by the Kurds but by the Turkish state. Any public demonstration of Kurdish identity is still officially interpreted as a potential threat against the state's "unitary" structure, that is, a structure inherently dominated by Turkish ethnic identity. Still, during this period, the Kurds challenged the official Turkish stand on the Armenian Genocide first by recognizing and acknowledging it, and then by apologizing to the Armenians for siding with the Turks against them. The first Kurdish apology to the Armenians took place on 24 April 2004.[48] The same apology was repeated five years later on the same day: the only Kurdish newspaper in Turkey printed in the Turkish language featured a large headline above its logo that read in Armenian, with Armenian lettering: "We Remember, We Share Your Grief."[49] Such acknowledgment sharply contrasted with the official Turkish stand as well as that of the dominant Turkish Muslim majority, which still insisted on denial.

The memoirs of one Kurdish intellectual captured the difficulties of living in Turkey as a Kurd.[50] In 1978, the memoir writer was elected the first independent socialist mayor of Diyarbekir only to be imprisoned for sixteen years after the 1980 military coup. He then left for Europe, returning in 2004. His wife was elected deputy to the Turkish national assembly in 1991, but she too ended up in prison for ten years when she insisted on reading a part of her swearing-in at the national assembly pertaining to the Kurds in Kurdish. Even though her parliamentary immunity should have protected her, the legal closure of her party and the subsequent removal of her political immunity led to her trial and imprisonment. The memoir comprises the long letters the writer sent to his wife while he was in prison. In all, they reveal not only the high degree of collective violence interwoven into the lives of Kurds in Turkey but also the ensuing social fragmentation of many Kurdish lives as family members are frequently imprisoned.

This period was also marked by the inflow of ethnic Turkish refugees from Bulgaria. The inflow started in 1985 and continued until 1989; during this time, approximately 160,000 arrived in Turkey, with 90,000 eventually returning to Bulgaria. The rest were settled predominantly in Bursa in western Turkey. The memoirs of one such refugee captured the high degree of nationalism present among all Diaspora communities, including the ethnic Turks living outside of Turkey.[51] The narrative of the entire memoir was based on demonstrating how truly Muslim and truly Turkish his community continued to be, an insistence that reveals how threatened the memoir writer must have felt upon arriving in Turkey. Such Turkish Bulgarian refugees faced prejudice and discrimination; they were not given official posts, and local ethnic Turks often refused to interact with them. The ones who did survive did so by rapidly assimilating and totally and systematically erasing their "difference."

In a sociological survey a colleague and I conducted in Bursa from 2001 to 2003 on the economic transformation of the Bursa textile industry, we were surprised to discover that in spite of the large inflow of Bulgarian refugees to the city, there was not a single social scientific study conducted on the course and impact of this significant immigration. This was the case because all the refugees emphasized their Turkish identity, silencing their Bulgarian origins in the process. Such flights of populations into Turkey also proceeded in the east. Iranians escaping from the Iran-Iraq War arrived in 1985, only to be followed in 1991 by the Iraqi Kurds escaping massacres conducted by the Iraqi state in northern Iraq. Many of these either eventually returned to Iraq, as in the case of the Iraqi Kurds, or else continued on to Europe, as in the case of the Iranians. In all, then, domestic social polarization escalated along ideological, ethnic, and religious axes, and those social groups who attempted to seek refuge in Turkey were not integrated into the body politic.

Escalating Late Republican Collective Violence and the Assassination of Hrant Dink

It is not accidental that the collective violence during this period initially occurred along the axes of polarization discussed earlier, namely, against the political opposition, the Kurds, the Alewites, and the non-Muslims. And with the exception of the violence against the Kurds, the violence was not overt but instead covert, that is, executed by extralegal paramilitary armed bands very similar to the Special Organization of the CUP. Assassinations of prominent leaders of these social groups were frequently undertaken and then blamed on the groups themselves; in almost all cases, the assassins could never be identified, thereby escaping punishment by impunity. Only in the relative liberalization after the first half of the decade of the 2000s did it become evident that such state-sanctioned paramilitary bands had committed this violence.

Against Public Intellectuals

From the late 1970s to the late 1990s, dozens of public figures were assassinated with impunity.[52] At the time, the media discussions of the assassinations could never pinpoint who the assailants were, except to argue that they were politically motivated; the leftists and rightists blamed each other. Two contemporaneous memoirs document the manner in which prominent individuals negotiated and interpreted such violence.[53] One Turkish official argued that the 1979 assassination of journalist Abdi İpekçi was executed because the victim "always tried to support the social forces stabilizing the country through democratization." "It was thought that his assassination would upset Turkey's stability," the writer continued. "On the night he was killed, all the lights were on at the offices of the general chief of staff in Ankara, but what was desired did not occur, and Turkey did not plunge into total disorder." Hence, the memoir writer insinuated that the secret armed bands of the military were behind the assassination, aiming to plunge the country into disorder with the intent to justify and legitimate the military coup that was eventually carried out. The memoir of a leftist Turkish intellectual revealed not only the violence she and her friends were subjected to but also the reasons behind the student movements.[54] According to the writer, the 1970s youth movement against the state started as follows:

> [The Turkish youth] were able to gain the support of the populace in undertaking public activities such as protesting the visit of the American fleet.... When [the state and the military] could not contain such democratic mass movements [however], provocations and the unaccounted murders of many leaders ensued.... In all, these movements could not accomplish much because they could not unite, instead becoming fragmented without a particular vision that could have mobilized the masses.

The memoir writer stressed the gradual fracturing of all student movements due to state repression, a political fragmentation that undermined youths' ability to participate in the system. Indeed, "the youth were never given a voice in running the country, and were instead provoked and repressed," the memoir writer concluded.

Such political agitation intended to sustain the authoritarian hold of the republican leadership over the country continued with a series of bombings in public spaces.[55] Especially through the 1980s and into the 1990s, such bombings by unknown assailants were accompanied by violence executed by allegedly radical leftist and rightist groups, often penetrated and coerced into action by state informants.[56] Contemporaneous memoirs penned by such radical rightist and leftist militants do not exist, since many of them ended up murdered. An exception, however, is the memoir of a rightist militant.[57] He first recounted why he became militant, stating that "there were some of our heroes who had turned into flags for us for having engaged in fights in big cities against the communists.... In those days, I wanted to become like one of those dead or living heroes." Such hero worship instigated by the exclusionary nationalism of the state led to the involvement of the memoir writer in violent activities he did not at all discuss, only stating that he had to leave İstanbul, escaping to Erzurum:

> Because of the incidents I had become engaged in, I had to go to Erzurum; while I was there, the Kahramanmaraş [massacres of the Alewites] took place and martial law was proclaimed. The seeds of violence that had been planted for years had now taken a form impacting the masses. It was so sad that the same people who just fifty years ago

> had been fighting shoulder to shoulder against the [Western] occupying forces had now started shooting each other.

As the memoir writer eventually and secretly returned to İstanbul, he observed the populace sharply divided into those who, having established a wealthy and protected lifetsyle, did not experience any violence, and those in the poor neighborhoods whose lives were fully immersed in such violence:

> When I went to İstanbul, I often took one of the public buses traveling along the Bosporus shores, [then] returning on the last bus. During those summer nights, whenever I saw the lights pouring from the seaside mansions, the high society whose laughter could be heard from the streets, the groups of girls and boys [cruising around], the expensive cars, the wealth and the splendor, I became aware of the existence of other worlds and other lives. While the world in which I had become embedded contained blood, gunpowder, fear, tears, police, and torture, this new world I had just started to get acquainted with was [instead] filled with happiness, entertainment, music, dance, wealth, and prosperity.... The violence that had scorched my world had not impacted these places. In the worlds of my contemporaries cruising in their latest model cars, the risk of being caught, the fear of the police, and the anxiety of getting shot did not exist. None of the realities that had destroyed my country, making my nation shed tears of blood, had penetrated here. The fire only burned the hearts of the poor, forlorn, desperate, and suffering people of Anatolia. When I saw the tranquil lives of the Bosporus residents, I was angered on the one hand and envious on the other.... If we had all been able to make use of the provided opportunities and possibilities, perhaps a larger portion of society would achieve that comfortable life in a decade.

Such societal comparisons and ensuing future aspirations reveal the origins of rightist and leftist political radicalism. Unbeknownst to each other, both radical militant groups aspired to the same vision, for inclusion in the pristine domain established, monitored, and sustained by the republican leadership on a members-only basis: just like Sultan Abdülhamid II's practice, only those who promised not to engage in politics and thus not challenge the status quo were permitted to accumulate wealth and lead luxurious yet sequestered lives. Those who chose to engage in political opposition were repressed, imprisoned, or murdered; and the fragmentation into the leftist and rightist political camps prevented these two radical sides from perceiving the similarities beyond their publicly disparate visions, leading them instead to gradual containment and extinction, through arrest, imprisonment, and sometimes death by hanging.[58]

Against the Alewites

During this period, the inherent prejudice and discrimination encountered by the Alewites, a religious group practicing Shiism instead of the dominant Sunni practice, also came to the forefront.[59] In republican Turkey, in spite of the presence of a substantive Alewite population, the Turkish state exclusively supported and advocated the Sunni version of Islam. Only the Sunni religious organizations received substantial financial support from the state and its governments. The economially and politically unstable environment of the time polarized the relationship between the Sunni and Alewite Turks, erupting in collective violence against the Alewites in 1978, 1980, 1993, and 1995. The first instance, in 1978, occurred in Kahramanmaraş. As the leftist-rightist divide mapped onto the Sunni-Shiite one, the Alewites united with the leftists against the Sunnis, who naturally collaborated with the rightists. The ensuing popular clashes led to 104 deaths, mostly from among the Alewites. This violence provided yet another justification for the ensuing military coup. Initially, about 804 people of mostly radically rightist orientation were arrested, tried, and imprisoned, with sentences ranging from death by hanging to long-term imprisonment. Yet, none of the capital punishment sentences were executed, and the rest of the prisoners were released in 1991. It is especially significant that some later became deputies to the national assembly, demonstrating once again the inherent lack of accountability.

The same collective violence replicated itself during the summer of 1980 in Sivas, engulfing the cities of Sivas and Çorum in flames. This violence likewise occurred right before the advent of the military coup. The collective violence against the Alevis continued in 1993; the Madımak Hotel in Sivas, hosting many Alewites and leftists during an annual Alewite festival, was attacked and burned down by radical rightist and Sunni militants, leading to a death toll of thirty-seven. The violence also diffused into the major cities containing many recent immigrant neighborhoods from Alewite-dominated provinces. In 1995, three Alewite coffeehouses in the Gazi neighborhood in İstanbul were raided by radical religious militants, who shot many of the coffeehouse patrons. Contemporaneous memoirs do not contain any information on this inherent yet not often publicly addressed violence.

Against the Kurds

The most numerically significant collective violence of this time period was committed against the Kurds. It took two forms: direct armed conflict and indirect political repression. Direct armed conflict occurred between the state forces and the PKK during which many local Kurdish leaders were also assassinated by state-controlled paramilitary bands. Indirect political repression took the form of closing down Kurdish organizations and political parties. A decade after its foundation in 1974, the PKK undertook its first official raid in 1984, ending in the trial of PKK members in Mardin, where twenty-two Kurds were sentenced and executed by hanging. The skirmishes between the PKK and the Turkish forces continued throughout the rest of the 1980s all the way to the present, transforming into a civil war in the process. In 1986, the Turkish military destroyed the PKK camps, leading to PKK attacks especially in Hakkari, one resulting in twenty-five deaths among the local populace. In 1989, as the PKK activities continued, the Turkish military started to empty out 5,000 Kurdish villages by force, leading to their forced migration into major cities in the east and west. Violent PKK activities targeting state security forces continued in 1991, gradually spreading to major cities where the Kurds now dwelled. In İstanbul, shops, commercial malls, and the Chamber of Commerce bombed. During the following year, the PKK security force clashes led to the killing of 600 PKK members in one incident. During the 1990s, many Turkish soldiers, especially the gendarmerie responsible for maintaining order in the rural areas, were also killed in these skirmishes. Subsequently, their families became publicly active, demonstrating against the PKK during the "funerals of the martyrs." Rather than containing such ethnic polarization, the Turkish state and the military instead instigated it, often supporting and mobilizing the grieving families of Turkish soldiers into staging such public demonstrations. Kurdish families became increasingly fractured; some young family members were recruited into the PKK, while other family members had to serve in the Turkish military, thereby often ending up fighting against each other. Those Kurdish families aiding the PKK were severely punished by the Turkish state and military, which consciously chose to overlook the fact that such families could not have refused aid to their own family members now serving in the PKK. The military operations against the PKK escalated from 1995 to 2008, with the Turkish military often crossing Turkey's borders with Iraq and Syria, attempting to destroy the PKK camps stationed there. Clashes during the Kurdish celebration of Nevruz[60] became routinized, happening almost annually in the east between the locals and the Turkish military and security forces. The Turkish state eventually decided to symbolically contain Nevruz by declaring it a national holiday. Yet the subsequent state repression, with the military dictating the terms of the Nevruz celebrations, failed to contain the violence. During the same time, prominent Kurdish businessmen and intellectuals also started to be assassinated by secret paramilitary Turkish bands. The PKK militants retaliated during the first half of the decade of the 2000s, starting to bomb the summer resorts in the west, thereby attempting to undermine Turkey's tourist industry.

Also significant during this time was the political violence committed against the Kurds. The parties they established in an attempt to participate in the political system were banned, and their democratically elected deputies arrested, tried, and imprisoned in 1994 and then again in 2009. Yet the year 2009 also witnessed the emergence of official attempts to undertake a "democratic opening (Demokratik Açılım)"; violent military repression was complemented by peaceful negotiations especially with locally prominent Kurdish organizations. Official decisions such as lifting the bans on the public use of Kurdish language, songs, and names and the establishment of Kurdish television stations and language courses were significant in somewhat reducing the violence.[61] Some PKK members returned to Turkey due to the amnesty issued by the Turkish state. Still, the frustrations of the Kurdish populace of Turkey once again escalated with the recent closing down of the Kurdish party that had been democratically elected to the Turkish national assembly. Contemporaneous memoirs do not yet cover these recent activities.

Against the Non-Muslims and Hrant Dink

During this period, violence against non-Muslims persisted in the form of raids and attacks on their religious establishments, and murders of non-Muslim religious clergy residing in Turkey.[62] The most significant violence of the period was the 2007 assassination of journalist Hrant Dink by assailants and a plot that is still legally unaccounted for.[63] Why and how did Dink become the target of such violence? I argue that Dink's public stand on three issues led the radical segments within the republican leadership involved in extralegal, paramilitary activities to mark him for destruction. These issues, which Hrant publicly challenged, were the exclusionary nature of Turkish nationalism, the official discriminatory Turkish state policy against non-Muslim minorities, and the continued lack of accountability for past collective violence committed against the Armenians.

About two decades after establishing a successful chain of bookstores Hrant with his brothers in 1979, he founded, along with friends, the Turkish-Armenian bilingual newspaper *Agos* in 1996. Becoming the editor in chief of *Agos* provided Hrant with the public space to discuss Turkey's social problems; his newspaper editorials and frequent appearances on television then turned him into a public intellectual. His visibility also brought dangers along with it, however, in the form of frequent death threats. The Turkish state, taking issue with his critical stand, started to harass Hrant through the legal system. In 2002, the public prosecutor filed a lawsuit against him, on the grounds of challenging Turkey's unity.[64] Dink had taken issue with the Turkish national anthem, stating the following:[65]

> Since my childhood, I have been singing the national anthem along with you. Recently, [I realized that] there is a section I can no longer sing, and I have to remain silent [instead]. You sing, and I'll join you later. It is: *Smile at my heroic race....* Where is the heroism of this race? We are

> trying to form a concept of citizenship [based] on national unity and a heroic race. For example, if it were *Smile at my hard-working people. . .*, I would sing it louder than all of you, but it is not. Of the oath *I am Turkish, honest and hard-working,* I like the "honest and hard-working" part, and I shout it loudly. The *I am Turkish* part, I try to understand as *I am from Turkey.*

Hrant's editorial thus challenged the ethnically defined boundaries of the nation, one that let in only the Turks, excluding all others, non-Turks and non-Muslims alike. Such public discussion of ethnic boundaries made the inherent exclusion visible, thereby indirectly undermining the naturalized dominance of the ethnic Turks. The republican leadership did not acknowledge and agree with Hrant's aspiration to include everyone in Turkey within the boundaries of the nation but instead focused on his articulation of the excluded, legally interpreting it is a threat to the (ethnic) unity of the republic. Hrant was eventually acquitted from this first charge.

This lawsuit was followed by another in 2004. This time, Hrant had written an editorial in *Agos* criticizing the Diaspora Armenians, arguing that it was time for them to rid themselves of their inherent enmity against all Turks.[66] He based his argument on a Turkish nationalist phrase first uttered by Mustafa Kemal (Atatürk) during his 1927 "Speech" to the Turkish youth, where he argued that the republic was to face many internal and external threats that the Turkish youth would fight, finding the necessary power to do so "with the noble blood they as Turks had in their veins."[67] Addressing the Armenian Diaspora instead, Hrant stated that their blood had been poisoned with their hatred of the Turks and recommended that the Armenian Diaspora "replace such poisoned blood, with fresh (constructive) blood associated with the Armenian republic." He was basically asking the Diaspora Armenians to cease their hatred of the Turks and commence to pour fresh blood and resources into the Armenian republic. Hence Hrant's statement did not criticize the Turks, and a panel of legal experts assigned by the court actually attested that this was indeed the case. Nevertheless, the Turkish court tried him and sentenced him to six months in prison, a sentence that was then suspended because Dink did not have a criminal record.[68] It was this legal injustice that initially led liberals within Turkey and other like-minded people outside the country to start mobilizing in support of Hrant.

Also in 2004, Hrant published an editorial on the first republican female pilot, Sabiha Gökçen, who had also been an adopted daughter of Mustafa Kemal Atatürk. Hrant claimed, based on numerous interviews and documents, that Gökçen was of Armenian descent; her parents having been murdered in 1915, she was subsequently adopted from an orphanage.[69] This indirect reference to Turkey's violent past caused a nationalist outcry. First, the Turkish military issued a strong disclaimer, taking issue with the "stain placed upon one of their own." Then, the offices of the *Agos* newspaper were physically attacked; the ultranationalist National Action Party members arrived in the hundreds, protesting Hrant, shouting at him to leave the country if he did not love it the same way they did.[70] Hrant himself traced the escalation of official state violence against him to this editorial he had written on Gökçen.[71] Increasing numbers of Turkish newspapers started to turn Hrant into a target, in the process closely identifying him with the 1915 massacres against the Armenians on the one hand and with sedition on the other. This is how addressing the violence embedded in Turkey's past slowly turned Hrant into a public target of violence, the violence that had been so often practiced by the republican leadership. In 2006, another lawsuit was filed against Hrant, this time charging him with "denigrating Turkishness," based on an interview in which he referred to the 1915 massacre of Armenians in the Ottoman Empire as genocide.[72]

In addition to indirectly destabilizing the ethnic underbelly of Turkish nationalism and getting legally harassed as a consequence, Hrant also did not hesitate to publicly discuss the official, inherently destructive Turkish state policy against the non-Muslim minorities. He argued that the policy consisted of the systemic exercise of prejudice and discrimination against all non-Muslims with the intent to eliminate their existence in Turkey.[73] As an Armenian who had chosen in spite of all adversity to remain on his ancestral lands, Hrant first drew attention to the origins of such a stand, stating that the Armenian issue only became a taboo after the 1920s when the CUP cadres, namely, the perpetrators, started to penetrate into the republic.[74] He then continued:

> It is claimed [by the Turkish state] that the Armenian issue was closed at [the] Lausanne [Treaty in 1923]. No, the Armenian issue did not start in 1915 and it did not end with the Republic.... According to the Lausanne records, 300,000 Armenians transitioned to the Turkish Republic; 170,000 in Anatolia and 130,000 in İstanbul. Yet the current population of Armenians in Turkey is between 50,000 and 60,000. If the Armenian issue was terminated at Lausanne, why didn't the number of Armenians in Turkey reach, [as it would have with natural population increase], 1.5 million in the ensuing eighty years?... Their population was instead reduced... because the fundamental state policy was the reduction of minorities. Read the ninth report of the RPP to see what had been planned to reduce the number of minorities during the single-party period [from 1923 to 1950].... [Minorities experienced] many offenses like the 1942 wealth tax and the 6–7 September incidents in 1955. Then, the 1970s witnessed the ASALA events. Many [Armenian] migrations [out of Turkey] occurred [as a consequence].

> The [state] policy to reduce the minorities has continued to this day. [State] policies targeting minority foundations and schools ensured that minorities did not expand, did not develop. Armenian place names were changed; it was not only the people who left, their buildings were also destroyed. Many Armenian schools and churches were torn down, transformed into other things, [becoming] sports complexes, mosques, state buildings. They were distributed among the [Turkish Muslim] populace. No trace remained of anything. The [official] operation to erase the traces [of the Armenian presence] continued throughout republican history.

Thus, in addition to articulating a chronology of collective violence continuing unfettered from the empire to the republic, Hrant also publicly declared in no uncertain terms that there was an official, discriminatory Turkish state policy explicitly targeting the non-Muslims. Many scholars and intellectuals in Turkey always knew informally that this was indeed the case, but few had talked about it in public. And they had started to talk about it during the same time Hrant did, but those few were ethnic Turks, inherently protected by the state; Dink was not.

Finally, in addition to exposing Turkish official exclusion and discrimination, Hrant also discussed what such an official stand had translated to in practice. All the wealth, goods, and properties the Armenians had left behind were still unaccounted for. The Turkish state had silenced and repressed such discussions that would have ultimately incriminated the state, destabilizing its hegemony. He specifically noted in the same interview:

> When the Armenians left Turkey, they did not carry their wealth and properties on their backs. Yet the new recently published [official] claim states that "the government back then was so well-intentioned that it protected everything the Armenians had left behind, establishing special commissions to record all their wealth. Once the Armenians returned from the deportation, their propeties were going to be given back to them; there are records [to this effect]." Please, let them... say "Here are the documents distributing the Armenian properties back to them. They got everything back, they were paid." What happened to the civilization, to the wealth generated by a society that was thousands of years old; who acquired all these?... This is one of the fundamental problems of Turkey. Indeed, the issue of Armenian properties is the scariest, most horrid issue of Turkey. The properties of all Armenians who did not return within the specified period went to the [Turkish state] treasury. Laws were promulgated and executed [to that effect] so Turkey took legal precaution.... [If an official investigation into

> abandoned Armenian properties were to be undertaken], incredible injustices would be revealed. If one were to ask "how were the properties left behind by the Armenians distributed; who got what?" this would create an immense shock... because a [false] history forcibly taught to the country would collapse. The idea that would subsequently spread into society would be that if this history was wrongfully told, so could other things [be likewise wrong]. A most significant transformation would ensue.

Hrant thought that holding the state accountable for its past violence would liberate the Turkish state and society, furthering democratization. At the same time, however, such accountability would have also destabilized the status quo, further undermining the hegemony of the republican leadership. Hrant was certain that the relative liberalization in Turkey with the application of EU legal norms would enable him to bring these issues to the public sphere. Yet radical segments within the state and military thought and decided otherwise, violently destroying him instead.

On Counterviolence Initiatives

After the first half of the decade of the 2000s, the relative liberalization enabled the Turkish public sphere to become a forum for the investigation of past collective violence in general and the unaccounted assassinations in particular. Such civilian-driven initiatives deciphering past violence had four significant turning points in 1996, 2005, 2007, and 2008. All these years were marked by public scandals that documented the complicity of the state, its governments, and the military in secretly engaging in paramilitary violence with the intent to destabilize society, thereby sustaining and legitimizing the status quo.

Prior to 1996, the most significant public media coverage articulating the close connection of the Turkish state with illegal activities centered on the activities of an ultranationalist assassin, Mehmet Ali Ağca. He became internationally renowned through his unsuccessful assassination attempt on the pope in 1981, only to be caught and imprisoned in Italy. While serving his nineteen-year sentence, however, Ağca declared that he had initially escaped from the Turkish prison with the aid of a former Turkish minister, also providing the name of a liberal Turkish journalist who had aided him. Ağca had done so, he claimed, because he was a mercenary.[75] A decade later, in 1996, while Turkey was politically unstable, transitioning from one coalition government to another, the incoming prime minister publicly accused the outgoing one of being unable to account for significant funds. The ensuing extensive media discussion revealed that the point of contention pertained to the "secret funds" the Turkish state had for allocating monies to its extralegal activities. Identical to the former CUP use of secret funds, this practice too had evidently continued unchanged in the transition from the empire to the republic. The documentation of where the monies went and how they were employed emerged through the ensuing 1996 Susurluk scandal: a car crash occurring at a location in Turkey called Susurluk revealed that among the crash victims were the İstanbul deputy chief of police, a deputy of the national assembly, and a contract killer on Interpol's red list, all on their way to see the interior minister.[76] The scandal publicly demonstrated, for the first time, the existing connections among the state, the military, and organized crime. Especially noteworthy among this odd assortment of characters was the contract killer, a member of the secret paramilitary bands established through the cooperation of the military and the state.

It is important to note that such bands increased in number and were turned into independent units in the aftermath of the 1980 military coup. Coup leader, general chief of staff, and later president Kenan Evren had actively instigated the establishment of such bands with the intent to take revenge against the Armenian ASALA and JCOAG terrorists who were assassinating Turkish diplomats with impunity. Those recruited into the bands were, just like the SO bands before them, imprisoned ultranationalist militants. The state literally aided them in their escapes from prison, supplied them with new identities, cash, and arms, and then sent them abroad to engage in covert action. Contemporaneous memoirs of an ultranationalist militant confirmed this connection, as the writer recounted:[77]

> I think it was 1989 when I was in prison and... a journal... had published [an article] about the infighting that had started at the MİT [Milli İstihbarat Teşkilatı, Turkish National Intelligence Agency] when an undercover operation was conducted against the Armenian terrorist organization ASALA; [the ultranationalist militant] Abdullah Çatlı [who died in the Susurluk car crash] and his friends had undertaken these operations. I too had read these, but did not know the inside story.... I asked Çatlı years later, receiving the response that "they wanted to sacrifice us to the game they had going on among them [at MİT]." When I asked about what conditions had been stipulated for carrying out the operations, he did not want to respond, saying [instead] "forget it, everything remains in the past." Not a single word came out of his mouth pertaining to what they had undertaken.

These illegal bands carried out their initial operations in France and Lebanon, bombing Armenian sites and murdering some of the terrorists. They then started to investigate the possible Armenian-PKK connections on the one hand

and drug trafficking through which such groups financed their operations on the other. In the east of Turkey, the PKK, Turkish security forces, and the military had all eventually become involved in drug trafficking to raise funds for their activities. It was alleged that the turf war among these four groups over the drug trade had enabled the scandal to become public: especially the security forces that had been shortchanged at this juncture did not cover up the car crash but made it public to settle their score with the other three groups. Yet the only additional casualty was the prime minister, who resigned after the scandal; the only surviving victim, who was the deputy of the national assembly, was released without receiving a sentence. During the trials, it became evident that the armed band had also been involved in many extrajudicial murders, including the assassinations of seven Kurdish businessmen with alleged PKK connections.[78] For the first time, the urban populace took civic action: they protested the scandal by turning off all the lights in their dwellings for "one minute of darkness" they had all been plunged into.

About a decade later, in 2005, the Susurluk Scandal was followed by the 'Şemdinli Incident, this time revealing the intimate connection between the Turkish military and illegal operations. In the southeastern town of Şemdinli in Hakkari, a former PKK member's bookstore was bombed, causing one death. The local populace identified and chased the car, allegedly containing the three assailants. Not only did the assailants belong to the military, but their car was also registered to the local gendarmerie commander.[79] The three assailants were initially tried and sentenced at civilian courts. Yet the military courts then took over the case, claiming that the military identities of the assailants necessitated such a move. Subsequently, all three assailants were freed by the military court. Hence, not only were the perpetrators punished, but to add insult to injury, the civilian judges and prosecutors initially trying the case bore the brunt of the violence, losing their jobs on the allegation that they had "destroyed the honor of their occupation as state officials."

Merely two years later, in 2007, the Diary Scandal broke when the private diaries of the commander of the Turkish naval forces were published in a journal. The diaries recorded in minute detail the significant role of the military top command in instigating state-assisted violence with the intent to carry out a military coup. It appeared that some top-ranking generals within the military had been so incensed by the JDP's electoral victory that not only had the highest-ranking military commanders of the Turkish air, ground, and naval forces and of the gendarmerie planned three unsuccessful coup attempts, but they had done so against the objections of the Turkish general chief of staff.[80] Their discussions of the coup attempts revealed the many extrajudicial activities the Turkish military engaged in to destabilize the country and legitimate their subsequent military intervention. Such activities included engaging in psychological warfare through assassinations to aggravate public opinion against the JDP, talking to prominent journalists to instigate their taking public action in the media against certain prominent liberals and democrats, and, finally, getting the military-controlled NGOs to stage mass demonstrations against the JDP. The following passage reveals, through the admiral's own words, the degree of Turkish military involvement in politics:

> [While discussing the first coup attempt] . . . we decided to form an action plan on our own . . . upon the suggestion of the commander of the gendarmerie forces. We were first going to take control of the media, so I was going to invite M.Ö. for that purpose. [Then] . . . [we would] keep in contact with the university presidents, arranging students to engage in demonstrations . . . act in unison with the unions. . . . get posters hung in the streets . . . contact [civilian] associations, inciting them against the [JDP] government. We were going to do all of this across the country. . . . [While discussing the second coup attempt], gathered at the headquarters of the gendarmerie, the gendarmerie commander had shared with the group the preparations I had been [previously] shown on Tuesday, having them [also] listen to a number of voice recordings belonging to some high-ranking government officials. Most of these were JDP advisers . . . sharing their ideas on how they planned to handle the Cyprus problem. At the end of the briefing, the commander of the air forces and the commander of the gendarmerie started pressing for [undertaking] a coup on March 10. . . . The gendarmerie commander's aim is to become the commander of the land forces. . . . The current commander of the land forces told me that the gendarmerie commander was digging a pit [within which to bury] the general chief of staff. I thought the gendarmerie commander was acting somewhat unfairly and too ambitiously. . . . [While discussing the third coup attempt] we gathered at my house at 2:00 p.m. with the commanders of the air forces, the navy, the army, and the gendarmerie. . . . The second topic again turned out to be the same one, that "we should topple these fellows." The gendarmerie commander and the air guy are pressing too much for this. The gendarmerie commander cannot get [the coup idea] out of his head, repeating the same thing every two words. So does the air guy. If we don't want to give Cyprus away, the latest time [for a coup] is 9 April 2004. Whatever we must do, we should do before that.

Given that these diaries had been written in 2004 and became public in 2007, many scholars then looked back and analyzed the public events of the preceding three years, in the process identifying the many instances of violence committed by the Turkish military. Public trials prosecuting these commanders were also slow, as the military once again wanted to try them in its own courts.

A year later, assassination attempts directed at the Council of State by an allegedly ultrareligious militant on the one hand and against a nationalist conservative newspaper on the other, undertaken with the intent to destabilize Turkey, were carefully investigated. The investigations into these acts of violence produced the 2008 Ergenekon trial. The deep-rooted, secret, and illegal paramilitary activities that had been aided and abetted by the radical secularist segments within the Turkish state and the military with the intent to topple the democratically elected JDP were finally investigated by public prosecutors who had the full support of the government and the military.[81] The inherent, deep-rooted, violent streak of exclusionary nationalism embedded within the Turkish state and military thus started to surface.[82]

It is apt to conclude this section by returning to the collective violence committed against Hrant Dink. During the still ongoing trials attempting to identify the command structure that is deeply embedded within the top echelons of the Turkish state and the military, Hrant's lawyer articulated the complicity of the Turkish state, government, and military in Hrant Dink's assassination:[83]

> By the end of 2005 [two years before Dink was murdered], everyone in the entire town [of Pelitli, where the murderers are from] knew that Dink was going to be killed. Both the police and the gendarmerie knew. The police informant told the security forces that Dink was going to be murdered. Eleven months prior to the murder, the intelligence director of the Trabzon police wrote to the İstanbul police chief that the murderer was going to kill Dink. The murderer stated that the police informant had provided him with the money and the arms. "A group within the security directed us. The state used us. We did this for the state upon the promise that we would be protected," [the murderer said]. All those who were tried pointed their fingers at the state.... [Yet] at the trial, permission was granted [by the state] to only investigate three state officials, one in the security forces and two in the gendarmerie. It is [also] unclear as to whether [even] lawsuits will be [eventually] filed against them. The security director who wrote stating that the murder was going to be committed has been removed from his position. Clues are being hidden from the public prosecutors. This is a very serious crime.... Due to the government's determination, the actual assassins and their immediate circle were caught, but the real perpetrators [within the state and the military issuing them the command] have still not surfaced.

Such unaccounted collective violence has not only undermined the trust of the populace in their state and government but also destroyed the moral fabric of society. Given such explicit documentation of official involvement in past collective violence, why do the Turkish state and society not extend this pattern to understand and acknowledge the collective violence committed against the Armenians in the past? It is in this context that the ASALA and JCOAG assassinations of Turkish diplomats become significant in that these events were officially employed to legitimate past violence against the Armenians.

Legitimating Event: The ASALA and JCOAG Assassinations of Turkish Diplomats, 1974–85

The ASALA and JCOAG murders were undertaken with the intent to bring the Armenian issue and especially the Armenian Genocide to the attention of the world community. What the perpetrators did not fully consider was the adverse impact of such violent attacks on Turkish state and society, one that did not lead to acknowledgment but instead staunch denial. And this adverse reaction was actualized as follows: First, the republican leadership immediately used these assassinations as proof of the constant external threat they had alleged Turkey was under, a threat that necessitated and legitimated its continued presence in the citizens' lives. Thus, enabling the leadership to prioritize national security and with it increased military spending, the assassinations indirectly curtailed the citizens' political and civic rights and liberties. Another undesirable impact was the establishment of secret paramilitary bands to seek vengeance, thereby aiding the development of a "deep state" acting with impunity beyond the reach of law. These assassinations also indirectly legitimated the continued prejudice, discrimination, and repression of the non-Muslims of Turkey in general and the Armenians in particular. Given that the Turkish diplomatic community was so badly hit by the assassinations, the most significant long-term consequence was the production of an entire cohort of Turkish diplomats whose friends had been violently murdered, leading them to take an anti-Armenian stand, strongly opposing any engagement in bettering Turkish-Armenian relations for decades to come.

Contemporary memoirs reveal that the Turkish authorities were aware of the increased activities among militant Armenian groups as early as 1967. One Turkish diplomat noted that during his time in Ankara in 1967–68, the reports sent by the Turkish ambassador in Lebanon stated that the Armenians were making extensive preparations to attack Turkey. Yet the diplomat dismissed such a possibility, claiming the Armenian issue was eventually going to disappear.[84] Such a stand was based exclusively on the diplomat's perception regarding the public disappearance of the Armenian issue within Turkey. Yet it did not take into account what transpired outside of Turkey, overlooking the fact that the lack of official acknowledgment would lead memories of past violence and injustice to be passed down through generations of Armenian survivors, preventing them from grieving their trauma and loss on the one hand and leading them to feel escalated anger and frustration on the other.[85]

The initial attacks of the Armenian groups against the Turkish state commenced abroad, in the United States, in 1972; Armenian Diaspora members became increasingly confrontational in their protests against the Turkish foreign offices.[86] Physical violence commenced in January 1973 when the Turkish consul general and the consul in Los Angeles were murdered by an elderly Armenian who intended to draw attention to the Armenian Genocide through his violence.[87] The ensuing Turkish diplomatic correspondence was just as telling. The victims were immediately considered martyrs, and the act was immediately interpreted as yet another indication of the work of those intending to harm the Turkish state and nation. Ensuing correspondence among civilian Armenians, the Armenian patriarchs, and responses of the diplomatic community declared the violence a tragedy, also noting that the Armenian tragedy in the past had emerged due to the discord sown between the Turks and Armenians by the Great Powers. In his memoirs, one Turkish diplomat mourned the loss of the murdered general consul, remembering how he had met the victim in the past.[88] The ensuing trial necessitated the US public prosecutor to research the history of the Armenian issue; he contacted the Turkish consulate for reference material depicting the Turkish perspective. Yet all that the Turkish Foreign Ministry could find was a single brochure, revealing that the Turkish state had indeed considered the Armenian issue closed for all intents and purposes.[89] At the US court, the public defendant continually tried to bring up the matter of past injustices, yet the public prosecutor focused only on the present, finding the defendant guilty of first-degree murder.

Why had such violent action emerged at this particular juncture? The 1970s marked the transition into old age of those Armenians who had been eyewitnesses and surviviors of the massacres committed against them and their families. The Ottoman and subsequent Turkish denial of the collective violence prevented them from grieving the immense trauma they had suffered, leaving their wounds open, keeping their emotions trapped in the past, and passing their anger and frustration onto the next generation, thereby committing the latter to live with the nightmare of unacknowledged pain and suffering as well. This perhaps explains the continuation of such violence for a decade. Of course, the Armenians who resorted to such violence overlooked the fact that violence begets violence, never leading to a peaceful end result. By taking justice into their own hands and by murdering innocent Turkish officials whose only fault was to be citizens and representatives of the Turkish state, they further polarized and alienated a whole generation of Turks in general and the Turkish Foreign Ministry officials in particular.

The detailed analysis undertaken by one retired Turkish diplomat of his "martyred" colleagues enables the chronicling of the Armenian terrorist violence in detail.[90]

The Year 1975

The preceding 1973 violence has long been considered the act of an individual Armenian with no known connection to any particular Armenian radical groups.[91] Therefore, the violence that occurred from 1975 to 1985 is often regarded as the decade of radical Armenian violence, where the violence was executed by two radical Armenian groups, the Armenian Secret Army for the Liberation of Armenia and the Justice Commandos of the Armenian Genocide.[92] The first assassination of a high-level Turkish diplomat occurred in the fall of 1975: Turkey's Austrian ambassador was murdered in Vienna by three assailants who raided the embassy with automatic weapons.[93] In spite of the Armenian Liberation Organization assuming responsibility for the assassination, the Turkish state and media suspected the Greek state, given that the murder occurred right after the 1974 Cyprus invasion. This violence was followed by another incident only two days later: Turkey's French ambassador and his driver were murdered in Paris by automatic weapon fire. This time, both ASALA and JCOAG claimed responsibility, stating their intent was to draw world attention to the condition of the Armenians.[94] Turks living in France protested the violence, while the Turkish diplomats compared the way the two assinations were officially handled by Austria and France, noting the much lower diplomatic significance given to the murder by the French. These initial accounts of the first systemic violence by Armenian terrorists provide several insights. First, it was unclear which group assumed responsibility, since both ASALA and JCOAG took credit. Second, the Turkish state was initially unwilling to attribute the violence to these groups, interpreting it instead as a Greek reaction to the Cyprus invasion, thereby silencing the agency of the Armenians and with it the focus on past events. Third, the Turkish authorities paid extreme attention to the official reaction of different Western European states to these acts, gauging from the funeral ceremonies the level of respect they showed toward the Turkish state.

The ensuing discussions in the Turkish national assembly revealed that under the shadow of the Cold War, the Turkish state and government still concentrated on locating the assailants not among the Armenians but instead among Turkish leftists and communists.[95] The Turkish media were nationalist in their reaction; rather than looking into what had happened and why, they immediately identified with the victims and focused not on the assailants but instead on the muted French reaction, which, they argued, demonstrated once again Western hypocrisy and duplicity when confronted by Muslim deaths. The foundations of the Turkish official narrative on the Armenian issue emerged slowly thereafter, strongly influenced by the Turkish state rhetoric. Many of those who personally knew these two ambassadors and attended their funerals later attained important state positions such as that of the general chief of staff, ambassadors, and foreign minister.[96] As a consequence, an entire generation of Turkish state authorities was negatively impacted by this contemporary violence. One retired diplomat recounted in his memoirs the situation at the Turkish embassy in Austria when he arrived there as an embassy official:[97]

> The embassy was in a state of total shock. The bullets on the wall and the broken glass were still in evidence... the smell of gunpowder persisted.... Still the [current] ambassador... was most imperturbable, and kept his cool a couple of years later—when ambassador to the Vatican, he was able to withstand a similar Armenian attack.... After these two tragedies, an order came [from Ankara] to report all suspicious activities to the ministry.... [We were all so much on edge] that once when the wireless operator... took a fall making a lot of noise in the process, we were all shocked, certain that bombs had gone off.... The arriving [Austrian] police initially treated him as a terrorist.

The morale within the Turkish diplomatic corps plummeted as everyone started to live their lives in a state of constant anxiety. The last violence of 1975 occurred on 18 December as the Turkish embassy in Beirut was attacked with rockets and one person killed, with ASALA claiming responsibility.

At this juncture, the memoirs of the Armenian terrorist Monte Melkonian, who carried out many of these attacks, provide additional confirmation of the violence. Melkonian noted:[98]

> ASALA carried out... the four bombings... against the Turkish diplomatic corps and private interests in Beirut.... Then, [the Dashnak] party's bureau secretly set up a rival assassination squad. And so it came to pass that in October 1975—two and a half months after the Secret Army's first operation—the JCOAG gunned down the Turkish ambassador in Vienna. A couple of months later, on 16 February 1976, Hagop Darakjian shot and killed with a silenced pistol Oktar Cirit, the first secretary at the Turkish embassy in Beirut. With this, ASALA and JCOAG began in earnest their competition to chalk up the most number of dead diplomats. Soon, the JCOAG mounted assassination and

> bombing operations in Paris, Vatican City, and Madrid, claiming the lives of two more Turkish ambassadors, two family members, and two chauffeurs.... Hagopian, however, turned his rival's successes to the advantage of ASALA: as soon as he got wind of a JCOAG attack, he would phone the press agencies to claim credit for it in the name of ASALA.

Melkonian's account reveals the origins of the initial ambiguity over the real assailants where both groups claimed responsibility. Yet the Turkish state was much more inclined view ASALA as the main assailant because its leftist connections extending beyond the Armenian cause to destroy all sources of imperialism, a stand that legitimated its violence not only against the Turks because of what they had committed in their own past but also against other Western powers, including the United States. ASALA's leftist connections also enabled the Turkish state and government to take on and destroy the Turkish leftists. To this day, the Turkish state and society constantly refer to all these attacks as ASALA attacks, thereby minimizing the significant role in the violence played by the JCOAG.

Yet what was the nature of the relationship between ASALA and JCOAG on the one hand and Armenian organizations on the other? An ASALA statement sent to an Armenian Diaspora newspaper in the United States attempted to clarify its connection to the leadership of the Armenian Revolutionary Federation (ARF), previously known as the Dashnak Party.[99] ASALA and JCOAG were militant organizations that broke off from the Dashnak. ASALA was especially upset that the ARF attempted to take credit for these acts of violence, publishing articles condemning the ARF stand.[100] There was still confusion within the Armenian Diaspora over who was actually undertaking these attacks. One thing was clear, however: they all had Dashnak connections, in the past or at present. This in turn demonstrates the destructive nationalism inherent in the ARF, spewing hatred toward the Turkish state and the Turks, a stand that evidently led some radical segments to splinter, undertaking such wanton acts of violence. Later, in 1982, there were indications that ASALA and JCOAG collaborted on some acts of violence.[101] Already by 1980, articles began to appear in the Diaspora newspapers condemning the violence on two grounds: it had started to transform the image of Armenians "from rug merchants to terrorists," and it aroused public sympathy for the Turks by harming innocent people who bore no personal responsibility for the genocide.[102] Still, in 1982, the prelacy annual assembly failed to endorse a statement condemning terrorism due to the presence of ARF members.[103] Such violence finally ceased in 1986.[104]

The Year 1976

The previously mentioned assassination of Turkey's first secretary at the Lebanese embassy was the first act of violence committed in 1976.[105] Actually, the person who accosted the fleeing assailant and the one who took the victim to the hospital were both Armenians as well.[106] ASALA once again sent a note taking responsibility, claiming that the first secretary was a secret Turkish agent, sent from Vienna to Beirut after the Austrian ambassador's assassination. Yet a Turkish diplomat refuted this claim, stating that the secretary was sent to Beirut three weeks before the assassination. The investigations into the assassination did not produce any conclusive results. Hence, the perpetrator, in this case Hagop Darakjian, was never held accountable for the murder he committed, thereby ironically repeating the pattern of murders with unknown assailants that had until now been confined to violence committed by secret Ottoman and then Turkish paramilitary bands.

The Year 1977

On 9 June 1977, Turkey's Vatican ambassador was assassinated in Rome.[107] As he was getting out of his car, the ambassador was caught in the crossfire of two assailants in front of the embassy's residence; he was taken to the hospital, where he lost his life. Although the ambassador had been assigned protection by the Turkish state as well as the Italian police, he had refused them both, starting instead to carry a gun himself. Having previously served in Lebanon, he had been perhaps the only Foreign Ministry official who had any knowledge of Armenian revolutionary groups. The Turkish newspapers revealed that the ambassador had received a threat from the Armenians in March 1977 as well. Both the Turkish state and government still refused to acknowledge the Armenian assailants, publicly presenting the assassination as an attack against the Turkish state and nation.[108] Yet the Turkish newspapers identified the murderers as belonging to an Armenian organization. International newspapers discussed the past Turkish violence leading to these attacks, also pointing out that the Turkish state and government suspected the communists or the Maoist Turkish Liberation Army members.[109] The Turkish authorities continued to project the roots of the violence elsewhere, on anyone but the Armenians. When the Italian newspapers wrote a year later declaring the investigation closed due to lack of evidence, which they later rescinded, one Turkish journalist penned an article. After noting how incensed he was at this violence, he targeted the Armenians of Turkey, who had no connection to it:[110]

> Then there are some duties that fall onto our Armenian citizens who live in our homeland in comfort and who are said to be about thirty thousand.... They all have friends, acquaintances among the Armenians who live in other countries. They have to write letters to these, warning them. It should not be forgotten that just like people, the patience of nations also has a limit.

Similar to the CUP mentality that had blamed the violence of a few Armenians on all Armenian subjects of the empire, to then violently punish the latter, this Turkish journalist was also placing the blame on Armenians in Turkey who had nothing to do with the violence. In addition, the article contained a veiled threat against the Turkish Armenians, revealing once again how violence often led to the harassment of unprotected innocents.

The Year 1978

Three assailants opened fire in Madrid on the car of Turkey's ambassador to Spain.[111] The ambassador was not in the car; instead, his wife, his brother-in-law, who was a retired ambassador, and the Spanish driver lost their lives, the first two at the site of the incident and the last at the hospital. JCOAG claimed responsibility. The investigation conducted on the Armenian community in Spain, which consisted of about 100 people, revealed that the assassins must have arrived from the outside—as indicated by their poor Spanish on the phone—and the murders remained unsolved. Even though the Turkish authorities were incensed at such unsolved murders, it should be noted that it is extremely challenging for a state's security forces to solve murders committed by assailants who come from abroad and leave immediately after the violence. Because there often are no local connections, the authorities have difficulty getting any leads toward solving such murders. Once again, in their public statements, none of the Turkish state officials who condemned this abhorrent act directed at the Turkish state and nation mentioned the Armenians.[112] Three other instances of violence that also occurred in 1978, all claimed by ASALA, did not lead to any loss of life.[113]

The Year 1979

This year witnessed an escalation in radical Armenian violence, and the Turkish official rhetoric condemning these acts also became increasingly well articulated.[114] During the fall of 1979, the twenty-seven-year-old son of Turkey's ambassador to the Hague was killed in an armed attack, with the JCOAG claiming responsibility. One Turkish memoir writer and diplomat, who had also delivered the news of his son's death to the ambassador, provided additional details on the murder.[115] The fact that the last two assassinations had murdered not the diplomats but instead members of their families agitated Turkish state and society even more. A program on Dutch television acknowledged the past Armenian massacres but also pointing out that undertaking such violence in return was not right. Once again, the murder remained unsolved.

The then Turkish ambassador to the United States, later increasingly active in spearheading the nationalist anti-Armenian stand in Turkey, wrote a letter to the Foreign Ministry, recommending an official course of action. He suggested that Turkey engage in counteraction through front organizations "that do not bear the insignia of the Turkish state."[116] He also suggested that such a reaction should have both public overt and private covert components. The Special Organization tradition of employing armed bands to execute extrajudicial violence was thus once again suggested, again targeting Armenians. At this juncture, another diplomat also presented a report, attempting to identify Armenian violence through history in a linear continuum.[117] He also stated that at the time, the dominant state view was that foreign intelligence services were behind the assassinations. This assessment concurred with those of many Turkish officials who were certain that the instigation did not start and end with the Armenian assailants but that other states were possibly involved, probably the Soviet Union and perhaps even the United States. It is noteworthy that just as had been the case throughout the history of the Armenian subjects in the empire, the Armenians were once again denied agency for the acts they committed, and the origins of the issue was once again removed from the domestic to the international arena as other powers were blamed for the actions of these Armenian terrorists.

The second violence occurred at the end of the year as Turkey's tourism counselor in Paris was attacked and murdered by an assailant while buying a newspaper across from his office building.[118] The call taking responsibility for the killing stated it was an act of the JCOAG, not the ASALA, thereby revealing the rivalry that had started between the two terrorist groups. It was also at this juncture that the Turkish official stand grew more militant and vengeful, stating that the Turkish state would "not let the spilled blood remain on the ground."[119] Yet, the Turkish state continued to conjecture that there were other states behind the violence. The Turkish media increasingly drew parallels to the violence Turks had been subjected to in the past at the hands of Armenians; they also criticized the French state and government for once again not catching the assailants and not adequately condemning the violence.[120] There were also numerous attacks during the year that did not result in a loss of life, since the Western states and the Turkish government had taken additional security measures.[121] Also significant was the first domestic retaliation in Turkey: the church of the Armenian Apostolic Patriarchate was bombed.

According to the contemporaneous memoirs of a Turkish diplomat, for the first time in 1979, the Turkish state and the Foreign Ministry started to discuss what course of action to take in order to counter the Armenian violence. Their initial debate was over how to classify the violence, whether to approach all current separatist violence against Turkey all at once, thereby uniting the violence of militant Kurds with that of the militant Armenians, or forming separate desks for each. They decided to put the Kurdish issue aside for the time being. On the Armenian issue, three decisions were reached: to prepare a "totally scientific and objective" white book, to establish a Turkish lobby in the United States, and to form Turkish research centers in foreign countries, all funded by the state.[122] As the succeeding years would indicate, however, not everything went according to plan.

The Year 1980

The year commenced with the assassination of the administrative attaché of Turkey's embassy in Athens, Greece.[123] Both the attaché and his fourteen-year-old daughter were killed, his wife and older son were wounded, and only his younger son was uninjured. When the attack occurred, the family had been returning from a seaside trip. The older son chased after the assailant, yet another person came to the latter's aid, and the two escaped in opposite directions by mixing into the crowds. ASALA claimed responsibility. In this case, the memoirs of the perpetrator Monte Melkonian are available, narrating the murders he committed as follows:[124]

> Two weeks had passed since Monte had first arrived in Athens, and he still had not carried out an operation. He walked up to the car, raising his 7.32 mm pistol and shooting the driver and the other passenger in the front seat. He then twisted around to fire into the shapes in the back seat. As he turned from the car to make his escape, a young man pulled himself out from the back seat, holding his gunshot wound, sprinting after his assailant. Bystanders joined in the chase. Dashing across a busy street, Monte . . . shook off his pursuers.

It is evident from Melkonian's account elsewhere that it was sufficient for him that the car carried Turkish diplomatic plates; he did not care who he actually murdered. Indeed, it was only on the following day that the Armenian assassin discovered the identities of his Turkish victims, finding out that he had killed a fourteen-year-old child:

> When Alec later asked Monte why in the world he had shot the boy and the girl in the back seat, his comrade snapped, "I wasn't going to leave

> witnesses to identify me." ... There was never any question in Monte's mind that the girl's father ... was a legitimate target.... When I learned that my brother had pointed a pistol ... and shot dead a fourteen-year-old girl, I could not shake the conviction that it would take a lot for him to ever redeem himself. As time passed, his expressions of regret became less glib. Five years after the shooting, he described it as a counterproductive and indefensible crime, the likes of which should not be repeated, and for the next thirteen years he would attempt to prevent others from committing similarly cruel acts. This would be a gesture of his compensation. But the compensation would never be adequate. When Monte returned to Lebanon from Greece, I noticed that he had lost his smile.

This narration reveals the ever-expanding boundaries of destructive violence: as many innocent victims and children were also sacrificed, the allegedly noble cause employed to justify such violence quickly lost its luster. As in the case of the victim's son, the survivors of such violence quickly became radicalized as well, thereby reproducing and multiplying the possibility of such violence occurring in the future. Once again, because Melkonian arrived from Lebanon to commit the murders and then left immediately afterward, it was impossible for the Greek authorities to capture the assailant.

The reaction of the Turkish state authorities was understandably furious. The Turkish official stand once again did not openly condemn the Armenian terrorists, employing Turkish nationalism instead by posing the violence in terms of protecting the fatherland. Once again, the assailants were referred to as unidentified "foreigners." Yet the Turkish Foreign Ministry started to take more systematic action, requesting that Turkey's NATO allies issue a joint declaration condemning the last murder; Britain, the United States, Germany, Belgium, and Luxembourg did, and NATO eventually did as well. Also condemning the attack was Shnork Kalustian, the Armenian patriarch in Turkey, who expressed the grief the Armenian community in Turkey felt, damning the perpetrators. The patriarch's statement reveals the great pressure the Armenians of Turkey came under as a consequence of such violent acts. The Turkish newspapers instead put the blame squarely on the Greek state.[125] The Greek newspapers responded in kind, reporting that the victim was an officer of the Turkish secret service tracking down Armenians and was therefore number one on the Armenian militants' blacklist. The idea of such a blacklist drew an analogy to Operation Nemesis whereby the Dashnak had assassinated the top CUP perpetrators of the Armenian massacres, but the one scholarly work on the latter states that "these perpetrators are not the heirs of the heroes of Musa Dagh or Sardarabad or Operation Nemesis.... The guilt of the ancestors must not lie forever on the decendants... making the facts known is more important than shedding blood for blood, generation after generation."[126] One Turkish diplomat was duly scandalized that the Greek press investigated not the assailant but the victim. This murder also remained unresolved, infuriating the Turkish state and society even more and escalating the threats made against the assailants.

The second case of violence during this year occurred far away in Sydney, Australia; Turkey's consul general and his security guard policeman were murdered by two assailants on a motorcycle; the two victims were on their way to work in the morning, about to get into their car. The consul died on the spot, and the policeman died later at the hospital.[127] Once again, the JCOAG claimed responsibility, specifically pointing out that ASALA was not involved. Given the 1980 military coup in Turkey, the general chief of staff delivered the official public statement. With this assassination, for the first time after five years, Turkish state and society finally became convinced that this violence was primarily carried out by Armenian militants. All of Turkey's ambassadors in the West started to pressure the countries they served in to get official recognition for the committed violence.[128] Local Armenian archbishops and the patriarch in Turkey started to systematically issue press releases on behalf of their communities, indirectly replicating the symbolic separation of the Armenians from the nations of the states in which they lived. Given the escalating number of such acts of violence with almost no assailants captured and punished, the Turkish media became even more emotional in their coverage. Some still sought other, greater powers and insidious plans behind the violence, while others started to delve into the violence in Turkey's past, yet one where the Turks remerged not as the perpetrators but as the victims not only at present but also in the past.[129] The journalists also increasingly recommended covert action to punish the perpetrators, thereby publicly legitimating extralegal violence.[130] There were continuous attacks during the rest of the year, mostly executed by ASALA, yet none resulted in the loss of lives.[131] Still, there were numerous failed attacks on Turkish diplomats. The attack on the Turkish ambassador to Switzerland was noteworthy because for the first time in five years, the assailant was caught.[132] Some within the Armenian Diaspora mobilized, collecting money for the assailant's defense, conducting a media campaign on his behalf, and writing to authorities.[133] The trial took place two years later, with the court finding him guilty only of being an accomplice in the plot to assassinate the Turkish ambassador.[134] Such Armenian complicity further increased the Turkish state and society's identification of the perpetrators with the entire Armenian Diaspora.

The year 1980 was also significant in the development of the Turkish state strategy against the Armenian militant violence. In his memoirs, one Turkish diplomat who closely participated in this endeavor described what transpired in detail. A month after the September 1980 military coup, the diplomat met with a general in relation to the collection of existing archival documentation on the past collective violence committed against the Armenians, including those in the American, British, and French archives as well as published books and documentation in the Ottoman archives. The last were all transliterated by retired diplomats who knew the script. All the archival material covering the period between the Armenian rebellions (1895–96) and the end of World War I (1918) was gathered in Ankara, the republican capital. This sole focus on past Armenian seditious activity rather than researching the full range of Armenians as social actors revealed the inherent bias of the official research project. In addition, only official documents were collected, leaving out other significant sources like memoirs, oral histories, and eyewitness accounts and thereby indirectly reproducing the inherent bias. Once the transitional government was formed after the 1980, the next step of this official project was to establish the Internal Security Coordination Council, a committee that brought together all the relevant officials and their organizations but failed to generate significant results.[135]

The Year 1981

The year commenced with the assassinations of Turkish officials in France.[136] Three Turkish officials (two counselors of labor and religious affairs at the Turkish embassy in Paris and one bank representative) were attacked by two assailants while getting into their car in front of the labor attaché's office. One was killed on the spot, and another died at the hospital; the third was not wounded. ASALA claimed responsibility just as the Turkish state delivered a protest note to France for not properly protecting the Turkish diplomats. One memoir writer who was a diplomat recounted that the military generals ruling Turkey at the time wanted to cease all relations with France, yet he convinced them to instead start a media campaign publicizing the Turkish sentiments.[137] This time, the United States, NATO, the European Council, the British government, Germany, and Austria all condemned the murders, revealing a shift in the stand of these Western states toward the Turkish state and away from the Armenian cause. Turkey delivered an official note of protest to France, and the Turkish ambassador in France held talks with the French authorities criticizing their stand.[138]

At this point, relations between France and Turkey reached their most critical point as the French ambassador in Turkey had to go to France to receive instructions. In Turkey, for the first time, about 3,000 Turkish women silently marched to the French embassy in Ankara with signs that read, "Is this Armenian terrorism or French terrorism?" "Why do the French protect the murderers?" and laid a black wreath on the embassy door in protest. It was also at this juncture that the French government sent a television crew to Turkey to make a film reflecting the Turkish sentiments. At the same time, the Turkish state began to work on a television series "to explain and teach the Turkish populace about the true character of the Armenian problem."[139] A seven-episode television series was created under the leadership of a retired ambassador. Turkish state officials also started to recruit French citizens and mobilize the Turkish Diaspora to promote the official Turkish stand in France. Hence, both the media and the Turkish Diaspora started to mobilize around this issue at this juncture.

During the second attack that year, the secretary of the Turkish consul general in Geneva, Switzerland, lost his life; he was shot by an assailant as he left his office after work.[140] ASALA claimed responsibility, and for the first time, the assailant was arrested after the attack with a gun and a bomb, subsequently receiving a fifteen-year prison sentence. At the secretary's funeral, the deputy foreign minister mentioned the Armenian assailant and then immediately added that the Armenians had subverted historical reality, thereby acknowledging the past but only with the intent to refute it. He then added that "the Turks had never committed any murders against innocent people."

In the third attack that year, four Armenian assailants occupied the premises that housed the Turkish consulate general and the cultural attaché in Paris, taking fifty-six people hostage, killing the security guard who attempted to prevent attack, and wounding the consul general. One wounded assailant was also taken to the hospital.[141] ASALA members who had carried out the attack demanded the release of many prisoners from Turkish jails.[142] The Turkish ambassador noted that his government did not recognize the terrorist group, which claimed to be an Armenian organization, and had no intention to negotiate. Yet ASALA's claims demonstrated the attention with which the Armenian militants followed the incidents in Turkey; their willingness to also speak on behalf of the Kurdish prisoners was duly noted by the Turkish officials.

During the ensuing trials, it emerged that all four assailants, born in Beirut, were young, around twenty-two years of age.[143] Eash was given a seven-year prison sentence. Among them, one assassin hanged himself in jail halfway through his sentence. Memoirs of an Armenian assassin provide additional information on how these four Lebanese Armenian militants had been trained:[144]

> [ASALA leader] Hagopian soon assigned [Monte Melkonian] the task of training four volunteers for a spectacular "armed propaganda" mission in a European capital. The operation would go by the code name Van, an ancient citadel that lay in ruins in Turkey. Calculating that the Van operation would "strengthen the progressive tendencies inside ASALA," Monte... focused on the task at hand with grim determination. Throughout August and September, [the four] trained at a new camp they had set up at Tellet el-Wardeh, the Hill of Roses, on the coast of southern Lebanon.... The four recruits had already received

> considerable commando training by late summer, when Monte accelerated the training to Olympic pace: running, calisthenics, group maneuvers, karate, pistols, special weapons, and explosives. On September 24, 1981, the training paid off. They entered the foyer of the Turkish consulate... held the grenades over their heads, and proceeded to take over the consulate, room by room.

The celebratory manner in which Melkonian narrated the violence demonstrates the lack of empathy toward those in the consulate. Because the assailants ended up receiving relatively short prison sentences, this court verdict once again led to widespread resentment in Turkey toward France. The Turkish officials' criticisms of the French media for their pro-Armenian coverage continued as well. One Turkish diplomat stated that this raid reminded him of the 1896 Ottoman Bank Raid, thereby connecting past and present Armenian violence.[145] In Turkey, the Armenian patriarch once again expressed his sadness, also organizing mass for the police officer at the Armenian church in İstanbul.

At this juncture, the Turkish official narrative on what had happened in 1915 emerged for the first time in its entirety. The interior minister fully delegitimated the collective violence committed against the Armenians in the past as follows:

> In 1915, the Armenians had been provoked by foreign forces set on tearing Turkey apart. Because of [such] outside instigation in 1915 at our eastern front, some of our Armenian citizens had been led to create terror and savagery on others, and still others had been encouraged to collaborate with the enemy. The roads behind the front had been rendered insecure, and the provisioning of the army was paralyzed. The government of the time was forced to make the rear of the war front more secure and prevent the terror created by one group, taking [the necessary] precautions. Those who want to intentionally subvert this historical reality to use it for their alleged and imagined aims are greatly mistaken and negligent.

Such a narrative accepted, without any changes, the official CUP stand, thereby demonstrating how the emerging Turkish official narrative reproduced the former CUP one. The Turkish state also increasingly mobilized its official historians to travel abroad, promoting the Turkish official explanation of past violence.[146] There was pressure put on the Lebanese ambassador to contain the Armenian militant activities but to no avail.[147] This exchange points to the additional power Turkey had as a state in negotiating with the various other states; the Armenian Diaspora had to instead argue on the basis of moral conscience and ethical principles that often got waylaid when the real interests of particular states trumped them. During the rest of the year, there were once again unsuccessful attacks against Turkish diplomats.[148] Also during this year, the secret paramilitary armed bands established after the 1980 military coup in Turkey with the intent to take revenge from the Armenians arrived in France, bombing local Armenian centers and churches, thereby demonstrating once again the futile and misguided nature of such violence.[149] The memoir of an Armenian assailant reveals that the Armenian bands were initially misled by these bombings, blaming each other.[150]

The year concluded with an attack on the second secretary in Turkey's Rome embassy, who survived with minor wounds.[151] The secretary, who later served as a deputy in the national assembly and then as a minister, had been walking on the street when he was attacked; he returned fire, thereby escaping death. The memoir of the Armenian perpetrator who carried out the attack described what transpired:[152]

> [The assailant crossed] the street, approaching the embassy staff car.... The Turkish embassy second secretary Gökberk Ergenikon [*sic*] [who was] at the wheel of his car noticed him approaching. The Turk started rolling up his window, going for his 9 mm pistol. Monte pulled his 7 mm from his jacket and pointed the silencer through a diminishing three- to four-inch opening in the window. Ergenikon fired a shot, hitting Monte in the left forearm, and knocking [Monte's] first shot off target. As the window closed, Monte squeezed off several more shots, but the 7 mm slugs did not pierce the bulletproof glass. He knew he had only grazed his target with his first shot, but it was no use to try to finish the job. The failed assassin buried the hand of his bleeding arm deep in his jacket pocket, sprinting from the scene.

Interestingly, the assailant was caught by the police, but the victim failed to identify him in a lineup, thereby leading to his release. It is significant to note that the assailant's forged passport had been provided by the Palestinian terrorist Abu Nidal. The memoirs of a Turkish diplomat confirmed the same identification procedure, noting that the victim had hesitated between the last two persons at the lineup, leading to the perpetrator's release.[153]

During this year, militant Armenian attacks against particular sites spread to the United States, and some of the violence was committed against rich Armenians with the intent to raise money for the revolutionary groups, thereby repeating once again the earlier Dashnak pattern employed during the Ottoman period. Yet it was evident that groups in the United States had also started to engage in violence on their own, independent from their Lebanese counterparts.[154] Meanwhile, attacks outside the United States continued without any loss of life.[155]

The Turkish authorities continued to organize around the Armenian issue, developing their project in the United States with two specific aims: forming a Turkish lobby and establishing Turkish research centers to promote the Turkish official stand on the Armenian issue. The memoirs of a Turkish diplomat also noted the necessity of writing "a scientific work on the Armenian problem," explaining the need for this as follows: [156]

> Even though many [works on the Armenian issue] have been written since then, at that time, no one in Turkey had any substantive knowledge on the Armenian problem. [This was the case] because the topic had not been discussed or studied either at schools or even at universities. This may appear unbelievable, but I personally met some Turkish academics who believed in the truth of the imaginary Armenian claims.

Indeed, the diplomat's focus on this lack eventually led him to write the definitive work illustrating the official Turkish stand on the Armenian problem.[157] Yet, he also engaged in additional activities during the year, briefing the Turkish president on the Armenian issue, getting approval to formulate a single committee overseeing the activities relating to the issue, and preparing a brochure on the "Armenian Problem." In the brochure, explicitly prepared for Turkish state officials, the diplomat made two significant corrections to the official narrative. He stated that the deportations of Armenians had indeed taken place, and that crimes had indeed been committed during the process. Hence, the official narrative of denial started to be increasingly fine-tuned. Yet, as in all nationalist narratives, past incidents were selected in a manner that silenced the aspects of the past that did not bolstering the official narrative, highlighting instead only the aspects that did.[158] In addition to penning these works, the diplomat also wanted to mobilize and recruit local Turkish academics to the cause, thereby germinating the origins of the idea of "official" historians promoting the Turkish narrative. He explained what transpired at the meeting as follows:[159]

> We wanted to pass on the task of writing a white book to those who truly owned this topic, namely, the Turkish academic scholars and historians. We also had a hard time finding people to send to the programs organized overseas at various television and radio stations where the Turks were invited as well. It might have been beneficial to send people who did not have official state appointments, ones who were preferably academics. The things uttered by those who had official positions were considered a repetition of the [official Turkish] state policy. With these purposes in mind, we wrote letters to the Ankara, İstanbul, Hacettepe, and Boğaziçi universities, inviting them to send representatives to a

> meeting at our ministry.... In response, it [emerged] that 31 scholars would be attending.... We awaited the opportunity to conduct such a meeting with great pleasure. Yet only 15 scholars showed up. I am not going to write the names of those who either attended or did not because it became evident that we would not be able to get any serious help from those who showed up. Among the ones who did attend, rather than stating what they could do [for us], they instead chose to tell [us] what to do. That day, only two scholars stated that they could attend meetings outside Turkey. Eventually, a few more scholars started to both attend such meetings and also write about this issue, yet this first meeting was seriously a source of great sadness for us. As a consequence of our being unable to find any academic scholar willing to write [on this issue], the writing of the white book was left on my shoulders, the initial owner of this idea.

The resistance among the majority of Turkish academics attending the meeting to become the promoters of the official state position is noteworthy. Instead of taking action against such attempts, however, these academics merely withdrew, thus protesting through their silence. The escalating political repression the scholars were under, especially in the aftermath of the 1980 military coup, might have been the primary cause of their silence. Also significant is the stand of the Turkish state authorities. Rather than allowing scholars to independently hold their own workshops and conferences to research the Armenian issue, the official committee instead invited them to a state institution, namely, the Turkish Foreign Ministry; it therefore must have become evident to the invited scholars that the intent was not to conduct research but instead to support the already formulated official stand. That is probably why half of those who stated they would attend did not show up.

This initial negative academic response led the Turkish authorities to take two additional steps. First, they formed an immediate committee that appeared to have scholarly bearing, recruiting scholars who did not work on the Armenian problem but instead specialized in entirely different fields like economics and medicine. In addition, they included deputies and generals in the committee; also forced to attend were many Turkish non-Muslims, probably to make the committee more "representative." Second, this initial unsuccessful official outreach into the top echelons of Turkish academia did eventually lead to some scholars from second- and third-tier academic institutions joining their ranks, ones who were either retired or else young, ambitious, set on furthering their careers, and taking advantage of the resources the state offered them.

The Year 1982

The militant Armenian violence in the United States escalated as another consul general was assassinated in Los Angeles; while stopped at a red light on his drive to work, he was killed by two assailants.[160] The consul general had been active in organizing those taking a stand against the Armenian violence; he had also written to the California Parole Board, requesting denial of parole for the assailant who had murdered the previous Los Angeles consul general. He too had refused protection, stating that he did not want the guards to suffer his own fate. An American passing by also died from a heart attack. JCOAG claimed responsibility. At the crime scene, a witness pursued the assailants to a car and wrote down their license plate number; they were therefore quickly found and arrested. One was a California native, and the other was a Lebanese citizen who escaped, only to be killed later during the Lebanese civil war. One American academic commented on this act of violence that:[161] "The genocide issue had been festering in third- and fourth-generation Armenians for years; these largely young people cannot abide by the nonaction of their fathers and mothers. They do not see why they should be nice citizens when they see other governments committing acts of terrorism on behalf of political causes."

The trial of the captured assailant lasted two years, concluding initially in a sentence of life imprisonment without parole; the sentence was later changed to twenty-five years in an appeal agreement in which he finally confessed to the killing. The assassination led the Turkish ambassador to the United States, who had previously suggested to the Foreign Ministry to take covert action against the Armenian assailants, to hold a press conference at the embassy. The ambassador first made a lengthy announcement about how the Armenian claims were false, then answered questions about this particular murder. Hence, the Turkish state authorities were increasingly employing the media attention created by the Armenian militant violence to their advantage, taking every opportunity to communicate the official Turkish narrative of past violence, denying the Armenian claims in the process by pointing out all the Turks who had been murdered by the Armenians.[162]

The second attack occurred five months later when Boston's honorary consul general of Turkey was killed in his car with a single gunshot to his head.[163] He had been active in promoting the Turkish official stand, appearing frequently on US television.[164] The Turkish state had asked the United States to provide protection for the consul general but had been turned down. The JCOAG claimed responsibility for this killing. In their reaction to the assassination, the Turkish state and government identified the assailants, for the first time, as Armenian "terrorists," also referring to their violence as "Armenian terrorism." The speech the foreign minister delivered at the Turkish national assembly demonstrated the increased virulence of the Turkish official discourse, one that accused all the organizations supporting the Armenian assailants of racism against the Turks. The minister claimed that the Turkish state had initially been hesitant to discuss the violence in their past "in order not to open old wounds"; yet from now on, they had decided to engage in full propaganda to reveal the Armenian distortion of history. The Turkish ambassador to the United States drew an additional connection between the Armenian violence and the terrorism that American officials were being subjected to throughout the world, thereby equating this particular act with terrorism at large. Such a connection subsequently led the US State Department to include ASALA on its list of terrorist organizations. By this time, Turkish state and society had begun to perceive the Armenian assailants and the Armenian Diaspora as one and the same perpetrator.

The third attack occurred a month later. The administrative attaché of Turkey's Lisbon embassy and his wife had left the embassy where they worked to have lunch at home; they were met with gunfire in front of their apartment building. The attaché died immediately, and his wife, who had been shot in the head, went into a coma; she was flown to Turkey, where she was kept alive on life support, only to die seven months later.[165] The assailant was not caught, so the murders once again remained unsolved. The official Turkish statements now fully took on the Armenian militants; while condemning them for their violence, the statements also continued to delegitimate the Armenian claims. This time around, the grieving in Turkey spread further into society; messages of protest were received from the chambers of commerce, workers' unions, and many citizens, all indicating that "the indignation and hatred of the [Turkish] nation had escalated, their patience overwhelmed," and that "they hoped the state and the nation would do everything possible."

Yet this was not the end of the violence incurred by the Turkish state and society. The violence was brought home to Turkey two months later when two ASALA assailants undertook an armed attack at the Ankara Esenboğa Airport, resulting in eight casualties and seventy-two injuries.[166] For the first time, the statement of the assailants articulated the land demands of some Armenians from the Turkish state, asking the return of the ancestral lands of the Armenians where they had once lived during Ottoman times. The assailants also warned of future attacks if the eighty-five prisoners held at various prisons in the United States, Canada, England, Sweden, and Switzerland were not released.[167] Only one of the Armenian assailants was apprehended and put on trial, recanting his violence but to no avail. He was put to death by the Turkish state.[168] This violence and the ensuing trial in Turkey also demonstrated the extreme stress the Armenians of Turkey had been placed under; three days after the attack, a Turkish citizen of Armenian descent publicly set himself on fire in protest, dying immediately.[169]

The attacks continued; three weeks later, the military attaché at the Turkish embassy in Canada was killed in an armed assault. The general staff colonel had departed from his house in a car only to be assassinated at a traffic light by two armed men; one man stepped out of a car, shooting the attaché with eleven bullets.[170] JCOAG claimed responsibility. At the time, the Turkish ambassador to Canada was the one who had lost his only son to an Armenian assassination three years earlier. The Turkish state officials were once again furious, increasingly turning through their official rhetoric all the Turks into victims and all the Armenians into perpetrators. Also, Lebanon was identified for the first time as the base of all Armenian terrorism.

The attacks continued unabated; a mere month later, while entering his apartment building, the administrative attaché of the Turkish consulate general in Bourgos, Bulgaria, was killed by an assailant.[171] Even though a few people chased the assailant, he was able to escape by mixing in with the crowd. Yet the assassin left behind a single glove, a gun with the words "Turkish diplomat, Armenian" written on it, and a paper with the following message in English: "We killed the Turkish diplomat. JCOAG." Turkish state officials called on the Bulgarian ambassador, expressing their shock that the murder for the first time took place in a socialist country where the security forces were so well organized. Numerous attacks without loss of life occurred during the year as well. This year also marked the invasion of Lebanon by Israeli forces during the summer, forcing the ASALA to move its activities elsewhere, probably going underground because there was "hardly any country in the world outside of Lebanon which would tolerate the open presence of such a group."[172] Israeli intelligence officers were reported as being intent on uprooting the centers of all extremist groups; Israeli gunfire destroyed the ASALA headquarters in the bombed-out Muslim section.

During the same year, the memoirs of a Turkish diplomat noted that he visited the United States with the intent to mobilize the Turkish Diaspora into establishing a lobby, and to form Turkish research centers that would disseminate the official Turkish position.[173] During his travels, he also met with the owner of an Armenian weekly. The latter stated that most American Armenians were against the violence, but whenever the weekly published editorials to that effect, its employees immediately received death threats.[174] The diplomat engaged in lobbying activities as well, meeting first with the Jewish lobby. He did so in order to emulate its activities and to rally the Jewish lobby to the Turkish side, especially given its political strength in the United States. The diplomat also claimed that the Jewish lobby ought to support the Turkish state as the only Muslim country that had established official relations with Israel.[175] He also researched the lobbying activities of the Armenians, attempting to sever the connection between the Jewish and Armenian lobbies. Those members of the Jewish lobby who supported the uniqueness of the Holocaust drew upon the diplomat's visit to exclude the Armenian Genocide from the Holocaust Museum. The Turkish ambassador to the United States was officially given the task of organizing the Turkish lobby, eventually leading to the formation of the American Turkish Assembly of America (ATAA).[176]

The diplomat narrated the activities he undertook in establishing Turkish research centers in the United States, thereby revealing the origins of the Institute for Turkish Studies (ITS), which is still in existence today. He initially focused on the idea of establishing endowed chairs in Turkish studies, noting that "with this purpose in mind and with the support of the National Security Council, I had placed 3 million dollars to the budget." This money was then employed to instead establish the ITS, although endowed chairs in Turkish studies funded by the Turkish state at various US universities later followed as well.[177] The diplomat's meeting with prominent US scholars specializing in Turkey convinced him to establish an institute instead of endowed chairs.[178] The scholars and the diplomat subsequently agreed on appointing Heath Lowry as the first ITS director.[179] The diplomat concluded by providing a list of things to be done:[180]

> [There should be] exhibits on Turkey, and there is also almost no Turkish history taught at the US universities: Turkish chairs need to be established, and American scholars in the social sciences have to be hosted in Turkey [where they should receive] help in conducting research. The third activity is to distribute beneficial scientific and literary works in the United States, with the Turks in the United States helping with the translation efforts.... There should also be publications about how the Jews were helped by the Turks... as it should not be forgotten that there are 5 million Jews in the US as opposed to 500,000 Armenians.

Hence, the Turkish state initially focused on writing an official version of past events; it then expanded into media propaganda, followed by the establishment of lobbying activities and research institutes promoting the official narrative.

The Year 1983

At the beginning of the year, two armed assailants attacked Turkey's ambassador to Yugoslavia, wounding the ambasador in the head and also injuring his driver.[181] The ambassador went into a coma, dying two days later; his wounded driver survived. The Yugoslav security agents accompanying the Turkish ambassador fired back at the attackers; a Yugoslavian student passing by lost his life, and another Yugoslavian was wounded.[182] A retired Yugoslavian colonel had also drawn his gun, firing at the assailants, wounding one of them and getting wounded in the process.[183] The Turkish coverage of the slain ambassador reveals that he had been especially promising and well liked, destined to become a future foreign minister. He had previously served at NATO, leading NATO circles to immediately condemn the assassination. Both Armenian assailants of Lebanese origin were taken into police custody. Some members of the Armenian Diapora brought expert witnesses to the trial in an effort to argue that the past collective violence had generated the present one, but the issue of the Armenian Genocide was not admitted in court.[184] Both assailants were sentenced to twenty years of imprisonment, the longest sentence they could have received in a Yugoslav court.[185] The reaction in the Turkish media reached new heights, with one newspaper referring to the assailants as "dogs." In addition, given the lack of significant research and knowledge on the violence committed against the Armenians in Turkey's past, journalists started to assume the role of public arbiters of the Armenian issue, relying almost exclusively on the official narrative in the process. Because the slain diplomat was unmarried and his parents were deceased, he was adopted by the media and the state as the "son of the Turkish nation."

Four months later, the administrative attaché at the Turkish embassy in Brussels was attacked and murdered as he was getting into his car in front of his house.[186] The assailant escaped, leaving behind his jacket and gun. Three groups—ASALA, JCOAG, and the Armenian Revolutionary Army—all claimed responsibility. The memoir of another Turkish diplomat who served Belgium for four years, from 1982 to 1986, provides additional detail about both the assassination and its impact on other Turkish officials.[187] "Among the bitter events that cast a shadow over the beauty of my years in Belgium, the Armenians getting out of control and engaging in assassinations and terrorist activities throughout Europe and also in Belgium ranked at the top," the diplomat noted. He continued to describe what transpired as follows:

> I was given the news that our young and hard-working administrative attaché Dursun Aksoy was martyred by Armenian terrorists in front of his house as he got into his car. I immediately went to the scene of the incident. I found my dear friend Dursun Aksoy lying motionless in a pool of blood, his head fallen on the driving wheel. The murderers had escaped and they have not been found to this day. After a sad ceremony, we sent Aksoy's body to the fatherland. . . . Among the Armenian activities, the attacks against the tourism and press attaches, and the Turkish Airlines bureau, the detonating bombs, the broken glass are all in front of my eyes even today. The sad part is that the instigators of none of these activities were ever discovered by the Belgian police. Whenever we pressured the authorities, we got the response "Belgium is a tiny

> country; it must be that the instigators escaped as soon as they undertook these activities."

Such violence thus remained forever etched in the memory of the Turkish diplomats who were eyewitnesses, had served with the victims, or had attended school with them. And the circle of violence kept expanding through the years, bringing many under its grip. The diplomat's account of a failed attempt that is not included in the official narrative of the Turkish Foreign Ministry indicates that such occurrences were probably quite numerous, constantly increasing the anxiety of all Turkish officials working abroad. The Turkish authorities started to refer to "Armenian barbarity," escalating their tone, only to conclude that all such actions were futile because the Turkish state and society were increasingly set in their resolve. Once again, the United States, NATO, the European Security Council, Germany, and, interestingly, also the Palestinian Liberation Organization all condemned the assassination.

A day later, a bomb exploded in front of the Turkish Airlines office at the Orly Airport in Paris, killing eight—two Turks, four French, one American, and one Swede—and wounding sixty-three; twenty-eight of the wounded were Turks. This attack was later referred to by Turkish state and society as the "Orly Massacre." Afterward, in an attempt to contain possible damage, many airports moved arriving and departing Turkish flights to distant corners. These murders also remained unresolved. Because the assassination had occurred on the last day of the holy month of Ramadan, the Turkish newspapers drew upon the connection to note that their holiday had been besmirched by blood. The Armenian patriarch in Turkey also gave a long interview, condemning the last two attacks as inhumane and un-Christian and reiterating that the Armenians in Turkey lived in "peace and security with rights and opportunities equal to that of the Turkish nation, the nation to which they all fully belonged."

Ten days later, the Turkish embassy in Portugal was occupied, with the wife of the embassy counselor and their son taken hostage.[188] Before the late-arriving Portuguese security forces could storm the building, the bombs that the assailants had placed went off. The wife subsequently died from the wounds she received during the incident, while the son escaped with minor injuries. In his memoir, one Turkish diplomat referred to this incident by drawing a parallel, once again, to the 1896 raid of the Ottoman Bank by Armenian revolutionaries.[189] The five assailants, who were subsequently killed by the Portuguese security forces, were nineteen to twenty years old.[190] The Turkish Foreign Ministry and the media united in condemning the attacks, claiming that the Armenian terrorists were going to roast in the fire they had ignited and insisting that not a single handspan of Turkish land would ever be given away.

While the wife's death received ample coverage, there was almost no mention of the Portuguese policeman or the five assailants who had also died. In the United States, a special memorial rally for the five youths killed in Lisbon was held in Watertown, Massachusetts, by the local ARF. Also in Tehran, thousands of Armenians took to the streets, memorializing the heroism of the five young Armenian men, who had become "martyrs" in the attack.[191]

During the same year, the Armenian Diaspora started to report on the secret paramilitary activities of the Turkish state outside Turkey. An article written on the event of the kidnapping and murder of Apraham Ashjian, a top Dashnak leader and head of the ARF security forces, pointed out that "Turkey appears to have finally chosen the strategy of tracking down and killing all those Armenian youths who are suspected of belonging to the two Armenian underground groups, ASALA and the JCOAG."[192] The article then argued that an additional three Armenians had also been murdered by the Turkish paramilitary armed band.[193] The article concluded by stating that the intelligence division of the Israeli occupying forces in Lebanon was cooperating with the Turkish secret police regarding Armenian terrorism. Information on the Armenian militant groups captured during the Israeli army's sweep of Lebanon was probably passed on to Turkey, leading the latter to dispatch armed bands to track down and murder the ASALA members. In the case of Ashjian, however, it later became evident that he was murdered by other Armenians.

Also during the same year, the JCOAG sent a message to the world public, explaining why it had undertaken such a violent route to acknowledgment.[194] This message began by first stating:

> We, the sons of the Armenian people, the descendants of one and a half million innocent victims of the Genocide of 1915 perpetrated by the Turkish government, we who have been scattered all over the globe for more than sixty-five years as a result of mass deportation and have been deprived of our right of self-determination and have lived under constant threat of losing our identity and, being fully aware of our responsibilities, wish to draw the attention of American, West European, and world opinion.

The message then argued that the violence the JCOAG engaged was not at all different from the violence that the Western states engaged in. The rest of the statement reiterated the JCOAG's resolve, stating that it had engaged in such violence because of the Turkish state's refusal to hold any dialogue on the Armenian Genocide. It is fascinating that the JCOAG could not comprehend that its own violence not only failed to generate any dialogue: for at least the following two decades, it instead bolstered and legitimated the Turkish refusal and resistance to engage in such dialogue.

The Year 1984

The attacks continued during this year as well.[195] In the spring, a couple working at the Tehran embassy were murdered: the businessman husband of Turkey's Tehran embassy secretary was driving her to the embassy when they were attacked by two assailants riding on a motorcycle. The assassins opened fire on the couple as they drove past the car.[196] The husband later died at the hospital. The call claiming responsibility for the attack for ASALA also noted that the attack had been undertaken to protest the arrival of Prime Minister Turgut Özal in Iran for a series of talks. The Armenians in Iran also held marches protesting the arrival of the Turkish prime minister; in his memoir, a Turkish diplomat likened these marches in Iran to the 1895 Kumkapı protest, once again drawing a parallel between past and present Armenian public acts.[197] In his message to Iran, the Turkish foreign minister warned the Iranians not to be exploited by the Armenians, thereby risking the destruction of their good ties with Turkey. The Turkish media were once again full of fury. In an interesting and constructive turn, however, the Turkish prime minister pointed out that it was wrong to reach decisions through one's emotions, and that reason ought to prevail. Yet he could not prevent one Turkish newspaper from remarking that in spite of visiting Iran to improve trade relations, the prime minister was instead returning from his trip with a coffin.

Two months later, the deputy labor attaché at the Turkish embassy in Austria was killed by a car bomb, with the blast also wounding two people.[198] The Armenian Revolutionary Army claimed responsibility. The assailants were never found in this case either. In his memoir, a Turkish diplomat drew an analogy between this bomb and the bomb Armenian revolutionaries had employed in 1905 with the intent to assassinate Sultan Abdülhamid II.[199] The history of Turkey's past was thus increasingly employed, but not with the intent to analyze what had happened. Instead, the Armenian past violence was selectively employed to legitimate the victimhood of the Turks. Turkish embassy officials protested that the Austrian media constantly referred to past historical events, as if to justify the recent murders. They were also upset that the Austrian state did not publish an official condemnation of the attack. Noting that the slain attaché was the fortieth victim of Armenian terror, both the Turkish state and the media severly condemned the attack; the media discussions were dominated by how venegeance against Armenian militant violence ought to be carried out.

Five months later, the Turkish director at the UN Vienna bureau was ambushed and assassinated while driving to work in his car. He was not actually a Turkish diplomat but a UN employee who happened to be Turkish.[200] The Armenian Revolutionary Army claimed responsibility. The perpetrator was also not found. Turkish authorities again had a run-in with the Austrian television reporters for referring to the past violence. Interestingly, the Turkish ambassador to Austria who spearheaded these discussions was the son of a perpetrator who had once engaged in violence against Armenians in 1915.[201] A Turkish diplomat noted in his memoir that every year, the 2,000 Armenians living in Vienna held a ceremony at the tomb of Franz Werfel, the author of *Forty Days of Musa Dagh*, a book that chronicled the 1915 Armenian massacres and subsequent resistance.[202] Hence, not only was the past collective violence committed against the Armenians not acknowledged, but the instances of Armenian violence in the past were brought forward instead.

During the same year, Western authorities stepped up their investigation of especially those Armenians of Lebanese or Iranian origin entering their countries. They did so to reduce the risk of further assassinations of Turkish officials and increasingly refused entry to known ARF members and officers.[203] The article discussing such refusals noted that since the Israeli invasion of Lebanon, JCOAG had moved its headquarters to Athens while continuing its search for another location. It also became clear that the ARF official who had been denied entry conducted business with the Soviet Union, with one Dashnak source claiming that the business was a cover for supplying arms to militant Armenians. Also discussed was the conflict within JCOAG as members could not decide where to carry out their next act of violence. While two ARF members had made a deal with the CIA not to engage in terrorism in the United States during the Los Angeles Olympics, the other member objected vehemently, arguing that terrorism should take place wherever the circumstances allowed. The latter's stand led to his liquidation, although care was taken to publicly portray the murder as if the Turks had carried it out.

The Year 1985

The loss of their Lebanese base decreased the ability of the radical Armenian militant groups to recruit and train Armenian youths for attacking Turkish officials and buildings. They could no longer remain there only to travel overseas for the attacks, often returning without being caught. As a consequence, the violence against the Turkish officials gradually abated. Still, in late winter, the Armenian Revolutionary Army militants raided and occupied the Turkish embassy in Ottowa, Canada.[204] The assailants, all Canadian citizens, were then convinced to turn themselves in to the police, stating in the process that they had two claims: the return of the Armenian lands occupied by Turkey and the Turkish acknowledgment of the genocide. All three were sentenced to twenty-five years in prison without parole. The Turkish government also established a fellowship in the name of the murdered Canadian security guard.[205] After the attack, Prime Minister Brian Mulroney's conservative government reviewed Canada's counterterrorism capabilities, which eventually led to the creation of Canada's top-secret commando unit, Joint Task Force Two. In the talk the Turkish foreign minister gave at the special section of the cemetery now dedicated to all the victims of the Turkish Foreign Ministry, he appealed to the Armenian communities throughout the world, asking them to assess what the recent violence had produced other than bringing death and destruction for all. He asked members of the Armenian Diaspora to put the past behind them as the Turks had done with the Australians whom they had fought against in World War I. In doing so, the foreign minister equated amd legitimated the Turkish violence committed during conventional warfare with the massacres that the Armenian civilians had suffered at the hands of the Ottoman government that should have protected them in the first place. There were no other casualties in the other instances of violence that occurred during this year.[206] As the trial of the three Armenian militants ended in Canada, so did the decade of militant Armenian violence against Turkish officials.[207]

The year also witnessed increased infighting among the militant Armenian groups, thereby providing yet another clue as to why the violence against the Turkish diplomats had ceased. One of the ARF founders was abducted by members of another Armenian militant group who claimed they were soon going to release the names of all the "Armenian agents" operating in Lebanon, France, and Germany. The body of the abducted founder was never recovered. Then, two leaders of the newly founded Revolutionary Movement, who also happened to be the local leaders of the Dashnak Party in Lebanon, were assassinated. The movement had invited all Dashnak members to sever their ties with the party or face death, irrespective of age or sex; these leaders had not done so and were therefore murdered. The internal strife within the Dashnak Party revealed that the ARF had created the JCOAG in an attempt to prevent Armenian youths from leaving the party with the intent to join ASALA. Yet the involved leaders had then disagreed on how much collaboration there should be between ASALA and JCOAG. In settling their differences, another ARF member was assassinated in 1986.[208] In analyzing this internal violence, a contemporaneous US report stated that the Armenian nationals in Beirut were heavily involved in drug trafficking with the intent to raise funds for JCOAG activities, thereby revealing another source of income of the radical Armenian militant groups.[209] Yet the violence within the Dashnak Party continued, leading many members to leave Lebanon to instead settle in the Soviet Republic of Armenia. In 1999, a splinter group took over the Armenian parliament, killing three top-level deputies in the process and justifying the violence in the name of patriotism.[210]

The Aftermath

Although militant Armenian violence had gradually abated by the mid-1980s, the anxiety at Turkish diplomatic posts about the possibility of such violence continued, leading to the issuance of an ever-increasing number of security precautions. One Turkish diplomat noted in his memoir that not only was the embassy building he served in equipped with bulletproof glass and an alarm system, but in order to be able to use the guns they were given, he and his wife continually practiced shooting at a firing range. His views toward all Armenians had also become polarized; many were now regarded as potential security risks for simply being an Armenian. When the ambassador found out that a Turkish policeman at the embassy had mistreated a man protesting for waiting in line for a long time, he had the personal life of the policeman investigated only to find out the latter was living with an Armenian woman, although he had a wife and children back in Turkey. The ambassador immediately had the policeman returned to Turkey.[211]

Yet not all Turkish diplomats held such polarized views toward all Armenians. A case in point is provided by the memoir of another Turkish diplomat and ambassador.[212] He narrated that there was one Armenian who was employed as the armed attendant of the Turkish consulate, one who did everything at the consulate and was well liked by everyone. The ambassador then described the impact the Armenian militant violence had on their relations, stating that this Armenian employee condemned the violent perpetrators as much as he did. Yet a letter of denunciation from a member in the consulate led the Turkish Foreign Ministry to start sending letters to the ambassador, asking if it should remove the Armenian employee given that the latter posed a security threat. The ambassador persisted, responding that he would entrust his life to this Armenian employee, thereby allowing the man to keep his job.

The final incident relating to Armenian militant violence occurred in 2001 when a cache of high explosives and firearms and a dusty trench coat were discovered in a storage facility in Bedford, Ohio, a suburb of Cleveland.[213] The unit, which was opened after rental fees had gone unpaid for six months, had initially been rented under three false names and addresses. American agents traced the ownership of the unit to the chairman of the Armenian National Committee of America, who evidently led a double life, also serving as a top JCOAG leader. Yet some members of the Armenian Diaspora raised money for his defense, claiming that the pro-Turkish elements in the US government had singled him out for persecution. He was eventually sentenced to thirty-seven months in prison, the maximum allowed under sentencing guidelines.

In summary, this militant Armenian violence undertaken during the 1975–85 decade did not accomplish the intended aim of genocide recognition; instead, it enabled the Turkish state and its governments to develop an official discourse of denial based on the selective use of the Ottoman and Turkish past, not with the intent to acknowledge the inherent violence against the Armenians but instead to portray all Armenians as violent perpetrators and all Turks as innocent victims. As a consequence, the possibility of genocide recognition was delayed for at least three decades. It is telling that in Turkish collective memory, whenever the possibility of peaceful negotiation with the Armenians comes up, the first connection that immediately surfaces is the one made to the violent assassinations of Turkish diplomats in the recent past. Hence in Turkey, these recent violent incidents served to rationalize the fervent Turkish nationalist denial of the collective violence committed against the Armenians in the more distant past.

Fourth Denial: Late Republican Denial of Responsibility for Violence Committed against the Armenians

The official Turkish denial of responsibility for the collective violence committed against the Armenians was the last step of multilayered denial throughout history, one that initially commenced in 1789 with the advent of Ottoman modernity. During the first phase, lasting from 1789 to 1907, the domestic origins of the Armenian problem were denied as the issue was blamed almost entirely on the intervention of the Western powers in the empire's affairs. The next phase of CUP rule from 1908 to 1918 was marked by the denial of the act as all Armenian imperial subjects were forcibly removed from their ancestral lands under the facade of an official deportation. During the third nationalist phase, spanning 1919 to 1974, the denial of the actors commenced as the republic was manned and eventually led, with the exception of Mustafa Kemal Atatürk, by those perpetrators who had successfully transitioned into the republican era with impunity. The final phase, from 1975 to 2009, was instigated by the ASALA and JCOAG assassinations targeting Turkish diplomats. In a defensive move that commenced in 1981, Turkish state officials in general and the diplomats at the Foreign Ministry in particular developed an official counternarrative that actually delegitimated and negated the Armenian claims. These officials selectively focused on the past, homing in exclusively on the incidents of Armenian violence to thereby portray the Turks not as perpetrators but as victims. As a consequence, it became easier to argue that what had occurred in the past had been "mutual massacres." By doing so, however, the Turkish official stand actualized the last stage of denial, namely, the denial of responsibility for the collective violence committed against the Armenians.

Evolution of Turkish Official Denial

This book's primary focus on memoirs enables the analysis of the Turkish collective memory in general and the emergence of the Turkish official narrative of denial in particular.[214] Especially the memoir of one diplomat demonstrated how the official Turkish narrative of the denial of responsibility came into being.[215] I argue here that such an official denial narrative is predicated on two strategic moves: selectivity and silencing followed by decontextualization. In the first strategic move, pertinent historical actors and acts fitting the official narrative of denial were selected while others contradicting the narrative were silenced. A case in point is the diplomat's discussion of Armenian land demands, where he stated:

> "Turkey is still keeping the Armenian lands under occupation!"...And this addled terrorist had decided to free [these lands]. "And no one asks him 'What Armenian lands are you talking about?" A thousand years ago when the Turks conquered Anatolia, there was no Armenian soil, but the Byzantine Empire. The Byzantine state had not left any Armenian land to the Ottomans. [Then], there was no place called "Armenian land" in the Ottoman Empire. The Turkish Republic did not inherit such "Armenian land" from the Ottoman Empire. In Anatolia, "Armenian land" or "Armenian homeland" solely existed in the retarded imaginations of Armenian terrorists.

As the diplomat temporally bounded Anatolian history with the arrival of the Turks, he overlooked the earlier kingdoms the Armenians had established on these lands, thereby silencing Armenian history in the process. In terms of what happened later, one cannot possibly argue that there were "Turkish lands" during the Ottoman Empire, since the concept of nationalism did not yet exist; all lands belonged to the sultan. Yet new interpretations of space emerged with nationalism, among both the Armenians and the Turks. Selectively reinterpreting history from the standpoint of the present, the diplomat reaffirmed the Turkish presence and claims over Anatolia while silencing and delegitimating the presence and claims of the Armenians that are equally valid.

The next inherent element of the official Turkish narrative, "decontextualization," emerges from the memoirs of two prominent Turkish diplomats. The first one, narrating the assassinations of diplomats, connected this recent militant

Armenian violence to the past Armenian violence committed during World War I as follows:[216]

> Armenian terror is nurtured by racist propaganda that distorts history and that indifferently claims all sorts of lies and slander about Turkey and the Turks. Our experience with Armenian terrorism and propaganda is not new. Armenian organizations resorted to the same methods at the end of the 19th and the beginning of the 20th centuries when they reached their political desires by murdering hundreds of thousands of Turks in Anatolia with hair-raising savagery. They then tried to convince the world that these bloodthirsty murders had been committed against them.

Even though the diplomat accused Armenian racist propaganda of distorting history, he then ironically continued to engage in a similar act of distortion. He thus removed historical facts from their temporal context, thereby making a causal connection between past and present Armenian violence, a connection that selectively focused on particular acts performed under very different circumstances and in very different time periods.

Likewise, in his memoir, the second diplomat summarized the main elements of the Turkish official narrative in a formal note he sent to the entire top echelon of the Turkish state and government, stating:[217]

> The current Armenian propaganda does not mention the events leading to the deportation decision…instead, only the murder of 1.5 million Armenians…is emphasized without even bringing up the term deportation. [This figure]…overlooks all the Western works written after the war…[citing] the total Armenian population in Turkey [as 1.5 million]….The deportation was [solely] conducted from the eastern and central Anatolian provinces….The highest number of those who lost their lives during the deportation is about 500,000….Right after the Lausanne Treaty, the Armenians in the United States prevented the approval of an individual treaty between Turkey and the United States….Anti-Turkish activities then somewhat lessened during World War II and…dissipated by the Korean War. There was no apparent reason for such attacks to occur.

This explanation brings up the valid point that the official Armenian narrative is also selective; it does not adequately discuss the historical context and especially overlooks the Armenian massacres of the Turks and Kurds that occurred in the eastern and southern provinces at the end of the war and during the Allied occupation. At this juncture, the Armenians probably massacred around 60,000 Turks and Kurds in the east, and this needs to be acknowledged by the official Armenian narrative, especially since none of the perpetrators undertaking this destructive act has been punished either. Concerning the total number of Armenians massacred, the official Ottoman statement of the Damad Ferid Pasha government was 800,000, a figure probably closer to what transpired than the often-cited higher figure of 1.5 million by the Armenian organizations or the lower figure of 500,000 that the diplomat cites. In addition, by emphasizing the act of deportation and then claiming that this act occurred only in the eastern and central Anatolian provinces, the diplomat carefully omits the violence ensuing from the deportations as well as the fact that they occurred from almost all the regions of the central imperial lands. Given this emergence of the official narrative of denial through selectivity and silencing on the one hand and decontextualization on the other, what is the current state of denial in Turkish state and society? I next analyze current denial by the Turkish state and government in education, in the Turkish media, and outside Turkey.

In the 1980s, the Turkish diplomats at the Foreign Ministry and the officers in the military carried out the initial groundwork on the official Turkish narrative in relation to the Armenian claims by selectively combing through archival documentation. In the 1990s, their work was gradually centralized and institutionalized under the aegis of the Turkish Historical Society (TTK), where a specific directorship for Armenian research was established. The TTK then recruited personnel to conduct this research, individuals who were selected primarily for their knowledge of the Ottoman script. Such personnel often did not have access to or interest in the international theoretical and empirical developments in the field of history in particular and the social sciences in general. As a consequence, they unquestioningly reproduced in their research the narrow ontological and epistemological parameters initially set by the retired diplomats and officers.

Two scholars among these have been especially active in informing the Turkish public about the Armenian issue. One is Yusuf Halaçoğlu, who served as the TTK director for fifteen years from 1993 to 2008; the other is Kemal Çiçek, the TTK director of Armenian research since 2002. What unites both scholars is their passion for sustaining and reproducing the initial official Turkish narrative they inherited from the Foreign Ministry and the military. Their main contribution to this narrative has been the rearrangement of the numbers, increasing the number of Turkish deaths by Armenians while decreasing Armenian deaths by Turks with the intent to equate the two numbers to claim everyone suffered, thereby delegitmating and eliminating the Armenian claims for justice. The following discussion is based on the newspaper interviews they gave in 2007 and 2009.[218] In 2009, for instance, the TKK director presented the following official narration:

> The research Yusuf Halaçoğlu conducted at the Ottoman, UN, US, German, French, British, and Russian archives has revealed that the Armenians murdered 532,000 Muslims whereas the number of Armenians who died during the deportations was around 47,000. Of these, 37,000 perished due to hunger, illness, and the strain of travel; 8,000 were killed by Arab, Kurdish, and Turkish bandits on the deportation routes, and 1,500 were unregistered deaths. In addition, 67 state officials were tried and executed for failing to protect the deported Armenians.

First, one should note that Halaçoğlu does not know any foreign languages, so it would be impossible for him to personally conduct research in the UN, US, German, French, British, and Russian archives; he probably relied on information gathered by others. Second, given that the Armenian population at the end of the Ottoman Empire was around 1.5 to 2 million, and given that a typical Ottoman household of the period comprised five members, including the women, children, and the elderly, the figure Halaçoğlu cites would imply that one in every three Armenians murdered Muslims, which is not only improbable but actually impossible. Third, in terms of the Armenian deaths, given that about 300,000 Armenians survived the massacres, and given that there were initially 1.5 million Armenians in the empire, it is difficult to account for what happened to the rest. Fourth, even though the CUP government tried some of the perpetrators, it did so not to punish them for the crimes they committed but instead for keeping the plundered Armenian wealth for their personal use. Halaçoğlu engages in such falsification for the denial of responsibility.

In his interview, Kemal Çiçek presented the counterevidence his division collected with the intent to delegitimate the Armenian claims. He commenced by taking on the issue of the number of Armenian deaths, claiming this time that only around 200,000 to 300,000 Armenians died, with the rest escaping to neighboring countries. He specifically noted:

> There are 150 million documents in the [Ottoman] archives. Of these 100,000 have been cataloged, revealing that the Ottomans had not committed genocide.... [In all] a minimum of 200,000 and a maximum of 300,000 Armenians died due to armed band attacks and illness. Yet because of the... lack of [state] oversight [due to war conditions], many Armenians escaped from the convoys, ending up in Russia, Georgia. and Iran. 350,000 to 400,000 Armenians escaped to the Caucasus.... In 2005, we researched the world archives to determine where the Armenians went. We saw that 1,300,000 Armenians survived the deportations.... After removing the Armenians from their homes,

> the Ottomans determined with circulars how many convoys would be formed, the road they would pass through, and the precautions taken to protect, but did not follow through due to war conditions.... The Ottomans took precautions sending telegrams to all the governors, ordering them to ensure the deportations were carried out properly with the accompaniment of many guards, and without any attacks and losses; the state found protective families for the orphans, giving them money to take care of them. There are hundreds of documents on these matters.... In the past, we did not know that the [Ottoman] state was so protective of the Armenians, establishing hospitals and orphanages [for them], and when they did not have sufficient funds, permitting Armenian aid organizations to help the camps and the convoys.... Even though there was misuse by the soldiers, about 1,700 Turks were tried for their poor treatment of Armenians, plundering their properties, raping girls, committing [other] sexual crimes. During 1915–17, four military courts were established, trying and hanging sixty-seven. A total of 1,347 were sentenced to exile and forced labor.

The main fundamental fallacy Kemal Çiçek commits in his approach to historical research is that in interpreting archival documents, he fails to differentiate state rhetoric from subsequent action. He assumes that what was stated in the official documents was actually, entirely, and fully carried out. Yet contemporaneous memoirs illuminate what happened on the ground, revealing not only that such precautions were not carried out but also that the perpetrators were not punished for the crimes they committed against the Armenians. In addition, he is not willing to provide any documentation to support his claims, especially the one alleging that 1.3 million Armenians survived the deportations. Yet, Çiçek is able to get away with such false allegations because his audience is not the international scholarly community but the Turkish public; his intent is not to engage in scholarly research but to generate an official rhetoric for domestic consumption. It is not accidental that none of these official historians are able to participate in international academic gatherings, for their research would not withstand any scientific scrutiny. Yet, such official historians are nevertheless able to influence and shape the Turkish domestic interpretations of what happened in the past in relation to the Armenians.

Indeed, the stand of these official historians has adversely impacted the outlook of the current JDP government. Given his various explanations regarding the past violence committed against the Armenians, it is evident, for instance, that Prime Minister Tayyip Erdoğan was briefed by members of Turkish Historical Society.[219] After criticizing the Armenian Diaspora for accusing the Turks of genocide, Erdoğan recently noted that "his ancestors could not have committed genocide so it did not take place." By making such a claim, the Turkish prime minister reveals that he was uninformed about the current state of genocide literature in general and Hannah Arendt's distinction of guilt from responsibility in particular: Prime Minister Erdoğan is of course not personally guilty of the violence committed in Turkey's past against the Armenians, but he is nevertheless responsible for that violence, as a human being, as a Turkish citizen, and also as the top-ranking official of the country. He is responsible as a human being because his failure to acknowledge that violence destroys the moral fabric of Turkish society and the trust of the people of Turkey in the future of humanity. He is responsible as a Turkish citizen and a state official because his failure to acknowledge that violence normalizes and reproduces it within Turkish state and society.

During this period, two activities stood out in the educational sphere in relation to denial, one within formal education and the other in civic education. In formal education, the Education Ministry undertook an official decision in line with EU membership requirements: in Turkish history textbooks, all references to the "baseless" or "so-called Armenian Genocide" were to be replaced instead by "1915 events."[220] In spite of such a modest move toward the elimination of prejudice from the history textbooks, however, two months later, it was reported that a film on the Armenian violence in the past entitled *Sarı Gelin: Ermeni Olayının İçyüzü* (*Blonde Bride: The Inside Story of the Armenian Incidents*)," prepared by the Turkish general chief of staff and referred to in public as the "documentary of hatred," was still being shown in schools.[221] These schools had also been asked by officials to report on students' reactions to the film. This public act had come to the attention of parents because of the fear and anxiety it had produced on their children. When the incident was thus brought to the attention of the Turkish media, the education minister argued that he had ordered such showings to be stopped. Yet, district education directorates claimed that they had not received such an order.[222] Hence, in spite of some attempts by the Turkish state and government, such nationalist documentaries were still circulated, thereby perpetrating denial.

The other activity focused on civic education, entailing the frequent conferences, panels, and workshops on the Armenian issue that were held throughout the country in conjunction with the Turkish Historical Society.[223] At such occasions, alongside the official TTK historians, state officials like the governor and military officers like the local commander gave lectures on this issue. They collectively engaged in denial, arguing that the Muslim suffering in the past was never addressed and there was nothing in the Turkish past that one needed to apologize for.[224] The persistent continuation of these educational activities especially in the provinces systematically undermines the EU membership requirements that are intent on promoting acknowledgment, not denial.

During this time, the mainstream Turkish media initially reacted to the ASALA and JCOAG assassinations of Turkish diplomats by fully adopting the official state narrative. The journalists then retrospectively applied this violence to Turkey's past to argue that, historically, the Turks had always been victims and the Armenians perpetrators, thereby effectively dismissing responsibility for past violence once again. After the cessation of the militant Armenian violence in 1985, the Turkish media continued to discuss the Armenian issue on three temporalities: whenever countries throughout the world legally adopted the genocide resolution, when a genocide resolution made its way to the US Congress, and at the annual genocide commemorations held on 24 April.

The most significant theme emerging in such discussions was the issue of restitution and reparation. Various journalists reiterated time and again that they personally were not ready to give even a handspan of their fatherland to the Armenians and were likewise not at all interested in paying reparations. A case in point is the editorial of one such journalist who stated:

> Occasionally the naive or those representing [Western] imperialism arrogantly argue: "What would it cost? If the [Armenians] want it so much, let us accept [the genocide]. We did not commit genocide, the Ottomans did." These arrogant people thus ask us to accept that our ancestors were like the Nazi murderers. Okay, you naive people, don't you know that the Turkish republic is the descendant of the Ottoman Empire?... If you once acknowledge, then see what will happen next? From demands for restitution to land.... Is this paranoia? Come on!

Dismissing those who insist on acknowledgment as naive, arrogant, and representers of Western imperialism, the journalist immediately adopted a defensive stand. He then eliminated the possibility of acknowledgment by coupling the genocide with the Holocaust on the one hand and with the possibility of ensuing reparations on the other. It is significant that Turkish journalists often approach the issue of the Armenian Genocide as an imposition on Turkish state and society, one that would solely benefit the Armenians. In doing so, they do not take into account the positive constructive impact such recognition would have on Turkish state and society: First, recognition would further democratize the country by challenging the current normalization of violence. Second, it would mend the moral fabric of Turkish state and society that has been impaired by denial, since denial ultimately destroys one's faith in humanity. Third, recognition is an ethical issue, one that enables a collectivity to take responsibility for past violence with the intent that no such violence would reemerge in the future. As such, recognition would enable the peaceful solution of all the problems Turkey has with the Kurds, Alewites, and non-Muslims.

The Turkish official narrative has also diffused among the Diaspora Turks living outside Turkey, especially within those segments that uncritically adopt, promote, and defend Turkish state interests at all costs. Such defense emerges in academic, political, and legal contexts. Academically, some independent researchers in Europe replicate the nationalist stand by undertaking research to demonstrate that other nations committed far worse crimes against humanity, and by organizing activities commemorating the assassinations of prominent CUP leaders.[225] One invitation to such a commemoration of CUP leaders, inviting people to stand in attendance in Berlin with a one-minute silence, reads:

> The honorable children of the Turkish nation, the sensitive period we live in demonstrates that the existence of our nation and state is under threat. The historical scenarios obstinately pressured by Western imperialists to humiliate the Turk and erase his existence from Anatolia in the past are also being carried out today. Through various channels, such pressures have been turned into tools of political pressure against the Turk and his nation.... We need to be conscious of the debt of gratitude we the Turks have toward those [statesmen such as Sait Halim Pasha, Talat Pasha, Cemal Pasha, Dr. Bahaeddin Shakir, and Azmi Bey]...who prevented the liquidation of the Turkish existence in Anatolia.

Associating Turks with honor, the invitation reiterates the nationalist stand that Turks, Turkey, the Turkish nation, and the Turkish fatherland are all under continuous attack by Western imperialists intent on destroying the Turk. In this context, the top CUP leaders who destroyed the Armenians emerge as the saviors of all Turks. Such prioritization of Turkish interests to the exclusion of everything else legitimates all ensuing violence. Likewise, the academic work that points out the collective violence embedded in other countries' pasts fails to take into account that all such countries, including Argentina, Japan, and the United States, are trying to acknowledge, not deny, such past violence.

In the related sphere of education, since the 2006 French adoption of a bill proposing punishment to anyone denying the Armenian Genocide, there have been instances of students of Turkish origin engaging in denial. In France, in spite of teachers' attempts to the contrary, one thirteen-year-old Turk was suspended from school for writing that even if the genocide happened, the Armenians deserved it.[226] Such a stand at such a young age demonstrates the diffusion of denial across generations. In the legal sphere, after the passage of a similar law in Switzerland, a Turkish nationalist politician specifically traveled there with the intent to be punished by denying the Armenian Genocide. He was indeed convicted, but the sentence was then reduced to a monetary fine. It is no accident that the same politician is currently in jail for engaging in illegal activities against the government.[227] In the sphere of politics, since Holland had passed a similar law, three Turkish-Dutch candidates running for political office were removed from the 2006 general elections because of either denying or refusing to publicly declare that the Armenian Genocide had happened. Such a stand may reflect not only the personal stands of these candidates but also the dominant norm among their Turkish voters, revealing once again the social penetration of the official narrative.[228] The legal adoption of such laws has generated significant debate among scholars as well. Such laws indeed prevent the diffusion of prejudice and discrimination to the public, thereby promoting tolerance. Yet they also inhibit the public discussion of prejudice and discrimination, thereby eliminating the opportunity to alter individual denialist stands.

In the United States, the impact of the Turkish official narrative becomes evident at the intersection of legal, academic, and civic spheres. In the civic sphere, the American Turkish Assembly of America was established and funded by the Turkish state during the 1975–85 decade of Armenian militant violence against the Turkish diplomats with the express intent to create a Turkish lobby in the United States countering the Armenian lobby. As such, the ATAA has diffused the official Turkish narrative at every opportunity, explicitly targeting the education of the Armenian Genocide at US schools and universities, and employing legal means to argue that the inclusion of the Turkish narrative is a First Amendment right. Yet the US educational and legal systems have so far consistently dismissed the lawsuits initiated by the ATAA.[229] Another significant medium the ATAA employs for diffusing the official Turkish narrative is the online Turkish Forum. I became the target of an attack by the Turkish Forum in 2006 when, at a talk I gave at the University of Toronto, I publicly apologized to the Armenians for the past collective violence by stating, "Personally, I am not guilty, but responsible for what happened in the past." In an e-mail posted on the Forum, one of its board members vilified me. I had to get my university's legal counsel to write protest letters to all the involved parties, including the Chicago Turkish consulate and the Turkish embassy, forcing them to apologize.

In summary, the current Turkish official narrative on the collective violence committed against the Armenians developed during the militant Armenian assassinations of Turkish diplomats, projecting this recent victimization of Turks onto the past with the intent to deny responsibility for committing violence against the Armenians. This narrative penetrated into many spheres of state and society in Turkey as well as among the Turkish Diaspora. In the last two decades, however, this official narrative has increasingly been challenged both within and outside Turkey. With the intent to end this book on a positive note, I next outline the recent challenges to the contemporary Turkish denial of responsibility.

Recent Challenges to the Late Republican Denial of Responsibility

Many Turkish intellectuals, journalists, and academics have started to independently delve into the Armenian issue to gradually construct a narrative of counterdenial, discovering in the process that the origins of such a stand extend back in history. I shall review here three spheres of knowledge production and reproduction where the Turkish official narrative has begun to be contested and countered: newly transliterated or penned texts, activities at newly established private universities, and public interpretations of a new generation of Turkish journalists and intellectuals.

Especially after the 1928 script reform, the politics of transliteration had severely limited the access of ensuing generations to any historical texts that contradicted the official republican narrative. Ensuing censorship and repression also prevented generations of republican citizens from penning and publishing their own texts. After the relative liberalization in the late 1990s and the first half of the decade of the 2000s, there has been an explosion of oppositional transliterated texts and memoirs. Especially the publication of oppositional memoirs gradually diffused from covering the experiences of the oppositional Turkish Muslim majority to include the memoirs, and thereby the voices, of other excluded groups, like the non-Muslims and the Kurds. A case in point is the 2003 publication of the 1915 deportation memoirs of Manuel Kırkyaşaryan, edited by the Turkish scholar Baskın Oran and published by the scholarly press İletişim.[230] For the first time, the actual account of an Armenian survivor narrating the massacres he and his community suffered was introduced to the Turkish public sphere. In addition, the forewords and introductions written for such memoirs enabled additional Turks to also engage and relate their own experiences and impressions on the Armenian suffering. A case in point is the introduction to the memoir by Bayar Karakaş, an Armenian of Turkey now settled in the United States and writing about his father's past.[231] The introduction commences with the description of a group of young people who met in the Karakaş home, with one among the Turks delivering, during a history debate, a patriotic speech about the "alleged" Armenian massacres. The Karakaş family, who had of course not disclosed their origin, had listened from the next room, remaining silent and then sending the young people trays of food with great hospitality. The introduction continues:

> The humane warmth of this [Armenian] family, the way they distanced themselves from that rancor, their ability to surpass the pain and anger created by the injustices they experienced always deeply impressed me. Those who commit injustices never say "I am unjust." Unfortunately,

> it is often the case that those suffering injustice demonstrate greatness by first extending their hand toward those who have committed the injustice. Both the pain and pride of being human are embedded in this truth... [of] human enlightenment. Despite all the darkness that surrounds us, we should not be afraid of our light, our luminosity. Yet we are afraid of even [that]. It is so sad that we are not afraid of our darkness instead. Our darkness does not scare us, frightening us even when dark and uncaring people and systems surround us. Being unafraid of light ought to be the sole criteria of humanity. Next to a very deeply felt pain, such an attitude bestows upon one the distinction of feeling the dignity of being human.

Addressing the emotions surrounding justice and injustice, and adopting the contrasting imagery of light and darkness, the introduction written by an ethnic Turk thus invites the reader to choose human enlightenment, and thereby the luminous acknowledgment of the collective violence committed against the Armenians in the Turkish past.

The publication of such non-Muslim memoirs has been accompanied by memoirs of Turks and Kurds yearning for the past when they lived together with their non-Muslim neighbors, often recalling it as an experience that had enriched their lives. Such memoirs went against the grain of the hegemonic Turkish nationalist narrative that refused to even acknowledge the non-Muslim presence, except to exclude, marginalize, and denigrate. A case in point is the memoir of Hüseyin Irmak, a Kurd who spent his childhood in Kurtuluş, İstanbul, surrounded by non-Muslims in general and Armenians and Greek Rum in particular. He concluded his memoir with this paragraph:[232]

> How do Niko, Taso, Nahabet, Varujan, Kirkor, Arman, Yasef, Niso, Kamer, Takvor, Arto, Hacik, Verjin, Suzi, Şeli, Süzer, Korin, İrma, and Agop remember the past? Do they recall their childhoods like us? Do they remember those days, the Kurtuluş of those days with a sad smile on their faces?... Who knows where they are now?... Where is the fatherland of those people who had to leave? Why did they turn their yearnings into folk songs, their hearts into songs? Why did the local populace... exclude them? Why did they have to live torn-up lives, lost hopes, sorrow, separation, and yearning? Why did they have to grieve so deeply?... It would have been so nice if they had stayed here, on the land of their ancestors.... Could they have not found a remedy other than departure, migrating to the uncertainties of unknown lands? Why do so many of those who remain behind feel the need to use a Turkish name in addition to their own real one? What kind of a feeling must it

> be to use for a lifetime a name that is not actually one's own?...Now Kurtuluş is so faded, so dilapidated that one cannot help but be sad....One can no longer hear *mama, yaya, ahcik, yegur, ela, kalaysi, kalimera, kalispera, oley, madam, musu, matmazel.* We, their friends, were not the ones at fault for their departure.

Such memoirs of yearning recognize the past that once was in its human richness, then move on to consider how and why it was wiped away, empathizing with the losses and thereby easing the road to acknowledgment. The common theme across all such memoirs is the prioritization of humanity above all else, of relating to each other first as humans. In all, the memoirs not only contain knowledge of the past but also point the way to a brighter future in Turkey.

In the 1990s, the establishment of private universities was perhaps the most significant development in the production of knowledge outside Turkish state control. Currently, of the 146 universities in Turkey, only about 20 percent are privately funded. In spite of their relatively small proportion, however, these private universities have created new, independent public spaces for the research, discussion, and diffusion of new interpretations of Turkey's past. Indeed, many have held conferences, workshops, and panels taking a critical approach to the past, willing in the process to analyze the violence embedded within.[233] Academics at these universities have also started to collaborate with local civic organizations and nonprofit foundations, analyzing textbooks, collecting oral histories, and promoting tolerance.[234] Among such civic nonprofit foundations, many have recently taken the initiative to educate the Turkish public by annually commemorating 24 April 1915; they hold vigils, recognizing and mourning the deported Armenians.[235] The text accompanying the 2009 commemoration read as follows:

> The Armenian poets, writers, musicologists, lawyers, journalists, and physicians who were taken away by the arrests starting in İstanbul on 24 April 1915, leading many never to return, is being commemorated by the activities of the human rights organization....During these arrests, 220 Armenians including the most prominent representatives of Ottoman thought, arts, literature, and culture were taken away from their homes, most dying on deportation routes....The 24 April 1915 arrests marked the beginning of the process, leading to the material and spiritual destruction of Armenian society...[this] is a grave loss not only for the Armenian society, language, and culture, but also for us. We consider it our duty to commemorate them. The life stories and examples from the works of the three great poets of the Armenian language Siamanto, Taniel Varujan, and Rupen Savag and the poet, writer, lawyer, and socialist deputy Krikor Zohrab will be presented.

It is significant that the text acknowledges that the loss belonged to all, including the Turks; the massacres not only diminished the spirit of the Armenian community but intellectually impoverished the Turks as well. This public activity of the human rights organization then transformed into an annual event, gradually spreading to major cities throughout Turkey. On the same date, a separate commemoration was held at the Hrant Dink burial site in the Armenian cemetery in İstanbul.[236] Such human rights communities also employ Internet technology to maintain constant communication with each other and their members, mobilizing when necessary.[237] During the last decades, books and articles on non-Muslims in general and Armenians in particular have increased significantly as well.[238] The rise in the number of the members of the Armenian Diaspora returning to visit their ancestral lands also promotes the development of a common vision of a common past, and hopefully a common future.

During the last two decades, many articles and editorials appearing in the Turkish media have also helped generate a counterdenial narrative. Every year on 24 April, more and more articles and editorials appear that emphasize what this date meant and ought to mean for the Turks. A case in point is a 2007 editorial by journalist Semih İdiz, who notes: [239]

> We struggle with the "antipathy" whirpool of the Armenian issue. We do not say "let the genocide be officially recognized"; for those who believe it, let them do so, but also let those who do not express their views as well. Yet it is evident that unless we manage to nurture "empathy" and view the 1915 events from a more humane perspective, we will not be able to generate "sympathy" on this matter. Meanwhile, our efforts to imprison those who openly express their views on this issue do not serve any purpose other than increasing "antipathy." One cannot help but think that there ought to be a more rational road that needs to be taken.

Another journalist, Hüseyin Aygün, approaches the Armenian issue through self-reflection, drawing on his past personal experiences in which he witnessed, much to his surprise, discrimination against Armenians.[240] Indeed, looking into one's own past from such a vantage point often highlights many such events, experienced but duly unforgotten. I too had many similar experiences when I lived in Turkey during the first twenty-five years of my life. Looking back, I recalled one particular incident, when a grocer at whose store my family used to shop proudly told me that it was an honor to serve me because I was an ethnic Turk, "unlike those dirty Armenians." At the time, I remained silent, but I nevertheless tried to get my family to switch to another grocer. Now, whenever I encounter such prejudice, I immediately speak out.

At this juncture, one also needs to note how the counternarrative can be bolstered unintentionally, as in the case of the 2008 publication of Talat Pasha's diary by the conservative journalist Murat Bardakçı, who also happens to be a popular amateur Ottoman historian.[241] Even though Bardakçı had most of the documentation he had acquired from Talat Pasha's widow in his possession for the last twenty-six years, he could not publish the diary back then, he stated, because "ten years ago Turkey would not even accept the argument that the Armenian deportations had occurred... claiming instead that only some rebellions had taken place.... Then, things gradually progressed. In the 1980s, the academics who defended the official Turkish position at international courts warned me to make sure I did not make them public." According to the diary thus published, Bardakçı stated that the figures in the diary noting the number of Armenians at the beginning and end of the deportations indicated that a total of 972,246 Armenians were deported, a much larger figure than the ones claimed by official historians. What is most significant, however, is Bardakçı's severe yet correct ensuing criticism of the historians defending and promoting the official Turkish narrative:

> The [official historians] have been publishing stuff for years, getting funds from the secret funds and elsewhere, but they still do not have a single publication accepted outside Turkey. The publications are like mud, nonsensical; they employ terms like "immoral Armenians," and "they attacked us and we massacred them."... Those who have adopted the "rejection of the Armenian issue" as a professional duty, then going on to influence [Turkish] state authorities, must cease their activities. We suffered a lot from such people... because none of them ever follow what goes on in the world; they are not aware of anything.... We need to publish things that will be taken seriously by the international community; we need to approach issues with academic neutrality, thereby escaping ridicule. Other than the initial publication of Esat Uras's *The Armenian Question* in 1950 and now [my book], we have not been able to move forward by taking even a single step.... I have for years contended that the [Ottoman] archives are open to the public, but some significant documents cannot be found [because] they have been hidden away. The population registers are not there; there ought to be forty of them, but they are not there. The deportation registers are closed; some even contend that they do not exist. These two very significant collections of documents are not open to the public because of the pressures put on by those who are more royalist than the king.... You cannot convince anyone without those registers. It is for this reason that astute scholars stay away from this topic.... The ones opening these

> collections should not be the prime minister or the general chief of staff either. Some people are misleading them, telling them there are no such registers. This enables [such people] not to work on them, because they are afraid to do so.

It is significant, however, that Bardakçı's book was silenced in the Turkish media, with only a few newspapers willing to engage the book and comment on its implications. Academic and journalist Murat Belge wrote specifically about this silence to then address the Turkish state and its official narrative:[242]

> If you really want to do something constructive, stop shouting in a manner that does not convince anyone that "It did not happen! It did not happen!," instead using your efforts to construct a law that adequately defines what is what.... The book confirmed and reaffirmed once again what we already knew and kept stating... and [did so] from the mouth of Talat Pasha. Actually Talat Pasha did not say "this did not happen," either. There was no one back then who claimed "it did not happen." Everyone knew about it. The defense of Talat Pasha was not that it did not happen, but that "if I had not done so to the [Armenians], they would have done so to my people [the Turks]." That is what he had said. So what are the official authorities who are in total silence going to say now? They probably will not claim Talat Pasha lacked mathematical skills.... Truth is like this; you cannot keep it secret, it kicks to eventually emerge into broad daylight.

While the state authorities in Turkey working on the Armenian issue have indeed recently been silent, an increasing number of independent scholars have started to empirically research what happened, when, and most important, who the involved perpetrators were and what happened to them in the aftermath of the violence.

A case in point is the recent work of Sait Çetinoğlu.[243] In his extensive 2007 article on the perpetrators of the Armenian massacres exiled to Malta, Çetinoğlu not only analyzed the Malta exiles name by name but then traced their transition into the republican period, discussing the state and government positions each subsequently assumed. He revealed that most of the perpetrators not only were not punished or held accountable for their crimes but actually were rewarded by the republican state and governments with significant posts.[244] Çetinoğlu also inspected the 1955 budget containing the names of those given annual salaries from the category of "serving the fatherland." He did so to document those perpetrators who were rewarded by the Turkish republic, coming up with a list of twenty-five names.[245] Çetinoğlu added that the wives of many members of the

CUP central committee and SO members also received annual salaries from the Turkish republican state. Tracing the descendants of these perpetrators, he argued that many of their children also continued to occupy significant state posts throughout the republican period.[246] In addition, he compiled a list of all those righteous Turks who opposed the CUP deportation order and ensuing massacres, only to lose their lives or their posts.[247]

Next, Çetinoğlu undertook a thorough analysis of the abandoned Armenian properties. He did so because of the connection he surmised between these properties and Hrant Dink's murder, stating that "the process that targeted and intentionally led Hrant Dink to his death contains, in addition to his being an Armenian, three significant factors: acknowledging what happened to the Armenians in 1915 as genocide; Armenian orphans; and what happened to the Armenian properties." Çetinoğlu then delved into the archival records of the Settlement and Tribes Directorate (İskan ve Aşair Umum Müdürlüğü), noting that such records were very carefully kept because the Ottoman government "was much more careful in punishing those Turks who turned the national profit accruing from the confiscation of Armenian properties to their own personal profit; it did not at all investigate those who massacred the Armenians." During his search in the Ottoman archives, Çetinoğlu noted that the lists composed by abandoned properties commissions did not exist "as they were probably intentionally cleaned out." Yet, he still managed to find three lists of abandoned Armenian properties, from Kilis, Antioch/Belen in Turkey, and Cisr-i Şugur, now part of Syria. That the lists of these Armenian properties from three small towns were standardized led him to conjecture that the CUP government center had provided a blueprint for all local authorities to follow. The list from Kilis that he provided reads as follows:

> Deported [Armenian] population: Total 3879 (1917 women, 1762 men); Value of abandoned movable and immovable goods: 1,944,000 kurush; Value of livestock and grains: 124,816 kurush; Value of trade goods: 65,271 kurush; [Adding to] Total value: 190,087 kurush; Amount of abandoned [Armenian] properties: olive press: 4, bakery: 3, inn: 3, shop: 93, residence: 395; [Adding to] Total value: 1,678,348 kurush; The number of abandoned [Armenian] tilled lands: Poplar groves included in the register: 11,955; gardens confiscated as of today: 62; olive groves recorded as of today: 33,548; orchards included in the register as of today: 257,627. It is additionally presented [to the higher authorities] that this list records the private [Armenian] properties and lands... as indicated. It is certified that this list corresponds to the records of the Abandoned Properties Commission. 4 January 1915.

Çetinoğlu also documented the confidential correspondence pertaining to the ensuing official fight over the abandoned Armenian properties: the local postal directorate, the military command, and the quartermaster corps all made demands, trying to wrest some away from the others. Additional correspondence also revealed the great benefit that the Ottoman military accrued from this tragedy; the correspondence stated that "as the residences and shops left by the Armenians are surveyed, the dry goods, belongings, and material needed by the Ottoman military should be forwarded to them." Çetinoğlu then noted that he had contacted the Finance Ministry, the Directorate of National Properties (Milli Emlak Genel Müdürlüğü), and the Adana treasurer (Defterdar), where such abandoned properties were one of the most concentrated, only to be told that they had no such records. This negative response was the end result of the discussions that had taken place at the Turkish national assembly some eighty years earlier, on 16 April 1924, when the issue of how to legally register the Armenian and Greek Rum properties came up. It was argued that "the Armenians caused the destruction in the east... and the Greek Rum in the west... their cost to the [Turkish] nation should be recovered by including all their abandoned properties and goods... within [our national resources], [yet] we could not have openly stated these belonged to the Armenians and the Greek Rum... so we came up with various formula... to do so [basically not recording their origin]." This law silencing the confiscated and plundered Armenian and Greek Rum properties stayed in effect from 1924 to 1988, thereby obfuscating the origins of these properties that were taken over by local Turkish notables or the Turkish state. Çetinoğlu conjectured that since all the republican leaders had participated in this plunder, the Turkish state and its governments have been extremely wary of the Armenian issue, duly generating an official denial narrative to cover up this violent process.

It is apt to end this chapter with another significant incident in 2008 because of the manner in which it brought together the official narrative with the emerging counternarrative, demonstrating that the nationalist rhetoric of the Turkish authorities in relation to the Armenians no longer remains unaddressed. In 2008, at a talk delivered at a ceremony honoring the seventieth anniversary of the death of Mustafa Kemal Atatürk organized at the Turkish embassy in Brussels, defense minister Vecdi Gönül stated that the Turkish nation-state only came into being as a consequence of the deportations of the Armenians and Greek Rum. He explicitly noted: [248]

> If the existence of the Greek Rum in the Aegean region and of the Armenians in many regions of Turkey had continued as before, would it have been possible to maintain the same [Turkish] national state today? I do not know how to explain to you the significance of the population

> exchange undertaken with Greece, but its significance would become evident if one analyzes the former population balances. Even today, we cannot deny the contributions of those [Turks, Muslims] disadvantaged by those [non-Muslims] who considered themselves victimized by the deportations. The principles at the advent of the Turkish republic were extremely significant in turning Turkey into a modern, civilized, and enlightened country.

Hence, the minister identified and justified the violence committed against the Armenians by identifying it as one of the foundation stones of the Turkish nation-state. In the past, such nationalist statements would not have made any ripples in the Turkish media. Yet this was not the case in 2008; numerous editorials and articles emerged immediately, severely criticizing the defense minister. One journalist stated that during the nation-building process, there were many discriminatory and even racist actions by the Turkish state against the minorities, but that such mistakes were eventually recognized and acknowledged by at least those who possessed a brain. He then continued:[249]

> The 1915 Armenian deportation is a grave disgrace of the CUP that through all of its policies led the Ottoman Empire to its death. Today, none of those who are Turkish citizens should have the responsibility of shouldering this disgrace. Yet by owning up to this horrid event, the defense minister is not aware that he is harming the entire Turkish populace. He is not aware how his statements are going to be used in the genocide debates.... He is unaware that... Bulgaria... and Germany... could employ the same argument... to deport all the Turks living there.... Also, someone sharing the defense minister's mentality may emerge, claiming "look, we have solved the Armenian issue through deportations, so we can also resolve the Kurdish issue through deportations as well."... Let this minister go to his house right away, buy some decent books to improve [his knowledge] to understand what is happening in the world in 2008.

Another journalist drew attention to the mentality behind the defense minister's statements, one predicated on Turkish nationalism that placed "us" before "them, often converging with paranoia, leading the Turks to then wrongfully consider themselves as eternal victims, thereby overlooking the past instances when they were indeed the perpetrators.[250] In an interview, one scholar commented that the defense minister had literally admitted to having committed religious and ethnic cleansing and then continued:[251]

> From the foundation of the [Turkish] nation until now, there was no space for those who were not Muslim; in addition, even those Muslims outside Turkey would be accepted into the nation [only] if they were Turkified, giving up their identities in the process.... The important thing is to draw lessons from what happened.... In the aftermath of the Armenian deportations, the economy of east Anatolia collapsed irrevocably... the population exchange likewise caused severe economic damage.... those expelled [Armenians and Greek Rum] had been the bourgeoisie and artisans who had accumulated capital. So the operation under question was not one of transforming the capital from the non-Muslims to the Turks, but instead one of plunder. The Turks were unable to transform what they confiscated into capital because they did not have the necessary skills and knowledge... further weakening Turkey as a consequence.

Still another scholar elaborated on what would have happened if the non-Muslims had not been forcefully expelled, arguing that "western Anatolia would not have had barren mountains, but instead cultivated gardens; Anatolia would have been extremely civilized and democratized with thousands of schools; Islam would not have emerged as the hegemonic religion, as it would have been balanced out by a multiplicity of faiths." As a consequence of such forced deportations, he concluded, "Turkey's industrialization process was set back at least fifty years."[252]

In another interview, a young scholar carefully argued and documented that the population exchange with Greece had been a form of ethnic cleansing for Turkey, one that led "one in four Greek Rum in the refugee camps to lose their lives.... Since 1.5 million Greek Rum were submitted to the exchange, about 200,000 ended up dying." He added that ethnic cleansing was a Unionist project, one that nevertheless "remained in practice until the 1950s.... Turkey would have been much more civilized had the Greek Rum and Armenians stayed."[253] The civilian activist group Young Civilians (Genç Siviller) also put out a special press release, protesting the statement of the minister:

> We understand you have no respect toward the deaths of our hundreds of thousands of Greek Rum and Armenians with whom we [once shared] the country. At least remove your hands from the necks of the handful that have remained behind. Such statements you make bring fear, leading to the assassinations of those promoting peace [like Hrant Dink].... What are you defending, Vecdi Gönül?... Are you defending those perpetrators who raped and murdered hundreds of thousands of [Greek Rum and Armenians] to then confiscate their properties and goods?... Isn't so much death enough for you?... This country

> does not belong to you, Vecdi Gönül.... Yet you might be right on one account.... If those Unionists with whom you share the same worldview had allowed, we the Armenians, we the Greek Rum, we the Kurds, we the Circassians, we the Assyrians, we the Turks, all of us who are not bothered by our difference, but instead celebrate it, we all could have tilled our fertile lands together, singing our songs altogether.... Obey the laws you have written. Do not incite people against one another. First, apologize to all our people you hint are not "truly modern, civilized, and enlightened," and then resign from the seat you have latched on for a century. Do so, because we do not have a single victim left to sacrifice to your destructive clutches.

All these statements reveal the manner in which many scholars, intellectuals, and journalists in Turkey have started to challenge the official narrative predicated on denial, gradually formulating a counternarrative in the process, one that ought to lead to eventual acknowledgment, if not by the Turkish state and its governments, certainly by Turkish society. I want to conclude the discussion of the denial of responsibility with another commentary on the minister's statement, one written by Hrant Dink's son, Arat Dink. Following in his father's footsteps, he gave voice to the Armenians of Turkey, bringing forward their perspective once again:[254]

> Of course the saddest point is that most of what the minister says was unfortunately true. So what if it is true, why is that a problem? The minister is right, but he is right for the wrong reasons. He hurls around our chests filled with the touchy poignance we had hidden in the attics and basements of our hearts, ones we carry along wherever we go. From the route to the consolation that "everyone suffered a lot back then," he suddenly veers into one of "what happened was a good thing." He thus recounts what happened correctly, but at the same time, he also says what happened was right.... So what does the defense minister defend? That our absence would be better, that deportations and population exchanges were good for Turkey.... Hasn't he ever passed by the house of conscience?

Conclusion

When I completed the first draft of this book, I consciously decided not to write a conclusion because the denial of the Turkish state and society of the collective violence committed against the Armenians continues on in Turkey today. I wanted to capture that awkward, unsatisfactory state of incompletion that the lack of closure produces and has produced for almost a century for the Armenian victims and their descendants. I promised to write the final chapter if and when Turkish state and society finally acknowledged this foundational violence located in their past. Such a response rightfully privileges the victims of the collective violence as it should.

Colleagues pointed out that I should also address the perpetrators, since I have mainly intended this book for them, to comprehend what has happened in their past according to my reading of it. Having been born and raised in Turkey, I came to respect the communal compassion and care I experienced while increasingly becoming aware of and challenging the inherent discriminatory exclusion practiced against the community of Turks. In Turkey today, acknowledging the Armenian Genocide is primarily viewed as a public act that is forced upon the Turks by the West and the Armenians; it is widely believed that the acknowledgment will benefit these parties alone. I argue the contrary in this book, pointing out how the way collective violence infused into Turkish republic corrupted and undermined public ethics. While Turks still abide by moral standards in their personal lives, all complain about the lack of trust and respect in public life. Unless Turkish state and society come to terms with the collective violence embedded in their past, they will not be able to recover such trust and respect in their own state and society. And they will not have hope in the future because they still do not believe in humankind, in the goodness of others. They do not, because their sense of justice has been undermined: many perpetrators who have committed heinous crimes still walk around free, not held accountable for their destructive acts by the state, government, and its presumably independent legal institutions. As long as such perpetrators are not punished and thereby held accountable for what they committed, Turkish state and society will not recover their sense of justice and with it hope in a better future.

I want to end with a note to my colleagues because this book attempts to study collective violence in history through a sociological lens. Through this research, I have become aware of how significant and yet underexamined emotions are in studying phenomena like violence and denial. I have tried to include affective elements alongside structural ones to articulate how collective denial emerges and reproduces itself in states and societies. The denial provides some sense of why many states and societies face so many challenges in accomplishing equality for all their citizens and, as such, hopefully takes us one step further than the functionalist approaches often employed to explain continuity. Resistance to change is complex, emerging in spite of the constant attempts of states and societies to change and to do so for the better. Perhaps the theoretical employment of structural and affective elements on the one hand and the methodological use of resources like memoirs on the other may help capture the often wide discrepancy between what states and societies intend and what they actually accomplish.

What to do next? Empirically, I am interested in seeing how the collective violence I studied here was employed within the Turkish republic against another, this time Muslim group, namely, the Kurds. Another research venue would be to comparatively analyze similar instances of foundational violence, such as that conducted against the native peoples in the United States and in many countries in Europe and South America. Only when we understand and come to terms with such collective violence embedded in all of our pasts can we create a better future for our descendants.

Appendix A

CONTEMPORANEOUS MEMOIRS EMPLOYED IN THE BOOK

- Abdurrahman Şeref Efendi [1823–1925]
  - 1978 [1923] *Tarih Musahabeleri (Conversations on History)*. Ankara: Ministry of Culture and Tourism.
  - 1996 [1892] *Son Vak'anüvis Abdurrahman Şeref Efendi Tarihi: II. Meşrutiyet Olayları, 1908–1909 (The History of the Last Official Chronicler Abdurrahman Şeref Efendi: The Events of the Second Constitution, 1908–1909)*. Ankara: TTK.
- Abdülhamid Han-ı Sani [1842–1918]
  - 1985 [1924] *Hatıra Defteri (Diary of Memories)*. Ed. İsmet Bozdağ. İstanbul: Pınar.
  - 1987 *Siyasi Hatıratım (My Political Memories)*. İstanbul: Pınar.
  - 1994 *Saray Hatıraları (Palace Memories)*. Ed. A.N. Galitekin, İstanbul: Nehir.
- Adıvar, Halide Edip [1883–1964]
  - 1963 *Mor Salkımlı Ev (The House with Wisteria)*. İstanbul: Atlas.
  - 2005 [1962] *Türkün Ateşle İmtihanı: İstiklal Savaşı Hatıraları (The Trial of the Turk by Fire: Memories of the Independence Struggle)*. İstanbul: Özgür.
- Ağaoğlu, Ahmed [1869–1939]
  - 1994 [1940] *Serbest Fırka Hatıraları (Memories of the Free Party)*. İstanbul: İletişim.
- Ağaoğlu, Samet [1909–82]
  - 1998 [1958] *Babamın Arkadaşları (The Friends of My Father)*. İstanbul: İletişim.

- Ahmed Cevdet Paşa [1822–95]
  - 1986 [1933] *Tezakir (Notes)*. 4 vols. Ankara: TTK.
- Ahmed Hilmi, Şehbenderzade Filibeli [1865–1913]
  - 1991 [1913] *Muhalefetin İflası: Hürriyet ve İtilaf Fırkası (The Bankruptcy of the Opposition: The Liberty and Entente Party)*. İstanbul: Nehir.
- Ahmed İzzet [Furgaç] Paşa [1864–1937]
  - 1993 *Feryadım (My Cry)*. İstanbul: Nehir.
- Ahmed Mithat Efendi [1844–1912]
  - 2004 *Üss-i İnkılap: Kırım Muharebesinden II. Abdülhamid Han'ın Cülusuna Kadar (The Foundations of Transformation: From the Crimean War [1856] to the Accession of Abdülhamid II [1876])*. İstanbul: Selis.
- Ahmed Muhtar Paşa, Gazi [1839–1919]
  - 1996 [1912] *Anılar: Sergüzeşt-i Hayatım (Memoirs: My Life Adventure)*. 2 vols. İstanbul: Tarih Vakfı Yurt Yayınları.
- Ahmed Rasim [1865–1932]
  - 1976 *İki Hatırat Üç Şahsiyet (Two Memoirs and Three Personalities)*. İstanbul: Çağdaş.
- Ahmed Rıza Bey [1859–1930]
  - 1988 *Meclis-i Mebusan ve Ayan Reisi Ahmed Rıza Bey'in Anıları (Memoirs of Ahmed Rıza Bey, the Head of the Ottoman Parliament and Senate)*. İstanbul: Arba.
- Ahmed Ubeydullah [Hatipoğlu] Efendi [1858–1937]
  - 2002 *Malta, Afganistan ve İran Hatıraları (Malta, Afghanistan and Iran Memoirs)*. İstanbul: Dergah.
- Akgiray, Hasan Basri [1918–2011]
  - 2003 [2000] *Gereği Düşünüldü: Anılar (It Has Been Considered: Memoirs)*. İstanbul: Kaynak.
- Akıncı, İbrahim Ethem [1889–1950]
  - 1978 [1936] *Demirci Akıncıları (The Demirci Raiders)*. Ankara: TTK.
- Akkılıç, Abdülhalim [1891–1960]
  - 1994 *Askerin Romanı: Emekli Süvari Albay Abdülhalim Akkılıç'ın Savaş ve Barış Anıları (The Prose Narrative of a Soldier: The War and Peace Memories of Retired Cavalry Colonel of Abdülhalim Akkılıç)*. Gemlik: Körfez. Published by son Yılmaz Akkılıç [1933–2010]
- Akyavaş, A. Ragıp [1890–1969]
  - 2002 *Tarih Meşheri: Hatırat (Display of History: Memoir)*. 2 vols. İstanbul: Diyanet Vakfı.
- Aldan, Mehmed [1923–2012]
  - 1992 *Mülki İdarede bir Ömür: Anılar (A Lifetime in Civil Service: Memories)*. Ankara: Erk.
- Ali Kemal [1867–1922]
  - 1985 *Ömrüm (My Life)*. Published by son Zeki Kuneralp. İstanbul: İsis.

- Ali Rıza Bey, Balıkhane Nazırı [1842–1928]
  - 1975 [1970] *Bir Zamanlar İstanbul (İstanbul Once upon a Time)*. İstanbul: Tercüman.
- Alican, Fikri [1930–]
  - 2000 *Koca Meşenin Gölgesi (The Shadow of the Great Oak Tree)*. İstanbul: Doğan.
- Altay, Fahrettin [1880–1974]
  - 1998 *İmparatorluktan Cumhuriyete (From the Empire to the Republic)*. Ed. Taylan Sorgun. İstanbul: Kamer.
- Altınay, Ahmed Refik [1881–1937]
  - 1998 [1919] *İki Komite İki Kıtal (Two Committees Two Massacres)*. İstanbul: Temel.
- Amça, Hasan Çerkes [1884–1961]
  - 1958 *Nizamiye Kapısı (The Nizamiye [School] Gate)*. İstanbul: M. Sıralar.
  - 1989 [1958] *Doğmayan Hürriyet: Bir Devrin İçyüzü 1908–1918 (The Unborn Freedom: Inside Story of an Era 1908–1918)*. İstanbul: Arba.
- Anter, Musa [1917–92]
  - 1999 [1990] *Hatıralarım (My Memoirs)*. İstanbul: Avesta.
- Apak, Rahmi [1889–1969]
  - 1988 *Yetmişlik bir Subayın Hatıraları (Memoirs of a Seventy-Year-Old Colonel)*. Ankara: TTK.
- Aray, Suat [1902–]
  - 1959 *Bir Galatasaraylının Hatıraları: Mektebi Sultanide Saltanattan Cumhuriyete (Memories of a Galatasaray Graduate: From Empire to the Republic)*. İstanbul: Yayınevi.
- Arıkan, İbrahim [1893–]
  - 2007 *Osmanlı Ordusunda Bir Nefer (An Enlisted Man in the Ottoman Army)*. İstanbul: Timaş.
- Arıkoğlu, Damar [1889–1969]
  - 1961 *Hatıralarım (My Memories)*. İstanbul: n.p.
- Arseven, Celal Esat [1876–1971]
  - 1993 *Sanat ve Siyaset Hatıralarım (My Memoirs Pertaining to Fine Arts and Politics)*. İstanbul: İletişim.
- Arslan, Emir Şekip [1869–1946]
  - 2005 *Bir Arap Aydınının Gözüyle Osmanlı Tarihi ve 1. Dünya Savaşı Anıları (Ottoman History and the Memoirs of WWI from the Viewpoint of an Arab Intellectual)*. İstanbul: Çatı.
- Aşcıdede Halil İbrahim [1828–ca. 1906]
  - 1960 *Hatıralar (Memoirs)*. İstanbul: İstanbul Ansiklopedisi.
- Atatürk, Mustafa Kemal [1881–1938]
  - 1991 [1983] *Karlsbad Hatıraları (Karlsbad Memories)*. Ed. Afet İnan. Ankara: TTK.

- 1998 [1961] *Atatürk'ün Özel Mektupları (The Private Letters of Atatürk)*. İstanbul: Kaynak.
- Atay, Falih Rıfkı [1893–1971]
  - 1938 [1932] *Zeytindağı (Olive Mountain)*. İstanbul: Remzi.
  - 1999 [1963] *Batış Yılları (The Years of Decline)*. İstanbul: Bateş.
  - 2004 [1961] *Çankaya*. İstanbul: Pozitif.
- Avar, Sıdıka [1901–79]
  - 1986 *Dağ Çiçeklerim: Anılar (My Wild Flowers: Memories)*. İstanbul: Öğretmen.
- Ayaşlı, Münevver [1906–99]
  - 1990 [1973] *İşittiklerim, Gördüklerim, Bildiklerim (What I Heard, I Saw and I Knew)*. İstanbul: Boğaziçi.
- Aykaç, Fazıl Ahmed [1883–1967]
  - 1991 [1923] *Kırpıntı (Clippings)*. İstanbul: Arba.
- Aykan, Cevdet [1925–]
  - 2003 *Demokratik Süreç ve Anılar (Memoirs and the Democratic Process [in Turkey])*. Ankara: Grafiker.
- Ayni, Mehmed Ali [1868–1943]
  - 1945 *Hatıraları (Memoirs)*. İstanbul: Türkiye.
- Aznavour, Charles [1924–]
  - 2005 *Geçmiş Zaman Olur ki (Once upon a Time)*. İstanbul: Aras.
- Bahar (Morhaim), Beki [1926–2011]
  - 2003 *Efsaneden Tarihe Ankara Yahudileri (The Ankara Jews from Legend to History)*. İstanbul: Pan.
- Balkan, Fuat [1887–1970]
  - 1998 *İlk Türk Komitacısı Fuat Balkan'ın Hatıraları (The Memoirs of the First Turkish Komitadji [Underground Revolutionary Activist] Fuat Balkan)*. İstanbul: Arma.
- Bardakçı, Cemal [ca. 1887–1981]
  - 1945 *Toprak Davasından Siyasi Partilere (From Land Conflict to Political Parties)*. İstanbul: Işıl.
  - 1991 [1942] *Devşirmelerle Sığıntılardan ve Mütegallibededen Neler Çektik? (How We Suffered from Converts, Parasites, and Tyrants?)*. Bolu: Vilayet Matbaası.
- Bardakçı, İlhan [1926–2004]
  - 1975 *Taşhan'dan Kadifekale'ye (From Taşhan to Kadifekale)*. İstanbul: Milliyet.
- Barutçu, Faik Ahmed [1894–1959]
  - 1977 *Siyasi Anılar (Political Memories)*. İstanbul: Milliyet.
- Başar, Ahmed Hamdi [1897–]
  - 2007 [1945] *Hatıraları (His Memoirs)*. 2 vols. Ed. Murat Koraltürk. İstanbul: Bilgi University.

- Başgil, Ali Fuat [1893–1967]
  - 1990 *Hatıraları (His Memoirs)*. İstanbul: Boğaziçi.
- Batur, Muhsin [1920–99]
  - 1985 *Anılar ve Görüşler (Memoirs and Opinions)*. İstanbul: Milliyet.
- Bayar, Mahmut Celalettin [1883–1986]
  - 1965 *Ben de Yazdım (I Too Wrote)*. 7 vols. İstanbul: Baha.
- Baytın, Arif [1880s?–]
  - 1946 *İlk Dünya Harbinde Kafkas Cephesi: Hatıralar (The Caucasus Front during the First World War)*. İstanbul: Vakit.
  - 2007 *Sessiz Ölüm: Sarıkamış Günlüğü (Silent Death: Sarıkamış Diaries)*. Revised reprint. İstanbul: Yeditepe.
- Baytok, Taner [1936–]
  - 2005 *Dış Politikada Bir Nefes: Anılar (A Breath in Foreign Politics: Memoirs)*. İstanbul: Remzi.
- Bedirhan, Mehmed Salih [1873–]
  - 1998 *Defter-i Amalım (My Notebook of Wishes)*. İstanbul: Belge.
- Behmoaras, Liz [1950–]
  - 2005 *Bir Kimlik Arayışının Hikayesi (The Story of a Search for Identity)*. Istanbul: Remzi.
- Belli, Mihri [1916–2011]
  - 2000 [1989] *İnsanlar Tanıdım: Mihri Belli'nin Anıları (I Met People: The Memoirs of Mihri Belli)*. İstanbul: Doğan.
- Belli (Tarı), Sevim [1925–]
  - 1994 *Boşuna mı Çiğnedik? Anılar (Did We Tread for Naught? Memoirs)*. İstanbul: Belge.
- Benlioğlu, Abdurrahman [1903–79]
  - 2004 *Hatıraları (Memoirs)*. İstanbul: General Chief of Staff.
- Bereketzade İsmail Hakkı [1851–1918]
  - 1997 [1913] *Yad-ı Mazi (Remembrance of the Past)*. İstanbul: Nehir.
- Berkem, Süreyya Sami [1890–1968]
  - 1960 *Unutulmuş Günler (Forgotten Days)*. İstanbul: Hilmi.
- Berkes, Niyazi [1908–88]
  - 1997 *Unutulan Yıllar (The Forgotten Years)*. Ed. Ruşen Sezer. İstanbul: İletişim.
- Beşe, Hüseyin Atıf [1880s?–]
  - 2004 *Dedem Hüseyin Atıf Beşe (My Grandfather Hüseyin Atıf Beşe)*. Prepared by Güliz Beşe Erginsoy. İstanbul: Varlık.
- Beyatlı, Yahya Kemal [1884–1958]
  - 1973 *Çocukluğum, Gençliğim, Siyasi ve Edebi Hatıralarım (My Childhood, Youth, Political and Literary Memoirs)*. İstanbul: Baha.
  - 1975 *Tarih Musahabeleri (Conversations in History)*. İstanbul: Fetih Cemiyeti.

- 1997 *Yahya Kemal'in Hatıraları (The Memoirs of Yahya Kemal)*. İstanbul: Fetih Cemiyeti.

- Bilgiç, Sadettin [1920–]
  - 1998 *Hatıralar (Memories)*. İstanbul: Boğaziçi.
- Binark, Nermidil Erner [1925–]
  - 2000 *Şakir Paşa Köşkü: Ahmet Bey ve Şakirler (The Şakir Paşa Mansion: Ahmet Bey and the Şakirs)*. İstanbul: Remzi.
  - 2004 *Sadece Anı Değil (Not Only Memories)*. İstanbul: Remzi.
- Biren, Mehmed Tevfik [1876–1956]
  - 1993 *II. Abdülhamid, Meşrutiyet ve Mütareke Devri Hatıraları (Memoirs of the Abdülhamid II, Constitutional and Armistice Periods)*. İstanbul: Arma.
- Bleda, Mithat Şükrü [1872–1956]
  - 1979 *Bir İmparatorluğun Çöküşü (The Decline of an Empire)*. İstanbul: Remzi.
- Bolayır, Ali Ekrem [1867–1937]
  - 1991 *Hatıraları (His Memoirs)*. Ed. Kayahan Özgül. İstanbul: Kültür Bakanlığı.
- Borçbakan, Ali Cevat [1876–1966]
  - 2005 *Hatıraları (Memories)*. Ed. Saime Yüceer. Bursa: Uludağ Üniversitesi.
- Bozok, Salih [1881–1941]
  - 1985 *Hep Atatürk'ün Yanında (Always beside Atatürk)*. İstanbul: Cağaloğlu.
- Bölükbaşı, Rıza Tevfik [ca. 1869–1949]
  - 1993 *Biraz da Ben Konuşayım (It Is My Turn to Talk)*. Ed. A. Uçman. İstanbul: İletişim.
- Burak, Ratip Tahir [1904–76]
  - 1961 *Hapishane Hatıraları (Prison Memoirs)*. İstanbul: Güven.
- Cabi Ömer Efendi [ca. 1749–]
  - 2003 *Cabi Tarihi—Tarih-i Sultan Selim-i Salis ve Mahmud-u Sani (Cabi Chronicle: The History of [Sultans] Selim III and Mahmud I)*. Vol. 2. Ankara: TTK.
- Cavid Bey [1875–1926]
  - 2000 *Felaket Günleri: Mütareke Devrinin Feci Tarihi (Disastrous Days: The Terrible History of the Armistice Period)*. 2 vols. İstanbul: Temel.
- Cebesoy, Ali Fuat [1882–1968]
  - 1998 [1953] *Milli Mücadele Hatıraları (Memoirs of the National Struggle)*. İstanbul: Temel.
- Cemal Paşa [1872–1922]
  - 1933 *Hatıralar ve Vesikalar (Memories and Documents)*. Ankara: Vakit.
  - 1959 *Hatıralar (Memories)*. İstanbul: Selek.
  - 1977 *Hatıralar: İttihat ve Terakki, I. Dünya Savaşı Anıları (Union and Progress and First World War Memories)*. İstanbul: Çağdaş.

- Cemaleddin Efendi, Şeyhülislam [1848–1919]
  - 1990 [1917] *Siyasi Hatıralarım (My Political Memoirs)*. İstanbul: Nehir.
- Çalıka, Hurşit [1887–1963]
  - 1992 *Ahmet Rifat Çalıka'nın Anıları (Memoirs of Ahmet Rifat Çalıka)*. İstanbul: n.p.
- Çambel, Hasan Cemil [1877–1967]
  - 1987 [1960] *Makaleler Hatıralar (Articles, Memoirs)*. Ankara: TTK.
- *Çanakkale Hatıraları (Dardanelle Memoirs)*
  - 1964 İstanbul: Arma, two volumes.
- Çarıklı, Hacim Muhittin [1881–1965]
  - 1967 *Balıkesir ve Alaşehir Kongreleri ve Hacim Muhittin Çarıklı'nın Kuvayı Milliye Hatıraları (1919–1920) (The Balıkesir and Alaşehir Congresses and the National Force Memoirs of Hacim Muhittin Çarıklı [1919–1920])*. Ankara: Ankara University Press.
  - 2005 *Babam Hacim Muhittin Çarıklı (My Father Hacim Muhşttşn Çarıklı: The Life Story of a Member of the National Forces [Kuvay-ı Milliyeci])*. İstanbul: Boğaziçi Üniversitesi Yayınevi.
- Çerkes Ethem [ca. 1883–1948]
  - 2000 [1955] *Anılarım (My Memoirs)*. İstanbul: Berfin.
- Çerkezyan, Sarkis [1916–2009]
  - 2003 *Dünya Herkese Yeter (The World Is Big Enough for Everyone)*. Ed. Y. Gedik. İstanbul: Belge.
- Çetinkaya, Ali [1878–1949]
  - 1993 *Ali Çetinkaya'nın Milli Mücadele Dönemi Hatıraları (The Memoirs of Ali Çetinkaya on the Era of the Independence Struggle)*. Ankara: TTK.
- Çolak, İbrahim [1879–1944]
  - 1996 *Milli Mücadele Esnasında Kuva-yı Seyyare Kumandanlığıma ait Hatıratım (My Memoir on Commanding the Mobile Military Forces during the National Struggle)*. Ed. O. Hülagü. İstanbul: Emre.
- Damadyan, Mihran [1863–1945]
  - 2009 *Bir Komitecinin İtirafları (Confessions of a Komitaji)*. Istanbul: Timaş.
- Davudoğlu, Ahmed [1910s?–]
  - 1979 *Ölüm Daha Güzeldi (Death Was More Beautiful)*. İstanbul: Kitsan.
- Deleon, Jak [1951–2005]
  - 1993 *Pera Hatıratı (Pera Memoir)*. İstanbul: Gözlem.
- Delilbaşı, Nizamettin [1880s?–]
  - 1946 *Hatıralarım (My Memoirs)*. İstanbul: Türkiye Yayınları.
- Demirer, Hüseyin (Hisene Emin) [1919–83]
  - 2008 *Ha Wer Delal (Emine Perixanenin Hayatı) (The Life of Emine Perixane)*. İstanbul: Avesta.

- Denker, Arif Cemil [1888–1945]
    - 1992 *İttihatçı Şeflerin Gurbet Maceraları (The Adventures Abroad of the CUP Leaders)*. İstanbul: Arma.
    - 1998 I. Dünya Savaşında Teşkilat-ı Mahsusa (The Special Organization during World War I). Istanbul: Arba.
    - 2005 *Sürgün Hayatlar (Exiled Lives)*. İstanbul: Emre.
- Derin, Haldun [1912–]
    - 1995 *Çankaya Özel Kalemini Anımsarken, 1933–1951 (Remembering the Presidential Private Secretariat, 1933–1951)*. Ed. Cemil Koçak. İstanbul: TTV.
- Dersimi, Nuri [ca. 1893–1973]
    - 1992 *Dersim ve Kürt Milli Mücadelesine Dair Hatıratım (My Memoir Concerning Dersim and the Kurdish National Struggle)*. Ankara: Özge.
    - 1997 *Hatıratım (My Memoir)*. İstanbul: Doz.
- Diken, Şeyhmus [1954–]
    - 2002 *Sırrını Surlarına Fısıldayan Şehir: Diyarbakır (Diyarbakır, the City That Whispers Its Secrets to Its Forts)*. İstanbul: İletişim.
- Dikerdem, Mahmut [1916–93]
    - 1989 *Hariciye Çarkı (The Grindstone of the Turkish Foreign Ministry)*. İstanbul: Cem.
- Dirik, Kazım [1881–1941]
    - 1998 *Babam General Kazım Dirik ve Ben (My Father General Kazım Dirik and I)*. Ed. Orhan Dirik. İstanbul: YKY.
- Doğan, Avni [1892–1965]
    - 1964 *Kurtuluş Kuruluş ve Sonrası (Independence, Establishment [of the Republic] and Aftermath)*. İstanbul: Dünya.
- Doğrugüven, Uğur [1910s?–]
    - 2003 *Şaşkın Kuşak (The Bewildered Generation)*. İstanbul: Nokta.
- Duhani, Said [–1970]
    - 1984 [1982] *Eski İnsanlar, Eski Evler: 19. yüzyıl sonundaBeyoğlu'nun Sosyal Topoğrafyası (Old Houses, Old People: The Social Topography of Pera at the End of the 19th Century)*. İstanbul: Turing.
- Duru, Kazım Nami [1876–1967]
    - 1957 *İttihat ve Terakki Hatıralarım (My Memoirs of the Union and Progress)*. İstanbul: Sucuoğlu.
    - 1959 *Arnavutluk ve Makedonya Hatıralarım (My Memoirs of Albania and Macedonia)*. İstanbul: Sucuoğlu.
- Ekdal, Müfid [1918–]
    - 2003 *Eski Bir İhtilalciden (Hasan Amça) Dinlediklerim (Things I Listened to from an Old Revolutionary Hasan Amça)*. İstanbul: Kitabevi.

- El-Kazımi, Mehmed Avnullah [1868–1914]
  - 2005 [1910] *Son Müdafaa Divan-ı Örfi ve Avnullah el-Kazımi (Avnullah el-Kazımi the Last Defense and the Tribunal).* Ed. Osman Selim Kocahanoğlu. İstanbul: Şehir.
- Erden, Ali Fuad [1883–1957]
  - 2003 [1920] *Birinci Dünya Harbinde Suriye Hatıraları (Memoirs of Syria during WWI).* İstanbul: İş Bankası.
- Erdoğan, Fahrettin [1874–1958]
  - 1998 [1954] *Türk Ellerinde Hatıralarım (My Memoirs in Turkish Lands).* Ankara: Ministry of Culture.
- Erendoruk, Ömer Osman [1934–2006]
  - 2007 *Bir Başkadır Bizim Eller: Hatıralar, Gözlemler (Our Lands Are Different: Memories and Observations).* İstanbul: Çağrı.
- Ergeneli, Adnan [1912–]
  - 1993 *Çocukluğumun Savaş Yılları Anıları (The War Year Memories of My Childhood).* İstanbul: İletişim.
- Erkanlı, Orhan [1924–]
  - 1972 *Anılar, Sorunlar, Sorumlular (Memories, Problems and Those Responsible for Them).* İstanbul: Baha.
- Erkin, Feridun Cemal [1900–1980]
  - 1986 [1980] *Dışişlerinde 34 Yıl (34 Years at the Foreign Ministry).* 3 vols. Ankara: TTK.
- Ertuğrul, Muhsin [1892–1979]
  - 1989 *Benden Sonra Tufan Olmasın! (Let There Be No Deluge after Me!).* İstanbul: Eczacıbaşı Vakfı Yayınları.
- Ertürk, Hüsamettin [1890s?–]
  - 1957 *İki Devrin Perde Arkası (Two Eras behind the Scenes).* İstanbul: Hilmi.
- Esatlı, Mustafa Ragıp [1896–]
  - 2004 [1933] *İttihat veTerakki Tarihinde Esrar Perdesi: Yakup Cemil Niçin ve Nasıl Öldürüldü? (Curtain of Mystery in the History of the Union and Progress: How and Why Was Yakup Cemil Killed?).* İstanbul: Örgün.
- Esendal, Memduh Şevket [1883–1952]
  - 2003 *Oğullarıma Mektuplar (Letters to My Sons).* Ankara: Bilgi.
- Eti, Ali Rıza [1887–1965]
  - 2009 *Bir Onbaşının Doğu Cephesi Günlüğü (1914–1915) (The Eastern Front Diary of a Corporal, 1914–1915).* Ed. Gönül Eti. İstanbul: İş Bankası.
- Eyüboğlu, İsmet Zeki [1925–2003]
  - 1999 *Anılar (Memories).* İstanbul: Pencere.
- Eyüp Sabri [Akgöl] [1884–1953]
  - 1978 *Bir Esirin Hatıraları (The Memoirs of a Captive).* İstanbul: Tercüman.

- Fani, Ali İlmi [1867–1922]
  - 1998 *Bir 150'liğin Mektupları (Letters of One of the 150 (Exiled by the Nationalists)*. Ed. Abdullah Uçman. İstanbul: Kitabevi.
- Fatma Aliye Hanım [1862–1924]
  - 1994 [1916] *Ahmed Cevdet Paşa ve Zamanı (Ahmed Cevdet Pasha and His Time)*. İstanbul: Pınar.
- Felek, Burhan [1889–1982]
  - 1974 *Yaşadığımız Günler (The Days We Lived Through)*. İstanbul: Milliyet.
- Fethi Naci [1927–2008]
  - 1999 *Dönüp Baktığımda (When I Look Back)*. İstanbul: Adam.
- Gerede, Hüsrev [1886–1962]
  - 2002 *Hüsrev Gerede'nin Anıları: Kurtuluş Savaşı, Atatürk ve Devrimler (Memoirs of Hüsrev Gerede: The War of Independence, Atatürk and the Reforms)*. Ed. Sami Önal. İstanbul: Literatür.
- Gilmanoğlu, Fatih Kerimi [1870–1945]
  - 2001 *İstanbul Mektupları (İstanbul Letters)*. İstanbul: Çağrı.
- Giz, Adnan [1914–89]
  - 1988 *Bir Zamanlar Kadıköy (Kadıköy Once upon a Time)*. İstanbul: İletişim.
- Gökalp, Ziya [1875–1924]
  - 1965 *Limni ve Malta Mektupları (Letters from Lemnos and Malta)*. Ankara: TTK.
- Güley, Ferda [1916–2008]
  - 1990 *Kendini Yaşamak (To Live Oneself)*. İstanbul: Cem.
- Günday, A. Faik Hurşit [1884–]
  - 1960 *Hayatım ve Hatıralarım (My Life and Memories)*. İstanbul: Çelikcilt.
- Gündem, Naci [1906–]
  - 2002 [1955] *Günler Boyunca: Hatıralar (Along the Days: Memoirs)*. İzmir: Belediye.
- Günsav, Bekir Sami [1879–1934]
  - 1994 *Kurtuluş Savaşı Anıları (Memories of the Independence Struggle)*. Ed. Muhittin Ünal. İstanbul: Cem.
- Günyol, Vedat [1911–2004]
  - 1990 *Uzak Yakın Anılar (Memories Near and Far)*. İstanbul: Belge.
- Gürün, Kamuran [1934–2004]
  - 1994 *Akıntıya Kürek: Bir Büyükelçinin Anıları (Rowing against the Current: The Memoirs of an Ambassador)*. İstanbul: Milliyet.
  - 1995 *Fırtınalı Yıllar: Dışişleri Müsteşarlığı Anıları (The Tempestuous Years: The Memories as the Permanent Undersecretary of the Foreign Ministry)*. İstanbul: Milliyet.
- Güvemli, Fevzi [1903–72]
  - 1999 *Bir Zamanlar Ordu: Anılar (Ordu Once upon a Time: Memories)*. Ankara: Kültür Bakanlığı.

- H. Raci Efendi [1860s?–]
  - 1990 [1910] *Tarihçe-i Vak'a-i Zağra: Zağra Müftüsünün Anıları (History of the Zağra Incident: Memoirs of the Mufti of Zağra).* İstanbul: Timaş.
- Haçeryan, Garabet [1876–]
  - 2005 *Bir Ermeni Doktorun Yaşadıkları: Garabet Haçeryan'ın İzmir Güncesi (The Things an Armenian Physician Lived through: The İzmir Diary of Garabet Haçeryan).* Ed. Dora Sakayan. İstanbul: Belge.
- Haker, Erol [1930–]
  - 2004 *İstanbul'dan Kudüs'e Bir Kimlik Arayışı (Search for an Identity from İstanbul to Jerusalem).* İstanbul: Kitap.
- Hasan Rami Paşa [1842–1923]
  - 1997 [1908] *Bahriye Nazırının Hatıraları (Memoirs of the Naval Minister).* Ankara: Military Command of the Naval Forces.
- Hayrullah Efendi [1818–66]
  - 2002 *Avrupa Seyahatnamesi (European Travelbook).* Ankara: Kültür Bakanlığı.
- Hovhannesyan, Sarkis Sarraf [1740–1805]
  - 1997 *Payitaht İstanbul'un Tarihçesi (The History of the Imperial City İstanbul).* Ed. Elmon Hançer. İstanbul: Tarih Vakfı.
- Hüseyin Avni Bey [1876–1921]
  - 1999 *Hüseyin Avni Bey: Sakarya Şehidi Binbaşı (Hüseyin Avni Bey: The Sakarya Martyr and Colonel).* Ankara: Atlas.
- Hüseyin Kazım Kadri [1870–1934]
  - 1991 *Meşrutiyet'ten Cumhuriyete Hatıralarım (My Memoirs from the Constitutional Period to the Republic).* Ed. İsmail Kara. İstanbul: İletişim.
  - 1992 *Balkanlar'dan Hicaz'a İmparatorluğun Tasfiyesi: 10 Temmuz İnkılabı ve Netayici (The Liquidation of the Empire from the Balkans to the Hijaz: The July 10th Revolution and Its Consequences).* Ed. Kudret Büyükcoşkun. İstanbul: Pınar.
- Hüseyin Nazım Paşa [1854–1927]
  - 2003 *Hatıralarım: Ermeni Olaylarının İçyüzü (My Memoirs: The Inside Story of the Armenian Incidents).* Ed. Tahsin Yıldırım. İstanbul: Selis.
- Irmak, Hüseyin [1961–]
  - 2003 *Yaşadığım Kurtuluş (The Kurtuluş [Neighborhood in İstanbul] I Lived In).* İstanbul: Aras.
- İbrahim Temo [1865–1939]
  - 1987 [1939] *İbrahim Temo'nun İttihat ve Terakki Anıları (The Union and Progress Memoirs of İbrahim Temo).* İstanbul: Arba.
- İğdemir, Uluğ [1900–1994]
  - 1976 *Yılların İçinden (From Within the Years).* Ankara: TTK.

- İhmalyan, Vartan [1913–87]
  - 1989 *Bir Yaşam Öyküsü (A Life Story)*. İstanbul: Cem.
- İlden, Köprülülü Şerif [1877–]
  - 1998 *Sarıkamış (The Sarıkamısh Battle [during World War I])*. Ed. Sami Önal. İstanbul: İş Bankası.
- İmre, Halil [1910s?–]
  - 1976 *Bir Ömür Üç Kitap (One Life Three Books)*. İstanbul: Ayyıldız.
- İz, Mahir [1895–1974]
  - 1990 [1975] *Yılların İzi (The Imprint of the Years)*. İstanbul: Kitabevi.
- İzbudak, Veled Çelebi [1869–1953]
  - 1946 *Hatıralarım (My Memoirs)*. İstanbul: Türkiye Yayınevi.
- Kadri Cemil Paşa (Zinar Silopi)
  - 1991 [1969] *Doza Kurdistan (Kürdistan Davası): Kürt Milletinin 60 Yıllık Easretten Kurtuluş Savaşı Hatıraları (The Kurdish Cause: Memories of the Kurdish Nation's Liberation from 60 Years of Enslavment)*. Ankara: Öz-Ge.
- Kahraman, Hayreddin [1934–]
  - 2008 *Bir Varmış Bir Yokmuş (Once upon a Time)*. 3 vols. İstanbul: İz.
- Kalaç, Ahmed Hilmi [1887–1966]
  - 1960 *Kendi Kitabım (My Own Book)*. İstanbul (?): Yeni Matbaa.
- Kalkavanoğlu, İlyas Sami [1890s?–]
  - 1957 *Milli Mücadele Hatıralarım (My Memories of the Independence Struggle)*. İstanbul: Ekicigil.
- Kamil Paşa, Kıbrıslı Mehmed [1833–1914] and Küçük Mehmed Said Paşa [1830–1914]
  - 1991 *Anıları ve Polemikleri (Memoirs and Polemics)*. Ed. Gül Çağalı-Güven. İstanbul: Arba.
- Kansu, Mazhar Müfit [1873–1948]
  - 1966 *Erzurum'dan Ölümüne Atatürk'le Beraber (With Atatürk from Erzurum until His Death)*. Ankara: TTK.
- Kant, Albert [1900s?–]
  - 2003 *Bir Yahudinin Anıları (Memoirs of a Jew)*. İstanbul: Kastaş.
- Kapancızade Hamit Bey [1878–1928]
  - 2008 *Bir Milli Mücadele Valisi ve Anıları: Kapancızade Hamit Bey (An Independence Struggle Governor and His Memoir: Kapancızade Hamit Bey)*. Ed. Halit Eken. İstanbul: Yeditepe.
- Karabekir, Cemal [1880s?–]
  - 1991 *Maçka Silahhanesi Hatıraları: İstiklal Harbi Kahramanları (Memoirs of the Maçka Armory: Heroes of the Independence War)*. Ed. Aykut Kazacıgil. İstanbul: Nehir.

- Karabekir, Kazım [1882–1948]
  - 1982 *İttihat Terakki Cemiyeti: Neden Kuruldu, Nasıl Kuruldu, Nasıl İdare Olundu? (The Committee of Union Progress: Why and How Was It Established and Administered?)*. Ed. Faruk Özerengin. İstanbul: Özerengin.
  - 1992 [1933] *İstiklal Harbimizin Esasları (The Principles of Our Independence War)*. Ed. Faruk Özerengin. İstanbul: Timaş.
- Karakaş, Bayar [1900s?–]
  - 2003 *Nazir: Anadolu'dan Okyanus Ötesine (Deputy: From Anatolia across the Ocean)*. İstanbul: Belge.
- Karaman, Sami Sabit [1877–1923?]
  - 2002 [1949] *İstiklal Mücadelesi ve Enver Paşa: Trabzon ve Kars Hatıraları (The Independence Struggle and Enver Pasha: The Trebizond and Kars Memoirs)*. İstanbul: Arma.
- Karaosmanoğlu, Yakup Kadri [1889–1974]
  - 1969 *Gençlik ve Edebiyat Hatıraları (Memories of Youth and Literature)*. Ankara: Bilgi.
  - 1987a [1938] *Bir Sürgün (An Exile)*. İstanbul: İletişim.
  - 1987b [1927] *Hüküm Gecesi (The Night of Judgment)*. İstanbul: İletişim.
- Karaveli, Orhan [1930–]
  - 1999 *Bir Ankara Ailesinin Öyküsü (The Story of an Ankara Family)*. İstanbul: Pergamon.
- Karay, Refik Halid [1888–1965]
  - 1964 *Minelbab İlelmihrab (From the Front Door to the Apse)*. İstanbul: İnkılap ve Aka.
  - 1996 [1990] *Bir Ömür Boyunca (During a Lifetime)*. İstanbul: İletişim.
- Kartal, Kinyas [1900–1988]
  - 1987 *Erivan'dan Van'a Hatıralarım (My Memories from Erivan to Van)*. Ankara: Anadolu Basın Birliği.
- Kaygusuz, Bezmi Nusret [1890–1961]
  - 1955 *Bir Roman Gibi ([Life That Reads] Like a Novel)*. İzmir: İhsan Gümüşayak.
- Kazancıgil, Yekta [1916–]
  - 1989 [1980] *Dünden Bugüne Hatıralar (Memories from Yesterday to Today)*. İstanbul: Kervan.
- Kerkük, Mahmut Nedim [1879–1940]
  - 2002 *Hatıratım 1334 (1918) (My Memoir 1918)*. Ed. Ali Birinci. Altınküre: İstanbul.
- Kestelli, Raif Necdet [1881–1937]
  - 2001 [1913] *Uful, Osmanlı İmparatorluğunun Batışı: Edirne Savunması (Extinction, the Demise of the Ottoman Empire: The Edirne Defense)*. Ed. Veliye Özdemir. İstanbul: Arma.

- Kevirbiri, Salihe [1920s?–]
  - 2005 [2002] *Karapete Xaco: Bir Çığlığın Yüzyılı (Karapete Xaco: The Century of a Scream)*. İstanbul: Elma.
- Kıbrıslızade Binbaşı Osman Bey [1820s?–]
  - 1996 *Hatıraları ya da 19cu Yüzyıl'da Doğu'da İngilizler (Memoirs or the British in the East during the 19th Century)*. İzmir: Akademi.
- Kıdwai, Şeyh Müşir Hüseyin [1878–1937]
  - 1991 *Paris Sulh Konferansı ve Osmanlıların Çöküşü (The Paris Peace Conference and the Demise of the Ottomans)*. Ed. Ahmed Zeki İzgör. İstanbul: Nehir.
- Kılıç Ali [1888–1971]
  - 1955 *Kılıç Ali Hatıralarını Anlatıyor (Kılıç Ali Recounts His Memoirs)*. İstanbul: Sel.
  - 1997 [1955] *İstiklal Mahkemesi Hatıraları (Memoirs of the Independence Courts)*. İstanbul: Cumhuriyet.
  - 2005 *Atatürk'ün Sırdaşı Kılıç Ali'nin Anıları (The Memoirs of Kılıç Ali, Atatürk's Confidante)*. Ed. Hulusi Turgut. İstanbul: İş Bankası.
- Kılıç, Altemur [1924–]
  - 2005 *Kılıçtan Kılıça: Bir Dönemin Tanıklığı (From One Kılıç to Another: The Witnessing of an Era)*. İstanbul: Remzi.
- Kırcı, Haluk [1958–]
  - 1998 *Zamanı Süzerken (While Sifting through Time)*. İstanbul: Burak.
- Kırımer, Cafer Seydahmet [1889–1960]
  - 1993 [1970] *Bazı Hatıralar (Some Memories)*. İstanbul: Emel.
- Kırkyaşaryan, Manuel [1906–97]
  - 2005 *M. K. Adlı Çocuğun Tehcir Anıları: 1915 ve sonrası (The Deportation Memoirs of a Child Named M.K.: 1915 and Its Aftermath)*. Ed. B. Oran. İstanbul: İletişim.
- Korle, Sinan [1914–96]
  - 1990 *Cam Sarayda Kırk Yıl: Sinan Korle'nin Birleşmiş Milletler Anıları (Forty Years in the Glass Palace: The United Nations Memoirs of Sinan Korle)*. İstanbul: Yanar.
- Kuran, Ahmed Bedevi [1884–1966]
  - 1945 *İnkılap Tarihimiz ve Jön Türkler (Our Revolutionary History and the Young Turks)* İstanbul: Tan.
  - 1948 *İnkılap Tarihimiz ve İttihat Terakki (Union and Progress and Our History of Revolution)*. İstanbul: Tan.
  - 1976 *Harbiye Mektebinde Hürriyet Mücadelesi (Freedom Fight at the War Academy)*. İstanbul: Çeltüt.
- Kuşçubaşı, Eşref [1873–1964]
  - 1999 *Hayber'de Türk Cengi (Turkish Battle at Khayber Pass)*. İstanbul: Arba.

- Kut, Halil Paşa [1881–1957]
    - 1972 *Bitmeyen Savaş (The Unending War)*. İstanbul: Yedigün.
- Kutay, Cemal [1909–2006]
    - 1966 *Tarih Sohbetleri (History Conversations)*. 6 vols. İstanbul: Halk.
    - 1975 *Örtülü Tarihimiz (Our Covered History)*. 2 vols. İstanbul: Hilal.
- Madanoğlu, Cemal [1907–93]
    - 1992 [1982] *Anılar 1911–1953 (Memoirs 1911–1953)*. İstanbul: Evrim.
- Mahmud Celaleddin Paşa [1838–99]
    - 1970 *Madalyonun Tersi (The Other Side of the Medallion)*. İstanbul: Gür.
- 1979 [1908] *Mir'at-ı Hakikat (The Mirror of Truth)*. Ed. İsmet Miroğlu. İstanbul: Tercüman.
- Mahmud Şevket Paşa [1856–1913]
    - 1988 *Sadrazam ve Harbiye Nazırı Mahmud Şevket Paşa'nın Günlüğü (The Diary of the Grand Vezier and Minister of War Mahmud Shevket Pasha)*. İstanbul: Arba.
- Makal, Mahmut [1930–]
    - 1979 *Köy Enstitüleri ve Ötesi (Village Institutes and Beyond)*. İstanbul: Çağdaş.
- Mardin, Yusuf [1916–94]
    - 1988 *Kocataş Yalısı Anılarım (My Memoirs of the Kocataş Mansion)*. İstanbul: Güryay.
- Masar, İlhami [1900–]
    - 1974 *Bir Ömür Boyunca (Through One Life)*. İstanbul: Boğaziçi.
- Mehmed Arif Bey, Miralay [1882–1926]
    - 1987 [1921] *Anadolu İnkılabı: Milli Mücadele Anıları, 1919–1923 (The Anatolian Revolution: Memoirs of the National Struggle, 1919–1923)*. Ed. Bülent Demirbaş. İstanbul: Arba.
- Mehmed Memduh Paşa [1839–1925]
    - 1990 *Tanzimattan Meşrutiyete (From the Tanzimat to the Constitutional Revolution)*. Ed. Hayati Develi. İstanbul: Nehir.
- Mehmed Rauf, Leskovikli [1875–1931]
    - 1991 [1909] *İttihat ve Terakki Ne İdi? (What Was the Union and Progress?)*. Ed. Bülent Demirbaş. İstanbul: Arba.
    - 2001 *Mehmed Rauf'un Anıları (Memoirs of Mehmed Rauf)*. Ed. Rahim Tarım. İstanbul: Özgür.
- Mehmed Selahaddin Bey [1880s?–]
    - 1989 *İttihat ve Terakki'nin Kuruluşu ve Osmanlı Devletini Yıkılışı hakkında Bildiklerim (Things I Know about the Establishmnet of the Committee of Union and Progress and the Demise of the Ottoman Empire)*. Ed. Ahmed Varo. İstanbul: İnkılap.
- Melek, Faik [1924–]
    - 1994 *Hepsi Geldi Geçti: Dışişlerinde 43 Yıl (All Those Who Passed Through: 43 Years at the Foreign Ministry)*. İstanbul: Milliyet.

- Melek Hanım [1870s?–]
  - 1996 *Haremden Mahrem Hatıralar (Intimate Memoirs from the Harem)*. Ed. İsmail Yergüz. İstanbul: Oğlak.
- Menteşe, Halil [1874–1948]
  - 1986 *Osmanlı Meclisi Mebusan Reisi Halil Menteşe'nin Anıları (The Memoirs of Halil Menteşe, the President of the Ottoman Assembly)*. Ed. İsmail Arar. İstanbul: Hürriyet.
- Mevhibe Celaleddin, Prenses [1887–1952]
  - 1987 [1953] *Geçmiş Zaman Olur ki: Prenses Mevhibe Celaleddin'in Anıları (Once Upon a Time: Memoirs of Princess Mevhibe Celaleddin)*. Ed. Sara Korle. İstanbul: Çağdaş.
- Mevlanzade Rıfat [–1930]
  - 1992 *Mevlanzade Rıfat'ın Anıları (Memoirs of Mevlanzade Rıfat)*. Ed. Metin Marti. İstanbul: Arma.
  - 1993 *İttihat Terakki İktidarı ve Türk İnkılabının İçyüzü (The Union and Progress Rule and the Inside Story of the Turkish Revolution)*. İstanbul: Yedi İklim.
  - 1996 *31 Mart: Bir İhtilalin Hikayesi (March 31st: The Story of a Revolution)*. Ed. Berire Ülgenci. İstanbul: Pınar.
  - 2000 *Türkiye İnkılabının İçyüzü (The Inside Story of the Turkish Revolution)*. İstanbul: Pınar.
- Mimaroğlu, M. Reşad [1881–]
  - 1946 *Gördüklerim Geçirdiklerimden (From What I Saw and Went Through)*. Ankara: Ziraat Bankası.
- Mithat, Ali Haydar [1872–]
  - 1946 *Hatıralarım 1872–1946 (My Memoirs, 1872--1946)*. İstanbul: Mithat Akçit Yayını.
- Mithat Paşa [1822-1884]
  - 1997 [1908] *Midhat Paşa'nın Hatıraları (Memoirs of Mithat Pasha)*. Ed. Osman Selim Kocahanoğlu. 2 vols. İstanbul: Temel.
- Mizancı Murad [1853–1914]
  - 1994 [1910] *Mücahade-i Milliye: Gurbet ve Avdet Devirleri (National Strife: The Abroad and Return Eras)*. Ed. Faruk Gezgin. İstanbul: Nehir.
  - 1997 [1908] *Hürriyet Vadisinde Bir Pençe-i İstibdat (The Clutches of Autocracy in the Valley of Freedom)*. Ed. Ahmed Nezih Galitekin. İstanbul: Nehir.
- Muhiddin Bey [1890s?–]
  - 2003 *Yaver: Muhiddin Beyin Hatıraları (Aide [of Enver Pasha]: The Memoirs of Muhiddin Bey)*. Ed. Yusuf Gedikli. İstanbul: Ufukötesi.
- Mümtaz, Ahmed Semih [1890s?–]
  - 1946 *Hatıralarım (My Memoirs)*. İstanbul: Türkiye Yayınevi.

- Münim Mustafa [1880s?–]
    - 1998 [1940] *Cepheden Cepheye (From One Frontier to Another)*. İstanbul: Arma.
- Naciye Sultan [1896–1957]
    - 2002 *Acı Zamanlar: Enver Paşa'nın Eşi Naciye Sultan'ın Hatıraları (Bitter Times: The Memoirs of Naciye Sultan, the Wife of Enver Pasha)*. Ed. O. Gazi Aşiroğlu. İstanbul: Burak.
- Nadir Nadi [Abalıoğlu] [1908–91]
    - 1964 *Perde Aralığından (From amidst the Curtains)*. İstanbul: Cumhuriyet.
- Natanyan, Boğos [1850s?–]
    - 2008 *Sivas 1877*. Ed. Arsen Yarman. İstanbul: Bir Zamanlar Yayıncılık.
- Nesimi, Abidin [1941–]
    - 1977 *Yılların İçinden (From within the Years)*. İstanbul: Gözlem.
- Numanzade, Ömer Faik [1872–1937]
    - 1976 *Kafkasya'dan İstanbul'a Hatıralar (Memoirs from the Caucasus to İstanbul)*. Ed. Fazıl Gökçek. İzmir: Akademi.
- Nur, Rıza [1879–1943]
    - 1991 *Moskova/Sakarya Hatıraları (The Moscow/Sakarya Memoirs of Doctor Rıza Nur)*. İstanbul: Boğaziçi.
    - 1992 [1967] *Hayat ve Hatıratım (My Life and Memories)*. 4. vols. Ed. Abdurrahman Dilipak. İstanbul: İşaret.
- Nutku, Emrullah [1902–]
    - 1977 *Denizlere Özlem (Yearning for the Seas)*. İstanbul: Su.
- Oğuz, Burhan [1919–]
    - 2000 *Yaşadıklarım Dinlediklerim: Tarihi ve Toplumsal Anılar (Things I Lived and Heard: Historical and Social Memoirs)*. İstanbul: Simurg.
- Okday, İsmail Hakkı [1900s?–]
    - 1975 *Yanya'dan Ankara'ya (From Yanya [in the Balkans] to Ankara)*. İstanbul: Sebil.
- Oker, Ahmed Fevzi [1887–1974]
    - 2004 *Cumhuriyet'i Kuranların Sessizliği: Hilmi Oker [1887–1974] (The Silence of Those Who Founded the Republic: Hilmi Oker)*. Istanbul: Chiviyazıları.
- Okyar, Fethi [1881–1943]
    - 1980 *Üç Devirde Bir Adam (One Man during Three Eras)*. Ed. Cemal Kutay. İstanbul: Tercüman.
- Orbay, Hüseyin Rauf [1881–1964]
    - 1965 *Hatıraları ve Söyleyemedikleri ile Rauf Orbay (Rauf Orbay with His Memories and What He Could Not Say)*. Ed. Feridun Kandemir. İstanbul: Sinan.

- 1992 *Yüzyılımızda bir İnsanımız: Hüseyin Rauf Orbay (One of Our People in Our Century: Rauf Orbay)*. 2 vols. Ed. Cemal Kutay. İstanbul: Kazancı.
- 2000 *Cehennem Değirmeni: Siyasi Hatıralarım (Hell's Mill: My Political Memoirs)*. 2 vols. İstanbul: Emre.

- Orhan, Celaleddin [1900–]
  - 2001 *Bir Bahriyelinin Anıları: 1914–1981 (The Memoirs of a Naval Officer, 1914–1981)*. İstanbul: Kastaş.
- Osmanoğlu, Ayşe [1887–1960]
  - 1984 [1960] *Babam Abdülhamid (My Father Sultan Abdülhamid)*. İstanbul: Selçuk.
- Ökte, Faik [1902–82]
  - 1950 *Varlık Vergisi Faciası (The Disaster of the Wealth Tax)*. İstanbul: Nebioğlu.
- Ölçen, Mehmed Arif [1893–1958]
  - 1994 *Vetluga Irmağı: Çarlık Rusyasında bir Türk Savaş Tutsağının Anıları, 1916–1918 (The Vetluga River: The Memoirs of a Turkish Prisoner of War in Tsarist Russia, 1916–1918)*. Ankara: Ümit.
- Öngör, Sami [1920s?–]
  - 1987 *Geçen Yılları Düşündükçe: Anılar (Thinking about the Years Past: Memories)*. İstanbul: Tekin.
- Örgeevren, Ahmed Süreyya [1889–1969]
  - 2002 *Şeyh Sait İsyanı ve Şark İstiklal Mahkemesi: Vesikalar, Olaylar, Hatıralar (The Sheikh Said Rebellion and the Eastern Independence Court: Documents, Incidents, Memories)*. Ed. Osman Selim Kocahanoğlu. İstanbul: Temel.
- Öz, Erdal [1935–]
  - 2003 *Defterimde Kuş Sesleri (Bird Chirps on My Notebook)*. İstanbul: Can.
- Özoğuz, Esat [1900s?–]
  - 1934 *Adana'nın Kurtuluş Mücadelesi (The Independence Struggle of Adana)*. İstanbul: Ülkü.
- Paker, Esat Cemal [1900s?–]
  - 2000 [1952] *Kırk Yıllık Hariciye Hatıraları (Forty Years of Foreign Service Memoirs)*. İstanbul: Remzi.
- Peker, Nurettin [1893–1987]
  - 1955 *İstiklal Savaşı: İnebolu Kastamonu ve Havalisi (The Independence Struggle: Inebolu-Kastamonu and Their Vicinity)*. İstanbul: Gün.
- Ragıp Bey, Başkatipzade [1889–1950]
  - 1996 *Tarih-i Hayatım: Kayserili Başkatipzade Mülazım Ragıp Bey'in Tahsil, Harp, Esaret, Kurtuluş Anıları (The History of My Life: The Memoirs of*

Lieutenant Başkatipzade Ragıp Bey of Kayseri Comprising Education, War, Captivity and Liberation). Ed. Bülent Varlık. Ankara: Kebikeç.

- Resneli Niyazi [1873–1913]
  - 1975 [1910] *Balkanlarda bir Gerillacı: Hürriyet Kahramanı Niyazi Bey'in Anıları (A Guerrilla in the Balkans: Memoirs of the Freedom Hero Niyazi Bey)*. İstanbul: Çağdaş.
- Reşit Paşa, Mustafa [1858–1924]
  - 2001 *İstiklal Savaşında Reşit Paşanın Hatıraları (The Memoirs of Reşit Pasha during the Independence War)*. Ed. Adnan Şenel. Ankara: Berikan.
- Rey, Ahmed Reşit [1870–1956]
  - 1945 *Gördüklerim Yaptıklarım, 1890–1922 (Things I have Seen and Done, 1890–1922)*. İstanbul: Türkiye.
- Saatçıgil, Enver [1915–]
  - 1993 *Geçen Günlerim, Olaylar ve Hatıralar (My Days Past, Events and Memories)*. İzmir: Mopak ve Tükelmat.
- Sabancı, Sakıp [1933–2004]
  - 1985 *İşte Hayatım (Here Is My Life)*. İstanbul: Aksoy.
  - 2004 *...bıraktığım yerden Hayatım (My Life from Where I Left It)*. İstanbul: Doğan.
- Sabis, Ali İhsan [1882–1957]
  - 1992 [1951] *Harp Hatıralarım (My War Memoirs)*. 6 vols. İstanbul: Nehir.
- Sadeddin Paşa [–1921]
  - 2003 *Sadeddin Paşa'nın Anıları: Ermeni-Kürt Olayları, Van 1896 (Memoirs of Sadeddin Pasha: Armenian-Kurdish Incidents, Van 1896)*. Ed. S. Önal. İstanbul: Remzi.
- Sağlam, Tevfik, Dr. [1882–1963]
  - 1991 [1959] *Nasıl Okudum (How I Got Educated)*. İstanbul: Nehir.
- Sağlar, Eşref [1910s?–]
  - 1976 *Yaşam Öykülerim veya Bana Göre Ben ve Çevrem (My Life Stories or I and My Surroundings According to Me)*. İstanbul: Güryay.
- Said Paşa, Ali [1885–1922]
  - 1994 *Saray Hatıraları: Sultan Abdülhamid'in Hayatı (Palace Memoirs:T the Life of Sultan Abdülhamid II)*. İstanbul: Nehir.
- Sait Hurşid [1927–]
  - 1999 *Son Vapuru Kaçıranlar (Those Who Missed the Last Boat)*. Ed. Bülent Varlık. İstanbul: İletişim.
- Sav, Ergun [1933–]
  - 1992 *Diplodramatik Anlatılar (Diplodramatic Narratives)*. İstanbul: Bilgi.
  - 2000 *Diplomaturka: Bir Diplomat-Yazarın Anıları (Diplomaturca: Memoirs of a Diplomat and Writer)*. İstanbul: Bilgi.

- Sazak, M. Emin [1882–1960]
  - 2007 *Emin Bey'in Defteri: Hatıralar (Emin Bey's Notebook: Memories)*. Ed. Himmet Kayhan. Ankara: Tolkun.
- Scognamillo, Giovanni [1929–]
  - 1990 *Bir Levantenin Beyoğlu Anıları (The Pera Memoirs of a Levantine)*. İstanbul: Metis.
- Sedes, İzzet [1928–]
  - 2005 *Siz Türk müsünüz!: Babıaliden Avrupa Konseyi koridorlarına anılar, olaylar, portreler (Are You Turkish! Memories, Events and Portraits from the Seat of Government to the Hallways of the European Council)*. İstanbul: Doğan.
- Selahattin Adil Paşa [1882–1961]
  - 1982 *Hayat Mücadeleleri (Life's Struggles)*. İstanbul: Zafer.
- Serdi, Hasan Hişyar [1905–85]
  - 1994 *Görüş ve Anılarım, 1907–1985 (My Views and Memoirs, 1907–1985)*. Ed. Hasan Cuni. İstanbul: Med.
- Sertel, Yıldız [1922–]
  - 1994 *Annem: Sabiha Sertel Kimdi, Neler Yazdı? (My Mother: Who Was Sabiha Sertel and What Works Did She Pen?)*. İstanbul: YKY.
- Sertel, Zekeriya M. [1890–1980]
  - 1968 *Hatırladıklarım (What I Remember)*. İstanbul: Yaylacık.
  - 2000 *Hatırladıklarım (What I Remember)*. Revised new updated edition. İstanbul: Remzi.
- Sevük, İsmail Habib [1892–1954]
  - 1937 *O Zamanlar: 1920–1923(Those Days, 1920–1923)*. İstanbul: Cumhuriyet.
- Sezen, Halit [1906–89] and Ibrahim Erturan [1904–90]
  - 1999 *İki Kardeşten Seferberlik Anıları (General Mobilization Memoirs of Two Brothers)*. Ed. Yıldırım Sezen. Ankara: Kültür Bakanlığı.
- Sırma, İhsan Süreyya [1944–]
  - 1986 *Birkaç Sahife Tarih (A Few Pages of History)*. Konya: Selam.
- Simavi, Lütfi Başmabeynci [1880s?–]
  - 1965 *Osmanlı Sarayının Son Günleri (The Last Days of the Ottoman Palace)*. İstanbul: Hürriyet.
- Sorguç, İbrahim [1897–1974]
  - 1996 *Kaybolan Filistin ve İstiklal Harbi Hatıratı (The Lost Palestine and the Memoir of the Independence Struggle)*. İzmir: İzmir Yayıncılık.
- Soydan, Mahmut [1883–1936]
  - 2007 *Ankaralı'nın Defteri: Milli Mücadele Tarihine dair Notlar (Notebook of Ankaralı: Notes on the National Independence Struggle)*. İstanbul: İş Bankası.

- Soyer, Dündar [1910s?–]
  - 2000 *Cumhuriyetle Adım Adım Olaylar, Anılar (Incidents and Memories Step by Step with the Republic)*. İstanbul: Büke.
- Söylemezoğlu, Galip Kemali [1873–1955]
  - 1949 *Hariciye Hizmetinde Otuz Sene, 1892–1922 (Thirty Years in the Service of the Foreign Ministry, 1892–1922)*. İstanbul: Maarif.
  - 1957 *Yok Edilmek İstenen Millet (The Assassination of a People)* [title translation from the French original]. İstanbul: Selek.
- Sunata, İ. Hakkı [1892–]
  - 2003 *Gelibolu'dan Kafkaslara: Birinci Dünya Savaşı Hatıralarım (From Galipoli to the Caucasus: My World War I Memoirs)*. İstanbul: İş Bankası.
- Süleyman Nazif [1870–1927]
  - 1957 *Hatıralar (Memories)*. Ed. Hilmi Yücebaş. İstanbul: Dizerkonca.
  - 1978 [1915] *Batarya ile Ateş (Battery and Fire)*. Ed. Sabahaddin Ardıç. İstanbul: Tercüman.
  - 1979 [1924] *Malta Geceleri, Fırak-ı Irak ve Galiçya (Malta Nights, Separation of Iraq and Galicia)*. Ed. İhsan Erzi. İstanbul: Tercüman.
- Süleyman Şefik Paşa [1890s?–]
  - 2004 *Hatıratım, Başıma Gelenler ve Gördüklerim: 31 Mart Vak'ası (My Memoir, Things I Encountered and Saw: March 31 Incident)*. Ed. Hümeyra Zerdeci. Istanbul: Arma.
- Şahabettin, Cenap [1870–1934]
  - 2002 *Afak-ı Irak: Kızıldeniz'den Bağdat'a Hatıralar (Iraqi Horizons: Memories from the Red Sea to Baghdad)*. Ed. Bülent Yorulmaz. İstanbul: Dergah.
- Şahingiray, Mehmed Reşid, Dr. [1873–1919]
  - 1992 *Sürgünden intihara Dr. Reşid Bey'in hatıraları (From Exile to Suicide: Dr. Reşid Bey's Memoirs)*. Ed. Ahmed Mehmetefendioğlu. İzmir: Ahmed Mehmetefendioğlu.
  - 1997 *Hayatı ve Hatıraları (His Life and His Memoirs)*. Ed. Nejdet Bilgi. İzmir: Akademi.
- Şaul, Eli [1916–]
  - 1999 *Balat'tan Bat Yam'a (From Balat to Bat Yam)*. Ed. Rıfat Balı. İstanbul: İletişim.
- Şerif Paşa [1865–1944]
  - 1990 *Şerif Paşa, Bir Muhalifin Hatıraları: İttihat Terakkiye Muhalafet (Sherif Pasha, the Memoirs of an Opponent: Opposition to the Union and Progress)*. İstanbul: Nehir.
- Tahmiscizade Mehmed Macid [1860s?–]
  - 1977 *Girit Hatıraları (Crete Memoirs)*. Ed. İsmet Miroğlu. İstanbul: Tercüman.

- Tahsin Paşa [1858–1934]
  - 1931 *Abdülhamid: Yıldız Hatıraları (Abdülhamid: The Yıldız Memoirs)*. İstanbul: Muallim Ahmed Halit.
- Talat Paşa [1874–1921]
  - 2005 [1946] *Ermeni Vahşeti (The Armenian Atrocities)*. Ed. Nurer Uğurlu. İstanbul: Örgün.
- Talu, Ercümend Ekrem [1886–1956]
  - 2005 *Geçmiş Zaman Olur ki: Anılar (Once upon a Time: Memoirs)*. Ed. Alaattin Karaca. İstanbul: Hece.
- Tanpınar, Ahmed Hamdi [1901–62]
  - 1973 *Sahnenin Dışındakiler (Those outside the Stage)*. İstanbul: Büyük Kitaplık.
- Tansel, Selahattin [1900s?–]
  - 1973 *Mondros'tan Mudanya'ya Kadar (From the Mondros Armistice Treaty [signed at the end of the Great War] to the Mudanya Treaty [signed at the end of the Independence Struggle])*. 3 vols. Ankara: Başbakanlık.
- Tarcan, Selim Sırrı [1874–1957]
  - 1946 *Hatıralarım (My Memoirs)*. İstanbul: Türkiye Yayınevi.
- Tarhan, Abdülhak Hamit [1852–1937]
  - 1994 *Hatıraları (His Memories)*. Ed. İnci Enginün. İstanbul: Dergah.
  - 1995 *Mektupları (Letters)*. Ed. İnci Engünün. İstanbul: Dergah.
- Tarhan, Lüsyen [1893–1966]
  - 2006 *Karlar Altında Nevbahar: Hatıralar (New Spring under the Snow: Memoirs)*. Ed. İhsan Safi. Istanbul: Dergah.
- Tengirşenk, Yusuf Kemal [1878–1969]
  - 1967 *Vatan Hizmetinde (In the Service of the Fatherland)*. İstanbul: Bahar.
- Tepeyran, Ebubekir Hazım [1864–1947]
  - 1982 *Belgelerle Kurtuluş Savaşı Anıları (Memoirs of the War of Independence with Documents)*. İstanbul: Çağdaş.
  - 1998 *Hatıralar (Memoirs)*. Ed. Faruk İlikan. İstanbul: Pera.
- Terziyan, Nubar Alyanak [1909–94]
  - 1995 *Ne İdim Ne Oldum (What I Was What I Became)*. İstanbul: İletişim.
- Tesal, Reşat Dürrü [1911–]
  - 1998 *Selanik'ten İstanbul'a Bir Ömrün Hikayesi (The Story of a Life from Salonica to İstanbul)*. Ed. Ruşen Sezer. İstanbul: İletişim.
- Tokgöz, Ahmed İhsan [1868–1942]
  - 1993 [1930] *Matbuat Hatıralarım (My Memoirs of the Press)*. Ed. Alpay Kabacalı. İstanbul: İletişim.
- Tomruk, Ahmed Esat [ca. 1893–1966]
  - 2000 *İngiliz Kemal: Milli Mücadele Dönemi Hatıraları (Kemal, the English Man: Memoirs of the Independence Struggle Era)*. Ed. Zekeriya Türkmen. Ankara: Kültür Bakanlığı.

- Tonguç, Faik [1880s?–]
    - 1999 [1960] *Birinci Dünya Savaşında bir Yedeksubayın Anıları (The Memoirs of a Reserve Officer during World War I)*. İstanbul: İş Bankası.
- Topuzlu, Cemil [1868–1958]
    - 1982 [1951] *İstibdat, Meşrutiyet, Cumhuriyet Devirlerinde 80 yıllık Hatıralarım (My Eighty Years of Memories during the Eras of Autocracy, Constitution and the Republic)*. İstanbul: Tıp Fakültesi Yayınları.
    - 1988 [1951] *80 Yıllık Hatıralarım (My Eighty Years of Memories)*. İstanbul: Topuzlu.
- Tör, Ahmed Nedim Servet [1871–1947]
    - 2000 *Nevhiz'in Günlüğü: Defter-i Hatırat (The Diary of Nevhiz: The Book of Memories)*. İstanbul: Yapı Kredi Yayınları.
- Tör, Vedat Nedim [1897–1985]
    - 1976 *Yıllar Böyle Geçti (The Years Went By Like This)*. İstanbul: Milliyet.
- Tufan, Osman Paşa [1889–1944]
    - 1998 *Osman Tufan Paşa'nın Kurtuluş Savaşı Hatıraları (The Independence War Memoirs of Osman Tufan Pasha)*. İstanbul: Arma.
- Tuğaç, Hüsamettin [1889–]
    - 1975 [1966] *Bir Neslin Dramı (The Drama of a Generation)*. İstanbul: Çağdaş.
- Tunalı, Ali [1890–1975]
    - 2005 *Vatana Hizmette 70 Yıl: Ali Tunalı (1890–1975) (Seventy Years in the Service of the Fatherland: Ali Tunalı 1890–1975)*. Ed. Bülent Varlık. İstanbul: Tarih Vakfı.
- Tükel, Sükuti [1900s?–]
    - 1953 *Tatlı ve Acı Hatıralar (Sweet and Bitter Memories)*. İzmir: Piyasa.
- Türkgeldi, Ali Fuat [1867–1935]
    - 1949 *Görüp İşittiklerim (Things I Saw and Heard)*. Ankara: TTK.
    - 1987 *Mesail-i Mühimme-i Siyasiyye (Significant Political Issues)*. 3 vols. Ed. Bekir Sıtkı Baykal. Ankara: TTK.
- Uçuk, Cahit /Cahide Üçok [1911–2004]
    - 1995 *Bır İmparatorluk Çökerken: Anılar (Memoirs as an Empire Crumbled)*. İstanbul: YKY.
- Ulunay, Refii Cevat [1890–1968]
    - 1999 *Sürgün Hatıraları (Memoirs of Exile)*. Ed. H. Hüsnü Kılıç. İstanbul: Arma.
- Uran, Hilmi [1886–1957]
    - 1959 *Hatıralarım (My Memories)*. İstanbul: Ayyıldız.
- Us, Asım [–1967]
    - 1964 *Gördüklerim, Duyduklarım, Duygularım: Meşrutiyet ve Cumhuriyet Devirlerine ait Hatıralar ve Tetkikler (What I Saw, Heard and*

Felt: Memories and Analyses about the Constitutional and Republican Eras). İstanbul: Vakit.
    - 1966 *Asım Us'un Hatıra Notları (Memory Notes of Asım Us)*. İstanbul: Vakit.
- Uşaklıgil, Halid Ziya [1869–1945]
    - 1965 [1940] *Saray ve Ötesi: Son Hatıralar (The Palace and Beyond: Last Memories)*. İstanbul: İnkılap Aka.
    - 1987 [1936] *Kırk Yıl: Anılar (Forty Years: Memories)*. Ed. Şemsettin Kutlu. İstanbul: İnkılap.
    - 1990 *Nesl-i Ahir: Son Kuşak (The Last Generation)*. Ed. Şemsettin Kutlu. İstanbul: İnkılap.
- Üçok, Ahmed Kemal [1910s?–]
    - 2002 *Görüp İşittiklerim, 1931–36 (Things I Have Seen and Heard, 1931–36)*. Ankara: Okuyan Adam.
- Ünüvar, Veysel General [1890s?–]
    - 1997 [1948] *Kurtuluş Savaşında Bolşeviklerle Sekiz Ay, 1920–1921 (Eight Months with the Bolsheviks during the Independence Struggle)*. İstanbul: Göçebe.
- Vahideddin, Nevzat [1861–1926]
    - 1999 *Yıldız'dan San Remo'ya (From the Yıldız (Palace) to San Remo)*. Ed. Yücel Demirel. İstanbul: Arma.
- Va-Nu, Müzehher [1901–67]
    - 1997 [1975] *Bir Dönemin Tanıklığı (Witnessing an Era)*. İstanbul: Sosyal.
- Vardar, Galip [ca. 1890–1958]
    - 1960 *İttihat ve Terakki İçinde Dönenler (Things That Went On within the Union and Progress)*. Ed. Samih Nafiz Tansu. İstanbul: İnkılap.
- Velidedeoğlu, Hıfzı Veldet [1904–92]
    - 1977 *Anıların İzinde (In Pursuit of Memories)*. 2 vols. İstanbul: Remzi.
- Yalçın, Hüseyin Cahit [1875–1957]
    - 1943 *Talat Paşa (Talat Pasha)*. İstanbul: Yedigün.
    - 1976 *Siyasi Anılar (Political Memoirs)*. İstanbul: İş Bankası Yayınları.
    - 2001 [1936] *Tanıdıklarım (The People I Know)*. İstanbul: YKY.
    - 2002 [1944] *İttihatçı Liderlerin Gizli Mektupları (Secret Letters of the Unionist Leaders)*. Ed. Osman Selim Kocahanoğlu. İstanbul: Temel.
- Yalman, Ahmed Emin [1889–1972]
    - 1997 [1970] *Yakın Tarihte Gördüklerim ve Geçirdiklerim (What I Saw and Experienced in Recent History)*. 2 vols. İstanbul: Pera.
- Yeğena, Ali Münif [1874–1951]
    - 1996 *Ali Münif Bey'in Hatıraları (Memoirs of Ali Münif Bey)*. Ed. Taha Toros. İstanbul: İsis.
- Yener, Şakip Sabri [1888–1973]

- 1958 *Gaziantebin Yakın Tarihinden Notlar (Notes from the Recent History of Gazianteb)*. Gaziantep: Gaziyurt.
- Yergök, Ziya Tuğgeneral [1877–1949]
  - 2005 *Sarıkamış'tan Esarete (1915–1920) (From Sarıkamış to Captivity, 1915–1920)*. Ed. Sami Önal. İstanbul: Remzi.
  - 2006 *Harbiye'den Dersim'e (1890–1914): Askeri Öğrencilik, Erzurum, Erzincan ve Dersim Harekatı (From Military School to Dersim [1890–1914]: Military Student Years, and the Erzurum, Erzincan and Dersim Operations)*. Ed. Sami Önal. İstanbul: Remzi.
- Yiğit, İbrahim Süreyya [1880–1952]
  - 2004 *Atatürk'le Otuz Yıl (Thirty Years with Atatürk)*. Ed. Nuyan Yiğit. İstanbul: Remzi.
- Yoldaş, Cemil Zeki [1896–1934]
  - 1992 *Kendi Kaleminden Teğmen Cemil ZekiYoldaş: Anılar, Mektuplar (Lieutenant Cemil Zeki Yoldaş from His Own Pen: Memoirs, Letters)*. Ed. Engın Berber. İstanbul: Arba.
- Yunus Nadi [Abalıoğlu] [1880–1945]
  - 1955 *Ankara'nın İlk Günleri (The First Days of Ankara)*. İstanbul: Sel.
- Yücel, Mehmed Lütfi [1881–1956]
  - 2006 *Hatıralarım (My Memoirs)*. Ed. Arif Suavi Okay. İstanbul: Günaydın.
- Yüzbaşı Cemal [Savaşkan] [1877–1948]
  - 1996 *Arnavutluk'tan Sakarya'ya Komitacılık: Anılar (Memoirs: Militia Activities from Albania to Sakarya)*. Ed. Kudret Emiroğlu. İstanbul: Kebikeç.
- Zana, Mehdi [1940–]
  - 1995 *Sevgili Leyla: Uzun Bir Sürgündü O Gece (Dear Leyla: That Night Was a Long Exile)*. İstanbul: Belge.
- Zarifi, Yorgo L. [1880–1943]
  - 2005 *Hatıralarım: Kaybolan bir Dünya, Istanbul 1800–1920 (My Memories: A World Lost, Istanbul 1800–1920)*. Ed. Karin Skotiniyadis. İstanbul: Literatür.
- Zobu, Vasfi Rıza [1902–92]
  - 1977 *O Günden Bu Güne Anılar (Memories from That Day to This One)*. İstanbul: Milliyet.

Appendix B

ANALYSIS OF THE DEPUTIES OF THE FIRST TURKISH NATIONAL ASSEMBLY

Name	***Birthplace (Origin)***	***Profession***	***CUP Member-Ship***	***Position In 1915–17***	***Deputy Of***	***Terms Served***
Abdullah Faik (Çopuroğlu)	Adana (Anatolian)	Religious scholar	No	Deputy in Ottoman assembly	Adana	I, II
Eşref (Akman)	Yanya (non—Anatolian)	Physician	No	Adana health inspector	Adana	I
Mehmet Hamdi (İzgi)	Adana (Anatolian)	Religious mufti and merchant	No	Member of Adana General Assembly	Adana	I
Zamir Damar (Arıkoğlu)	Adana (Anatolian)	Landowner and merchant	Yes; CUP Adana council member	Landowner and merchant in Adana	Adana	I, II, IV, V Seyhan, VI, VII
Zekai (Apaydın)	Bosnia (non-Anatolian)	Government official	No	Mersin governor 1915, Kayseri 1916, Eskişehir 1917; accused of Armenian deportations and escaped[5]	Adana	I, II Aydın,III–V Diyarbekir

Ali Rıza (Topçu)	Amasya (Anatolian)	Government official, then farmer	No	Mayor of Amasya; member of General Assembly	Amasya	I
Ali Rıza (Özdarende)	Amasya (Anatolian)	Religious scholar and mufti	No	Mufti of Amasya	Amasya	I, II
Bekir Sami (Kunduh)	Tokat (non-Anatolian origin)	Government official	No	Aleppo governor	Amasya	I, II Tokat
Asım (Sirel)	Amasya (Anatolian)	Physician	No	Chief physician at Sivas Military Hospital	Amasya	I, III–V Samsun
Ahmet Hamdi (Apaydın)	Erzurum (Anatolian)	Government official	No	Established school for war orphans	Amasya	I
Mehmet Ragıp (Topala)	Amasya (Anatolian)	Legal profession	No	Member of Amasya lower court	Amasya	I
Ömer Lütfi (Yasan)	Amasya (Anatolian)	Military officer	No	In the army, Erzurum	Amasya	I, II
Ahmet Rüstem	Midilli (non-Anatolian)	Government official	No	Ottoman ambassador in Washington	Ankara	I
Ali Fuat (Cebesoy)	İstanbul	Military officer	No	In the army—Caucasus, Bitlis, Van, Palestine	Ankara	I, II, IV–XI
Şemsettin (Bayramoğlu)	Ankara (Anatolian)	Religious sheikh	No	In Ankara	Ankara	I

(*Continued*)

Name	*Birthplace (Origin)*	*Profession*	*CUP Member-Ship*	*Position In 1915–17*	*Deputy Of*	*Terms Served*
Atıf (Taşpınar)	Ankara (Anatolian)	Religious scholar	No	Member of Ankara General Assembly	Ankara	I
Mustafa (Beynam)	Ankara (Anatolian)	Religious scholar	No	Professor at Kocabey medrese	Ankara	I
Mustafa Hilmi (Çayırlıoğlu)	Ankara (Anatolian)	Landowner and merchant	No	Deputy in Ottoman assembly	Ankara	I, II
Mustafa Kemal (Atatürk)	Salonica (non-Anatolian)	Military officer	No	In the army—Dardanelles, Bitlis, Baghdad	Ankara	I–V
Ömer Mümtaz (Tanbi)	Adıgey (non-Anatolian)	Police superintendent	No	Deputy in Ottoman assembly	Ankara	I, II
Şakir (Kınacı)	Ankara (Anatolian)	Merchant	No	Ankara mayor	Ankara	I–VI
Ali Vefa (Seyhanlı)	Cyprus (non-Anatolian)	Government official	No	Head official of İslahiye, Çerkes, Maan	Antalya	I
Halil İbrahim (Özkaya)	Antalya (Anatolian)	Teacher and lawyer	No	Drafted, fought in Dardanelles, Caucasus	Antalya	I
Hamdullah Suphi (Tanrıöver)	Istanbul	Writer and professor	No	Professor in Istanbul	Antalya	I, II İstanbul, III, VII, IX, X
Hasan Tahsin (Sürenkök)	Antalya (Anatolian)	Government official	No	Employee in Postal Office Headquarters	Antalya	I
Mustafa (İbrişimoğlu	Antalya (Anatolian)	Government official	No	Mayor of Antalya; member of board of directors	Antalya	I

Rasih (Kaplan)	Antalya (Anatolian)	Religious scholar	No	Member of Antalya standing committee	Antalya	I–VI, VII Maraş, VIII
Hilmi Bey	Artvin (Anatolian)	Military officer, farmer merchant	Yes;[1] SO member	Farmer and merchant in Artvin	Ardahan	I
Osman Server (Atabekoğulları)	Ahıska (non-Anatolian)	Engineer and lawyer	No	Fought Armenians with militia forces	Ardahan	I
Abdülkadir Cami (Baykurt)	İstanbul	Military officer	Yes	In the army—where?	Aydın	I, II
Ahmet Şükrü (Yavuzyılmaz)	Denizli (Anatolian)	Religious scholar	No	Mufti of Sarayköy	Aydın	I
Sadık Bey	Aydın (Anatolian)	Merchant	No	Nazilli mayor; member of board of directors	Aydın	I
Mazhar (Germen)	Aydın (Anatolian)	Physician	No	Drafted, health inspector, chief physician of Eskişehir hospital	Aydın	I–VIII
Mehmet Emin (Erkut)	Aydın (Anatolian)	Religious scholar	No	Mufti of Bozdoğan	Aydın	I
Mehmet Esat (İleri)	Gümülcine (non-Anatolian)	Religious scholar	No	Teacher at Aydın lyceum	Aydın	I, II Menteşe

(*Continued*)

Name	*Birthplace (Origin)*	*Profession*	*CUP Member-Ship*	*Position In 1915–17*	*Deputy Of*	*Terms Served*
Hasan Tahsin (San)	Salonica (non-Anatolian)	Government official	No	Head official of Çal	Aydın	I–V
Ahmet Akif (Suner)	Artvin (Anatolian)	Merchant	No	Fought Armenians	Batum	I
Ahmet Fevzi (Erdem)	Artvin (Anatolian)	Religious scholar	No	Student at İstanbul Law School	Batum	I
Ahmet Nurettin	Çürüksu (Anatolian)	Religious scholar	No	Unknown?	Batum	I
Ali Rıza (Acara)	Acara (non-Anatolian)	Religious scholar	No	Fought against the Russians	Batum	I
Mehmet Eyüp (Dinç)	Artvin (Anatolian)	Merchant and contractor	No	Fought as militia with Russians, Armenians	Batum	I
Mehmet Atıf (Bayazıt)	Rhodes (non-Anatolian)	Government official	No	Head official of Bilan 1915; governor of Tarulula 1916, Dardanelles, Karabiga 1917	Bayazıt	I
İbrahim Refik (Saydam)	İstanbul	Physician	Yes; present in Tripoli[6]	General Headquarters health inspector	Bayazıt	I, II–VI İstanbul
Mehmet (Onay)	Bayazıt (Anatolian)	Religious scholar	No	Migrated to Istanbul	Bayazıt	I
Süleyman Sudi (Acarbey)	Bayazıt (Anatolian)	Government official	Yes; SO member	Participated with band in Armenian massacres in Ardahan	Bayazıt	I, II

Şevket (Bayazıt)	Bayazıt (Anatolian)	Government official	No	Chief secretary of Erzurum 1915, governor of Çimin, Kemerik, Yavi 1916–18	Bayazıt	I
Ahmet Hamdi(Dumrul)	Dardanelles (Anatolian)	Merchant	No	Merchant in Ayvacık	Biga	I
Hamit (Karaosmanoğlu)	Isparta (Anatolian)	Government official	No	Public prosecutor and judge?	Biga	I
Mehmet (Dinç)	Dardanelles (Anatolian)	Government official, merchant	No	Member of General Assembly; Standing Council of Biga	Biga	I, II, III Çanakkale
Arif Hikmet (Özdemir)	Bitlis (Anatolian)	Government official	No	Police superintendent?	Bitlis	I, VIII
Derviş (Sefunç)	Bitlis (Anatolian)	Landowner and merchant	No	Fought with own militia in Van	Bitlis	I
Hüseyin Hüsnü (Orakçıoğlu)	Bitlis (Anatolian)	Government official	No	Bitlis head secretary of board of directors	Bitlis	I
Resul Sıtkı	Bitlis (Anatolian)	Government official (knew Armenian)	No	Bitlis population director 1914; Mardin director of refugee affairs 1916	Bitlis	I, II
Sadullah Fevzi (Eren)	Bitlis (Anatolian)	Government official (knew Armenian)	No	Deputy in Ottoman assembly	Bitlis	I, II

(*Continued*)

Name	*Birthplace (Origin)*	*Profession*	*CUP Member-Ship*	*Position In 1915–17*	*Deputy Of*	*Terms Served*
Şaban Vehbi (Öztekin)	Bitlis (Anatolian)	Government official	No	Employed at military post headquarters	Bitlis	I
Yusuf Ziya (Koçoğlu)	Bitlis (Anatolian)	Merchant	No	In Bitlis?	Bitlis	I
Mehmet Cevat Abbas (Gürer)	Niş (non-Anatolian)	Military officer	Yes	In the army, Dardanelles Bitlis, Baghdad	Bolu	I–V
Abdullah Sabri (Aytaç)	Zonguldak (Anatolian)	Religious scholar	No	Mufti of Devrek	Bolu	I
Fuat (Umay)	Kırklareli (non-Anatolian)	Physician	No	Government physician in Kırklareli	Bolu	I, II–VIII Kırklareli
Nuri (Aksu)	Filibe (non-Anatolian)	Government official	No	Head of finance office and mayor of Düzce	Bolu	I
Mehmet Şükrü (Gülez)	Bolu (Anatolian)	Government official and merchant	Yes; CUP Bolu director, council member	Lawyer and merchant in Bolu	Bolu	I–V
Abdülvahap Efendi	Bolu (Anatolian)	Religious scholar	No	Teacher at Darülhilafet	Bolu	I
Tunalı Hilmi	Eskicuma (non-Anatolian)	Physician	Yes	Head official of Gemlik 1915, inspector at Directory of Refugees 1916	Bolu	I, II, III Zonguldak
Yusuf İzzet (Met)	Yozgat (of non-Anatolian origin)	Military officer	No	In the army, Caucasus	Bolu	I

Halil Hulusi	Burdur (Anatolian)	Religious scholar	No	Mufti of Burdur	Burdur	I
Şevket Bey	Serfice (non-Anatolian)	Government official	No	Head official of Burdur 1915	Burdur	I
Mehmet Ali Ulvi	İstanbul	Government official	No	Governor of Kerbela, Kangırı, Kayseri 1915–17	Burdur	I
İsmail Suphi (Soysallıoğlu)	İstanbul	Government official and journalist	Yes?; CUP newspaper editor	Journalist and teacher in İstanbul	Burdur	I
Mehmet Akif (Ersoy)	İstanbul	Government official	Yes,SO member	In Riyadh 1915, rest unknown?	Burdur	I
Veliyüddin (Saltıkgil)	Buldan (Anatolian)	Government official	No	Deputy in Ottoman assembly	Burdur	I
Muhittin Baha (Pars)	Bursa (Anatolian)	Government official and teacher	No	Teacher at Bursa lyceum	Bursa	I, V Ordu, VI–VIII Bursa
Mustafa Fehmi (Gerçeker)	Bursa (Anatolian)	Religious scholar	No	Mufti of Karacabey	Bursa	I–VIII
Necati (Kurtuluş)	Skopje (non-Anatolian)	Military officer	Yes, SO member[6]	CUP Ankara regional representative and official secretary	Bursa	I, II
Mehmet Emin (Erkul)	Grebene (non-Anatolian)	Physician	No	Director of Bursa Health Department	Bursa	I

(*Continued*)

Name	*Birthplace (Origin)*	*Profession*	*CUP Member-Ship*	*Position In 1915–17*	*Deputy Of*	*Terms Served*
Hasan Fehmi	Denizli (Anatolian)	Government official	No	Head of Bursa Court of Appeals	Bursa	I
Osman Nuri (Özpay)	İstanbul	Lawyer	No	Director of Bursa General Assembly	Bursa	I, II
Servet (Akdağ)	Kastamonu (non-Anatolian origin)	Religious scholar	No	Religious preacher of Bursa	Bursa	I
Emin (Geveci)	Bafra (Anatolian)	Government official	No	Lawyer in Samsun	Canik	I, IV Samsun
Ahmet Hamdi (Yalman)	Ünye (Anatolian)	Teacher	No	Director of education in Adana 1915, Bursa 1916	Canik	I, II–VIII Ordu
Ahmet Nafiz (Özalp)	Konya (Anatolian)	Government official	No	Prosecutor in Canik lower court 1915, Samsun court legal councilor 1917	Canik	I
Süleyman (Boşnak)	Samsun (Anatolian)	Merchant	No	Merchant in Canik?	Canik	I
Mehmet Şükrü (Fırat)	Kemaliye (Anatolian)	Merchant	No	Secretary of Samsun Chamber of Commerce	Canik	I
Mehmet İhsan (Eryavuz)	İstanbul	Military officer	Yes; founded CUP Edirne branch	In the army, fought at western and eastern fronts	Cebelibereket	I–III
Faik (Öztrak)	Tekirdağ (non-Anatolian)	Government official	No	Head official Uzunköprü 1915, governor Nablus 1917	Cebelibereket	I, II–VIIITekirdağ

Rasim Celalettin (Öztekin)	Monastır (non-Anatolian)	Military officer	No	In the army, in İstanbul	Cebelibereket	I, II ErtuğrulIII, IV Kütahya
Behçet (Kutlu)	Çankırı (Anatolian)	Religious scholar	No	Deputy in Ottoman assembly	Çankırı	I
Neşet (Akkor)	Payas (Anatolian)	Government official (knew Armenian)	No	Drafted and served?	Çankırı	I, VIII Aydın
Said (Üçok)	Çankırı (Anatolian)	Merchant	No	Merchant in Çankırı	Çankırı	I
Tahir Aşık (Musuloğlu)	Çankırı (Anatolian)	Merchant	No	Merchant in Çankırı	Çankırı	I
Mehmet Tevfik (Durlanık)	Çankırı (Anatolian)	Religious scholar	No	Teacher and preacher in Çankırı	Çankırı	I, II
Müştak Bey	Erzurum (Anatolian)	Government official	No	Erzurum head engineer of public works	Çankırı	I
Yusuf Ziya (İsfendiyaroğlu)	Çankırı (Anatolian)	Government official then merchant farmer	No	Merchant farmer in Çankırı	Çankırı	I–VI
Abdurrahman Dursun (Yalvaç)	Tokat (Anatolian)	Teacher	No	Principal at Bolu 1915, Ankara 1916 lycees	Çorum	I
Hüseyin Ferit (Torumküney)	İstanbul	Government official (knew Armenian)	No	Director of financial administration Diyarbekir 1915, Kastamonu 1917	Çorum	I, II

(*Continued*)

Name	*Birthplace (Origin)*	*Profession*	*CUP Member-Ship*	*Position In 1915–17*	*Deputy Of*	*Terms Served*
Mehmet Haşim (Apaydin)	Erzurum (Anatolian)	Government official	No	Konya chief accountant 1915, granary official 1916–17	Çorum	I
Mehmet Fuat (Tek)	İstanbul	Government official	No	Erzurum government inspector 1915	Çorum	I
Hasan Sıddık (Mumcu)	Merzifon (Anatolian)	Government official	No	Zile head of finance 1915–16	Çorum	I
Abdullah İsmet (Eker)	Çorum (Anatolian)	Government official	No	Deputy in Ottoman assembly	Çorum	I, VIII
Hakkı Behiç (Bayiç)	İstanbul (non-Anatolian origin)	Government official	Yes, SO member[4]	Governor of Isparta 1915, Ertuğrul 1916, Nablus 1917; on court list for crimes related to Armenian massacres[2]	Denizli	I
Hasan (Tokcan)	Denizli (Anatolian)	Religious scholar	No	Mufti of Acıpayam	Denizli	I
Hüseyin Mazlum (Bababalım)	Denizli (Anatolian)	Religious scholar	No	In Denizli	Denizli	I
Mustafa Nuri (Tavaslıoğlu)	Denizli (Anatolian)	Merchant farmer	No	In Tavas	Denizli	I
Necip (Buldanlıoğlu)	Denizli (Anatolian)	Merchant	No	Merchant in Denizli	Denizli	I

Yusuf (Başkaya)	Denizli (Anatolian)	Government official	Yes; CUP İzmir council member	CUP Denizli official secretary; Standing Council member	Denizli	I–VII
Abdülhak Tevfik (Gençtürk)	Tunceli (Anatolian)	Government official	No	Secretary Çemişgezek lower court 1915–16, Dersim examining magistrate 1917	Dersim	I
Diyab (Yıldırım)	Tunceli (Anatolian)	Tribal leader	No	In Dersim	Dersim	I
Hasan Hayri (Konko)	Dersim (Anatolian)	Tribal leader	No	In the army, eastern front	Dersim	I
Mustafa (Öztürk)	Tunceli (Anatolian)	Tribal leader	No	In Dersim	Dersim	I
Mustafa Zeki (Saltuk)	Elazığ (Anatolian)	Tribal leader	No	In the army, Eastern front	Dersim	I
Ahmet Ramiz (Tan)	Tunceli (Anatolian)	Tribal leader	No	In the army, Eastern front	Dersim	I
Fevzi (Pirinççioğlu)	Diyarbekir (Anatolian)	Landowner, merchant	No	Deputy in Ottoman assembly; imprisoned by the British forArmenian massacres	Diyarbekir	I, II
Şükrü (Aydındağ)	İstanbul	Military officer	No	In the army, fought in Iraq, Iran	Diyarbekir	I

(*Continued*)

Name	*Birthplace (Origin)*	*Profession*	*CUP Member-Ship*	*Position In 1915–17*	*Deputy Of*	*Terms Served*
Abdülhamit Hamdi (Bilecen)	Diyarbekir (Anatolian)	Religious scholar and teacher	No	Teacher at Diyarbeeir lyceum	Diyarbekir	I
Kadri Abdülkadir Ahmet (Kürkçü)	Diyarbekir (Anatolian)	Military officer	No	In the army, inspector of provisions in the East	Diyarbekir	I, II Siverek
Mustafa Akif (Tütenk)	Diyarbekir (Anatolian)	Teacher	No	Diyarbekir secretary of estates in mortmain 1915	Diyarbekir	I
Mehmet Kadri (Üçok)	Diyarbekir (Anatolian)	Government official (knew Armenian)	No	Head official of Palu 1915; governor of Mardin 1917	Diyarbekir	I
Zülfü (Tiğrel)	Diyarbekir (Anatolian)	Government official	No	Deputy in Ottoman assembly; imprisoned by the British forArmenian massacres	Diyarbekir	I–VI
Cafer Tayyar (Eğilmez)	Priştine (non-Anatolian)	Military officer	No	In the army?	Edirne	I, II
Kazım (Karabekir)	İstanbul	Military officer	Yes[4]	In the army, Iran, Dardanelles, Iraq, Caucasus, Erzincan	Edirne	I, II, V–VIII İstanbul
Mustafa İsmet (İnönü)	İzmir (Anatolian)	Military officer	Yes[4]	In the army, Dardanelles, Palestine	Edirne	I–IV, V–XIV Malatya
Mehmet Faik (Kaltakkıran)	Edirne (Rumelian)	Government official	No	Deputy in the Ottoman parliament; imprisoned and deported to Malta[3]	Edirne	I–VI

Mehmet Şerafettin (Aykut)	Edirne (Rumelian)	Lawyer, journalist	No	Published newspapers; imprisoned and deported to Malta[3]	Edirne	I, IV–VI
Muhittin (Çöteli)	Elazığ (Anatolian)	Landowner	No	Elazığ member of General Assembly	Elazığ	I–III
Mehmet Naci (Karaali)	Elazığ (Anatolian)	Government official	No	Konya director of finance	Elazığ	I, II
Hasan Tahsin (Berk)	Salonica (non-Anatolian)	Government official	No	Adana auditor 1915, Baghdad director of public property 1916	Elazığ	I, III–V
Hüseyin (Gökçelik)	Elazığ (Anatolian)	Government official	No	Police superintendent of Diyarbekir	Elazığ	I–IV
Mustafa Şükrü (Çağlayan)	Elazığ (Anatolian)	Government official	No	Secretary, Elazığ lower court of appeals	Elazığ	I
Mehmet Fevzi (Celayır)	Keban (Anatolian)	Government official	No	Head of finance at various districts	Elazığ	I
Mustafa Rasim (Tekin)	Malatya (Anatolian)	Government official, teacher at Armenian school	No	Antep secretary of board of directors	Elazığ	I

(*Continued*)

Name	*Birthplace (Origin)*	*Profession*	*CUP Member-Ship*	*Position In 1915–17*	*Deputy Of*	*Terms Served*
İbrahim Hakkı (Akgün)	Elazığ (Anatolian)	Government official	No	Drafted, at eastern front	Ergani	I
Mahmut (Sığnak)	İstanbul	Landowner	No	Landowner in Palu	Ergani	I
Mehmet Emin (Giray)	Elazığ (Anatolian)	Government official	No	Mayor of Palu	Ergani	I
Ahmet Nüzhet (Saracoğlu)	Tunceli (Anatolian)	Government official	No	Muhundu district director	Ergani	I
Rüştü (Bulduk)	Elazığ (Anatolian)	Landowner	No	Landowner in Palu	Ergani	I
Ali Sırrı (Özata)	Tunceli (Anatolian)	Government official	No	Tax collection office chief: Mazgirt 1915, Siverek 1916	Ergani	I
Halil (Işık)	Bilecik (Anatolian)	Military officer, then teacher	No	Drafted and fought in?	Ertuğrul	I, II
Mustafa Kemal (Güney)	Bilecik (Anatolian)	Government official	No	Aydın, Dörtyol examining magistrate 1915, Kütahya lower court member 1916	Ertuğrul	I
Ahmet (Lakşe)	Mostar (non-Anatolian)	Landowner	No	In İnegöl	Ertuğrul	I
Necip (Soydan)	Bursa (Anatolian)	Government official	No	To Erzurum governorship 1915, head official of Çemişgezek 1916, Haran Raka 1917	Ertuğrul	I

Ahmet Hamdi (Aksoy)	İzmir (Anatolian)	Landowner and journalist	Yes	CUP Çatalca official secretary	Ertuğrul	I, II–V İzmir
Mehmet Emin (Lekili)	Bursa (Anatolian)	GovernmentOfficial	No	Unemployed during 1915–19?	Erzincan	I
Hüseyin (Aksu)	Erzincan (Anatolian)	Tribal leader	No	Fought Russians with own militia	Erzincan	I
Osman Fevzi (Topçu)	Erzincan (Anatolian)	Religious scholar	No	Preacher at Erzincan mosque	Erzincan	I
Mehmet Tevfik (Kütükbaşı)	Erzincan (Anatolian)	Government official	No	Administrator of Selepur and Mollakendi 1915	Erzincan	I
Fevzi (Baysoy)	Erzincan (Anatolian)	Religious scholar	No	Resisted Russians in Erzincan	Erzincan	I
Zihni (Orhon)	Erzurum (Anatolian)	Military officer	No	In the army, Russian front	Erzurum	I, VI–VIII Kars
Asım Vasfı (Mühürdaroğlu)	Erzurum (Anatolian)	Merchant	Yes, SO member	Conducted guerrilla warfare against Russians; imprisoned by British but escaped	Erzurum	I, III, IV
Celaleddin Arif	İstanbul	Lawyer and professor	No, but defends CUP members accused of massacres[4]	President of İstanbul Bar Association	Erzurum	I

(*Continued*)

Name	*Birthplace (Origin)*	*Profession*	*CUP Member-Ship*	*Position In 1915–17*	*Deputy Of*	*Terms Served*
Hüseyin Avni (Ulaş)	Erzurum (Anatolian)	Lawyer	Yes,SO member[4]	Drafted, fought Russians in the East	Erzurum	I
İsmail Naim (Arslan)	Erzurum (Anatolian)	Military officer	No	In the army: conscription department Kayseri 1917, Erzurum 1918	Erzurum	I
Mehmet Salih (Yeşiloğlu)	Erzurum (Anatolian)	Religious scholar, then merchant	No	Merchant in Bursa	Erzurum	I
Mustafa Durak (Sakarya)	Erzurum (Anatolian)	Government official	No	Ankara police chief 1915, Adana 1917; there when Ankara massacres occurred[4]	Erzurum	I, V, VI
Mehmet Nüsret (Son)	Erzurum (Anatolian)	Religious scholar	No	Mufti of the army, Caucasus	Erzurum	I
Süleyman Necati (Güneri)	Bingöl (Anatolian)	Lawyer and teacher	Yes; CUP Erzurum school teacher, pro-CUP newspaper editor[6]	Principal of UP Konya school	Erzurum	I, V Zonguldak
Abdullah Azmi (Torun)	Eskişehir (Anatolian)	Religious scholar and lawyer	No	Deputy in Ottoman assembly	Eskişehir	I, II Eskişehir
Emin (Sazak)	Eskişehir (Anatolian)	Landowner and merchant	No	Mihaliççik president of Chamber of Commerce	Eskişehir	I–VIII

Eyüp Sabri (Akgöl)	Monastır (non-Anatolian)	Military officer	Yes; CUP founding member, SO member[6]	Worked for SO/TM and imprisoned by the French	Eskişehir	I, V–VIII Çorum
Veliyullah (Bayraktar)	Mangalya (non-Anatolian)	Merchant	No	Mayor of Eskişehir 1915	Eskişehir	I
Halil İbrahim (Sipahioğlu)	Eskişehir (Anatolian)	Merchant	No	Mayor of Eskişehir 1917	Eskişehir	I
Hüsrev Sami (Kızıldoğan)	Gümülcine (non-Anatolian)	Military officer	Yes, SO member	Worked for SO/TM in Trabzon and Caucasus[4]	Eskişehir	I, V–VI Kars
Mehmet Niyazi (Çamoğlu)	Eskişehir (Anatolian)	Merchant	No	Merchant in Eskişehir	Eskişehir	I
Abdurrahman Lami (Ersoy)	Kilis (Anatolian)	Government official	No	Aleppo director of estates administration 1916	Gaziantep	I
Mehmet Ali (Cenani)	İstanbul	Landowner	Yes	CUP deputy in Ottoman assembly;imprisoned by the British for Armenian massacres	Gaziantep	I–III
Mehmet (Şahin)	Gaziantep (Anatolian)	Religious scholar	No	Gaziantep director of orphans	Gaziantep	I–VIII

(Continued)

Name	*Birthplace (Origin)*	*Profession*	*CUP Member-Ship*	*Position In 1915–17*	*Deputy Of*	*Terms Served*
Ali (Kılıç)	İstanbul	Military officer	No	In the army, Dardanelles, Caucasus	Gaziantep	I–V
Ragıp (Yoğun)	İstanbul	Government official	Yes	CUP Hicaz secretary	Gaziantep	I
Mehmet Yasin Sani (Kutluğ)	Urfa (Anatolian)	Landowner	No	Farming in Gaziantep	Gaziantep	I
Celal Nuri (İleri)	Dardanelles (Anatolian)	Journalist	No	Published newspapers in Istanbul	Gelibolu	I, II, III–IV Tekirdağ
Ali Vasıf (Telli)	Erzurum (Anatolian)	Military officer	No	Commander of gendarmerie Van, Musul, Diyarbekir	Genç	I
Mehmet Celal (Saracoğlu)	Adana (Anatolian)	Government official	No	Head official of Palu, deputy governor of Genç	Genç	I
Ali Haydar	Diyarbekir (Anatolian)	Physician	No	Headed military hospitals in the East	Genç	I, II
Fikri Faik (Güngören)	Elazığ (Anatolian)	Government official	No	Bursa police chief	Genç	I
İbrahim Fikri (Ergun)	Bitlis (Anatolian)	Government official	No	Postal clerk	Genç	I
Hamdi (Yılmaz)	Siirt (Anatolian)	Government official	No	Trial clerk, notary, court bailiff at Genç	Genç	I
Mehmet Şükrü (Üçüncüoğlu)	Gümüşhane (Anatolian)	Government official	No	Mayor of Torul	Gümüşhane	I

Mustafa (Darman)	Gümüşhane (Anatolian)	Pharmacist	No	Pharmacist in Eskişehir	Gümüşhane	I
Hasan Fehmi (Ataç)	Gümüşhane (Anatolian)	Landowner	No	Deputy in the Ottoman parliament	Gümüşhane	I–VIII
İbrahim Ruşen (Oktar)	Gümüşhane (Anatolian)	Government official	No	Director of Gümüşhane Prison	Gümüşhane	I
Veysel Rıza	Gümüşhane (Anatolian)	Government official	Yes	CUP deputy in Ottoman assembly	Gumushane	I, II
Ziya Bey	Gümüşhane (Anatolian)	Government official	No	Kelkit director of finance	Gumushane	I
Mazhar Müfit (Kansu)	İstanbul	Government official	No	Governor of Mersin, İzmit, Balıkesir	Hakkari	I, II-V Denizli, VI-VII Çoruh
Mehmet Tufan (Ülker)	Hakkari (Anatolian)	Government official	No	Fought with own militia forces in the East	Hakkari	I
Mehmet Cemal (Mersinli)	Mersin (Anatolian)	Military officer	No	In the army; imprisoned and deported to Malta for possible crimes against Armenians[3]	Isparta	I, VI İçel
Mehmet Tahir (Küçür)	Isparta (Anatolian)	Government official	No	Drafted, fought at Macedonian, Euphrates fronts	Isparta	I

(*Continued*)

Name	*Birthplace (Origin)*	*Profession*	*CUP Member-Ship*	*Position In 1915–17*	*Deputy Of*	*Terms Served*
İbrahim (Demiralay)	Isparta (Anatolian)	Religious scholar and farmer	No	Member of Isparta lower court	Isparta	I–VI
Hüseyin Hüsnü (Özdamar)	Isparta (Anatolian)	Religious scholar	No	Member of city board of directors 1915; Mufti of Isparta 1916	Isparta	I–VI
İsmail Remzi (Berkun)	Isparta (Anatolian)	Government official	No	Mayor of Yalvaç	Isparta	I
Mehmet Nadir (Süldür)	Isparta (Anatolian)	Government official	No	Lawyer in Isparta	Isparta	I
Ali Rıza (Ataışık)	Antalya (Anatolian)	Religious scholar	No	Mayor of Mut; Adana General Assembly member	İçel	I
Ali Sabri (Güney)	İçel (Anatolian)	Government official	No	Kadi of Tarsus	İçel	I
Haydar Lütfi (Aslan)	İçel (Anatolian)	Government official	No	Haifa lower court president 1915, Beirut justice of the peace 1916	İçel	I, VIII
Mehmet Alim Naim (Ulusal)	İçel (Anatolian)	Religious scholar	No	Lawyer in Silifke	İçel	I
Mehmet Sami (Arkan)	İçel (Anatolian)	Merchant	No	Merchant in İçel	İçel	I
Ahmet Şevki (Göklevent)	İçel (Anatolian)	Government official	No	İçel lower court clerk	İçel	I

Ahmet Ferit (Tek)	Bursa (Anatolian)	Military officer	Yes; 1909 CUP deputy Ottoman assembly	In Sinop in exile	İstanbul	I, II Kütahya
Ahmet Mazhar (Akifoğlu)	İzmit (Anatolian)	Merchant	No	Drafted, fought at?	İstanbul	I, II
Ahmet Muhtar	Çanakkale (Anatolian)	Government official	No	Deputy diplomat at Lahey	İstanbul	I, II, IV Kastamonu
Ahmet Şükrü (Oğuz)	İstanbul	Military officer	Yes; aide of Enver pasha	In the army, Dardanelles, Austria, Germany, İstanbul	İstanbul	I
Ali Fethi (Okyar)	Pirlepe (non-Anatolian)	Military officer	Yes[4]	Deputy in Ottoman assembly; imprisoned and deported to Malta for not taking action against Armenian massacres[3]	İstanbul	I–III, V–VII Bolu
Selahattin Bey	İzmir	Teacher	Yes?	Teacher at İzmir UP lyceum	İstanbul	I
Ali Rıza (Bebe)	Sinop (Anatolian)	Military officer	No	Head of provisions	İstanbul	I, II, III Cebelibereket
Abdülhak Adnan (Adıvar)	Gelibolu (Anatolian)	Physician	No	Director of public health	İstanbul	I, II, VIII
Hacı Arif (Marlali)	Antalya (Anatolian)	Government official	No	Member of İstanbul Municipal Assembly	İstanbul	I

(*Continued*)

Name	*Birthplace (Origin)*	*Profession*	*CUP Member-Ship*	*Position In 1915–17*	*Deputy Of*	*Terms Served*
Hüseyin Hüsnü (Işık)	Kocaeli (Anatolian)	Religious scholar	Yes, removed from office for CUP ties	Mufti of Gebze	İstanbul	I
Mehmet Neşet (Özercan)	İstanbul	Government official	No	Head official Cisr-i Mustafapaşa 1915, Süveyde 1917; refugee inspector 1916	İstanbul	I, II, III Aksaray
Numan Usta	Köstence (non-Anatolian)	Laborer	Yes[6]	Worker at the Zeytinburnu military factory; imprisoned and deported to Malta for possible crimes against the Armenians[3]	İstanbul	I
Ali Enver (Tekand)	Rhodes (non-Anatolian)	Teacher	Yes?; teacher at CUP İzmir school	Principal of UP Izmir lyceum	İzmir	I
Süleyman (Bilgen)	Aydın	Religious scholar	No	Religious scholar in Aydın	İzmir	I
Mahmut Esat (Bozkurt)	Aydın (non-Anatolian origin)	Legal profession	No	Studying law in Switzerland	İzmir	I–VII
İbrahim Refet (Bele)	Salonica (non-Anatolian)	Military officer	Yes[4]	In the army, communications officer, Palestine	İzmir	I, VI–VIII

Hasan Tahsin (Uzer)	Salonica (non-Anatolian)	Government official	Yes, SO member[10]	Governor of Erzurum 1915, Syria 1916; involved in deportations from Erzurum[8]	İzmir	I, II Ardahan III–V Erzurum, IV Konya
Mustafa (Bengisu)	İzmir (Anatolian)	Physician	No	In the army, Dardanelles, Syria	İzmir	I, V Çanakkale VI İzmir
Süleyman Efendi	İzmir (Anatolian)	Religious scholar	No	In İzmir	İzmir	I
Yunus Nadi (Abalıoğlu)	Muğla (Anatolian)	Journalist	Yes[7]	CUP Deputy in Ottoman assembly	İzmir	I, III–VI Menteşe, Muğla
Mehmet Fuat (Carım)	Aleppo (non-Anatolian)	Government official	No	Director of Bornova district 1915, Karesi legal director 1916, Gönen, Adapazarı head official 1917; fought against Armenians there	İzmit	I
Abdullah (Tezemir)	Adapazarı (Anatolian)	Religious scholar, then merchant	No	Director of Adapazarı Emniyet Bank	İzmit	I
Halil Ibrahim (Gürsoy)	İznik(Anatolian)	Landowner	No	Mayor of İzmit, member of General Assembly	İzmit	I
Hamdi Namık (Gör)	Monastir (non-Anatolian)	Government official	No	Secretary general of Menteşe 1915, Karesi 1917	İzmit	I
Tahir (Barlas)	Istanbul	Government official	No	Head official Hınıs 1915, Mazgirt 1916, Arapgir 1917	İzmit	I

(*Continued*)

Name	*Birthplace (Origin)*	*Profession*	*CUP Member-Ship*	*Position In 1915–17*	*Deputy Of*	*Terms Served*
Hüseyin Sırrı (Bellioğlu)	Cyprus (non-Anatolian)	Government official	No	Governor of Kerbela 1915, Amasya 1916	İzmit	I, IV Kocaeli
Ali (Çetinkaya)	Afyon (Anatolian)	Military officer	Yes[12]	In the army, in Iraq, Bitlis, Monastır, Kiğı, Rumelia; imprisoned and deported to Malta for crimes against Armenians[3]	Karahisarısahip	I–VIII
Hasan Hulusi (Kutluoğlu)	Samsun (Anatolian)	Military officer	No	In the army, provisioning, Iraq, Iran	Karahisarısahip	I
Mehmet Şükrü (Koç)	Afyon (Anatolian)	Government official	No	Public prosecutor, judge in Aleppo Kilis	Karahisarı sahip	I
Mustafa Hulusi (Çalgüner)	Denizli (Anatolian)	Religious scholar	No	Kadi of Kütahya and head of lower court	Karahisarı sahip	I
Ahmet Nebil (Yurteri)	Afyon (Anatolian)	Religious scholar and merchant	No	In Afyon	Karahisarı sahip	I
Halil Hilmi (Bozca)	Afyon (Anatolian)	Government official	No	Saruhan lower court member	Karahisarı sahip	I
İsmail Şükrü (Çelikalay)	Afyon (Anatolian)	Religious scholar	Yes	Teacher at the Darülhilafe medrese	Karahisarı sahip	I
Ömer Lütfi (Argeşo)	İstanbul	Military officer	No	In the army, Palestine	Karahisarı sahip	I

Ali Sururi (Tonuk)	Karahisar (Anatolian)	Government official, lawyer	No	Lawyer at Mesudiye	Karahisarı şarki	I, II
Memduh Necdet (Erberk)	İstanbul	Military officer	No	In the army, Dardanelles, Bolu, Samsun	Karahisarışarki	I
Mesut (Benli)	Artvin (Anatolian)	Government official	No	Head official of Zaho	Karahisarı şarki	I
Mehmet Vasfi (Secer)	Karahisar (Anatolian)	Religious scholar aand government official	Yes	Member, Sivas General Assembly, Turkish teacher	Karahisarı şarki	I
Mustafa Sırrı (Serdaroğlu)	Ordu (Anatolian)	Government official	No	Merchant farmer in Karahisar	Karahisarı şarki	I
Abdülgafur (İştin)	Balıkesir (Anatolian)	Religious scholar	No	Teacher at the Darülhilafe medrese	Karesi	I
Hüseyin Hacim Muhittin (Çarıklı)	Uşak (Anatolian)	Government official	Yes, SO member[4]	Izmir police chief 1915, Akhisar head official 1916, Havran governor 1917	Karesi	I, II–III Giresun, IV–VIII Balıkesir
Hasan Basri (Çantay)	Balıkesir (Anatolian)	Government official	Yes?; published CUP newspaper in Balıkesir	Journalist, teacher at the Darülhilafe medrese	Karesi	I
İbrahim Cevdet (Yörük)	Balıkesir (Anatolian)	Landowner and merchant	No	Merchant in Balıkesir	Karesi	I, IV Balıkesir

(*Continued*)

Name	*Birthplace (Origin)*	*Profession*	*CUP Member-Ship*	*Position In 1915–17*	*Deputy Of*	*Terms Served*
Kazım (Özalp)	Köprülü (non-Anatolian)	Military officer	Yes, SO member[4]	In the army, gendarmerie commander in Van, Caucasus, Iran, Azarbaijan	Karesi	I, II–VIII Balıkesir IX Van
Mehmet Vehbi (Bolak)	Balıkesir (Anatolian)	Government official	No	Deputy in Ottoman assembly	Karesi	I, II
Ali Rıza (Ataman)	Kars (Anatolian)	Landowner	Yes?; fought Armenians in a secret committee	Exiled to Siberia by the Russians	Kars	I
Cavit (Erdel)	Edirne (non-Anatolian)	Military officer	No	In the army, Caucasus	Kars	I
Fahrettin (Erdoğan)	Divriği (Anatolian)	Merchant	Yes?; fought with the Armenians	Exiled to Orenburg by Russians, escaped, fought again with the Armenians	Kars	I
Abdülkadir Kemali (Öğütçü)	Osmaniye (Anatolian)	Government official	Yes	Joined the army, imprisoned during armistice in relation to Bursa?	Kastamonu	I
Mehmet Besim (Fazlıoğlu)	Kastamonu (Anatolian)	Journalist	Yes?; editor of CUP Kastamonu newspaper	Chief clerk at Ottoman assembly	Kastamonu	I
Suat (Soyer)	İzmir (Anatolian)	Physician	No	Inspector at Kastamonu, Bolu mobile hospitals	Kastamonu	I, IV

Mehmet Hulusi (Erdemir)	Kastamonu (Anatolian)	Religious scholar	No	Imam of the Istanbul Hoca Piri mosque	Kastamonu	I
Hüseyin Sabri (Dura)	Kastamonu (Anatolian)	Government official, then merchant	No	Merchant, member of Standing Committee	Kastamonu	I
Ahmet Rüştü (Çolakoğlu)	İnebolu (Anatolian)	Engineer	No	Deputy in Ottoman assembly	Kastamonu	I
Mehmet Murat	Kastamonu (Anatolian)	Government official, then lawyer	No	Lawyer in Kastamonu	Kastamonu	I
Yusuf Kemal (Tengirşenk)	Kastamonu (Anatolian)	Legal scholar	No	Appointed to inspect 1909 Adana incidents; president of Justice Ministry Inspection Council	Kastamonu	I, II-VIII Sinop
Ahmet Hilmi (Kalaç)	Kayseri (Anatolian)	Government official and teacher	No; but proposed law forKemal Bey hanged for Armenian massacres	Deputy for Şarki Karaağaç governor during Armenian unrest in 1914; chief secretary of Sivas 1915; went to Austria 1916 for overwork, head official in Karaman 1917; on court list for crimes related to Armenian massacres[2]	Kayseri	I, II, VII

(*Continued*)

Name	*Birthplace (Origin)*	*Profession*	*CUP Member-Ship*	*Position In 1915–17*	*Deputy Of*	*Terms Served*
Mehmet Alim (Çınar)	Kayseri (Anatolian)	Religious scholar	No	Preached in Istanbul, İzmir, Sivas	Kayseri	I
Mehmet Atıf (Tüzün)	Artvin (Anatolian)	Government official	No	Drafted as an officer, served in?	Kayseri	I, III-IV Rize, V–VIII Çoruh
Osman (Uşşaklı)	Kayseri (Anatolian)	Merchant and accountant	No	Deputy inspector at Ziraat Bank	Kayseri	I
Rıfat (Çalıka)	Kayseri (Anatolian)	Government official	No	Mayor of Kayseri	Kayseri	I
Remzi (Akgöztürk)	Kayseri (Anatolian)	Religious scholar	No	Mufti of Kayseri	Kayseri	I
Sabit (Gözügeçgel)	Kayseri (Anatolian)	Merchant and journalist	Yes; CUP Kayseri secretary	General Assembly and Standing Committee member	Kayseri	I, II
Ali Cevdet (Alişiroğlu)	Kırşehir (Anatolian)	Government official	No	Examining magistrate and court member, Kırşehir General Assembly member	Kırşehir	I
Ahmet Müfit (Kurutluoğlu)	Kırşehir (Anatolian)	Religious scholar and lawyer	No	Mufti of Kırşehir; tried during the armistice period?	Kırşehir	I
Rıza (Silsüpür)	Kırşehir (Anatolian)	Merchant	Yes	tried during the armistice for Armenian massacres in Keskin	Kırşehir	I

Sadık (Sevtekin)	Samsun (Anatolian)	Government official	No	President of lower court Gümüşhane 1915, Kırşehir 1917; Düzce public prosecutor 1916	Kırşehir	I
Ahmet Cemaleddin	Nevşehir (Anatolian)	Religious scholar	No	Fought in the East with his own militia	Kırşehir	I
Yahya Galip(Kargı)	İstanbul	Government official	No	Director of finance Kastamonu 1915, Aleppo 1916; Ankara chief of finance 1917	Kırşehir	I–III, IV–VI Ankara
Abdülhalim Çelebi	Konya (Anatolian)	Religious scholar	No	In Konya	Konya	I
Bekir (Sümer)	Konya (Anatolian)	Religious scholar and merchant	Yes	Founded Akşehir electric and textile companies	Konya	I–III
Halil Kazım Hüsnü	Konya (Anatolian)	Teacher and merchant	Yes	Konya General Assembly and Standing Council member	Konya	I–IV
Mehmet Vehbi (Çelik)	Karaman (Anatolian)	Religious scholar	No	Teacher in Konya	Konya	I
Musa Kazım (Onar)	Karaman (Anatolian)	Religious scholar and lawyer	No	Lawyer in Konya	Konya	I–III

(*Continued*)

Name	Birthplace (Origin)	Profession	CUP Member-Ship	Position In 1915–17	Deputy Of	Terms Served
Ömer Vehbi (Büyükyalvaç)	Isparta (Anatolian)	Religious scholar	Yes	Teacher in Konya	Konya	I, II
Hulusi (Göksu)	Karaman (Anatolian)	Government official	No	Mayor of Ermenek; General Assembly and Standing Council member	Konya	I
Bekir Refik (Koraltan)	Sivas (Anatolian)	Government official	No	Public prosecutor Karaman 1915, legal councilor Konya 1916, prosecutor of court- martial	Konya	I–IV,VI–XI İçel
Arif (Baysal)	Konya (Anatolian)	Government official	No	Chief court clerk of Konya	Konya	I
Mehmet Rıfat (Saatçi)	Konya (Anatolian)	Religious scholar and merchant	Yes	Founded National Economy and Trade Banks	Konya	I
Takiyeddin Fikret (Onuralp)	İstanbul	Physician	No	In the army,?	Kozan	I, II–III Ertuğrul
Hüseyin (Çelik)	Kozan (Anatolian)	Landowner and religious scholar	Yes; CUP Kozan president	Mayor of Kozan	Kozan	I
Mustafa Fevzi (Çakmak)	İstanbul	Military officer	No	In the army, Caucasus, Palestine	Kozan	I, II İstanbul, VIII

Reşit (Ronabar)	Damascus (non-Anatolian)	Government official	Yes	Governor of Kastamonu 1915, deputy in the Ottoman parliament 1916	Kozan	I
Mustafa Elvan (Cantekin)	Çorum (Anatolian)	Physician	No	In the army, Ankara, İstanbul, Dardanelles commander of wounded dispatch, chief physician of Afyon military hospital	Kozan	I, II–VIII Çorum
Besim (Atalay)	Uşak (Anatolian)	Teacher	No	Director of education Maraş 1915, İçel, Niğde 1916–17	Kütahya	I, II–IV Aksaray, V–VII Kütahya
Yusuf Cemil (Altay)	İzmir(Anatolian)	Merchant	Yes	Member of Kütahya General assembly	Kütahya	I
Mehmet Ali Cevdet Izrab (Barlas)	Gaziantep (Anatolian)	Educator	No	Principal of Kütahya Teacher's School	Kütahya	I–III
Haydar Bey	Serez (non-Anatolian)	Government official	Yes	UP deputy in Ottoman assembly	Kütahya	I
Ragip (Soysal)	Uşak (Anatolian)	Merchant and teacher	No	Teacher at Uşak medrese	Kütahya	I–III
Seyfi (Aydın)	Kütahya (Anatolian)	Religious scholar	No	Mayor of Kütahya	Kütahya	I, II

(*Continued*)

Name	*Birthplace (Origin)*	*Profession*	*CUP Member-Ship*	*Position In 1915–17*	*Deputy Of*	*Terms Served*
Abidin (Atak)	Serbia (non-Anatolian)	Physician	Yes, SO member[7]	In Iran, as SO member; then in Elaziz, Erzurum, Erzincan, and Kayseri	Lazistan	I
Esat (Özoğuz)	Hopa (Anatolian)	Government official	No	Chief clerk of Adana	Lazistan	I, II–IV Rize, V–VII Kars
Mehmet Necati (Memişoğlu)	Rize (Anatolian)	Religious scholar and lawyer	Yes	Joined the army as imam in Trabzon, Macedonia	Lazistan	I
Osman Nuri (Özgen)	Rize (Anatolian)	Engineer	No	Unknown?	Lazistan	I
İbrahim Şevki (Tüzün)	Arhavi (Anatolian)	Religious scholar	No	Kadi of Baghdad, then Musul	Lazistan	I
Ziya Hurşit	Rize (Anatolian)	Engineer	No	Teacher in Eskişehir lyceum	Lazistan	I
Mustafa Fevzi (Bilgili)	Malatya (Anatolian)	Religious scholar	No	Member of General Assembly and Standing Council	Malatya	I
Bedir (Fırat)	Adıyaman (Anatolian)	Tribal leader	No	In Malatya	Malatya	I, II, III Kars
Garip (Taner)	Malatya (Anatolian)	Landowner	No	Fought against Russians with his own militia	Malatya	I
Lütfullah (Evliyaoglu)	Malatya (Anatolian)	Religious scholar and lawyesr	No	Head official in Eğin Vezirköprü Malazgirt Hızan	Malatya	I

Resit (Ağar)	Adıyaman (Anatolian)	Landowner	No	Member of the lower court	Malatya	I, II, III–V Gaziantep
Hüseyin Sıtkı (Gür)	Karaman (Anatolia)	Government official	No	Public prosecutor of lower court of Tokat	Malatya	I
Hasip (Aksüyek)	Maraş (Anatolian)	Government official	No	Examining magistrate of Maraş	Maraş	I
Hasan Refet (Seçkin)	Maraş (Anatolian)	Religious scholar	No	Maraş director of orphan affairs	Maraş	I
Mehmet Rustu (Bozkurt)	Maras (non-Anatolian origin)	Government official and farmer	No	Aleppo and Maras General Assembly and Standing Council member	Maraş	I
Mehmet Tahsin (Hüdayioğlu)	Maraş (Anatolian)	Landowner	No	Administrative Council, General Aseembly, and Standing Council member	Maraş	I, II
Paso Yakup Hamdi (Bozdağ)	Maraş (Anatolian)	Tribal leader	Yes	Fought in region with own militia	Maraş	I
Arslan (Toğuz)	Maraş(non-Anatolian origin)	Government official	No	Police chief in Tripoli	Maraş	I
Esad (Önen)	Mardin (Anatolian)	Government official	No	Head secretary of Aleppo, Mardin Population Directorate	Mardin	I

(*Continued*)

Name	*Birthplace (Origin)*	*Profession*	*CUP Member-Ship*	*Position In 1915–17*	*Deputy Of*	*Terms Served*
İbrahim (Turan)	Mardin (Anatolian)	Government official	No	Various official posts in Mardin?	Mardin	I
Mithat (Ulusal)	Mardin (Anatolian)	Government official	No	Siverek Administrative Council member 1915, Hazro district director 1917	Mardin	I
Derviş Bey	Mardin (Anatolian)	Government official	No	Governor of Bucak district	Mardin	I, II
Hasan Tahsin	Mardin (Anatolian)	Government official	No	Deputy head official of Savur	Mardin	I
Mehmet Necip (Güven)	Mardin (Anatolian)	Clerk	Yes	Director, Mardin Ziraat Bank	Mardin	I, II
Ahmet Tevfik Rüştü (Aras)	Dardanelles (Anatolian)	Physician	Yes, SO member	Member of Supreme Council of Public Health and Hygiene	Menteşe	I, II–V İzmir
Ethem Fehmi (Arslanli)	Crete (non-Anatolian)	Government official	No	Out of commission during the war	Menteşe	I
Hamza Hayati (Öztürk)	Muğla (Anatolian)	Landowner	No	In Muğla	Menteşe	I
Mahmut Nedim	Adıgey (non-Anatolian)	Military officer	No	In the army, in the East	Menteşe	I
Rıfat (Börekçi)	Ankara (Anatolia)	Religious scholar	No	Mufti of Ankara	Menteşe	I
Ahmet Sadettin (Özsan)	Muğla (Anatolian)	Government official	No	Unknown?	Menteşe	I

Fahrettin (Altay)	Albania (non-Anatolian)	Military officer	No	In the army, Dardanelles, Romania, Palestine	Mersin	I, II İzmir, VII Burdur
Muhtar Fikri (Gücün)	Muş (Anatolian)	Landowner	Yes	Farming in Adana;deported after the 1909 Adana incident for provocation and guilt; prepared list of Armenians to be deported in 1915[6]	Mersin	I
Huseyin Salahattin (Köseoğlu)	İstanbul	Military officer	No	In the army, Caucasus	Mersin	I
İsmail Safa (Özler)	Adana (Anatolian)	Government official and teacher	Yes	Joined the army; deported after the 1909 Adana incident for provocation and guilt; prepared list of Armenians to be deported in 1915[6]	Mersin	I, II Adana, VI Seyhan
Hüseyin Hüsnü (Konay)	Konya (Anatolian)	Military officer	No	Head of Istanbul military tribunal investigation, served in Rumelia and Aydin	Mersin	I, III Konya, IV–V Tokat
Yusuf Ziya (Eraydın)	Mersin (Anatolian)	Agriculturalist	No	Drafted, Dardanelles, eastern front	Mersin	I

(*Continued*)

Name	*Birthplace (Origin)*	*Profession*	*CUP Member-Ship*	*Position In 1915–17*	*Deputy Of*	*Terms Served*
Abdülgani (Ertan)	Bitlis (Anatolian)	Government official	No	Head clerk at lower court of Hızan 1915, Samsun 1917	Muş	I
Ahmet Hamdi (Bilgin)	Siirt (Anatolian)	Government official	No	Head clerk of Mus tax administration	Muş	I
İlyas Sami (Mus)	Muş (Anatolian)	Landowner and religious scholar	No	Deputy in Ottoman assembly; arrested during armistice for Armenian massacres	Muş	I, II, III Bitlis, V Çorum
Kasım (Dede)	Muş (Anatolian)	Landowner and merchant	No	Joined the army as a private on eastern front	Muş	I
Mahmud Said (Yetgin)	İstanbul	Government official	No	Director of Sason, Silvan lower courts, public prosecutor of Mus	Muş	I
Osman Kadri (Bingöl)	Muş (Anatolian)	Government official	No	Principal of orphanage in Diyarbekir, official of refugee affairs	Muş	I, II
Rıza (Kotan)	Muş (Anatolian)	Landowner and merchant	No	Member of General Assembly, Standing Council	Muş	I, II
Mehmet Ataullah (Atay)	Nevşehir (Anatolian)	Government official	No	Head official of Karaman 1915; governor of Yozgat 1916, Maraş 1917	Niğde	I–III

Ahmet Hakkı (Sütekin)	Nevşehir (Anatolian)	Military officer	No	Retired in 1915 and returned to Niğde	Niğde	I
Mustafa Hilmi (Soydan)	Niğde (Anatolian)	Religious scholar	No	Lawyer, member of General Assembly 1915	Niğde	I
Mustafa (Soylu)	Niğğe (Anatolian)	Government official	No	Head clerk of education office; teacher	Niğde	I
Zeynelabidin Abidin (Bayhan)	Niğde (Anatolian)	Government official	Yes	Member of General Assembly	Niğde	I
Mustafa Vehbi (Çorakçi)	Niğde (Anatolian)	Merchant	No	Merchant in Niğe	Niğde	I, II Aksaray
Rüstem (Hamsioğlu)	Erzurum (Anatolian)	Farmer	No	Farmer in Oltu	Oltu	
Yasin (Haşimoğlu Akdağ)	Erzurum (Anatolian)	Teacher	No	In Erzurum	Oltu	
Hüseyin Avni (Zaimler)	Monastır (non-Anatolian)	Military officer	No	In the army, put down Haçin, Maraş Armenian rebellion ın 1915, retired 1918, hid when sought by British during the Armistice	Saruhan	I, II–III Cebelibereket
İbrahim Süreyya (Yiğit)	İstanbul (non-Anatolian origin)	Government official	Yes	Governor of Gelibolu, Kırkkilise 1915, Karesi 1916, İzmit 1917	Saruhan	I, II–VIII Kocaeli

(*Continued*)

Name	*Birthplace (Origin)*	*Profession*	*CUP Member-Ship*	*Position In 1915–17*	*Deputy Of*	*Terms Served*
Mahmut Celaleddin (Bayar)	Edremit (non-Anatolian origin)	Clerk	Yes; CUP Bursa, İzmir Secretary; SO member[4]	Unknown?	Saruhan	I, II–VII İzmir, VIII–XI İstanbul
Mustafa Necati (Uğural)	İzmir (Anatolian)	Lawyer and teacher	No	Teacher and lawyer in Izmir	Saruhan	I, II–III İzmir
Ömer Lütfi (Ünlü)	Manisa (Anatolian)	Farmer	No	Farmer in Manisa	Saruhan	I
Mehmet Refik Şevket (Ince)	Polihinit (non-Anatolian)	Lawyer	No	Drafted, in provisions and as legal council	Saruhan	I, IV–VI Manisa, IX
Reşit Bey	Balıkesir (non-Anatolian origin)	Military officer	Yes; SO member	Fought as SO member at various fronts	Saruhan	I
Mehmet Reşat (Kayalı)	Manisa (Anatolian)	Government official	No	Positions in the Finance Ministry	Saruhan	I, II
Mustafa Sabri (Baysan)	Denizli (Anatolian)	Religious scholar	No	Kadı of Siverek	Siirt	I
Nuri (Payam)	Siirt (Anatolian)	Merchant	No	Member of Siirt municipal council	Siirt	I
Halil Hulki (Aydın)	Siirt (Anatolian)	Religious scholar	Yes; CUP Siirt president, member of CUP central committee	In Siirt	Siirt	I–VI

Kadri (Oktay)	Siirt (Anatolian)	Landowner	No	Head clerk at the court in Pervari	Siirt	I
Necmettin (Bilgin)	Siirt (Anatolian)	Government official	No	Chief accountant Bitlis 1915, Siirt 1917	Siirt	I
Salih (Atalay)	Siirt (Anatolian)	Religious scholar	No	Siirt court clerk	Siirt	I
Abdullah (Karabina)	Sinop (Anatolian)	Merchant	No	Mayor of Boyabat, General Council member	Sinop	I
Rıza (Nur)	Sinop (Anatolian)	Physician	Yes	In exile in Egypt	Sinop	I, II
Hakkı Hami (Ulukan)	Sinop (non-Anatolian origin)	Lawyer	No	Lawyer in Sinop	Sinop	I
Mehmet Şerif (Avgan)	Kırklareli (non-Anatolian)	Government official	No	Retired, in Kastamonu	Sinop	I
Rıza Vamık (Uras)	Monastır (non-Anatolian)	Military officer	No	Commander of gendarmerie at Şarki Karahisar	Sinop	I
Mehmet Sevket (Peker)	Sinop (Anatolian)	Government official, then lawyer	No	Lawyer in Sinop	Sinop	I
Mustafa Taki (Doğruyol)	Sivas (Anatolian)	Government official	No	Teacher at Sivas lyceum	Sivas	I
Mehmet Rasim (Başara)	Sivas (Anatolian)	Teacher	No	Deputy in the Ottoman parliament	Sivas	I–V

(*Continued*)

Name	*Birthplace (Origin)*	*Profession*	*CUP Member-Ship*	*Position In 1915–17*	*Deputy Of*	*Terms Served*
Kara Vasıf (Karakol)	Yemen (non-Anatolian)	Military officer	Yes; within CUP, SO member[4]	In the army: Malazgirt, Tutak, retires in 1916; imprisoned and deported to Malta for crimes against Armenians[4]	Sivas	
Emir (Marsan)	Sivas (non-Anatolian origin)	Landowner	No	Animal husbandry in Uzunyayla	Sivas	I
Hüseyin Rauf (Orbay)	İstanbul	Military officer	Yes, SO member[4]	Department head at Naval Ministry; imprisoned and deported to Malta for not stopping crimes against Armenians[3]	Sivas	I, II, VI İstanbul
Mehmet Ziya (Bacanak)	Sivas (Anatolian)	Military officer	No	In the army, Caucasus	Sivas	I
Mustafa Hayri (Sığırcı)	Sivas (Anatolian)	Government official	No	Accounting clerk	Sivas	I
Yusuf Ziyaettin (Başara)	Sivas (Anatolian)	Government official	No	Principal, Sivas School of Industry	Sivas	I–VII
Abdülgani (Ensari)	Mardin (Anatolian)	Military officer	No	In the army, Caucasus	Siverek	I, II Mardin
Bekir Sıtkı (Ocak)	Diyarbekir (Anatolian)	Religious scholar	No	Member of General Assembly	Siverek	I

Mehmet Sırrı (Tayanç)	Siverek (Anatolian)	Government official	No	Clerk of estates in mortmain of Siverek	Siverek	I
İhsan (Sağlam)	Trabzon (Anatolian)	Military officer	Yes; joined exec. council of Teceddüd Party	Deputy in Ottoman assembly	Siverek	I, II Ergani
Mustafa Lütfi (Azer)	Azarbaijan (non-Anatolian)	Teacher	No	Principal, Urfa School of Industry	Siverek	I
Ahmet Hamdi (Mütevellioğlu)	Tokat (Anatolian)	Landowner	No	In Tokat	Tokat	I
İzzet (Gence)	Tokat (Anatolian)	Landowner	No	In Tokat	Tokat	I
Mustafa Vasfi (Süsoy)	Tokat (Anatolian)	Military officer	No	In the army, Dardanelles, Palestine, Bitlis	Tokat	I–IV
Nazim (Resmor)	Erzurum (Anatolian)	Government official	Yes	Retired in 1915	Tokat	I
Mehmet Rıfat (Arkun)	Tokat (Anatolian)	Government official	No	Chief secretary of Çorum, Amasya	Tokat	I
Ali Şükrü Bey	Trabzon (Anatolian)	Military officer and journalist	No	İstanbul or Trabzon	Trabzon	I
Celalettin (Akyar)	Trabzon (Anatolian)	Religious scholar and merchant	No	Teacher in Samsun 1916, Amasya 1917	Trabzon	I
Mehmet (Engin)	Trabzon (Anatolian)	Government official	Yes[1]	Deputy in Ottoman assembly	Trabzon	I, II

(*Continued*)

Name	*Birthplace (Origin)*	*Profession*	*CUP Member-Ship*	*Position In 1915–17*	*Deputy Of*	*Terms Served*
Hasan Hüsnü (Saka)	Trabzon (Anatolian)	Government official	No	Clerk in Finance Ministry 1915, 1917; Eskişehir region economic director 1916	Trabzon	I–IX
Hüsrev (Gerede)	Edirne (non-Anatolian)	Military officer	No	In the army, eastern front 1915, Germany 1917; participated in quelling 1909 Adana Incidents.	Trabzon	I, II Urfa, V Sivas
Hamdi (Ülkümen)	Serez (non-Anatolian)	Lawyer	No	Unknown?	Trabzon	I–VI
Ahmet Faik (Aybay)	Trabzon (Anatolian)	Government official	No	Sivas court of appeals	Trabzon	I
Hamit (Kapancı)	Rhodes (non-Anatolian)	Government official	Yes	Governor of Diyarbekir 1915, Interior Ministry Inspection Council	Trabzon	I
İzzet (Eyüboğlu)	Trabzon (Anatolian)	Government official	No	Deputy in Ottoman assembly	Trabzon	I, II
Mehmet Recai (Baykal)	Ordu (Anatolian)	Military officer	No	In the navy	Trabzon	I, II–IV Ordu
Salih Hayali	Urfa (Anatolian)	Teacher	Yes; CUP regional inspector, Urfa secretary	Urfa General Assembly, Standing Council member	Urfa	I

Ali Saib (Ursavaş)	Revandiz (non-Anatolian)	Military officer	No	Commander of gendarmerie Aleppo 1915, Deyr-i Zor 1917	Urfa	I, II Kozan, III–VI Urfa
Pozan Bey	Urfa (Anatolian)	Tribal leader	No	Unknown?	Urfa	I
Hakkı (Ungan)	Van (Anatolian)	Government official	No	Director of record office 1915, deputy governor 1917	Van	I–VII
Hasan Sıddık (Haydari)	Van (Anatolian)	Tribal leader	No	Fought Russians with own militia, exiled to Russia until 1918	Van	I
Haydar Hilmi (Vaner)	Serbia (non-Anatolian)	Government official	No	Governor of Musul 1915, Bitlis, Diyarbekir 1917; on court list for crimes related to Armenian massacres[2]	Van	I
Tevfik (Demiroğlu)	Van (Anatolian)	Government official	No	Van Population Director 1915	Van	I
Yusuf Bahri (Tatlıoğlu)	Yozgat (Anatolian)	Landowner	Yes	Clerk at the Administration of Tobacco Monopoly	Yozgat	I
Mehmet Feyyaz Ali (Ust)	Yozgat (Anatolian)	Government official	Yes	Clerk in estates in mortmain 1915; arrested in 1919 for Armenian massacres	Yozgat	I

(*Continued*)

Name	*Birthplace (Origin)*	*Profession*	*CUP Member-Ship*	*Position In 1915–17*	*Deputy Of*	*Terms Served*
Rıza (Ersoy)	Yozgat (Anatolian)	Government official	Yes; active in İstanbul during armistice[7]	Resigned from government service in 1915 and attended personal affairs	Yozgat	I
Ahmet (Baydar)	Yozgat (Anatolian)	Government official	No	Mayor of Yozgat	Yozgat	I
İsmail Fazıl (Cebesoy)	Crete (non-Anatolian)	Military officer	No	Retired in 1914 to İstanbul	Yozgat	I
Mehmet Hulusi (Akyol)	Yozgat (Anatolian)	Religious scholar	No	Drafted, unknown?	Yozgat	I
Süleyman Sırrı (İçöz)	Yozgat (Anatolian)	Government official	No	Head official of Hacle, Koyulhisar, Darende 1915–17; on court list for crimes related to Armenian massacres[2]	Yozgat	I, II Bozok, III–VIII

The information cited in this table is primarily extracted from *The Turkish Parliamentary History*, the official publication of the Turkish national assembly. The only cases that were not included were those that *The Turkish Parliamentary History* had stated to be ones on which there was no documentation due either to ambiguity in the appointment (in the transition of the assembly and the government from İstanbul to Ankara) or to the death of the person before arrival in Ankara. Other sources are indicated in the following notes.

1 Osman Selim Karahanoğlu, *Atatürk'e Kurulan Pusu* (İstanbul: Temel, 2003), 457, 526.

2 "The 'Deportation-Related' Deputies at the Court Martial under a State of Siege," *Alemdar*, 15 April 1920, 2. I thank Taner Akçam for providing this information. See also, German war documents 1916-12-04-DE-001 from the Political Archives of the German Foreign Office located in Berlin, Germany.

3 Salahi Sonyel, *Malta Sürgünleri (Malta Deportees)*. (İstanbul: Bilgi, 1985).

4 Emel Akal, *Milli Mücadelenin Başında Mustafa Kemal, İttihat Terakki ve Bolşevizm (Mustafa Kemal, Union and Progress, and Bolshevism at the Onset of the Nationalist Struggle)* (*İstanbul*: Tüstav, 2002). Specific information on Orbay is provided on page 136; Okyar, 145; Karabekir, 152; İnönü, 153; Bele, 155; Özalp, 157; Kara Vasıf, 171; Hacım Muhittin, 222; Bayar, 231; Hüsrev Sami, 259; Hüseyin Avni, 299; Celaleddin Arif, 299 n. 41; Eyüp Sabri, 307; and Hakkı Behiç, 318.

5 Damar Arıkoğlu, *Hatıralarım (My Memoirs)*, (İstanbul, 1961), 151.

6 *Ali Münif Bey'in Hatıraları (Ali Münif Bey's Memoirs)* (İstanbul, 1996), 78. See also declassified German war documents 1915-09-10-DE-011.

7 Hüsamettin Ertürk, *İki Devrin Perde Arkası (Two Eras behind the Scenes)* (İstanbul, 1957), 34–35, 77, 202–3, 238, 327; and Eşref Kuşçubaşı, *Hayber'de Türk Cengi (Turkish Battle at Khayber Pass)* (İstanbul, 1999), 212.

8 Ahmed Refik Altınay *İki Komite İki Kıtal (Two Committees Two Massacres)*. (İstanbul, 1998), 174.

9 Declassified German war documents 1915-07-08-DE-001-E, 1915-08-23-DE-013-E, and 1916-01-31-DE-003-E.

10 Declassified German war documents 1915-09-05-DE-001-E-T.

11 Eyewitness account of Nuri Dersimi, *Dersim ve Kürt Milli Mücadelesine dair Hatıratım (My Memoir on Dersim and the Kurdish National Struggle)* (Ankara, 1992), 93.

12 Mustafa Ragıp *İttihat Terakki Tarihinde Esrar Perdesi (Curtain of Mystery in the History of the Union and Progress)*. İstanbul 2004, p. 234.

NOTES

Preface

1. I thank Speros Vryonis for the information on why Armenians near the imperial capital actually knew Greek. At the time, the Greek Rum were not being deported because during World War I, Greece had not yet declared which side it was going to be on. The Young Turk government as well as its German and Austro-Hungarian allies did not want to alienate Greece by deporting the Greek Rum, that is, Greeks living in the empire. I am also grateful to Helin Anahit for providing the additional information on how some of the family attended Greek schools.
2. Burawoy 2007: 55.
3. Massey 2007: 145–57.
4. The Ottoman Empire reigned from 1299 to 1922, to be then replaced on its central lands in 1923 by the Turkish nation-state. Hence, the period studied here covers both the imperial and national political systems, leading to the use of the term "Ottoman-Turkish" when the analysis pertains to both contexts. The two political systems are conjoined because many of the cultural, economic, political, and social processes continued uninterrupted from the Ottoman Empire to the Turkish republic.

Introduction

1. See Milburn and Conrad 1996: 5–13, 179–84, for a fuller discussion.
2. See in particular Cohen 2001; Zerubavel 2006. See also Schmitt et al. 2008; Edelstein, Nathanson, and Stone 1989.
3. Bandura 1999, 2002.
4. See Van Dijk 1992; see also Bowers 1997; Markowitz and Rosner 2002; Warry 2007; Fourie and Meyer 2010; Weicks 2011; Duchinski and Hoffman 2011; Todd, Bodenhausen, and Galinsky 2012; and Nelson 2013.
5. See in particular Meyer et al. 1997.
6. See, for instance, Hegarty 2004; Altman 2006; Curry 2007; Rivera 2008; Tsutsui 2009; Seu 2010; McGovern 2013.
7. See Bilali 2013.
8. See Çalı 2010.
9. Trimikliniotis 2012.
10. Margree and Bhambra 2011.
11. See Adam 2011 for a fuller discussion.
12. Lipstadt 1993.
13. See in this context Bischoping 1997, who rightfully argues that many do not know the civil liberties discourse adequately to counter denialism. In addition, there is a debate regarding

whether to appear with deniers publicly because if one does not, lies go unchallenged, but if one does, their credibility is enhanced. Stern (1993: 15) states that most Jewish organizations do not participate in such debates. Another debate centers on the issue of criminalization of Holocaust denial; the French state recognized the Holocaust as a crime against humanity and criminalized denial with the 1990 Gayssot law, but scholars are once again divided on whether to present the denialist stand in public, with the intent to change the views of the deniers, or to suppress it because of the damage it would do to others if it is publicly available.

14. Hovannisian 1986, 2004; the quotation is from Hovannisian 2004: 3. See also Melson 1986.
15. Hovannisian 2004: 5–31.
16. Hovannisian 1986: 112, 120–22.
17. Charny 1992, 2001. See also Auron 2003.
18. Charny 2001: 6–7.
19. Stern 1993: 86–88.
20. See, in particular, Smith, Markusen, and Lifton 1995; Smith 1991.
21. For an argument similar to the Turkish one I make earlier in the context of Serbia, see Byford 2008.
22. Zerubavel 2006: 2–3, 47–59, 74–78. See also Sheriff 2000.
23. Akerström 1991: 68–71.
24. Trouillot 1995: 26–27.
25. Zerubavel 2006: 14–15.
26. Ibid., 33–45.
27. Hallsworth and Young 2008: 135–39.
28. Byford 2008: 126–29.
29. Baumeister and Hastings 1997: 280–91. See also Vinitzky-Seroussi 2001 for a discussion of how Yitzhak Rabin memorial day selectively sanctifies Rabin's image and biography while individualizing, depoliticizing and bypassing the discussion of the assassination itself.
30. For an extensive discussion of the concept of boundaries in the social sciences, see Lamont and Molnar 2002.
31. Zerubavel 2006: 80–87.
32. See Giesen 2004: 116–18 for an excellent discussion of the trauma of the Holocaust in Germany across generations.
33. Zerubavel 2006: 33–45.
34. Power 2002.
35. See Curry 2007, who develops the concept in the context of El Salvador.
36. Fine 2006, 2007.
37. Hirschman 1977.
38. See, for instance, Levin and Rabrenovic 2007, who trace the sociological analysis of crime back to Quetelet, Durkheim, Simmel, Marx, and the Chicago school.
39. Moore 1966; Tilly 1992.
40. Arendt 1969: 37, 39.
41. Mazower 2002: 1158
42. Stone 1999: 371, 375.
43. Dona 1986: 227–29.
44. Stone 1999: 371.
45. Dona 1986: 227–28.
46. Ibid., 228–29; see also the discussion in Appadurai 1998: 225–26; and Makdisi and Silverstein 2006: 7–8.
47. Meyer 2008.
48. Bauman 1989.
49. Wimmer 2002, 2006.
50. Brubaker 2002, 2004.
51. Mann 2005.
52. The definition is loosely based on the one provided by Levin and Rabrenovic 2007: 332, although they focus not on the perpetrators or the victims but instead on the act.
53. Bourdieu 1984, 1991.

54. See Guhin and Wyrtzen 2013 for a discussion of how such violence of knowledge works in the case of imperialism.
55. McGovern 2013.
56. Ben-Yehuda 1997.
57. Grayson 2012.
58. Gingeras 2010a, 2010b.
59. Wimmer 2006: 337.
60. Robben and Robben 2012: 306, 309, 311.
61. Gerlacht 2010: 4–5.
62. Pappe 2006: 3.
63. Winks and Neuberger 2005: 1.
64. Mouzelis 2012: 207.
65. Dona 1986: 227.
66. Pomeratz 2000.
67. Mignolo 2011.
68. Eisenstadt 2000.
69. Gaonkar 2001.
70. Therborn 2003.
71. Bhambra 2007. Even though in her book Bhambra solely emphasizes connected histories in the reformulation of modernity, I took the liberty of terming her model "connected" modernities.
72. Dona 1986. I see this model as a slight variation on Bhambra, where the focus is not as much on the states and societies as on the nature of interaction among them.
73. Sen 2000; see also the excellent discussion in Fernée 2012: 72.
74. Siegel 2012. See also Barker, Harms, and Lindquist 2014: 12 for further discussion of modernity as lifestyle.
75. Chatterjee 2004, 2011. The concept of "our" modernity is introduced and discussed by Shome 2012: 202–4. Shome highlights the significance of contextualism, that is, the framework within which modernity takes shape, whereas I emphasize the uniqueness of the meaning that ensues from the application of such a framework.
76. Koselleck 1985: 16–17.
77. Bevernage 2012: 2–3.
78. Connerton 2008: 63–64.
79. Bauman 1989.
80. Hall 1992a, 1992b; see also the discussion in Stone 1999: 376.
81. Lawrence 1999: 24.
82. Vazquez 2011: 27.
83. Escobar 2004: 15.
84. Progress is perhaps the most destructive component of Western modernity. Not only is it constantly redefined, but it changes the conception of time; it is predicated on the inherent value judgment of self-righteousness in enacting all it sees fit in the context of institutions, including violence. Interestingly, autonomy oddly complements progress at times because it instigates creativity. Yet the two clash when they entail disparate future visions, at which point the structurally stronger vision of progress crashes the physically fragile autonomy. Peter Wagner (2012: 151) defines "social progress in terms of inclusion and individualization, material progress as better satisfaction of human needs, and political progress as enhancement of the capacity to resolve problems through collective action."
85. Joel Hahn (2001: 11) articulates this inherent tension as "conflict between two equally basic cultural premises: vision of an infinitely expanding rational mastery and the individual and collective aspiration to autonomy and creativity." With the discovery of culture, a shift occurred from the objective to the subjective as "modernity becomes as much a state of mind as a set of objective historical processes…hence modernity is a product of contradictory conflicting processes."
86. Bozdoğan and Kasaba 1997.
87. Kaya 2004; see also Kaya 2012.
88. Kaya and Tecmen 2011: 13–36; see also Ichijo 2011.

89. Bozdoğan and Kasaba 1997: 3, 13.
90. Kaya 2004: 58–59, 122.
91. For a fuller discussion, see Calhoun 2001: 46–47.
92. Goffman 1963; see also Rivera 2008: 615 for an excellent discussion.
93. Goodwin, Jasper, and Poletta 2001: 10. See also Kaindaneh and Rigby 2012: 158.
94. See Wisecup, Robinson, and Smith-Lovin 2007: 106 for a more extensive discussion.
95. Hoggett and Thompson (2012: 2–3) note that "affect concerns the more embodied, unformed and less conscious dimension of human feeling, whereas emotion concerns the feelings which are more conscious since they are more anchored in language and meaning. An affect such as anxiety is experienced in a bodily way, while an emotion such as jealousy is directed toward objects (a lover, a rival) which give it meaning, focus and intentionality."
96. See Marcus et al. 1995: 1 for a fuller discussion.
97. Cunningham 2012: 142.
98. Butler 2004: xvii–xix.
99. Kamper 2001: 67. See also Levin and Rabrenovic 2004.
100. Thoits 1985.
101. Northcott 2012: 69–70.
102. Collins 2001: 40–41; see also Zerubavel 2006: 6.
103. Cunningham 2012: 141.
104. See Rosenwein 2002: 821–45 for a historical approach to emotions, and Goodwin, Jasper, and Poletta 2001: 1–24; and Wisecup, Robinson, and Smith-Lovin 2007: 106–16 for a sociological approach. The preceding discussion combines elements from these three depictions.
105. Such stereotyping of human action as being based on either reason or emotion was also the case regarding the political behavior of women and slaves in that neither social group was deemed capable of having reason.
106. Langman 2006: 66.
107. Billig 1995.
108. Branscombe and Doosje 2004.
109. Giesen 2004: especially 115–18.
110. Milburn and Conrad 1996: 168.
111. Sewell 2005; see pages 81–123 for the discussion of the three temporalities. The ensuing quotation is from page 90.
112. Sewell defines historical events as "a ramified sequence of occurrences that . . . is recognized as notable by contemporaries, and that . . . results in a durable transformation of structures" where a structural transformation comprises "changes in cultural schemas, shift of resources, and the emergence of new modes of power" (2005: 228). See also Fraser 2006: 129–32 for a discussion of the concept.
113. Historical events (1) rearticulate structures; (2) constitute cultural transformations as historical actors unknowingly introduce new conceptions of what really exists, what is good, and what is possible; (3) are shaped by particular conditions such as particular meanings, accidents, and causal forces, namely, "the structure of conjuncture"; (4) are characterized by heightened emotion that not only signifies the extent of dislocation, articulation, and destabilization but also actually contours the very course of events; (5) constitute acts of collective creativity as the ordinary routines of everyday life and sanctions of existing power relations are all put to doubt, making possible new options—albeit within the framework of structurally available forms of thought and practice; (6) are punctuated by rituals whereby the social actors mark them as such to then attempt to align everyone present with the newly posited ultimate source of power, producing in the process a profound sense of community that bestows upon the rituals their psychological and social power; (7) produce more events as the structural transformation cascades throughout the entire social system, often marked by waves of panic; (8) need to gain authoritative sanction in order to become definitive, where such sanction is often offered or challenged by both the event in question and the particular institutional nodes in which the affected power is concentrated (which is often the state); (9) are spatial as well as temporal processes in that they necessitate spatial concentration to generate episodes of collective effervescence that then expand spatially; and (10) are fractal, with many overlapping and interpenetrating small ruptures ultimately located within

a vast structural transformation, which necessitates their boundaries to be determined through an act of judgment. Sewell 2005: 232–62.

114. Deleuze ([1969] 2004: 7) initially conceptualizes formulation of transformations "not as things or facts, but events." I do not think it is accidental that Deleuze is French, thereby inherently drawing upon the historical experience of the French Revolution.
115. See, in particular, Abbott 1990, 1992.
116. See especially Aminzade 1992.
117. See Griffin 1992: 403–27.
118. Sewell's choice of this particular historical event contains both strengths and weaknesses. This structural transformation is so radical that the inherent social processes crystallize to become articulated into a clearly visible historical event, one closely studied and extremely well documented through continuous research. In addition, as this historical event permeates human history, it helps generate and form similar events elsewhere throughout the world. Yet it is exactly this dramatic quality that also forms its weakness.
119. Sewell 2005: 230.
120. The use here of the eventful approach therefore differs from Sewell's conceptualization in that the analysis focuses on "failed" ruptures as opposed to successful ones that liberate and democratize social systems where the temporal boundaries in identifying such ruptures extend from 1789, marking the advent of systematic Ottoman modernity, to the present, thereby partially problematizing the issue of post hoc judgment employed in the identification of ruptures. In this context, see also Jost and Hunyady 2005: 260–65.
121. Norgaard 2006: 392.
122. Wertsch 2002: 13–15.
123. Pennebaker and Banasik 1997: 10.
124. The Balkan League consists of united Bulgarian, Greek, Montenegrin, and Serbian forces.
125. Even though the Russians had come close to the Ottoman capital of Constantinople in the aftermath of the 1877–78 war, once again instigating a flood of Muslim refugees from the Russian empire and the Balkans, they were regarded as mere "occupiers." In addition, their military expansion was immediately contained by France and Great Britain through subsequent treaties. Yet the Balkan warfare was much more significant because these former subjects claimed these territories to belong to their nation.
126. Had there been no forced deportations and massacres, there should have been, with natural population growth, approximately 15 to 20 million Armenians in Turkey today.
127. See Şimşir 2000. This first case is discussed on pages 86–87, 106. It has been argued, however, that ASALA and JCOAG, as well as Yanikian before them, actually drew upon the example of Solomon Tehlirian, who assassinated Talat Pasha in Berlin in 1921.
128. Irwin-Zarecka 1994: 9.
129. Wertsch 2002: 23–24.
130. Ibid., 51; Conway 1997: 21.
131. Wessel and Moulds 2008: 289.
132. Pennebaker and Banasik 1997: 4.
133. Schuman and Corning 2000; Schuman and Scott 1989; Schuman and Rodgers 2004; Griffin 2004.
134. Ben-Ze'ev and Lomsky-Feder 2009.
135. Irwin-Zarecka 1994.
136. For instance, forgetting past violence prevailed from the end of World War II to the end of the Cold War, but forgetting has recently been replaced by remembering as states and societies attempt to come to terms with the collective violence embedded in their pasts. Bevernage 2012: 8–9.
137. Fine and McDonnell 2007.
138. Ibid., 171.
139. Griffin and Bollen 2009.
140. Jansen 2007; Gill 2012: 29–30.
141. Vinitzky-Seroussi 2002: 30; see also Teeger and Vinitzky-Seroussi 2007.
142. Ram 2009: 366–70.
143. Marques, Paez, and Serra 1997: 253–75.

144. Kofta and Slawuta 2013: 54–55.
145. Connerton 2008: 63–64.
146. Olick 2003.
147. Bilali 2013: 18.
148. Douglas 1986.
149. See Terzioğlu 2001 for a detailed discussion of such Ottoman personal miscellanies (*mecmu'a*).
150. Ahmet Mithat Efendi's *Menfa*, first published in 1876, is the first Western-style autobiography in Turkish literature; it recounts his memoirs in exile in Rhodes. Sevük 1940: vol. 2, 187.
151. Birinci 2001: 1–10. Birinci cites the earlier memoirs of Barbaros Hayreddin Pasha, Macunzade Mustafa, Zaifi, and Me'mun Bey; Osman Agha of Temeshvar and the *sheikhul islam* Feyzullah Efendi in the seventeenth century; and the seaman who wrote under the pen name Talati in the eighteenth century. In the nineteenth century, multiple examples abound, including Keçecizade İzzet Molla (1785–1829), Bozoklu Akif Pasha, and Muallim Naci.
152. Lewis 1991: 20.
153. Kara 2001: 107.
154. Ibid., 118.
155. Adak 2001: 130–32.
156. Akyıldız, Kara, and Sagaster 2007: 9–15.
157. Glassen 2007: 143–56.
158. See especially Tilly 1985.
159. Even though the actual number of writers cited in Appendix A is 309, I also count my own memories of my life in Turkey as a memoir, bringing the total up to 310.
160. See especially Said 1978, 1993.
161. Wimmer and Feinstein 2010.
162. The Greek Rum that had been dominant in the earlier centuries lost their dominance as trust in them eroded after the 1820 Greek independence; many lost their prominent positions in society. The other non-Muslim category of Jews had been dominant in the fifteenth and sixteenth centuries when their commercial connections with Europe were still strong after their 1492 expulsion from Catholic Spain; they were also much smaller in number and were not as spread out across the empire as were the Greeks and Armenians.

Chapter 1

1. Sadeddin 2003.
2. Ibid., 20, 44–46.
3. Ibid., 47–49.
4. Ibid., 21–22, 50.
5. Ibid., 65.
6. Ibid, 65–67.
7. Ibid. 66.
8. Ibid. 66–67.
9. It could be argued that the Balkan States were more advantaged in this respect because, unlike the majority of Armenian subjects, many did indeed fight in special auxiliary units of the Ottoman military.
10. For a more detailed discussion of the Ottoman rule, see Göçek
11. The use of the term "Greek Rum" to refer to the Greek Orthodox in the empire separates them from the Greek Orthodox who lived in Greece, which gained its independence in 1821. I therefore refer to the Greek Orthodox living in Ottoman imperial lands as Greek Rum.
12. According to the account of Başkatipzade Ragıp Bey, for instance, many Muslim tradesmen started to pay bribes in order to enroll in *medreses* (Islamic institutes of higher education) and thus avoid their military duty. See Ragıp 1996: 20–21. Delilbaşı (1946: 59) likewise noted that the Muslim populace tried its hardest to avoid military service.
13. The actual terms employed by Fuad Pasha are "*millet-i Islamiye, devlet-i Türkiyye, salatin-i Osmaniyye, and payitaht-ı İstanbul.*" See Ahmet Cevdet 1986: vol. 1, 85.

14. With the establishment of the Turkish republic, the first two characteristics (Muslim and Turkish) were sustained at the expense of the last two (Ottoman and İstanbul).
15. Abdurrahman Şeref 1978: 51. For other depictions, see also Şehbenderzade 1991: 31; Tahmiscizade 1977: 50–51.
16. For other depictions of the structural divide, see, for instance, Arıkoğlu 1961: 36–37; Atay 1938: 42–44; 1999: 12; Hüseyin Nazım 2003: 282; Kalaç 1960: 93–96; Bereketzade 1997: 237–38, 251; Okyar 1980: 105–6; Orbay 1992: vol. 1, 2901; Esat Cemal 2000: 11; Topuzlu 1982: 17; 2002: 40; and Berkes 1997: 51.
17. Tokgöz 1993: 29. See also the experiences of those who decided to go into fine arts, such as Rey (1945) and Muhsin Ertuğrul (1989), and those who decided to become a physician, such as Topuzlu (1982).
18. Sertel 2000: 16.
19. Nur 1992: vol. 1, 87–88, 91; Selahattin Adil 1982: 16; Yergök 2006: 23.
20. Yergök 2006: 23.
21. See, for instance, Zarifi 2005: 30, 32.
22. The demonstration of this phenomenon is especially evident at the schools attended by mostly Muslim Turkish children. Amça 1958: 93–94; Kuran 1976: 23; Başkatipzade 1996: 20–21.
23. Atay 1999: 5–6. See also Apak 1988: 100.
24. Masar 1974: 50–51.
25. I employ the terms "majority" and "minority" sociologically in terms of how much each social group controls the resources that are considered valuable by a particular society.
26. See, for instance, Tarhan 1994: 176; Bölükbaşı 1993: 33; Mümtaz 1946: 21, 93; Adıvar 1963: 103; and Sadeddin 2003: 86, 96.
27. Cabi Ömer 2003: vol. 2, 803–6. The Turkish words are "*Durup da Ermeni keferesi gibi kamçıyla döğüp.*"
28. Attending schools run by non-Muslims provided to be especially challenging to the authors Adıvar (1963: 13, 85) and Uşaklıgil (1987: 126–27), who both faced pressure from Muslim relatives and neighbors to discontinue their attendance.
29. See, for instance, Melek Hanım 1996: 9, 11, 23; Zarifi 2005: 130–33; and Duhani 1984: 33–34 for accounts of how the physical well-being, wealth, and property of non-Muslims were violated with impunity. The same violent practice was employed against Muslims as well, but due to their formal and often informal familial connections to the sultan's household, unlike the non-Muslims, they or their descendants had a much better chance of eventually recovering their wealth and property and thereby their social standing in Ottoman society.
30. It should be noted that the pasha then seated the monk at the chair closest to him and talked about various things for two hours. Tepeyran 1998: 79.
31. Hovhannesyan 1997: 8, 20, 24, 33–34, 37, 45–46, 52, 55, 59, 61.
32. Ibid., 8, 20, 24, 33–34, 37, 52, 55, 61.
33. Ibid., 8, 20.
34. Scognamillo 1990: 26. For similar discussions, see Yalçın 2001: 139; Giz 1988: 138–39; Duhani 1984: 12.
35. See, for instance, Yalçın 2001: 139.
36. See, for instance, Giz 1988: 138–39.
37. For living in separate villages, see Haçeryan 2005: 13–5; for mixed living, see Aykan 2003: 40–41; Öngör 1987: 9; and Tunalı 2005: 3–4.
38. Behmoaras 2005: 54–55. See also Zarifi 2005: 97; and Ahmet Cevdet 1986: vol. 4, 202.
39. Cabi Ömer 2003: 769, 877–78, 927–28, 947, 1007, 1015, 1055.
40. Ibid., 872.
41. The blood libel accusations that the Christian subjects lodge against the Jews are a case in point. As Bahar noted (2003: 39, 43–44), these cases were swiftly acted upon as those inciting these groundless accusations were speedily punished by the Ottoman state. Likewise, Aşcıdede (1960: 64) recounted that in 1868 in Erzincan, the rumor of increased animosity between the Muslims and Christians was contained when a Muslim leader gathered the Muslim populace at the big mosque and delivered a sermon counseling them.
42. See Ahmed Muhtar 1996: vol. 1, 104–5.

43. Aksan 1993: 54–55.
44. Ibid., 58–59.
45. Davison 1954: 855.
46. Aksan 1993: 58–59.
47. Shaw 1962: 292–93.
48. Levy 1971: 32.
49. Melson 1982: 504.
50. Shaw 1962: 51–53.
51. Findley 1972: 396.
52. Masters 1992: 579.
53. There were later attempts to recruit non-Muslims into the army, but the first total recruitment occurred during the 1912–13 Balkan Wars.
54. It should be noted, however, that Ottoman minorities were actually most active in the Foreign Ministry and did serve in prominent posts. Their inability to either form or reproduce social networks with their Muslim counterparts through marriage largely inhibited them, however, from translating their activity into social and political power as their Muslim counterparts were able to.
55. Among these merchants, there were significant differences in the stipulations for the two religions: Ottoman Muslim applicants had to be "men of high moral and religious character [*ehl-i arz ve dindar*], something apparently not required of their non-Muslim colleagues... a Muslim merchant had the right to bequeath his patent to his oldest son and, of course, did not have to pay the [poll-tax]." Masters 1992: 585–86.
56. Even though Sultan Mustafa IV reigned in the interim, his brief rule of fourteen months (May 1807 to November 1808) did not have a significant impact on the empire.
57. Karpat 1972: 253–54.
58. Sadık Rıfat Pasha, regarded as the author of the decree, had based it on his initial observations of Europe during his ambassadorship in Vienna, arguing that in order to be civilized, a state had to provide for individuals' security of life, possessions, and honor; additionally, law and justice had to be the main principles of administration. For a more detailed discussion, see Seyitdanlıoğlu 2009.
59. Two contemporaneous sources assert that Mustafa Reşid Pasha prepared the reform decree to gain Europe's support and to also contain Mehmed Ali Pasha; see Mahmud Celaleddin 1979: 32; Fatma Aliye 1994: 54–55.
60. The Paris Treaty negotiations at the end of the 1856 Crimean War against Russia, during which the Ottoman Empire had to seek the support of Britain and France, stipulated certain conditions regarding Ottoman non-Muslims. They did so because European powers were dissatisfied, like the reformist Ottoman officials, with the rate of reform enacted after the 1839 edict.
61. Türkgeldi 1987: vol. 1, 41, 47, 76–78, 92, 94–98, 111, 114, 121, 139–46; Ahmet Cevdet 1986: vol. 1, 67–74, 76–82.
62. See, for instance, Mümtaz 1946: 102; Yergök 2006: 196; Nutku 1977: 51–54; Arseven 1993: 123; Fatma Aliye 1994: 101–2; Ahmet Cevdet 1986: vol. 1: 20–23; Masar 1974: 5.
63. As a consequence, the discharge of privates, especially in distant locations like Yemen, was constantly delayed, leading them to serve up to eight years. Selahattin Adil 1982: 94.
64. Süleyman Şefik 2004: 15–18; see also 23–30. For other similar accounts of corruption, see Ahmet Muhtar 1996: vol. 1, 11, 23; vol. 2, 8–9, 273–74; Sadeddin 2003: 60, 73–74, 131–34.
65. See, for instance, Tepeyran 1998: 205–9.
66. The most serious attempt to integrate the non-Muslim subjects into the military took place in the aftermath of the 1856 reform decree as Mithat (1997: vol. 1, 202–16) established Christian volunteer battalions in the Balkans. The pasha then constituted a battalion of volunteer Christian soldiers, added a cross to the crescent on their flag, and paraded them in İstanbul. After the proclamation of the 1876 constitution, volunteer battalions were formed in major cities like the capital, Salonica, and Izmir. For a description of such activities, see also Mahmud Celaleddin 1979: 209–10. The ensuing quotation is from Abdülhamid 1985: 112.
67. In his memoirs, Tunalı (2005: 25–27, 28–31, 38–39) provided a summary of these attempts.

68. This system was abolished in 1909 when the School for Arms Production (İmalat-i Harbiye Nazari Mektebi) was established instead.
69. See, for instance, Süleyman Şefik 2004: 124–27.
70. See, for instance, Karabekir 1982: 357.
71. Natanyan 2008: 27–28, 34, 83, 87; Mahmud Celaleddin 1979: 100.
72. For a detailed discussion, see Ahmet Cevdet 1986: vol. 1, 20–23.
73. Mithat 1997: vol. 1, 172.
74. Kamil and Mehmed Said 1991: 201–4.
75. Arseven 1993: 99, 102.
76. Mithat 1997, vol. 1, 33–35, 43–58, 114–15, 143–49, 164–68, 174; vol. 2, 37. Even though Mithat Pasha advocated the rule of law, he himself was not very keen on its application when it contradicted his own interests; upon becoming the grand vizier, he wanted the sultan to exile such conservative officials from the empire. See especially Mithat 1997, vol. 1, 207 n. 92.
77. He replicated these measures in Baghdad as well, building a rice factory, parks, a water fountain for the water needs of the populace, gaslit streetlamps, and a tramway.
78. In addressing the scale of economic reforms, the pasha further noted that even though the Ottoman state should directly undertake large-scale projects such as the building of railroads, canals, and ports, it should nevertheless delegate engagement in trade to local actors, who would then be overseen by state-appointed officials.
79. In all, "30 Austrian, 24 Russian, 20 French, 8 Italian, 5 German, 4 British, and 2 Indian postal services" were in operation. Abdülhamid 1985: 116.
80. See, for instance, Kalaç (1960: 7–10), recounting his first encounters with a train, a kerosene lantern, and a gramophone.
81. For instance, Sazak (2007: 40) stated that the elderly fervently opposed the 1888–93 extension of the railway from the imperial city to Eskişehir, arguing that "wherever trains arrive, so do infidels! . . . and this state of affairs deeply saddened [the elderly]."
82. Tokgöz 1993: 33.
83. Arseven 1993: 99, 102.
84. Bahar 2003: 52–53.
85. Fatma Aliye 1994: 101–2; Mevhibe Celaleddin 1987: 110.
86. See, for instance, Nutku (1977: 62–67) for a discussion of the concession to pilot at the İstanbul port and Bosporus.
87. Zarifi 2005: 158–59; Mithat 1997: vol. 1, 21 n. 1; Us 1966: 12.
88. Hovhannesyan 1997: 64.
89. The 1881 *Annuaire* listed the names of many Armenian tradesmen and professionals residing at the capital. Deleon 1993: 49–79.
90. Greek Rum businessman Yorgo Zarifi's grandfather helped establish these two institutions. Zarifi 2005: 64.
91. Tokgöz 1993: 206.
92. Hayrullah 2002: 196–97; Fatma Aliye 1994: 61.
93. Anter 1999: 331–33.
94. Natanyan 2008: 367.
95. Deleon 1993: 49–79; Natanyan 2008: 367.
96. See, for instance, the case of Vahan Surinyan Bey. Ali Kemal 1985: 142.
97. See, for instance, Sazak 2007: 58–60; Kuran 1976: 8.
98. See, for instance, Yergök (2006: 111), stating that his uncle's business greatly suffered upon the death of "Dikran, the owner of the store next to my uncle's who helped him more than a brother, bought goods for him and sold his goods, picked him up in the mornings to bring him to the store."
99. In the history of the Ottoman Empire, this period is often identified as the First Constitutional Period.
100. Both the representatives of the Great Powers and Ottoman officials like Mithat Pasha concurred that the reforms had not been properly executed. Mahmud Celaleddin 1979: 49–50, 133–35, 140–41, 165–66, 176; Mithat 1997: vol. 1, xiii–xiv, 73–74, 329–31) noted that in

spite of the reforms, the state "had not altered anything in its traditional order" (*nizamat-ı kadimesinden hiçbirsey tebdil etmemişti*).

101. Natanyan 2008: 36–39.
102. Bedirhan 1998: 64; Ahmed Muhtar 1996: vol. 1, 63–64.
103. Natanyan 2008: 42–43, 71–73.
104. See Klein 2011 for a full discussion.
105. Mahmud Celaleddin 1979: 32; Fatma Aliye 1994: 54–55.
106. Ahmet Cevdet 1986: vol. 1, 67–74, 76–82.
107. Mithat 1997: vol. 1, xxx–xxxi. See also Natanyan 2008: 83, 87.
108. It is for this reason that historian Altınay (1998: 156) concurred that such reforms would be ineffective "if the Turks do not develop their culture the way minorities did."
109. Abdurrahman Şeref 1978: 59; Ahmet Cevdet 1986: vol. 1, 67–73; Hayrullah 2002: 190.
110. The Rum, for instance, who regarded themselves as the most privileged among the minorities, realized that they would permanently lose their advantaged stand. For the unhappiness of the non-Muslims, see Natanyan 2008: 40–41.
111. Ahmet Cevdet 1986: vol. 1, 67–74, 76–82.
112. According to Section 16 of the Ayastefanos Treaty and Section 61 of the Berlin Treaty, both signed at the end of the 1878 war with Russia, Britain even assigned consuls to the eastern provinces to monitor the reforms: Colonel Wilson was sent to Sivas, Major Trotter to Erzurum, Captain Clayton to Van, and Captain Cooper to Kayseri.
113. Mithat 1997: vol. 2, 23–24.
114. See, for instance, Dersimi 1992: 56.
115. Temperley 1933: 158. The ensuing quotation in the text is from the same page.
116. See, for instance, the skeptical account of one Ottoman official discussing this state of affairs. Kadri 1992: 133–34.
117. See the discussion by Kamil 1991: 193–96.
118. Sultan Abdülhamid II told Mithat Pasha that his priorities were "the preservation of the land mass of the empire as well as the security and immortality of the state." Mithat Pasha 1997: II: 314, 316. The exact term is "*temamiyet-i mülkiye-i devlet; devlet-i aliyyenin selamet ve bekası.*"
119. Ibid., 34.
120. Mithat Pasha (ibid., 28, 97) remarked that "our system is not based on freedom and liberty. No laws regulate the rights of the populace. Yes, we too have laws, courts, organizations, but we do not have a power that protects the direction and continuity of these developments.... Unless there is a power protecting the things done by a person or a company, all of it could disappear in an instant." The pasha therefore continued to emphasize that "a populace can only be expected to act civilized, improve, develop, and reach happiness and prosperity if the use of their rights and liberties is protected by a general law [i.e., a constitution]."
121. Fatma Aliye 1994: 58, 77; Hayrullah 2002: xvii.
122. See, for instance, the experiences of Mithat 1997: vol. 1, 34–35; Hayrullah 2002: 28.
123. Ahmet Cevdet 1986: 11, 13.
124. Fatma Aliye 1994: 50–51; Kaygusuz 1955: 18, 24–25.
125. See, for instance, the experiences of Beyatlı 1973: 27–28; Uşaklıgil 1987: 103, 128–29; and Kuran 1976: 14–15.
126. See, for instance, Orhan 2001: 15.
127. Uşaklıgil 1987: 103, 128–29.
128. Kaygusuz 1955: 18, 24–25.
129. Aray 1959; Selahattin Adil 1982: 83; Orbay 1992: vol. 1, 43; II, 84.
130. Amça 1958: 17.
131. Apak 1988: 13; Amça 1958: 17, 89, 144–45.
132. Orbay 1992: vol. 1, 243.
133. Amça 1958: 17, 89, 144–45.
134. Especially the education offered at the school of public administration (*mülkiye*) was significant in relation to what they learned in the new fields of economics and finance from Ottoman minorities such as Portakal Paşa and Sakızlı Ohannes Efendi. Uran 1959: 12–13. See also Tokgöz 1993: 31.

135. Ayni 1945: 9, 47. See also Nesimi 1977: 24–25.
136. Tarcan (1946: 28) recounts the director telling him, "Son, these are not a tribe, but vermin!" The exact words are "*aşiret değil haşarat.*"
137. Arseven 1993: 14–16.
138. Natanyan 2008: 244, 264.
139. Uşaklıgil 1987: 111–15.
140. For a detailed discussion, see Yener 1958: 13, 32.
141. Gerede 2002: 59–60.
142. Uşaklıgil 1987: 101–3.
143. See the accounts of Nur 1992: vol. 1, 219; Sağlam 1991: 55–56, 109, 119, 137–38.
144. For a fuller discussion, see Findley 1989.
145. Orbay 1992: vol. 1, 276. See also Söylemezoğlu 1949: 54–59.
146. Tengirşenk 1967: 77–78.
147. Sağlam 1991: 55–56, 109, 119, 137–38.
148. Arseven 1993: 90; İzbudak 1946: 46.
149. At the capital, the books published would be sent to the Education Council for approval; the books printed at the provinces were instead inspected by the governors, who, after ascertaining that the contents were not detrimental to property and the nation, forwarded them to the Sublime Porte.
150. Kaygusuz 1955: 21.
151. Amça 1958: 103–4; Sağlam 1991: 58; Kuran 1976: 15; Rey 1945: 41; Nutku 1977: 48–49.
152. Kuran 1945: 125, 143, 166–67.
153. One such newspaper press the Ottoman state tried to purchase belonged to Nişan Sironyan in Marseilles.
154. Numanzade 1976: 34–35.
155. Kuran 1976: 27–28, 30, 48, 51–52, 63–65, 90; İbrahim Temo 1987: 15–18, 49; Mehmed Selahaddin 1989: 21–22; Mehmed Rauf 1991: 29, 33, 77.
156. The specific words used are "*Cemiyetimiz halis bir Türk cemiyetidir*" and "*İslamlığa ve Türklüğe düşman olanların hiçbir vakit fikrine tebaiyet etmiyecektir.*" Kuran 1945: 221; 1948: 203.
157. Even though the initial reform-minded officials of the empire had been called "Young Ottomans," the present use of "Young Turks" in its stead also signaled a move toward employing a potentially ethnic identity to unify all Ottoman opponents to the existing regime.
158. Kaygusuz 1955: 15–16.
159. Kuran 1948: 194–97.
160. Kuran 1945: 27–29, 150–54; İbrahim Temo 1987: 137.
161. Kutay 1975: vol. 1, 21 n. 1; Beyatlı 1973: 206–7; 1975: 97. The terms employed for these paramilitary fighters are *fedayi* or *komitacı*.
162. Beyatlı 1975: 97.
163. Kuran 1945: 168, 170–71, 234–43. The exact terms employed were "*hukuk-u hilafet ve saltanat.*" See also Kaygusuz 1955: 16.
164. The Armenians also added that what was considered sacred by the Turks of the empire did not concern them; they, however, did not oppose such a stand either.
165. Kuran 1945: 221; 1948: 203.
166. See, for instance, Tarcan 1946: 22–23; Yergök 2006: 87; Sağlam 1991: 72–74; Duru 1957: 5, 8, 11, 13, 15; Karabekir 1982: 166–80.
167. Uran 1959: 19–20.
168. Fatma Aliye 1994: 64.
169. See, for instance, Öngör (1987: 28–29) regarding the use of new headgear by men.
170. Arseven 1993: 132.
171. Uşaklıgil 1987: 168.
172. Arseven 1993: 130–32.
173. The Turkish term is *karşıya dadanmak*. Atay 1999: 14–15.
174. Uşaklıgil 1987: 111–15.
175. Süleyman Şefik 2004: 78; Orbay 1992: vol. 1, 243.
176. Hayrullah 2002: xiv, 187–88.
177. Arslan 2005: 227; Abdurrahman Şeref 1978: 21.

178. Zarifi 2005: 33–36, 43. See also Türkgeldi 1987: vol. 3, 9–10; Arslan 2005: 240–60; Mümtaz 1946: 34.
179. Mahmud Celaleddin 1970: 199–200.
180. The Ottomans referred to this war as the "93 War" because it occurred in the year 1293 of the Muslim *hijri* calendar that commences with the migration of the prophet Muhammad from Mecca to Medina in the year 622.
181. See Abdülhamid 1985: 93–94; H. Raci 1990: 14–16, 56, 68, 70–71, 79, 91, 147. The quotations are located on pages 91 and 130. See also Ali Rıza 1975: 27–28; Kırkyaşaryan 2005: 46 n. 9.
182. Süleyman Şefik 2004: 37.
183. Alican 2000: 9–10; Said 1994: 26; Hüseyin Nazım 2003: 72–73; Tanpınar 1973: 27–28, 46–48; Selahattin Adil 1982: 327.
184. Topuzlu 1982: 27; Süleyman Nazif 1978: 35–36; Tepeyran 1998: 175.
185. Atay 1999: 8; Uşaklıgil 1990: 82; 1987: 631–32; Adıvar 1963: 119.
186. Süleyman Nazif 1957: 78.
187. See, for instance, Tarcan 1946: 6–7; Güvemli 1999: 1–3; İmre 1976: 9–10, 21; Kutay 1966: vol. 1, 61; Amça 1958: 93–94.
188. See, for instance, Ayaşlı 1990: 18–19; Atay 1999: 18–19.
189. Uşaklıgil 1990: 216; 1987: 557.
190. Arseven 1993: 130–32.
191. Atay 1999: 14–15, 18–19.
192. Amça 1989: 112.
193. Derin 1995: 9
194. Atay 1999: 3–4. The term Atay employed was *eğreti vatan.*
195. Ahmet Cevdet 1986: vol. 1, 9, 11.
196. Mizancı Murad 1994: 99–100.
197. Arslan 2005: 228–29.
198. Apak 1988: 7, 19.
199. Atay 1999: 14–15, 18–19.
200. Uşaklıgil 1987: 547–48.
201. Kuran 1976: 55–59.
202. Apak 1988: 7, 19.
203. Uşaklıgil 1987: 615–17, 621, 624–25; Paker 2000: 20; Söylemezoğlu 1949.
204. Mahmud Celaleddin 1979: 51.
205. Tükel 1953: 161.
206. See, for instance, Amça 1958: 64–65.
207. Yergök 2006: 68; Süleyman Şefik 2004: 110; Kırımer 1993: 42.
208. Kaygusuz 1955: 16; Kıbrıslızade 1996: 13–14; Kuran 1976: 5; Uşaklıgil 1987: 164–65, 202.
209. Sazak 2007: 100–105.
210. Hüseyin Nazım 2003: 164–65.
211. Gerede 2002: 69.
212. Anter 1999: 331–33. The exact wording Anter used was "*Babam Ermeni üstünlüğünden çok rahatsız oluyordu.*"
213. See, for instance, Natanyan 2008: 88–89, 168–9, 280, 300, 302–14, 368.
214. Natanyan 2008: 52–56, 58–61, 88. For more information, also refer to Somel 2001: 80.
215. Natanyan 2008: 258, 297, 300; Erdoğan 1998: 27, 29.
216. Kırkyaşaryan 2005: 46 n. 9, 48; Natanyan 2008: 356, 371–72.
217. Natanyan 2008: 383; Kadri 1991: 135–36.
218. See, for instance, the account of Us 1966: 88–90.
219. Erdoğan 1998: 27, 29.
220. Mehmed Memduh 1990: 171.
221. Sadeddin 2003: 24–25, 38–40, 42–44, 57.
222. It is possible that the authorities did not have many informants within the community, and/or the community closed itself up.Hüseyin Nazım 2003: 16, 138, 218, 221, 226, 283.
223. Akyavaş 2002: vol. 2, 95.
224. Natanyan (2008: 73–75) noted that of the 115 members of the Ottoman assembly during the first term (March–June 1877), 46 (40 percent) were non-Muslims; during the second

term (December 1877–February 1878), of the 106 members, non-Muslims constituted 44 percent, with 47 members, while Muslim participation declined. Of these non-Muslim members, 13 were Armenian deputies comprising 28 percent of non-Muslims, and 12 percent of the total number of deputies. The Armenian deputies were Viçen Holas, İstepan Aslanyan, Serviçen, Hovhannes Allahverdi, Sebuh Maksud, Simon Maksud, Aliksan Sakayan, Agop Kazazyan, Rupen, Misak Kharacıyan, Hamazasb Ballaryan, Agop Şahinyan, and Agop Frenkyan.

225. Arslan 2005: 262.
226. Dersimi 1997: 404.
227. Arslan 2005: 262.
228. The ensuing Armenian unrest at the imperial city is referred to in the Ottoman sources as the "Kumkapı" incident, since the Armenian patriarchate was located in that neighborhood and the protests originated there as well.
229. Hüseyin Nazım 2003: 14–16; Arslan 2005: 262; Kamil 1991: 174; Rey 1945: 16–19.
230. For an extensive discussion of these Hamidiye regiments, see Klein 2011.
231. Tepeyran 1998: 533.
232. Hüseyin Nazım 2003: 107–9, 112–19, 121–24, 127–32.
233. Ibid.
234. Arslan 2005: 263–24.
235. Bleda 1979: 56–62.
236. Kamil 1991: 188. The exact words of the sultan are *"urulsun dedi isem katliam edilsin demedim."*
237. The demonstration took on the term "Babıali," namely, the Ottoman seat of government, because the Armenian protesters aimed to march there peacefully, expressing their discontent with the episodic violence.
238. Narrations of the demonstrations abound in the contemporaneous memoirs of Muslim Turkish officials. See, for instance, Said 1994: 10; Kamil 1991: 195, 369; Hüseyin Nazım 2003: 17–34; İzbudak 1946: 37–38; Söylemezoğlu 1949: 86.
239. Hüseyin Nazım 2003: 17–34, 45–49.
240. Kamil 1991: 195, 369; Tahsin 1931: 43–45, 57.
241. The following sources provide for numerous accounts of the violence committed by Muslims against Armenian subjects: Rey 1945: 16–19; Uşaklıgil 1987: 410–11; İbrahim Temo 1987: 41; Hüseyin Nazım 2003: 27–28; Ahmet Rasim 1976: 130–33; Akyavaş 2002: vol. 2, 62; Mizancı Murad 1994: 24–30; Sazak 2007: 44–47.
242. Karay 1996: 101; Tokgöz 1993: 205; Beyatlı 1973: 65; Selahattin Adil 1982: 24.
243. İbrahim Temo 1987: 45; Karabekir 1982: 467–68.
244. Dersimi 1992: 48–53.
245. Çerkezyan 2003: 11, 157–58, 17. See also, Hüseyin Nazım 2003: 182, 188; Yergök 2006: 57–59.
246. Rey 1945: 16–19; Yeğena 1996: 47; Ahmet Cevdet 1986: vol. 3, 120–21.
247. Sadeddin 2003: 20–21, 30–31, 48–49, 74, 108, 114, 135, 148–49. For other similar violent behavior of the Merzgi and Hartush tribes, see 124–25.
248. Even during Sadeddin Pasha's visit, the local Armenians were so scared that when he attempted to redistribute the plundered goods, they did not claim the goods that were actually theirs; "the goods therefore remained in the hands of a traitor called Talat Bey, the Agha of the Battalion. I have not yet reached a conclusion on the investigation I am conducting on this matter," he concluded.
249. Zarifi 2005: 366–70; Hüseyin Nazım 2003: 178.
250. Kadri 1991: 128.
251. Erdoğan 1998: 32; İlden1998: 22.
252. Hüseyin Nazım 2003.
253. Orbay 1992: vol. 1, 253–54.
254. Abdülhamid 1985: 13. See also Tahsin 1931: 112, 116, 157–60, 189–225; Orbay 1992: vol. 1, 547; Üçok 2002: 260–61; Söylemezoğlu 1949: 86, 89.
255. Paker 2000: 21.
256. Masar 1974: 62–64.
257. See, for instance, Karabekir 1982: 210, 221–26, 224, 228, 254–58, 273, 281–83, 317 for a detailed description of commiting such crimes that he termed "honorable duty."

258. Bayar 1965: I, 673–74; Ertürk 1957: 40; Sadeddin 2003: 77, 104; Üçok 2002: 497–98.
259. Çerkezyan 2003: 166–67.
260. Hüseyin Nazım 1993: 35–42, 150–52, 236, 239–40, 245–46.
261. Indeed, Sultan Abdülhamid himself (1985: 87) stated that "the children of my fatherland have always been very precious to me. I forgave the crimes of so many and I knowingly overlooked their faults. How could I ever get them drowned in the sea? Not only is it murderous to do so, but it is murder to even think about it."
262. Even though it was "highly concentrated in space to enable collective effervescence," it ultimately produced "a prodigious expansion in spatial reach of what are initially local phenomena." Sewell 2005: 259, 260.
263. Sewell argues that "historical events are never instantaneous happenings: they always have a duration, a period that elapses between the initial rupture and the subsequent structural transformation." Ibid., 229.
264. Tahsin 1931: 62–63; Duhani 1984: 119.
265. Mehmed Rauf 1991: 58, 177–78, 262.
266. Karabekir 1982: 35.
267. Aşcıdede (1960: 87) then likened the raid and ensuing unrest to the Janissary rebellions of the past.
268. Said 1994: 110–14.
269. Sazak 2007: 45–47.
270. İzbudak 1946: 38–40.
271. Uşaklıgil 1987: 505–8.
272. Sazak 2007: 45–47.
273. Ibid., 45–47.
274. Hüseyin Nazım 2003: 267–96.
275. Kerkük 2002: 30–32, 68.
276. See İzbudak (1946: 38–40), where he stated that he heard thousands of Armenians were massacred. The exact wording in Turkish is "*Sair Ermeni milletinden ahali tarafindan öldürülen binlerce Ermeninin haddi hesabı yoktur dediler.*"
277. The Greek Rum gave shelter to the Armenians at their houses and churches. Zarifi 2005: 368–70.
278. Yalman 1997: I: 40.
279. Natanyan 2008: 420–24.
280. Simavi 1965: 153.
281. Kuran 1945: 31–32.
282. İbrahim Temo 1987: 54–55.
283. Zarifi 2005: 366–70.
284. Atay 1938: 7.
285. Abdülhamid 1987; 1994.
286. Kamil 1991: 188, Rey 1945: 16–19.
287. Abdülhamid 1994: 250; 1987: 65–66, 69, 80–82, 85–86.
288. Mithat 1997: vol. 1, 332.
289. Abdülhamid 1987: 72, 80–82; 1985: 56–58.
290. Mizancı Murad 1994: 61.
291. Kadri1991: 124–26.
292. Kuran 1945: 167.
293. Ahmet Muhtar 1996: vol. 2, 281–82.
294. Tepeyran 1998: 324–25.

Chapter 2

1. Altınay 1998: 135–37.
2. Ibid., 165, 169.
3. Ibid., 60–61.
4. Ibid., 161.

5. Ibid., 162–63.
6. Ibid., 164.
7. Ibid., 165.
8. Ibid., 165–66.
9. Ibid., 168, 170, 178–80.
10. Ibid., 170–71.
11. Ibid., 169.
12. Ibid., 189–90.
13. Ibid., 184–87.
14. Ibid., 187–88.
15. It should be noted that prominent members of the CUP and Turkish republican leadership, including Enver, Talat, and Cemal Pashas, Mithat Şükrü Bleda, Kazım Karabekir, Rauf Orbay, and Mustafa Kemal Atatürk, all originated at this location.
16. The King of England Edward VII met with the Russian tsar Emperor Nicholas on the waters of the Bay of Reval in the Gulf of Finland on 9 June 1908. Even though it was stated that no new alliance was formed, the meeting still marked the first visit by the English king to Russia where it was rumored that they discussed many world issues.
17. Kaygusuz 1955: 35; Ahmed Rıza 1988: 19–20.
18. Bleda 1979: 48.
19. Karabekir 1982: 391.
20. Rey 1945: 79–80; Süleyman Şefik 2004: 159; Ayni 1945: 52.
21. Karabekir 1982: 359. See also Bleda 1979: 52–53.
22. Tarcan 1946: 30–39; Kalaç 1960: 19–24.
23. Karabekir 1982: 359.
24. Tarcan 1946: 42–43.
25. Karabekir 1982: 376; Duru 1957: 29.
26. Ahmed Rıza 1988: 26. See also İbrahim Temo 1987: 183.
27. Ahmed Rıza 1988: 26.
28. Karabekir 1982: 389–90.
29. Bleda 1979: 54; Günday 1960: 17.
30. Rey 1945: 103–4.
31. Felek 1974: 55.
32. Kalaç 1960: 19–21.
33. Tengirşenk 1967: 106; Söylemezoğlu 1949: 170–71.
34. Başar 2007: vol. 1, 67–68, 71. See also Atay 1999: 16.
35. Ayni 1945: 52. See also Karabekir 1982: 392, 398; Kalaç 1960: 25–26; Süleyman Şefik 2004: 158.
36. Ahmed İzzet 1993: 9–10; Atay 2004: 131–32; Aykaç 1991: 32, 55; İz 1990; Biren 1993: 120.
37. Atay 2004: 130.
38. Aykaç 1991: 55.
39. Mahmud Celaleddin 1970: 82–83.
40. Aykaç 1991: 39–40.
41. Hüseyin Kazım Kadri 1992: 38.
42. Gündem 2002: 21. See also Karabekir 1982: 19–20.
43. Hüseyin Kazım Kadri 1992: 21.
44. Sertel 1968: 9; 2000: 32.
45. Yalçın 1943: 39.
46. Amça 1989: 103.
47. This political practice of the army protecting the constitution, the state, or the nation continued unabated from the empire to the republic and is still partially in existence to this day.
48. Günday 1960: 17.
49. The term the pasha employed was *nev'i şahsına münhasır bir diyardır.* Kutay 1966: vol. 2, 143–44.
50. Adıvar 1963: 127.
51. Atay 1938: 51. The quotation is on page 22.
52. Ayni 1945: 60–61.

53. Dersimi 1992: 55; 1997: 49–50.
54. Cemaleddin 1990: 43–44.
55. Mizancı Murad 1994: 99–100.
56. Sertel 1968: 11–13.
57. If he had defined the nation ethnically, Gökalp would have been the first to be excluded from such a definition, since he was Kurdish.
58. Beyatlı (1997: 44, 46–48) stated that "the consciousness of our own nation had to be awakened, a national movement generated, and Turkism had to be comprehended."
59. Ahmed Hilmi1991: 43–44.
60. İz 1990: 102–3.
61. Sevük 1937: 91.
62. Yalçın 1943: 10, 13; 2001: 41.
63. Karaosmanoğlu 1987b: 172.
64. Gilmanoğlu 2001: 19.
65. Erden 2003: 79.
66. Sertel 1968: 46.
67. Karaosmanoğlu 1969: 25.
68. Atay 1938: 21–22.
69. Yalman 1997: 260–62.
70. Denker 1998: 272. The Turkish term is *laftan anlar*.
71. Kalaç 1960: 57–58.
72. Selahattin Adil 1982: 92, 94.
73. Mahmud Celaleddin 1970: 47.
74. Selahattin Adil 1982: 92, 94.
75. See, for instance, Amça 1989: 42–43; Apak 1988: 92.
76. Tarcan 1946: 40–41.
77. Ibid.; Kuran 1976: 121, 144–47.
78. See, for instance, Amça 1989: 43.
79. Yalçın 1943: 21–23; Kalaç 1960: 76.
80. Cemaleddin 1990: 117, 120.
81. Duru 1957: 52. The exact wording is "*Osmanlı ülkesinde hürriyeti meşrutiyeti kurmak için elde bulundurulabilecek biricik idraklı kuvvet ordudaki genç mektepli zabitlerdi.*"
82. Tör 2000: 127.
83. See, for instance, Baytın 1946: 18.
84. Kadri 1991: 65.
85. Cemaleddin 1990: 129–30.
86. İlden 1998: 37, 53, 61, 123, 128–29, 182.
87. Ibid., 26–30.
88. See, for instance, Mehmed Memduh 1990: 162–63; Yergök 2006: 228–29.
89. See, for instance, Velidedeoğlu 1977: vol. 1, 51.
90. Kalaç 1960: 30–31.
91. Akyavaş 2002: vol. 1, 20.
92. Topuzlu 1988: 102; Mahmud Şevket 1988: 147, 165.
93. See, for instance, İmre 1976: 31.
94. Kalaç 1960: 46–48.
95. My own paternal grandfather traveled to Germany under such auspices.
96. Uşaklıgil 1965: 356, 362–63; Kalaç 1960: 119.
97. Selahattin Adil 1982: 198.
98. Kalaç 1960: 86.
99. See, for instance, Biren 1993: 52, 55.
100. See Gilmanoğlu (2001: 320–21) for a more detailed discussion.
101. According to the 1912 *Annuaire* published at the capital (Deleon 1993: 95–168), there was a spectrum of Armenian tradesmen and professionals, as well as many companies established by them.
102. Giz 1988: 30–31; Atay 1999: 62; Esendal 2003: 179; Yalman 1997: 311–13; Yergök 2006: 239–41, 243.

103. Gilmanoğlu 2001: 317–21.
104. Selahattin Adil 1982: 102.
105. Topuzlu 1982: 141; 2002: 164–65, 167–69.
106. Yalman 1997: 320–23, 331. See also Uşaklıgil 1965: 392.
107. Gilmanoğlu 2001: 320–21. See also Mardin 1988: 100, 105; Yüzbaşı Cemal 1996: 37.
108. Uçuk 1995: 235.
109. Kalaç 1960: 56, 62; Sazak 2007: 98, 111–12.
110. Madanoğlu 1992: 300–302.
111. Yiğit 2002: 51.
112. Süleyman Nazif 1957: 18.
113. Erden 2003: 300–302.
114. Başar 2007: vol. 1, 21, 78–9, 134–36.
115. Esatlı 2004: 470–72, 608–9.
116. See Duru 1957: 71, 76–77 for the quotation.
117. Kadri 1992: 96, 98–101.
118. Kalaç 1960: 56, 62.
119. Peker 1955: 257.
120. Kutay 1966: vol. 1, 86–87, 92–93, 97, 102.
121. Zobu 1977: 27–40; Ertuğrul 1989: 117, 123, 135–36; Giz 1988: 70–87, 218–19.
122. Arseven 1993: 20, 62, 126–27.
123. Nutku 1997: 182–83.
124. Orhan 2001: 19.
125. See, for instance, the accounts of Söylemezoğlu (1949: 78–79) and Tanpınar (1973: 52–55) recounting such experiences.
126. Topuzlu 1988: 42, 66.
127. Gündem 2002: 16.
128. Mevlanzade 1992: 25.
129. Söylemezoğlu 1949: 8–9.
130. Orbay 1992: 129.
131. Kuran 1976: 110–12, 114–17; 1945: 267; Duru 1959: 35.
132. Mevlanzade 1992: 22–23, 111–12.
133. Felek 1974: 45; Aykaç 1991: 15.
134. Mahmud Celaleddin 1979: 139, 147, 153, 157; Kuran 1945: 262–66, 264, 268–69.
135. İmre 1976: 126–28.
136. Yalçın 1976: 42.
137. Kuran 1948: 259.
138. Kaygusuz 1955: 56, 64–65, 72, 74–75.
139. İz 1990: 113. See also Altınay 1998: 149.
140. Karay 1996: 12, 46–47.
141. Temo 1987: 190; Yergök 2006: 213; Yalçın 1976: 78.
142. Kutay 1966: vol. 2, 232.
143. Kuran 1976: 118–19, 159, 163.
144. Rey 1945: 110–13; Temo 1987: 204–8.
145. Ahmed Hilmi 1991: 37.
146. Şerif 1990: 12–13.
147. Felek 1974: 83; Masar 1974: 95; Nur 1992: vol. 1, 267, 280–81; İlden 1988: 23; Ali Kemal 1985: 78. The disastrous Ottoman military defeat during the 1912 Balkan Wars has often been attributed to this political divide. See, for instance, Apak 1988: 67, 70; Aykaç 1991: 41; Bölükbaşı 1993: 10–17; and Berkem 1960: 9.
148. Rey 1945: 191; Uşakligil 1965: 318; Amça 1989: 19–24.
149. Kaygusuz 1955: 83.
150. Karaosmanoğlu 1987a: 141–47.
151. See, for instance, Nur 1992: vol. 1, 335.
152. Kuran 1945: 325–35; Karaosmanoğlu 1969: 163–66.
153. Kuran 271, 283–84, 287.
154. Kalaç 1960: 88.

155. Esatlı 2004: 384, 390–91, 397.
156. Karaosmanoğlu 1969: 278, 300–305.
157. Yalçın 1943: 17. As the CUP attempted to control these branches, they appointed young officers over civilians. See also Esatlı 2004: 437; Aykaç 1991: 41, 45; Kadri 1992: 29; Süleyman Şefik 2004: 177.
158. Ahmed İzzet 1993: 9–10; Yalman 1997: 316; Esatlı 2004: 168, 247–51, 315, 317; Aykaç 1991: 36–37.
159. Denker 1998: 9, 11.
160. Aykaç 1991: 45–46; Gilmanoğlu 2001: 48; Cemaleddin 1990: 38.
161. Mehmed Memduh 1990: 104–5, 113.
162. Temo 1987: 188–89; Fani 1998: 13.
163. Kaygusuz 1955: 46.
164. Kalaç 1960: 119.
165. Karaosmanoğlu 1987a: 125.
166. Aykaç 1991: 52–53.
167. Arslan 2005: 272, 274.
168. Uşaklıgil 1987: 655.
169. Kuran 1948: 259, 263. See also Amça 1989: 171, 176; Kılıç 1997; 2005: 21–22; Felek 1974: 57.
170. Simavi 1965: 428–29; Mahmud Şevket 1988: 18, 54, 77, 178.
171. Yalman 1997: 104. See also Nur 1992: vol. 1, 328–29.
172. Biren 1993: 112, 120; Uşaklıgil 1965: 217–18.
173. Yalçın 1943: 43.
174. Rey 1945: 131–32; Yalman 1997: 96–98.
175. Kutay (1966: vol. 2, 14; 1975, 86, n. 94) noted that the SO, then attached to the War Ministry, had organized files on the activities of some Rum and Armenian deputies.
176. Cemaleddin 1990: 43–44.
177. Yalçın 2001: 155–57; Söylemezoğlu 1949: 56.
178. Duru 1957: 36, 50.
179. See, for instance, Karay 1996: 21; Sazak 2007: 73–76; Kutay 1966: vol. 1, 21, n. 1.
180. Kadri 1992: 69, 71–72, 136–37. See also Aykan 2003: 41.
181. Mahmud Şevket 1988: 116, 162–63, 184–85.
182. Süleyman Nazif 1957: 111.
183. Bleda 1979: 120; Biren 1993: 10; Yalçın 1943: 46; Beyatlı 1973: 171; Orbay 2000: 184; Tanpınar 1973: 205; Kuran 1948: 287–88; Yalman 1997: 61–62.
184. In the case of World War I, for instance, he was certain of German success; he also thought the war would last only a few months. Bleda 1979: 104–6.
185. Serdi 1994: 118; Karaosmanoğlu 1969: 124; Yücel 2006: 89–90; Okday 1975: 224–25.
186. Yücel 2006: 93, 127.
187. Us 1966: 30–31.
188. Ahmed Rıza 1988: 41–43.
189. Orbay 1992: vol. 2, 232–33.
190. Yalçın 1943: 26–29.
191. Başar 2007: vol. 1, 75–77. See also Borçbakan 2005: 73–74.
192. Süleyman Şefik 2004: 87.
193. See, for instance, Tör 2000: 92; Tarcan 1946: 62; İmre 1976: 25; Serdi 1994: 50–52.
194. See depictions of the inequality between Muslim and non-Muslim neighborhoods also in, for instance, Güvemli 1999: 108, 117; Sunata 2003: 239–40; Uran 1959: 65–66; Sevük 1937: 20.
195. See, for instance, Gilmanoğlu 2001: 153, 216.
196. The account further stated that a small incident like the braying of a camel in the middle of the marketplace led shops to be closed down for fear of a possible disturbance. See Rey 1945: 107–8.
197. Tonguç 1999: 22–23, 28, 88.
198. Tarcan 1946: 35–36; Kutay 1966: vol. 2, 237.
199. Kuran 1948: 287–88.

200. Kartal 1987: 9–10; Şahingiray 1997: 97–98.
201. See, for instance, Karabekir 1982: 448–49, 453; Masar 1974: 15–16; Karaveli 1999: 15, 23, 36–37, 45; Okyar 1980: 94; Simavi 1965: 282–83.
202. Kuran 1948: 261–62. See also Ertürk 1957: 64–65.
203. Bleda 1979: 27.
204. Duru 1957: 27.
205. Resneli 1975: 134, 150, 251–58; Bleda 1979: 36, 38–41.
206. Resneli 1975: 151–52, 158–59; Bleda 1979: 41–42; Ekdal 2003: 17; Duru 1957: 28–29.
207. Duru 1957: 32–33; Bleda 1979: 50.
208. Karabekir 1982: 336–37, 367.
209. Uşaklıgil 1987: 685–87.
210. Yalçın 1976: 41–42.
211. Ibid., 402.
212. Paker 2000: 44.
213. Nur 1992, vol. 1, 280–81, 285–86, 288–90, 322–23; Uşaklıgil 1965: 310.
214. Mehmed Selahaddin 1989: 100, 102.
215. Atay 2004: 131–32. See also Ulunay 1999: 13.
216. Orbay 1992: vol. 2, 230, 257; Cemal 1977: 19, 29–31.
217. "And I personally felt great anxiety about this," Orbay (1992: vol. 2, 230, 257) continued, "for it was hard in world history to find examples of concomitant success in the same hands of politics and defense of the homeland."
218. Yergök 2006: 198; Uşaklıgil 1987: 685–87.
219. Yalman 1997: 201–2; 1970: vol. 3, 379–81.
220. See, for instance, Nur 1992: vol. 1, 316–17.
221. Mehmed Selahaddin 1989. It should be noted that *feda* also meant sacrifice in Turkish, thereby seamlessly translating into CUP activities.
222. Nesimi 1977: 34.
223. Yalçın 1943: 41.
224. Balkan 1998: 10.
225. Ali Kemal 1985: 513.
226. Vardar 1960: 208, 297–98.
227. Orbay 2000: 232.
228. Esatlı 2004: 168–69, 179, 203, 207.
229. Balkan 1998: 12, 37.
230. Nur 1992: vol. 1, 290.
231. Amça 1989: 66–67.
232. İz 1990: 98; Kalaç 1960: 34–35; Yalman 1997: 100, 124; Nur 1992: vol. 1, 324; Kuran 1945: 276–83; Karaosmanoğlu 1987a: 42–43, 56, 71, 127–28, 134; Süleyman Şefik 2004: 161, 163; Duru 1957: 51; Felek 1974: 11; Adıvar 1963: 130, 132, 134.
233. Aykaç 1991: 49, 65, 69.
234. Rey 1945: 139.
235. Erden 2003: 267.
236. Karay 1996: 24–25, 58–59; Ali Kemal 1985: 74, 76–77, 429; Ahmed Rıza 1988: 43.
237. Altınay 1998: 151.
238. İz 1990: 178.
239. Nur 1992: vol. 1, 335.
240. Both Denker (1998: 286–87) and Atatürk (1991: 47–49) recount the murder of Silahçı Tahsin, an SO member who did not obey orders.
241. Kutay 1975: vol. 1, 21 n. 1, 333.
242. Nesimi 1977: 36–37.
243. Ibid., 109–11.
244. Ibid., 205–9; Topuzlu 1988: 91.
245. See, for instance, Bayar 1965, vol. 5, 1573.
246. Denker 1998: 9, 11, 18.
247. Yalçın 2001: 30, 32.
248. Denker 1998: 9, 11. See also Esatlı 2004: 179–80, 298.

249. Sabis 1992: vol. 2, 212–13; Nesimi 1977: 37.
250. Vardar 1960: 283–86; Esatlı 2004: 50, 179–80, 281–92. Different memoirs list these men as having assignments at different regions; the one presented in the text attempts to provide a composite picture based on the varied accounts.
251. Atay 1938: 35–36; Denker 1998: 13–14, 119–20, 126.
252. See, for instance, Akkılıç 1994: 17, 20.
253. Mevlanzade 2000: 119. See also Denker 1998: 88, 102–3.
254. Denker 1998: 20–26, 77, 102–3, 137.
255. Kuşçubaşı 1999: 23, 79, 224, 227–28. See also Ekdal 2003: 33.
256. Sabis 1992: vol. 2, 399.
257. Ibid., 277, 291.
258. Denker 1998: 20–26, 77, 102–3, 137.
259. Ibid., 137.
260. See, for instance, İlden 1998: 133, 164–66, 248, 264.
261. Sabis 1992: vol. 2, 310, 402.
262. Denker 1998: 240, 246, 261.
263. Mevlanzade 1993: 125–38; see also Denker's (1992: 140) recollection.
264. Mevlanzade 2000: 126–27.
265. Dersimi 1992: 79, 84–85, 92–93.
266. Nesimi 1977: 43–47, 58–60, 103, 141, 146, 48, 151, 198–99.
267. Kalaç 1960: 97–99.
268. Bloxham 2005.
269. For accounts of the counterrevolution, see Nur 1992: vol. 1, 295–96; Mevlanzade 1992: 21, 38–42, 130–31, 157; Selahattin Adil 1982: 98; Süleyman Şefik 2004: 168–70, 176, 184–85, 188; Şerif 1990: 27, 31, 48–49, 233; Orbay 2000: 201.
270. Tengirşenk 1967: 113.
271. Mevlanzade 1992: 21, 38–42, 130–31, 157.
272. See, for instance, Topuzlu 1988: 88; Karaosmanoğlu 1987a: 25.
273. Bölükbaşı 1993: 224–25; Felek 1974: 11.
274. For contemporaneous eyewitness accounts of the Adana massacres, see also Tengirşenk 1967: 120–24; El-Kazımi 2005: 74–75; Adıvar 1963: 138–39; Arıkoğlu 1961: 42–57; Çerkezyan 2003: 19–22.
275. Mevlanzade 1993: 139–43, 153, 159, 164. Mevlanzade argued that he had to narrate everything as it happened because, as the prophet Muhammad dictated, "he who is silent in front of injustice is a mute devil."
276. Yeğena 1996: 46–55, 70–71.
277. Günday 1960: 30–50.
278. Cemal 1959: 349–55.
279. Yeğena 1996: 46–55, 70–71. Günday 1960: 30–50 concurred with Cemal Pasha's figures.
280. For Antioch, see El-Kazımi 2005: 77–89, 113; for Lazkiye, see Ayni 1945: 72–77; for Aleppo, see Rey 1945: 106–7, 218, 221, 224; for Kayseri, see Biren 1993: 29–35.
281. Duru 1957: 54; Kadri 1991: 135–36.
282. For contemporaneous accounts of the Bab-ı Ali raid, also see also Akyavaş 2002: vol. 2, 83; Bleda 1979: 74–75; Kuran 1945: 318–19; Yalman 1997: 233.
283. Esatlı 2004: 322, 330, 333, 356. See also Orbay 1992: vol. 2, 292–93.
284. Rey 1945: 177, 201–3. See also Esatlı 2004: 44–45; Çambel 1987: 112; Kalaç 1960: 78.
285. Orbay 2000: 75–76, 214–15.
286. Dersimi 1992: 37–38.
287. Kalaç (1960: 67, 79–84, 89–90, 93–96, 135) proudly noted that in Sivas, where he and Muammer Bey served as officials, "there was no sacrifice and renunciation" they would not engage in "for the sake of the fatherland and country."
288. Mahmud Şevket 1988: 95, 135, 160, 163, 184, 190, 198; Söylemezoğlu 1949: 243–44, 267.
289. Üçok 2002: 260–61, 497–98.
290. For various accounts of Mahmud Şevket Pasha's assassination, also see Mahmud Celaleddin 1970: 110, 112; Felek 1974: 234–34; Esatlı 2004: 15, 19; Abdülhamid 1985: 155.
291. Ulunay 1999: 9, 41–42, 62, 67.

292. Karaosmanoğlu 1987a: 278, 300–305.
293. Menteşe 1986: 12, 175. In approaching all issues, domestic and foreign, the CUP, Uşaklıgil (1965: 271) argued, "preferred to approach them with the use of force and violence."
294. Kuşçubaşı 1999: 220–21, 249.
295. For the pogroms against the Greek Rum, also see Kutay 1966: vol. 1, 65–83; *Çanakkale* 1964: 49, 56; Yalçın 1976: 420, Yalman 1997: 233; Orbay 1992: vol. 2, 146.
296. Uran 1959: 68–79.
297. Şahingiray 1997: 21.
298. Sunata 2003: 72–73.
299. Çarıklı 2005: 20, 27.
300. Uran 1959: 68–79; Kuşçubaşı 1999: 220–21, 249.
301. Bayar 1965: vol. 7, 1545, 1568–69, 1574–95.
302. Kuşçubaşı 1999: 220–21, 249.
303. Uran 1959: 68–79.
304. Ulunay 1999: 100.
305. Uran 1959: 68–79.
306. Kuşçubaşı 1999: 220–21, 249. The original Turkish is "*stratejik noktalarda kümelenmiş ve dış menfi tesirlere bağlı gayri-Türk yığınların tasfiyesi.*"
307. Nur 1992: vol. 2, 323.
308. Kant 2003: 17, 26–29, 32–42.
309. For varying accounts of the empire's entering the war, see Bleda 1979: 77–79; Erdoğan 1998: 60–62, 64–68, 83; Güvemli 1999: 34–36; Kant 2003: 17, 26, 31–37, 40–42; Atay 1938: 57, 67, 120; 2004: 127, 130, 135, 262; Yalçın 2001: 48, 50–51, 243; Uşaklıgil 1965: 388, 390, 392; Cebesoy 1998: 16–17; Oker 2004: 22, 33; Simavi 1965: 341–43; Tör 1976: 154–55; Yalman 1997: 253, 331.
310. See, for instance, the accounts of Beyatlı 1997: 126–28; 1973: 130–32; Ulunay 1999: 194.
311. Amça 1989: 185–86, 192.
312. Atatürk 1998: 48–49, 100, 103, 111; Kuran 1948: 302–3.
313. Apak 1988: 95–96; Kut 1972: 146.
314. For accounts of the battles in the east in general and the Sarıkamış battle in particular, see also Apak 1988: 106, 125–26; Akkılıç 1994: 110, 115, 117–19, 121–25, 131–32, 147, 155–57; Serdi 1994: 135–37, 142; Sunata 2003: 477–84, 490, 510–12, 530–31, 546, 558.
315. Sunata 2003: 324–25, 352–55, 366, 408, 410.
316. General Ahmet Fevzi Pasha, who criticized the Ottoman attack against the Russians in the dead of winter, was quickly removed through the intervention of Bahaeddin Şakir. See Baytın 1946: 49–51; Yergök 2005: 53.
317. Sabis 1992: vol. 2, 44; Erdoğan 1998: 102, 110, 155–58; Tonguç 1999: 41, 47, 54, 71, 76–77, 112, 136–37, 140–41, 169, 175–76, 182–89, 194, 210; Sunata 2003: 324–25, 352–55, 366, 408, 410.
318. Apak 1988: 114, 118–21; Sabis 1992: vol. 4, 174, 189, 249, 254, 257; Kut 1972: 227–29; Uran 1959: 95–96; Erdoğan 1998: 160–61, 165–67, 172–86, 189, 193; Nur 1991: 27–28, 31.
319. Aykan 2003: 38–39; Tuğaç 1975: 26, 179, 196, 199–200, 203–4; Bahar 2003: 70.
320. For accounts of the war at the Dardanelles, see *Çanakkale* 1964; Selahattin Adil 1982: 270, 295–96; Süleyman Nazif 1978: 81; Tör 2000: 183, 192.
321. Esatlı 2004: 288; Vardar 1960: 286–88.
322. Yalçın 1976: 233.
323. For accounts of the Canal expedition, see *Çanakkale* 1964: 58; Cebesoy 1998: 18, 20–21; Günday 1960: 102–3, 120.
324. Beyatlı 1973: 136–37, 139–40.
325. Atay 1938: 75.
326. Arslan 2005: 326–76. See also Adıvar 1963: 192–93.
327. Mevlanzade 1993: 22–24; Yalçın 2001: 47, 63, 71–83; 1976: 235–36.
328. Abdülhamid 1985: 128.
329. Kadri 1992: 123–25. See also Mevlanzade 1993: 122–24.
330. Velidedeoğlu 1977: vol. 2, 218–29.

331. Atay (2004: 488–90) reiterated that the non-Turks and non-Muslims in Anatolia approached 40 percent of the population before the war, and then stated that "had this calamity not occurred, the National Force movement could not have taken root."
332. Altınay 1998: 142–48, 156–57, 190, 197–99, 205.
333. The specific Turkish terms Atay employed were "*elde kalan vatanı milli yurt olarak yoğurmak ve kurtarmak.*" Atay 1999: 59; 2004: 488–90.
334. See, for instance, Beyatlı 1973: 171; Vardar 1960: 306, 313–14; Menteşe 1986: 215–16.
335. Yalçın 2001: 83. See also Yalçın 1976: 235–36; 2001: 47; Vardar 1960: 306, 313–14.
336. Altınay 1998: 142–48, 156–57, 197–99, 205.
337. Ibid., 190.
338. Oğuz 2000: 51; Binark 2000: 44, 46; Ragıp Bey 1996: 56–56; Denker 1998: 48–49, 51, 58; Dersimi 1992: 43–45, 48–53; Kartal 1987: 20–21; Uran 1959: 91; Altınay 1998: 174–76.
339. Oğuz 2000: 51.
340. Binark 2000: 44, 46.
341. Uran 1959: 91.
342. Altınay 1998: 174–76.
343. Ragıp Bey1996: 56–57. In relation to Erzurum, see also Denker 1998: 48–49, 51, 58.
344. Dersimi 1992: 43–45, 48–53. See also the account of Kartal 1987: 20–22.
345. Güvemli 1999: 5, 18–19, 24–29.
346. Ulunay 1999: 197–99, 233; Akkılıç 1994: 17, 20; Karay 1996: 219.
347. Adıvar 1963: 184–87; Altınay 1998: 177; Binark 2000: 30 n. 1, 47; Üçok 2002: 497–98; Duru 1957: 64–65.
348. Adıvar 1963: 184–87.
349. Ahmed Rasim 1976: 177.
350. Üçok 2002: 497–98.
351. Binark 2000: 30 n. 1, 47.
352. Duru 1957: 64–65.
353. Orbay 1992: vol. 3, 88. See also Selahattin Adil 1982: 283.
354. Altınay 1998: 157–58, 178–79; Çerkezyan 2003: 23–24; Sazak 2007: 63, 100–105; Aykan 2003: 41–43; İhmalyan 1989: 16–17.
355. Altınay 1998: 157–58.
356. İhmalyan 1989: 16–17.
357. Tonguç 1999: 369.
358. Sazak 2007: 63, 100–105.
359. Aykan 2003: 41–43.
360. Çerkezyan 2003: 23–24.
361. Çalıka 1992: 17–33; Yeğena 1996: 77–79; Cemal 1959: 361–62; Kırkyaşaryan 2005: 14–17, 32–38, 45–81, 96, 126–33, 145, 157.
362. Çalıka 1992: 17–33.
363. Yeğena 1996: 77–79.
364. Cemal 1959: 361–62.
365. Kırkyaşaryan 2005: 14–17, 32–38, 45–81, 96, 126–33, 145, 157.
366. Apak 1988: 149–45; Sunata 2003: 105, 290–91, 304–7, 322; Dersimi 1997: 71–72, 85–86; 1992: 46–47; Kevirbiri 2005: 46, 49, 57, 68, 71–72, 82; Serdi 1994: 129–30.
367. Dersimi 1997: 71–72, 85–86; 1992: 46–47.
368. Kevirbiri 2005: 46, 49, 57, 68, 71–72, 82.
369. Serdi 1994: 129–30.
370. Apak 1988: 149–50.
371. Sunata 2003: 105, 290–91, 304–7, 322.
372. Cemal 1959: 361; Anter 1999: 223, 265, 331–33; Zana 1995: 61–64; Bleda 1979: 56–62; Karakaş 2003: 27, 32–34, 37, 48–50, 65–67; Nesimi 1977: 40–46; Serdi 1994: 123–31; Şahingiray 1992: 131–32; 1997: 22–34, 86–117, 168–71.
373. Anter 1999: 223, 265, 331–33.
374. Nesimi 1977: 40–46; Serdi 1994: 123–31.
375. Zana 1995: 61–64.
376. Karakaş 2003: 27, 32–34, 37, 48–50, 65–7.

377. Şahingiray 1992: 131–32; 1997: 22–34, 86–117, 168–71. See also Bleda 1979: 56–62.
378. Selahattin Adil 1982: 331; Binark 2000: 10, 37–42; Erden 2003: 144–46.
379. Erden 2003: 144–46.
380. Selahattin Adil 1982: 331; Binark 2000: 10, 37–42.
381. Çambel 1987: 136–39; Amça in Ekdal 2003: 19–24, 35, 154–55, 326–27; Atay 1938: 77–79, 81–83, 97–99; Altınay 1998: 174–76; Nur 1992: vol. 1, 328–29; Çerkezyan 2003: 37–41, 142–43; Günday 1960: 138, 152–54, 189; Adıvar 1963: 194–99, 206, 209, 217, 228–29, 233; Felek 1974: 176–77.
382. Erden 2003: 119, 142–43, 148–53, 156–59, 164, 266–76, 281–82, 296, 328, 348–49; Cemal 1959: 359–63; 1977: 443–44.
383. Çambel 1987: 136–39.
384. Atay 1938: 81–83. See also Felek 1974: 168–71; Cemal 1959: 361–62.
385. Erden 2003: 151.
386. Atay 1938: 78–79.
387. Erden 2003: 152.
388. Atay 1938: 58–59.
389. Erden 2003: 39, 267; Altınay 1998: 172–74; Nur 1992: vol. 1, 328–29.
390. Erden 2003: 276.
391. The memoirs citing the just Turks belong to Ferda Güley; Garabet Haçeryan; Ahmet Emin Yalman; Vedat Günyol; Abdülhalim Akkılıç; and Abidin Nesimi.
392. Güley 1990.
393. Haçeryan 2005: 92.
394. Yalman 1997: 400.
395. Günyol 1990.
396. Akkılıç 1994: 39–43.
397. For an extensive discussion, see the references in the earlier section to the work of Nesimi.
398. Apak 1988: 88; Mahmud Şevket 1988: 67; Tör 2000: 103–4; Rey 1945: 142; Tahmiscizade 1977: 29.
399. Ahmed İzzet 1993: 51.
400. Adıvar 1963: 59–60; Bleda 1979: 63–65; Kutay 1966: vol. 2, 7; Karaosmanoğlu 1969: 75–76; Atay 1999: 22; Ayni 1945: 22; Cemaleddin 1990: 49, 52, 56, 64–67.
401. Adıvar 1963: 59–60.
402. Karaosmanoğlu 1969: 75–76.
403. Cemaleddin 1990: 49, 52, 56, 64–67.
404. Atay 1999: 22.
405. Ayni 1945: 22.
406. Atay 1999: 42–43; Masar 1974: 70; Esatlı 2004: 147; Topuzlu 1982: 118–19, 124; 2000: 143–44; Yücel 2006: 10; Rey 1945: 142; Gündem 2002: 12–13.
407. Atay 1999: 42–43.
408. Topuzlu 1982: 118–19, 124; 2000: 143–44.
409. Masar 1974: 70; Esatlı 2004: 147.
410. Rey 1945: 142.
411. The poem was by Enis Rıza Bey, who wrote under the pseudonym Aka Gündüz.
412. Gündem 2002: 12–13.
413. Simavi 1965: 328–29; Kaygusuz 1955: 111; Gilmanoğlu 2001: 27; Esatlı 2004: 167–70; Mahmud Şevket 1988: 18, 29–30, 43–44, 53–54, 91; Atay 1999: 43; Akkılıç 1994: 47–50, 55, 84, 87; Arslan 2005: 303; Atatürk 1991: 56–57; Ayni 1945: 22; Erdoğan 1998: 51–53; Madanoğlu 1992: 12–13; Mahmud Celaleddin 1970: 56; Orbay 1992: vol. 2, 275–80; Rey 1945: 146, 160–61, 171–72; Tör 2000: 11–12; Yücel 2006: 35, 61, 64–65, 88; Yüzbaşı Cemal 1996: 25; Duru 1957: 52–54.
414. Simavi 1965: 328–29.
415. Erdoğan 1998: 51–53.
416. Mahmud Celaleddin 1970: 56; Orbay 1992: vol. 2, 275–80; Akkılıç 1994: 47–50, 55, 84, 87.
417. Atatürk 1991: 56–57; Esatlı 2004: 167–70; Rey 1945: 146, 160–61, 171–72.
418. Esatlı 2004: 167–70.
419. Atay 1999: 43.

420. Rey 1945: 146.
421. Akkılıç 1994: 59, 70, 91–92, 96, 101.
422. Tör 2000: 11–12.
423. Arslan 2005: 316.
424. Selahattin Adil 1982: 27–32.
425. Mahmud Şevket 1988: 18, 29–30, 43–44, 53–54, 91.
426. Rey 1945: 146, 160–61, 171–72.
427. Ayni 1945: 22; Yücel 2006: 35, 61, 64–65, 88; Yüzbaşı Cemal 1996: 25.
428. Rey 1945: 171–72.
429. Gilmanoğlu 2001: 27; Orbay 1992: vol. 2, 275–80.
430. Rey 1945: 171–72.
431. Duru 1957: 52–54.
432. Mahmud Şevket 1988: 18, 29–30, 43–44, 53–64, 91. See also Ahmet İzzet 1993.
433. Gilmanoğlu 2001: 27; Akkılıç 1994: 59, 70, 91–92, 96, 101; Apak 1988: 85; Atay 1999: 5; Balkan 1998: 10; Çambel 1987: 108; Sertel 2000: 41–42.
434. Gilmanoğlu 2001: 27.
435. Akkılıç 1994: 59, 70, 91–92, 96, 101.
436. Apak 1988: 85.
437. Atay 1999: 5; Balkan 1998: 10.
438. Çambel 1987: 108.
439. Selahattin Adil 1982: 56.
440. Topuzlu 1988: 48; Bereketzade 1997: 303–9; Mahmud Şevket 1988: 51, 135; Vardar 1960: 262.
441. Topuzlu 1988: 48; Vardar 1960: 262.
442. Adıvar 1963: 177–78; Amça 1989: 118; Akyavaş 2002: vol. 1, 57; Ali Kemal 1985: 17–18; Arslan 2005: 305, 314; Bereketzade 1997: 303–9; Karaosmanoğlu 1969: 75–76; İmre 1976: 9–10, 21; Gilmanoğlu 2001: 51, 91, 127–29; Mahmud Şevket 1988: 51, 135; Sertel 2000: 67; Tanpınar 1973: 27–28; Tesal 1998: 23–24, 148; Topuzlu 1988: 148; Vardar 1960: 262.
443. İmre 1976: 9–10, 21.
444. Sertel 2000: 67.
445. Tesal 1998: 23–24, 148.
446. Karay 1996: 75–76.
447. Adıvar 1963: 177–78; Akyavaş 2002: vol. 1, 57.
448. Karay 1996: 75, 83, 127, 138.
449. Amça 1989: 118; Ali Kemal 1985: 17–18; Tanpınar 1973: 27–28.
450. Amça 1989: 118.
451. Ali Kemal 1985: 17–18.
452. Tanpınar 1973: 27–28.
453. Mahmud Şevket 1988: 51, 135.
454. Kaygusuz 1955: 111; Adıvar 1963: 177–78; Akkılıç 1994: 95; Altay 1998: 63; Bleda 1979: 63–65; Denker 2005: 201; Dersimi 1997: 30–31; Ertürk 1957: 120–21; Esatlı 2004: 183; Kestelli 2001: 24, 79, 88, 103; Orbay 1992: vol. 2, 299; Sertel 1968: 28; Tükel 1953: 4–6; Uşaklıgil 1965: 365; Vardar 1960: 213, 221; Kutay 1966: vol. 2, 203.
455. Altay 1998: 63.
456. Tükel 1953: 4–6; Kestelli 2001: 24, 79, 88, 103.
457. Tükel 1953: 4–6.
458. Ertürk 1957: 120–21.
459. Denker 2005: 201.
460. Bleda 1979: 63–65.
461. Apak 1988: 86; Adıvar 1963: 162; Ahmed Hilmi 1991: 83–84; Altınay 1998: 138–39; Ahmed İzzet 1993: 51; Arslan 2005: 316; Bleda 1979: 67; Karaosmanoğlu 1987a: 209; Gilmanoğlu 2001: 172; Masar 1974: 46–47; Kestelli 2001: 14; Orbay 1992: vol. 1, 562; Simavi 1965: 330; Söylemezoğlu 1949: 14; Süleyman Nazif 1978: 59; Tahmiscizade 1977: 46, 125; Tör 2000: 70.

462. The Henry Herbert Asquith cabinet in Britain had declared in August 1912, right before the advent of the Balkan War, that the status quo in the Balkans would be kept regardless of the result of the war. "Evidently, Mister Asquith's declaration was just a precaution against the possible victory of the Turks," Adıvar (1963: 162) commented.
463. Apak 1988: 86.
464. Gilmanoğlu 2001: 172.
465. Süleyman Nazif 1978: 59.
466. Tahmiscizade 1977: 46, 125.
467. Kestelli 2001: 14.
468. Arslan 2005: 316.
469. Söylemezoğlu 1949: 14.
470. Tör 2000: 70.
471. Kalaç 1960: 83–84.
472. Simavi 1965: 330.
473. Masar 1974: 46–47.
474. Adıvar 1963: 177–78.
475. Sertel 1968: 28.
476. Kutay 1966: vol. 2, 203; Esatlı 2004: 183; Orbay 1992: vol. 2, 299.
477. Akkılıç 1994: 95; Uşaklıgil 1965: 365; 1960: 213, 221.
478. Adıvar 1963: 177–78.
479. Dersimi 1997: 30–31.
480. Atay 1999: 43, 48; Bleda 1979: 100–101; Esatlı 2004: 273; Kadri 1992: 130; Kalaç 1960: 77–78; Gilmanoğlu 2001: 69, 144–45; Kestelli 2001: 77, 113; Kuran 1976: 39; Mahmud Celaleddin 1970: 78; Masar 1974: 46–47; Orhan 2001: 37; Süleyman Nazif 1978: 85; Tanpınar 1973: 54, 57; Tengirşenk 1967: 127–28; Tokgöz 1993: 216; Tör 2000: 122–23, 192; Vardar 1960: 255.
481. Bleda 1979: 100–101.
482. Kalaç 1960: 77–78.
483. Tanpınar 1973: 54, 57.
484. Esatlı 2004: 273.
485. Atay 1999: 43, 48.
486. Tör 2000: 122–23, 192.
487. Vardar 1960: 255.
488. Kestelli 2001: 77, 113.
489. Hüseyin Kazım Kadri 1992: 130; Kuran 1976: 39; Gilmanoğlu 2001: 69, 144–45; Tör 2000: 122–23, 192; Kalaç 1960: 77–78.
490. Hüseyin Kazım Kadri 1992: 130.
491. Kuran 1976: 39.
492. Gilmanoğlu 2001: 69.
493. Karaosmanoğlu 1969: 219.
494. Masar 1974: 46–47.
495. Tör 2000: 122–23, 192; Kalaç 1960: 77–78.
496. Tör 2000: 122–23, 192.
497. Atay 1999: 43, 48; Tengirşenk 1967: 127–28; Mahmud Celaleddin 1970: 78; Tokgöz 1993: 216; Orhan 1999: 37.
498. Atay 1999: 43, 48.
499. Mahmud Celaleddin 1970: 78.
500. Tengirşenk 1967: 127–28.
501. Tokgöz 1993: 216.
502. Orhan 2001: 37.
503. Bölükbaşı 1993: 226; Denker 2005: 108, 110, 112, 133–40, 148–49; Erden 2003: 154–55; Yalman 1997: 404.
504. Bölükbaşı 1993: 226.
505. Denker 2005: 108, 110, 112, 133–40, 148–49.
506. Ibid., 139.
507. Ibid., 133–40.

508. Erden 2003: 154–55.
509. Ibid., 155.
510. Yalman 1997: 404.
511. Ölçen 1994: 63; Tuğaç 1975: 104–7; Kıdwai 1991: 24, 37–48; Şahingiray 1997: 26, 82–85, 95–96; Apak 1988: 149–51; Dersimi 1997: 65; Ali Haydar 1946: 291.
512. Ölçen 1994: 63.
513. Ibid.
514. Kıdwai 1991: 38.
515. Şahingiray 1997: 26, 82–85, 95–96.
516. Apak 1988: 149–51.
517. Haydar 1946: 291.
518. Dersimi 1997: 65; Kıdwai 1991: 24, 37–48.
519. Talat 2005: 89–90, 96–97, 111–17, 123–30, 131–215, 216–53; Bayar 1969: 2114; 1967: 1452, 1471, 1505–12; Şahingiray 1997: 26. See also Denker (1992: 114–15) for a reiteration of Talat's narrative.
520. Anter 1999: 73–74; Mevlanzade 2000: 117.
521. Mevlanzade 2000: 117.
522. Anter 1999: 73–74.

Chapter 3

1. Oğuz 2000: 463–65, 468–70.
2. The normal circulation of the newspaper was 20,000.
3. See Can Dündar's column in the *Milliyet* newspaper on 8 January 2006.
4. I heard my own father narrate the destruction as well. He protected and later financially helped his non-Muslim friend who owned the Baylan patisserie in Karaköy, the district where my father also had his business. The owner was his childhood friend from the Büyükada (Principo) Island located at the Marmara Sea.
5. Wimmer 2002: 4–5.
6. Their assets were seized, and members of the imperial family were given 2,000 pounds sterling each, as well as special one-way passports that could not be used to reenter the country. This law was only repealed in the 1990s.
7. Akyavaş 2002: vol. 2, 319, 321; Doğrugüven 2003: 111.
8. Initially, the CUP had decided that the central committee would pen the official CUP history. Yet the demise of the empire and the CUP, as well as the exile of the CUP leaders to Europe, technically opened the way for members to write their recollections.
9. Ayaşlı 1990: 5–6, 9.
10. Karabekir 1991: 5.
11. Berkes 1997: 158–59.
12. Atay 1999: 4. See also Atay 2004: 7.
13. He delivered his account in 1927 during the congress of the Republican People's Party for thirty-six hours straight. Interestingly, Mustafa Kemal had reflected on writing his memoirs earlier when he was still an Ottoman officer ailing in Karlsbad (1991: 60). The watchful stand he took in relation to revealing knowledge that might one day come to haunt him is very evident in his account.
14. For criticisms of Mustafa Kemal's speech, see, in addition to Karabekir, Kadri 1991: 165–66, 182, 193–96, 208, 290.
15. Ali Kemal 1985: 3, 5–6.
16. Arseven 1993: 140–43; Denker 2005: 55 n. 26, 153; Erdoğan 1998: 335; Arslan 2005: 399, 404; Öngör 1987: 159; Akkılıç 1994: 219–20.
17. Arseven 1993: 140–43; Denker 2005: 55 n. 26, 153; Arslan 2005: 399, 404.
18. Arseven 1993: 140–43.
19. See Derogy 1990 for a detailed description of Operation Nemesis, the latter word referring to the Greek goddess of revenge. The seven targeted people on the list were Talat, Enver, Cemal, Drs. Shakir and Nazim, Trabzon governor Cemal Azmi, and Constantinople police

commander Bedri Bey. Also assassinated were the former grand vizier Said Hilmi and Harutyun Mgirdichian, the Armenian informer who had supplied Talat with the names of the 300 deported and massacred Armenian intellectuals in İstanbul; the latter was murdered by Tehlirian as well.

20. Arseven 1993: 140–43.
21. Arslan 2005: 399, 404.
22. Öngör 1987: 159.
23. Akkılıç 1994: 219–20.
24. See especially Üngör 2011; Üngör and Polatel 2011; and Akçam 2012.
25. Atay 1999: 38; 2004: 359, 381–82; Güvemli 1999: 81; Öngör 1987: 9, 130–31; Arıkoğlu 1961: 64; Oğuz 2000: 257, 346, 448; İğdemir 1976: 189; Anter 1999: 331–33.
26. Atay 1999: 38; 2004: 359, 381–82.
27. Pertaining to northern Anatolia, memoirs provide evidence only on Ordu. After the population exchange, the whole town was immersed in silence for a very long time. Those Muslim Turks who arrived from Greece "did not at all measure up to those who had departed." Güvemli 1999: 81; Öngör 1987: 9, 130–31.
28. Arıkoğlu 1961: 64.
29. Oğuz (2000: 257, 346, 448) visited Kozan in 1952, keeping notes in a diary.
30. İğdemir (1976: 189) visited Dörtyol in 1925.
31. Anter 1999: 331–33.
32. To demonstrate how the same violent decision-making continued unabated during the republican era, one needs to comment on Jews, who were forcefully deported from Thrace in 1934 on grounds of posing a threat to national security. Öngör 1987: 9, 130–31.
33. Anter 1999: 33–34.
34. Karay 1964: 120–21; Örgeevren 2002: 156–57.
35. Karay 1964: 120–21.
36. Örgeevren 2002: 156–57.
37. Çalıka 1992: 21; Güvemli 1999: 30–31, 43, 47.
38. Çalıka 1992: 21.
39. Güvemli 1999: 30–31, 43, 47.
40. Kalkavanoğlu 1957: 36–37; Anter 1999: 131; Tufan 1998: 11–12.
41. Kalkavanoğlu 1957: 36–37.
42. Tufan 1998: 11–12.
43. Anter 1999: 131.
44. Yergök 2005: 260–61.
45. Bayar 1965: 1450; Çalıka 1992: 25; Cavid 2000: 14–15; Kalaç 1960: 144; Yener 1958: 42; Tufan 1998: 20–21, 79; Çerkezyan 2003: 23–24; Yergök 2005: 260–61; Bozok 1985: 206; Atay 2004: 293–94; Karaman 2002: 74; Balkan 1998: 171.
46. Çalıka 1992: 25.
47. Bayar 1965: 1450.
48. Cavid 2000: 14–15.
49. Kalaç 1960: 144.
50. Balkan 1998: 171.
51. Yener 1958: 42.
52. Tufan 1998: 20–21, 79.
53. Çerkezyan 2003: 42–45, 53–54, 103–5; İhmalyan 1989: 18. For similar prejudice and discrimination experienced by a Jew, see also Kant 2003: 56, 74, 127–29, 132–37, 159–66.
54. Çerkezyan 2003: 42–45, 53–54, 103–5.
55. İhmalyan 1989: 18.
56. When Mustafa Kemal sent his ailing mother to Smyrna for a change of weather, he instructed his aide (Salih Bozok) "to find an appropriate house... and let me know after you get it furnished; I will then send my mother. Yet make sure that the house you find does not belong to [Armenian] abandoned properties." See Mustafa Kemal 1998: 289. Mustafa Kemal probably did not know that the place he resided in in Ankara, still the Turkish Republican president's residence today, also belonged to an Armenian initially.

57. Anter 1999: 271.
58. Atay 2004: 293–94.
59. Karaman 2002: 74.
60. Beşe 2004: 199; Peker 1955: 257; Sorguç 1996: 103, 220; Yalman 1997: vol. 2, 9; Selahattin Adil 1982: 416–17; Anter 1999: 94, 300–301; Doğrugüven 2003: 58–59, 61, 69–70; Gerede 2002: 59–60; Yener 1958: 36, 38–39; Zobu 1977: 99, 181, 363, 357, 372–74, 403, 406; Güvemli 1999: 47, 57, 69; Duhani 1984: 105, 114, 117–18; Soyer 2000: 253; Avar 1986: 101.
61. Beşe 2004: 199.
62. Peker 1955: 257.
63. Sorguç 1996: 220.
64. Doğrugüven 2003: 58–59, 61, 69–70.
65. Selahattin Adil 1982: 416–17.
66. Yalman 1997: vol. 2, 9.
67. Avar 1986: 101; Anter 1999: 94, 300–301.
68. Gerede 2002: 59–60.
69. Anter 1999: 94, 300–301.
70. Yener 1958: 36, 38–39.
71. Zobu 1977: 99, 181, 363, 357, 372–74, 403, 406.
72. Güvemli 1999: 47, 57, 69.
73. Another state practice was to turn confiscated Armenian properties over to nationalist civil organizations like the Turkish Hearth. Zobu stated that in Bursa and Antalya, they performed in former churches that had been taken over by the local Turkish Hearths.
74. Doğrugüven 2003: 58–59, 61, 69–70.
75. Anter 1999: 94, 300–301.
76. Yener 1958: 36, 38–39. One wonders if Arif Efendi took the last name Kabakoğlu to further legitimate his illegal purchase.
77. Duhani 1984: 105, 114, 117–18.
78. İhmalyan 1989: 44–45; Belli 2000: 13; Kılıç Altemur 2005: 55.
79. İhmalyan 1989: 44–45.
80. Kılıç Altemur 2005: 55.
81. Belli 2000: 13.
82. Aldan 1992: 94, 124.
83. Tunalı 2005: 81–82, 91–92, 115–17, 139–43.
84. Nutku 1977: 62–67; Bardakçı 1975: 86–88, 107, 111; Tepeyran 1982: 123–26; Mehmed Arif 1987: 53; Çerkes Ethem 2000: 8; 1996: 12; Çolak 1996: 62; Tengirşenk 1967: 181–82, 236; Kut 1972: 330–31; Benlioğlu 2004: 13–14, 17; Kılıç Ali 2005: 208–9; Derin 1995: 100.
85. Nutku 1977: 62–67.
86. Bardakçı 1975: 86–88, 107, 111.
87. Mehmed Arif 1987: 53.
88. Çerkes Ethem 2000: 8.
89. Çolak 1996: 82; Tepeyran 1982: 123–26.
90. Tengirşenk 1967: 181–82, 236; Kut 1972: 330–31; Benlioğlu 2004: 13–14, 17.
91. Bardakçı 1975: 86–88, 107, 111.
92. Kılıç Ali 2005: 208–9; Derin 1995: 100.
93. Masar 1974: 119; Başar 2007: vol. 2, 176.
94. Başar 2007: vol. 2, 176.
95. Sazak 2007: 131–37.
96. Derin 1995: 100.
97. Kılıç Altemur 2005: 128, 135.
98. Ökte 1950: 23–25, 301.
99. Soyer 2000: 83–85.
100. Derin 1995: 100.
101. Establishing the Karabük heavy industry away from sources of steel and coal was a pertinent example of military prioritization. A similar example was the foundation of paper and chemical industries without attention to the nature of the country.

102. Tükel 1953: 52; Derin 1995: 100; Nutku 1977: 62–67; Kılıç Altemur 2005: 128, 135.
103. Haker 2004: 38–40.
104. Sağlar 1976: 210–11.
105. Tokgöz 1993.
106. Kutay 1966: vol. 5, 15–16.
107. Soyer 2000: 83–85.
108. Financial analyst Ökte (1950: 23–25, 301) presented a much more detailed picture of how economically strained the country had become: while the 1934 state revenues were 250,049 million lira and expenses 249,954 million lira (almost balanced), the 1944 revenues rose to 901,511 lira yet at a much slower rate than the expenses of 952,434 lira (showing a deficit of 40,923 million). The national defense expenses that had been 163,941 million lira (more than half of the revenues) in 1939 escalated in 1943 to 542,516 million lira (again more than half the revenues at a time when there was a deficit as well). The balance of trade also ran a deficit.
109. Barutçu (1977: 260–63) noted that domestic food provisioning became a major problem. The state's economic decision-making was based not on principles and foresight but instead on the daily pull of events. The situation worsened as a consequence. The Saracoğlu government took two years before it rationed food, leading to hoarding.
110. While the salaried who could not escape state control paid 53 percent of the taxes, the propertied, including the businessmen, who constituted 41 percent of the taxpayers, paid only 13.8 percent.
111. The agricultural sector, now mostly staffed by Muslim Turks, was much more protected by the state and government than the non-Muslims, who were now considered expendable foreigners; the latter were also frequently portrayed as profiteering at the expense of the rest. Poor state planning had produced such profiteering in the first place.
112. Barutçu 1977: 260–63; Yalman 1997: vol. 2, 378.
113. Ökte 1950: 23–25, 301.
114. Berkes 1997: 304.
115. İğdemir 1976: 82.
116. Başar 2007: vol. 2, 176.
117. Doğrugüven 2003: 112.
118. See, for instance, ibid., 116–17.
119. See, for instance, Kılıç Altemur 2005: 135.
120. Doğrugüven 2003: 100.
121. Başar 2007: vol. 2, 281.
122. Doğrugüven 2003: 112.
123. Derin 1995: 100.
124. See, for instance, ibid., 11.
125. Karaveli 1999: 148; Selahattin Adil 1982: 519; Tör 1976: 105; Bahar 2003: 62; Yener 1958: 33; Çerkezyan 2003: 90–91; Doğrugüven 2003: 100, 112, 116–17.
126. Tör 1976: 105.
127. Doğrugüven 2003: 100, 112, 116–17.
128. Bahar 2003: 62.
129. Karaveli1999: 148.
130. Selahattin Adil 1982: 519.
131. Yener 1958: 33.
132. Çerkezyan 2003: 90–91.
133. Derin 1995: 27, 110; Madanoğlu 1992: 283.
134. Derin 1995: 27, 110.
135. Madanoğlu 1992: 283.
136. Avar 1986: 386.
137. Haker 2004: 38–40.
138. Derin 1995: 27, 110.
139. Şaul 1999: 14.
140. Çerkezyan 2003: 91.
141. İhmalyan 1989: 34, 39.

142. Va-Nu 1997: 122–29; Berkes 1997: 387, 401, 406, 409, 456, 435, 475, 481; Şaul 1999: 80; İğdemir 1976: 24–25, 75, 195–96; Öngör 1987: 78; Binark 2004: 55–56; Sertel 1994: 228; Oğuz 2000: 337–38; Çambel 1987.
143. Va-Nu 1997: 122–29.
144. Berkes 1997: 387, 401, 406, 409, 435, 456, 475, 481. For a scholarly analysis of university expulsions, see Çetik 1998.
145. Öngör 1987: 78; Binark 2004: 55–56; Sertel 1994: 228.
146. Öngör 1987: 78.
147. Oğuz 2000: 337–38.
148. İğdemir 1976: 24–25.
149. Ibid., 75.
150. Kazancıgil 1989: 11.
151. İğdemir 1976: 237; Doğan 1964: 273; Kazancıgil 1989: 11; Makal 1979: 70, 89; Tör 1976: 39–40; Derin 1995: 114.
152. Makal 1979: 70.
153. Eyüboğlu 1999; Kahraman 2008.
154. The first opposition party, namely, the Progressive Republican Party (Terakkiperver Cumhuriyet Fırkası), lasted from 17 November 1924 to 5 June 1925, a mere seven months. The second opposition party, the Liberal Republican Party (Serbest Cumhuriyet Fırkası), was established on 12 August 1930 to be closed down on 17 November 1930, after a mere three months. The third opposition party, the Democrat Party (Demokrat Parti), was established much later, in 1946, to eventually rule the country from 1950 to 1960; it was ousted from power by the first military coup of the republic, with three of its leaders hanged in the process.
155. I differentiate the early republican use of religion in the 1920s and 1930s to institutionalize and legitimate secularism and other reforms from the later acknowledgment of Islam in the 1970s to the present as a viable political force.
156. Cavid 2000: 338; Bleda 1979: 154; Madanoğlu 1992: 284–85; Soydan 2007: 275; Tepeyran 1982: 46, 108–9; Çerkes Ethem 2000: 32; Reşit Paşa 2001: 107–8; Tansel 1973: vol. 3, 53, 69, 219–20; Atay 2004: 256–57; Mevlanzade 2000: 117–18; 1993: 160–62; Bardakçı 1975: 45; Karabekir 1991: 37, 57, 68–69, 82–83, 114, 117, 121, 146–49, 179–80; Mehmed Arif 1987: 17, 19, 23, 27; Derin 1995: 46; Ahmed İzzet 1993: 175.
157. Cavid 2000: 338.
158. Madanoğlu 1992: 284–85.
159. Soydan 2007: 275.
160. Tepeyran 1982: 46, 108–9.
161. Atay 2004: 256–57.
162. Derin 1995: 46; Ahmed İzzet 1993: 175.
163. Arıkoğlu 1961: 2.
164. Karabekir 1991: 24.
165. Mustafa Kemal 1991: 43.
166. Women were not included in this shift. Instead, the republican leaders served by example, attending public events, with women dressed in modern attire accompanying them.
167. Bahar 2003: 126–27; Haker 2004: 27, 32, 46; Doğrugüven 2003: 27–28; Şaul 1999: 27–31, 47–49; Derin 1995: 90; Ertuğrul 1989: 299–301; İğdemir 1976: 131; Scognamillo 1990: 110–11, 118, 121; Tör 1976: 80, 91, 94, 102; Va-Nu 1997: 137.
168. Derin 1995: 90.
169. Scognamillo 1990: 110–11, 118, 121.
170. Va-Nu 1997: 137.
171. Haker 2004: 32.
172. Şaul 1999: 27–31, 47–49.
173. Bahar 2003: 126–27.
174. Haker 2004: 27, 32, 46.
175. Berkes 1997: 158–59.
176. Süleyman Şefik 2004; Mevlanzade 1992, 1993, 1996, 2000; Sait Hurşid 1999: 49, 63, 77; Akkılıç 1994: 39, 43; Fani 1998: 44 n. 18; 60 n. 24, 118.

177. Ağaoğlu 1998: 194; Adıvar 2005: 158–59, 262–63, 270.
178. Kutay 1966: vol. 2, 280–89; see also Örgeevren 2002.
179. Tesal 1998: 74; Ağaoğlu 1998: 61, 65, 206; Aldan 1992: 61–63; Davudoğlu 1979: 169, 176.
180. Yiğit 2004: 170; Kılıç Altemur 2005: 82; Ayaşlı 1990: 82.
181. Sertel 2000: 121–22, 133; Ayaşlı 1990: 82; Berkem 1960: 144.
182. Tengirşenk 1967: 145; Kartal 1987: 9.
183. Ağaoğlu 1994: 58, 73, 188.
184. Binark 2004: 37.
185. Kazancıgil 1989: 11, 19.
186. Saatçıgil 1993: 28, 34–37, 51, 54, 58.
187. Soyer 2000: 137, 141; Saatçıgil 1993: 28, 58; Kılıç Altemur 2005: 61.
188. Bilgiç 1998: 41, 158, 190; Soyer 2000: 141; Kılıç Altemur 2005: 61; İmre 1976: 318–19, 337–39, 374–75, 382; Kazancıgil 1989: 53.
189. Kazancıgil 1989: 53.
190. Saatçıgil 1993: 93; Bilgiç 1998: 220; Öz 2003: 23.
191. Gerede 2002: 96; Ahmed İzzet 1993: 44; Velidedeoğlu 1977: vol. 1, 127, 135, 153–57; Kılıç Ali 1997: 16, 31; Selahattin Adil 1982: 345, 399, 401, 414; Sertel 1994: 110; Sazak 2007: 141; Kazancıgil 1989: 9, 21, 31; Orbay 2000: 214, 218, 220, 224; Aldan 1992: 16, 22, 24, 28, 35, 43–44, 49, 54, 60, 111, 137, 153–54, 201; Soyer 2000: 50–51; Dirik 1998: 122, 131; Oğuz 2000: 99, 248; Örgeevren 2002: 47, 50, 73, 100, 137, 139, 145, 151; Bleda 1979: 155–87; Tunalı 2005: 188–89; Başar 2007: vol. 2, 160–65.
192. Gerede 2002: 96.
193. Sertel 1994: 110.
194. Kazancıgil 1989: 9, 21, 31; Sazak 2007: 141.
195. Derin 1995: 86.
196. Tunalı 2005: 188–89.
197. Kazancıgil 1989: 9, 21, 31.
198. Başar 2007: vol. 2, 160–65.
199. Doğan 1964: 276.
200. Akgiray 2003: 184.
201. Kılıç Ali 1997: 16, 31; Selahattin Adil 1982: 345, 414; Velidedeoğlu 1977: vol. 1, 127, 135, 153–57; Ahmed İzzet 1993: 44.
202. Örgeevren 2002: 47, 50, 73, 100, 137, 139, 145, 151.
203. Bleda 1979: 155–87.
204. Aldan 1992: 16, 22, 24, 28, 35, 43–44, 49, 54, 60, 111, 137, 153–54, 201.
205. Orbay 2000: 214, 218, 220, 224.
206. Oğuz 2000: 99, 248; Erden 2003: 22; Soyer 2000: 50–51.
207. Selahattin Adil 1982: 399, 401.
208. Dirik 1998: 122, 131.
209. Memoirs of General Muhsin Batur reveal how enmeshed he was in politics as a military officer, an involvement he considered to be very natural.
210. Başgil (1990) criticized the state officials, arguing that "they had turned into cosmopolitan lords who looked down on the populace of this country as if they were colonial subjects."
211. Öz 2003.
212. Korle 1990.
213. Şaul 1999: 144–45.
214. Arseven 1993: 22, 40, 62–63, 65, 99, 101–2, 106, 108–9, 244, 305; Çerkezyan 2003: 27; Akgiray 2003: 184; Derin 1995: 41, 108; Sertel 2000: 110–11, 113; Yalman 1997: vol. 2, 271; Dikerdem 1989: 76, 162; Tör 1976: 66, 125, 136; Kılıç Altemur 2005: 128, 135; Başar 2007: vol. 2, 281; Burak 1961: 49; Şaul 1999: 144–45.
215. Arseven 1993: 99, 101–2, 106, 108–9.
216. Çerkezyan 2003: 27.
217. Derin 1995: 41, 108.
218. Akgiray 2003: 184.
219. Derin 1995: 41, 108; Sertel 2000: 110–11, 113.
220. Sertel 2000: 110–11, 113.

221. Arseven 1993: 22, 40, 244.
222. Yalman 1997: vol. 2, 271.
223. Tör 1976: 66, 125, 136.
224. Arseven 1993: 62–63, 65.
225. Kılıç Altemur 2005: 128, 135.
226. Arseven 1993Nayır 1965: 65, 99.
227. Kılıç Altemur 2005: 128.
228. Arseven 1993: 106, 108–9.
229. Başar 2007: vol. 2, 281.
230. Burak 1961: 49.
231. Dikerdem 1989: 76, 162.
232. Saul 1999: 144–45.
233. Tepeyran 1982: 19; Gerede 2002: 18, 20; Atay 2004: 148, 166; Tanpınar 1973: 187; Tunalı 2005: 77–79.
234. Paker 2000: 103; Cavid 2000: 147.
235. Adıvar 2005: 17–19; Apak 1988: 190.
236. Karay 1964: 97; Ahmed İzzet 1993: 17–18; Tonguç 1999: 355; Tepeyran 1982: 17.
237. Şahingiray 1997: 36, 121; Orbay 2000: 228; 1992: 564–67, 602.
238. Alongside the Turks, the Kurds and Arabs had also taken Armenian women and children into their households.
239. Şahingiray 1997: 36, 121; Yalman 1997: 564–67, 602; Orbay 2000: 228.
240. For Kars, Erdoğan 1998: 216–17, 257, 280, 310–12; for Adana, Kaygusuz 1955: 179–81, 200; Arıkoğlu 1961: 41, 120, 124; Özoğuz 1934: 22, 26–27, 44, 48, 73–75; for Maraş, Gerede 2002: 18, 20; for Antep, Eyüp Sabri 1978: 13, 20, 68, 86. See also Yalman 1997: 424; Tepeyran 1982: 45.
241. For Adana, Cebesoy 1998: 288–89; for Ankara, Bardakçı 1975: 61–63; for İzmir, Selahattin Adil 1982: 303; for Giresun, Nur 1991: I, 107–9, 133. See also Ünüvar 1997: 33, 37, 39–40, 48, 54, 61, 71, 79, 94, 108.
242. Orbay 2000: 243, 262; 1992: vol. 3, 211, 242, 272, 318–19; Tansel 1973: vol. 2, 36–37, 56, 62, 67, 82, 87, 95–97, 152; Kansu 1966: 18–19; Mustafa Kemal 1968: 126, 391, 415; Kılıç Ali 1955: 14, 18.
243. Kutay 1966 : vol. 2, 801–2, 812.
244. Ünüvar 1997: 39–40, 108.
245. For Adapazarı, Ahmed İzzet 1993: 110; for Ankara, Bardakçı 1975: 61–63; for Antep and Maraş, Kılıç Ali 2005: 103–5, 191, 116–17; for Kadirli, Haçin, and Kozan, Tufan 1998: 25, 40, 67–68, 70–74, 79–80, 83, 93, 95; for Zeytun, Selahattin Adil 1982: 329, 332–34, 338, 346, 372, 405; and for Kars, Erdoğan 1998: 216–17, 257, 280, 310–12.
246. Some non-Muslims at the imperial city, like Keresteciyan and translator David, actually helped the national forces. See, for instance, Dersimi 1997: 94; Ertürk 1957: 240–41; Beşe 2004: 58.
247. For İstanbul, Bölükbaşı 1993: 252–53; for Kayseri, Kansu 1966: 436, 492, 562; for Izmir, Haçeryan 2005: 41–42, 44–45, 48–52, 65–67, 70–71, 79–80, 95–96.
248. Atay 2004: 351.
249. Sevük 1937: 284–90.
250. Kırkyaşaryan 2005: 35 n. 7. See also Nur 1991: 67–70; 1992: vol. 1, 38–39, 73–74; vol. 2, 192–93, 205, 245, 259, 26; Borçbakan 2005: 252.
251. Nur 1991: vol. 1, 67–68; Yalçın 1976: 243; Atay 2004: 489–90. The exact terminology Atay employed is "*som bir Müslüman Türklük vatanı.*"
252. Tesal 1998: 103; Behmoaras 2005: 174, 186.
253. Şaul 1999: 27–28; Bahar 2003: 164–66; Çerkezyan 2003: 131.
254. Bahar 2003: 164–66; 171–81; Kant 2003: 172–78; Arseven 1993: 73; Başar 2007: vol. 1, 165, 169; Şaul 1999: 29–31, 47, 48 n. 25, 49, 81–82; Binark 2000: 49. See also İhmalyan 1989: 47; Güley 1990: 35, 44, 75–76; Çerkezyan 2003: 131, 202; Haker 2004: 16, 24, 34–35; Sağlar 1976: 210–11.
255. Atay 2004: 448; Ayaşlı 1990: 41, 52–53; Zobu 1977: 269–70, 277.
256. Oğuz 2000: 101–3, 363–64; Sağlar 1976: 210–11.

257. Şaul 1999: 51; Haker 2004: 33.
258. Doğrugüven 2003: 33, 204; Çerkezyan 2003: 131–4; Şaul 1999: 27–28. See also Haker 2004: 29; Bahar 2003: 164–66.
259. Esendal 2003: 105.
260. Şaul 1999: 29–31, 47, 48 n. 25, 49, 81–82; İhmalyan 1989: 47; Güley 1990: 35, 44, 75–76.
261. Haker 2004: 83–84, 88–91, 132–34, 141–44, 199, 220, 222–23.
262. Şaul 1999: 29–31, 81–82; Çerkezyan 2003: 131, 202.
263. Haker 2004: 16, 24, 34–35; Bahar 2003: 164–66.
264. Dirik 1998: 133–34.
265. Çerkezyan 2003: 131, 202; Haker 2004: 16, 24, 34–35.
266. Barutçu 1977: 368; Bardakçı 1945, 1991; Berkes 1997: 366; Bahar 2003: 94, 164–66.
267. Berkes 1997: 207; Oğuz 2000: 473–74; Alican 2000: 117, 121; Haker 2004: 83–84, 88–91, 132–34, 141–44, 199, 220, 222–23; İhmalyan 1989: 49.
268. Bahar 2003: 94, 164–66; Şaul 1999: 109–10, 114, 127–29.
269. Ökte 1950: 47–49, 77–78, 80, 120–24, 130.
270. Kant 2003: 189–93.
271. Şaul 1999: 109–10, 114, 127–29.
272. Kılıç Altemur 2005: 140; Oğuz 2000: 363–64, 469–70, 551; Haker 2004: 139. See also Erkin 1986: vol. 3, 31; Öngör 1987: 191–93.
273. The Turkish state explicitly settled the Aegean Islands containing Greek Rum populations with Muslims from the Black Sea region. Oğuz 2000: 551.
274. Natanyan's memoirs reveal that the Virgin Mary Church, the main church of Sivas, was dynamited and destroyed after the İnönü government (of the RPP) lost the elections, but before the Menderes government (of the DP) assumed power. The Sümerbank Inn was built in its place.
275. Şaul 1999: 112, 127–28.
276. Kılıç Altemur 2005: 140.
277. See, for instance, İmre 1976: 411.
278. Çerkezyan 2003: 203.
279. Denker 2005: 74.
280. Dersimi 1992: 99–100.
281. Karabekir 1991: 121, 179–80.
282. Bedirhan (1998) noted that the Kurdish rebellions during this period consisted of the 1920 Koçgiri rebellion, the 1925–27 Said Nursi and Sheikh Abdurrahman revolts, the 1927–30 Ağrı mountain rebellions, and the 1937–38 Dersim massacres. The final one occurred after the 1943 Mustafa Muğlalı incident in Özalp, Van, where the Turkish military commander shot thirty-three Kurds for engaging in smuggling across the border.
283. There was also a previous Kurdish rebellion in 1924 termed the Beytüşşebab rebellion. Serdi (1994: 103–9) stated that the Kurdish rebellions emerged in three clusters, from 1785 to 1882, 1905 to 1938, and 1943 to 1979.
284. Ağaoğlu 1998: 61, 65, 206.
285. Ibid., 206; Örgeevren 2002.
286. Anter 1999: 73–74.
287. Avar 1986: 37, 42–44, 100, 135, 196–99, 201, 255, 266, 287.
288. Karaveli 1999: 111–12.
289. Berkes 1997: 67.
290. Akkılıç 1994: 22–23.
291. Berkes 1997: 172–73.
292. Dikerdem 1989: 159.
293. Tepeyran 1982: 125–26.
294. Berkes 1997: 368; Bilgiç 1998: 21.
295. Çerkezyan 2003: 203; İhmalyan 1989: 5, 7. İhmalyan was imprisoned on trumped-up charges as well.
296. Va-Nu 1997: 72–74, 120–24, 129–32, 197; Sertel 1994: 212–13, 220–22.
297. Berkes 1997: 368.
298. Ibid.

299. Ibid., 72–74, 120–24, 129–32, 197.
300. Fethi 1999: 67, 122.
301. Dikerdem 1989: 159.
302. Kırcı 1998.
303. Biren 1993: 223–28.
304. Berkem 1960: 72–73; Nur 1991: 80–81.
305. Orbay 1992: vol. 2, 100, 102, 137; Bayar 1965: 55.
306. Kutay 1975: vol. 2, 796–97, 803, 808, 834, 894.
307. Ahmed İzzet 1993: 50.
308. Bayar 1965: 2114, 2132.
309. Biren 1993: 209, 223–28.
310. Yalman 1997: 402–3.
311. Ölçen 1994: 160–61; Arıkoğlu 1961: 64–71, 76, 78–81; Sazak 2007: 121–22, 131–37.
312. Yalçın 2002: 456; Bleda 1979: 115, 124; Cebesoy 1998: 42–43; Denker 2005: 35–37, 178, 365; 1992: 20, 131–32; Süleyman Nazif 1957: 105, 110.
313. Mahmud Celaleddin 1970: 172; Sertel 1968: 94–95; Binark 2000: 55.
314. Gerede 2002: 186–87; Çolak 1996: 16.
315. Tufan 1998: 16.
316. Tansel 1973: vol. 3, 8, 225–28, 238.
317. Orbay 2000: 276, 299. See also Karabekir 1991: 278, 299.
318. Çerkezyan 2003: 61–63; Akkılıç 1994: 219–20; Tansel 1973: vol. 3, 186, 229. See also Mehmed Arif 1987: 72 on İzmit; Tufan 1998: 19–21 on Kayseri; Sevük 1937: 278 and Özoğuz 1934: 27, 44, 91 on Adana; Akkılıç 1994: 228–30 on Haçin; Borçbakan 2005: 219 on Harput.
319. Gerede 2002: 56; Muhiddin 2003: 49, 56.
320. See, for instance, Kılıç Altemur 2005: 56.
321. Akıncı 1978: 2, 173, 278–79; Çetinkaya 1993: 10, 46, 67–68, 85; Tansel 1973: vol. 3, 152; Çarıklı 2005: 112–13; Selahattin Adil 1982: 300, 317; Altay 1998: 36–37; Kaygusuz 1955: 209; Atay 2004: 357; Bardakçı 1975: 123–24; Berkem 1960: 136–39; Haçeryan 2005: 78–79.
322. Nur 1991: 199–200.
323. Güvemli 1999: 52; Yalman 1997: 118–19.
324. Uçuk 1995: 327–29.
325. Zana 1995: 30–31.
326. Sazak 2007: 131; Tansel 1973: vol. 2, 150.
327. Atay 2004: 307; Kılıç Ali 1955: 107–10; Us 1966: 47, 51–53.
328. Mustafa Kemal 1998: 118–19. See also Berkem 1960: 161, 171–72; Çerkezyan 2003: 61–63.
329. Biren 1932: 372; Yüzbaşı Cemal 1996: 47; Karabekir 1991: 187; Çarıklı 2005: 96.
330. Another venue through which the national movement exercised violence was the independence courts established by the national assembly that had absolute power to try and execute without any legal recourse anyone opposing the struggle. See, for instance, Kılıç Ali 1997: 12–16, 31.
331. One significant reason for this ambiguity was the origin of republican leaders themselves in the national resistance committees, where they had executed violence with impunity. Barutçu 1977: 308.
332. Dikerdem 1989: 92.
333. Kılıç Altemur 2005: 100, 184; Barutçu 1977: 353; Orbay 2000: 169.
334. Kılıç Ali 2005: 305–8.
335. Ağaoğlu 1998: 185; Öz 2003: 143; Kılıç Ali 1955: 121; Orbay 2000: 169; Kılıç Altemur 2005: 31–33; Güley 1990: 431, 457–58.
336. Kılıç Altemur 2005: 100. See also Ağaoğlu 1998: 185.
337. Öz 2003: 143; Güley 1990: 431, 457–58.
338. Güley 1990: 457–58. See also Barutçu 1977: 353; Kılıç Ali 2005: 305–8; Va-Nu 1997: 150; Sertel 1994: 210; Kılıç Altemur 2005: 100; Öz 2003: 13–15, 143; Günyol 1990: 41–43.
339. Contemporaneous memoirs frequently commented on the case of the poet Nazım Hikmet (1902–63), perhaps the most famous person who was unjustly prosecuted and imprisoned.

He initially received a twenty-eight-year prison sentence for giving some books to military cadets who had asked for them in the first place, books that were at the time sold at all bookstores. After serving thirteen years, he was released, but both he and his friends were kept under constant surveillance. Upon learning that the state was fabricating new charges to imprison him again, he escaped to the Soviet Union in 1951, dying there in exile.

340. Aykan 2003: 43; Tükel 1953: 52. For the 1934 forced deportation, see Şaul 1999: 15–16; Kazancıgil 1989: 8–10. For the impact of World War II on Turkey, see Saatçıgil 1993: 13; Nadir Nadi 1964: 16–17; Behmoaras 2005: 195, 218–19, 286; and Madanoğlu 1992: 300–302. For the 1941 forced draft, see İhmalyan 1989: 52–53, 58–61, 67–69, 72–78; and Çerkezyan 2003: 113–16, 120–26. For the 1942 wealth tax, see Tükel 1952: 33 n. 1; Mardin 1988: 83, 170; Kant 2003: 174–75; Naci 1999: 39; Dirik 1998: 133–34; Derin 1995: 167; Berkes 1997: 243, 248, 269, 309, 352–54; Us 1966: 553–54; Barutçu 1977: 263, 304; Belli 1994: 130; Şaul 1999: 19–20, 91–93, 103–5; Yalman 1997: vol. 2, 375–76; and Uran 1959: 385–86. For the 1955 plunder, see Bahar 2003: 120, 184, 187; Belli 1994: 338, 365–66; Çerkezyan 2003: 189–95; Doğrugüven 2003: 241–43, 291; Kılıç Altemur 2005; Oğuz 2000: 463–65, 468–70; Scognamillo 1990: 26, 44; Sedes 2005: 17; Soyer 2000: 131–35; Terziyan 1995: 106–9; Va-Nu 1997: 197; and Yalman 1997: vol. 2, 324–26, 354. For the 1964 forced extradition, see Çerkezyan 2003: 195; Burak 1961: 157; and İhmalyan 1989: 97.
341. See, for instance, Aykan 2003: 43.
342. Kazancıgil 1989: 8–10; Şaul 1999: 15–16.
343. Tükel 1952: 52.
344. Madanoğlu 1992: 300–302; Nadir Nadi 1964: 16–17.
345. Behmoaras 2005: 195, 218–19, 286, Haker 2004: 45, 86–87, 140.
346. İhmalyan 1989: 52–53, 58–61, 67–69, 72–78.
347. Çerkezyan 2003: 113–16, 120–26.
348. Ibid., 189–95.
349. Berkes 1997: 243, 352–54; Us 1966: 553–54; Yalman 1997: vol. 2, 375–76.
350. Barutçu 1977: 263; Şaul 1999: 19, 105.
351. Barutçu 1977: 304; Uran 1959: 385–86; Kazancıgil 1989: 24–25.
352. Kant 2003: 174–75; İhmalyan 1989: 52–53, 72–78; Haker 2004: 45, 140.
353. Şaul 1999: 103–5; Tükel 1952: 33 n. 1; Fethi 1999: 39; Dirik 1998: 133–34; Bahar 2003: 120, 184, 187; Behmoaras 2005: 195, 218–19, 286; Belli 1994: 130.
354. Mardin 1988: 83, 170; Çerkezyan 2003: 189–95.
355. Soyer 2000: 131–35.
356. Çerkezyan 2003: 189–95; Terziyan 1995: 106–9.
357. Sedes 2005: 17; Yalman 1997: vol. 2, 324–26, 354.
358. Sedes 2005: 18; Soyer 2000: 131–35.
359. Bahar 2003: 120, 184, 187; Belli 1994: 338, 365–66; Çerkezyan 2003: 189–95; Doğrugüven 2003: 241–43, 291.
360. Behmoaras 2005: 218–19.
361. Taha Toros, who edited the memoirs of Ali Münif Yeğena (Yeğena 1996: 1), recounted that in the earlier version printed at the *Akşam* newspaper ın 1955, "because Ali Münif's name was mixed up with the Armenian deportation incident, some pertaining paragraphs from the memoir were taken out upon the suggestion of a military captain with a law degree."
362. As the Turks started traveling to the United Sates for their education or lived there as Turkish officials, they began to encounter the Armenian issue in their conversations. See, for instance, Sertel 1968: 94–95.
363. Berkes 1997: 56.
364. Binark's father, Ahmed Erner, who had been accused of Armenian massacre, was freed after being held in Malta; he then traveled to Buenos Aires in 1930 to start a business that was ultimately unsuccessful. Binark 2000: 73–76, 157.
365. Tör 1976: 4.
366. Erkin 1986: vol. 3, 31.
367. Öngör 1987: 191–3.
368. Ibid., 196–97, 203–5.
369. Erkin 1986: vol. 2, 87–88.

370. Belli 2000: 106–7.
371. Çerkezyan 2003: 195.
372. Ekdal 2003: 45–46.
373. Irmak 2003.
374. Bedirhan 1998; Zana 1995: 30–31; Anter 1999: 149–50; Avar 1986: 281–83; Kartal 1987; Örgeevren 2002: 16, 31, 37, 189, 196, 204, 225; Sağlar 1976: 228; Serdi 1994: 302–3, 325; Us 1966: 88, 91, 93.
375. Örgeevren 2002: 16, 225.
376. Kartal 1987: 12; Serdi 1994: 302–3, 325.
377. Us 1966: 88, 91.
378. Sağlar 1976: 228; Zana 1995: 30–31.
379. Avar 1986: 281–83.
380. Anter 1999: 149–50.
381. In her memoirs, their daughter Yıldız (1994: 212–13, 220–22) recounted the constant threat of violence and imprisonment her parents faced.
382. Soyer 2000: 145; Sedes 2005: 31; Kılıç Altemur 2005: 61, 105, 206, 210–18, 220, 229–30; Kazancıgil 1989: 4, 49, 52; Doğrugüven 2003: 359–60; Belli 1994: 365–66, 375; Başgil 1990: 17, 23, 39–48, 57, 90, 102–5; Erkanlı 1972: 12–22.
383. Soyer 2000: 145.
384. Kılıç Altemur 2005: 61, 230; Erkanlı 1972: 12–22.
385. Erkanlı 1972: 12–22.
386. Talat Aydemir and Fethi Gürcan, who led the second coup, were immediately hanged. Sedes 2005: 31; Belli 1994: 375.
387. Kazancıgil 1989: 4, 49, 52.
388. Doğrugüven 2003: 359–60.
389. Başgil 1990: 17, 23, 39–48, 57, 90, 102–5.
390. Öz's memoirs (2003: 143) also revealed the beatings and torture that took place in the Turkish prisons.
391. Doğrugüven 2003: 336, 358; Kılıç Altemur 2005: 40–43, 66, 116, 122, 124, 184; Ağaoğlu 1998: 67–68; Derin 1995: 103; Saatçıgil 1993: 21–23.
392. Derin 1995: 103; Kılıç Altemur 2005: 184; Ağaoğlu 1998: 67–68; Doğrugüven 2003: 336, 358; Orbay 2000: 169.
393. Kılıç Altemur 2005: 44, 184; Derin 1995: 103, 178–79; Başar 2007: vol. 2, 211.
394. Saatçıgil 1993: 21–23.
395. See, for instance, Kalaç 1960: 156; Ağaoğlu 1998: 90.
396. These two were also joined by the CUP and SO member and Diyarbekir governor Mehmed Reşid Şahingiray, a physician, who escaped from prison only to commit suicide upon realizing that he was about to be caught by the security forces.
397. Mevlanzade 2000: 117–18; 1993: 160–62; Kansu 1966: 419–20; Simavi 1965: 454–57; Denker 1992: 112–14.
398. Mevlanzade 2000: 117–18.
399. Simavi 1965: 454–57.
400. Kansu 1966: 419–20.
401. Denker 1992: 112–14.
402. Military tribunals were also established in İzmir, Bursa, Tekirdağ, Edirne, Samsun, and Antep, but the memoirs almost exclusively cover and comment on the military tribunal at the imperial capital.
403. Bayar 1965: 1673–74; Ahmed İzzet 1993: 15–16, 26, 31; Ertürk 1957: 220–21, 239–40; Kutay 1975: vol. 1, 334 n. 4; Tanpınar 1973: 328; Tepeyran 1982: 108–10, 125–26.
404. Bayar 1965: 1673–74.
405. Kutay 1975: vol. 1, 334 n. 4.
406. Tanpınar 1973: 328.
407. Ertürk 1957: 220–21.
408. Ahmed İzzet 1993: 15–16, 26, 31.
409. Tepeyran 1982: 108–10.
410. Kalaç 1960: 137.

411. Biren 1993: 133, 137, 153–54, 165–66; Ahmed İzzet 1993: 56–57, 65–66, 211–12; Nesimi 1977: 42–43; Cavid 2000: 75–77, 129, 138–39; Kalaç 1960: 137; Kansu 1966: 101.
412. Biren 1993: 137; Kansu 1966: 101.
413. Ahmed İzzet 1993: 55–56.
414. Nesimi 1977: 42–43.
415. Cavid 2000: 129.
416. See Biren 1993: 153–54 for the full list.
417. Cavid 2000: 129; Üçok 2002: 51–53.
418. Cavid 2000: 75.
419. Kutay 1975: vol. 2, 812; Ahmed İzzet 1993: 54; Atay 2004: 176–77; Kansu 1966: 101, 583–84; Süleyman Nazif 1978: 76, 100, 102, 108, 118; Sertel 1968: 66; Ertürk 1957: 306; Bayar 1965: 1520; Çalıka 1992: 24, 67.
420. Bayar 1965: 1520; Ahmed İzzet 1993: 54.
421. Sertel 1968: 66; Ertürk 1957: 306.
422. Çalıka 1992: 24, 67.
423. Kansu (1966: 583–84) argued that the tribunal further delegitmated itself by sentencing in absentia to death by hanging the leaders of the independence struggle, specifically Mustafa Kemal and Kara Vasıf, Ali Fuat Cebesoy, Alfred Rüstem, Adnan Adıvar, and Halide Edip.
424. Süleyman Nazif 1978: 108.
425. Atay 2004: 176–77.
426. Tengirşenk 1967: 190; Menteşe 1986: 237; Kut 1972: 271–72; Bayar 1965: 1468–72, 1525–30; Ertürk 1957: 370–71; Uran 1959: 115–17; Yiğit 2004: 91; Çarıklı 2005: 47–48; Günyol 1990: 35–37; Tufan 1998: 18, 24; Ergeneli 1993: 107.
427. Kut 1972: 271–72; Bayar 1965: 1468–72, 1525–30; Ertürk 1957: 370–71.
428. Uran 1959: 115–17; Tengirşenk 1967: 190; Menteşe 1986: 237; Ergeneli 1993: 107; Tufan 1998: 18, 24.
429. Çarıklı 2005: 47–48; Günyol 1990: 35–37.
430. Bayar 1965: 1468–72, 1525–30. See also Ertürk 1957: 370–71.
431. Uran 1959: 115–17; Tengirşenk 1967: 190; Ergeneli 1993: 107; Tufan 1998: 18, 24; Menteşe 1986: 237; Yiğit 2004: 91.
432. Çarıklı 2005: 47–48; Günyol 1990: 35–37.
433. Kansu 1966: 566; Binark 2000: 54; Yiğit 2004: 94–95; Okyar 1980: 278, 283–85; Yeğena 1996: 78–79, 96–100, 107; Gökalp 1965: 19; Yalçın 2001: 166; 1976: 206; Yalman 1997: 519, 524, 548, 556, 594, 618, 651, 664–65, 670; Bleda 1979: 127–28, 134–43; Borçbakan 2005: 209; and Eyüp Sabri1978: 21, 27–44, 65–67.
434. They only mention the CUP Diyarbekir deputies Feyzi (Pirinççioğlu) and Zülfi (Tiğrel), who had initially been exiled to Egypt in January 1919 to be then sent on to Malta on 23 July 1919. See Akça 2007: 25. For an extensive discussion of the Malta exiles, see Şimşir 1985.
435. Kansu 1966: 566.
436. Yiğit 2004: 94–95.
437. Binark 2000: 54.
438. Okyar 1980: 278, 283–85.
439. Yalman (1997: 519). Bleda (1979: 134–43) provided the only clue to who the real perpetrators were upon recounting how some of the exiled successfully escaped from the island. At some point, the British wanted to negotiate the release of twenty Malta exiles in exchange for the British war prisoners in the empire. Yet their one condition was that those exchanged would not be chosen from among the ones involved in the Armenian deportations. Bleda noted that "the ones among us who had been involved in the Armenian deportations amounted to 16 people, including commanders and governors among them. We were especially worried about Ali İhsan Sabis Pasha as his condition was more dangerous than the others." Yalman provided the names of some of those in this group, namely, "Cevdet Bey, Kırzade Mustafa Bey of Trabzon, Yunus Nadi Bey, Ali İhsan Paşa, Kemal Bey, Yakup Şevki Pasha, and many governors." The exiles bribed the local fishermen to take these sixteen to Italy by boat. The remaining Malta exiles were eventually freed in exchange for British prisoners without facing a court of justice.
440. Yalçın 2001: 166; 1976: 206; Yalman 1997: 618.

441. Yeğena 1996: 78–79, 96–100, 107.
442. Gökalp 1965: 19.
443. Yeğena 1996: 107; Borçbakan 2005: 209.
444. Eyüp Sabri(1978: 21, 27–44, 65–67) provided the only information on those local perpetrators in the provinces in Antep who were exiled to Egypt.
445. Berkem 1960: 42–43, 48–60; Sertel 1968: 71, 73; Tanpınar 1973: 300; Okyar 1980: 280; Menteşe 1986: 238; Bayar 1965: 1523; Binark 2000: 52; Çolak 1996: 21–23; Ertürk 1957: 29, 298–301; Üçok 2002: 51–53; Şahingiray 1997: 31–41, 80–81, 131–36, 146, 152, 155–58; Sabis 1992: vol. 4, 254, 257, 284, 325; Ertürk 1957: 308–10, 327.
446. Berkem 1960: 42–43, 48–60.
447. Sertel 1968: 71, 73.
448. Berkem 1960: 42–43, 48–60; Sertel 1968: 71, 73; Tanpınar 1973: 300; Okyar 1980: 280; Menteşe 1986: 238; Bayar 1965: 1523; Binark 2000: 52; Biren 1993: 195; Çolak 1996: 21–23; Ertürk 1957: 29, 298–301; Üçok 2002: 51–53; Şahingiray 1997: 31–41, 80–81, 131–36, 146, 152, 155–58; Sabis 1992: vol. 4, 254, 257, 284, 325; Ertürk 1957: 308–10, 327.
449. Okyar 1980: 280.
450. Atay 2004: 256–57.
451. Çolak 1996: 21–23.
452. Üçok 2002: 51–53.
453. Ertürk 1957: 29.
454. Menteşe 1986: 238.
455. Binark 2000: 52; Ertürk 1957: 298–301.
456. Tanpınar 1973: 300; Bayar 1965: 1523.
457. Süleyman Nazif 1957: 105, 110; Şahingiray 1997: 31–41, 80–81, 131–36, 146, 152, 155–58.
458. Süleyman Nazif 1957: 105, 110.
459. The exact sentence in Turkish is "*Hiçbir din, hiçbir mezheb ve mesleğin kabul etmeyeceği şenaati Reşid Bey gibi kimselerin yüzünden icra etmekle alem-i medeniyet bize 'mazlumların katili' nazarıyla bakıyor ve bu leke ecdadımızın kabrinden çocuklarımızın beşiğine kadar bergüzar kalacak.*"
460. The exact Turkish wording is "*Ermeni meselesinde benim ne kadar vazife-i vataniyemi ifa etdiğim meydanda iken yüzbinlerce lira çaldı, yedi gibi hezeyanlarla namusuma dokundular.*"
461. The statement in Turkish is "*Ben her zaman vazifemi telakki etdiğim emre imtisalen ifa etdiğime eminim.... Eğer bu milllete isnad olunan cürümleri yalnız benim naşımın imhası izale edecekse, şüphe etmeyiniz bir dakika bile tereddüd etmem ve intihar etmekden bir lahza cekinmem ve titremem!*"
462. Sabis 1992: vol. 4, 254, 257, 284, 325; Berkem 1960: 42–43, 48–60; Ertürk 1957: 29, 298–301.
463. Akça 2007: 46, 54, 57, 91, 93.
464. Sabis 1992: vol. 4, 325.
465. Ertürk's remarks (1957: 29, 298–301) on Nusret Bey capture the emerging nationalist rhetoric.
466. Berkem 1960: 42–43, 48–60.
467. Akça 2007; Akalın 1992.
468. Berkem 1960: 42–43, 48–60.
469. Günsav 1994: 17; Gerede 2002: 217; Atay 2004: 237, 256–57; Çalıka 1992: 15, 19, 21, 24–27; Erdoğan 1998: 258; Kalaç 1960: 138–43, 159, 165; Kansu 1966: 15–17; Sazak 2007: 100–105, 115–20; Uçuk 1995: 311–12; Arıkoğlu 1961: 151; Bayar 1965: 1648; Çolak 1996: 21–23.
470. The nine memoir writers who escaped to Ankara to avoid arrest were Hüsrev Gerede, İbrahim Çolak, Fahrettin Erdoğan, Eşref Çalıka, Falih Rıfkı Atay, Ahmed Hilmi Kalaç, Emin Sazak, Celal Bayar, and Mazhar Müfit Kansu. The other eight perpetrators mentioned in the memoirs are the former gendarmerie regiment commander Colonel Avni Bey, accused of the Adana deportation; General Halil Kut; Küçük Talat (Muşkara); Palu district governor Kadri; Siverek deputy İbrahim Vehbi Bey; Ebuhindili Cafer Bey of Erzurum; physician Fuat Sabit Bey, who had massacred the Armenians at the Kemah Pass; and the Kayseri district governor Zekai Bey.

471. Atay 2004: 237, 256–57.
472. Gerede 2002: 217.
473. Çolak 1996: 21–23.
474. Erdoğan 1998: 258.
475. Kansu 1966: 15–17.
476. Çalıka 1992: 15, 19, 21, 24–27.
477. Atay 2004: 237.
478. Kalaç 1960: 138–43, 159, 165.
479. Sazak 2007: 100–105, 115–20.
480. Uçuk 1995: 311–12.
481. Bayar 1965: 1648.
482. Çalıka 1992: 15, 19, 21, 24–27; Arıkoğlu 1961: 151.
483. Mustafa Kemal assumed the leadership of the independence struggle and also kept the CUP leaders away from Anatolia, thereby further distancing himself from the CUP. He did so to prevent the Allied forces from invading Anatolia. For further discussion, see Atay 2004: 374–75; Kut 1972: 281; Karay 1996: 8–10, 12.
484. Karabekir 1982: 19–20.
485. Atay 1999: 48.
486. Ahmed İzzet 1993: 59–60; Us 1966: 11, 30–31, 47; Oğuz 2000: 34–35; Mustafa Kemal 1998: 190, 202; Atay 2004: 172, 372–35, 400, 442–43, 481; Yalman 1997: 423; 1997: vol. 2, 89–90; Orbay 1965: 29, 31, 33; 1992: vol. 3, 69, 77, 187, 211, 293; Kut 1972: 259–61, 278–79, 281, 290–91, 305; Karaman 2002: 24, 27, 30, 32, 93; Yalçın 2002: 81, 95, 116–17, 136–37; Tükel 1953: 15; Kutay 1966: vol. 5, 152; Kılıç Ali 1997: 34; Denker 2005: i–iii, 27–28, 184; Ertürk 1957: 204, 307; Soydan 2007: 414; Karay 1996: 8–10, 12; Reşit Paşa 2001: 27–28; Rey 1945: 256, 258, 284; Kaygusuz 1955: 75, 143; Oker 2004: 34; İz 1990: 98; Soyer 2000: 30–31; Ağaoğlu 1998: 117.
487. Orbay 1965: 33; 1992: vol. 3, 77.
488. Denker 2005: 184; Kut 1972: 305.
489. Oğuz 2000: 34–35; Us 1966: 30–31.
490. See Borak's account in Mustafa Kemal's memoirs (1998: 190–202) for a more detailed account of the top CUP leaders' intentions, revealing that although they might have agreed upon Mustafa Kemal in the short term, their long-term intent was to eventually replace him to assume power themselves. See also Denker 2005: 184; Karaman 2002: 93; Kılıç Ali 1997: 34.
491. Ahmed İzzet 1993: 59–60.
492. Orbay (1965: 29–33; 1992: vol. 3, 69–77) stated that during the armistice period, those Unionists who had not been arrested kept meeting at the imperial capital, and Kazım Karabekir was the first one to instruct all military commanders to escape to Anatolia as soon as possible. Orbay explicitly noted that Karabekir and Mustafa Kemal then alighted in Anatolia to start the struggle "with the money financed by the CUP." The names of those accompanying Mustafa Kemal to Samsun, namely, Topçuoğlu Nazmi, İbrahim Süreyya, Osman Tufan, Çerkes Reşid, Çerkes Ethem, and Bekir Sami, indicate that they were not only former CUP members but also members of the Special Organization.
493. Rıza Tevfik (Bölükbaşı 1993: 51–52) noted that "even though the top [CUP] leaders had escaped, the organizations as well as the followers were in place in perfect order, holding the entire security organization in their hands except the police chief [himself]."
494. Başar (2007: vol. 1, 107–8, 167) stated that "even though the Unionist leaders had escaped after our defeat at the [World] war, Unionism had not died out"; those like "Kara Kemal and Kara Vasıf started to organize, overtaking existing national resistance units, and then meeting with Mustafa Kemal in İzmit as the sole representatives of the Turkish resistance."
495. Atay 2004: 176–77, 230, 375.
496. Reşit Paşa 2001: 27–28; Us 1966: 47; Rey 1945: 256–58, 284.
497. See, for instance, Yalçın 2002: 81, 95, 116–17, 136–37.
498. Karaman 2002: 24, 27, 30, 32, 93; Ertürk 1957: 204, 307; Yalçın 2002: 81, 95, 116–17, 136–37; Tükel 1952: 15.
499. Yalçın 2002: 95; Kutay 1966: vol. 5, 152.

500. Denker 2005: i–iii, 27–28, 184.
501. The former CUP members at the national assembly also believed for a while that they had enough power to contain the course of the struggle. See Karaman 2002: 24, 27, 30, 32; Yalman 1997: 423; 1970: vol. 2, 89–90.
502. Atay 2004: 400.
503. Many former CUP members defended the CUP. See Kaygusuz 1955: 75, 143; Oker 2004: 34; Atay 2004: 236; Soydan 2007: 414.
504. The CUP's attempts to wrest power away from Mustafa Kemal were best summarized by İz 1990: 98.
505. Ağaoğlu 1998: 117.
506. Nutku 1977: 44; Şaul 1999: 123.
507. Atay 2004: 176–77, 230, 375; Beyatlı 1975: 99–100; Nadir Nadi 1964: 48, 54, 57; Menteşe 1986: 239; Gerede 2002: 206; Yalçın 1943: 6; Kalaç 1960: 145; Haçeryan 2005: 82; Yalman 1997: 685–87; Başar 2007: vol. 1, 107–8, 167; Bölükbaşı 1993: 51–52; Bayar 1965: 2113–14, 2132; 1967: 1452; Bleda 1979: 192; Bozok 1985: 31; Kutay 1975: 130–32; 1967: vol. 5, 166–67; Ökte 1950: 59–60, 96–99, 101, 152; Duru 1957: 28–29; Resneli Niyazi 1975: 134, 150; Selahattin Adil 1982: 170–71.
508. Atay 2004: 176–77, 230, 375; Nadir Nadi 1964: 48, 54, 57.
509. Menteşe (1986: 239) argued that "there are very few Turks in Anatolia who are not somewhat connected to the [Armenian] deportation business." What upset Menteşe was not that these should be punished for their crimes, but that "they would take to the mountains to avoid punishment, thereby failing to protect the country."
510. Kalaç (1960: 145) remarked that the locally prominent merchants and the Unionists wanted by the military tribunal at the imperial capital put away their differences and "secretly decided to present a united front and to not inform on one another. After this decision, those wanted by the military tribunal saved themselves by either going into hiding or escaping somewhere else." He then remarked that "closing down the local CUP clubs did not turn out to be anything more than saving appearances." In Kayseri, even though the CUP club building had been shut down and its door sealed, its furnishings and documents were moved elsewhere through the efforts of Gözübüyük Sabit Bey, a radical Unionist. The CUP responsible secretary Cemil Bey, who had hidden somewhere, was kept safe.
511. Gerede (2002: 206) commented on how these perpetrators were actually pardoned with the advent of the independence struggle: "The month of November 1920 is a significant period… [in our] national history. In order to escape legal investigation, former convicts, murderers, and deporters (those who had engaged in bad deeds such as plunder, murder, and rape against the civilian caravans of Armenians who had rebelled behind our army during World War I and were being deported to Syria and Iraq by the CUP government) had withdrawn to the mountains with their armaments. These had [then] helped the national struggle, wanting [in return] to be honored with amnesty." Gerede then remarked that "one could not conduct business for a [national] holy cause with such men, and needed an organized army and soldiers with discipline and national conscience instead."
512. Beyatlı (1975: 99–100) commented on the character of these escapees, noting that "[during the republican era], the most forgotten CUP guerrilla fighters reemerged, turning into heroes applauded by the nation." Yalçın (1943: 6) concurred, pointing out that it was "easy to detain, imprison, deport, or even hang people in İstanbul, but in Anatolia… the mountains belonged to whoever grabbed his rifle and found a shrub (to hide in)." As a consequence, Yalçın stated he was not aware of "the existence of a single Unionist who then opposed the independence movement of Anatolia. Whatever had been left of the CUP after the [Great] war rushed to obey the orders of their national leader, sacrificing themselves as the pure children of the fatherland."
513. Bleda (1979: 135) recounted that Mustafa Kemal invited him to public service in 1935, asking him to run for a deputy position from Sivas. "For you, I was thinking Sivas because there is a post open there; should I have a telegram sent to Sivas right away?" Mustafa Kemal queried. He then made Bleda write a note stating, "I was the CUP general secretary and did not behave improperly in serving my country. This time, acting on Mustafa Kemal's trust in me,

I declare my candidacy for the deputyship of Sivas. I would like the necessary procedures to be undertaken." Bleda did indeed become the Sivas deputy.

514. Bozok (1985: 31) remarked that Mahmut Soydan, one of the two CUP assassins of Şemsi Pasha, later served, upon Bozok's intervention, as Mustafa Kemal's adjutant. Soydan then became the Siirt deputy until his death.
515. Duru (1957: 28–29) and Resneli Niyazi (1975: 134, 150) both noted that the other CUP assassin, Atıf Kamçılı, also went unpunished; he first became the director of the Ottoman State Tobacco Monopoly in Çankırı and then the Çanakkale deputy to the national assembly. Selahattin Adil Pasha (1982: 170–71) remarked that Kamçılı was then buried at the Hill of Eternal Freedom (Hürriyet-i EbediyeTepesi) as a hero of the Turkish republic.
516. Ahmed Rıfat Çalıka, a leading CUP member sought for his role in the deportations of the Kayseri Armenians, served at the Turkish national assembly from 1920 to 1923, also becoming the minister of justice from 1922 to 1923.
517. Kutay discussed Mustafa Abdülhalik Renda, arrested in relation to the Armenian deportations and massacres while serving as the governor of Bitlis and Aleppo. Upon his return from Malta, Renda was elected the Çorum deputy in 1924, then served as the minister of finance, defense and public works; in 1935, he became the president of the national assembly, and later, again, the minister of defense and state minister. Kutay also discussed the later successful republican careers of the Malta exiles; Hüseyin Rauf Bey (Orbay) and Ali Fethi Bey (Okyar) served as prime ministers, and Şükrü Kaya, Sabri Toprak and Zekai Apaydın became ministers. "The Malta exiles never wanted to remember their days there, and therefore their memories remained a mystery," he concluded.
518. Gerede 2002: 150; Kalaç 1960; Orbay 2000: 238–39; 1992: vol. 3, 253–54.
519. Ökte 1950: 59–60, 96–99, 101, 152.
520. Kılıç Ali 2005: 52, 96–97, 127; Kılıç Altemur 2005: 19, 150; Ertürk 1957: 200–201; Mevlanzade 2000: 163; Çerkezyan 2003: 196; Çolak 1996: 31–33, 38; Nesimi 1977: 39; Oğuz 2000: 49–50, 54, 92–93, 100; Kuşçubaşı 1999: 225; Balkan 1998: 49–55, 112–13, 133, 169; Yalçın 2005: 203–4; 1943: 51; Esendal 2003: 172–73; Duru 1957: 3–4; Erden 2003: 225; Ergeneli 1993: 107; Gerede 2002: 150; Hüseyin Avni 1999: 38 nn. 50, 51; Kalaç 1960; Orbay 2000: 238–39; 1992, III: 253–54; Tomruk 2000; Şahingiray 1997: 120 nn. 50–51, 121 n. 52, and 123 nn. 57 and 58.
521. Ertürk 1957: 200–201; Mevlanzade 2000: 163.
522. Nesimi 1977: 39.
523. Çolak 1996: 31–33, 38; Oğuz 2000: 100.
524. Kuşçubaşı 1999: 225.
525. Oğuz 2000: 49–50.
526. Esendal 2003: 172–73.
527. Kılıç Ali 2005: 52, 96–97, 127.
528. Erden 2003: 225; Oğuz 2000: 49–50, 54, 92–93, 100.
529. The best connection between the SO and the republic is illustrated by SO member Fuat Balkan's interaction with the former CUP and SO member, prominent republican prime minister, and second president of Turkey, İsmet İnönü. Balkan 1998: 49–55, 112–13, 133, 169. See also Kılıç Ali 2005: 52, 96–97, 127; Kılıç Altemur 2005: 19, 150; Çerkezyan 2003: 196.
530. Atay 2004: 176–77, 230, 375.
531. Haçeryan 2005: 82.
532. Yalçın 2005: 203–4; 1943: 51.
533. Şahingiray 1997: 120 n. 50, 51, 121 n. 52, 123 n. 57, 58.
534. Yalçın 2004: 268.
535. Kut 1972: 134; Selçuk 1993: 124.
536. *Takvimi Vekayi*, no. 2105.
537. *Takvimi Vekayi*, no. 3540.
538. Avcıoğlu 1974: 469.
539. See series 21, file M, no. 249.
540. Series 17, file H, nos. 571, 572.

Chapter 4

1. I should note that at other ensuing local conferences on the Armenian issue held by much less prominent universities in Turkey, the state often did not allow the host university to hold the conference unless it also invited these "official" historians advocating the Turkish state view. As a consequence, these universities ended up holding conferences where the faculty did not have the freedom to decide who to invite and why, turning in the process into a mouthpiece of the official denialist narrative. The same state officials also attempted to break their way into the workshops we organized as well. At the many WATS workshops we organized, we constantly received the applications of "official" historians who wanted to give papers, or the requests of "official" observers and/or Turkish consuls to participate in the workshop proceedings. We successfully resisted such efforts through constant vigilance; the most significant decision we took during the process was to hold the workshop closed to the public to prevent unwanted "official" participation. We did eventually establish one public session that we held at the beginning or end of the workshop, informing those who wanted to attend as to what we intended to do and why. Our aim was to hold an academic gathering devoid of any politics, where the attending scholars freely shared ideas as they saw fit.
2. Kerinçsiz had done so because the presidents of these two universities had been publicly visible from May to September 2005, defending the necessity to hold such an academic gathering. The Bilgi University president had not been with them because the university was in the process of electing a new president.
3. These were "imaginary" in that some businessmen obtained export permits from the state, thereby accessing foreign currency, but then kept this currency for their own use by establishing dummy corporations.
4. A program for transitioning into a strong economy was put into place only in 2001, leading to economic growth through the rest of the twenty-first century.
5. Sedes 2005: 37, 65, 67, 83, 110–11, 122–23, 141; Kazancıgil 1989: 65; Soyer 2000: 171, 266.
6. This trend in favor of politics at the expense of the economy has started to change only in the last decade as an increasing number of businesspeople have begun to pen their memoirs. These need to be further analyzed in yet another study.
7. Sedes 2005: 37.
8. Soyer 2000: 171, 266.
9. Kazancıgil 1989: 65.
10. The newspapers *Günaydın* and *Türkiye* were closed down in 1982, and *Cumhuriyet, Milli Gazete, Tercüman, Milliyet,* as well as the journal *Nokta* were closed in 1983. This was followed by the closure in 1988 of the journal *2000e Doğru* that printed the report of the National Intelligence Organization. In 1990, a newspaper was likewise shut down for printing an interview that opposed mandatory military service in Turkey, an action that revealed the strong influence of the military in such prohibitions.
11. For instance, the works of Server Tanilli, Henry Miller, and Ahmet Altan were banned in 1988.
12. Sedes 2005: 138, 151, 158.
13. Comparing Turkey's rankings in education and culture, Sedes (2005: 161) noted that "while per capita education spending was $2303 in Sweden, $1246 in France, $1125 in Germany, $446 in Portugal, $258 in Hungary it was only $69 in Turkey. This was the case even though 60% of Turkey's population was below 30 years, with 17 million between 15 and 25.... In reaching the European level of prosperity, Slovenia and Malta were at 69%, Czech republic 62%, Hungary 53%, Slovakia 47%, Poland 41%, Estonia 40%, Lithuania 39%, Letonia 35%; as to Romania, Bulgaria, and Turkey, all three were around 25%."
14. Sedes (2005: 161): "Europe's conception of 'minorities' has evolved through the 2000s and is very different from our conception.... Spain was silently forced to become more tolerant of its Protestants before getting admitted to the EC.... Had Greece applied to the EC today, it may not have been admitted, given its stand in relation to the Turkish minority, Muslims, and Catholics."
15. Soyer 2000: 253.
16. Within military circles, this coup was regarded with disdain because it was presumably carried out by second-tier officers left behind at the capital when the first-tier officers were in

the southeast fighting the Kurds. This coup also altered military priorities, with the threat of Islamic revivalism replacing Kurdish nationalism as the primary threat.

17. Turgut Özal's rightist Main Fatherland Party (Anavatan Partisi) shared votes with Erdal İnönü's Social Democratic Party (Sosyal Demokrat Partisi). A decade later, in 1992, the formerly shut-down political parties were allowed to reopen.
18. Also significant during this time was the 1994 establishment of the New Democracy Movement (Yeni Demokrasi Hareketi) under the leadership of businessman Cem Boyner. Many of my friends and I attended the initial meetings with great excitement. As the economically and socially liberal movement turned into a political party, however, it could not garner grass-roots support. The constant oppression of party members and especially party donors by the military and other state-supported parties led to its quick demise in 1997. Had this party been allowed to survive, it probably could have balanced the JDP's meteoric rise.
19. In addition to the ban of left-wing Workers Party of Turkey (Türkiye İşçi Partisi) and the United Communist Party of Turkey (Türkiye Birleşik Komünist Partisi), the religious National Order Party (Milli Nizam Partisi) was also banned in 1971, the Welfare Party (Refah Partisi) in 1998, and the Virtue Party (Fazilet Partisi) in 2001. Also banned were the Kurdish People's Labor Party (Halkın Emek Partisi) in 1993, the Democracy Party (Demokrasi Partisi) in 1994, the People's Democracy Party (Halkın Demokrasi Partisi) in 2003, and the Democratic Society Party (Demokratik Toplum Partisi) in 2009.
20. The 1990s witnessed the continuation of the skirmishes with Greece as indicated by the 1994 and 1996 Kardak island crisis, on an unpopulated insignificant small island that nevertheless became a point of contention in relation to the sea borders of the two countries. One of the 1995 EU conditions was for Turkey to pursue a peaceful solution to the Kurdish conflict, a condition that gradually transformed the country's outlook on the issue, thereby undercutting the influence of the Turkish military that benefited the most from the continuation of repression and violence. The kidnapping of a Turkish seaboat by Chechen rebels from Russia demonstrated how quickly Turkey was impacted by conflicts in neighboring countries. Also significant during this period was the signing of a mutual defense treaty with Israel as a consequence of which the two countries started close collaboration in the region. The attack on the World Trade Center in New York on 11 September 2001 once again polarized the relationships in the region. In 2003, the Turkish national assembly rejected the US notice to employ its military bases in Turkey to attack Iraq from the north, leading to a chill in their relations. Such a stand also demonstrated that Turkey had begun to make its own foreign policy decisions. Yet the ensuing terrorism also impacted Turkey as Al-Qaida carried out an attack in İstanbul in August 2004. Perhaps the most significant development during the first decade of the 2000s was the final negotiation of Turkey with the EU for future membership, a development that brought with it the democratization of the country as the legal system was liberalized and the control of both the state and the military on society reduced.
21. In the speech Barack Obama delivered at the Turkish national assembly, he first noted the significance of Turkey as a "critical ally," then lauded Mustafa Kemal and the republic he had founded on democratic principles. After articulating Turkey's contribution to Western wars as well as its participation in G-20 meetings as the eighteenth largest economy in the world, President Obama emphasized that the United States supported Turkey's bid to join the EU. It was in this context that Obama stressed that Turkey had to tackle its problems democratically, especially in "dealing with the past." Stating that the United States itself was still working on these issues, he lauded the "historic and courageous steps taken by the Turkish and Armenian leaders" toward a peaceful coexistence. He concluded by emphasizing Turkey's participation in containing terrorism. The speech led many, including Khatchig Mouradian in the *Armenian Weekly* on 8 April 2009 and Markar Esayan in *Taraf* on 6 April 2009, to praise President Obama for moving the political emphasis to human rights issues, away from the national security concerns that had for so long determined Turkey's foreign policy.
22. The signs of liberalization within the Turkish military became evident in 2008 with the appointment of İlker Başbuğ as the general chief of staff. Interested in academic research in general and social science research in particular, Başbuğ seemed more astute in analyzing and assessing the recent political, economic, and social developments in Turkey. As a consequence, he led the liberalization of Turkey by promoting peaceful negotiations with the Kurds and by questioning, for the first time, the dominant Turkish nationalism by redefining

Turkish national identity. In a speech delivered to the War Academies on 14 April 2009, he argued that Turkish identity ought to be defined not ethnically but instead spatially, as Mustafa Kemal Atatürk had once done, considering all citizens living within the geographical boundaries of Turkey as Turks. For the first time, Kurds were symbolically included in the definition of Turkish citizens; he also indirectly alluded to the PKK terrorists as children of the fatherland. Yet, he was still adamant about preserving the unitary political system that did not give political rights to the Kurds. Başbuğ nevertheless reiterated the danger of antisecular activities. For the full texts of Başbuğ's speeches, see http://www.tsk.tr/.

23. Sedes 2005: 37, 65, 67, 83, 110–11, 122–23, 141.
24. Bilgiç 1998: 281; Soyer 2000: 261–62.
25. Baytok 2005: 339.
26. TESEV, "Cognitions, Mental Frameworks and Institutions: The Judiciary," November 2007. For the full report, see http://www.tesev.org.tr/UD_OBJS/PDF/DEMP/YargidaAlgiveZihniyetKaliplariRaporu.pdf.
27. See http://www.sabah.com.tr/2008/09/06/haber,FCC6A6EF99DA49AAB3A00CF2037BF215.html.
28. Akgiray 2003: 221.
29. See Ercan Yavuz, *Today's Zaman*, 25 August 2007.
30. The legal grounds for the intervention were the JDP attempts to lift the headscarf ban that prevented covered female students from attending schools, a civic right that was thus taken away from them.
31. Having been a university student in Turkey during this time, I still remember the struggles of various political groups, ranging from the Maoists and Trotskyites all the way to social democrats, apportioning the public spaces at the university I attended: who put up which posters where became a big point of contention, as did the university canteens that were controlled by different political groups. The students were also active in preventing other students from attending classes, often to commemorate the deaths of their political allies that often occurred at other university campuses in Turkey.
32. In 1984, the entry of a female academic to her classes wearing a turban caused an uproar, leading to the expulsion during the same year of covered female students from many universities, including the Uludağ University in Bursa. In 1987, the state forbade the entrance of covered female students to any school. It was then that many covered students started to travel abroad to continue their education. Even though the constitutional court initially annulled the headscarf ban in 1989, the protests continued into the late 1990s, when the ban was once again put into practice. Perhaps most significant in this context was the 1999 Merve Kavakçı Affair. Kavakçı, who ran for a seat from the Virtue Party to be then democratically elected to the national assembly, was nevertheless prevented from being sworn in with her headscarf on. Booed at the national assembly by the secularist deputies and criticized by the then president Demirel and opposition leader Ecevit for not being "modern," Kavakçı eventually lost her position as a deputy because of a technicality: she had also become an American citizen without notifying the Turkish authorities, a move that effectively prevented her from holding public office in Turkey. Even though another female deputy belonging to the National Action Party also word a headscarf, she decided to take it off within the national assembly, thereby escaping expulsion. Interestingly, the headscarf is worn in the public sphere and is taken off in the privacy of one's home. With such an action, the public and private spaces became reversed, with the national assembly being redefined as private space. The turban crisis continued into the twenty-first century. In January 2000, Konca Kuriş, a headscarved religious activist, was murdered in eastern Turkey; her murder occupied the newspapers as many debated the boundaries of public participation by headscarved women.
33. Interestingly, many wives of the JDP members who were now in control of the government as well as the presidency, wore the headscarf; while they were informally prevented from attending public ceremonies where especially members of the staunchly secularist members of the military were present, they nevertheless became publicly visible in many other occasions they initiated. It is also interesting that while Prime Minister Tayyip Erdoğan publicly abided by the secular republican principles, he had to send his two headscarved daughters to the United States to continue their education. Likewise, the headscarved wife of Abdullah

Gül, who had initially filed a lawsuit with the European Court, had to withdraw the suit when her husband became the Turkish foreign minister.

34. In 1994, for instance, a man attending a public ceremony at Mustafa Kemal Atatürk's mausoleum started to shout, waving a Quran and inviting the attendees to Islam; he was summarily arrested and imprisoned for disturbing the public order and the secular principles of the republic. In 1996, as Necmettin Erbakan briefly assumed the position of prime minister as the leader of the coalition party, many university presidents marched to Mustafa Kemal Atatürk's mausoleum, swearing their allegiance to the secular principles of the republic. Perhaps significant in the domestic debate over religion was Erbakan's subsequent visit to Libya, where President Kaddafi severely criticized the suppression of religion in Turkey, a move that placed Erbakan, as a visiting dignitary of the Turkish republic, in a very difficult position. Continuing religious activities, including an invitation of the populace to sharia in Sincan in 1997, led a year later to a debate as to whether the military or the civilian government ought to take the lead in opposing public demonstrations of religion. In 1998, Tayyip Erdoğan, who was then a deputy of the Virtue Party, was imprisoned for ten months for delivering a public speech with religious undertones. His political rights were also removed, and were only restored by the national assembly years later. During this time, civic religious leader Fethullah Gülen, who had established a movement that included many schools and student dormitories in Turkey and abroad, was also tried in 1999 due to his alleged antisecular activities. While Gülen eventually left to settle in the United States, he was acquitted from this charge only in 2006. Gülen continues to live in the United States.
35. In 1990, fifteen officers were expelled from the military for engaging in religious activities; they were followed by yet another twenty-nine officers in 1996. Such expulsions from the military continue as especially the general chiefs of staff still define religion as one of the most significant dangers facing the Turkish republic.
36. Kahraman 2008.
37. Terziyan 1995: 9, 25, 69, 115; Çerkezyan 2003: 171–72; Irmak 2003: 93, 121–22, 127–29.
38. Terziyan 1995: 9, 25, 69, 115.
39. Interestingly, such silencing also occurred in the case of another famous actor, Ayhan Işık, who was also of Armenian origin but carefully silenced his ethnic identity.
40. Çerkezyan 2003: 171–72.
41. Irmak 2003: 93, 121–22, 127–29.
42. Akgiray 2003: 220.
43. See the Yonca Poyraz and Kezab Hatemi report for TESEV, Turkish Economic and Social Studies Foundation, entitled "Bir 'Yabancı'laştırma Hikayesi: Türkiye'de Gayrimüslim Cemaatlerin Vakıf ve Taşınmaz Mülkiyeti Sorunu (The Story of an Alienation: The Problem of Non-Muslim Communities in Turkey regarding Foundations and Immovable Property," 16 March 2009. See also Hrant Dink in the 2007 documentary *Swallow's Nest.*
44. See Tolga Korkut, *Bianet*, 14 May 2009. Korkut based his report on a study conducted by Professor Harun Tunçel, head of the Department of Human and Economic Geography at Fırat University, Elazığ. A count of all settlements, including town and city names, revealed that around 28,000 names were changed in total. The number of villages whose names were changed per province in Turkey was as follows: Erzurum (653), Diyarbakır (555), Van (415), Sivas (406), Kars (398), Siirt (392), Trabzon (390), Şanlıurfa (389), Elazığ (383), Ağrı (374), Erzincan (366), Gümüşhane (343), Muş (297), Kastamonu (295), Gaziantep (279), Tunceli (273), Bingöl (247), Tokat (245), Bitlis (236), Konya (236), Adıyaman (224), Malatya (217), Ankara (193), Samsun (185), Bolu (182), Adana (169), Antalya (168), Giresun (167), Zonguldak (156), Bursa (136), Ordu (134), Hakkâri (128), Hatay (117), Sakarya (117), İçel (112), Balıkesir (110), Kahramanmaraş (105), Rize (105), Çorum (103), Artvin (101), Amasya (99), Kütahya (93), Yozgat (90), Afyonkarahisar (88), Kayseri (86), Manisa (83), Çankırı (76), Eskişehir (70), Muğla (70), Aydın (69), İzmir (68), Sinop (59), Çanakkale (53), Denizli (53), Burdur (49), Niğde (48), Uşak (47), Isparta (46), Kırşehir (39), Kırklareli (35), Bilecik (32), Kocaeli (26), Nevşehir (24), İstanbul (21), Edirne (20), and Tekirdağ (19).
45. According to the story by BBC News on 8 March 2005, the Turkish state attempted to change the Latin names of three animals, namely, the red fox known as *Vulpes vulpes*

kurdistanica, the wild sheep called *Ovis armeniana* and the roe deer referred to as *Capreolus capreolus armenus*.

46. The Adıyaman deputy governor İdris Kurtkaya faced a lawsuit in 1985 for lauding the PKK in one of his public speeches, and journalist Mehmet Ali Birand, who conducted an interview with Öcalan in exile in 1988, was prevented by the office of the public prosecutor from printing his story in the Turkish newspapers. In 1989, the center right Social Democrat Populist Party (Sosyaldemokrat Halkçı Parti; SHP) removed one member from office for stating that the Kurds are a people separate from the Turks.
47. In 1995, Yaşar Kemal, a famous novelist of Kurdish origin, criticized the Turkish republic abroad in Germany, "blaming it for generating a system of repression and brutality." A year later, Kemal was sentenced to 1.5 years in prison for an article he wrote on Turkey.
48. The Kurdish newspaper *Ülkede Özgür Gündem* appeared on 24 April with the front-page headline "We Apologize," thereby marking the first instance of an apology to the Armenians in the press in Turkey.
49. See Ayşe Günaysu in the *Armenian Weekly*, 14 May 2009. The Kurdish newspaper is *Günlük*.
50. Zana 1995.
51. Erendoruk 2007.
52. The years 1978 and 1979 leading to the military coup witnessed the assassinations of five public figures. The assailants of deputy public prosecutor Doğan Öz, constitutional law professor Server Tanilli—who survived—and journalist Abdi İpekçi, were initially unknown, but it became evident over time that these were committed by state paramilitary organizations. Clandestine radical leftist groups like the Turkish Populace Freedom Organization (THKP-C) carried out the other two assassinations, murdering the lieutenant colonel who had shot and killed the leftist activist Hüseyin Cevahir and the police chief that had tortured and killed many leftist students. Such assassinations also continued in 1980 before the September military coup as three public figures were likewise killed. While writer Ümit Kaftancıoğlu and Deputy Mayor Bülent Demir were assassinated this time by radical rightist organizations like the Muslim Brothers (Müslüman Kardeşler Birliği), the assailants of the former prime minister Nihat Erim were once again unknown. The assassinations abated for a while in the 1980s in the aftermath of the military coup only to once again escalate in the 1990s. The year 1990 witnessed the assassinations of five public figures; while the assailants of the secularist Turkish intellectuals Muammer Aksoy and Bahriye Üçok and journalist Çetin Emeç were once again unknown, the two National Intelligence Organization officials Hiram Abbas and Ferdi Tamer were perhaps assassinated by radical leftist groups, once again in retaliation for their previously murdered leftist friends. The assassinations of the radical leftist groups continued in 1991 and 1992 as a retired major general, the former MIT director, the head public prosecutor of the State Security Courts, and former vice admiral Kemal Kayacan were murdered. In 1993, journalist Uğur Mumcu was assassinated by unknown assailants, yet the possibility of their belonging to radical religious groups led to public demonstrations declaring allegiance to secular republican principles. Likewise, in 1999, intellectual and academic Ahmet Taner Kışlalı was assassinated, with the murder once again being pinned on radical religious groups. The tide of assassinations ended in 2001 with the assassination of Üzeyir Garih, the prominent businessman of Jewish origins, whose assailants were once again unknown.
53. Sedes 2005: 15–16; Belli 1994: 311, 462–63, 494.
54. The Belli family had to leave Turkey for ten years from 1982 to 1992 because of the ensuing political unrest and possible arrest in the aftermath of the coup. Belli 1994: 311, 462–63, 494.
55. In 1978, bombs exploded at the Sirkeci boat dock in İstanbul, followed in 1979 with three similar public bombings, one at the Beyazıt public square, one at a coffeehouse, and the third at the Yeşilköy airport. Likewise, in 1983, a bomb exploded at the covered bazaar of Kapalıçarşı.
56. The radical leftist groups were accused, in 1979, of machine-gunning the headquarters of the ultranationalist National Action Party and, in 1980, of establishing "rescued zones," or zones freed of state presence. Such zones were then violently taken back by the state security and military forces. The period from 1989 to 1993 likewise witnessed the continuation of radical leftist violence by the Revolutionary Left (DEV-SOL) and the military arm of the

Marxist Leninist Communist Party of Turkey (TİKKO). In addition to bombs, raids, and machine-gunning the Police Academy, these two organizations also kept assassinating in vengeance the public officials who had killed their members. The same violence was replicated by the radical rightist groups belonging to the Muslim Brothers or similar paramilitary armed bands stated to have been formed within the Islamist National Salvation Party, organizations that also undertook political assassinations. Bombings in 1983 and 1991 were consecutively attributed to the Islamic Cause (İslami Dava) and Islamic Resistance (İslami Direniş) secret organizations. It was assumed that radical religious activists were also behind the machine-gunning of two beer halls, presumably for serving alcohol, a practice objected to by pious Islamists. The violence erupted at the May Day celebrations in 1996 against the leftist activists; dozens were killed in the ensuing chaos as bullets were fired into the gathered crowd. The assailants were again unknown but initially were linked to ultrarightist groups.

57. Kırcı 1998: 14, 120, 152.
58. For instance, in 1980, a radical leftist and a radical rightist militant faced death by hanging in the aftermath of the military coup. Likewise, in 1982, the leftist militants were tried by the state, with 186 petitions for death by hanging.
59. The centuries-long divide had initially emerged within Islam over the rules of succession after the prophet Muhammad. One group, later evolving into the Sunnis, advocated succession by election of the religious community. The other, later transforming into the Shiites, instead supported succession from within the Prophet's own family. The two religious groups had different practices, with the Shiites venerating the prophet's son-in-law Ali over the elected Abubakr, and also refusing to attend the Sunni mosques, instead establishing communal places of their own.
60. Nevruz celebrates the first day of the year and spring according to the Persian calendar. In Alevi Kurdish communities, the day also marked the birthday of the prophet's son-in-law Ali as well as the day when the prophet's daughter Fatma and Ali were married.
61. Also, for the first time, Kurdish was included among the living languages institute established at the Mardin Artuklu University.
62. The Neve Shalom synagogue in İstanbul was attacked in 1986, 1992, and 2003; twenty-two Turkish Jews died in the first attack, there were no casualties in the second attack, and twenty people died in the last attack. The responsibility for the first two attacks was claimed by radical groups operating from outside of Turkey, a Palestinian militant group and the Lebanon-based Shiite Muslim group Hezbollah. Even though a local Muslim militant group, the Great Eastern Islamic Raiders' Front (İslami Büyükdoğu Akıncılar Cephesi; İBDA-C), claimed responsibility, it was alleged that it did so with help from an international terrorist organization. Also, in addition to attacks on churches, in 2006, a Fidei Donum priest, Andrea Santoro, was assassinated in Trabzon.
63. Hrant Dink, a journalist of Armenian origin, was murdered on 19 January 2007 by Ogün Samast, a seventeen-year-old Turkish nationalist. After running a successful chain of bookstores with his brothers in 1979, about two decades later in 1996, Dink founded the *Agos* Turkish-Armenian bilingual newspaper along with friends. Under Hrant Dink's editorship, *Agos* focused on the treatment of the Armenian community in Turkey. It published articles and serials on the Armenian cultural heritage, carried news on the Republic of Armenia especially in relation to Turkey, and also covered human rights violations and democratization problems in Turkey. What distinguished Dink was his willingness to approach the problems of the Armenian community in Turkey within the larger framework of the problems the populace faced, especially as a consequence of the suppression of human rights and of civil liberties. At his funeral, about 100,000 to 200,000 protesters marched in protest of the assassination, chanting, "We are all Armenians" and "We are all Hrant Dink."
64. The legal accusations stemmed from a speech Dink had delivered at a panel hosted by the human rights NGO Mazlum-Der in Şanlıurfa. In his speech, Dink conveyed his reactions to singing the Turkish national anthem that assumed the entire populace of the republic to be ethnically Turkish, thereby erasing and silencing all other non-Turkish and non-Muslim groups living in Turkey.
65. *Hürriyet*, 20 January 2007.
66. *Agos*, 13 February 2004.

67. The Turkish phrase is "*muhtac olduğun kudret damarlarındaki asil kanda mevcuttur.*"
68. This gross injustice and legal violence led me to organize along with others the first signature campaign of international scholars protesting the sentence.
69. Dink interviewed a former Gaziantep resident, Hripsime Sebilciyan, who argued she was Gökçen's niece, that Gökçen was originally an Armenian named Hatun Sebilciyan. Hatun's father, Nerses Sebilciyan, had been murdered in 1915, leading Hatun to be taken in by an orphanage from where Mustafa Kemal adopted her in 1925. Late in her life, Gökçen herself also corroborated this alternate version of her life story.
70. The chant they sang in Turkish was "*ya sev ya terket,*" often employed against all who oppose Turkish ethnic nationalism.
71. Personal interview with Dink. Dink stated that he had collected much more information and documentation for the article, including many eyewitness accounts of those who had visited and talked to Gökçen before her 2001 death. Gökçen acknowledged that she was indeed Armenian. Dink was shocked by the fervor of the nationalist attacks where none of the concerned even considered that such a heritage made both Gökçen and Mustafa Kemal's ensuing protection of her all the more noble. Dink stated that, during this time, he was invited to the office of the İstanbul governor, where he was told that his life could not be protected if he continued to publish such provocative articles. Interestingly, the governor did not take any action against the ultranationalists who harassed him for expressing his views, but he reproved Dink, who had been the harassed party all along. Dink also stated that Gökçen was not the only public figure with Armenian ancestry; there were many others just as significant. For instance, he stated that, ironically, the founder and leader of the National Action Party, Alparslan Türkeş, was himself an Armenian orphan originally from Sivas; he had been adopted by a Turkish Muslim couple from Cyprus and later rose to prominence in the Turkish military and later politics. The lineage of the current party leader, Devlet Bahçeli, likewise contained Armenian ancestry. When I asked Dink why he did not publish this information, he replied: "You have seen the violence that occurred when I published an article about Gökçen. Can you fathom how much stronger the reaction would be if I had published the Armenian origins of Türkeş? They would literally bury me under the rabble of my own newspaper." Since they have indeed buried Dink, I find no reason to exclude such information.
72. The lawsuit was filed in September 2006 by the İstanbul Prosecutor's Office. Dink's interview with the Reuters news agency had taken place on 14 July 2006. Upset by this blatant legal suppression of freedom of expression, my friends and I once again organized a signature campaign of international scholars protesting the fact that a journalist was being prosecuted merely for expressing his views on the past.
73. Neşe Düzel, *Radikal*, 25 May 2005.
74. Dink noted that "the Armenian issue had not been a taboo until the 1920s as it was discussed in the Ottoman parliament, trials were held, books published and even monuments erected to the Armenian suffering." He then added that the Armenian issue started to turn into a taboo during the republican period because "after 1920, the Unionist cadres started to penetrate into the republican cadres, attaining significant state posts that in turn enabled them to shape the course of the republic."
75. The assassin was Mehmet Ali Ağca; he had killed journalist Abdi İpekçi in 1979. The name of the former Turkish minister was Tuncay Mataracı. After his nineteen-year imprisonment in Italy, Ağca was deported to Turkey, serving a ten-year sentence there as well, only to be released on 18 January 2010.
76. The crash occurred on 3 November 1996; the victims included the İstanbul deputy police chief (Hüseyin Kocadağ), a deputy who was also the leader of a powerful Kurdish clan (Sedat Bucak), and the leader of an ultranationalist militant group who, as a contract killer, had been on Interpol's red list (Abdullah Çatlı). The interior minister was Mehmet Ağar.
77. Kırcı 1998: 173.
78. Three reports were prepared in the wake of the scandal. The first was by the National Intelligence Organization. Yet suspicions about the truthfulness of the MİT report led to the commissioning of a second report, by Kutlu Savaş, the chairman of the Prime Minister's Inspection Board (Başbakanlık Teftiş Kurulu Başkanı). It should be noted that 12 of the 124

pages of this report were classified. Finally, a parliamentary investigatory commission headed by Mehmet Elkatmış published the 350-page *Susurluk Report* in April 1997.

79. The populace turned these assailants over to the police. The Van public prosecutor as well as the RPP Hakkari deputy, who had both been at the scene, conducted the preliminary investigations before the police or the military had a chance to cover things up. Subsequent investigation identified the car's owner as the Hakkari gendarmerie commander; documentation in the car's trunk revealed other violent actions the assailants had planned, thereby revealing the close connection between some segments within the military and extralegal violence. Even though the three assailants were initially tried and sentenced at civilian courts, the military courts took over the case, claiming the military identities of the assailants necessitated such a move. All three assailants were freed by the military court; those civilian judges and prosecutors initially trying the case were punished, losing their jobs, under the allegation that they had "destroyed the honor of their occupation as state officials." Meanwhile, Major General Yaşar Büyükanıt, who then became Turkey's general chief of staff, defended one of the assailants by arguing that the latter was "a good fellow."
80. The diaries belonged to Admiral Özden Örnek. The general chief of staff was Hilmi Özkök. These diaries were allegedly acquired by the Turkish security forces from the erased files on the admiral's computer. They were then sent to the prominent Turkish journal *Nokta* for publication. The military initially argued that the diaries were either forgeries or doctored; they then raided the journal's offices, removing all the computer equipment. Needless to say, the journal was shut down. Özkök, who had been the general chief of staff, refrained from making a public statement, thereby indirectly supporting the view that the diaries were indeed genuine.
81. The Turkish military supported the investigation when it became clear that these radical segments had also decided to take out the general **OK** chief of staff and the high-ranking commanders, thereby taking over the military as well. The government and the current military command structure therefore united in giving support to the investigations that eventually led to the arrest of especially many high-ranking retired army generals involved in extrajudiciary violent activities against prominent intellectuals, Kurdish leaders, and non-Muslims.
82. At the trials, files of many past violent acts were combined when it became evident that all were connected. In all, 75 arrested assailants were tried, and 119 assailants were tried without arrest. Among the arrested were Doğu Perinçek, the leader of the ultranationalist Workers' Party, retired brigadier general Veli Küçük, retired military captain Muzaffer Tekin, journalists Tuncay Özkan and Mustafa Balbay, Başkent university president and professor Mehmet Haberal, and the deputy director of the Special Operations Department İbrahim Şahin. Such a list of assailants once again demonstrated how ultranationalist elements had penetrated not only into the state and the military but also into the civilian sphere.

    See also the investigations of prominent journalists like Şamil Tayyar, who started to write a book on the secret paramilitary armed bands established within the state and the military. The interviews he gave to Neşe Düzel at the *Taraf* newspaper on 11 February 2008 and to Nuriye Akman on 7 April 2008 highlighted most of his findings. In the interviews, he drew the command structure of the extralegal organization referred to as the "deep state," placing retired general Doğu Silahçıoğlu at the number two position, with the top position also presumably belonging to a higher-up military officer, probably Çevik Bir, a member of the Turkish General Staff in the 1990s. Even though Tayyar noted that he knew who occupied the number one position at the moment, he refused to name him. Yet Tayyar did note that before the 1980 military coup, the number one position was occupied by General Turgut Sunalp, the same general who had run against Turgut Özal after the coup, only to lose. Tayyar further claimed that the military-based "Ergenekon" was the most centralized armed band, organized like an octopus with many tentacles; even though one can destroy the tentacles, he stated, the structure will survive insofar as the central body is not destroyed. Such secret paramilitary organizations were always headed and manned by retired military officers. Tayyar explained that the person occupying the number one position was elected from among those retired generals with influence and authority within both the military and the state. Tayyar alleged that the Susurluk scandal, the Şemdinli incident, Hrant Dink's assassination, and the violence conducted against non-Muslims were all operations of this clandestine structure. Likewise, gendarmerie commander Eşref Bitlis, who advocated a peaceful solution to the Kurdish issue, was assassinated in 1993 by this organization. In tracing the origins of this organization, Tayyar noted that "this virus is older than republican history, going all the way back to the Committee of Union and Progress."

83. Based on thousands of official documents and depositions, the journalists Timur Soykan and Demet Bilge Ergun from the *Radikal* newspaper wrote a book entitled *Slingshot: The Hrant Dink Murder—The Murderers of a Pigeon,* in which they concurred with this alleged complicity.
84. Taha Carım was the Turkish ambassador to Lebanon. When Carım had come to Ankara for vacation, he had met with Baytok, trying to draw the latter's attention to this dangerous possibility. Yet, Baytok recounted, "I was not of the same opinion and defended the view that the Armenian issue was going to gradually disappear over time" (2005: 25–26).
85. A case in point is that of the Armenian survivor Manuel Kırkyaşaryan (2003: 22), who throughout his later life was very healthy, with one exception: throughout his ninety-one-year life, he got always got up at two in the morning to check the doors and windows of the entire house as well as the sleeping family members and then would go back to sleep. This was the exact time when Kırkyaşaryan, at the age of nine in 1915 during the Armenian deportations, had found his father next to him dead.
86. On 24 April 1972, on the anniversary of the 1915 deportation and massacres of the Armenian intellectuals from İstanbul, the group removed the consulate sign, engaging in a skirmish with the consul. Later that year, on 29 October 1972, that is, on the anniversary of the foundation of the Turkish republic, a bomb threat was received from some Armenians before a Mevlana performance, leading to its termination halfway through. Soon afterward, on 4 November 1972, a group of Armenians attacked a meeting of the Turkish American Club organized on the occasion of the foundation of the Turkish republic. The date of the first assassination was 27 January 1973. The names of the murdered diplomats were Mehmet Baydar and Bahadır Demir, the consul general and the consul of Turkey. The assailant was Gurgen (Karakin) Mgirdich Yanikian, a seventy-seven-year-old American Armenian who had initially migrated from Turkey. Şimşir 2000: 84, 86–89, 93, 96–98, 105–8, 111–17, 228; Soyer 2000: 233.
87. Inviting Baydar and Demir to the Baltimore Hotel in Santa Barbara by stating that he wished to give to the Turkish state a watercolor painting of Sultan Abdülhamid by the Italian painter G. Fureli and one contemporaneous banknote, the photocopies of which he had already submitted as a gift, Yanikian then shot and killed the two Turkish diplomats in his hotel room. Arrested for murder and sentenced to life imprisonment, Yanikian was paroled ten years later and died shortly afterward. Two days before the incident, Yanikian had prepared and mailed to the major American newspapers a 100-plus-page text in Armenian stating that he was committing the murders "to avenge the events of 1915." This single incident, constituting the first assault by an Armenian against Turkish diplomats in recent history, was followed by a chain of attacks and murders soon after. A day before the murders, Yanikian had sent another note to the newspapers stating, "Armenians everywhere should pursue this tactic. This [is a] new type of war. I am ending my writing so that I can start taking my first step.... Perhaps my action would be effective in awakening the sleeping consciences of many."
88. Dündar Soyer recounted meeting Mehmet Baydar when visiting the United States.
89. The Santa Barbara deputy public prosecutor, having read the text Yanikian had prepared, started to research the history of the Armenian issue. He contacted the Turkish consulate in Los Angeles for recommendations and for reference material depicting the Turkish perspective. The Turkish embassy wrote to Ankara asking "to immediately dispatch works on the Armenian problem in English prepared by our [state] institutions to convey to the prosecutor." Yet there was not one such publication available. Bilal Şimşir conjectured that "the [Armenian] issue had been considered buried into history at Lausanne." Only one brochure prepared by Taha Carım in 1971 in English and French, based on a talk he gave, could be located and duly sent.
90. Şimşir 2000. Unless otherwise indicated, all the information on the assassinations comes from this source.
91. Still, it should be noted that Hasan Esat Işık, the Turkish ambassador to France, resigned in protest in 1973 when an Armenian monument to the genocide was erected in Marseilles.

Baytok (2005: 194) recounted in his memoirs that Işık did so by stating that he "could not carry the dishonor of being the Turkish ambassador to France during a time when such an act was carried out."

92. Şimşir 2000: 122–27, 137–52, 171–89, 228; Baytok 2005: 203–4.
93. The first act commenced on 20 February 1975 as the Turkish Airlines office in Beirut was bombed, leaving behind a letter by ASALA that took responsibility for the violence, stating that it was "going to fight against the imperialists for the righteous case of the Armenians, the attacks would target Turkey, Iran, and the United States, and that this was only the first step." The first assassination occurred on 22 October 1975; the assassinated ambassador was Daniş Tunaligil.
94. The ambassador's car, returning from a reception, was ambushed around 1:30 p.m. at the Bir Hakeim Bridge on the Seine River. The ambassador was İsmail Erez, and his driver was Talip Yener. The following day, the JCOAG distributed pamphlets in Paris and Bonn, also sending notices to the news agencies and embassies stating that the Turkish ambassadors in Paris and Vienna had been murdered "with the aim to draw the attention of the peoples of the world to the condition of the Armenians." The same day, someone contacted the Beirut bureau of the Agence France Press (AFP), declaring that the murders had instead been committed by ASALA, the Vienna murder by the martyr Bordikian (or Boulgidian) cell, and the Paris assassination by the Kurken Yanikian cell.
95. During the ensuing discussions at the Turkish national assembly, the foreign minister, İhsan Sabri Çağlayangil, stated that "there are some organizations active against us such as the Turkish Communist Party, Our Radio [Bizim Radyo], and the Radio of the Turkish Communist Party."
96. During Daniş Tunalıgil's funeral, General Necip Torumtay, who was later to become the chief of general staff, came from Turkey to accompany the plane. At the time, Şükrü Elekdağ, who was to later become the Turkish ambassador to the United States and a fervent critic of any reconciliation with the Armenians, was then the general secretary at the Foreign Ministry. Vahit Halefoğlu who was then the Turkish ambassador to Germany in Bonn, later became the foreign minister. Bilal Şimşir, who penned the definitive book on this violence, was himself a contemporary and friend of both the slain Tunalıgil and Erez; he later became a Turkish ambassador. As these two slain ambassadors had both attended the School of Public Administration, where they were friends with many others who later manned the entire Turkish state administration, their views of the Armenians became polarized through this personal loss.
97. Baytok 2005: 203–4.
98. Melkonian 2007: 78–79.
99. *Armenian Reporter,* 31 January 1980.
100. *Armenian Reporter,* 14 February 1980.
101. "ASALA Lends Support to Justice Commandos for LA Action," *Armenian Reporter International,* Feb 18 February 1982; "Affiliation of Attackers in 3 Incidents Subject of Wide Speculation," *Armenian Reporter International,* 6 October 1983.
102. On 16 October 1980, the *Armenian Reporter* declared it was time to find common ground because violence allegedly executed on behalf of all Armenians was very destructive.
103. "Prelacy Annual Assembly Fails to Endorse Statement on Terror," *Armenian Reporter International,* 10 June 1982.
104. In discussing ASALA activities in particular, Melkonian (2005: 88–89, 90–92) stated that even though many claimed to belong to the central committee, "behind the cowls and the pseudonyms was one man—Hagopian himself. Alec, Ajemian, and Monte begged him to form a real central committee, but Hagopian refused to relinquish his prerogatives as the sole decision-maker."
105. The first secretary's name was Oktar Cirit. The assassination took place at a miniature golf hall on Hamra Street in Beirut. Şimşir 2000: 195–99, 202–7.
106. An Armenian businessman, Serhad Serhadian, accosted and attempted to stop the assailant from escaping the scene of the crime but only managed to get his gun. Serhadian then helped a policeman take the wounded Cirit to the hospital. The taxi driver was another Armenian, Ohannes Kusurian.
107. The Italian police asked Semih Akbil, the Turkish ambassador to Italy, if the involvement of any Turks was suspected. Akbil replied that Armenian organizations ought to be investigated. Şimşir 2000: 212–13, 217–23, 228–31, 240–42.

108. Prime Minister Süleyman Demirel and President Fahri Korutürk both declared the incident "very heartrending." Demirel reiterated that these were "abhorrent attacks against the Turkish state and nation," not addressing the past violence against the Armenians that generated them or the Armenian identity of the assailants.
109. See the Italian *Il Messagero,* the Greek *Acropolis,* and the British *Financial Times* on the pertinent dates.
110. The journalist was Mithat Sertoğlu. The article appeared on 3 July 1978 in the *Dünya* newspaper.
111. The ambassador was Zeki Kuneralp; the violence occurred on 2 June 1978. Kuneralp's wife was Necla Kuneralp, his brother-in-law was Beşir Balcıoğlu, and his driver was Antonio Torres. Şimşir 2000: 246–54, 255–58, 261, 265.
112. Bilal Şimşir specifically noted that he attended the funeral because he had been friends with the family for many years; he then remembered the numerous debates he had with ambassador Kuneralp, who had told him not to exaggerate the Armenian propaganda that Bilal Şimşir was researching at the time. Kuneralp never recovered from the loss of his wife, dedicating to her the books he wrote during his retirement. The foreign minister at the time was Gündüz Ökçün, another Turkish official who was later going to play a significant role in rejecting the peaceful resolution of the Turkish Armenian problem. Interestingly, Ambassador Kuneralp's father had been Ali Kemal, one of the fiercest CUP opponents, who had recognized the collective violence of 1915 as one of the greatest sins of the CUP and protested it.
113. On 4 January 1978, a bomb was thrown at the car of Turkey's assistant press attaché Metin Yalman; on 10 March 1978, three small bombs exploded under cars owned by Turkish diplomats in Athens, slightly injuring a Turkish diplomat, two policemen, and a passerby. Finally, on 18 December 1978, an explosive device was thrown at the Turkish Airlines office in Geneva, with no resulting physical injuries.
114. Şimşir 2000: 217, 269, 274–83, 289–311.
115. The attack occurred on 12 October 1979; the son's name was Ahmet Benler, and his father, the ambassador, was Özdemir Benler. Bilal Şimşir stated that he lived through this tragedy as well, since he had just been appointed the first secretary to the Hague; he actually was the one who delivered the news of the son's death to the ambassador. Ahmet Benler was an only son, whose brother had died at a traffic accident in Switzerland at the age of nine. Having graduated from Grenoble University as an electrical engineer, Ahmet Benler was working on his PhD at Delft University at the time of his murder. At the request of the family, no official ceremony was conducted in Ankara, and since the Dutch government did not offer any transportation, Benler's body was flown by a Turkish plane directly to Marmaris, where the family had intended to retire. It should be noted that Günduz Ökçün was the Turkish foreign minister at the time of this murder as well. Bilal Şimşir noted that the chief of general staff Kenan Evren, who later became Turkey's president, also knew the Benler family well and ended up settling in Marmaris during his retirement as a consequence of his interaction.
116. The ambassador was Şükrü Elekdağ.
117. The ambassador was Bilal Şimşir. He traced the origins of the recent Armenian assassinations to the 1920s, "when the Armenians were after the CUP leaders in exile outside; Turkey, murdering them one by one."
118. The date of the attack was 22 December 1972. The murdered counselor was Yılmaz Çolpan. The attack occurred on the Champs Élysées.
119. See the interview with Prime Minister Süleyman Demirel on 24 December 1979 at the *Hürriyet* newspaper.
120. See pertinent discussions in the *Günaydın* newspaper by Can Polak; in the *Tercüman* newspaper by Ergun Göze; and in the *Dünya* newspaper by Ercümend Melih Özbay.
121. On 22 August 1979, the Geneva deputy consul general Niyazi Adalı was attacked, with three people wounded. On 19 October 1979, the first domestic retaliation to Benler's murder occurred in İstanbul as the church of the Armenian Apostolic Patriarchate was bombed. On 17 November 1979, three explosions took place in central Paris at the offices of Turkish Airlines, the Dutch airline KLM, and the German airline Lufthansa. Likewise, two bombs went off on 25 November 1979 in front of the Madrid offices of British Airlines and the American Trans World Airlines (TWA), with ASALA once again claiming responsibility.

On 23 December 1979, four bombs exploded in Rome, one in front of a refugee center that oversaw the transfer of many Armenians to the United States, and the other three in front of the Air France and TWA offices. Once again, ASALA claimed responsibility. Melkonian noted in his memoirs (2005: 80) that it was "Hagop Hagopian who helped coordinate the 1979 bombing of the Soviet Information Office in Paris and an Aeroflot Office in Brussels."

122. Gürün 1995: 322–23.
123. The name of the attaché was Galip Özmen; his daughter was Neslihan Özmen; his wife was Sevil Özmen; his wounded son was Kaan Özmen; and his unhurt son was Alper Özmen. Şimşir 2000: 317–33, 341–48, 356–65, 899–911, 913–20.
124. The memoirs of Monte Melkonian (2005: 84–85), the perpetrator, were recorded by his brother Markar.
125. See the editorial in *Günaydın* and the column of Ali Sirmen in *Cumhuriyet.*
126. Derogy 1990: 201.
127. The consul general was Şarık Arıyak, and his security guard policeman was Engin Sever.
128. The Turkish government once again had this murder brought to the attention of NATO, and its council condemned the murder. Then, pointing to the NATO decision, Turkey's US ambassador, Şükrü Elekdağ, pressured the US government to express its regrets and to employ the word "Armenian" in doing so. The US government appeared to have done so, according to the US declaration printed in the Turkish newspapers, but not in the US ones. Turkey's ambassador to Germany made a similar attempt, but it produced no result; Turkey's ambassador to Canada was able to get the Canadian foreign minister send a letter of condolence.
129. See, for instance, the pertinent column of Fahir Armaoğlu in *Tercüman.*
130. See Orhan Birgit in *Dünya;* Örsan Öymen in *Milliyet;* and Ergun Göze and Zafer Atay in *Tercüman.*
131. On 18 February 1980, a bomb in Rome damaged the offices of Swissair. On 10 March 1980, two bombs detonated at the Turkish Airlines office in Rome killed two and injured twelve passersby. The second bomb was calculated to kill or wound the onlookers who came to watch after the first bomb went off. On 3 October 1980, the Turkish Airlines office in Milan was bombed, causing some damage but no injuries. In his memoirs, Melkonian (2005: 88–89, 90–92) claimed responsibility for this last attack as well as an attack on the Mondadori Press office because the latter had violated an agreement concerning an interview with the ASALA leader Hagopian. Melkonian also listed a failed attack at the Hotel Beau-Site in Geneva on 3 October 1980, when two ASALA militants were injured, generating a new nickname for the group, namely, the "October 3rd Organization." Alec Yenikomchian was blinded as a consequence. From 12 October 1980 to 5 February 1981, Monte Melkonian carried out a total of eighteen bombings in the name of the October 3rd Organization in order to pressure the Swiss authorities to release Yenikomchian, and he was indeed hastily released. It is therefore probable that the 5 October 1980 bombing of the Alitalia office in Madrid, injuring twelve, the 12 October 1980 bombing of the Turkish Airlines office in London, the 10 November 1980 bombings in Rome (one at the Swiss Airlines office and the other at a Swiss tourist bureau), and the 19 November 1980 bombing of the offices of the Turkish Airlines in Rome were all executed by Melkonian.
132. On 6 February 1980, Doğan Türkmen, the Turkish ambassador to Switzerland, survived an attack in Bern when his car was fired upon as he was leaving the British embassy. The JCOAG claimed responsibility for the attack by phoning the AFP in Paris and Beirut. The assailant was identified as the French citizen Max Hrair Kilimdjian, a tobacco shop owner residing in Marseilles. As the guns were recovered from a creek and the rental car employees and others positively identified the assailant, the Swiss authorities decided they had sufficient evidence to request the French to arrest Kilimdjian. Unsuccessful attacks against the Turkish diplomats continued during the rest of 1980. On 17 April 1980, fire was opened on the official car of the Vatican ambassador Vecdi Türel, and both Türel and his security guard, Tahsin Güvenç, were wounded. Someone called the Reuter Agency in Beirut, declaring the JCOAG had committed the attack. The assailants were not found. Later, on 29 July 1980, two gunmen shot the TurkishcConsulate in Lyon, killing two people and seriously wounding two others, with ASALA claiming responsibility. On 26 September 1980, Selçuk Bakkalbaşı, the

press attaché of the embassy in Paris, was wounded in an armed attack as he entered his house; the police discovered him lying in the street, shot twice but still conscious. He was paralyzed as a result of the attack, for which ASALA claimed responsibility.

133. Bilal Şimşir explained that "the arrest and trial of Kilimdjian almost drove the Armenian fanatics insane. Already possessing a deep-rooted guerrilla tradition, the Armenians once again immediately formed a special committee [to support him]. A typical Armenian hullabaloo commenced. Even though we termed this Armenian rowdiness, it would be more correct to call it Armenian wildness. The Armenian committee started to howl like wasps poked in their nest. They were supporting a terrorist being tried for attempted first-degree murder. The tough thief was trying to outwit the homeowner. Monies were collected from the Armenian community through threat or goodwill, and a [public] campaign started to save [him]. Full-page ads were given to the French newspapers; telegrams were sent and letters written to the French authorities. A 6787-signature petition was sent to the French president and prime minister. Support was sought from foreign countries and marches took place in Marseilles. Ugly things were written on the walls of the Turkish consulate. Their slogan was: 'Max Hrair Klindjian: from Genocide to Jail.'"

134. See H. Kantzabed "Klindjian Solidarity Group Demonstrates in New York; Protests Imprisonment of French-Armenian,", *Armenian Reporter International*, 21 January 1982; "M. Hrair Klindjian, Given 2-Year Sentence for Attempt on Turkish Ambassador's Life, Set to Go Free This Week," *Armenian Reporter International*, 28 January 1982.

135. Gürün 1995: 205, 284–85.

136. The attack occurred on 4 March 1981. The counselors' names were Reşat Moralı and Tecelli Arı. The Anatolian Bank representative was İlkay Karakoç. All three men were graduates of the School of Public Administration, and among their cohort was Candan Azer, who later became an ambassador and also played a significant role in heading a state institute in Turkey researching the Armenian issue. Şimşir 2000: 394–97, 400–445, 458.

137. Gürün 1995: 340–43.

138. Ibid.

139. Ibid., 334–39.

140. The attack occurred on 9 June 1981; the secretary's name was Mehmet Savaş Yergüz. Born in 1949, Yergüz had attended the Saint Joseph Middle School and the Galatasaray Lyceum; he then graduated from the School of Journalism in Paris. The Geneva UN permanent representative at the time was Kamuran İnan, who later served as a deputy at the national assembly, and he returned his French Légion d'honneur medal in protest of the Armenian Genocide law that France passed in 2006. As Yergüz was buried in Fethiye, all the retailers closed their shops on the day of his funeral to protest the Armenian terror. The perpetrator was Mardiros Jangodjian, a Lebanese Armenian terrorist. Jangodjian's options were to either enter the Turkish consulate and detonate a bomb or kill an important consulate official. Because it was difficult to enter the well-protected consulate, he had chosen the latter option.He was released ten years later in 1991, settling in Marseilles.

141. The attack occurred on 24 September 1981. The security guard killed was Cemal Özen; the wounded consul general was Kaya İnal. The assailants resisted releasing Özen and İnal; Özen died within a couple of hours; İnal was released seven hours later, rushed to hospital, and saved.

142. The assailants stated that they were ASALA members; naming their operation "the Yeghia Keshishian Suicide Commandos Operation of Van," they made demands and kept siege for fifteen hours before surrendering to the French police. See "Public Rally in L.A. Slated for the Release of Father Yergatian," *Armenian Reporter International*, 24 November 1983.

143. The four Armenian assailants (Vazken Sako Seslian, Kevork Abraham Guzelian, Aram Avedis Basmadjian, and Agop Abraham Julfaian) were all born in Beirut; they were also very young, around twenty-two years of age.

144. Melkonian 2007: 97–98.

145. Şimşir 2000.

146. International relations professor Türkkaya Ataöv and the secretary of the Advisory Council of the Armenian Patriarchate, Dikran Kevorkian, went to France to testify as expert witnesses about 1915 and the conditions of Armenians in Turkey.

147. Gürün 1995: 295.
148. On 13 January 1981, a bomb exploded inside the car of Ahmet Erbeyli, the financial adviser of the Turkish embassy in Paris, though he escaped without injury. ASALA once again claimed responsibility. On 12 March 1981, a group of ASALA members trying to occupy the Turkish embassy in Tehran killed two guards in the process; two of the perpetrators were captured and later executed by the Iranians. ASALA claimed responsibility. The Copenhagen labor attaché Cavit Demir received minor arm wounds on 2 April 1981 when he was attacked in the elevator of the flat where he lived.
149. On 28 May 1981, a bomb exploded on the grounds of an Armenian community center in Paris, killing a neighbor's guard. A week later, on 4 June 1981, the French police dismantled a bomb planted at the entrance of an Armenian church; the next day a bomb exploded in front of another Armenian church in a suburb of Paris.
150. Melkonian (2005: 94) noted that his brother "Monte had begun to suspect that these bombings had not been the works of the 'Turkish fascists' who had supposedly taken credit for them, but of [ASALA leader] Hagopian and his provocateurs."
151. The attack took place on 25 October 1981. The second secretary was Gökberk Ergenekon.
152. Melkonian 2007: 98–100.
153. Gürün 1995: 355–57.
154. First, a small bomb exploded at a Carpeteria store on 1 January 1981, and the owners were threatened with more violence unless money was paid to ASALA. On 3 February 1981, the US police dismantled a bomb discovered on the doorstep of the Swiss consulate in Los Angeles. Because an Armenian group named the October 3rd Organization claimed responsibility, it is evident that Monte Melkonian, who was in Europe at the time, probably had some help from the local Armenian community in the United States. In November 1987, ASALA member Vicken Tcharkhutian admitted in federal court that he had put together both attacks.
155. On 15 September 1981, shortly before an explosion, a man was observed placing two plastic bags outside a building at the airport in Copenhagen, Denmark. Two people were injured in the attack, one of them seriously. ASALA claimed responsibility. On 3 November 1981, a bomb once again exploded at a Swissair office in Madrid, injuring three people, with ASALA claiming responsibility. On 15 November 1981, two banks were bombed in East Beirut. Although the damage was extensive, no one was injured. Once again, ASALA claimed responsibility.
156. Gürün 1995: 285–88, 290–97, 344–49, 352–53, 385–99, 402–3, 445.
157. The book, *The Armenian Files*, was written by Kamuran Gürün.
158. The biases in Gürün's corrective emerged at two points. First, he argued that if one wanted to "prove" that such deportations were necessary, it would be no problem to do so. The argument for the necessity of the Armenian deportations inherently accepted the argument of the CUP government without questioning it, thereby introducing a significant bias to the conclusion that was reached. Second, in discussing the crimes committed during the Armenian deportations, Gürün briefly touched on the stand of the Damad Ferit Pasha cabinet without going into details. If he had done so, he would have to reveal that the Damad Ferit Pasha cabinet not only condemned the previous CUP cabinet for executing extensive Armenian massacres but also officially and publicly stated the number of massacred Armenians to be 800,000. In addition, it was the same Damad Ferit Pasha cabinet that continuously insisted on bringing all the perpetrators to account for the crimes they committed.
159. The meeting with the Turkish academics took place on 18 December 1981.
160. The consul general was Kemal Arıkan; he was killed in late January. As Kemal Arıkan slumped over the steering wheel, the car drifted slowly across the street, hitting another car and then rolling into some trees. Previously, on 6 October 1980, two Molotov cocktails had been hurled at his residence, causing damage, probably as a consequence of his writing to the California Parole Board to deny the petition for the parole of Gourgen Yanikian, who had murdered two Turkish diplomats in 1973. Two months earlier, the consulate had been bombed with extensive damage but no personal injury. Arıkan's latest confrontation with the Armenians had occurred three weeks earlier; he drove to UCLA when the Armenian students of the university were staging a demonstration calling for the dismissal of Professor

Stanford Shaw "for distorting the truth and serving the interests of the Turkish state." Arıkan had been warned of a possible attack and had two guards, but he did not use them, stating that he did not want them to suffer his own fate; thus, he was unprotected at the time of the attack. An American passerby also died from a heart attack. A witness pursued the assailants to a car and wrote down the license plate number. Someone called the United Press International and claimed responsibility on behalf of the JCOAG, also pointing out that it had "carried out 14 actions until then." The quickly arrested assailants were Hampig Harry Sassounian, a nineteen-year-old American Armenian from Pasadena, and Krikor (Koke) Saliba; even though Saliba escaped to Lebanon, he was later killed in June 1982 during the Lebanese civil war. Şimşir 2000: 462–79, 488–89, 502–9, 511–12, 516–21, 530–48, 551–58, 561, 570–77, 584–96, 937–42. See also "Los Angles Turkish Consul General Assassinated in Ambush," *Armenian Reporter International*, 4 February 1982; "Mixed Reaction by California Armenians Reported Following Killing of K. Arikan," *Armenian Reporter International*, 4 February 1982.

161. The academic was Dickran Kouymjian, professor of Armenian studies at California State University. In 1982, Kouymjian also offered a course on the history and consequences of Armenian militancy since 1975. See "New Course Will Explore Armenian Political Violence," *Armenian Reporter International*, 2 December 1982.
162. Şükrü Elekdağ soon became the strongest public voice of the Turkish official narrative. Bilal Şimşir stated that the Turkish permanent undersecretary of the Foreign Ministry was also sent to Los Angeles, and both he and Elekdağ frequently gave interviews stating the Armenian claims about 1915 were a "big lie," thereby "balancing the Armenian perspective for the first time."
163. The attack took place on 5 May 1982. The name of the consul general was Orhan Gündüz. Gündüz had been a former captain in the Turkish military and later became a businessman. An honorary consul since 1971, he had been active in establishing a Turkish school in Boston and helping out the Turkish American community. His murder had been preceded by the bombing of his gift shop on 22 March 1982. Even though the Turkish state had asked for Gündüz's protection after the bomb attack, the US government did not provide it.
164. In his memoirs, Soyer (2000: 237) provided additional information on Gündüz.
165. The attack occurred on 7 June 1982. The slain attaché's name was Erkut Akbay, and his wife was Nadide Akbay. The couple left behind two young children aged five and eleven. Bilal Şimşir noted that he remembered quietly crying while he kept receiving telegrams from Lisbon, thinking about what would happen to these orphaned children.
166. The attack occurred on 7 August 1982.
167. Their statement noted that their attack was "against the Turkish fascist occupation of their lands," thereby articulating for the first time the land demands of some Armenians from the Turkish state. They also warned of additional suicide attacks in the United States, Canada, England, Sweden, and Switzerland unless eighty-five prisoners held in those countries were released within seven days. A caller to the press noted that the operation was staged by "the Martyr Kharmian Hayrik Suicide Squad." Who Hayrik had been was not further identified.
168. He was Levon Ekmekjian, a French national of Lebanese extraction, put on trial at the Ankara Martial Law Command Third Military Court; after being sentenced to death, he appealed the sentence but to no avail.
169. The Turkish citizen's name was Artin Penik.
170. The attack occurred on 27 August 1982. The name of the military attaché was Atilla Altıkat.
171. The attack took place on 9 September 1982. The murdered attaché's name was Bora Süelkan. See also "Killing of Turkish Diplomat Reported in Bulgaria," *Armenian Reporter International*, 16 September 1982.
172. ASALA had "operated out of the Western section of the Lebanese capital, [though] often holding press conferences in Palestinian held enclaves to the south of the capital." ASALA also "sponsored a daily radio program, published a well-edited periodical called *Hayastan* and lately presented its view in a daily column that appeared in the leftist Arab daily, *Sout Al Shaghyla* (*The Voice of the Workers* in Arabic)." "Armenian Radical Groups May Have to Clear Out of Beirut," *Armenian Reporter International*, 17 June 1982.
173. Gürün 1995: 344–49, 412–18, 433, 445.

174. Gürün mentioned Richard Hovannisian and the owner of the *Armenian Weekly*, "Bogosyan." Eminent Armenian historian Hovannisian was mentioned with envy in relation to his activities in Los Angeles, with Gürün (1995) remarking that "the ability of our [Los Angeles] consulate to engage in counterpropaganda is close to nill and limited to sending disclaimers to various newspapers." He met the *Armenian Weekly* owner, Bogosyan, in New York, learning that "the Armenians in the United States were generally against terrorism... yet when articles were published in his weekly to that effect, [Bogosyan] received death threats.... according to Bogosyan, the ones who support the terrorism are the Armenians who have recently migrated from Lebanon, and they are able to sustain their activities by collecting money through blackmail."
175. In New York, Gürün initially met with members of the Jewish lobby both to emulate them and also to draw them to the side of the Turkish state. Baron Rothschild arranged appointments with members of the World Zionist Organization, the World Jewish Congress, and the American Jewish Committee.
176. Şükrü Elekdağ was officially given the task of establishing a Turkish lobby and had already formed an umbrella organization more than twenty-five local organizations and associations. Eventually, this initial attempt led to the formation of the American Turkish Association of America, which, with significant financial support from the Turkish state and possibly from the US defense industry providing arms and armaments for the Turkish military, has taken the initiative in promoting the official Turkish stand at all costs. Both the ATAA and its offshoot, the Turkish Forum, provide anti-Armenian propaganda and also harass scholars, like myself, who refuse to do so.
177. Among such endowed chairs are the ones at Princeton University (held by Heath Lowry) and Portland State University (held by Birol Yeşilada); the chair at Indiana University (held by Kemal Silay) was indirectly financed by the Turkish military. Private Turks also established chairs at Harvard University (held by Cemal Kafadar) and New York University (held by Leslie Peirce). Attempts to establish such endowed chairs were also turned down at other universities such as the University of California, Los Angeles (UCLA).
178. Gürün (1995) recounted the conversations he had as follows: "I met with Professors Kemal Karpat, Halil Inalcik, Richard Chambers, and Frank Tachau, who suggested that such a center would be a better investment than endowed chairs; in addition to putting out publications, it could help [institute] Turkish studies in the United States as well as give fellowships to those academics coming to Turkey or going to the United States. Ambassador Elekdağ had found a candidate to head such a center. This is how I met professor Heath Lowry with whom I was about to have with time a close cooperation in Washington. Professor Lowry discussed in great detail the benefits such an institute would have.... Upon my return to Turkey, I had the 3 million dollars in the budget set aside to establish such an institute in the United States. The amount was to be deposited in a [local Turkish], bank and the institute would operate on the annual income accrued."
179. The ITS that was thus established recently faced trouble as many of its board members resigned when the eminent Ottoman historian Donald Quataert, who was also on the ITS board, was forced by the Turkish state authorities to resign. The resignation was instigated by a book review Quataert wrote in which he argued that the initial reticence of their generation of scholars to engage in research on the Armenian Genocide had adversely affected the field of Ottoman studies, a reticence, he then remarked, that was thankfully being corrected by a new generation of scholars.
180. Indeed, the ITS does provide funds for American graduate students and academics to conduct research in Turkey, even though the funded research often does not include controversial topics such as those concerning non-Muslims or the Kurds.
181. The attack occurred on 9 March 1983. The ambassador was Galip Balkar, and his driver was Necati Kaya. Şimşir 2000: 606–15, 620–31, 641, 657–58, 671–74, 680–83, 688, 694–97, 701–25, 733–42. See also "Turkey's Ambassador to Yugoslavia Seriously Wounded in Belgrade Attack Claimed by Justice Commandos," *Armenian Reporter International*, 10 March 1983; "Second Gunman in Belgrade Killing Arrested by Yugoslav Police," *Armenian Reporter International*, 24 March 1983.

182. The name of the killed Yugoslavian student was Zeljko Milivojevich, and the wounded one was Zorico Zolotich.
183. The name of the colonel was Slobodan Brajevich.
184. Assailant Haroutiun Kirkor Levonian, who had been wounded by the retired Yugoslav colonel, was at the hospital; the other assailant, Raffi Alexander Elbekjian, initially escaped only to be caught and arrested the same day. Both held Lebanese passports, and both had also entered Greece twice. As they were tried in prison, the Diaspora Armenians brought in expert witnesses such as Pierre Vidal Naquet, Gerard Chaliand, Garbis Agopian, Henri Nauqueres, Henri Leclerc, and Anahit Terminassian in an effort to narrate the past collective violence that had somehow generated the present one.
185. The defendants wanted the sentence translated into Armenian, then appealed it. Eventually, Elbekian's sentence was reduced by five years, and Levonian was actually released after four years because he had been disabled by the wounds he had received and was about to die. Yet Bilal Şimşir claimed that Levonian is still alive, living in Yerevan under the name Antranik Bogossian. After six years, Elbekian was forgiven by Slobodan Milošević and then settled in Beirut. In a later interview, Elbekian stated that they had chosen Balkar because of his anti-genocide statements and his bright future as the possible next prime minister of Turkey.
186. The name of the attaché was Dursun Aksoy; he was murdered on 14 July 1983.
187. Melek 1994: 166–67.
188. The attack occurred on 27 July 1983. The wife's name was Cahide Mıhçıoğlu, and her husband was Yurtsev Mıhçıoğlu; the first name Yurtsev means "love your country." The Mıhçıoğlus' had named their two surviving sons Yurtsay, that is, "respect your country," and Atasay, that is, "respect Mustafa Kemal Atatürk and/or your ancestors." Such symbolism demonstrates the degree of nationalism in Turkey. A month after this violence, Yurtsev Mıhçıoğlu died in a traffic accident in Turkey.
189. "Their grandfathers had also once raided the Ottoman Bank and spilled the blood of many innocent people," he stated, thereby stereotyping all the Armenians of the past and present, of all political inclinations, to draw a spurious connection between the past and present acts of violence. See Gürün 1995.
190. The assailants' names were Simon Yehneian, Sarkis Aprahamian, Vahe Navar Tagihitian, Setrak Onnik Agaminian, and Ara Hosvel Harvikian. They had arrived in two cars, opening fire; Tagihitian was then shot dead by returned fire. The rest of the assailants then decided to enter the embassy residence instead of the consulate, taking the mother and son hostage and placing bombs with the threat that they would blow up the place. Because the Portuguese Special Operation Team could only attack the embassy upon the decision of the Council of Ministers, the council met and approved the operation, and then the team stormed the building. Yet an explosion was heard, leading to the collapse of the first floor. The counselor's wife, one police officer, and five terrorists died as a consequence.
191. "Affiliation of Attackers in 3 Incidents Subject of Wide Speculation," *Armenian Reporter International*, 6 October 1983. A message left at the AP Lisbon bureau claimed that the Armenian Revolutionary Army had committed the attack.
192. "Beirut Armenians Stage Huge Demonstration for Release of Missing Top Dashnag, Apraham Ashjian," *Armenian Reporter International*, 13 January 1983; "Abducted ARF Leader in Beirut Feared Dead; Turks Accused of Murder," *Armenian Reporter International*, 27 January 1983.
193. The murdered Armenians were Minas Simonian, killed in Beirut, Lebanon; Noubar Yalemian, killed in Rotterdam, Holland; and Karnig Vahradian, killed in Athens, Greece.
194. "Justice Commandos Issue Message to Armenian People," *Armenian Reporter International*, 13 January 1983.
195. Şimşir 2000: 747–58, 762–63, 772–78, 782–96, 803–9, 811.
196. The attack occurred on 28 April 1984. The husband's name was Işık Yönder, and his wife was Şadiye Yönder. The couple had been living in Iran for fifteen years.
197. Providing a history of the Armenian attacks against the Turkish state in Iran, Şimşir noted that they commenced on 10 September 1980 with the ASALA bombing of the Turkish Airlines bureau. Then, on 23 April 1981, about 5,000 Armenians marched to the Turkish embassy, "exactly like they had done ninety years ago at the Kumkapı protest." After another

ASALA attempt to raid the embassy in April 1982, a series of attacks occurred on 28 March 1984.

198. The attack occurred on 20 June 1984. The name of the slain deputy attaché was Erdoğan Gözen. The bomb in the car parked in front of the embassy was so powerful that Gözen, whose body was completely burned, could be identified only from his wedding ring. One pedestrian and an Austrian policeman in charge of security at the embassy were wounded; all the windows of all the buildings on the street, including the embassy, were broken. The assailants' intention had been to detonate the bomb inside the embassy garage to cause additional damage, but Gözen had parked outside on that day.
199. Retired ambassador Şimşir once again drew a spurious analogy between this car bombing and the 1905 assassination attempt by the Armenians against Sultan Abdülhamid II.
200. The attack occurred on 19 November 1984. The slain director's name was Enver Ergun. Ergun, a fifty-two-year-old architect who had previously taught at New York University, was married and had a seventeen-year-old son. Having served in South America and Africa, he had been transferred to Vienna five years earlier.
201. The Turkish ambassador, Erdem Erner, was the son of Ahmet Erner, who had been accused of massacring thousands of Armenians in the southeastern provinces of the empire in 1915, when he had served there as an Ottoman official. See Binark 2004: 111.
202. See Şimşir 2000: 943–45, 955–56.
203. "Top Dashnag Leader Refused Entry into Britain," *Armenian Reporter International*, 29 November 1984.
204. The attack occurred on 12 March 1985. The Turkish ambassador was Coşkun Kırca. On that rainy day, the assailants had arrived with a U-Haul truck at seven in the morning, entering the embassy by jumping from the truck over the three-meter-high wall. After killing one of the Canadian guards with their twelve-gauge shot gun, they blew open the embassy's oak door with a homemade bomb, gaining entrance. As they went in, they threw a hand grenade that somehow did not explode. The embassy personnel called the Canadian police while the assailants went to the ambassador's bedroom taking as hostages his wife, his daughter, and the daughter's friend, who was sleeping over. Meanwhile, Turkish ambassador Coşkun Kırca jumped from the second floor into the garden, lying there with a broken right leg, arm, and pelvis. Police constable Michel Prud'Homme, who was the first to respond to the embassy call, dragged Kırca to the side of the house, out of the gunman's line of fire, an act that earned him the Medal of Bravery. Şimşir 2000: 943–45, 955–61; Nick Petter, "Turkish Diplomat Survived 1985 Embassy Siege: Ambassador Hurled Himself Out Window during Attack," *Ottawa Citizen*, 7 March 2005.
205. The name of the security guard was Claude Brunelle.
206. Hasan Servet Öktem and İsmail Pamukçu, the first secretary and deputy attaché of the Turkish embassy in Iran, were wounded in an armed assault in front of their houses on 29 March 1985. The two bombing incidents occurred in France; on 3 January 1985, a bomb was detonated in a flat above the AFP office, with ASALA claiming responsibility, and on 7 December 1985, a bomb exploded in two adjacent stores, injuring twenty-five as the Palestine Liberation Front, the Islamic jihad, and ASALA all claimed responsibility.
207. "Trial of Three Armenian in the Turkish Embassy Seizure in Ottawa Begins," *Armenian Reporter International*, 30 October 1986.
208. Sarkis Zeitlian, one of the alleged founders of the Armenian Revolutionary Army after the demise of the JCOAG, who had in the meanwhile also confessed to ordering the assassination of Apo Ashjian, was abducted along with his driver and bodyguard as he left the offices of the *Aztag* weekly located in West Beirut. It was alleged that the followers of Apo Ashjian, who had now formed the Revolutionary Movement, had carried out the abduction. A released photograph depicted Zeitlian in handcuffs with bruises on his left cheek; the accompanying statement alleged that Zeitlian had confessed to the Dashnak Party collaborating with the United States, Israel, and Turkey. The statement added that the Revolutionary Movement would soon publish the names of all "Armenian agents" operating in Lebanon, France and Germany. "ARF Splinter Group Releases Photograph of Sarkis Zeitlian; Promises New Confessions," *Armenian Reporter International*, 5 December 1985.

Also assassinated during this time by the newly founded Revolutionary Movement were Sarkis Aznavourian and Tatoul Saheyan, who were the local leaders of the Dashnak Party in Lebanon. The Revolutionary Movement had invited all the members of the Dashnak Party to sever their ties with it or face death, irrespective of age or sex. The article also provided more information about the conflict within the Dashnak Party. While the more radical and leftist Apo Ashjian had called for much closer cooperation between the JCOAG created by the ARF and ASALA, since both were pursuing the same goals, the more conservative Dashnak Party leadership strongly opposed any cooperation "as it was quite clear that the JCOAG had been created in order to keep disgruntled young party militants from switching to ASALA and [thus] abandoning party rank and file." This rift led the party leadership to eliminate Ashjian, fearing that "if the rift worsened, then the party secrets would leak out or somehow be exposed, something that could create a far deeper crisis within the ranks of the party." The article conjectured that this explanation "assumed a degree of credence in as much as the Dashnak press consistently either undermined or completely ignored ASALA activities." "Disappearance and Assassination of ARF Leaders in Lebanon: ARF Revolutionary Movement Claims Responsibility," *Armenian Reporter International*, 31 October 1985.

209. The US report on marijuana trafficking stated that, in 1980, "Noubar Sofoyan, an Armenian heroin and hashish trafficker connected with the … [JCOAG] was indicted in the US for heroin smuggling" to then reveal that "Sofoyan allegedly helped fund the 1976 bombing of a Turkish installation in Zurich." In 1981, he was arrested in Greece on drug charges, to be subsequently extradited to Lebanon and released, still remaining a fugitive. The report articulating the drug connection to the militant Armenian violence also explains the eventual US stand in support of the Turkish state. "Marijuana Trafficking," http://www.druglibrary.org/schaffer/govpubs/amhab/amhabc3a.htm
210. The gunmen's leader, Nairi Unanian, declared that theirs was "a patriotic action … a shake-up necessary for the nation to regain its senses." Dave Montgomery and Daniel Sneider, "Gunmen Take Over Armenian Parliament," *Milwaukee Journal Sentinel*, 28 October 1999.
211. Baytok 2005: 321–24.
212. Sav 1992: 81–87, 148–49.
213. The discoveries included 100 pounds of dynamite, blasting caps, and more, plus thirteen firearms, and a shopping bag full of ammunition, all found at a storage facility in Bedford, Ohio. An agent with the US Bureau of Alcohol, Tobacco, and Firearms eventually traced the gun to Mourad Topalian, who at the time was the chairman of the Armenian National Committee of America. The explosives were originally stolen from a Michigan drilling site in 1976, ending up in the hands of Armenian terrorists, with some later turning up at an Armenian youth camp in Franklin, Massachusetts. The long and extensive investigation led the US agent to believe that "Mourad Topalian had led a double life, that the respected community leader had been a key figure in the world of Armenian terrorism." By 1999, Topalian, who had turned fifty-six, had moved to Cleveland, taking a job as the vice president of Cuyahoga Community College. He was arrested for "conspiracy to traffic in firearms and explosives and to commit acts of terror against persons of Turkish descent." The prosecutors accused Topalian of ordering the theft of the explosives, sending followers to Beirut for weapons training, and directing the 1980 car bombing of Turkey's UN mission that had badly injured three passersby. They also alleged that the stolen explosives were used in two 1981 bombings, of the Turkish consulate in Los Angeles and the Orange County Convention Center. The investigators also thought that Topalian had served as a top JCOAG leader. His supporters raised over $300,000 in his defense, arguing that "pro-Turkish elements in the US government had singled him out for persecution." Topalian maintained his innocence of any terrorist activity, claiming he did not know the contents of the storage unit. Yet the federal officials remained unconvinced, stating that the FBI had suspected Topalian of ties to terrorist activity since 1983. He was eventually sentenced to thirty-seven months in prison, the maximum allowed under sentencing guidelines. After the 1982 murders of the Turkish officials in Boston and Ottawa, when a Cleveland newspaper asked the local Armenians how they felt about attacks on Turkish officials, Mourad Topalian had answered that "there are two victims, the one who got shot and the one who was pushed to that extreme." David E. Kaplan, "Following Terror's Forgotten Trail," *U.S. News & World Report*, 5 February 2001, 26.

214. Öngör 1987: 10–12; Masar 1974: 11; Apak 1988; Karaveli 1999: 199; Belli 2000: 106–7; Baytok 2005: 466–67; Gürün 1995: 286–88, 339, 406–11; Şimşir 2000: 450–51, 580–82, 907–8.
215. Gürün 1995: 286–88, 339, 406–11.
216. Şimşir 2000: 450–51, 580–82, 907–8.
217. Gürün 1995: 286–88.
218. *Radikal*, 27 September 2007, where Yusuf Halaçoğlu responded to the questions raised about the Armenian problem by Levent Yılmaz, a scholar teaching at l'École des hautes études in Paris and the private Bilgi University in İstanbul; *Zaman*, 27 April 2009, where Yusuf Halaçoğlu expressed his most recent views on the Armenian problem. The interview conducted by Fadime Özkan with Kemal Çiçek appeared at *Stargazete* on 26 October 2009. For their publications, see, for instance, Halaçoğlu 2001, 2006; Çiçek 2005.
219. See, for instance, Erdoğan's commentary at the speech he delievered regarding Turkish-Armenian relations at Chatham House, London, on 4 April 2009.
220. *Hürriyet*, 22 January 2009.
221. *Taraf*, 6 March 2009.
222. The education minister was Hüseyin Çelik. The Kadıköy district education directorate stated that it had received no such communication from the ministry.
223. See lpghaber.com, 16 March 2009.
224. The most recent instance of such an attempt within the time frame of this book took place in March 2009, when the Adana governor, İlhan Atış, organized a panel commemorating the centennial of the 1909 Adana incidents.
225. Sefa M. Yürükel, living in Norway, defines himself as "a researcher of genocide and terrorism, social anthropologist and ethnographer." Yürükel's two prominent activities have been the 2004 publication of his book *Crimes against Humanity in Western History* and the 2006 demonstration he organized to commemorate "those Turkish statesmen assassinated by the West and Armenians supported by Russia," "namely, Sait Halim Paşa, Talat Paşa, Cemal Paşa, Dr. Bahaeddin Şakir and Azmi Bey's."; for the announcement, see http://www.bg-turk.com/index.php?act=forum&do=view&id=3659, accessed 19 July 2010.
226. On 18 November 2009, Mustafa Doğan, a thirteen-year-old Turk, was suspended from a school in Nancy, France, for insisting that there was no Armenian Genocide. In 2006, the French National Assembly adopted a bill proposing punishment to anyone denying the Armenian Genocide. In a written exam, Doğan's history teacher had asked a question about the events of 1915 and the Armenian Genocide. Doğan, who had previously argued with the teacher over the issue, wrote, "Even if it did happen, they deserved it." The school's disciplinary committee suspended Doğan for two days, giving him an assignment on the Armenian Genocide. Doğan refused to do the assignment. Doğan's father stated that he also did not recognize the genocide, but he criticized his son for writing that the Armenians "deserved it." Ali İhsan Aydın, *Today's Zaman*, 18 November 2009.
227. On 8 March 2007, Turkish Labor Party leader and journalist Doğu Perinçek, currently in jail in Turkey for engaging in activities against the government, became the first person convicted by a court of law for denying the Armenian Genocide. He was found guilty by a Swiss district court in Lausanne. The prosecutor called for a six-month sentence, but it was then changed to a monetary fine. Even though Perinçek appealed the verdict, the conviction was upheld by the Swiss Federal Supreme Court on 12 December 2007.
228. On 26 September 2006, three Turkish-Dutch candidates, Ayhan Tonca, Osman Elmacı of the Christian Democratic Appeal (CDA), and Erdinç Saçan of the Labor Party (PvdA), were removed from the 2006 general elections because they "either denied or refused to publicly declare that the Armenian Genocide had happened." As a consequence of these removals, a large segment of the Turkish minority in Holland stated that they considered boycotting the elections. "Dutch Parties Expel Candidates for 'Armenian Genocide' Denial," *Zaman*, 28 September 2006; "Swiss Genocide Trial for Turk," BBC News, 6 March 2007.
229. In 1998, senator Tolman sponsored a law that required the Massachusetts Department of Education to establish guidelines for a high school curriculum on human rights and genocide. The subjects to be taught included the Holocaust, the Irish potato famine, and the Armenian Genocide. The education department's guidelines offered information and links

to scholarship about the Armenian tragedy. At first, there was also some material from a few scholars and Turkish groups who denied that the tragic events constituted genocide. Yet Tolman protested, leading state education officials to remove the dissenting material from the guidelines. In August 1999, the board of education sent a letter to the American Turkish Association of America, which had supported the inclusion of the dissenting material, arguing that "since the legislative intent of the statute was to address the Armenian Genocide, and not to debate whether or not this occurred, the Board and Department of Education cannot knowingly include resources that call this into question." By October 1999, the denial material was removed from the teacher's guide. Yet in 2005, the AATA solicited the assistance of two Boston-area teachers and a high school senior to file a case against the Massachusetts Department of Education accusing the state "of censorship and political interference for using the word 'genocide' to describe the massacres of the Armenians during World War I." They argued that the existing literature was one-sided, and that the Turkish side needed to be represented along with the Armenian side. On 10 June 2009, however, the US district court judge dismissed the case, stating that the plaintiffs "are not entitled to relief in federal court . . . except in limited circumstances, decisions concerning what should be taught must be made by state and local boards rather than by federal judges." Milton Valencia, "Armenian Genocide Lawsuit Rejected," *Boston Globe*, 13 June 2009.

230. Kırkyaşaryan 2005.
231. Karakaş 2003.
232. Irmak 2003.
233. For instance, since the 2007 assassination of Hrant Dink, especially Boğaziçi University and Sabancı University annually organize conferences, workshops, and panels on the anniversary of his murder. On 12 September 2008, that is, on the twenty-eighth anniversary of the 1980 military coup, Bilgi University also promoted a civilian initiative organized by the "70 million steps against the military coup," setting up a tribunal of conscience. At the tribunal, the attendants tried military commanders, explicitly criticizing the 1982 constitution for denying the basic rights of the Kurdish people and the Armenian, Assyrian, and Greek minorities of Turkey. Likewise, at Bilgi University a group of scholars have carried out a research project on the current state of the Armenians of Turkey, a project funded by the Turkish Social and Economic Studies Foundation (TESEV), as well as another project analyzing and comparing the norms and values of the Armenians in Armenia and Turkey. On 6–7 November 2009, that is, on the centennial of the Adana massacres of the Armenians, Boğaziçi, Bilgi, and Sabancı Universities, along with the Gomidas Institute and the International Hrant Dink Foundation, organized an international conference in İstanbul entitled "Adana 1909: History, Memory and Identity from the Perspective of a Century."
234. Burcu Soydan and Pınar Keleş, "Ders kitapları Sarı Gelin'e rahmet okutuyor" [School textbooks worse than Sarı Gelin], habervesaire.com, 21 February 2009; also see http://www.hyetert.com/prnhaber3.asp?Id=31492&Sayfa=1&DilId=1&A.
235. For instance, the İstanbul branch of the Human Rights Organization of Turkey started to commemorate 24 April in 2009 with a poster that read, "Armenian Intellectuals and 24 April 1915: They Were Arrested, Deported and Could Not Even Have a Gravestone." See http://www.ihd.org.tr/index.php?option=com_content&view=article&id=1351:ermeni-aydinlari-ve-1915-etkinligi-ihd-İstanbul-subesi&catid=55:duyurular&Itemid=194 (accessed 20 July 2010).
236. Around twenty people laid wreaths at the grave of Hrant Dink and at the memorial to the victims of the 1894–96 massacres. The 1909 Adana massacre victims were also commemorated by those present.
237. One needs to mention the Internet news source www.hyetert.com, which reviews and presents to its audience all news items on the Armenians that appear in Turkey as well as abroad.
238. According to the hyetert website, which has cataloged articles appearing on the Armenians in Turkey since 2001, the distribution of the number of such articles was as follows: 2001 (44); 2002 (29); 2003 (29) (excluding 21 articles on general health); 2004 (22); 2005 (22); 2006 (18); 2007 (36); 2008 (41); and 2009 (117), with a total of 358 articles published in the last nine years. Hence, after a small dip from 2001, when the possibility of Turkey's EU membership brought the minority question to the public agenda, until 2006, there has been

a steady rise in 2007 and 2008, leading to an explosion in 2009, when the number of such articles almost triples.

239. Semih İdiz, "Bu kez ABD ile soykırım krizi görünüyor" [This time genocide crisis immanent with the US], *Milliyet*, 18 October 2007.

240. Hüseyin Aygün, "Ermeniler ve 'Biz' Kavramı" [Armenians and the concept of "we"], *Birgün*, 30 August 2007.

241. Murat Belge, "Talat Paşa'nın ağzından" [From the mouth of Talat Paşa], *Radikal*, 9 January 2009; Bardakçı 2008.

242. Belge's editorial focused on the diary of Talat Pasha published by Murat Bardakçı. After noting that Bardakçı's earlier attempts to publish a series of articles based on the book in a mainstream newspaper was inexplicably cut off short—"a situation we are used to in Turkey," Belge remarked—the publication of this book is lauded as a very significant contribution. "That it is so is indicated by the fact that no newspaper other than *Milliyet* has written anything about it," he continued. Belge personally thought that about 600,000 of these Armenians were massacred.

243. Çetinoğlu 2009a, 2009b.

244. Malta exiles Ali Fethi Okyar and Rauf Orbay were appointed as republican prime ministers; Feyzi Pirinçcioğlu, Şükrü Kaya, Abdülhalik Renda, M. Şeref Aykut, Ali Seyit, Ali Cenani, and Ali Çetinkaya as ministers; four governors, including Hüseyin Aziz Akyürek, were Malta exiles as well. Van and Bitlis chief secretary Ali Rıza Ceylan, Sivas chief secretary, and Palu and Mardin subdistrict governor M. Kadri Üçok also became governors. Perpetrators like the Bitlis governor Mazhar Müfit (Kansu), Van governor Haydar Hilmi (Vaner), Trablusşam police chief Arslan Toguzata, General Deli Halit Paşa (Karsıalan), General Pertev Demrhan, militia leader Sarı Edip Efe, Ardahan deputy Hilmi, Eskişehir and Trablusşam deputy Ali Suuri, Ahmet Nazif Göker from the Supplies Ministry, Mustafa Maruf and Ahmet Faik Üstün from the deportation commission, Abdurrahman Şeref Uluğ from Diyarbekir, Halis Turgut, Hüseyin Tahir Güvendiren, Halil Rıfat Şabanoğlu, Rüştü Bozkurt, Tevfik Rüştü Aras, Refik Saydam, Memduh Şevket Esendal, Yenibahçeli Nail, and Şükrü Saracoğlu were the first ones to join the national forces of the independence struggle thereby avoiding punishment. Veli Necdet (Sünkıtay), the chief secretary of the Diyarbekir province in 1915, emerged in the 1930s as the director of the Ankara Chamber of Commerce; Edirne settlement director İbrahim Zağra became the mayor, also heading the Edirne Chamber of Commerce; deputy director of the deportation commission Ali Haydar Yuluğ became the Ankara mayor. [As for those transitioning to serve as republican deputies, these were] Malatya subdistrict governor Ahmet Faik Günday [to Ordu]; Midyat, Malatya, and Trablusşam deputy governor Mehmet Şükrü Yasin [to Çanakkale]; Sivas chief secretary and Yozgat subdistrict governor Mehmet Ata [also serving as interior minister]; İstanbul general director of prisons Hüseyin Emrullah Barkan; İsmail Sefa Özler, İsmail Müştak Mayokam, Mehmet Vehbi Bolak, Mehmet Fuat Carım, Ömer Adil Tiğrel, Mehmet Fehmi Alta, and Mazhar Germen. CUP vice director of intelligence Ahmet Esat Uras served as the chief of general security, governor, deputy and member of the Turkish Historical Society. Malta exile Hacı Adil Bey was appointed to the faculty at the İstanbul Law School; Malta exile M. Reşad became the head of the Council of State. Many, like the prominent Turkish businessman and industrialist pharmacist Mehmet (Eczacıbaşı), enriched themselves through confiscated Armenian properties; Bolu deputy Habip became a distinguished republican merchant, also known as the "bulghur king," and Kocaeli CUP responsible secretary Hoca Rıfat (Önen) became a newspaper publisher.

245. Perpetrators who were given annual salaries by the Turkish state for serving the fatherland: Urfa subdistrict governor Nusret, Boğazlıyan deputy governor Kemal, Gebze commander Yahya Kaptan, former naval minister Cemal Paşa, former prime minister Talat Paşa, former Diyarbekir governor Reşit (Şahingiray), *sheikulislam* Hayri (Ürgüplü), Ziya Gökalp, retired cannon major Rıza, Kırşehir deputy Mehmet Rıza (Silsüpür), Edirne deputy Faik Kaltakkıran, Gazianetp deputy Ali Cenani, İstanbul deputy Numan Usta, Muş deputy İlyas Sami, Bitlis governor Mazhar Müfit Kansu, Van governor and deputy Haydar Vaner, Fevzi Pirinçcioğlu, Arslan Toğuzata, Rüştü Bozkurt, Hacı Bedir, Mazhar Germen, Süleyman Sırrı İçöz, Rauf Orbay, Eyüp Sabri Akgöl, and Bekir Sami Kunduh.

246. General Fahri Özdilek, the deputy of SO commander Fuat Balkan, not only was one of the instigators of the 1960 coup but also was appointed as a senator in its aftermath. Likewise, after the 1960 coup, the son of Enver Pasha's cousin Hasan Tahsin Uzer, and the son of Fevzi Pirinççioğlu served as ministers, while Enver Pasha's brother-in-law Kazım (Orbay), the chief of general staff from 1944 to 1946, became the head of the national assembly. These perpetrators also married into each other's families, thereby becoming relatives.
247. Among those who lost their lives are the Diyarbekir junior official Ali Sabit Es-Süveydi and the Lice deputy governor Nesimi Bey. The Konya governor Celal, Kütahya subdistrict governor Faik Ali Bey, and Foça deputy governor Ahmed Ferid were dismissed from their posts. The Mardin subdistrict governor Mustafa Hilmi and the deportation commissioner Ali Fehmi Bey were murdered by unknown persons. Nabi Bey, an official at the Konya police station who was accused of committing massacres, was murdered by Armenian revolutionaries in Kars, where he had been hiding for two years.
248. "For the EU, Sarkozy and the UN, Turkey Is Already in Europe," *Brussels Journal*, 14 November 2008; NTV-MSNBC report, 10 November 2008.
249. Okay Gönensin, "O kafa hortladı" [That mentality has risen once again],Gazetevatan.com, 11 November 2008; Markar Esayan, "Vecdi Gönül'e teşekkür borçluyuz" [We owe gratitude to Vecdi Gönül], *Taraf*, 13 November 2008; Ecevit Kılıç, "Mübadele barışçıl olmadı 200 bin kişi hayatını kaybetti" [The [Greek-Turkish] population exchange was not peaceful, with 200,000 losing their lives], *Sabah*, 16 November 2008.
250. Yavuz Baydar, "What Lies Beneath? It's the Mentality, Stupid!," *Today's Zaman*, 11 November 2008.
251. Cengiz Aktar, "Bakan Gönül Etnik-Dinsel Temizliği İtiraf Ediyor, Ders Almıyor" [Bakan Gönül confesses ethnic and religious cleansing, refusing to draw any lessons], Bianet.com, 11 November 2008
252. Baskın Oran, "Kesin itiraf: 'Türk Milleti' = Müslüman Türkler" [Definite confession: Turkish Nation = Muslim Turks], *Radikal*, 16 November 2008.
253. Ecevit Kılıç, "Mübadele barışçıl olmadı 200 bin kişi hayatını kaybetti" [The (Greek-Turkish) population exchange was not peaceful, with 200,000 losing their lives], *Sabah*, 16 November 2008.
254. Arat Dink, "Yokluğum Türk varlığına armağan olsun" [May my Absence be a gift to the Turkish presence], *Taraf*, 14 November 2008.

SELECT BIBLIOGRAPHY

Abbott, Andrew 1990 "Conceptions of Time and Events in Social Science Methods: Causal and Narrative Approaches." *Historical Methods* 23: 140–50.

1992 "What Do Cases Do? Some Notes on Activity in Sociological Analysis." In *What Is a Case? Exploring the Foundations of Social Inquiry*, ed. Howard Becker and Charles Ragin, 53–82. New York: Cambridge University Press.

Abou-El-Haj, Rifa'at 1991 *Formation of the Modern State: The Ottoman Empire, Sixteenth to Eighteenth Centuries*. Albany: SUNY Press.

Adak, Hülya 2001 "Who Is Afraid of Dr. Riza Nur's Biography?" In *Autobiographical Themes in Turkish Literature: Theoretical and Comparative Perspectives*, ed. O. Akyıldız, H. Kara, and B. Sagaster, 125–41. Würzburg: Ergon-Verlag.

Adam, Heribert, ed. 2011 *Hushed Voices: Unacknowledged Atrocities of the 20th Century*. Berkshire, UK: Berkshire Academic Press.

Adams, J., E. Clemens, and A. S. Orloff, eds. 2005 *Remaking Modernity: Politics, History and Sociology*. Durham, NC: Duke University Press.

Akalın, Müslüm 1992 *Urfa Mutasarrıfı Şehit Nusret Bey'in Nemrut Mustafa Paşa divan-ı harbindeki savunması (The Defense of the Martyred Subprovincial Governor Nusret Bey at the Military Court Martial headed by Nemrut Mustafa Pasha)*. Urfa: İl Vakfı.

Akça, Bayram 2007 *1915 Ermeni Tehciri ve Urfa Mutasarrıfı Şehit Nusret Bey (The 1915 Armenian Deportation and the Martyred Nusret Bey, the Sub-provincial Governor of Urfa)*. Ankara: Atatürk Araştırma Merkezi.

Akçam, Taner 2012 *The Young Turks' Crime against Humanity: The Armenian Genocide and Ethnic Cleansing in the Ottoman Empire*. Princeton, NJ: Princeton University Press.

Akerström, Malin 1991 *Betrayal and Betrayers: The Sociology of Treachery*. New Brunswick, NJ: Transaction.

Aksakal, Mustafa 2008 *The Ottoman Road to War in 1914: The Ottoman Empire and the First World War*. Cambridge: Cambridge University Press.

Aksan, Virginia 1993 "Ottoman Political Writing, 1768–1808." *International Journal of Middle East Studies* 25/1: 53–69.

2007 *Ottoman Wars, 1700–1870: An Empire Beseiged*. Harlow: Longman/Pearson.

Aksan, Virginia H., and D. Goffman, eds. 2007 *The Early Modern Ottomans: Remapping the Empire*. Cambridge: Cambridge University Press.

Aktürk, Şener 2012 *Regimes of Ethnicity and Nationhood in Germany, Russia and Turkey*. Cambridge: Cambridge University Press.

Akyıldız, Olcay, H. Kara, and B. Sagaster 2007 "Introduction." In *Autobiographical Themes in Turkish Literature: Theoretical and Comparative Perspectives*, O. Akyıldız, H. Kara, and B. Sagaster, 9–15. Würzburg: Ergon-Verlag.

Altınay, Ayşe Gül, and Fethiye Çetin 2009 *Torunlar (Grandchildren)*. İstanbul: Metis.

Altman, Dennis 2006 "Taboos and Denial in Government Responses." *International Affairs* 82/3: 257–68.
Aminzade, Ronald 1992 "Historical Sociology and Time." *Sociological Methods and Research* 20/4: 456–80.
Appadurai, Arjun 1996 *Modernity at Large: Cultural Dimensions of Globalization*. Minneapolis: University of Minnesota Press.
1998 "Dead Certainty: Ethnic Violence in the Era of Globalization." *Public Culture* 10/2: 225–47.
Arendt, Hannah 1969 *On Violence*. New York: Harcourt.
Artinian, Vartan 1988 *The Armenian Constitutional System in the Ottoman Empire, 1839–1863: A Study of Its Historical Development*. İstanbul: n.p.
Astourian, Stephan 1996 "Testing World-System Theory, Cilicia (1830s–1890s): Armenian-Turkish Polarization and the Ideology of Modern Ottoman Historiography." PhD diss., UCLA.
Atasoy, Yıldız 2009 *Islam's Marriage with Neoliberalism: State Transformation in Turkey*. Houndmills: Palgrave Macmillan.
Auron, Yair 2003 *The Banality of Denial: Israel and the Armenian Genocide*. New Brunswick, NJ: Transaction.
Avcıoğlu, Doğan 1968 *Türkiye'nin Düzeni: Dün, Bugün, Yarın (The Order of Turkey: Yesterday, Today, and Tomorrow)*. İstanbul: Tekin.
Aymes, Marc 2007 "The Voice-Over of Administration: Reading Ottoman Archives at the Risk of Ill-literacy." *European Journal of Turkish Studies* 6: 1–41.
Bandura, Albert 1999 "Moral Disengagement in the Perpetration of Inhumanities." *Personality and Social Psychology Review* 3: 193–209.
2002 "Selective Moral Disengagement in the Exercise of Moral Agency." *Journal of Moral Education* 31: 101–19.
Barkan, Ömer Lütfi 2000 *Osmanlı Devletinin sosyal ve ekonomik tarihi (Social and Economic History of the Ottoman Empire)*. 2 vols. Ed. H. Özdeğer. İstanbul: İstanbul Üniversitesi Yayınları,
Barker, Joshua, E. Harms, and J. Lindquist, eds. 2014 *Figures of Southeast Asian Modernity*. Honolulu: University of Hawaii Press.
Barkey, Karen 1994 *Bandits and Bureaucrats: The Ottoman Route to State Centralization*. Ithaca, NY: Cornell University Press.
2008 *Empire of Difference: The Ottomans in Comparative Perspective*. Cambridge: Cambridge University Press.
Barnes, Marion 2012 "Passionate Participation: Emotional Experiences and Expressions in Deliberative Forums." In *Politics and the Emotions: The Affective Turn in Contemporary Political Studies*, ed. Paul Hoggett and Simon Thompson, 23–40. New York: Continuum.
Bauman, Zygmunt 1989 *Modernity and the Holocaust*. Ithaca, NY: Cornell University Press.
Baumeister, Roy, and S. Hastings 1997 "Distortions of Collective Memory: How Groups Flatter and Deceive themselves." In *Collective Memory of Political Events: Social Psychological Perspectives*, ed. J. Pennebaker, D. Paez, and B. Rime, 253–75. Rahwah, NJ: Erlbaum.
Bedjaoui, Yuocef, A. Aroua, and M. Ait-Larbi, eds. 1999 *An Inquiry into the Algerian Massacres*. Geneva: Hoggar, 1999.
Ben-Yehuda, Nachman 1997 "Political Assassination Events as a Cross-Cultural Form of Alternative Justice." *International Journal of Comparative Sociology* 38/1–2: 25–47.
Ben-Ze'ev, Efrat, and E. Lomsky-Feder 2009 "The Canonical Generation: Trapped between Personal and National Memories." *Sociology* 43/6: 1047–65.
Berezin, Mabel 2001 "Emotions and Political Identity: Mobilizing Affection for the Polity." In *Passionate Politics: Emotions and Social Movements*, ed. J. Goodwin, J. Jasper, and F. Poletta, 83–98. Chicago: University of Chicago Press.
Berkes, Niyazi 1976 *Türkiye'de Çağdaşlaşma (Modernization in Turkey)*. Ankara: Doğu-Batı.
Berntsen, Dorthe, and David C. Rubin 2012 "Introduction." In *Understanding Autobiographical Memory: Theories and Approaches*, ed. Dorthe Bernsten and David C. Rubin, 1–8. Cambridge: Cambridge University Press.
Bevernage, Berber 2012 *History, Memory and State-Sponsored Violence: Time and Justice*. New York: Routledge.
Bhambra, Gurminder 2007 *Rethinking Modernity: Postcolonialism and the Sociological Imagination*. London: Palgrave Macmillan.

Bilali, Rezarta 2013 "National Narrative and Social Psychological Influences in Turks' Denial of the Mass Killing of Armenians as Genocide." *Journal of Social Issues* 69/1: 16–33.

Billig, Michael 1995 *Banal Nationalism*. London: Sage.

Birinci, Ali 1998 "Hatırat Türünden Kaynakların Tarihi Araştırmalardaki Yeri ve Değeri" [The Place and Value of Sources Like Memoirs in Historical Research]. *Atatürk Araştırma Merkezi Dergisi* 41/14: 1–10.

2001 *Tarihin gölgesinde: meşahir-i meçhuleden birkaç zat (In the Shadow of History: A Few Persons from among the Unknown Famous*. İstanbul: Dergah.

Bischoping, Katherine 1997 "Responses to Holocaust Denial: A Case Study at the University of Michigan." *Contemporary Jewry* 18: 44–59.

Bloxham, Donald 2005 *The Great Game of Genocide: Imeperialsim, Nationalism, and the Destruction of the Ottoman Armenians*. London: Oxford University Press.

Bourdieu, Pierre 1984 *Distinction: A Social Critique of the Judgment of Taste*. Cambridge, MA: Harvard University Press.

1991 *Language and Symbolic Power*. Cambridge, MA: Harvard University Press.

Bowers, C. A. 1997 *The Culture of Denial: Why the Environmental Movement Needs a strategy for Reforming Universities and Public Schools*. Albany: SUNY Press.

Bozdoğan, Sibel, and Reşat Kasaba, eds. 1997 *Rethinking Modernity and National Identity in Turkey*. Seattle: University of Washington Press.

Branscombe, Nyla K., and B. Doosje, eds. 2004 *Collective Guilt: International Perspectives*. Cambridge: Cambridge University Press.

Braude, Benjamin, and B. Lewis, eds. 1982 *Christians and Jews in the Ottoman Empire: The Functioning of a Plural Society*. New York: Holmes and Meier.

Brubaker, Rogers 2002 "Ethnicity without Groups." *Archives Européennes de Sociologie* 43/2: 163–89.

2004 *Ethnicity without Groups*. Cambridge, MA: Harvard University Press.

Brummett, Palmira 2000 *Image and Imperialism in the Ottoman Revolutionary Press, 1908–1911*. Albany: SUNY Press.

Buğra, Ayşe 1994 *State and Business in Turkey: A Comparative Study*. Albany: SUNY Press.

Burawoy, Michael 2007 "For Public Sociology" and "The Field of Sociology: Its Power and Its Promise." In *Public Sociology: Fifteen Eminent Sociologists Debate Politics and the Profession in the Twenty-First Century*, ed. Dan Clawson et al., 23–64 and 241–58. Berkeley: University of California Press.

Burbank, Jane, and F. Cooper, eds. 2010 Empires in World History: Power and the Politics of Difference. Princeton, NJ: Princeton University Press.

Butler, Judith 2004 *Precarious Life: The Powers of Mourning and Violence*. London: Verso.

Byford, Jovan 2008 *Denial and Repression of Antisemitism: Post-Communist Remembrance of the Serbian Bishop Nikolaj Velimirovic*. Budapest: CEU Press.

Calhoun, Craig 2001 "Putting Emotions in Their Place." In *Passionate Politics: Emotions and Social Movements*, ed. J. Goodwin, J. Jasper, and F. Poletta, 45–57. Chicago: University of Chicago Press.

Campbell, B., and A. Brenner, eds. 2000 *Death Squads in Global Perspective: Murder with Deniability*. London: Palgrave.

Campos, Michelle U. 2011 *Ottoman Brothers: Muslims, Christians, and Jews in Early Twentieth-Century Palestine*. Stanford, CA: Stanford University Press.

Chakrabarty, Dipesh 2002 *Habitations of Modernity: Essays in the Wake of Subaltern Studies*. Chicago: University of Chicago Press.

Charny, Israel W. 1992 "The Psychology of Denial: A Contribution to the Psychology of Denial of Genocide—Denial as a Celebration of Destructiveness, an Attempt to Dominate the Minds of Men, and a 'Killing' of History." In *Genocide and Human Rights: Lessons from the Armenian Experience*, special issue of *Journal of Armenian Studies* 4/1–2: 289–306.

2001 "The Psychological Satisfaction of Denials of the Holocaust and Other Genocides by Non-extremists or Bigots and Even by Known Scholars." *Idea* 6/1: 1–20.

Chatterjee Partha 2004 *Politics of the Governed*. New York: Columbia University Press.

2011 *Lineages of Political Society*. New York: Columbia University Press.

Çiçek, Kemal 2005 *Ermenilerin Zorunlu Göçü, 1915–1917 (The Forced Deportation of the Armenians, 1915–1917)*. Ankara: TTK.
Cohen, Stanley 2001 *States of Denial: Knowing about Atrocities and Suffering*. Cambridge: Polity.
Collins, Randall 2001 "Social Movements and the Focus of Emotional Attention." In *Passionate Politics: Emotions and Social Movements*, ed. J. Goodwin, J. Jasper, and F. Poletta, 27–44. Chicago: University of Chicago Press.
Connerton, Paul 2008 "Seven Types of Forgetting." *Memory Studies* 1/1: 59–71.
Conversi, Daniele 2006 "Genocide, Ethnic Cleansing and Nationalism." In *The Sage Handbook of Nations and Nationalism*, ed. G. Delanty and K. Kumar, 320–33. London: Sage.
Conway, Brian 1997 "The Inventory of Experience: Memory and Identity." In *Collective Memory of Political Events: Social Psychological Perspectives*, ed. J. Pennebaker, D. Paez, and B. Rime, 21–45. Rahwah, NJ: Erlbaum.
2009 "Rethinking Difficult Pasts: Bloody Sunday (1972) as a Case Study." *Cultural Sociology* 3/3: 397–413.
Criss, Bilge 1999 *Istanbul under Allied Occupation, 1918–1923*. Boston: Leiden.
Cunningham, Michael 2012 "The Apology in Politics." In *Politics and the Emotions: The Affective Turn in Contemporary Political Studies*, ed. Paul Hoggett and Simon Thompson, 139–55. New York: Continuum.
Curry, Jane L. 2007 "When an Authoritarian State Victimizes the Nation: Transitional Justice, Collective Memory and Political Divides." *International Journal of Sociology* 37/1: 58–73.
Çağaptay, Soner 2006 *Islamism, Secularism and Nationalism in Modern Turkey: Who Is a Turk?* London: Routledge.
Çalı, Başak 2010 "The Logics of Supranational Human Rights Litigation, Official Acknowledgment, and Human Rights Reform: The Southeast Turkey Cases before the European Court of Human Rights, 1996–2006." *Law and Social Inquiry* 35/2: 311–37.
Çetinoğlu, Sait 2009a "Ermeni Emval-i Metrukeleri Üzerine (On the Armenian Abandoned Goods)." 8 June 2009, http://www.birikimdergisi.com/birikim/makale.aspx?mid=552&makale=Ermeni%20Emval-i%20Metrukeleri%20%DCzerine.
2009b "Malta Documents - Continuity of CUP and Turkish Republic." 15 July 2009, http://www.keghart.com/Cetinoglu-Malta.
Çizgen, Engin 1987 *Photography in the Ottoman Empire, 1839–1919*. İstanbul: Haşet.
Dadrian, Vahakn, and T. Akçam 2011 *Judgment at Istanbul: The Armenian Genocide Trials*. New York: Berghahn.
Danielian, Jack 2010 "A Century of Silence: Terror and the Armenian Genocide." *American Journal of Psychoanalysis* 70: 245–64.
Darling, Linda T. 1996 *Revenue-Raising and Legitimacy: Tax Collection and Finance Administration in the Ottoman Empire, 1560–1660*. Leiden: Brill.
2007 "Islamic Empires, the Ottoman Empire and the Circle of Justice." *Comparative Studies in Society and History* 49: 329–57.
Davison, Roderic H. 1963 *Reform in the Ottoman Empire, 1856–1876*. Princeton, NJ: Princeton University Press.
Deleuze, Gilles 2004 [1969] *The Logic of Sense*. London: Continuum.
Deringil, Selim 1998 *The Well-Protected Domains: Ideology and the Legitimation of Power in the Ottoman Empire, 1876–1909*. London: I.B. Tauris.
2009 "'The Armenian Question Is Finally Closed': Mass Conversions in Anatolia during the Hamidian Massacres of 1895–97." *Comparative Studies in Society and History* 51/2: 344–71.
Derogy, Jacques 1990 *Resistance and Revenge: The Armenian Assassination of Turkish Leaders Responsible for the 1915 Massacres and Deportations*. New Brunswick, NJ: Transaction Publishers.
Dona, Giorgia 1986 "Interconnected Modernities, Ethnic Relations and Violence." *Current Sociology* 61/2: 226–43.
Douglas, Mary 1986 *How Institutions Think*. Syracuse, NY: Syracuse University Press.
2007 "Forgotten Knowledge." In *Shifting Contexts: Transformations in Anthropological Knowledge*, ed. Marilyn Strathern, 13–29. London: Routledge.
Duchinski, Haley, and B. Hoffman 2011 "Everyday Violence, Institutional Denial and Struggles for Justice in Kashmir." *Race and Class* 52/4: 44–70.

Dussel, Enrique 2002 "World-System and 'Trans'-Modernity." *Nepantla: Views from the South* 3/2: 221–44.

Dündar, Fuat 2008 *Modern Türkiye'nin Şifresi: İttihat ve Terkkinin Etnisite Mühendisliği, 1913–1918 (The Cipher of Modern Turkey: Ethnic Engineering of the Committee of Union and Progress, 1913–1918)*. İstanbul: İletişim.

2010 *Crime of Numbers: Statistics and the Armenian Question, 1878–1918*. New Brunswick, NJ: Transaction.

Edelstein, E. L., D. Nathanson, and A. Stone, eds. 1989 *Denial: A Clarification of Concepts and Research*. New York: Plenum Press.

Eisenstadt, S. N. 2000 "Multiple Modernities." *Daedalus* 129/1: 1–29.

Emrence, Cem 2012 *Remapping the Ottoman Middle East: Modernity, Imperial Bureaucracy and the Islamic State*. London: I.B. Tauris.

Eren, Nuri 1963 *Turkey Today and Tomorrow: An Experiment in Westernization*. New York: Praeger.

Escobar, Arturo 2004 "Development, Violence and the New Imperial Order." *Development* 47/1: 15–21.

Faroqhi, Suraiya 1985 "Civilian Society and Political Power in the Ottoman Empire: A Report on Research in Collective Biography (1480–1830)." *International Journal of Middle East Studies* 17/1: 109–17.

Fein, Helen 1979 *Accounting for Genocide: National Responses and Jewish Victimization during the Holocaust*. New York: Free Press.

Fernée, Tadd Graham 2012 "Modernity and Nation-Making in India, Turkey and Iran." *International Journal of Asian Studies* 9/1: 71–97.

Findley, Carter V. 1972. "The Foundation of the Ottoman Foreign Ministry." *International Journal of Middle East Studies* 3/4: 388–416.

1989 *Bureaucratic Reform in the Ottoman Empire: The Sublime Porte, 1789–1922*. Princeton, NJ: Princeton University Press.

Fine, Gary Alan 1996 "Reputational Entrepreneurs and the Memory of Incompetence: Melting Supporters, Partisan Warriors and Images of President Harding." *American Journal of Sociology* 101/5: 1159–93.

2006 "The Chaining of Social Problems: Solutions and Unintended Consequences in the Age of Betrayal." *Social Problems* 53/1: 3–17.

2007 "The Construction of Historical Equivalence: Weighing the Red and Brown Scares." *Symbolic Interaction* 30/1: 27–39.

Fine, Gary Alan, and T. McDonnell 2007 "Erasing the Brown Scare: Referential Afterlife and the Power of Memory Templates." *Social Problems* 54/2: 170–87.

Finkel, Caroline 2006 *Osman's Dream: The Story of the Ottoman Empire, 1300–1923*. New York: Basic Books.

Fortna, Benjamin C. 2001 "Education and Autobiography at the End of the Ottoman Empire." *Die Welt des Islams* 41/1: 1–31.

2002 *Imperial Classroom: Islam, the State, and Education in the Late Ottoman Empire*. Oxford: Oxford University Press.

Fourie, Pieter, and M. Meyer 2010 *The Politics of AIDS Denialism: South Africa's Failure to Respond*. Surrey: Ashgate.

Frangoudaki, Anna, and Ç. Keyder, eds. 2007 *Ways to Modernity in Greece and Turkey: Encounters with Europe, 1850–1950*. London: I.B. Tauris.

Fraser, Mariam 2006 "Event." *Theory, Culture and Society* 23/2–3: 129–32.

Gaonkar, Dilip Parameshwar, ed. 2001 *Alternative Modernities*. Durham, NC: Duke University Press.

Genç, Mehmet 2000 *Osmanlı İmparatorluğunda devlet ve ekonomi (State and Economy in the Ottoman Empire)*. İstanbul: Ötüken.

Gerlacht, Christian 2010 *Extremely Violent Societies: Mass Violence in the Twentieth-Century World*. Cambridge: Cambridge University Press.

Giesen, Bernhard 2004 "The Trauma of Perpetrators: The Holocaust as the Traumatic Reference of German National Identity." In *Cultural Trauma and Collective Identity*, ed. J. C. Alexander, R. Eyerman, B. Giesen, N. J. Smelser, and P. Sztompka, 112–54. Berkeley: University of California Press.

Gill, Sandra 2012 "Recalling a Difficult Past: Whites' Memories of Birmingham." *Sociological Inquiry* 82/1: 29–48.

Gingeras, Ryan 2009 *Sorrowful Shores: Violence, Ethnicity, and the End of the Ottoman Empire, 1912–1923*. New York: Oxford University Press.

2010a "Beyond Istanbul's 'Laz Underworld': Ottoman Paramilitarism and the Rise of Turkish Organized Crime, 1908–1950." *Journal of Contemporary European History* 19/3: 215–30.

2010b "Last Rites for a 'Pure Outlaw': Clandestine Service, Historiography and the Origins of the Turkish 'Deep State.'" *Past and Present* 206: 121–44.

Glassen, Erika 2007 "The Sociable Self: The Search for Identity by Conversation (*Sohbet*)—The Turkish Literary Community and the Problem of Autobiographical Writing." In *Autobiographical Themes in Turkish Literature: Theoretical and Comparative Perspectives*, ed. O. Akyıldız, H. Kara, and B. Sagaster, 143–56. Würzburg: Ergon-Verlag.

Go, Julian 2013 "For a Postcolonial Sociology." *Theory and Society* 42: 25–55.

Goffman, Erving 1963 *Stigma: Notes on the Management of Spoiled Identity*. New York: Prentice-Hall.

Goodwin, Jeff, J. Jasper, and F. Poletta 2001 "Why Emotions Matter." In *Passionate Politics: Emotions and Social Movements*, ed. J. Goodwin, J. Jasper, and F. Poletta, 1–24. Chicago: University of Chicago Press.

Göçek, Fatma Müge 1987 *East Encounters West: France and the Ottoman Empire in the Eighteenth Century*. New York: Oxford University Press.

1993a "Ethnic Segmentation, Western Education, and Political Outcomes: Nineteenth-Century Ottoman Society." *Poetics Today* 14/3: 507–38.

1993b "Shifting the Boundaries of Literacy: Introduction of Western-Style Education to the Ottoman Empire." In *Literacy: Interdisciplinary Conversations*, ed. D. Keller-Cohen, 267–88. Princeton, NJ: Hampton Press.

1994 "Ottoman Provincial Transformation in the Distribution of Power." In *Scripta Hierosolymitana XXXV: Studies in Ottoman History*, ed. A. Cohen and Amy Singer, 31–41. Jerusalem: Magnes Press of Hebrew University.

1996 *Rise of the Bourgeoisie, Demise of Empire: Ottoman Westernization and Social Change*. New York: Oxford University Press.

2000 "The Politics of History and Memory: A Multidimensional Analysis of the Lausanne Peace Conference (1922–23)." In *Histories of the Modern Middle East: New Directions*, ed. H. Erdem, I. Gershoni, U. Wokoeck, 207–28. New York: Lynne Rienner.

2004 "Reconstructing the Turkish Historiography on the Armenian Deaths and Massacres of 1915." In *Looking Backward, Moving Forward*, ed. R. Hovannisian, 209–30. New Brunswick, NJ: Transaction.

2006a "Defining the Parameters of a Post-Nationalist Turkish Historiography the Case of the Anatolian Armenians." In *Turkey beyond Nationalism: Towards Post-Nationalist Identities*, ed. Hans-Lukas Kieser, 86–103. London: I.B. Tauris.

2006b "Reading Genocide: Turkish Historiography on the Armenian Deportations and Massacres of 1915." In *Middle East Historiographies: Narrating the Twentieth Century*, ed. Israel Gershoni, Amy Singer, and Hakan Erdem, 101–27. Seattle: University of Washington Press. 2006.

2007 "Turkish Historiography and the Unbearable Weight of 1915." In *Cultural and Ethical Legacies of the Armenian Genocide*, ed. Richard Hovannisian, 337–68. New Brunswick, NJ: Transaction.

2011a "In Search of the 'Righteous People': The Case of the Armenian Massacres of 1915." In *Resisting Genocide: The Multiple Forms of Rescue*, ed. Jacques Semelin, Claire Andrew, and Sarah Gensburger, 33–50. London: Hurst.

2011b *The Transformation of Turkey: Redefining State and Society from the Ottoman Empire to the Modern Era*. London: I. B. Tauris.

2012 "Postcoloniality, the Ottoman Past, and the Middle East Present." *International Journal of Middle East Studies* 44/3: 549–63.

Göçek, Fatma Müge, ed. 1998 *Political Cartoons in the Middle East*. Princeton, NJ: Markus Wiener.

2002 *Social Constructions of Nationalism in the Middle East*. New York: Columbia University Press.

Göçek, Fatma Müge, and D. Bloxham 2008 "The Armenian Genocide." In *The Historiography of Genocide*, ed. Dan Stone, 344–72. London: Palgrave Macmillan.

Göçek, Fatma Müge, and Ş. Hanioğlu 2001 "Ottoman Imperial Control: The First Ottoman Statistical Survey of 1897." In *Cultural Horizons in the Ottoman Empire and Turkish State*, ed. Jayne Warner, 87–98. İstanbul: Isis Press.

Göyünç, Nejat 1983 *Osmanlı İdaresinde Ermeniler (Armenians under Ottoman Administration)*. İstanbul: Gültepe.

Grayson, Kyle 2012 "The Ambivalence of Assassination: Biopolitics, Culture and Political Violence." *Security Dialogue* 43/1: 25–41.

Greenfeld, Liah 2006 "Modernity and Nationalism." In *The Sage Handbook of Nations and Nationalism*, ed. G. Delanty and K. Kumar, 157–68. London: Sage.

Griffin, Larry J. 1992 "Temporality, Events and Explanation in Historical Sociology: An Introduction." *Sociological Methods and Research* 20/4: 403–27.

2004 "Generations and Collective Memory Revisited: Race, Region, and Memory of Civil Rights." *American Sociological Review* 69/4: 544–57.

Griffin, Larry J., and K. A. Bollen 2009 "What Do These Memories Do? Civil Rights Remembrance and Racial Attitudes." *American Sociological Review* 74/4: 594–614.

Grimshaw, Alan 1970 "Interpreting Collective Violence: An Argument for the Importance of Social Structure." *Annals of the American Academy of Political and Social Science* 391: 9–20.

Guhin, Jeffrey, and Jonathan Wyrtzen 2013 "The Violences of Knowledge: Edward Said, Sociology, and Post-Orientalist Reflexivity." *Political Power and Social Theory* 24: 231–62.

Hahn, Joel S. 2001 *Modernity and Exclusion*. London: Sage.

Halaçoğlu, Yusuf 2001 *Ermeni Tehciri ve Gerçekler, 1914–1918 (Armenian Deportations and Truths, 1914–1918)*. Ankara: TTK.

2006 *Sürgünden Soykırıma Ermeni İddiaları (Armenian Allegations from Deportation to Genocide)*. İstanbul: Babıali Kültür.

Hall, Stuart 1992a "Introduction." In *Modernity and Its Futures*, ed. S. Hall, D. Held and T. McGrew, 1–12. Cambridge: Polity.

1992b "The West and the Rest: Discourse and Power." In n *Formations of Modernity*, ed. S. Hall and B. Gieben, 275–332. Cambridge: Polity.

Hallsworth, Simon, and T. Young 2008 "Crime and Silence: 'Death and Life Are in the Power of the Tongue' (Proverbs 18: 210)." *Theoretical Criminology* 12/2: 131–52.

Hanioğlu, Şükrü 2001 *Preparation for a Revolution: The Young Turks 1902–8*. New York: Oxford University Press.

Hegarty, Angela 2004 "Truth, Law and Official Denial: The Case of Bloody Sunday." *Criminal Law Forum* 15: 199–246.

Hirschman, Albert O. 1977 *The Passions and the Interests: Political Arguments for Capitalism before Its Triumph*. Princeton, NJ: Princeton University Press.

Hochschild, Arlie 1983 *The Managed Heart: Commercialization of Human Feeling*. Berkeley: University of California Press.

1990 "Ideology and Emotion Management: A Perspective and Path for Future Research." In *Research Agendas in the Sociology of Emotions*, ed. T. D. Kemper, 108–203. Albany: SUNY Press.

Hoggett, Paul 2009 *Politics, Identity and Emotion*. Boulder, CO: Paradigm.

Hoggett, Paul, and S. Thompson 2012 "Introduction." In *Politics and the Emotions: The Affective Turn in Contemporary Political Studies*, ed. Paul Hoggett and S. Thompson, 1–22. New York: Continuum.

Holmes, Mary 2012 "'Building on a Firm Foundation of Tolerance and Love?' Emotional Reflexivity in Feminist Political Processes." In *Politics and the Emotions: The Affective Turn in Contemporary Political Studies*, ed. Paul Hoggett and Simon Thompson, 115–36. New York: Continuum.

Hovannisian, Richard G. 1986 "The Armenian Genocide and Patterns of Denial." In *The Armenian Genocide in Perspective*, ed. Richard G. Hovannisian, 111–33. New Brunswick, NJ: Transaction.

2004 *Denial of the Armenian Genocide in Comparison with Holocaust Denial*. Yerevan: National Academy of Sciences.

Hovannisian, Richard G., ed. 1998 *Remembrance and Denial: The Case of the Armenian Genocide*. Detroit, MI: Wayne State University Press.

Ichijo, Atsuko 2011 "Introduction: Europe as Modernity." In *Europe, Nations and Modernity*, ed. Atsuko Ichijo, 1–10. Houndmills: Palgrave.

İnalcık, Halil 1964 "The Nature of Traditional Society: Turkey." In *Political Modernization of Japan and Turkey*, ed. Robert E. Ward and Dunkward A. Rostow. Princeton: Princeton University Press.

1973 *The Ottoman Empire: The Classical Age, 1300–1600*. New York: A.D. Caratzas.

1978 *The Ottoman Empire: Conquest, Organization and Economy*. London: Variorum.

İnalcık, Halil, and Donald Quataert, eds. 1999 *An Economic and Social History of the Ottoman Empire, 1300–1916*. Cambridge: Cambridge University Press.

Iniguez, Lupicino, J. Valencia, and F. Vazquez 1997 "The Construction of Remembering and Forgetfulness: Memories and Histories of the Spanish Civil War." In *Collective Memory of Political Events: Social Psychological Perspectives*, ed. J. Pennebaker, D. Paez, and B. Rime, 237–52. Rahwah, NJ: Erlbaum.

Irwin-Zarecka, Iwona 1994 *Frames of Remembrance: The Dynamics of Collective Memory*. New Brunswick, NJ: Transaction.

Jansen, Robert 2007 "Resurrection and Appropriation: Reputational Trajectories, Memory Work, and the Political Use of Historical Figures." *American Journal of Sociology* 112/4: 953–1007.

Jaspers, Karl [2000] 1947 *The Question of German Guilt*. New York: Fordham University Press.

Jost, John T., and O. Hunyady 2005 "Antecedents and Consequences of System-Justifying Ideologies." *Current Directions in Psychological Science* 14/5: 260–65.

Kaindaneh, Steven, and A. Rigby 2012 "Peace-Building in Sierra Leone: The Emotional Dimension." In *Politics and the Emotions: The Affective Turn in Contemporary Political Studies*, ed. Paul Hoggell and Simon Thompson, 157–79. New York: Continuum.

Kamper, Theodore 2001 "A Structural Approach to Social Movement Emotions." In *Passionate Politics: Emotions and Social Movements*, ed. J. Goodwin, J. Jasper, and F. Poletta, 58–73. Chicago: University of Chicago Press.

Kane, Anne 2001 "Finding Emotion in Social Movement Processes: Irish Land Movement Metaphors and Narratives." In *Passionate Politics: Emotions and Social Movements*, ed. J. Goodwin, J. Jasper, and F. Poletta, 251–66. Chicago: University of Chicago Press.

Kara, Halim 2001 "Relational Self-Narratives: Yakup Kadri Karaosmanoğlu's Autobiographical Writings." In *Autobiographical Themes in Turkish Literature: Theoretical and Comparative Perspectives*, ed. O. Akyıldız, H. Kara, and B. Sagaster, 107–23. Würzburg: Ergon-Verlag.

Karpat, Kemal 1972 "The Transformation of the Ottoman State, 1789–1908." *International Journal of Middle East Studies* 3: 243–281.

1985 *Ottoman Population, 1830–1914: Demographic and Social Characteristics*. Madison: University of Wisconsin Press.

Kaya, Ayhan, and A. Tecmen 2011 "Turkish Modernity: A Continuous Journey of Europeanization." In *Europe, Nations and Modernity*, ed. Atsuko Ichijo, 13–36. Houndmills: Palgrave.

Kaya, İbrahim 2004 *Social Theory and Later Modernities: The Turkish Experience*. Liverpool: Liverpool University Press.

2012 "Conceptualizing the Current Clashes between Modernist Republicans and Islamic Conservatives in Turkey." *Social Science Information* 51/1: 3–21.

Kévorkian, Raymond H. 1992 *Les Arméniens dans l'Empire Ottoman à la veille du genocide*. Paris: Editions d'art et d'histoire.

Klein, Janet 2011 *The Margins of Empire: Kurdish Militias in the Ottoman Tribal Zone*. Stanford, CA: Stanford University Press.

Kofta, Miroslaw, and P. Slawuta 2013 "Thou Shall Not Kill…Your Brother: Victim-Perpetrator Cultural Closeness and Moral Disapproval of Polish Atrocities against Jews after the Holocaust." *Journal of Social Issues* 69/1: 54–73.

Kongar, Emre 1985 *Toplumsal Değişme Kuramları ve Türkiye Gerçeği (Theories of Social Change and the Turkish Reality)*. İstanbul: Remzi.

Konuk, Kader 2010 *East-West Mimesis: Auerbach in Turkey*. Stanford, CA: Stanford University Press.

Koselleck, Reinhart 1985 *Futures Past: On the Semantics of Historical Time*. Cambridge, MA: MIT Press.

Köroğlu, Erol 2007 *Ottoman Propaganda and Turkish Identity: Literature in Turkey during World War I*. London: I.B.Tauris.
Krikorian, Mesrob K. 1977 *Armenians in the Service of the Ottoman Empire, 1860–1908*. London: Routledge and Kegan Paul.
Lamont, Michele, and Virag Molnar 2002 "The Study of Boundaries in the Social Sciences." *Annual Review of Sociology* 28: 167–95.
Langman, Lauren 2006 "The Social Psychology of Nationalism." In *The Sage Handbook of Nations and Nationalism*, ed. G. Delanty and K. Kumar, 66–83. London: Sage.
Lawrence, Philip 1999 "Enlightenment, Modernity and War." *History of the Human Sciences* 12/1: 3–25.
Le Bon, Gustav 1896 *The Crowd: A Study of the Popular Mind*. London: Unwin.
Levin, Jack, and G. Rabrenovic 2004 *Why We Hate*. Amherst, NY: Prometheus Books.
2007 "Sociology of Violence." In *21st Century Sociology*, ed. C. D. Bryant and D. L. Peck, vol. 2, 322–26. New York: Sage.
Levy, Avigdor 1971 "The Officer Corps in Sultan Mahmud II's New Ottoman Army, 1826–39." *International Journal of Middle East Studies* 2/1: 21–39.
Lewis, Bernard 1991 "First-Person Narrative in the Middle East." In *Middle Eastern Lives: The Practice of Biography and Self-Narrative*, ed. Martin Kramer, 20–34. Syracuse, NY: Syracuse University Press.
Lifton, Robert Jay 1986 *Nazi Doctors: Medical Killing and the Psychology of Genocide*. New York: Basic Books.
Lipstadt, Deborah 1993 *Denying the Holocaust: The Growing Assault on Truth and Memory*. New York: Free Press.
Lucas, Scott 2012 "Mobilizing Fear: US Politics before and after 9/11." In *Politics and the Emotions: The Affective Turn in Contemporary Political Studies*, ed. Paul Hoggett and Simon Thompson, 79–91. New York: Continuum.
Makdisi, Ussama, and P. Silverstein, eds. 2006 *Memory and Violence in the Middle East and North Africa*. Bloomington: Indiana University Press.
Mann, Michael 2005 *The Dark Side of Democracy: Explaining Ethnic Cleansing*. Cambridge: Cambridge University Press.
Marcus, George E., J. Sullivan, E. Theiss-Morse, and S. Wood 1995 *With Malice towards Some: How People Make Civil Liberties Judgments*. Cambridge: Cambridge University Press.
Mardin, Şerif 1962 *The Genesis of Young Ottoman Thought: A Study in the Modernization of Turkish Political Ideas*. Princeton, NJ: Princeton University Press.
1983 *Jön Türklerin Siyasi Fikirleri, 1895–1909 (Political Thoughts of the Young Turks, 1895–1908)*. İstanbul: İletişim.
Margree, Victoria, and Gurminder K. Bhambra 2011 "Tocqueville, Beaumont and the Silences in Histories of the United States: An Interdisciplinary Endeavor across Literature and Sociology." *Journal of Historical Sociology* 24/1: 116–31.
Markowitz, Gerald, and David Rosner 2002 *Deceit and Denial: The Deadly Politics of Industrial Pollution*. Berkeley: University of California Press.
Markusen, Eric 1992 "Comprehending the Cambodian Genocide: An Application of Robert Jay Lifton's Model of Genocidal Killing." *Psychohistory Review* 20/2: 145–69.
Marques, Jose, D. Paez, and A. Serra 1997 "Social Sharing, Emotional Climate, and the Transgenerational Transmission of Memories: The Portuguese Colonial War." In *Collective Memory of Political Events: Social Psychological Perspectives*, ed. J. Pennebaker, D. Paez, and B. Rime, 253–75. Rahwah, NJ: Erlbaum.
Massey, Douglas 2007 "The Strength of Weak Politics." In *Public Sociology: Fifteen Eminent Sociologists Debate Politics and the Profession in the Twenty-First Century*, ed. Dan Clawson et al., 145–57. Berkeley: University of California Press.
Masters, Bruce 1992 *Christians and Jews in the Ottoman Arab World: The Roots of Secterianism*. Cambridge, UK: Cambridge University Press.
Mazower, Mark 2002 "Violence and the State in the Twentieth Century." *American Historical Review* 107/4: 1158–78.
McGovern, Mark 2013 "Inquiring into Collusion? Collusion, the State and the Management of Truth Recovery in Northern Ireland." *State Crime* 2/1: 4–29.

Melkonian, Markar 2007 *My Brother's Road: An American's Fateful Joruney to Armenia*. London: IB. Tauris.

Melson, Robert 1982 "A Theortical Inquiry into the Armenian Massacres of 1894–1896." *Comparative Studies in Society and History* 24/3: 481–509.

1986 "Provocation or Nationalism: A Critical Inquiry into the Armenian Genocide of 1915." In *The Armenian Genocide in Perspective*, ed. Richard G. Hovannisian, 61–84. New Brunswick, NJ: Transaction.

Meyer, John, J. Boli, G. Thomas, and F. Ramirez 1997 "World Society and the Nation-State." *American Journal of Sociology* 103: 144–81.

Meyer, Jörg 2008 "The Concealed Violence of Modern Peace (-Making)." *Millenium—Journal of International Studies* 36/3: 555–74.

Middleton, David, and D. Edwards 1990 "Introduction." In *Collective Remembering*, ed. David Middleton and D. Edwards, 1–22. London: Sage.

Mignolo, Walter 2011 *The Darker Side of Western Modernity: Global Futures, Decolonial Options, Latin America Otherwise*. Durham, NC: Duke University Press.

Mikhail, Alan, and C. Philliou 2012 "The Ottoman Empire and the Imperial Turn." *Comparative Studies in Society and History* 54/4: 721–45.

Milburn, Michael A., and Sheree D. Conrad 1996 *The Politics of Denial*. Cambridge, MA MIT Press.

Mills, Amy 2010 *Streets of Memory: Landscape, Tolerance, and National Identity in Istanbul*. Athens: University of Georgia Press.

Moore, Barrington 1966 *Social Origins of Dictatorship and Democracy: Lord and Peasant in the Making of the Modern World*. Boston: Beacon Press.

Mouzelis, Nicos 2012 "Modernity and the Secularization Debate." *Sociology* 46/2: 207–23.

Nalbandian, Louise 1963 *The Armenian Revolutionary Movement: The Development of Armenian Political Parties Through the Nineteenth Century*. Berkeley: University of California Press.

Nelson, Jacqueline 2013 "Denial of Racism and Its implications for Social Action." *Discourse and Society* 24/1: 89–109.

Neyzi, Leyla 2010 *Speaking to One Another: Personal Memories of the Past in Armenia and Turkey*. Bonn: DVV International.

Norgaard, Kari Marie 2006 "'People Want to Protect Themselves a Little Bit': Emotions, Denial and Social Movement Nonparticipation." *Sociological Inquiry* 76/3: 372–96.

Northcott, Michael 2012 "The Liberalism of Fear and the Desire for Peace." In *Politics and the Emotions: The Affective Turn in Contemporary Political Studies*, ed. Paul Hoggett and Simon Thompson, 61–77. New York: Continuum.

Olick, Jeffrey 2003 "What Does It Mean to Normalize the Past?: Official Memory in German Politics since 1989." In *States of Memory*, ed. J. Olick, 259–88. Durham, NC: Duke University Press.

Ortaylı, İlber 1983 *İmparatorluğun en uzun yüzyılı (The Empire's Longest Century)*. İstanbul: Hil.

Ökçün, A. Gündüz 1997 *Osmanlı Sanayii, 1913, 1915 yılları sanayi istatistiki (Ottoman Industry Industrial Census of 1913, 1915)*. Ankara: DEI.

Özyürek, Esra, ed. 2007 *The Politics of Public Memory in Turkey*. Syracuse, NY: Syracuse University Press.

Pamuk, Şevket 2000 *A Monetary History of the Ottoman Empire*. New York: Cambridge University Press.

Pappe, Ilan 2006 *The Ethnic Cleansing of Palestine*. Oxford: Oneworld.

Pennebaker J., D. Paez, and B. Rime. 1997 "Preface." In *Collective Memory of Political Events: Social Psychological Perspectives*, ed. J. Pennebaker, D. Paez, and B. Rime. Rahwah, NJ: Erlbaum.

Pennebaker, J., and B. Banasik 1997 "On the Creation and Maintenance of Collective Memories: History as Social Psychology." In *Collective Memory of Political Events: Social Psychological Perspectives*, ed. J. Pennebaker, D. Paez, and B. Rime, 3–19. Rahwah, NJ: Erlbaum.

Philliou, Christine M. 2011 *Biography of an Empire: Governing Ottomans in an Age of Revolution*. Berkeley: University California Press.

Pomerantz, Kenneth 2000 *The Great Divergence: China, Europe and the Making of the Modern World Economy*. Princeton, NJ: Princeton University Press.

Power, Samantha 2002 *"A Problem from Hell": America and the Age of Genocide*. New York: Basic Books.

Quataert, Donald 1983 *Social Disintegration and Popular Resistance in the Ottoman Empire, 1881–1908: Reactions to European Economic Penetration*. New York: NYU Press.

1992 *Manufacturing and Technology Transfer in the Ottoman Empire, 1800–1914*. İstanbul: İsis.

2000 *The Ottoman Empire, 1700–1922*. New York: Cambridge University Press.

Ram, Uri 2009 "Ways of Forgetting: Israel and the Obliterated Memory of the Palestinian Nakba." *Journal of Historical Sociology* 22/3: 366–95.

Ramazani, Vaheed 2007 *Writing in Pain: Literature, History and the Culture of Denial*. New York: Palgrave Macmillan.

Reynolds, Michael 2011 *Shattering Empires: The Clash and Collapse of the Ottoman and Russian Empires, 1908–1918*. Cambridge: Cambridge University Press.

Riedler, Florian 2011 *Opposition and Legitimacy in the Ottoman Empire: Conspiracies and Political Cultures*. London: Routledge.

Rivera, Lauren A. 2008 "Managing 'Spoiled' National Identity: War, Tourism, and Memory in Croatia." *American Sociological Review* 73/4: 613–34.

Robben, Antonious, and C. G. M. Robben 2012 "From Dirty War to Genocide: Argentina's Resistance to National Reconciliation." *Memory Studies* 5/3: 305–15.

Rodrigue, Aron 1990 *French Jews, Turkish Jews: The Alliance Israelite Universelle and the Politics of Jewish Schooling, 1860–1925*. Bloomington: Indiana University Press.

Rosenwein, Barbara 2002 "Worrying about Emotions in History." *American Historical Review* 107/3: 821–45.

Said, Edward 1978 *Orientalism*. New York: Pantheon.

1993 *Culture and Imperialism*. New York: Knopf.

Salzmann, Ariel 2004 *Tocqueville in the Ottoman Empire: Rival Paths to the Modern State*. Boston: Brill.

2010 "Is There a Moral Economy in State Formation? Religious Minorities and Repertoires of Regime Integration in the Middle East and Western Europe, 600–1614." *Theory and Society* 39: 299–313.

Schmitt, Michael T., D. A. Miller, N. R. Branscombe, and J. W. Brehm 2008 "The Difficulty of Making Reparations Affects the Intensity of Collective Guilt." *Group Processes and Intergroup Relations* 11/3: 267–79.

Schudson, Michael 1992 *Watergate in American Memory: How We Remember, Forget, and Reconstruct the Past*. New York: Basic Books.

Schuman, Howard, and A. D. Corning 2000 "Collective Knowledge of Public Events: The Soviet Era from the Great Purge to Glasnost." *American Journal of Sociology* 105/4: 913–56.

Schuman, Howard, and W. Rodgers 2004 "Cohorts, Chronology and Collective Memories." *Public Opinion Quarterly* 68/2: 217–54.

Schuman, Howard, and J. Scott 1989 "Generations and Collective Memories." *American Sociological Review* 54/3: 359–81.

Schuman, Howard, V. Vinitzky-Seroussi, and A. D. Vinokur 2003 "Keeping the Past Alive: Memoires of Israeli Jews at the Turn of the Millenium." *Sociological Forum* 18/1: 103–36.

Sen, Amartya 2000 *Development as Freedom*. New Delhi: Oxford University Press.

Seu, Irene Bruna 2010 "'Doing Denial': Audience Reaction to Human Rights Appeals." *Discourse and Society* 21/4: 438–57.

Sevük, İsmail Habib 1940 *Avrupa Edebiyatı ve Biz* (*European Literature and Us*). 2 vols. İstanbul: Remzi.

Sewell, William H., Jr. 1996 "Historical Events as Transformations of Structures: Inventing Revolution at the Bastille." *Theory and Society* 25/6: 841–81.

2005 *Logics of History: Social Theory and Social Transformation*. Chicago: University of Chicago Press.

Seyitdanlıoğlu 2009 "Meclis-i Ali-i Umumi (The Supreme Conseil General) and the Transformation in the Ottoman Political Thought (1839–1876)." *Journal for the Study of Religions and Ideologies* 8/23: 107–23.

Shaw, Stanford J. 1962 *The Financial and Administrative Organization and Development of Ottoman Egypt*. Princeton, NJ: Princeton University Press.

1971 *Between Old and New: The Ottoman Empire under Sultan Selim III, 1789–1807*. Cambridge, MA: Harvard University Press.

Sheriff, Robin E. 2000 "Exposing Silence as Cultural Censorship: A Brazilian Case." *American Anthropologist* 102/1: 114–32.

Shissler, Holly 2003 *Between Two Empires: Ahmet Ağaoğlu and the New Turkey*. London: I. B. Tauris.

Shome, Raka 2012 "Asian Modernities: Culture, Politics and Media." *Global Media and Communication* 8/3: 199–214.

Siegel, Jerrold 2012 *Modernity and Bourgeois Life: Society, Politics and Culture in England, France, and Germany since 1730*. Cambridge: Cambridge University Press.

Şimşir, Bilal 1985 *Malta Sürgünleri (Malta Exiles)*. İstanbul: Bilgi.

Sluka, J., ed. 2000 *Death Squad: The Anthropology of State Terror*. Philadelphia: University of Pennsylvania Press.

Smith, Roger 1991 "Denial of the Armenian Genocide." In *Genocide: A Critical Bibliographic Review*, ed. Israel W. Charny, vol. 2, 63–85. New York: Facts on File.

Smith, Roger W., E. Markusen, and R. J. Lifton 1995 "Professional Ethics and the Denial of the Armenian Genocide." *Holocaust and Genocide Studies* 9/1: 1–22.

Sohrabi, Nader 2011 *Revolution and Constitutionalism in the Ottoman Empire and Iran*. Cambridge: Cambridge University Press.

Somel, Selçuk Akşin 2001 *The Modernization of Public Education in the Ottoman Empire, 1839–1908: Islamization, Autocracy and Discipline*. Leiden: Brill.

Spencer, Jonathan 2010 "Collective Violence." In *Handbook of Indian Sociology*, ed. V. Das, 472–83. New Delhi: Oxford University Press.

Stern, Kenneth 1993 *Holocaust Denial*. New York: American Jewish Committee.

Stone, Dan 1999 "Modernity and Violence: Theoretical Reflections on the Einsatzgruppen." *Journal of Genocide Research* 1/3: 367–78.

Suny, Ronald Grigor, F. M. Göçek, and N. M. Naimark, eds. 2011 *A Question of Genocide: Armenians and Turks at the End of the Ottoman Empire*. New York: Oxford University Press.

Şimşir, Bilal N. 2000 *Şehit Diplomatlarımız 1973–1994 (Our Martyred Diplomats, 1973–1994)*. 2 vols. İstanbul: Bilgi.

Taylor, Tony 2008 *Denial: History Betrayed*. Melbourne: Melbourne University Press.

Teeger, Chana, and V. Vinitzky-Seroussi 2007 "Controlling for Consensus: Commemorating Apartheid in South Africa." *Symbolic Interaction* 30/1: 57–78.

Temperley, Harold 1933 "British Policy Towards Parliamentary Rule and Constitutionalism in Turkey (1830–1914)." *Cambridge Historical Journal* 4/2: 156–191.

Terzioğlu, Derin 2001 "Autobiography in Fragments: Reading Ottoman Personal Miscellanies in the Early Modern Era." In *Autobiographical Themes in Turkish Literature: Theoretical and Comparative Perspectives*, ed. O. Akyıldız, H. Kara, and B. Sagaster, 83–99. Würzburg: Ergon-Verlag.

Tezcan, Baki 2010 *The Second Ottoman Empire: Political and Social Transformation in the Early Modern World*. New York: Cambridge University Press.

Therborn, Göran 2003 "Entangled Modernities." *European Journal of Social Theory* 6/3: 293–305.

Thoits, Peggy 1985 "Self-Labeling Processes in Mental Illness: The Role of Emotional Deviance." *American Journal of Sociology* 92/2: 221–49.

Tilly, Charles 1985 "War Making and State Making as Organized Crime." In *Bringing the State Back In*, ed. Peter Evans, D. Rueschemeyer, and T. Skocpol, 169–187. Cambridge: Cambridge University Press.

1992 *Coercion, Capital, and European States, AD 990–1992*. Cambridge: Blackwell.

Todd, Andrew R., G. V. Bodenhausen, and A. D. Galinsky 2012 "Perspective Taking Combats the Denial of Intergroup Discrimination." *Journal of Experimental Social Psychology* 48: 738–45.

Trimikliniotis, Nicos 2012 "Sociology of Reconciliation: Learning from Comparing Violent Conflicts and Reconciliation Processes." *Current Sociology* 61/2: 244–64.

Trouillot, Michel-Rolph 1995 *Silencing the Past: Power and the Production of History*. Boston: Beacon Press.

Tsutsui, Kiyoteru 2009 "The Trajectory of Perpetrators' Trauma: Mnemonic Politics around the Asia-Pacific War in Japan." *Social Forces* 87/3: 1389–1422.

Turner, Jonathan H. 2007 "Self, Emotions, and Extreme Violence: Extending Symbolic Interactionist Theorizing." *Symbolic Interaction* 30/4: 501–30.

Üngör, Uğur Ümit 2011 *The Making of Modern Turkey: Nation and State in Eastern Anatolia, 1913–1950*. Oxford: Oxford University Press.

2012a "Creative Destruction: Shaping a High-Modernist City in Interwar Turkey." *Journal of Urban History* 39/2: 297–314.

2012b "Orphans, Converts, and Prostitutes: Consequences of War and Persecution in the Ottoman Empire, 1914–23." *War in History* 19/2: 173–92.

Üngör, Uğur Ümit and Mehmet Polatel 2011 *Confiscation and Destruction: The Young Turk Seizure of Armenian Property*. London: Continuum.

Van Dijk, Teun A. 1992 "Discourse and the Denial of Racism." *Discourse and Society* 3/1: 87–118.

Vazquez, Rolando 2011 "Translation as Erasure: Thoughts on Modernity's Epistemic Violence." *Journal of Historical Sociology* 24/1: 27–44.

Vinitzky-Seroussi, Vered 2001 "Commemorating Narratives of Violence: The Yitzhak Rabin Memorial Day in Israeli Schools." *Qualitative Sociology* 24/2: 245–68.

2002 "Commemorating a Difficult Past: Yitzhak Rabin's Memorial." *American Sociological Review* 67/1: 30–51.

Vryonis, Speros 2005 *The Mechanism of Catastrophe: The Turkish Pogrom of September 6–7, 1955, and the Destruction of the Greek Community of Istanbul*. New York: greekworks.com.

Wagner, Peter 2012 *Modernity: Understanding the Present*. Cambridge: Polity.

Wagner-Pacifici, Robin, and B. Schwartz 1991 "The Vietnam Veterans Memorial: Commemorating a Difficult Past." *American Journal of Sociology* 97/2: 376–420.

Walker, Christopher 1990 *Armenia: The Survival of a Nation*. London: Routledge.

Wang, Qi 2008 "On the Cultural Constitution of Collective Memory." *Memory* 16/3: 305–17.

Warry, Wayne 2007 *Ending Denial: Understanding Aboriginal Issues*. Toronto: Broadview Press.

Watenpaugh, Keith D. 2006 *Being Modern in the Middle East: Revolution, Nationalism, Colonialism, and the Arab Middle Class*. Princeton, NJ: Princeton University Press.

Weicks, Deidre 2011 "Silence and Denial in Everyday Life: The Case of Animal Suffering." *Animals* 1: 186–99.

Wertsch, James W. 2002 *Voices of Collective Remembering*. Cambridge: Cambridge University Press.

Wessel, Ineke, and M. L. Moulds 2008 "How Many Types of Forgetting? Comments on Connerton." *Memory Studies* 1/3: 287–94.

Williams, Robin M., Jr. 2003 *The Wars Within: Peoples and States in Conflict*. Ithaca, NY: Cornell University Press.

Wimmer, Andreas 2002 *Nationalist Exclusion and Ethnic Conflict*. Berkeley: University of California Press.

2006 "Ethnic Exclusion and Nationalizing States." In *The Sage Handbook of Nations and Nationalism*, ed. G. Delanty and K. Kumar, 334–44. London: Sage.

Wimmer, Andreas, and Y. Feinstein 2010 "The Rise of the Nation-State across the World." Online supplement to the article in *American Sociological Review* 75/5: 764–90.

Winks, Robin W., and J. Neuberger 2005 *Europe and the Making of Modernity, 1815–1914*. New York: Oxford University Press.

Wisecup, Allison, D. T. Robinson, and L. Smith-Lovin 2007 "Sociology of Emotions." In *21st Century Sociology*, ed. C. D. Bryant and D. L. Peck, 106–16. New York: Sage.

Wouters, Cas 2012 "The Slippery Slope and the Emancipation of Emotions." In *Politics and the Emotions: The Affective Turn in Contemporary Political Studies*, ed. Paul Hoggett and Simon Thompson, 199–216. New York: Continuum.

Yalçın, Kemal 2004 *Seninle Güler Yüreğim (Rejoice My Heart)*. Köln, Germany: Author.

Zerubavel, Eviatar 2006 *The Elephant in the Room: Silence and Denial in Everyday Life*. Oxford: Oxford University Press.

Zürcher, Erik J. 1986 "Young Turk Memoirs as a Historical Source: Kazim Karabekir's Istiklal Harbimiz." *Middle Eastern Studies* 22/4: 562–70.

2010 *The Young Turk Legacy: From the Ottoman Empire to Atatürk's Turkey*. Leiden: Brill.

INDEX

"n." indicates material in endnotes. "t" indicates material in tables